Private Woman, Public Stage

PRIVATE WOMAN, PUBLIC STAGE

Literary Domesticity in
Nineteenth-Century America

MARY KELLEY

New York   Oxford
OXFORD UNIVERSITY PRESS
1984

Copyright © 1984 by Oxford University Press, Inc.

Library of Congress Cataloging in Publication Data

Kelley, Mary, 1943–
    Private woman, public stage.

    Bibliography: p.
    Includes index.
    1. American fiction—Women authors—History and
criticism. 2. Women in literature. 3. American
fiction—19th century—History and criticism.
4. Popular literature—United States—History and
criticism. 5. Women authors, American—19th
century—Bibliography. 6. Women—United States—
Books and reading. 7. Women—United States—History—
19th century. I. Title.
PS374.W6K4   1984   813'.3'099287   83-17325
ISBN 0-19-503351-5

Printing (last digit): 9 8 7 6 5 4 3 2 1

Printed in the United States of America

For
ROBERT
who made everything possible

Preface

Writing from Savannah, Georgia, on 19 March 1819, a woman told her sister in Boston about witnessing a *lady singer* from New York City named Mrs. French who had been holding a series of concerts. "Her character and manner as a *public* performer is *unique*," she wrote.

> Her public concerts are marked by this peculiarity that she enters the room with a private party, for she is greatly noticed, and seats herself with the other ladies. When the company has assembled, she is led to the piano by private gentlemen of the first respectability, and after every song, again takes her place among the ladies, one of whom keeps a shawl ready to throw over her.

The woman did not claim to be "personally acquainted" with the singer, but she did "think her manner pleasing and respect her highly." The pleasing and respected Mrs. French and her husband belonged to the "first circle" of society in New York City, said the woman, but the husband had failed financially "to an immense amount" and was an "invalid" as well. When Mrs. French had discovered that her husband's affairs were "irretrievable," she had begun "singing publicly, to liquidate his debts, and educate her children." Having left their children behind, Mrs. French and her husband had traveled "Southerly" for the concerts and, so the woman had heard, along the way creditors had not hesitated "to present their claims to her," with the result that "she has expended her great profits upon them."[1]

The author of the letter was the twenty-four-year-old Caroline Howard. Boston-born and eminently respectable herself, she was visiting in Savannah prior to her marriage to the Harvard-trained clergyman Samuel Gilman. After the two were married, they would establish residence in Charleston, South Carolina, where the newly ordained husband would become minister to the first Unitarian church in the South and where they would maintain their home for the remainder of their years.

Caroline Howard's report on the lady singer was as striking as the event itself, because Caroline Howard *Gilman*—for it was under her married name that she later became identified to her country—had unknowingly foretold her own future as much as she had told about the lady singer, and had foreshadowed a peculiar phenomenon in nineteenth-century American society. Gilman and the eleven other private domestic women I have chosen for this study became popular, commercially successful writers of novels, stories, and miscellaneous prose. They, like the lady singer, were "greatly noticed" and found their female selves unexpectedly transformed into public figures, economic providers, and creators of culture. The twelve women were Maria Cummins (1827–1866), Gilman (1794–1888), Caroline Lee Hentz (1800–1856), Mary Jane Holmes (1825–1907), Maria McIntosh (1803–1878), Sara Parton (1811–1872), Catharine Maria Sedgwick (1789–1867), E.D.E.N. Southworth (1819–1899), Harriet Beecher Stowe (1811–1896), Mary Virginia Terhune (1830–1922), Susan Warner (1819–1885), and Augusta Evans Wilson (1835–1909). Beginning with Catharine Maria Sedgwick's first novel in 1822, they issued the largest number of their best-selling works in the 1850s, 1860s, and 1870s, and some of their books continued to sell widely into the early decades of the twentieth century.

I have proposed that these female writers be designated *literary domestics*, for in both their published prose and their previously neglected letters, diaries, and journals these women reported on their own phenomenon and became unwitting witnesses to both the public event and their own private experiences. When these women were not ignored, which was the case for decades, historians and literary critics have not known what to do with them. Significantly, we have witnessed a new form of effacing the female past. For the most part these women writers have been dubbed the "sentimentalists" or the "scribbling women." But those terms have a pejorative and ahistorical quality about them, calling to mind maudlin, unthinking celebrants of a cloyingly intimate and blissful homelife. That has in turn primarily served to raise the question of whether such creatures of emotion could ever have written books or, in fact, whether they ever existed. It has contributed to the overlooking of their importance in American history, particularly in the history of American women. As if to counter that tack, a few critics have portrayed these women as subversives, as promulgators of quasi-revolutionary manifestos with the expressed purpose of liberating women from their domestic captivity. Rather than paper dolls, we have paper tigers. But in either case the portrayal is static and one-dimensional, leaving us with cardboard cutouts. The result has been not only to place them outside of history—recalling the fact that until recently most women have been outside of history—but also implicitly to deny the existence of positive and substantive elements in the domestic experience and thus in women's experience. Given the fact that the literary domestics were women of the home who functioned in untraditional, unfeminine fashion, it is not altogether surprising that historians and critics have not known how to either characterize them or place them properly in history. Nevertheless, it is necessary to understand them as historical figures in the social and cultural context of the nineteenth century.[2]

Actually, in their published prose the literary domestics inadvertently revealed to the public much of the woman's act in private. This was a phenomenon that initially drew my interest, and as I became more and more attuned to it, I became increasingly aware that these women offered valuable insights into the condition of women generally in the nineteenth century. Their perspective was private and familial, their allegiance was to the domestic sphere, but they were also women who, out of step with their culture's past, wrote in public and necessarily wrote about private, domestic, female lives. Their best-selling books had in common the subject of women in and of the home. They focused upon the young female reared for and looking toward marriage; the adult woman as wife and mother; and the woman alone, whether unmarried, separated, or widowed. Theirs was a prose of heroines with only a sprinkling of heroes; a prose mostly of women, whether married or single, who like themselves—and often they drew upon the lives of their selves—were intimately involved with and derived their identity from the domestic sphere. Their public prose reflected the concerns, even obsessions, of their privately recorded thoughts, just as their letters, diaries, and journals documented what was for them the bewildering, anxious reign of private women as public, popular writers. Theirs was, perhaps, as complete and as significant an integration of private individual with published writing as has existed. It is as if creators and heroines alike invite us as readers of history to better understand the quotidian of nineteenth-century American women.

Seven of these women were born in New England, five in Massachusetts alone; one was born in New York City, one in Washington, D.C., and three in the South. But like Caroline Howard's lady singer, and in step with an expanding nation and an increasingly mobile society, a number of them moved far from home, in both southerly and northerly directions. Gilman and Caroline Lee Hentz, both born in Massachusetts, went south; Hentz spent her adult years in North Carolina, Alabama, and Georgia. Mary Virginia Terhune and Maria McIntosh, born in Virginia and Georgia respectively, lived most of their adult lives in New York City and environs. And others like Mary Jane Holmes, born in Massachusetts, and Sara Parton, born in Maine, did not stay in one locale; Parton lived in Boston and New York City, Holmes briefly in Kentucky and then in Brockport, New York.

All of the literary domestics were white Protestants, and all could claim social respectability in the first half of the nineteenth century. Regarding those for whom it can be determined, and for the most part it can only be determined through their male lineages, familial distinction could be traced to male leaders of early colonial settlements, merchants, major landholders, clergymen, military officers, statesmen, and withal gentry's gentlemen. Following the Revolution and the resulting diminution of privilege and dispersal of power, a more complex democratic society began to emerge. Labeled in relatively undiscriminating fashion a predominantly middle-class, bourgeois, or even mass society, nineteenth-century America nontheless did have various male elites. Generally, these women were daughters of those exercising leadership as merchants, clergymen, lawyers, educators, or journalists, and most of them became wives of men of similar rank and profession.[3]

But for females to be associated with socially elite elements of society constituted a different experience from that of their male counterparts, dictated a different social image, and necessitated a different evaluation of self. Born in Massachusetts and educated in private schools in Boston, Albany, and New York City, Catharine Maria Sedgwick, the first of the literary domestics to become nationally known, had as distinguished a family pedigree as any of them. Even so, Sedgwick was profoundly aware that her status in society was radically different from that of a male social equal, so-called. In a letter written to a Professor Potter of Schenectady, New York, in 1838, Sedgwick was addressing herself to the well-being of female domestic servants when she wrote that as Mme. de Staël had said of " 'genious' " that it " 'has no sex,' " she, Sedgwick, desired to prove that "neither has it any condition." Her desire notwithstanding, Sedgwick knew better, and her words could have applied equally well to the dilemma of her own social condition and that of her female kind. Certainly the perspective was rooted in the minds of her female kind. While it was her desire, she wrote to Professor Potter, to see "the humblest stimulated to the cultivation and enjoyment of their intellectual faculties," she wished also to "have them feel that a dutiful performance gives dignity to the lowest office." She could not help but believe that it would be far better for a female domestic servant to find "exercise for mind and heart in the prescribed duties of her station" than to anguish over the fact that her "intellectual faculties" were going "to waste because they are not devoted to what is esteemed their highest exercise."[4]

It was undoubtedly more than Sedgwick's observation of female domestic servants that led her to claim to have "seen many persons disturbed with longings for something out of their condition when they would have been made happy by a right appreciation of what was within it." And it was the peculiar irony of the circumstances of her own female kind, that is, a blend of social superiority and gender inferiority, that induced her to hedge, "I do not mean by this that I would discourage a taste for letters in working men and women." After all, she as much as anyone knew that "books are sure and unfailing friends and like all friends their value is more fully realized in the shade than in the sunny places of life."[5]

As popular writers, as public figures, economic providers, and creators of culture, the literary domestics in a very real sense left the "shade" for the "sunny places of life." Certainly that distinguished them from the overwhelming majority of their female contemporaries from all elements of society. But they were torn between a desire "for something out of their condition" and a conflicting and contradictory desire for "a right appreciation" of their condition. And that implied a linkage to American women generally. Anomalies in a man's world, they found that their ability to appreciate themselves in the public sphere was hampered by their ambiguous regard of themselves in the woman's private sphere. Beset by a lingering conviction that private domestic women were the "humblest" performing the "lowest office," they nevertheless sought "dignity" through "dutiful performance" in the private domestic sphere. Reluctant and fearful to claim more, they condemned any woman for doing less.

That these twelve women became best-selling writers in the nineteenth century was a radical development in American history. Swept up by the cultural and economic creation of a national publishing industry, they found themselves enmeshed in starkly incongruous circumstances. As literary domestics they had an identity in common with other women in their society even though their experiences were uncommon, and their reactions to those experiences highlighted a prevailing female condition. Because the gulf between a private domestic existence and a public literary career was immense, they found themselves in a world they did not know and that did not know them. Paradoxically, they both traversed that gulf and failed to bridge it. They published, but often under the cloak of anonymity. From their literary income they supported or contributed to the support of themselves and their families, yet felt compelled to justify that support on the basis of domestic need. And, most significantly, they struggled in their tales to assess and place a value on women's lives while disparaging and dismissing their own literary efforts.

Without realizing it, Caroline Howard had implied as much in her description of the lady singer, who remained in her eyes a private domestic woman. The witness, soon to be a writer, set the scene in the presentist language of a novelist, set the scene and made it appear timeless and unchanging. The lady singer enters the public room accompanied by a "private party" and sits with "other ladies," is led to the piano by "private gentlemen," and after each performance again "takes her place among the ladies," where she is covered by "a shawl." It is as if, symbolically, the lady singer has never appeared in public and has never been paid for a song that was never sung. But private domestic woman or not, the lady singer did sing her songs in public. And so did the literary domestics, private domestic women themselves. Although one can only speculate about why the literary domestics were best-selling authors, about why the large majority of their thousands of readers were most likely women, it may be that like Caroline Howard those readers recognized common private elements in the public prose, responded to familiar discordant strains.

This is an attempt to answer the question of how the literary domestics could have been so visibly onstage in their own time and yet remain invisible to the historical audience. I have tried to be a witness to what transpired both on the stage and behind the scenes, to ask and answer not only what happened but why it happened. This is a historical study, not, as the term is commonly understood, a literary one. It is not an examination of literary aesthetics or a work of literary criticism. But if one does not forget that these writers were women of the nineteenth century, it will become evident that I could not write about the women without referring to the prose. To evaluate their lives is in a sense necessarily to evaluate their literature. And I would hope that this evaluation will invite and stimulate further explorations involving creative methodologies as well as alternate perspectives on the historical and literary study of women.

Although the literary domestics told their story to the world in public and doubtlessly over and over again to themselves in private, they have yet to be understood, just as they failed to understand themselves fully. Drawing upon both their public prose and their private papers as well as a variety of other historical documents, I have attempted to construct their story anew in the hope of achieving a better understanding. As a historian it is not my task to invent tales, but every historian has to sift, arrange, and organize materials with the objective of revealing both discrete and shared elements in a total picture. Just as the literary domestics did, I have tried to write and view from within, but unlike them I have sought to observe from without, from as detached a perspective as possible. I have tried to be sensitive to the nuance of their days, true to the tenor of their times, and accurate as to the ideas of their age. In some respects every chapter of this book save the first is dominated by the central issue of domesticity, just as the ideology of domesticity in nuance, tenor, and idea dominated the lives of women in the nineteenth century. But like a photographer in the darkroom, I have attempted to develop a series of negatives taken from multiple angles, in the belief that a greater clarity will be the result.

It is necessary to pierce the glaze, the surface gleam, the hard gloss painted over these women's lives by what was then the new American publishing industry in order to recognize their self-reinforcement of and resistance to the enculturation of their minds and beings. Conscious of the accomplished males in their families' past and present, they pondered the mystery of their silent foremothers. Stimulated by the broadened educational opportunities proffered elite daughters of the nineteenth century, they were confused by the contradiction of an unavoidable domestic destiny. When as secret writers they were suddenly transformed into public figures; when as dependent women they gained economic power; and when, suffering from a sense of their intellectual inferiority, they became creators of culture, they were forced to confront and grapple with conflict, ambivalence, and guilt. The enclosed web of domesticity guaranteed that the struggle of the writer would constitute an extension of the struggle of the woman, that tales of women consumed in selfless service would fill their pages, and that the woman embattled in the home would appear in like guise before the world. Not surprisingly, when the literary domestics sought to locate themselves in relation to the nineteenth-century movement for women's rights they looked to woman's past and to their own present, as well as to woman's future. In a sense, theirs was a journey out of time.

When Caroline Howard looked at the lady singer she found her "manner pleasing." That was to speak of recognition. But she also said, "[I] respect her highly." In unlikely ways, the literary domestics were concerned with both recognition and respect. This is implicit in a comment by one of them, Mary Virginia Terhune, that originally suggested to me the designation "literary domestic." "It is my ambition," Terhune declared, "to relieve literary domesticity from the odium that rests upon it."[6] This is a study of the paradoxical ambition of literary domesticity.

M.K.

July 1983
Hanover, N.H.

Acknowledgments

Beginning with the early, tentative stages of investigation and continuing through the completion of this book, I have been helped by many. Stow Persons initially suggested that I pursue this subject. I have profited greatly from his guidance, insights, and encouragement. Linda Kerber's excellent counsel and her ongoing support have been highly important. Many individuals set aside time amidst the demands of teaching and writing to read all or parts of earlier versions of the manuscript. The suggestions made and exchanges shared influenced my thinking and strengthened the book. In this regard I am grateful to Martin Duberman, Colette Gaudin, Kirk Jeffrey, Anne Goodwyn Jones, Judith McGaw, Sharon O'Brien, Patricia Palmieri, and Catharine Stimpson. Others including Jere Daniell, Carl Degler, Michael Ermarth, Annette Kolodny, Marysa Navarro, Louis Renza, Brenda Silver, and Barbara Miller Solomon shared their specialized knowledge and helped me develop and clarify my ideas on a number of topics. Generally, my colleagues in the Department of History at Dartmouth College benefited me in providing a supportive and stimulating environment for the exchange of ideas.

The *New England Quarterly*, *American Studies*, *Signs: Journal of Women in Culture and Society*, and Iowa State University Press furnished valuable forums for an exploration of ideas during the years in which this book was being written. In particular, I thank Hamilton Cravens for his aid and advice as well as his adept editorship of *Ideas in America's Cultures: From Republic to Mass Society*. Individuals at Oxford University Press made the process of publication a gratifying experience. Nancy Lane who first inquired about the book played a key role at the outset; Tessa DeCarlo assiduously and skillfully copy edited the manuscript; Leona Capeless managed the final stages with admirable professionalism. Most noteworthy, Sheldon Meyer has been to me what he has been to many before: the exemplary editor who gave enthusiastic, strong, and timely support and for that I am deeply grateful. My parents, George and June Bremer, made a more intangible but significant contribution. They have been unstinting in their loyalty, affection, and encouragement. I shall always be indebted to them. Susan Macvicar's support and friendship have sustained me for nearly two decades. The years spent on this study were no exception. Richard and Joyce Darilek, Nancy Frankenberry, Lloyd and Mary Michaels, Wylie and Sallie Sypher, Radford Rigsby, and Laura Rigsby have always stood ready to aid me in times of need.

A fellowship from the Newberry Library helped launch this book. I am indebted to Richard H. Brown, Director of Research and Education, and to Lawrence W. Towner, President of the Newberry Library, both of whom were generous in their personal and financial support throughout the year that I spent at the Newberry. Two Faculty Research Awards from the Research Foundation of the City University of New York sustained further research and writing, while a Faculty Fellowship from Dartmouth College afforded me an uninterrupted period for writing. Dartmouth College's Faculty Research Committee helped defray expenses generally and made possible the exemplary research assistance of Lisa Rudman. The college also provided a timely grant for costs incurred in typing the final version of the manuscript. I had particularly good fortune in securing two typists who were as able as they were dedicated. Gail Patten brought care and precision as well as abundant skills, while Virginia Church who took on the task at a critical juncture demonstrated an efficiency that was matched by good humor.

That scholars rely heavily upon archivists and librarians is obvious. Not only have I been especially dependent because manuscript sources provided the primary basis for this study, but I have also benefited immeasurably from the assistance of knowledgable and unfailingly helpful staffs wherever I have gone. I am especially pleased to record my appreciation to Barbara Haber and Eva Moseley at the Arthur and Elizabeth Schlesinger Library, Radcliffe College; Mary-Elizabeth Murdock at the Sophia Smith Collection, Smith College; Diana Royce and Ellice Schofield at the Stowe-Day Memorial Library and Historical Foundation; Aimée Bligh, Elva Bogert, and Winifred Collins at the Massachusetts Historical Society. I am also grateful to the staffs at the Henry E. Huntington Library; American Antiquarian Society; Essex Institute; New-York Historical Society; Constitution Island Association; Boston Public Library; Historical Society of Pennsylvania; Library of Congress; South Carolina Historical Society; New York Public Library; Pierpont Morgan Library; William R. Perkins Library, Duke University; Sterling Memorial Library, Yale University; Alderman Library, University of Virginia; Houghton Library, Harvard University; South Caroliniana Library, University of South Carolina; Wollman Library, Barnard College; Southern Historical Collection, University of North Carolina. I was aided greatly by librarians at Baker Library at Dartmouth College who lightened many a task. In particular, Patricia Carter was indefatigable in locating materials through Interlibrary Loan Service, and Virginia Close never faltered before the most challenging queries.

Words cannot adequately express the debt to my husband. Robert provided the strongest and most constant support in my metamorphosis from beginning student to committed historian. His contribution to this study has been more specific but equally important. Not only has he participated in seemingly endless conversations, helped shape various ideas, and contributed to every word, but he has willingly set aside his own writing to do so. No greater gift could have been offered by an artist whose commitment is as intense and deep as his. The dedication signifies this book as an undertaking fully shared.

M.K.

Contents

PART I: PECULIAR CIRCUMSTANCES

Chapter 1:   *The Fanny Fern*   3

Chapter 2:   Fame Never Was   28

Chapter 3:   The Season of Instruction   56

Chapter 4:   Rights of the Mind, Duties to the
Sphere   74

PART II: THE NOTICE OF THE WORLD

Chapter 5:   Secret Writers   111

Chapter 6:   No Happy Woman Writes   138

Chapter 7:   Buying My Time   164

Chapter 8:   A Man's Clothing   180

PART III: WARFARE WITHIN

Chapter 9:   The Crisis of Domesticity:
A Crisis of Being   217

Chapter 10: The Great Question of
             Moral Life   250

Chapter 11: Preachers of the Fictional Page   285

Chapter 12: A Right Regard for Womanhood:
             A Word or Two on All Sides   316

Epilogue   336

Notes   343
Bibliographical Note   398
Index   401

Part I

PECULIAR CIRCUMSTANCES

1

The Fanny Fern

A letter from a freight conductor in the 6 September 1873 issue of the *New York Ledger*, a weekly paper, reported the sighting a month before of a railroad parlor car pulling into Cleveland's Union Depot. There was nothing unusual about seeing a railroad car in the American countryside, which signified in itself that the economic and physical face of the land had been transformed in a few decades. But the freight conductor's parlor car indicated other changes in America, in the nation's social and cultural fabric. This was no ordinary railroad car. Rather, this was a "magnificent parlor car" and, wrote the conductor, it "thrilled me as I read" the name it bore, "FANNY FERN," encircled by a golden wreath. As unlikely as the name was, even more strange was the fact that the railroad car heralded a writer, and a female writer at that. Oddly enough, "Fanny Fern" had died not long before, and there yet remained three months until the first anniversary of her death. Whether or not the conductor was surprised by this apparently unexplained appearance, he did not say. But he did write that "as I looked at it, the many truths she has written came to my mind, and I said to myself, FANNY FERN's name is one that will be remembered long as memory lasts."[1] It is possible that the parlor car was touring the country not as a memorial to "Fanny Fern" but in celebration of her birth, which had been in July 1811, and had only just arrived in Cleveland when the freight conductor saw it. In any case, it was appropriate that he wrote to the *New York Ledger*, for the *Ledger* had issued most of "Fanny Fern's" prose for almost two decades, and it was the *Ledger*'s editor and proprietor, Robert Bonner, who had promoted "Fanny Fern" from an early stage in her literary career.

Any history of American business inventiveness, commercial gimmickery, or just plain corn would do well to include the story of Bonner, who knew much more about celebrating life than mourning death. A Scotch-Irish immigrant who had come to this country in 1839 at the age of fifteen, the ambitious Robert Bonner quickly learned everything he could about

3

journalism and publishing. Beginning with a position as a printer's devil for the *Hartford Courant*, Bonner moved from there to the *American Republican*, where he worked as an assistant foreman and proofreader, and thence to the *New York Evening Mirror*. It was at the *Mirror* that Bonner's apprenticeship blossomed into a career, as he filled the roles of printer, subeditor, and writer. By 1851, when he was twenty-seven, he had also accumulated the money to purchase the *Merchant's Ledger*, a weekly business sheet begun in 1846. Made up of four pages measuring twenty-two by fourteen inches, with five columns to the page, the *Merchant's Ledger* printed a little news, classified advertisements, and financial and business information. Only a small portion of its space was devoted to stories and poetry for the family.[2]

After Bonner's purchase the sheet was never the same. By 1855 he claimed to have increased the number of copies sold twenty times. But Bonner's pioneering of America's first successful family story paper had only just begun. Only a year later the *Ledger* reached a circulation of 180,000, the highest of the time, and eventually climbed to 350,000. When Bonner retired in 1887 and transferred the operation of the *Ledger* to his three sons, it was estimated that he handed them property valued at $2 million, some $1 million in the *Ledger* alone, for which he had originally paid $500.[3]

Bonner accomplished his remarkable feat through basic changes in the *Ledger*'s content and extensive advertising of his paper. "New York" was substituted for "Merchant's" in the title in 1855, and business columns and advertising space were gradually made less prominent, until by 1856 the paper was filled almost exclusively with fictional serials, stories, sketches, poetry, editorials, correspondence, and miscellaneous items. Supposedly guided by the policy of printing nothing that "the most pious old lady in a Presbyterian church" would find objectionable, Bonner proclaimed that his paper "was meant for the family" and was "neither sectarian nor political." "Abolitionist" and even "Democrat" were forbidden words. His ploy was to recruit the services of famous writers by paying them liberally. Eventually included in his entourage were William Cullen Bryant, Henry Wadsworth Longfellow, Henry Ward Beecher, George Bancroft, James Parton, and, with an eye to a female audience, Harriet Beecher Stowe, Mary Virginia Terhune, and E.D.E.N. Southworth. Bonner had little difficulty recruiting writers when he paid such munificent sums as the $30,000 advanced to Beecher for his novel *Norwood* or the $3,000 paid Longfellow for a single poem. Five thousand was presented to Dickens for "Hunted Down," the only story the novelist wrote for an American publication, and another $5,000 was paid to Tennyson, again for a single poem.[4]

From the outset Bonner's stock-in-trade was advertising. One day he took a full page in the *New York Tribune*, and in one week he bought so much advertising space in the *New York Herald* that the size of the paper was doubled. The promotional sums spent were phenomenal for the period. In one particular year Bonner spent $100,000. Twenty-five thousand was lavished on Southworth's "The Island Princess," a novel that ran serially in the *Ledger*'s columns before it was reprinted in book form as *The Lady of the Isle*. "It pays to advertise when you've got a good thing and want people to know it," said Bonner upon his retirement. One way he made people "know it" was to have printed on the page of a newspaper just a few lines heralding an author's story, stating that the complete tale could be found in the *Ledger*'s pages. He is credited as well with being the first to resort to the stratagem of printing a few chapters of a tale in another publication, only to end it suddenly with the information that an interested reader would have to buy the latest issue of the *Ledger* in order to complete the adventure.[5]

Bonner's policy of combining famous writers with innovative advertising was probably never employed more ingeniously than with "Fanny Fern." "Fanny Fern" was the pseudonym of Sara Parton, and it was a pen name already known to thousands of American readers by the time Bonner obtained her services. Short sketches by Parton had appeared in many of the nation's newspapers in the early 1850s, and in 1854 the house of Derby and Miller had published her first volume of sketches, titled *Fern Leaves from Fanny's Portfolio*. In less than a year from the date of publication over 80,000 copies were sold. A second series of sketches followed shortly after, along with a juvenile volume whose title, *Little Fern Leaves for Fanny's Little Friends*, once more displayed Parton's delight in alliteration. The combined sale of the latter two volumes was 62,000.[6]

Bonner was not the first to conduct a huge campaign to promote Parton's work. The same year that the volumes of sketches addressed to adults and children appeared, Parton signed a contract with Mason Brothers for her first novel, *Ruth Hall*. Noteworthy among the clauses was the firm's agreement "to use extraordinary exertions" in publicizing the novel with the hope that it might "exceed the sale of any previous work." While Mason Brothers did not succeed in reaching that goal with their three-stage campaign, it cannot be said that their venture was a failure: *Ruth Hall* sold more than 50,000 copies within eight months. Mounted toward the end of 1854, stage one concentrated upon prepublication publicity announcing the forthcoming appearance of the novel and predicting great success for it. Utilizing favorable comments from critics, stage two involved repeated claims that the forecast was proving truer than expected. And in stage three the publisher ran six daily advertisements in February 1855 proclaiming "THE MOST SUCCESSFUL AMERICAN BOOK: RUTH HALL." The same technique was employed again in April of that year.[7]

Thus when Bonner recruited Parton for the *Ledger* in 1855 he was, in typically shrewd fashion, benefiting from an already successful show. But it would not have been in character for Bonner merely to climb aboard Parton's bandwagon for the ride. After all, he had a good thing and he wanted people to know it. Accordingly, the 19 May 1855 issue of the *Ledger* printed an editorial with banner headlines: "GREAT ATTRACTION: New Story for the Ledger, by FANNY FERN: Great Plans for the Future!" It had been four years, began the editorial, since the *Ledger* had come under new management, four years since it had stated in its very first issue the determination "to devote the strength and vigor of the morning of our manhood to the upbuilding and advancement of the LEDGER." No one could doubt, it stated proudly, recalling the increase in circulation already achieved, that that effort had proved to be "*eminently successful!*" But if others were satisfied with the *Ledger*'s progress, "we confess, we are not." The editorial continued, "We are ambitious—perhaps a little too much so—and have an ardent desire to extend our influence," to become the weekly paper with the highest circulation in the United States. The paper was already "cheap," it noted, selling for three cents a copy and one dollar a year, so that "the poor as well as the wealthy, can buy it."

The intention was to provide a "GREAT FEATURE by combining the highest order of attraction and excellence with our cheapness, and in that way make a paper that would be universally sought for and read." Efforts had already been made in that regard through the initiation of correspondence with some of America's most prominent writers in order to recruit them for the *Ledger* "without any regard to price!" And now, it announced, with trumpets blaring and banners waving, "the most popular authoress in this or in any other country—FANNY FERN, is now engaged in writing a Tale for the *Ledger*." In order to bring the woman writer to the *Ledger*, "we have to pay by far the highest price that has ever been paid by any newspaper publisher to any author." The price, of course, went unmentioned; said the editorial, "if we mentioned the amount, we presume some people would consider us 'half-cracked' for paying such an enormous price to any author." But that was no matter, for "we know that *something* cannot be obtained for *nothing*; and that a Good Article is worth a Good Price." Thus was stated what was probably Bonner's own personal logo as well as his policy for the *Ledger*.

Appearing on the first page under the leadline "Great Original Tale by Fanny Fern," the serial began running in the *Ledger* in the 9 June 1855 issue. It was titled "Fanny Ford: A Story of Everyday Life," and, said the *Ledger*, it was "Written expressly for the New-York Ledger, at a greater expense than was ever before incurred by a newspaper publisher, and will not be issued as a book." Sara Parton was paid $1,000 for the story. In 1856 she began writing a column exclusively for the *Ledger* and continued doing so until her death in 1872.[8]

Robert Bonner gave Parton's literary bandwagon his own vigorous push in 1855. In 1873 the freight conductor spotted the parlor car *Fanny Fern*. However, neither Parton's career nor the *Fanny Fern* would have rolled had the nation and the economy not experienced massive growth and expansion since 1820. Those changes made possible and provided the structure for the creation of a national publishing industry. Two of the more striking results were the commercialization and democratization of literature. In fact, literary economics had roughly paralleled the economic development of the nation. In a sense the appearance of the railroad parlor car symbolized those developments. Moreover, the *Fanny Fern* in its own right announced to the nation that the literary domestics, who believed in the dictum that woman's place was in the home as wife and mother, nevertheless had stepped into a public arena traditionally ruled by men and had achieved a distinctive measure of success there.

By the time that the literary domestics had exited the public stage they knew they had been noticed. Starting with Catharine Maria Sedgwick's first few efforts in the 1820s, followed by Caroline Howard Gilman and Caroline Lee Hentz in the 1830s, Maria McIntosh, E.D.E.N. Southworth, and Harriet Beecher Stowe in the 1840s, and Maria Cummins, Mary Jane Holmes, Sara Parton, Mary Virginia Terhune, Susan Warner, and Augusta Evans Wilson in the 1850s, these twelve, who were among the most commercially successful of the literary domestics, came to dominate a substantial literary marketplace.

The degree of the literary domestics' popularity was unique and staggering. It was only in the 1820s that changes in the publishing world made it possible for a writer—male or female—to contemplate reaching a national audience. There was little to compare between what existed before that time and what came after. There had been neither a national publishing industry nor what legitimately could have been called a profession of authorship in the United States before the third decade of the nineteenth century. Numerous factors had hindered the growth of American publishing before that time. A lack of capital typical for an underdeveloped country, high production costs, an inefficient system of distribution, poor transportation, and an absence of a predictable market were among the obstacles. But once those difficulties had begun to be solved a new publishing empire emerged in the United States, grew with the nation, and provided for women in America an opportunity such as they had never confronted before. Given their private domestic heritage, it truly could be said that these women were in strange company in a strange public world.[9]

Until well into the nineteenth century, publishing in America had been a provincial, risky business. Mathew Carey's firm, founded in 1785, was the only eighteenth-century venture that lasted long into the nineteenth century. Of those houses established before 1820 only Harper flourished beyond midcentury. Lacking its own commercially viable publishing, the young republic revealed its cultural dependence upon England as American booksellers welcomed reprints of British fiction. It was an advantageous arrangement for England, as it gave British publishers a profitable dumping ground for their remainders, and the market on this side of the Atlantic was flooded with imports. But it was hardly a situation designed to encourage the promotion of American fiction. There was little incentive for a publisher to share the profits with an author, to pay for the copyright of a work, or, for that matter, to undertake the gamble of an expensive and cumbersome process of manufacturing when cheap imported reprints were available. The situation was not ideal for the American publisher either. In the absence of international copyright laws, pirated editions of foreign works also inundated the American scene, and publishers engaged in a frantic struggle with one another to reach the marketplace first with competing reprints of the same work.[10] But the one who suffered the greatest loss was the American author. Before 1820 common practice compelled the author to pay manufacturing costs, with the publisher or bookseller acting as distributor on a commission basis. If nothing else, it could be said that the British aristocratic tradition of writing for neither money nor a vulgar public but as a demonstration of learning and genteel status was being sustained. A significant profit for a writer and a large reading audience for a book were highly unlikely.

A combination of circumstances changed that situation dramatically. The need to import most materials and tools for the production of books began to lessen at the opening of the nineteenth century. The chronic lack of capital from which most publishers still suffered in 1800 was gradually overcome by midcentury. There were also revolutionary developments in strictly mechanical factors such as presses, typecasting and typesetting, and paper. In fact, the technological explosion in printing in the second quarter of the century represented the greatest advance in that field since the fifteenth century. Whereas in the eighteenth century books had cost at least two and a half to more than three times as much as they do today, American publishers in the nineteenth century developed the ability to produce large quantities of books cheaply.

Economic growth and technological advancement also enhanced publishers' ability to market books. Specialization had been all but unheard of in the eighteenth century, and a variety of confused and inefficient relationships existed among printers, publishers, and booksellers well into the next century. Prior to the third decade of the nineteenth century, publishing was generally decentralized and local in nature. Writers employed the services offered by the printer in their own town, and sales were thereby confined to limited localities. This was transformed by the transportation revolution and the emergence of publishing centers distinguished by large houses with sophisticated methods of distribution and promotion. Enjoying access to river and ocean transportation, Philadelphia and New York City emerged as the dominant centers, and were joined by Boston after the introduction of the railroad obviated its geographical disadvantage. By the 1840s more than 90 percent of the fiction published in this country issued from one of these three centers.

Along with the trend toward centralization and improvements in methods of distribution, there were important developments in the promotion of books. Publishers began offering generous discounts to booksellers as an inducement to rapid movement of their stocks. They also entered upon campaigns which featured covert as well as overt advertising of their products in magazines. Publishers sent review copies—and handy notices for use by the harassed editor who did not have the time to read and evaluate the work himself. "Puffing," favorable or exaggerated publicity, was simply a technique of advertising, and publishers had their own stables of puffers, those less-than-critics hired to write laudatory reviews or blurbs for their publisher's books. With the growth of the industry the practice was not of minor consequence. In Mary Virginia Terhune's novel *Phemie's Tempta-tion*, published in 1869, the heroine, Phemie Hart, learns of the practice in painful fashion when she secretly writes and anonymously publishes her own novel, which proves to be an unexpected success. Although her husband Robert is a partner in the very firm that issues her novel, she manages to keep her secret even from him. When she finally tells him of her venture, thinking that he will be pleased, she is surprised to find that he is jealous of and mortified by her success. Looking over a pile of favorable reviews, husband Hart turns to Phemie and says, " 'If you were familiar as I am with the machinery of critic-making, you might not treasure them so carefully.' " The firm, he tells her, has spent a " 'ridiculously large sum in advertising, which includes puffing.' " In case she was unaware of the fact, he informs her, " 'We have a first-class puffer connected with our establishment,' " and her wonderful reviews " 'were undoubtedly paid for by the firm at so much per line.' "[11]

Puffing offered to the ambitious a ready opportunity to engage in the game of quid pro quo. Rufus Wilmot Griswold, journalist, critic, and at one point editor of *Graham's Magazine*, obviously wanted to extend his influence in literary circles as well as to receive a return for favors when he wrote to James T. Fields of Boston's Ticknor and Fields to say, "Did you see what a puff I gave Tennyson [then published by Ticknor and Fields] in the Sat Eve Post?" Griswold was quick to assure Fields that "I puff your books, you know, without regard to their quality."[12] Before Sara Parton had published a word, her brother, Nathaniel Parker Willis, was already a well-known poet and a leading editor and journalist, but rather than assist her he sought to blunt her literary aspirations and was highly critical. In Parton's roman à clef, *Ruth Hall*, published in 1855, he received due recompense. Willis, who helped foster his own reputation as a bit of a dandy, is satirized in the novel as Hyacinth Ellet, the vain, foppish, and unscrupulous editor of *Irving Magazine* who is very much in the center of the literary establishment's " 'Mutual admiration-society.' " The character of Horace Gates, one of Ellet's hired-hand writers, was based upon James Parton, who married

Sara Parton a year after *Ruth Hall* was published and who began his career as a journalist and biographer with Willis's *Home Journal*. Says Horace about his service as a " 'pliant tool' " for Ellet's magazine, " 'I am ordered to puff every "influential paper in the Union," to ward off attacks on the Irving Magazine, and the bait takes, too, by Jove.' "[13]

Willis himself knew very well how to set out bait. In 1844 he wrote to the poet James Russell Lowell, enclosing a favorable review he had written of Lowell's poetry with the note, "You will find a hasty notice of your poems on the last page which," he said, is "calculated (I think) eminently to serve you."[14] And in another undated letter he approached the publisher James T. Fields about the possibility of publishing his own literary efforts, adding, "Meantime, however, my friend Morris, who has been buying and selling of me, sold me to another customer—or rather to the old one—and Scribner takes my new series."[15] As can be seen in the examples of Robert Bonner and Mason Brothers, periodicals and publishing houses also began advertising their wares in newspapers throughout the country and thereby gained both publicity and generally favorable notices.

Another development favorable to both publisher and author was the appearance of subscription libraries throughout the United States. During the first third of the nineteenth century much of the reading audience looked to subscription libraries to meet their literary needs. Many libraries purchased at least one copy of most novels published, so a minimum sale was thereby assured. Periodical publishing eventually displaced the subscription libraries, and literary magazines like *Graham's Magazine,* established in 1841, and Bonner's *New York Ledger* also helped to place authorship on a more solid basis. The passage of copyright laws aided authors as well, however belatedly and imperfectly. The first copyright statute, passed by the General Court in Massachusetts in 1672, protected booksellers, not writers. After a protracted struggle, the first law for writers was passed in 1790. It offered only fourteen years of protection, with possible renewal for the same number of years. The failure to apply the law to foreign works placed American authors at an economic disadvantage by encouraging the flow of pirated editions from abroad, but at least a modicum of protection had been granted them.

Simultaneously, the audience for literature increased substantially. Beginning in 1790, when there were nearly four million people in the United States, the population doubled every twenty-five years into the twentieth century. The democratic goal of universal literacy in the new republic was translated into broadened opportunities for education, with the result that approximately 90 percent of the adult white population, men and women, entered the literate category during the first part of the nineteenth century.[16] By the 1840s America had the largest reading audience ever produced. That a mass market for books was being created can be seen in the rise in gross income derived from trade in books, from $2,500,000 in 1820 to $12,500,000 by 1850.[17]

Publishing was becoming big business. In fact, the transition from the late eighteenth century to the third decade of the next century has been described by one historian of publishing as the "ascendancy of commercialism over culture." Although there were efforts to maintain a façade of gentility in what had been a profession of gentlemen, publishing more and more became a competitive, commercial scramble. Another historian has characterized it as "a game of dog-eat-dog. Men with more instinct for fortune-hunting than for bookmaking plunged into the publishing business and swam out quickly."[18]

But whether America suffered culturally or gained, for the first time the American writer could consider the possibility of linking creative effort with vocation. Previously forced to confine themselves to an audience restricted by locality and literacy, American writers by the middle of the century could command a geographically national and broadly based audience, and some could hope realistically to garner an adequate income for their efforts. It was the writers of fiction who first gave substance to the term "best-seller." Their native ancestry could be traced to Francis Hopkinson's twenty-nine-page political satire *A Pretty Story*, published in 1774, which has been called the first fictional effort in America. William Hill Brown's *The Power of Sympathy*, which appeared anonymously in 1789, was the first American novel published in the United States. Both Charles Brockden Brown, whose novels appeared at the turn of the century, and Susannah Rowson have been called America's first professional novelists, but neither was able to live on earnings from writing. And Rowson was British, not American, having come to this country in 1793 when she was thirty-one. In fact, most of Rowson's fiction was set in England, and *Charlotte Temple*, the most famous of her novels, was first published in England in 1791 before going on to command a reasonably wide readership in the United States after its publication here in 1793.[19]

Three decades later, Washington Irving became the first American writer to receive adequate wages. The decade of the 1820s also saw James Fenimore Cooper's *The Spy* become the first American novel to enjoy significant commercial success. The year was 1821. Apparently it was an event that surprised both author and publisher. British fiction was ruling the day, led by Scott's Waverley novels, when Charles Wiley of Wiley and Halsted decided to risk publication of Cooper's novel. Cooper himself had set the manuscript aside for a time before submitting it. But the immediate "success" of the novel led Wiley to write Cooper with the exciting news that 100 copies each had been sold to two booksellers. It was hoped that they would be purchased before six months elapsed, for after that time they could be returned to the publisher. Fifty copies had been sold to yet another bookseller and 24 to several others. A number had been retailed by Wiley's firm, and 600 had been distributed on a commission basis. Surprise must have turned to amazement when, within four months, two additional editions of 3,000 and 5,000 copies were warranted.[20] The third decade of the nineteenth century, then, constituted the first stage in the serious publishing of American novels. Beginning in the twenties the rate of growth in American fiction published in this country was phenomenal. From 1820 to 1829, 128 novels appeared; that was almost forty more than had been published in the previous fifty years, and five times the number published in the previous decade. More than double that number, 290, appeared in the 1830s, and the total more than doubled again in the 1840s, to nearly eight hundred.[21]

One year after Cooper's *The Spy* had been issued, Catharine Maria Sedgwick published *A New England Tale*. Sedgwick was the first of the literary domestics to make her appearance. By the end of the 1850s all twelve had entered stage front. Each would be brought into the camp of the commercial giants, publishers such as Harper, Ticknor and Fields, Putnam, T. B. Peterson, and Lippincott, which distributed their literary wares through outlets extending beyond the Northeast to the southern and midwestern states. In the literary marketplace all of the literary domestics would prove best-selling authors in their time, and most would be major money-makers— for their publishers, at least, if not always for themselves. Some would have to struggle initially to get into print, but once they appeared there would be no denying their commercial success. Some would sell outright the copyright to their works, thus limiting their financial gain from the sales of their books. Not all would be prolific in their output. But for the most part when their volumes appeared they sold, and as the years passed and as the market grew with the country, the sales figures and the dollar signs got larger and larger.

In her time, Catharine Maria Sedgwick did splendidly. Shortly before *A New England Tale* appeared in the spring of 1822, Sedgwick's brother Henry Dwight Sedgwick, or Harry, as he was called, who frequently served as her intermediary with publishers, wrote to his brother-in-law William Minot to express his concern regarding the commercial fate of the novel. "Everything depends upon first impressions," he said, and added, "I have not much confidence in the bookseller employed and a great deal often depends upon that." But he need not have worried, for the novel was far more successful than they had anticipated. Shortly after the novel was issued he wrote to Catharine that Bliss and White, the publisher, had reported that "it was going off very rapidly, and much beyond their expectations, and would soon be entirely exhausted." In a few days, said Harry, bubbling with enthusiasm, he would send Catharine the draft of a preface for the second edition. In June he was still urging that a second edition be printed. "I think there can be no doubt that a new edition will sell," he wrote Catharine. At any rate, he emphasized, "I think if a Second edition is to come out, it should come out at once. If people cannot get books when they want them, they borrow, or the want goes over." Less than four months after the initial appearance of the novel, the second edition was out.[22]

The sales of *Redwood*, issued in 1824 again by Bliss and White, enabled Harry to continue in his role of eager reporter. "*Redwood* sells very well," he wrote Catharine in October, "about 1100 are gone. The sale is certainly increasing." Harry predicted that Catharine's subsequent works would sell as well or better than any of Cooper's or Irving's, and perhaps even rival Scott's. Less than two months later he informed her that "the booksellers are all teasing me to know when another work will come from the author of 'Redwood.'" He added that they now agreed with his earlier predictions in regard to Cooper and Irving. Three years after *Redwood* the booksellers' curiosity was satisfied with the appearance of *Hope Leslie*.[23]

Total figures for sales as well as for Sedgwick's income from her writing are not available, but there can be little doubt that for a pioneer she did well. Random figures from her personal papers testify to that. She noted in her journal that *Hope Leslie*, originally published by White, Gallaher and White, brought $1,100 for the first edition of 2,000 copies. While it is difficult to compare the money values of 150 years ago with those of today, we can get some idea from a letter Sedgwick wrote only the year before, attempting to restrain some of her brothers' financial ventures, in which she stated that her brother Charles and his family could live "comfortably" on $1,500 a year. And though the Sedgwicks were not among the very wealthy, they did indeed live "comfortably." Regarding sales figures, the publisher George Palmer Putnam noted that anything exceeding 2,000 was rare. And when Sedgwick's *Clarence* was published in 1830 by Carey and Lea, Sedgwick wrote to her brother Charles that she had received $1,200 for the first edition, again of 2,000. Although Sedgwick typically displayed little confidence in her ability to earn money, she expressed satisfaction with the latter amount. Convinced that the publisher had paid her as much as it could afford, considering that British works still dampened the market for American authors, she wrote Charles that she had been told that "the cheap reprints of popular English novels have reduced the value of copyright productions as much as Hope Leslie has raised the reputation of mine." Sedgwick continued to write and sell through the 1830s. *Home*, published by James Munroe in 1835, went through twelve editions in two years and by 1846 was in its twentieth edition. Other works by Sedgwick included *The Linwoods* (1835), *The Poor Rich Man, and the Rich Poor Man* (1836), and *Live and Let Live* (1837), all issued by Harper. In 1841 Sedgwick noted that since 1835 she had received from Harper $6,027.05, to the penny. That did not include income from other publishers and from magazines, annuals, and collections in which she appeared. Whatever she may have thought, Sedgwick's books sold.[24]

Sedgwick was the pioneer of these twelve literary domestics. Two followed in the thirties, three in the forties, and six in the fifties. The last was an extremely successful decade for both the literary domestics and the publishing industry. In fact, the heyday of Caroline Lee Hentz, E.D.E.N. Southworth, and Harriet Beecher Stowe, all of whom had begun publishing prior to that decade, can be said to have begun in the fifties. Southworth's first novel appeared in 1849, and Stowe would wait until the stunning reception accorded *Uncle Tom's Cabin* in 1852 to publish widely. Hentz's first novel, *Lovell's Folly*, was issued in 1833, and it was not until 1846 that her second, *Aunt Patty's Scrap Bag*, appeared. But when her husband's illness made her the sole financial supporter of her family, she produced from 1850 to 1856 (the last seven years of her life) the startling total of nine novels and six collections of stories, including what was probably the most autobiographical of her works, *Ernest Linwood*, which appeared almost on the day of her death.

Caroline Howard Gilman came after Sedgwick. In 1832 Gilman began editing and contributing to her literary paper, the *Rose-Bud, or Youth's Gazette* in Charleston, South Carolina. Gilman claimed that her publication, which had subscribers in northern cities like Boston and Philadelphia as well as in the South, was the first juvenile newspaper in the country; it was at least one of the first. A year after its initial appearance its name was changed to the *Southern Rose-Bud*, and, as it noted, its content was "adapted in many points to mature readers." In 1835 the name was shortened to *Southern Rose*. The periodical lasted seven years, with Gilman as editor throughout. She called it "a pet of mine," and no wonder, because her own fiction, poetry, and miscellaneous prose were serialized in its pages and compiled for publication as separate volumes. Gilman's primary fictional works were *Recollections of a Housekeeper* (1834), *Recollections of a Southern Matron* (1838), and *Love's Progress* (1840), all three published by Harper.[25]

It is likely that though her books sold well, Gilman made less money than any of the other writers. One culprit was the Panic of 1837 and its aftermath. In April of 1838 Gilman wrote to her sister, Harriet Fay, that she had been "exceedingly busy this winter and spring in preparing for the press," but that she was apprehensive that the "commercial blight" would have an adverse effect on publication. In June she wrote her sister that according to some "New York puffs" her book *The Poetry of Travelling in the United States*, a volume more prose than poetry describing two excursions in the North and the South, was apparently to be published shortly by S. Colman of Boston. "I half tremble," she said, "it is so long since I have seen or even thought about it." Her concern was warranted. Less than a month later she wrote to her sister again saying, "In answer to your anxiety about us, I am glad to tell you that my literary affairs are *simply at a stand*." What followed was a litany of her publishing woes. Even the "Rose," her paper, was at a temporary standstill, as her publisher "was fearful of failing." Regarding that matter, they would wait "until the country is more settled." Meanwhile, she continued, "The Harpers have had The Southern Matron *stereotyped* for two months, but have been afraid to risk its publication." A series of juvenile books to be issued by B. B. Hussey were "in press" but were being held back for "New Year presents." And although S. Colman apparently had the *Poetry of Travelling* ready, she said, "I do not know when he will publish."[26]

All of the books were eventually published that year and were commercial successes, but other culprits, namely the publishers themselves, kept Gilman's income to a minimum. Whether the Gilmans were poor bargainers or whether the publishers in question withheld payments because of the dim economic outlook is not known. But a letter written not long after by Gilman's husband, the Reverend Samuel Gilman, to his sister, Louisa Gilman Loring, tells the sad tale. "The Harpers paid Mrs. G. only $200 for the first edition of the Matron," wrote Samuel, "though 2000 were entirely sold in six months," and they had "put 2000 more to press, for which nothing has yet been received." As for the *Poetry of Travelling*, that edition of 1,500 had also been sold in six months, but as yet S. Colman had sent the Gilmans only $100. Even worse, however, was the fate of *Recollections of a Housekeeper*, for which the panic of 1837 could not be blamed. That book had been published in 1834 and, he said, "The Harpers have never given Mrs. G. but 50 dollars for the Northern Housekeeper, though it was stereotyped, and sold everywhere." In fact, he added, "I believe it is a standing sale book everywhere." Meanwhile they had received only $50 for her miscellany, *The Ladies Annual Register*. "I hear of the booksellers' liberality sometimes," said Samuel, "but for a popular author, Mrs. G. has experienced as little of it as [author and abolitionist Lydia Maria] Child used to."[27]

Gilman also wrote and edited a number of volumes of poetry, but those too probably brought her little income. For example, in May of 1851 she wrote to James Munroe, the publisher of her *Verses of a Lifetime*, saying that the fifty copies she had received from him had been distributed among booksellers in Charleston and she stood ready to handle trade in Columbia and Savannah, Georgia. "I shall not rest in my efforts," she said, "until you can pronounce yourselves clear of the expense of the Edition, as I feel deeply pained at the idea of involving anyone in pecuniary loss." Nearly a year later, in February, she sent Munroe fifteen dollars and said that she hoped "to forward you the remainder in the course of the season, on the fifty copies sent me April last." But she also expressed her irritation that she had been charged for twenty-four copies that she had assumed had been given her as "presentation copies." She asked that he investigate the matter.[28]

In 1851 Gilman had also written to Rufus Wilmot Griswold, who among his other literary endeavors acted as a mediator for authors, to solicit his aid in her efforts to publish a uniform edition of her prose "before my departure from this world—an edition that my family may love to see." Profit was not her motive; she claimed that she would be satisfied simply to avoid more expense. Time and money had already been expended "in securing volumes along with copyright." Gilman's immediate concern was not that her works were no longer selling—they were—or that she was receiving no income from current sales, although that did rankle her. Rather, it was that Harper the publisher of *Recollections of a Housekeeper, Recollections of a Southern Matron*, and *Love's Progress*, held both the stereotypes and the copyrights to those works and, as Gilman complained to her nephew, was "satisfied with their profits, and care nothing about their shabby appearance." As proof of her claim, she noted that *Recollections of a Housekeeper*, first published twenty years earlier and still "with a steady sale, has not shared in a single modern external improvement." Gilman therefore wanted to gather these volumes together in order to publish for family and friends a limited edition apparently separate from and obviously more attractive in appearance than Harper's single volumes. As she wrote her nephew, "I have some pride in leaving for my family and connections a collection, which shall not shame their libraries." As part of the edition Gilman also wanted to reprint two other volumes of prose that were not out of print. To be included in the projected edition were *Tales and Ballads*, originally published in 1834 and reprinted in 1838, 1839, and 1844, and *The Poetry of Travelling*.[29]

What Gilman probably desired from Griswold was that he pressure Harper to be amenable to her requests. From her nephew what she wanted was a loan of at least $300 to help her purchase the stereotypes from Harper, along with 700 copies of *Recollections of a Southern Matron*. That accomplished, her plan then was to negotiate a publishing arrangement for the limited edition with another firm. How much pressure Griswold may have brought to bear upon Harper is not known. But the nearly sixty-year-old Gilman showed no mercy to her poor nephew: "Now, my dear nephew, how much can you risk for *the honor of the family* and to have a smiling set of books go down to posterity? You observe that gain is entirely out of the question with me, and a loss is pretty certain to you." Obviously, complete candor was also in the offering.[30]

Maria McIntosh was next in line. Like a number of the other literary domestics, she eventually published with several houses, including D. Appleton, J. P. Jewett, and Harper. But also like some of them, she had to struggle to get her first book into print. Two years elapsed before *Blind Alice*, part of a five-volume series that was a great success and came to be known collectively as "Aunt Kitty's Tales," found a publisher in 1841. Later, among other volumes, *Two Lives*, issued in 1846, went through seven editions in less than four years, and *Charms and Counter-Charms*, published in 1848, saw six editions in the same number of years.[31]

Mary Virginia Terhune, Susan Warner, E.D.E.N. Southworth, and Sara Parton all made their first commercial splash in the 1850s, but not without initial struggles. In 1854 Adolphus Morris, owner of the principal bookstore in Richmond, Virginia, received what would prove to be bad advice from John R. Thompson, editor of the *Southern Literary Messenger* and later literary editor of the *New York Evening Post*. Thompson told him not to publish "upon speculation" a manuscript titled "Alone." But *Alone* was a first in two senses: it was Mary Virginia Terhune's initial effort as a novelist, and it was her initial success in a long line of immensely successful publications. Terhune had written the novel at age sixteen and rewritten it at twenty-two. On the advice of her father, Samuel Pierce Hawes, she submitted it to Morris, his friend and business associate, for consideration. Morris gave it to editor Thompson to read, and after glancing through a few pages, Thompson had said, in essence, don't publish it unless someone else pays for it. Reminiscent of publishing prior to the 1820s, that someone else was Terhune's father, and thus the novel first appeared in Richmond under the imprint of "A. Morris." Shortly afterward, Terhune wrote her close friend Virginia Eppes Dance to tell "Dear Eppes" that "two editions have been 'run off' already, and another is now in press—unprecedented success in this part of the world—or so they tell me." Similar news regarding the success of the first edition must have surprised Thompson and made Morris regret that he had not negotiated a deal more favorable to himself. That he was not one simply to brood over past errors was indicated by Terhune's telling Dance that "I clear expenses and make several hundreds on the first edition—have no risk in the ensuing ones and share the profits."[32]

The story of *Alone* did not end in Richmond. The following year Terhune's father, obviously the ideal in paternal benevolence, took the novel to New York and arranged to have J. C. Derby reissue it in 1855. Derby also published Terhune's second novel, *The Hidden Path*, that same year. Again Terhune wrote to "Dear Eppes," to say that "I may afford to rest now for a little while, from active labor, since my last book has already reached its fifteenth thousand and is still, as speculators say—'going up,' while 'Alone' has received a new impetus from the success of its younger sister." That impetus was such that *Alone* eventually sold more than 100,000 copies. In all Terhune wrote and published more than twenty-five novels, not to mention innumerable stories, essays, and sketches that appeared in magazines, journals, and newspapers. Her greatest publishing success came with the appearance of *Common Sense in the Household, A Manual of Practical Housewifery* in 1871. *Common Sence* offered culinary aid to the housewife, aid that Terhune would say was "fit to supply what American women lacked and sorely needed," but it also proffered brief, pungent, critical comment on woman's position in the home, similar to the commentary that Terhune interspersed throughout her novels. The volume went through ten editions in as many months and, according to Terhune, eventually exceeded the million mark in sales.[33]

Susan Warner received help from her father, too, although at first it appeared that it would be unavailing. Warner finished *The Wide, Wide*

World at the end of the summer of 1849, set it aside for a while, and then her
father, Henry, took it to a publisher for its first reading. It was rejected. In
fact, it was refused by nearly all of the leading firms in New York City.
Harper, for one, returned the manuscript with "Fudge" written on one of the
pages. Finally it was given to George Palmer Putnam, who took it to his
summer home on Staten Island and handed it to his mother for a judgment. It
was apparently a tale that suited her taste. Shortly thereafter mother
reportedly told son, "If you never publish another book, publish this."
Putnam dutifully obeyed, but until the book's appearance he fretted that it
might be too long, and he communicated his worries to Warner. She recorded
her response in her journal: "Oh my book! If this should fail, I might not be
able to go on writing. God's will be done." Her words contained an unwitting
prophecy. The novel finally appeared in December 1850, and for the first
couple of months it appeared that the judgment of Putnam's mother would
not be confirmed and his worries would be. However, according to the
memoirs of the publisher J. C. Derby, Putnam's mother tried to brighten her
son's spirits by telling him " 'that the book was so good, she was sure that
Providence would aid him in the sale of it.' " Finally, as Derby tells it, the
first favorable review of the book came out in Providence, Rhode Island.[34]

The news from Putnam then began to change. Noting in her journal of
February 1851, "The edition is all sold out and Mr. Putnam is talking of
another," Warner proudly declared, "Nine weeks since published; and sold
with great liking. He has had repeated orders for more copies from Boston
and Providence." In fact, the edition had not been totally depleted, but the
news did remain favorable. In April, Putnam wrote Warner, "Of the 'Wide,
Wide World' I have printed 1,500 copies, and about 1,400 copies of these
are sold, I believe, so that a new edition of 750 or 1,000 copies has already
been ordered. This I consider very good success." Putnam also admitted his
surprise: "I certainly did not anticipate the half of it. Your book has indeed
been received with remarkable interest in various quarters, and I consider it
to have been '*a hit*' in a special and emphatic sense of the word." As it turned
out, Putnam's anticipation was more in error than his original doubts. Just as
Charles Wiley and Bliss and White had seriously underestimated the
potential of Cooper's *The Spy* in 1821 and Sedgwick's *A New England Tale*
in 1822, so thirty years later Putnam had little idea just how big a hit he had.
Either errors in the judgment of future sales of books were chronic
occurrences in the publishing world or publishers had yet to recognize the
phenomenal strides both the country and the publishing industry had made.
The Wide, Wide World sold more than 40,000 copies in less than a year and
went through thirteen editions in two years; Putnam's son, George Haven
Putnam, claimed that sales eventually exceeded a million copies. It was
reprinted sixty-seven times. J. C. Derby, combining amazement with a
businessman's admiration and envy, noted thirty years after the appearance
of the novel that it was still selling. When Warner's second novel, *Queechy*,

was issued in 1852, she wrote in her journal that it was boxed and ready to be sent from Putnam's store, "a greater start than any book ever out of the store." Warner went on to publish additional novels with Putnam, as well as others with Lippincott, D. Appleton, and Robert Carter. George Haven Putnam reported in the first decade of the twentieth century that there was still continued demand for Warner's novels.[35]

Warner must have made a reasonable income, but again less than one might imagine, because she sold her copyrights and thereby denied herself the returns from royalties. To hear the Warner sisters tell it, they barely scratched out a living. In the late 1860s Susan complained that she wanted "to stop this selling of copyright—but it is difficult." It was difficult because money was needed immediately. As Anna said, "My sister kept the copright of none of her later books, because we could not wait for the slow publishing returns. Each story was sold as soon as written—sometimes, indeed, by installments. Very unwillingly we did it, but there seemed no other way." But copyright had not been sold for *The Wide, Wide World*. George Palmer Putnam, for example, paid Warner $4,500 for six months' sales in 1853. Of course, the novel did not remain forever a best-seller. Nevertheless it sold, and sold for years.[36]

Practically all of the literary domestics appeared in a wide variety of periodicals—literary monthlies or quarterlies, weekly story papers, or newspapers—in which they published stories, sketches, and essays, and frequently serialized their novels before they appeared in book form. A number of these writers also began their careers in such publications. Paralleling the development of the publishing industry as a whole, more and more of these publications entered the literary marketplace and garnered large sales in the two decades before the Civil War. Some periodicals, of course, had begun earlier. *Godey's Lady's Book* first appeared as a monthly miscellany in 1830; the *North American Review* in 1815; and the *Saturday Evening Post* in 1821. But the appearance of story papers like the *Flag of Our Union* (1845), *New York Weekly* (1855), and Bonner's *New York Ledger* (1855), and of literary monthlies like *Harper's* (1850), *Putnam's* (1853), and *Atlantic* (1857) were testimony that at midcentury the market for writers was flourishing as never before.

Policies instituted by editors at various magazines also benefited authors. George R. Graham furthered the economic foundations of the American literary profession with his decision to pay writers four to twelve dollars for a page of prose and ten to fifty dollars for a poem printed in *Graham's Magazine*. Established in 1842, *Graham's* scale was liberal for a time when many writers had to be satisfied with merely seeing their work in print. Graham was also one of the first magazine publishers to copyright his pages. While *Putnam's*, a decade later, began by paying its contributors an average price of only three dollars a page for prose, it did pay some writers from five to ten dollars a page and from ten to twenty-five dollars a poem. However,

Putnam's most important contribution was the restriction of its pages to American authors, in conscious and direct opposition to *Harper's*, which had begun its existence by relying heavily upon the reprinting of British material. The policies of both *Putnam's* and *Harper's* demonstrate that American writers were still bedeviled by their British counterparts.[37]

Periodical publishing and serialization of novels became such a significant economic factor by the 1850s that editors could attempt to exercise dictatorial power in questions of content, length, number of installments, and deadlines. Of course, depending upon the writer's popularity and thus economic clout, the writer could attempt to resist. The experience of E.D.E.N. Southworth is a case in point. Southworth's first publication, "The Irish Refugee," appeared in the *Baltimore Saturday Visitor* in 1846. At her death in 1899, obituaries in the *New York Times, New York Journal,* and *Washington Star* claimed that she received no compensation for the story, but her son, Richmond Southworth, later wrote the *Star* stating that in fact she had received fifteen dollars for it. The next year Southworth began submitting stories to the *National Era*, an antislavery journal in Washington, D.C., which had absorbed the *Visitor*. The *Era* serialized Southworth's first novel, *Retribution*, in 1849, the same year that she began writing for the *Saturday Evening Post*.[38]

It was the latter magazine and its editors, particularly Henry Peterson, with whom Southworth carried on a running battle. Southworth must have realized from the beginning that Peterson was an editor with a heavy hand and peremptory manner. The tone and content of a letter she received from him the first year made that clear. Apparently responding to a query of Southworth's about the editorial policy of the *Post*, or perhaps having read her first submission and already indicating disapproval, Peterson haughtily informed her that if she had read the magazine, she would have known that "it is conducted in no straight-laced system." He quickly added, "I bear in mind of course that what I publish is to be read by wives and daughters and children." It was Peterson's unflinching opinion that anything that appeared in print should be suitable for the entire family: "And do you think, my dear madam, that *any* writer ought to write that—perhaps I ought to say any *novel* writer—which is not suitable to place on the parlor table of a family to be read by young and old." Subsequently Southworth exacerbated an already difficult relationship with Peterson and the *Post* because she repeatedly exceeded the prescribed length in her serialized novels, and failed to meet deadlines as well. Time and time again the *Post* would print notices that a story of Southworth's was "much longer than . . . we desired," or that it "was far too long notwithstanding its great merits," or that they regretted that a novel had "not concluded this week, according to promise." [39]

Merit—or popularity—apparently withstood editorial pressure, and the stormy relationship between the two parties continued until it was finally severed in 1857—but not without a parting skirmish. Southworth had promised the *Post* a final novelette, and the *Post* kept promising its appearance to readers from 29 November 1856 to 11 April 1857. It never appeared. The explanation is found in a letter of Peterson's to Southworth dated December 1856. Peterson revealed that whatever charm he may have originally possessed, it had totally vanished, or that, finally dropping all pretense, he was completely exasperated with Southworth. However unsuccessful, Peterson made every effort to intimidate Southworth into giving him what he wanted. Contemptuous, callous, and patronizing, he criticized her latest installment, saying that it "would not do without great alterations—indeed it would not." Demanding that Southworth not, "for heaven's sake, fall into your old blunder again," he slashed, cut, changed, and sent her "the proofs of the parts I have altered—generally by omitting." He also ordered her to "alter the plot." Even as it stood, Peterson did not think the piece was "unobjectionable"—but, he said haughtily, it "may pass." The problem seemed to be the old one: Southworth went on at too great length. He had warned her repeatedly about that fault, said Peterson, and yet she seemed unable to change her ways. Once again it appeared that her story was wandering out of control, although, he added witheringly, he was not certain he could determine how far the tale had progressed. Choosing to exploit any insecurity she may have felt and trying mightily to bully her, Peterson angrily charged that the unedited piece "would have ruined both you and the Post," and again damned its "extreme length." "You have given me a *deal* of *trouble*, and anxiety," he wrote, and ended on a threatening note: "Whatever you may *think* about these matters, I *know* that I am correct. I stand between you and literary perdition."[40]

By the spring of 1857 Southworth had written the *Post* to inform them that her story would not be forthcoming. The *Post* reacted, in turn, by telling its readers of that fact and claiming that, anyway, "our readers were growing very dissatisfied with her productions." The *Post* statement concluded with the words, "We may simply add here, that we think our readers will admit, before the year is out, that they have lost nothing in the way of interest or amusement by this withdrawal." The piece was unsigned, but Peterson had probably had his final say.[41]

So far as Southworth's popularity with readers was concerned, Robert Bonner did not share Peterson's opinion. In fact, Peterson's stated opinion may not have been his true, private one. And whether Peterson severed relations with Southworth or she with him is open to question. What is certain is that Southworth's literary salvation was not in Peterson's hands. By the fall of 1856 the redoubtable Bonner already had made his move to gain her services for the *New York Ledger*, and to gain them exclusively. Unlike Peterson, Bonner chose to flatter Southworth rather than browbeat her. Writing to her on 10 October that he had read many of her stories and, more, that "my wife has read all of them," he offered his unequivocal opinion that "there is no female author either on this or the other side of the Atlantic, who can write so excellent a story." Eager to obtain her services, he emphasized that he did not *"practice economy on authors"* and offered to pay her on *"your own terms* . . . [at] double the amount" she had ever received from any other source—"I care not what that amount might be."[42]

Not surprisingly, Southworth responded immediately and favorably, and Bonner, not one to dally, pounced, writing again only twelve days after his original inquiry. In the second letter he sought to capture Southworth for the *Ledger* alone. He did not wish, he informed her, to interfere with any arrangements she had made previously. But beyond what she had already promised others, he wanted everything she wrote for the *Ledger*, again *"at your own terms.* Can I have it?" He then explained the reasons for his policy of restricting those under contract with the *Ledger*. Like everything else, the arrangement was directed toward the promotion of his paper. More specifically, it was related to Bonner's innovative advertising and his "desire to have the benefit of the author's increased popularity." Obviously, he concluded, "I could not afford, of course, to advertise any author's story so extensively, if he were at liberty to write his next Tale for Tom, Dick or Harry."[43]

Southworth and Peterson's *Post* said good-bye in 1857, but there can be little doubt that rather than being pushed, she had leapt. Her original contract with Bonner and the *Ledger* called for twenty pages a week for forty dollars, a lucrative contract for the time. Bonner later increased his payment to fifty dollars a week. By 1867 the amount had reached seventy-five dollars weekly. Correspondence between the two suggests that each contract was made for a specific number of years, and the amount paid Southworth continued to rise with each new contract. In addition to her weekly salary, Bonner on occasion also paid Southworth for the copyright to an individual novel, including the $1,000 he gave her for *The Hidden Hand*. What is more, Bonner assured Southworth that if she became ill and unable to write, her salary would continue, even if she were incapacitated for an extended period of time.[44]

After her death, the *Washington Star* estimated that Southworth had made $6,000 a year from her writing at one stage in her career, probably not an exaggerated figure. Southworth published her fiction serially in Bonner's *Ledger* for thirty years, until the late 1880s, and her correspondence reveals that by 1867 she was making nearly $4,000 from the *Ledger* alone. She also published her fiction in book form with T. B. Peterson. Theophilius B. was still her publisher in 1877 when he issued an edition of her novels in forty-two volumes. Southworth herself noted in 1895, four years before her death, that a "cheap" edition of her books was still being sold by Layton and Company at twenty-five cents a volume.[45]

Publishers had power, but the growing battle for multiplying literary dollars also meant that they had to compete with each other. They could be pressured to pay, if the will was there on the part of the literary domestics.

Sara Parton had been induced to bring her act to Bonner's tent two years before Southworth. However, even the free-spending Bonner had been bargained up, as had others before him. From her first payment of fifty cents for a story, to six dollars a week total from two papers (the Boston *Olive Branch* and the Boston *True Flag*), to a substantial increase from them, plus double whatever they were paying her from the New York *Musical World and Times*, Parton had gradually improved her bargaining and financial position in negotiations with publishers. She was well prepared, then, to push Bonner's offer up the financial ladder. Typically, Bonner's first offer of $25 an installment for a story was high for the time, and Parton would have been well advised to accept it. She not only rejected it, she also rejected subsequent offers of fifty and then seventy-five dollars. Parton finally accepted Bonner's offer of one hundred dollars. Reportedly without having read a line, Bonner gave Parton a check for $1,000 for her ten-installment "Great Original Tale."[46]

Bonner treated Parton as well as he did Southworth. After supplying the *Ledger* with weekly columns for fourteen straight years, without missing a single week, Parton wrote Bonner expressing her sense of achievement and pride. "Can it be possible that it is as long as that?" responded Bonner. To mark the occasion he enclosed a check as a bonus or, what he thought would be less offensive to Parton, an initial payment for something else he would like from her in addition to the weekly columns. Still mindful of his Presbyterian old lady, Bonner asked that she send him short pieces in response to items that she might see in the newspapers, "particularly if the subject happens to be about husbands, wives, mothers, girls, or babies." Always the opposite of a Peterson, he said that she should not feel "obliged to do it," and that the timing and number were her decision: "If you should send me no more than five during the next year or two, I'll be satisfied, and if you should send me fifty, I'll take them just the same." Besides producing further volumes of fictional, often autobiographical sketches, and a second partly autobiographical novel, *Rose Clark*, Parton continued to write for the *Ledger* until her death in 1872. On 26 October 1872 the following announcement appeared in the *Ledger*: "DANGEROUS ILLNESS OF FANNY FERN—FANNY FERN is extremely ill—we fear hopelessly, and of an incurable disease. We know that this announcement will carry immeasurable sorrow to the hearts of our readers, and that their warmest sympathy will be extended to the gifted authoress in her hour of suffering." Despite all of the advances in printing it was still the nineteenth century, and a weekly newspaper had to be put to bed long before publication date. Parton had actually died on 10 October, but it was not until the 2 November issue that the *Ledger* contained the black-bordered announcement. The 9 November issue, again with a black border, printed a long obituary written by Bonner. A year later, on 30 November, Parton's daughter Ellen Eldredge wrote to Bonner to thank him for the monument he had placed at Parton's grave in Mount Auburn

Cemetery in Cambridge, Massachusetts. It is not known if Bonner was responsible for the railroad parlor car that was sighted in Cleveland earlier that year.[47]

Maria Cummins's literary career was cut short by her death at the age of thirty-nine, within twelve years of the appearance of her first novel, *The Lamplighter* (1854). During that period she produced four novels; the last, *Haunted Hearts*, appeared in 1864. But in that brief span she proved a hardy competitor in the literary marketplace. On the Sunday following her death in 1866 the Reverend Nathaniel Hall said in his sermon delivered at the First Church in Dorchester, Massachusetts, "Never before, I suppose, did a writer among us, if anywhere, flame into such sudden popularity—a popularity calling for edition upon edition of her work." Cummins signed her first contract with John P. Jewett and Company, calling for her to be paid 10 percent royalties on every volume, sold at one dollar a copy. Twenty days after *The Lamplighter*'s publication Jewett issued a broadside announcing that it had already sold 20,000 copies. Sales rose to 40,000 within eight weeks of publication, and by the end of 1854 the figure reported was 73,000. With Cummins's sudden fame came demand. The editor of the Boston *Gazette* wrote to ask if she would supply a story for fifty dollars, while the *American Union*, claiming a circulation of 30,000 weekly, requested that she state her terms. For her second novel, *Mabel Vaughan* (1857), Cummins signed again with Jewett at the same terms, but with *El Fureidis* (1860) she moved to Ticknor and Fields and received 15 percent royalties, with a copy still priced at a dollar a volume. Her last novel was published by J. E. Tilton, from whom she received thirty cents a copy. The publisher's copyright for Cummins's first two novels lasted twenty-eight years, and by the 1880s her novels began to appear in cheap quarto editions selling at twenty-five cents apiece. Regardless of the form in which *The Lamplighter* was issued, it continued to sell into the twentieth century.[48]

Both Mary J. Holmes and Augusta Evans Wilson also began publishing in the 1850s, but they did not become extraordinary commercial successes until the next decade. The numbers vary for Holmes, but after a slow beginning they were all large. Had Daniel Appleton known what was to come, D. Appleton and Company, a latecomer to fiction reportedly because of Daniel's aversion to it, might not have ceased publishing Holmes after issuing her first two novels, *Tempest and Sunshine* (1854) and *English Orphans* (1855). Holmes wrote nearly forty novels and, next to Harriet Beecher Stowe, was probably the biggest money-maker of the literary domestics. At her death in 1907 more than two million copies of her books reportedly had been sold. Miller, Orton and Company published Holmes's next three novels, but her popularity did not become striking until G. W. Carleton became her publisher in the 1860s. Carleton's sales undoubtedly were promoted by the prior serialization of Holmes's novels in the *New York Weekly*, which paid her from $4,000 to $6,000 for serial rights. Carleton issued the novels in book form for sale generally on railroads and steamboats. George W. Alexander, reportedly the oldest bookseller of his period in New York City, claimed that he frequently had orders to bind 50,000 copies at a time of Holmes's books. By 1889 *The Woman's Story*, a collection of biographical sketches of "successful" women of the century, said Holmes's income ranged from $10,000 to $15,000 a year.[49]

On 22 February 1863 Augusta Evans Wilson wrote to the publisher West and Johnston, of Richmond, Virginia, to say that as she had "a very decided preference for your house, above all others in the Confederacy" she was "much gratified, that we have been able to enter into satisfactory arrangements concerning the publication of my books." Specifically, Wilson had agreed to a contract for her third novel, *Macaria* (1864), calling for "$1,000 cash" in advance and 10 percent royalty for every copy sold. Unfortunately for Wilson, the Civil War played havoc with her "arrangements" and she received very little in royalties from West and Johnston for *Macaria*. But she need not have been concerned about the effects of the Civil War, at least in terms of the commercial success of her literary career, for one year after the war's conclusion her all-time best-seller, *St. Elmo*, appeared. Wilson's first novel, *Inez* (1855), the publication of which was probably made possible by a subsidy paid Harper by her uncle, was not a commercial success. Helped by her subsequent popularity, however, even *Inez* was being issued by eight different publishers as late as 1912. Her second effort, *Beulah* (1859), rapidly gained success, with 22,000 copies printed in the first nine months. The Civil War then intervened and crippled West and Johnston's marketing operations for *Macaria*. Meanwhile, two copies of the novel were smuggled north. One copy went to J. C. Derby, who obtained it from a blockade runner via Cuba. Derby, who had previously published *Beulah* under the imprint of Derby and Jackson, was no longer directly involved with publishing himself, so he arranged for an edition of *Macaria* with J. B. Lippincott. Unfortunately, another pirated copy of the novel had been obtained by a Michael Doolady, who had beaten Derby and Lippincott to the presses and was nearly ready to issue an edition of 5,000 copies, supposedly with no intention of paying a penny to *Macaria*'s Rebel author. But Doolady's machinations were discovered, and Derby and Lippincott were able to prevail upon him to pay Derby in trust whatever royalties were due Wilson.[50]

In June 1866, after the war, Wilson wrote a friend that she was "hard at work, writing a new novel, which I hope to publish this fall." The book, she thought, was "the best thing I have ever written, and if the public will only agree with me, I shall be *profoundly gratified*." The novel was *St. Elmo*, and whatever the public's judgment of its quality, Wilson must have been more than gratified by the sales: for the first four months after publication the publisher, G. W. Carleton, kept running notices in the pages of the New York *Tribune* apologizing for not keeping up with orders for the book, and at the end of those four months announced that already one million people had read *St. Elmo*. This was not insignificant in a year when the country's population was estimated at thirty-six million. Obviously Carleton was doing its best to promote sales, but there must have been more truth than puffery in its claims, for the firm also reissued *Macaria* and paid Wilson a $15,000 advance for her next novel, *Vashti* (1869). After the successes of both *St. Elmo* and *Vashti*, Carleton, on his own, changed Wilson's contract for *Macaria*, agreeing to pay her a higher return on sales. Each of Wilson's novels went into many editions, and as of 1884 one of her publishers stated that she had received nearly $100,000 for her fiction.[51]

Uncle Tom's Cabin, one of the all-time best-sellers, made Harriet Beecher Stowe one of the most commercially successful of the literary domestics. Her first volume of sketches, *The Mayflower*, was published in 1843, almost a decade before the famous antislavery novel launched her career as a writer. Within a year after *Uncle Tom's Cabin* had been serialized in the *National Era* and published by John P. Jewett, Stowe wrote Eliza Cabot Follen that she had received $10,000 from the first three months' sales alone and that she presumed that "as much more is now due." Before the passage of three years the novel had climbed past the 300,000 mark. Little wonder that by the late 1860s she would be arguing with her major publisher, James T. Fields of Ticknor and Fields, that his initial offer of $6,000 for the first edition of *Oldtown Folks* (1869) hardly seemed enough. Hadn't she received $7,500 for *The Minister's Wooing*? she asked—and *that* had been published ten years earlier. And wasn't she getting offers from magazines in both England and America of $2,000 each for stories much shorter in length? In fact, Stowe's correspondence with Fields and with various members of her family in the decades after the publication of *Uncle Tom's Cabin* indicates that she earned at least $10,000 a year from her writing.[52]

The literary domestics' success and their impact upon the marketplace were striking. The 14 August 1858 issue of the *American Publishers' Circular* listed seventeen works which it said were "among the greatest successes" in recent publishing. Seven of the titles represented the efforts of Cummins, Parton, Stowe, and Terhune. These four were included in a table prepared by the *Boston Post* in 1860 of "the most popular and widely circulated" authors; so was Susan Warner. By 1871 nearly three-fourths of all the novels published that year came from the pens of women. If information supplied by the *Nation* and *Publishers Weekly* in the next year was any indication, the literary domestics were still more than holding their own: the three authors whose works were said to be most in demand at public libraries were Southworth, Hentz, and Holmes, in that order.[53]

From the surprising success of Catharine Maria Sedgwick's *A New England Tale* in the 1820s to midcentury and beyond, the literary domestics had a public, national impact. Even Sedgwick, in the early days, received varying and widespread notice. From a country physician who wrote her saying he had prevailed upon his Unitarian minister to give a copy of *Home* to every couple he married, to news she received about the impact of her writing on a factory girl, to a message relayed from Chief Justice John Marshall praising her works, Sedgwick learned of the fame she was achieving. Similar attention would be gained by those who followed. With the publication of her *Recollections of a Housekeeper*, Caroline Howard Gilman spoke about receiving "thanks and congratulations from every quarter," and she attributed her book's popularity "to the fact that it was the first attempt, in that particular mode, to enter into the recesses of American homes and hearths." The year after Maria Cummins's first novel was published, Mary Virginia Terhune wrote that Cummins's "*The Lamplighter* was in every home, and gossip of the personality of the author was seized upon greedily by press and readers." Terhune herself, Augusta Evans Wilson, and Susan Warner expressed in letters and journals their "earnest thanks," "personal gratitude," and "great pleasure" at receiving letters praising their prose. E.D.E.N. Southworth claimed that she had "always tried to please the multitude and satisfy the cultured; and with what success others may judge." Judging for herself, Southworth proudly boasted, "Among all the people that I have met, and they have been many, and among all the thousands that have written to me, I have never found one who has not read some of my books, and I have never heard of one." Before dismissing Southworth's extravagant rhetoric as absurd, one must remember that her sales have been estimated to be the greatest of any female author in American history.[54]

The railroad parlor car rolling in "Fanny Fern's" memory was not the only manifestation of a public mania associated with the fortunes of the literary domestics. When Southworth was in London from 1859 to 1862, she found the fame of her heroine Capitola from *The Hidden Hand* furthered by the appearance of Capitola hats, suits, and boots. (It would seem that the subtitle of the novel, *Capitola the Madcap*, was most opportune.) Not to be outdone, Americans appropriated Augusta Evans Wilson's *St. Elmo* as the name for objects as disparate as female academies, a cigar, a Southern punch, steamboats, and thirteen towns stretching from New York to California. Perhaps it was appropriate also that the literary domestics were attended with such publicity, considering that the rise of the American publishing industry in the young republic accorded these twelve private domestic women a public stature such as never before had befallen the American woman.[55]

2

Fame Never Was

"Nay, fame never was a woman's Paradise, yet," Susan Warner wrote in her journal on 2 August 1851. Implicit in the ambiguity of Warner's words were several truths. Most immediate was that Warner, a published writer at the age of thirty-two, had been introduced to fame. Her first novel, *The Wide, Wide World*, was already an assured publishing success, although the full magnitude of its commercial success was as yet unrealized. At the very least she was well on her way to establishing herself as a popular writer. More than a month earlier she had completed a draft of *Queechy*, her second novel, which would prove to be another best-seller. Ever since she had been hard at work copying it by hand, putting it in presentable form for her publisher. She had yet to finish her task, although she had done little else for weeks but rewrite and copy, neglecting other "duties." Three days before, she had noted in her journal that for "too long" she had not written in it. She had been too busy with her novel. Expending her last drops of energy in drops of ink, one per word, she had managed to put down, "One gets tired, and how then write journal?" Not that there was little to say. As Warner herself admitted, "I have had a world of things I might have written—praises from every quarter, and multitudinous." Obviously, she was experiencing fame. What was unusual was that Warner was a woman, a woman who had recognition and reputation beyond the home.[1]

But what Warner acknowledged on other occasions was that the praise, apart from that of relatives and friends, had come to "Elizabeth Wetherell," her public literary pseudonym, and not to Susan Warner, the private domestic woman. And that was how she wanted it. "Mere personal fame seems to me a very empty thing to work for," she had written to an editor earlier that year.[2] Herein was a paradox, namely that Susan Warner simultaneously was and was not "Elizabeth Wetherell." It suggested an ambivalent dual identity which pointed to a larger historical paradox involving women and the world beyond the home. The private female voice was being heard in a public setting. It was a phenomenon that would engage all of the literary domestics in a relatively brief span of time. By the end of the 1850s, the decade in which Warner published her first novel, all of them would see print, and all would either be on the verge of bestsellerdom or have already achieved it. Considering what had been and what was the experience of American women, it was an extraordinary development. As Warner's words suggested, it was antithetical to what had been woman's historical experience, that is, that "fame never was." Not surprisingly, although these women achieved fame, as private women they were uncomfortable in the world beyond the home. At best they felt ambivalent, at worst that they simply did not belong there. Their conflicted, often adverse reactions to their status as writers amounted to a recognition that fame, in particular fame in the literary marketplace, was not and was not supposed to be "a woman's Paradise, yet." In a number of ways their words and actions suggested a profound sense of wonder that they had arrived at the gates of paradise, guilt that they had passed through.

Rather than a historical development, the act of these creators of fantasy stepping upon a stage before a huge audience seemed itself a fantasy. The literary domestics responded as if they felt a time change had occurred and misplaced them in another world. What had happened did not seem real. With the publication in 1827 of Catharine Maria Sedgwick's third novel, *Hope Leslie*, Sedgwick found that her fame had grown to such an extent that it could no longer be ignored. It was nearly a quarter of a century prior to the day when Susan Warner wrote in her journal of a "Paradise" that was not woman's. "My fond friends," Sedgwick wrote in her journal of that year, "expect a great accession of fame to me." But, she wondered, "fame—what is it?" She recoiled at the thought that once again she would be exposed to the critical "breath of man," adding, "oh God let me look to thee for thy approbation!" In July of the same year she wrote to her brother Robert to say that she had been receiving "what honestly seems to me extravagant praise of 'Hope Leslie.'" "I trust I shall not be elated by it," she added. There was little danger of that. That same July Sedgwick vacationed in Saratoga Springs, New York, where she was bathed in attention and praise. She was not, however, about to bask contentedly. Rather, as she noted in her journal, having been "introduced to the multitudes at the springs who paid this compliment to what they deemed my literary success," she sought to eschew illusions and keep herself in her accustomed place. She recognized the difficulty of escaping the "intoxication of flattery" in a place like Saratoga Springs, where those who paid obeisance to her "vanity" did so merely "to gratify their own." Nor did she hide from herself the fact that she felt "a pleasure in being able to command a high station" wherever she went, or that she enjoyed giving pleasure to others by acknowledging their "notice and attentions." But it was clear that Sedgwick felt as if she were impersonating someone else.[3]

At the end of 1835, Sedgwick recorded in her journal that she had received the usual "congratulations about my book." She felt that it had "proved more generally acceptable than anything I have before written." The reference was probably to her novel *The Linwoods*, although *Home* and *Tales and Sketches* had also appeared that year. But the specific volume to which she was referring did not actually matter. Certainly it did not matter to Sedgwick. To her there was something odd about the congratulations she had received, as if the plaudits had little relation to her own sense of female identity. Her "*author's* existence," she observed, had "always seemed something accidental." She had written the books; indeed, she had published eight by the time she dubbed her career an accident. Her volumes proved undoubted commercial successes, and Sedgwick had become a public figure. But thirteen years of success notwithstanding, she would reflect in her journal that everything about her authorship still seemed somehow spurious, as if it should not have happened. All of that, she wrote, felt "extraneous and independent of my inner self." She could not dismiss the fact that the gulf between her private domestic life and her public literary career was immense.[4]

In Augusta Evans Wilson's novel *Beulah* (1859), after Beulah Benton is revealed "by accident" to be the pseudonymous "Delta," the author of several articles, her "humble home" is invaded by the "leading *literati*" of the locale. The implication is that the invasion is a dangerous one, threatening corruption of both home and person. In fact, Beulah's female person is already in peril. "Her successful career, thus far, inflamed the ambition which formed so powerful an element in her mental organization," wrote Wilson, "and a longing for Fame took possession of her soul." Beulah is warned by Dr. Guy Hartwell, the man who becomes her husband by the end of the novel, that she is risking personal destruction. " 'Ambition such as yours,' " he says, " 'which aims at literary fame, is the deadliest foe to happiness.' " What he means is that it is unnatural for a woman and threatens *her* happiness, and he says as much: " 'Man may content himself with the applause of the world, and the homage paid to his intellect; but woman's heart has holier idols.' " Having already had his proposal of marriage rejected, Guy has little hope that Beulah will find his words persuasive, but he cannot resist expressing scorn for her and her proposed career. He accuses her of being a " 'proud, ambitious woman, solicitous only to secure eminence as an authoress.' " He has asked for her " 'heart,' " he says to her, but alas, " 'you have none to give.' " The apparently final blow is struck with his parting words: " 'Make yourself a name; bind your aching brow with the chaplet of Fame, and see if ambition can fill your heart.' " Yet although it is with seeming finality that he says, " 'Good bye, dear child,' " the parting is only temporary. Wilson, the popular author, is on Guy's side, and the novel ends with Beulah properly forsaking literary fame and taking her rightful place beside Guy as his wife.[5]

Had the literary domestics been sons rather than daughters of socially and culturally elite families in the early American republic, they would not have experienced this disjunction between the public and the private. Not only would theirs have been the world beyond the home, they would have been trained for and expected to enter the ranks of the professional, commercial, and political leadership of their communities and country. Generally, the literary domestics' forefathers and fathers had done so, as did the men they married, and they assumed that their sons would follow suit. To have been a male in their families' pasts was frequently to have been visible, active, successful, and (in American fashion) titled. It was the female's destiny to marry one of those males and thereby share in the social standing of his family. Of course, if the bride's origins were more distinguished, she could enhance those of her bridegroom's. But once a woman married, a wealthy cultured widow acknowledges in Caroline Lee Hentz's novel *Ernest Linwood* (1856), " 'the husband either exalts, or lowers, a wife to the position he occupies' "; to state the matter differently, " 'She loses her own identity in his.' "[6]

Not all the details of the family lineages of the literary domestics are known. There are gaps and obscurities. More can be said about some than others. But what is known testifies that their origins were not humble. At least eight of these women, whether on the paternal or maternal side, had distinguished male forebears as far back as the country's colonial beginnings. Maria Cummins's father, David, a graduate of Dartmouth, class of 1806, a lawyer and judge of the court of common pleas of Norfolk County, Massachusetts, was a descendant of Isaac Cummins, who settled Ipswich, Massachusetts, and owned a considerable amount of land there before 1638. Cummins's mother, Mehitable Cave, was the granddaughter of Dr. Thomas Kittridge, who came from a family of physicians located in Andover, Massachusetts.[7] Both of Susan Warner's parents traced their ancestry to colonial Ipswich. Her mother, Anna Bartlett, came from a family that was particularly well established, socially and financially. Anna's father maintained summer residences in Providence, Rhode Island, where Anna was born, and in Newport, as well as a permanent home in Jamaica, Long Island, New York. Warner's father, Henry, was a descendant of William Warner, who first settled in Ipswich in 1637. Henry was born in Canaan, New York, where his Warner and Whiting forebears had been prominent citizens for decades. His father, Jason, was a member of the New York state legislature in the first decade of the nineteenth century. After working in publishing and teaching, Henry attended Union College and became a prosperous lawyer in New York City. He published a *Discourse on Legal Science* and *Liberties of America*, on the role of a citizen in a republic. His brother, Warner's uncle Thomas, was chaplain and professor of geography, history, and ethics at the United States Military Academy at West Point.[8]

Caroline Lee Hentz, the daughter of John and Orpah Danforth Whiting, was a descendant of Samuel Whiting, who arrived in Boston in 1636 and became the first minister in Lynn, Massachusetts. Her father was a colonel in the Revolutionary War and owned a bookstore in Lancaster, Massachusetts, until his death in 1810. Three of Hentz's brothers were also military men. One, Henry, who reputedly was an author himself, served in both the War of 1812 and the Mexican War and became a brigadier general.[9] Mary Virginia Terhune traced her ancestry to colonial Virginia as well as Massachusetts. Her mother, Judith Anna Smith, was the daughter of a well-to-do planter, Captain William Sterling Smith, who was one of the original elders of the First Presbyterian Church of Richmond, Virginia, and a lineal descendant of the brother and heir of Captain John Smith of Jamestown. Terhune's father, Samuel Pierce Hawes, born in Dorchester, Massachusetts, included among his ancestors Robert Pierce, who arrived in Massachusetts Bay in 1630 and built the family homestead in Dorchester ten years later. After an apprenticeship with merchants in Boston, Terhune's father moved to Richmond and established himself as a prosperous merchant. A military man, magistrate, and politician, he was a leading Whig in local and state politics.[10]

The maternal side of Catharine Maria Sedgwick's family stemmed from the Williamses and Dwights, who were among the "River Gods" of the eighteenth-century Connecticut River Valley. Sedgwick's grandmother Abigail Williams was the half-sister of Ephraim Williams, who left a bequest for the founding of Williams College, and Abigail's son from her first marriage became the college's third president. Sedgwick's mother, Pamela, was the daughter of Abigail Williams and her second husband, Joseph Dwight, a general in the Massachusetts provincial forces that fought in the French and Indian War. Sedgwick's father, Theodore, was the great-great-grandson of Robert Sedgwick, who came to Massachusetts in 1635, was appointed commissioner general of Jamaica in 1654, and died there from yellow fever in 1656. Theodore, who began his studies at Yale in 1761, was expelled in his last year for " 'boyish gaieties,' " although he did receive his degree in 1765. He then prepared for the ministry before turning to the law and doing an apprenticeship with his second cousin Mark Hopkins of Great Barrington, Massachusetts, a prominent lawyer and the grandfather of yet another president of Williams. After serving in both houses of the Massachusetts General Court, Theodore became a congressman and Speaker of the U.S. House of Representatives, a United States senator, a justice of the Supreme Judicial Court of Massachusetts, and a prominent figure in the Federalist party. Sedgwick's four brothers became distinguished lawyers and political writers.[11]

The Beechers emigrated with John Davenport, a London clergyman, to New Haven, Connecticut, in 1638. Harriet Beecher Stowe's father, Lyman Beecher, the son of a prosperous blacksmith, prepared for the ministry at Yale and became a leading evangelical in antebellum America. Roxana

Foote, Stowe's mother, came from a family that had enjoyed prominence for generations. The Footes had come from Massachusetts to Connecticut with Thomas Hooker's congregation in 1636. Roxana's grandfather, General Andrew Ward, served under Washington during the Revolutionary War, and her father, Eli Foote, was a wealthy lawyer and merchant. All of Stowe's seven brothers became clergymen, including the celebrated minister and lecturer Henry Ward Beecher.[12]

Little is known of the ancestors of Sara Parton's mother, Hannah Parker, but the lineage of her father, Nathaniel Willis, can be traced. Parton's paternal line in this country extended back to George Willis, who was born in England in 1602 and came to the Massachusetts Bay Colony in 1630. He was admitted to the Freeman's Oath in 1638 and elected deputy to the General Court. Parton's grandfather, also named Nathaniel Willis, was part-owner and editor of the militant *Independent Chronicle* of Boston during the Revolutionary era and served in the war under General John Sullivan. In 1784 he left Massachusetts to establish newspapers in the Virginia towns of Winchester, Shepardstown, and Martinsburg, as well as in Chillicothe, Ohio. Parton's father followed a similar path. In Portland, Maine, he published the *Eastern Argus*, begun in 1803 "in support of the measures of Mr. Jefferson's administration." In Boston "Deacon" Willis, as he was called, established the *Recorder*, later the *Boston Recorder*, which he claimed was the first religious newspaper in the world. Finally, he also founded and edited a juvenile paper, the *Youth's Companion*, in Boston. His sons, Parton's brothers, continued and expanded upon the family's journalistic tradition. The oldest, yet another Nathaniel Willis, became one of the leading American poets and editors of his time, wrote drama, fiction and criticism, founded the literary *American Monthly Magazine*, was a correspondent and editor of the *New York Mirror*, and as an outgrowth of the *Mirror* cofounded the *Home Journal*, a weekly magazine that eventually became *Town and Country*. Parton's younger brother, Richard Storrs Willis, a poet and composer, was editor of the *Musical World and Times* and author of *Our Church Music*.[13]

E.D.E.N. Southworth's ancestors were part of Leonard Calvert's group that first settled Maryland at St. Mary's in 1632. They were landed proprietors and held important posts for generations in the colonial government. All that is known of Southworth's father, Captain Charles Lecompte Nevitte, is that he was of French descent, hailed from Alexandria, Virginia, and was an importer and owner of a fleet of ships. Shortly after he died from a wound suffered in the War of 1812, Southworth's mother married Joshua L. Henshaw of Boston, who had come to Washington to serve as secretary to Daniel Webster.[14] The maternal was the obscure half of Maria McIntosh's ancestry. Her mother, Mary Moore Maxwell, was a widow when she became the fifth wife of Lachlan McIntosh, who had played a central role in the settlement of Georgia during the 1730s. Lachlan himself became a member of Georgia's colonial elite. A prominent planter who had amassed more than fourteen thousand acres by the 1770s, he first served as a brigadier general responsible for Georgia's troops during the Revolution and then was appointed commander of the Western Department by Washington. A brother of Maria's, James M. McIntosh, became a captain in the Navy, while her nephew, John Elliot Ward, was an envoy extraordinary and minister plenipotentiary to China.[15]

There are a number of blank pages in the family histories of Caroline Howard Gilman and Mary Jane Holmes. Gilman's father, Samuel Howard, was a shipwright of unknown origins, but he was prosperous and could claim distinction, or at least notoriety, from his participation in the Boston Tea Party. Gilman's mother, Anna Lillie, brought him the more respectable type of status. She was descended from the Breck family, branches of which were prominent in Boston and Philadelphia during the colonial and Revolutionary eras. Her father, Theophilos Lillie, was a Massachusetts merchant, a Loyalist importer of tea who could not have been particularly pleased with his son-in-law's exploits in Boston's harbor.[16] As for Holmes, aside from her parent's names, Preston and Fanny Olds Hawes, of Brookline, Massachusetts, almost nothing is known of her family except that their ancestors were supposedly established in New England at an early date. But Holmes's uncle, Joel Hawes, was a well-known New England evangelical and minister of the First Congregational Church in Hartford. Hawes's published sermons also made him a fairly popular writer in the 1840s. That he shared with his niece the desire to shape character is obvious from titles such as "Lectures to Young Men" and "Looking Glass for Ladies; or, The Formation and Excellence of Female Character."[17] Not much is known about Augusta Evans Wilson's family, either. Her father, Matthew Ryan Evans, left his father's plantation in South Carolina and prospered for a period as a merchant in Columbus, Georgia. He was supposedly a distant relative of the influential branches of the Crenshaw and Calhoun families of South Carolina. Wilson's mother, Sarah Howard, was the descendant of Nehemiah Howard, a wealthy planter in colonial South Carolina. Wilson's maternal grandfather, John Howard, was also an affluent planter from Georgia, and a major during the Revolution.[18]

Four of these daughters—Cummins, McIntosh, Sedgwick, and Warner—remained unmarried. That, of course, was an anomalous and difficult situation for a nineteenth-century woman, who above all else was expected to become a wife and mother. Those who deviated were statistical oddities during a century in which nine out of ten women married. Their deviance can be measured in social as well as numerical terms. The spinster was a forlorn, alternately ignored and disparaged figure in a society that was at a loss as to how to deal with her except to tuck her away in the home of her parents or siblings. Cummins died at the relatively young age of thirty-nine. Sedgwick tried to cope with her spinsterhood through surrogate relationships with brothers and their children, an experience in which she gained much and suffered much. The financial losses of their families may have diminished the marital eligibility of McIntosh and Warner. Still, McIntosh was thirty-four when her inheritance was lost in the Panic of 1837. Warner, however, was only sixteen when the Panic dealt her wealthy father irreversible losses, and there is evidence to suggest that her marital prospects were adversely affected.

Not surprisingly, the eight who did marry looked to the fields of religion, education, science and letters, and commerce and law for their spouses. The majority chose husbands whose education included college, during years in which less than 1 percent of the population attended institutions of higher learning.[19] These, then, were males from whom leadership and distinction were expected. Seven of the eight married men who met these expectations and achieved some renown in their vocations. Little is known of South-worth's husband of two years, Frederick Hamilton Southworth, an obscure inventor from Utica, New York. Three married ministers, two of whom distinguished themselves in other professions as well.

Terhune, who counted twenty male relatives in the ministry, took another for her husband with her marriage to Edward Payson Terhune, a graduate of Rutgers, a Presbyterian minister from New Jersey, and himself the son of a clergyman. After a first pastorate at Charlotte Court-House, Virginia, Terhune held positions in Newark, New Jersey; Springfield, Massachusetts; and Brooklyn, as well as abroad, including the appointment to the chaplaincy of the American Chapel in Rome. Stowe chose a minister as well. Her husband, Calvin Stowe, had been valedictorian of his class at Bowdoin College before completing his studies at Andover Theological Seminary. Primarily an educator and biblical scholar, Stowe held professorships of Greek at Dartmouth, biblical literature at Lane Theological Seminary, and religion at both of his alma maters. He was also appointed commissioner for investigating European public schools, and his *Report on Elementary Instruction in Europe,* published in 1838, had a significant influence on America pedagogy. Gilman's husband, Samuel Gilman, graduated from Harvard College and then chose Andover's theological rival, Harvard Divinity School, for further study. His first position was his last. Ordained as the minister of the newly established Archdale Street Church in Charleston, South Carolina, he served what was the first Unitarian church in the South until his death. Samuel Gilman was an author and poet as well. His most famous effort in the latter regard was the ode "Fair Harvard," written for exercises celebrating the 200th anniversary of the founding of the college. His essays appeared in the *North American Review*, the *Christian Examiner*, and the *Southern Quarterly Review*.

Hentz married a man who also displayed varied talents. Born in Versailles, France, Nicholas Marcellus Hentz emigrated with his family after his father, a lawyer and politician, was forced to flee France by the fall of

Napoleon. Hentz studied medicine in France and at Harvard, was a linguist, and pioneered the study of American entomology; in particular, he was a celebrated arachnologist, or spider specialist. His *Spiders of the United States* was considered the authoritative source on the subject until the end of the nineteenth century. In addition, he published in the *Journal of the Boston Society of Natural History, Silliman's Journal,* and the *Journal of the Philadelphia Academy of Arts and Sciences.* His efforts in fiction resulted in a historical novel with the unlikely title of *Tadeuskund, the Last King of the Lenape.* Hentz taught at the Round Hill School for boys in Northampton, Massachusetts, with the historian George Bancroft, and was Professor of Modern Languages and Belles Lettres at the University of North Carolina.

Sara Parton married three times. Her first husband was Charles H. Eldredge, an officer of the Merchants' Bank of Boston and the son of Dr. Hezekiah Eldredge, a former president of the Massachusetts Medical Society. Eldredge died nine years after their marriage. Her second marriage to Samuel P. Farrington, a Boston merchant, ended in divorce after three years. Her third husband, to whom she remained married until her death, was James Parton, a leading American biographer and journalist. Born in Canterbury, England, Parton began his career in journalism in the United States as a writer and editor for the *Home Journal,* which as mentioned had been established by Sara's brother. He also contributed essays on contemporary political, social, and economic topics to a wide variety of journals, including Robert Bonner's *New York Ledger,* the *North American Review,* and the *Atlantic Monthly.* Among his biographies were studies of Horace Greeley, Benjamin Franklin, and Voltaire.

The last two women chose husbands who became prominent in their communities. Mary Jane Holmes's husband, Daniel Holmes, was a Yale graduate of the class of 1848 and received an M.A. from the University of Rochester in 1853. He was first a teacher and then became the pioneer lawyer in Brockport, New York, where he served in a variety of village and county offices, including justice of the peace and justice of sessions. He was as well the secretary and treasurer of the New York State Normal School organized there in 1867. Finally, he was vestryman and senior warden of St. Luke's Episcopal Church. Augusta Evans Wilson was the oldest to marry, and when she did at age thirty-two she chose a husband almost thirty years her senior. Colonel Lorenzo M. Wilson of Mobile, Alabama, whose title was apparently honorary, was a prosperous financier and at the time of their marriage an officer and director of Mobile's leading bank, director of the Mobile and Montgomery Railroad, and principal stockholder in the city's streetcar line.

The literary domestics could find in their family histories widespread evidence of "distinguished" men. For the most part they would maintain that tradition of distinction by marrying males of accomplishment. But the absence of "distinguished" women, in fact the invisibility of females in their ancestry, contributed to and heightened their insecurity and sense of illegitimacy as public writers. Searching for their own identity, they sought to rescue their female forebears from their silent past and prove their being. However, if the literary domestics looked too far back they found simply names, if they found anything at all, and knew only that these were the names of wives and mothers. Sensing that as writers, as intellectual figures they were anomalies in their society, the literary domestics sought to reassure themselves of their own legitimacy by looking to their families' histories if not for literary predecessors, at least for female intellectual mentors. Usually they could look no farther back than to their mothers, although the more fortunate could glimpse their grandmothers or at least fantasy about them. The need to emphasize the intellectuality of their female forerunners was revealing in its own right. Indeed, the effort to demonstrate that, if there had been no female writers in their families before them, there at least had been wives and mothers involved in the life of the mind underlined their own insecurity. It pointed as well to recognition of the fact that these foremothers had been anomalies before them. In short, for the literary domestics to look to the sources of their beings was in circular fashion to find themselves.

Caroline Lee Hentz's last novel, *Ernest Linwood*, published the year of her death in 1856, stands almost as a parable of the literary domestics' attempts to know themselves by looking to those who went before. There is fantasy; there are gaps and awkward posturings, inconsistencies and insecurities; and there is no way to demonstrate with certainty that Hentz's portrayal of the daughter-mother relationship in the novel is autobiographical. Nothing is known of Hentz's mother but a name. Nor is it known how much Hentz herself, born in 1800, remembered about her mother, Orpah Danforth Whiting. What is known is that Hentz's father died when she was ten, and when *Ernest Linwood* opens, the mother and her twelve-year-old daughter live alone. The father is mysteriously absent, perhaps dead. It can also be shown that in the fictional daughter's marital relationship, the major focus of the novel, Hentz drew heavily upon the psychological and emotional relationship she had with her own husband.[20] There are additional autobiographical overtones in the fact that the fictional daughter, Gabriella Lynn, both the heroine and the first-person narrator of the novel, has aspirations to write and also to teach school. Hentz did both. An underlying theme of the novel concerns Gabriella's need to know more of herself and what her role as a woman can and should be, reflected in her search for answers to the mysteries of the past of her mother, Rosalie Lynn. Integral to Gabriella's search is her struggle to deal with her ambivalent, insecure sense of herself as an intellectual being. But in that respect the tale of her mother's past is not long, clear, or reassuring. In fact, Hentz's treatment of the subject, awkward and groping in both form and content, reflects her sense that she had little of a decided or positive nature to say.

Hentz opens the novel with the narrator Gabriella's words: "With an incident of my childhood I will commence the record of my life. It stands out in bold prominence, rugged and bleak, through the haze of memory." The incident involves the reading of her poetry for the first time, at age twelve, to her classmates and teacher at school. Scorned and ridiculed for her efforts, Gabriella returns home and declares to her mother, Rosalie, "'I will never write any more...I will never more expose myself to ridicule and contempt.'" Rosalie's response apparently reflects her own experience as a female and stands as both an explanation of the incident and a warning that Gabriella can expect the same in the future. Her words seem to prophesy the future of the adult woman as measured by what her own life has become. Had I known, Gabriella's mother tells her, that you intended to read your poetry to an audience outside your home, to someone other than your mother, "'I would have warned you of the consequences. The child who attempts to soar above its companions is sure to be dragged down by the hand of envy. Your teacher saw in your effusion an unpardonable effort to rise above himself—to diverge from the beaten track. You may have indulged too much in the dreams of imagination. You may have neglected your duties as a pupil.'" It is easy to see in the female pupil who diverges from the beaten track, who neglects duties, the adult woman who deviates from her prescribed role as wife and mother. The girl who inadvertently challenges her male teacher can also be equated with the woman writer whose success angers and threatens her male counterparts. The reference to indulgence in "the dreams of imagination" suggests another bit of indulgence on the part of Hentz the author, as she goes beyond the parameters of the novel and invites the reader to regard the commentary as self-commentary on Hentz's status as a female writer in her society. At this moment in the novel daughter and mother appear likely personae of Hentz.[21]

What little encouragement Rosalie has to offer Gabriella, if encouragement it is, is that she continue writing, if only "'for my gratification and your own.'" But what about Rosalie's cynicism? One can easily guess the source, but Hentz's introduction of the subject at the outset leads one to expect further explanation and elaboration. Nevertheless, for most of the nearly five-hundred-page novel Hentz leaves the subject alone—dangling. A few pages later, Gabriella does relate another cynical outburst on the part of Rosalie. "Suppressing a deep sigh," the mother encourages the daughter to continue her education so that she can achieve a modicum of status as a teacher and support herself: "'It is the most honorable path to independence

a friendless young girl can choose,'" declares Rosalie and, she adds
pointedly, "'almost the only one.'" Associated with the nurture of children,
teaching gained legitimacy in the nineteenth century as a pursuit for women.
But the very fact that it was "almost the only" possibility highlights the
significance of the dictum that woman's place was actually in the home.
Aside from these comments, the remainder of the novel leaves the subject
aside for the most part. Inadvertently, Hentz testifies to her inability to say
more (and to say anything positive) about woman as intellectual in a society
that restricts her to the home and demeans her as a thinking being, if it
regards her in that light at all. By failing to elaborate on the subject after
introducing it, Hentz inadvertently draws attention to it.[22]

What little else of substance that is offered on the subject comes
approximately a third of the way through the novel when Gabriella reads a
manuscript that Rosalie, now dead, has left for her. The ironies, allusions,
and parallels, twisted tightly together like the strands of a rope, are almost
too numerous to unravel. Author Hentz, again perhaps with autobiographical
allusions, explores the theme of a daughter with literary aspirations seeking
self-knowledge and encouragement by exploring her mother's secret past; the
heretofore nearly invisible, silent past of the dead mother is partially revealed
by means of a secret manuscript written by the mother herself; and just as
author Hentz—by way of fictional mother to fictional daughter to herself—
becomes a writer thrice removed, so we become readers twice removed as
Gabriella reads the manuscript within the manuscript.

Supposedly the means by which we and Gabriella are provided with
answers to questions concerning Rosalie's past, the manuscript tells us first
that she knows little of her own mother because she died giving birth to
Rosalie. There is apparently no limit or end to the tricks the past plays upon
women. All Rosalie does know is that her mother "'was one of those gentle,
dove-like, pensive beings, who nestled in her husband's heart, and knew no
world beyond.'" It need hardly be added that neither did the world know her.
More important, the image that Hentz inadvertently projects is that of a
thinking woman engulfed by her wifely status, to wit, the "pensive being who
nestled in her husband's heart." Naturally, the father is a distinguished
young captain in the military, a man described as "'always engrossed with
the duties of a profession which he passionately loved.'" He pays little
attention to his daughter, but Rosalie stands in awe of him, particularly when
he appears on military parade looking like "'one of the demigods of the
ancient world.'" The images of male and female are familiar, and the
contrast between them, in experience and self-identity, could not be more
stark.[23]

From this stage onward, the tale within a tale enlightens us regarding the
direction Rosalie's life took, but not before, with little apparent relevance to
that direction, we and Gabriella are informed by Rosalie that she herself was
strikingly intelligent, curious, and involved in the expansion of her mind. It is

the only invitation offered in the novel to look into Rosalie's intellectual past; indeed, it is the only indication that she had such a past. She possessed, she says, the "'avidity of a hungry and unoccupied mind.'" Left alone with no one to "'direct my tastes,'" she developed "'a remarkable love of reading.'" What she read was fiction or, as she describes it, "'some wild, impassioned romance.'" Thus, completing the tripartite symmetry of writer to reader, yet another tale is unfolded to yet another reader, suggesting that the further one delves into the history of women the more fiction one encounters. So intense were her reading habits, Rosalie writes, that she came to be known as "'the little bookworm,'" the "'prodigy'" even. But at the same time, with no sense of irony on Hentz's part, we are told that she also was called the "*dream-girl*" (italics Hentz's), and we immediately recall the twelve-year-old Gabriella engaged in her "dreams of indulgence."[24]

Even if Hentz does not intend that it should be so, we are led invariably to the conclusion that Rosalie's intellectual awakening as a child was nothing more than a disconnected interlude in her life, an interlude that had no bearing on her later adult experience, at least no positive bearing. The point is reemphasized—again, with no ironic commentary intended—when Rosalie adds, "'But while my imagination was preternaturally developed, my heart was slumbering, and my soul unconscious of life's great aim.'" Implicit here is the assumption that she is preoccupied intellectually only because her heart is not yet preoccupied with the love of man. The young female has yet to recognize that woman's "great aim"—a phrase that will be repeated several times in relation to Gabriella—is to love the male, to marry him, and to bear and nurture his children. A life of the mind is irrelevant or superfluous in that scenario, at worst impossible, at best possible only with determined effort. But Hentz is merely foreshadowing Rosalie's romantic involvement and marriage, and she continues her chronology apace by abruptly leaving the subject of Rosalie's precociousness and curiosity. In perfunctory fashion, Rosalie concludes, "'Thus unguarded by precept, unguided by example, I was sent from home to a boarding-school, where I acquired the usual education and accomplishments obtained at fashionable female seminaries.'" With unintended irony compounded, Hentz brings Rosalie's education to an end in more ways than one. As the daughter of a distinguished father, she receives the typical training at a fashionable school, but the implication is that the education amounts to little and Hentz will treat the subject no further. Only of Rosalie's married life will Hentz say more, just as Gabriella's literary aspirations are left aside for the melodrama of her married life.[25]

In her novel *Beulah*, Augusta Evans Wilson equated the search for examples of "Female Heroism" with an attempt to find "among the dusky annals of the past . . . instances of confirmation . . . that female intellect was capable of the most exalted attainments, and that the elements of her character would enable woman to cope successfully with difficulties of every class." Insecure as literary figures and plagued by the guilty fear that they might indeed be intruders, unlawful interlopers in what was properly a male intellectual realm, the literary domestics looked to the past for some confirmation of female intellectual attainment. Sara Parton claimed a literary inheritance from her mother, Hannah Parker Willis, declaring that "'all the capability for writing which I possess—be it little or much—came from her.'" Parton's father, a journalist and editor, would have been the obvious source of influence, so it is particularly striking that it was her mother to whom homage was paid. Still, Hannah Willis could provide Sara the example that her husband could offer only his sons, who also became writers. Defensively, as if to buttress the validity of her own literary activities, Parton asserted that her mother "'had she lived at this day, would have been a writer worthy of mention.'"[26]

Writing to Kate Sanborn in 1883, Mary Virginia Terhune acknowledged her "'genuine pleasure in tracing what authorly gifts I have back to my maternal grandmother, Mrs. Judith Smith of Olney, Virginia, a woman of rare intellectual and personal gifts.'" Why a grandmother rather than a mother? Simply because Terhune's mother was to her a pale reality beside the more vivid and compelling image of a grandmother whose character could be imagined from documents left in Terhune's possession. For Terhune her mother was apparently an almost invisible presence, despite the fact that she lived until Terhune was well into her forties. When she does appear in Terhune's recollections, the impression left is negative. For example, she is described as the "weaker-willed wife" unable to adapt to a temporary decline in the family's fortunes.[27]

Terhune was more fortunate than most in her search for a female model. Papers and memorabilia did exist, and for her quest she had only to go back to the next generation. The reality of the mother could be set aside for a *storied* grandmother. Terhune had never personally known her revered grandmother, this Judith Smith of the eighteenth century, as she had died before Terhune's birth. But, she eagerly informed Kate Sanborn, she had books from her grandmother's library and many of the letters, both of which testified to Judith Smith's intellectual stature, and if there was any doubt about Terhune's likeness to her grandmother, well, she claimed, "'my very hand writing and voice are said to resemble hers.'" Published more than a quarter century after the letter to Sanborn, Terhune's autobiography revealed again how important the cherished image of her grandmother had been to her. Terhune insisted that Judith Smith had been a woman "remarkable in her day for intellectual vivacity," the possessor of "musical skill and literary tastes." Proof of that could be seen in those whom she chose for companionship: "Her chief associates of the other sex were men of profound learning, distinguished for services done to Church and State." Anxious to support her conviction with more concrete evidence, Terhune pointed proudly to a collection of 142 letters showing that her grandmother's chief correspondent had been the Reverend Drury Lacy, D.D., who was a professor at Hampden Sydney College at the time and a man "destined to become the progenitor of a long line of divines and scholars."[28]

Recognizing that she had "dwelt at length" in her autobiography upon her grandmother, Terhune tendered an explanation. It was simply "because of my solemn conviction that I inherited what humble talent is mine from her." But Terhune's need obviously gave birth to and shaped her conviction. Her "fancy" (as she also called her "conviction") that she had inherited her grandmother's intelligence and ability possessed for her, she said, "a sweet and weird charm." It enabled her daily to "renew my courage," and, she added, it made her "a better woman." She was willing to admit that "my fantasy may be a figment of the imagination." But she declared, "I cherish it with a tenacity that tells me it is more." Terhune's "tenacity" was a measure of her need to create the fantasy.[29]

The literary domestics' emphasis upon the intellectual capacity of the women in their families' past reflected their need to link themselves to models who had gone before and to acquire reassurance in the present. Inadvertently, it suggested as well recognition that women were not commonly regarded in those terms in either the past or the present. Woman's role as wife and mother, past and present, was assumed, and given their knowledge of woman's past and their own sense of themselves as private beings primarily committed to woman's role within the home, the literary domestics could be expected to describe their foremothers in terms of woman's traditional qualities and role. But by the same token, their insecurity as intellectual figures led them to emphasize the mental capacities and characteristics of their foremothers. Just as Hentz's fictional mother, Rosalie, is said to be more than simply intelligent or bright, in fact a "prodigy," so Terhune wrote about her grandmother as a woman of "rare" gifts. At the very least, such characterizations attached the *preternatural* to the natural. When Augusta Evans Wilson became a commercially successful novelist, she lauded her mother, Sarah Skrine Howard. To one biographical chronicler, Mary Forrest, she wrote that her mother was "'in every sense, my Alma Mater, the one to whom I owe everything, and whom I reverence more than all else on earth.'" Wilson imparted to another chronicler the understanding that she regarded her mother as a woman both of "great moral and intellectual worth."[30]

But the literary domestics' stress on the intellectual more than the moral suggested an attempt to alter their society's regard of the past and rebut prejudices of the present. Terhune mentioned her grandmother's exemplary "moral graces" but dwelt upon her "intellectual vivacity." Inadvertently, however, that was to reinforce the notion that intellectual qualities in a woman were unusual, while moral qualities were expected. Also implicit was that society did not regard the role of wife and mother as one requiring abilities of the mind. Moreover, awareness of what Terhune in *Eve's*

Daughters labeled the "influence of traditions" suggested that if women, particularly married women, enjoyed any intellectual life they did so in the face of what Wilson in *Beulah* called "the trials which hedge woman's path." One such trial might result from marrying a man of inferior intelligence. Terhune suggested as much when she was unable to resist implying that her grandmother had had such an experience in her marriage to a gentlemanly planter. Before her marriage, Terhune's grandmother allegedly had enjoyed the intellectual companionship of a number of men, and while she had maintained contact with some of them after marriage, the contacts were fewer, with the result that her grandmother, said Terhune, "must, sometimes, have missed her erudite admirers, and wished in her heart that the worthy planter were, intellectually, more in tune with herself." Obviously, too, the daily demands of domesticity could stand in the way. Supporting the claim that her mother would have been a writer had she lived in a different age, Sara Parton said of her mother's experiences: "'In those days women had nine children—her number, and stifled their souls under baskets of stockings to mend and aprons to make.'" Whatever the trials, the most basic, underlying all the rest, was the fact that woman, unlike man, was generally restricted, in mind and body, to the home.[31]

The literary domestics, then, offered tributes to the intelligence of their female forerunners that inadvertently spoke to a female life of the mind absorbed by or forcibly attached like an appendage to the female life of the home. A graphic and detailed example is provided by the correspondence of Harriet Beecher Stowe's mother, Roxana Foote Beecher, in conjunction with the *Autobiography, Correspondence, Etc., of Lyman Beecher, D.D.*. The latter might more accurately be called the "Beecher biographies," for it actually constitutes a joint effort on the part of numerous individuals in the Beecher-Foote clan, representing both the paternal and maternal sides of Harriet Beecher Stowe's family. Certain parts of the volumes were written separately; others apparently were composed when the family gathered to record their recollections together; and still others stemmed from family letters. Father Lyman's life is certainly addressed, but included as well are numerous references, anecdotes, and miniportrayals that tell inter alia much about Stowe's female intellectual mentors. From grandmothers to aunts to her mother, it is abundantly clear that Stowe indeed had intellectual exemplars of her own sex.

Stowe had her own personal experiences to reflect upon, but what she could not and did not recall herself she could and did learn from others. As she wrote in regard to her mother, "'During all my childhood, I was constantly hearing her spoken of, and, from one friend or another, some incident or anecdote of her life was constantly being impressed on me.'" The same could have been said regarding her grandmothers. As a matter of fact, Stowe could have learned much merely by reading the "Beecher biographies," which she herself helped prepare. For example, she wrote about her grandmother Foote: "'Her mind was active and clear; her literary taste just, her reading extensive.'" More telling, however, was Stowe's portrait of the elderly but lively woman: "'My image of her in later years is of one always seated at a great table covered with books, among which nestled her work-basket.'" Needless to say, the workbasket beneath the books contained the grandmother's sewing and knitting materials.[32]

Stowe erred in the biographies with her statement that she was between three and four years old when her mother died. Actually she was five when Roxana died of consumption in 1816. Whatever her age, Stowe was so young that "'my personal recollections of her [were] therefore but few.'" Significantly, those few recollections involved moments of maternal care, devotion, and wisdom, and one instance "'of her reading to the children one evening aloud Miss Edgeworth's "Frank," which had just come out, I believe, and was exciting a good deal of attention among the educational circles of Litchfield.' " Here Stowe's memory failed her once more, because Maria Edgeworth's novel *Frank* was published in England in 1822, six years after Roxana's death. But again, the error has little significance. It is likely that Roxana read an earlier novel of Edgeworth's to Stowe and the other Beecher children. Either that, or memory for Stowe became indistinguishable from tales heard. Certainly the ingredients of the event were familiar in the life of Roxana, in her education as a daughter, in the education of her children, and in her continuing efforts at self-education as a mother amidst her circle of domestic life and duties.[33]

Catharine Beecher, Stowe's older sister, recalled a number of tales heard about their mother. Roxana had grown to maturity in the eighteenth century. Hers was a childhood and youth that combined the duties of domesticity with achievements in learning. In particular, Catharine told of a French gentleman who became an intimate friend of the Footes and took special interest in the young daughter, Roxana: "'with his aid she learned to write and speak French fluently. He loaned her the best French authors, and she studied as she spun flax, tying the books to her distaff.'" Just as revealing were the letters written by Roxana herself when she was still the unmarried daughter. In one written following the death of her father, Eli Foote, after mother and children had gone to live in Nutplains, Connecticut, with her maternal grandfather, General Andrew Ward, Roxana related that "'I generally rise with the sun, and, after breakfast, take my wheel which is my daily companion, and the evening is generally devoted to reading, writing, and knitting.'"[34]

At still another family round table that included Stowe, more details culled for the Beecher biographies—actually in this instance the Roxana Foote Beecher biography—filled out a familiar picture. Lyman said that when he first visited the Ward's home in Nutplains, the girls were all out at the spinning mill. "From the homage of all about her, I soon perceived that Roxana was of uncommon ability." "'And there,'" Stowe interjected, repeating what she had been told, "'those girls used to spin, read novels, talk about beaux, and have merry times together.'" This was likely, Lyman responded, adding, "All the new works that were published at that day were brought out to Nutplains, read, and discussed in the old spinning-mill. When Miss Burney's Evelina appeared, Sally Hill rode out on horseback to bring it to Roxana. A great treat they had of it." It was a pattern that had been established in the eighteenth century and, with slight alterations, would continue when Roxana married four months before the nineteenth century commenced. The young, unmarried Roxana tying books to her distaff, reading novels in the spinning mill—both are appropriate metaphors. Both symbolize the nurture of the girl and forecast the life of the married woman.[35]

In 1798 Roxana Foote responded to Lyman Beecher's proposal of marriage. Lyman had no doubts and was eager for the union. But Roxana had other thoughts. "Are there no jarring differences that would interrupt our felicity were we united?" she asked. Something whispered to her, she said, " 'Beware Roxana that you deceive yourself,'" that she make the mistake of thinking that she was under the "'guidance of judgment solely,'" and above all, "'keep fancy aloof.'" At the moment, she admitted, regarding "this state of uncertainty I see no way of extricating myself from it but one." Nevertheless, she added, "there is a kind of certainty that may be more disagreeable than uncertainty." A year later Roxana was no longer uncertain. Lyman had already left for his first pastorate in East Hampton, on New York's Long Island, and Roxana sent a letter after him. "You know Beecher," she wrote, "that your happiness is mine," and if the two could be separated, she said, "yours is the first and dearest object of my wishes." A half century later, long after Roxana's death, Lyman wrote on the outside of that very letter the following words: "Read again December 1854—*Oh what a chasm of time* and what scenes between!!!" Whatever his thoughts may have been, Lyman's words recalled in ironic fashion those of Roxana's before their betrothal. The remainder of her life as a married woman was bounded by a relatively few years and divided from Lyman by a chasm of circumstances. Roxana Foote married Lyman Beecher in September 1799 and died in the same month seventeen years later. The seventeen years were filled with the demands of domesticity, which included most prominently the birth of nine children and the care of the eight who survived infancy. (As Sara Parton—born in the same year, 1811, as Harriet Beecher Stowe—said, that was the number in those days.) The first child was born in 1800, a year after marriage; the last in 1815, a year before Roxana's death.[36]

If any doubts remained in Roxana's mind, she learned not long after marriage what the nature and boundaries of her life would be. Not much more than a year after her wedding Roxana wrote a letter to her sister, Harriet, that was a plea for contact. Isolation, intellectual at least, had already set in. Roxana had not heard a word from home, and it was difficult to get a word out. Meanwhile, "the principal business I have done is to prepare three meals in a day." And what of Lyman? He was not at home. He had wasted no time beginning a career that would eventually bring him national prominence as one of the leading evangelicals of his generation. Then as later, he was off preaching and lecturing. While Roxana set and cleared tables, her husband, whom she characterized as "everybody's man," "preached seven or eight times in a week" every week of the winter. In her letter Roxana provided an itinerary of Lyman's travels, followed by the statement "I have not in the least exaggerated, and you may therefore suppose he has not had much leisure to attend to other business."[37]

Roxana did not enjoy much leisure either, but her duties were different. She put the house in order, cooked, spun material for stockings and knit them, and mended clothes. And there was contact with people, albeit interaction of a particular type. She visited members of Lyman's congregation, and there was a constant stream of visitors connected with the business of the parish, visitors who stayed until late in the evening so that, she wrote Harriet, "I find it difficult to seize a moment to write." This, apparently, was one of those moments. A month later she again spoke of her isolation to Harriet and of her effort to end it, to wit, with the very letter she was writing. She had heard of an opportunity to send a letter and had "therefore seated myself with my breakfast table half cleared and Catharine in my lap who is quite ill since yesterday." It might not be so impossible a situation, she said, if she "had a mother or a sister" that she could visit without having to "prepare for an India voyage"—and, she hinted, "I should be glad if I could hear from my friends." At the end of the next year's winter she wrote Harriet to see if it would be possible for their sister, Mary Hubbard, to spend that summer with her. Meanwhile, she was finding the antics of her two children, Catharine and William, "amusing," she said. "Most people I suppose would soon become tired" of them but, she told Harriet, they "contribute to enliven many a gloomy moment."[38]

Despite the consuming demands of her domestic duties and her cultural deprivation and isolation, Roxana did struggle to nourish some semblance of a life of the mind. But it was not easy, and it was done in an intellectual vacuum. Mary Hubbard, who lived with the Beechers for most of their time in East Hampton, described the situation six years after Lyman and Roxana had settled on Long Island. Her letter to Lyman's sister, Esther Beecher, noted, "'We get no paper, and know no more of the affairs of the world than if we were not in it. Here we are so still, so quiet, so dull, so inactive, that we have forgotten but that the world goes on the same way.'" But the threat was there: "'A kind of torpor and apathy seems to prevail over the face of things.'"[39]

The same year that Mary penned her mournful epistle, the increasing number of children in the household led directly to Roxana's best and practically only opportunity to give her intellectual endeavors a recognizable name and structure, namely, becoming a schoolteacher. Lyman's income was not sufficient to meet the needs of a family that now included four children. Husband and wife, therefore, advertised for "scholars," that is, students, and established "a select school." Naturally they enrolled their own sons and daughters. Lyman participated in directing the school, but Roxana apparently was the primary teacher. As the educated daughter of a socially prominent family, she had the training to be able to offer courses in "the higher English branches" and French, as well as in drawing, painting, and embroidery. Chemistry, "a new science," must have been offered, too, as Catharine recalled her mother and her Aunt Mary studying Lavoisier's *Chemistry* together, attempting a number of experiments, "'sometimes with the most ludicrous results.'" The school prospered and, for the most part, was profitable. It provided a new occupation for Roxana, even if it did cease with the family's removal to Litchfield, Connecticut, a few years later. But her new role as teacher did not mean that Roxana could abandon her primary obligation. As Mary wrote, "'This, with the care of the family, takes all her time.'" It was probably the only period in her married life that Roxana's psychological tug-of-war gave any semblance of a contest.[40]

Motivated by the promise of a larger salary for Lyman and less isolation for both of them, the move to Litchfield was made in 1810. Lyman went to Litchfield first in order to negotiate the terms of his new pastorate, necessitating a lengthy absence from East Hampton. Roxana wrote him to say, "I assure you I feel myself to be very lonesome and more than ever sensible that it is not 'good to be alone.'" That was probably a way of saying that she was also sensible that it was good that they were moving to Litchfield. For the time and for its size, Litchfield was a place bustling with cultural, political, and religious activity. An atypically large proportion of its inhabitants were prominent politicians, wealthy lawyers, and highly success-ful merchants. It had its literary societies, its Federalist-Democrat squab-bles, and its Congregational-Episcopal controversies of varying shades. And it boasted as well Judge Reeve's Litchfield Law School, the nation's first and already famous law school, and Miss Sarah Pierce's School for Young Ladies, also famous by the time the Beechers arrived. Catharine Beecher would claim that the first five years of Lyman's tenure in Litchfield, the period that ended with Roxana's death, were the happiest in his life, and that Roxana during that time "'sympathized thoroughly with him in all his tastes and employments.'" Noteworthy, too, was the fact that Roxana's reputation as a teacher had apparently preceded her. It was said she was "a good influence in forming [children's] characters," and soon after her arrival Miss Pierce approached her about taking some of the students under her wing. The request involved boarding the students rather than teaching them, but the Beechers, still in need of income, happily obliged.[41]

Nevertheless, the evidence suggests that the governing malady of her life had followed Roxana to Litchfield. In January of 1811, not long after their arrival, she wrote Esther Beecher saying that her letter would be necessarily short due to "several vexing circumstances." They were familiar ones. First, of course, Lyman was away preaching, this time in New Hartford. He had gone during extremely cold weather and had not chopped enough wood before his departure. She had company, a clergyman stranger. And then there was "Catharine sick; George almost [sick] . . . Rachel's finger cut off, and she crying and groaning with pain." Was it too much to expect that she could find time for reading? "I average perhaps one page a week, besides what I do on Sundays. I expect to be obliged to be contented (if I can) with the stock of knowledge I already possess, except what I can glean from the conversation of others." She had been able to read in the *Christian Observer* and the *Edinburgh Review* of the discovery that "fixed alkalies are metallic oxyds." She complained to Esther, "I think this is all the knowledge I have obtained in the whole circle of arts and sciences of late." If Esther had been more fortunate, "pray let me reap the benefit."[42]

More than three years later the story had not changed. Two letters written in the month of November told the latest installment. The Beechers had recently moved into a new house, and so even more household organizing and renovation were required. To her brother, Samuel Foote, Roxana wrote that they were in "an unfinished state." She had painted and papered some rooms, with more still to be done, and they still needed some doors and windows. However, at least they had tried their Russian stove and found that "two fires warm six rooms." More importantly, she wanted company and urged Samuel to pack himself up, along with her mother or perhaps sister Harriet, and come along. There were a number of things that might amuse him there, not to mention the fact that "I have a new philosophical work you may study, and some new poems you may read." In a following letter to Harriet, written while "sitting upon my feet, with my paper on the seat of a chair, while Henry is hanging round my neck, and climbing on my back, and Harriet is begging me to please to make her a baby," she explained that she had been expecting to visit her in a sleigh with the children, but had not yet heard from others or been outdoors to see for herself if there was sufficient snow for the journey.[43]

Though Lyman was frequently away, when home he was not aloof from Roxana. In many respects they apparently shared a great deal, including intellectual concerns. Some of Catharine's strongest early memories were of husband and wife eating in the sitting room, discussing various topics of the day or, as another example, reading together in the *Christian Observer* the writings of Macaulay, Wilberforce, Hannah More, and others. And the little three-year-old girl who had wanted her mother to make her a baby would later express the belief, perhaps encouraged by all those tales, that "'the communion between her and my father was a peculiar one. It was an intimacy throughout the whole range of their being.'" Whether Harriet Beecher Stowe only imagined this communion or knew it to be, as portrayed

y her it certainly seemed to serve Lyman's needs and being more than
\oxana's. Lyman had his career, and he was shaping that career. He needed
nd drew upon his wife for support. Stowe, for example, wrote that "'there
/as no human mind in whose decisions he had greater confidence'" than
\oxana's: "'Both intellectually and morally he regarded her as the better and
tronger portion of himself...'" Better and stronger, but in terms of
\yman's life.[44]

Roxana willingly played her role as a clergyman's wife as much as was
ossible for her. But even in that respect hers was, Stowe suggested, a nearly
ivisible presence. Roxana was a shy person who could not speak before
ompany or strangers "'without blushing.'" Possessing "'great natural
ensitiveness and even timidity,'" Roxana was unable to perform in the
xpected manner the duties associated with her position. For example, she
id not lead the weekly female prayer meetings. Stowe's proud judgment or
'impression,'" an impression given her by others, was that her mother's
ilent influence had more impact than the audible deeds of others. The
amily's idealized memory of a woman "'little known by personal acquaint-
nce in the parish'" was of a female figure revered in particular for "'her
eputation as a woman of talent and culture,'" and for "'her diligent devotion
ɔ her numerous family.'" It was a familiar duality in the minds, and the
ves, of the literary domestics.[45]

n a certain respect, the mother of Catharine Maria Sedgwick, Pamela
)wight Sedgwick, represented a special case in the history of the literary
omestics' foremothers. The wife of a "distinguished" man, Pamela was
herished in memory by her daughter as a woman of virtue and intelligence.
ut plagued throughout her married life by recurring mental illness, Pamela
'as frequently incapable of performing her role as a dutiful and accom-
lished wife and mother. Nevertheless, even in her particular circumstances
iere were familiar elements. Isolated at home throughout much of her
iarriage while her husband was away attending to public duties, groping
lone in her own dark history with her singular burden, Pamela exemplified
i a special way woman's mundane malady. To say the least, her somber
gure left troubled recollections in the memory of her daughter, who must
ave found it difficult indeed to reconstruct a model for emulation.

Early in the 1850s Catharine Maria Sedgwick was asked by William
Iinot, her nephew by marriage to Sedgwick's beloved niece, Kate Sedgwick
Iinot, to write her autobiography for their daughter Alice. During the years
/hen Kate, the daughter of Sedgwick's brother Charles, had grown to
iaturity, Sedgwick, without children of her own, had related to her as mother
ɔ daughter. After Kate married and had her own daughter, Sedgwick eagerly
ansferred her motherly affections to her grandniece, Alice. That her
eminiscences should be written for a second "daughter" was appropriate. It

was equally appropriate that Sedgwick began with a nostalgic portrayal o
her own mother and father. She acknowledged to "My Dear Little Alice" he
"earnest desire to brighten the links of the chain that binds us to those wh(
have gone before, and to keep it fast and strong."[46]

In securing and strengthening that chain, Sedgwick was bridging
approximately three-quarters of a century, from the latter years of th(
eighteenth to the middle of the nineteenth century, and linking her mother t(
a great-granddaughter. In fact, Sedgwick went a step further when she
proudly wrote that her own grandmother, Abigail Williams Dwight, mothe
of Pamela, had been a woman "much celebrated in her day for he
intelligence and character." Sedgwick revered the memory of Pamela, a
well, but it was a reverence tinged with sadness. Fondness was shadowed by
regret in Sedgwick's comment that the signal characteristics of her mother'
person and life had been "her wisdom, her conjugal devotion—and self
negation." As this characterization indicates, Pamela's person was dominated by and had little significance apart from her life as a married woman and
mother of ten children, seven of whom survived to adulthood. It was
apparently a circumstance that cost Sedgwick's mother dearly.[47]

Daughter Catharine passed on to grandniece Alice her cherished belie
that the "union" of Pamela and Theodore Sedgwick had been "a very perfect
one, reverence, devotion with infinite tenderness on her side—respect,
confidence and unswerving love on his." How "perfect" a relationship it was
for Pamela is questionable in light of several mental breakdowns she suffered
during the marriage. The relationship may not have been the direct cause o
the breakdowns, but it apparently aggravated them. According to Sedgwick
her mother "knew she was most tenderly beloved and held in the very highes
respect by my father—But her physical strength was not equal to the
demands on her—and her reason gave way." Sedgwick thought that she
could recall two or three "periods of insanity," but was not certain how long
each period lasted, "for I was too young to remember anything but being told
that my mama was sick and 'sent away to a good doctor.' " Just as it is
obvious that more than Pamela's physical strength gave way, the demands
with which she could not cope were clearly other than physical as well.[48]

Describing Pamela as "intellectually superior," Sedgwick also suggested
that this characteristic had been reinforced by her mother's "long 'partnership' with a superior mind occupied in great affairs." The reference, o
course, is to Theodore and his highly successful political career, which
included positions as U.S. senator and Speaker of the House of Representatives. Even so, it was those "great affairs" that took Theodore away from
Pamela on numerous occasions and thus left the "partnership" to wither and
Pamela to suffer in isolation. The effect, admitted Sedgwick, was severe and
terrible: "Her long separations from my father seem to have been utmost
cruel to her." For the daughter that was an admission of, but not a judgment
upon, a basic source of her mother's trials.[49]

Pamela Dwight married Theodore Sedgwick in 1774. She was Theodore's second wife, his first having died three years previously from smallpox one month before she was due to give birth to their first child. Almost from the time he was admitted to the Massachusetts bar in 1766, when he was nineteen, Theodore was deeply involved in political life. An ardent supporter of the Revolution, he also briefly held two military positions during the war, first as a military secretary with the rank of major to Major General John Thomas and then as commissioner of supply for the northern department of the Continental Forces from 1775 to 1778. Sedgwick was elected a representative to the Massachusetts General Court in 1780 and again in 1782 and became a state senator in 1784 and 1785. In 1785 and 1787 he was a delegate to the Continental Congress. In 1789 he began a twelve-year period in the national legislature as a congressman and a senator, ending as Speaker of the House. From 1802 to the end of his life he served as a justice of the Supreme Judicial Court of Massachusetts.[50]

Three years after their marriage, Pamela wrote to Theodore that she had been "fairly well except for frequent turns of the headache." In subsequent years her headaches would be linked again and again with periods of severe depression and irrationality. Pamela's mental illness and Theodore's absences from home would also continue to be linked, particularly in the last fifteen years of her life. In 1780 Pamela wrote to her friend Elizabeth Mayhew to say that she had experienced "but little health for this two years past," but had "been mending in my health for two months past." She noted as well her recent disappointment that a trip to Boston with Theodore had been canceled because her husband's business had taken him elsewhere. In later correspondence with Mayhew, Pamela made oblique but suggestive references to her experience as a wife and mother. She jokingly inquired in 1782 if the single Mayhew was ever going to "take the dark leap." A year later she wrote that she had had to forgo another trip to Boston with Theodore. This time it was Pamela's business that had made time away impossible: she neither wanted nor felt it appropriate to leave her three children. She also spoke of the death of her eight-month-old baby, saying, "May you my Dear never feel the bitterness of such a misfortune." It was the second time that Pamela had lost a child. A planned visit to Mayhew in the winter of 1785 was canceled because, as Pamela phrased it, "my dear we that have committed ourselves in the family way, find the small circle of domestic concerns engross almost all our attention and constitute us either happy or miserable." That same year a third child had died in infancy.[51]

Theodore went to New York City in 1789 as a representative to the First Congress under the newly ratified Constitution. In January Pamela wrote to him, having "snatch[ed] a moment" from a crying infant and despite the "noise" of other "ungoverned children," which she said was "as distracting to the brain as a confused din of arms to a . . . soldier." She had felt "very sensible pain" at his departure, she wrote, but had attempted to conceal it so as not to give pain to him. She alluded as well to suffering of a more serious nature. "When I reflect on my own imbecility and weakness," she said, "I think with the poet that you have lost your mate and been joined by one from a barbarous land." Less than a month later, in response to Theodore's inquiry about her health, Pamela sought to assure him that she was well except for a simple cold. But the truth surfaced in another fashion. She had been "so long of little use" to her children, she said, that "I often lament the poorness of my constitution as that ever deprives me of that power that would render me useful."[52]

If Pamela could not feel or be useful in her sphere, she had no doubt that Theodore could in his, and she supported him in his endeavors in political life. In July she told him that it was the "earnest wish of my heart that you may succeed in your generous purpose and be made a blessing to your country." Two weeks later she asked him to "forgive me" if her letters interrupted "your more important concerns." The self-deprecating tone of her letters, her sense of inferiority, did not change, and her burden of loneliness and isolation grew. The wife as lover pined for her bedmate. In anticipation of Theodore's homecoming in August she wrote to him, "The time, I flatter myself, is not far distant when I may expect your return—my Bed is decked with tapestry—but shall be covered with linen clean and white and perfumed with love." Pamela also felt the strain of having to meet the absorbing burden of domesticity by herself. Nine months later she wrote to complain of "living like a widow and being at the same time a nurse." The latter was undoubtedly a reference to the birth five months before of Catharine Maria, the Sedgwick's ninth child, six of whom were still living. Pamela complained again a month later, only to end with an apology. Disappointed that Theodore's return was to be delayed yet again, she wrote, "I sicken at the thought of your being absent for so long a time." He had been gone for a very long period but, she said, she could not reconcile herself to "this vale of Widowhood." It was growing "more and more disagreeable" to her every day—"My children want a father." Nevertheless, she abruptly concluded, she should not write or speak of the subject too often because "it is too much for me to contemplate" and she did not want to "willingly grieve you with my troubles."[53]

Pamela's constant flow of correspondence to her frequently absent husband stayed the same course. She missed him, but she did not want to burden him with her loneliness. She struggled, inadequately she felt, with her domestic cares, but she did not want to trouble him or distract him from his more important duties. In 1791 a tenth child was born, and her mother, Abigail, Catharine's revered grandmother, died. Regarding Abigail's death, Pamela wrote Theodore to say, "I have no Female Friend to whom I can look for aid and protection," but, she added, "do not think my dearest love that I mean to murmur or complain."[54]

Less than two months later Pamela wrote to Theodore in Philadelphia to beg him to come home and at the same time to tell him to stay away. The letter was short. It told Theodore that she had sunk deeply into herself, that he had once again lost his mate. She had received his latest letter, she said, and even her "imbecillity" could not stop her from speaking about her state. Friends had sought to make her understand that she was ill, "but this I have no reason to Believe," she said. Yet she made Theodore believe: "but shall I tell can I tell you that I have lost my understanding . . . " What was she to think, what could she think, she wondered, "what is my shame what is my pain what is my confusion to think of this what Evils wait my Poor Family without a guide without a head." She wanted him home for the children, for "their sakes," but not for his or hers; "for your sake I wish you not to come you must not come it would only make us both more wretched." She begged him to "make yourself easy don't be anxious about a creature utterly worthless to herself and to you." She sought deliverance—"It may please God to give me reason and a disposition to improve that Reason to some good purpose"—and if it came, she concluded, "you will then hear again from your once affectionate and even obliging Pamela Sedgwick."[55]

Two days later, Theodore wrote a friend to thank him for information about Pamela's state. His "anxiety and distress," he said, were somewhat relieved. But if more encouraging reports were not forthcoming he would return home, except that he would only go "at a time when my presence shall give the greatest support to dear Mrs. Sedgwick." A week later he wrote again to the same friend or perhaps to a doctor to say that he would probably return in a few weeks, maybe even in a few days because, he said, "my anxiety with respect to Mrs. Sedgwick is almost incapable of restraint." Three months later Pamela was still ill, and she wrote Theodore that "you desire me to write you and I must obey altho I cannot write anything that will or can give you the least pleasure."[56]

Pamela recovered from that particular breakdown. Or perhaps it is more accurate to say that she rallied until her health failed again, for that remained the pattern until she died in 1807. However, as the recoveries grew weaker and the breakdowns more severe, the Sedgwick family, including the children, came to recognize that her condition was at best chronic. During Theodore's frequent and often lengthy absences Pamela continued to urge him to fulfill his obligations to his country; for example, in late 1792 she wrote that she knew he could not be long from his duties "without feeling a disappointing and painful void—as a fond Mother does when she is by some misfortune Detached from the care of her family." That was, of course, a thinly veiled allusion to her poor health and her resultant failure to meet her responsibilities in the home. Pamela did not stop bemoaning Theodore's absences, and after a while his letters, in essence, constituted for her his presence. She felt like a "poor wanderer," she wrote in 1798, and were it not for his letters "come to cheer my drooping spirits I should sink into the deepest gloom." Naturally, her recurring mental illness depressed her. Most of all she felt useless. What "dependent creatures" we are, she said to Theodore in a letter written in 1789, "sure of no one thing in the world," not even of "being able to govern our own tempers and dispositions or of reducing our feelings under the control of reason." And in another letter written in the same year she owned that "my own unworthiness is the cause of depressing my spirits—but I will not dwell on this Painful subject." Theodore did as much as he could to reassure and comfort her. He too was a frequent correspondent, and in his letters he expressed his love for her, cautioned her to care for her health, and urged her to continue sending letters to him.[57]

With the election of Jefferson in 1800, Federalist Theodore's days in elective office were ended. By this time the Sedgwick children, including Catharine, had grown old enough to help in the care of their mother. And they were old enough to recognize the significance of the end of an era. In February 1801 eleven-year-old Catharine wrote to her father to mark the occasion of his leaving Congress forever. That day, she said, "shall in my own mind [be] celebrated forever." Yes, she continued, "as long as I live I shall reflect on that dear time when my Dear Pappa left a public life to live in a retired one with his Dear wife and children." There was Theodore's tenure on the Supreme Judicial Court of Massachusetts for the last eleven years of his life, however, and for a man of affairs there would always be the necessity of trips from home. At any rate, hope for Pamela's complete recovery had long dimmed. In 1804 she suffered another breakdown that left her completely irrational. Again her sanity returned, but from 1805 to her death two years later she remained a semi-invalid.[58]

As painful as the memory of her mother's mental breakdowns was to Catharine Maria Sedgwick, she did not blame her father. She was conditioned as much as her mother had been to the principle and tradition of the separation of duties and spheres on the basis of gender. In the autobiographical memoir she wrote for her grandniece Alice, Sedgwick pointedly quoted from one of her mother's letters to her father. In that letter Pamela said to Theodore that he should decide for himself whether he should remain in public life, despite the problems his career caused her and the pain inherent in their separations. Pamela concluded her letter by saying, "'Submission is my duty and however hard I will try to practice what reason teaches me I am under obligations to do.'" Sedgwick believed, she told Alice, that her mother "never again expressed one word of remonstrance or dissatisfaction." In Sedgwick's mind her father had his public duty to perform, unfortunate though the consequences may have been.[59]

Sedgwick recalled " 'Papa's going away' and 'Papa's coming home'—The dreadful cloud that came over our home when Mama was sick." But she accepted it as necessary and proper that "My father felt it to be his duty to remain in public life at any private sacrifice—at the expense of his domestic happiness, his homelove which was his ruling passion." She also felt that it was difficult for her father to be away from home whatever the circumstances. "My father," she wrote, "was domestic in his disposition—out and out social—he could not endure solitude unless he was intensely involved in business." But that was exactly the point: he had his business, while his wife had only the solitude. They had separate destinies. Two years before Pamela's death, Sedgwick had written her that while "Papa certainly is equalled by no person in the world," she thought that it was "impossible for any human creature to possess more exalted virtue" than her mother. Always defending her father to Alice in the course of sadly recalling the predicament of her mother, Sedgwick, again inadvertently, touched upon the crux of the problem: "My father was absorbed in political life—but his affections were at home—My mother's life was eaten up with calamitous sickness." That was to say that while Theodore was absorbed in his career, the object of his affections was at home absorbed with maladies.[60]

3

The Season of Instruction

For the literary domestics even more than their female predecessors, a particular sense of place preempted and distorted questions of intellectual being and created minds beset by conflict and contradiction, by doubt and confusion. Just as they wrestled with the ambiguous images of their foremothers as intellectual figures, so they struggled with their own insecurities and uncertainties, with their own unsettled self-images. It is not surprising that some felt the need to create idealized fantasies. It was no accident if they found in their foremothers mirror images of themselves.

From the beginning, the signals the literary domestics received from their society were not designed to encourage young women in formulating uniformly self-respecting and clear conceptions of themselves as intelligent beings. Those signals that invited comparisons between female and male educational training or that heightened the contrast between the lives envisioned for the literary domestics and those of their male counterparts were neither consistent nor reassuring. Women's educational experiences went no further than home and seminary, and no future was promised beyond the web of domesticity. Male social equals were readied for attendance at colleges like Harvard, Yale, and Dartmouth, preparatory to apprenticing for careers in law and commerce, to pursuing further studies in medicine and theology, or to establishing themselves in fields such as education, journalism, or the arts. Envisioning their daughters as the future wives of men who would exercise leadership in their communities and as the mothers of sons destined to follow in the paths of their fathers, elite families encouraged daughters to acquire culture, and the literary domestics availed themselves of the increasing educational opportunities their families and communities provided females in the early decades of the nineteenth century. But because the governing rationale was more domestic and social than intellectual, the learning was frequently superficial or, if substantive, nevertheless disconnected from objectives beyond itself. And regardless of the educational benefits daughters of culturally conscious families derived from their circumstances, it was impossible to forget that the cultivation of female minds was only secondarily important.

Given the inflexible premises about adult male and female activities and roles, to be performed within clearly defined public and private spheres, respectively, intellectual aspirations and ambitions on the part of females generally were regarded as gratuitous, perhaps abnormal. Even for daughters of prominent families intellectual accomplishment was more symbolic and ornamental than functionally purposeful. As a result, intellectual efforts by females were almost certain to be undirected and unchanneled, and just as likely to be diluted and undermined. It was hoped that males of the cultured and socially responsible elements of society would become recognized, responsible public figures in their communities. Earmarked from the outset as potential future leaders, young men knew they were expected to have ambitions and to prepare for future public responsibilities. In stark contrast, a young woman could not fail to understand early that her future would be as a subordinate, supportive, and nurturing figure within the confines of domesticity, that her life and status as an adult would be dependent upon and circumscribed by a male's social standing. The prospects for a career independent of the home were less than promising, to say the least. If she were to enjoy any life of the mind, there could be little doubt that it would have to be maintained in the face of unavoidable obstacles, under special circumstances, and rarely as a primary or even integral part of her overall life. Intellectual stimulation and fulfillment promised to be intermittent for the woman who had to pursue her endeavors in isolation, in opposition to social directives, or in spite of the demands of domesticity.[1]

The sources for those signals in nineteenth-century America had long been in place. During the colonial era the intellectual training of a female was accorded little consideration, certainly less than that of a male. Spurred by the new nation's republican experiment, females in early nineteenth-century America did enjoy increased educational opportunities, but the purpose and significance of those academic offerings were largely subsumed or compromised by the domestic orientation of their lives. Colonial women received less education, and as a consequence their lives were less shrouded in ambiguity. No women attended the nine colonial institutions of higher learning, and primary education, whether public or private, was not only rudimentary in the seventeenth and eighteenth centuries, but also made clear distinctions on the basis of gender.

The evidence indicates that New England's public schools generally excluded girls until the latter half of the eighteenth century, and even then offered them only a separate and lesser education. Girls, for example, tended to receive their schooling in sessions held either during the summer, at the conclusion of the regular schooling offered boys, or during the rest of the year in hours after boys had been dismissed for the day. A quasi-private alternative open to girls as well as boys became available from the seventeenth century onward with the appearance of dame schools. These schools offered an education that was for the most part elementary, emphasizing the alphabet, or when more ambitious including some spelling, reading, writing, and ciphering. But roles envisioned for adulthood fundamentally affected the curriculum. Although the dame opened the doors of her home to both sexes, her primary objective was the preparation of boys for entrance into the public schools. Guided by a dame who was probably more literate in the domestic and ornamental than the liberal arts, girls interspersed their ABCs with sewing and knitting. By the middle of the eighteenth century, families who could afford the tuition were able to offer their daughters additional education, but it was no less gender-determined. Building upon the distinctions established in the dame schools, institutions known as adventure schools offered girls in towns and cities instruction in social accomplishments such as dancing, along with a smattering of academic education.[2]

Fragmentary evidence indicates that the middle colonies did offer primary schooling for girls on nominally the same basis as boys. But those colonies also established patterns based on gender, with dame and adventure schools emphasizing domestically and socially oriented curricula for girls similar to those of their New England counterparts. The southern colonies' overwhelmingly rural character and widely scattered population contributed to different structural patterns of education. Public or private institutions were less important than more informal means of providing learning. Girls from sufficiently affluent families were schooled by tutors who resided in or visited their households and offered them instruction considered appropriate for daughters of the elite. Planters' daughters were the recipients of an education that stressed domestic and social accomplishments, rather than the knowledge and skills requisite for the more advanced academic learning that was offered planters' sons. The same emphasis characterized dame and adventure schools that emerged in the South after the middle of the eighteenth century.

In colonial America, then, factors such as period, locale, and social or economic status were less significant for females than gender in deciding the content and character of the schooling offered them. Institutions were shaped and guided by prevailing expectations concerning the roles children were to assume as adults. Boys could look forward to playing a number of public roles. For girls the sine qua non was that they would become wives and mothers.[3]

Throughout the colonies, household education was generally more important than the schooling offered by formal institutions. Not only were educational institutions in the formative stages of development, but the family as the principal unit of social organization had traditionally served as the basic means for education for life. The family's role was codified in colonial legislation that systematized household education and made parents legally responsible for the instruction of their children. It was in the home, of course, that children received their earliest conceptions of themselves and intimations of their world. Just as the household had greater significance as a school for life, so the instillment of values was considered more important than the teaching of academic skills. In socially elite homes in particular, the development of character was regarded as a more crucial enterprise than the development of mind. This reflected less an anti-intellectual bias than a belief that the moral and spiritual qualities of the individual should receive greater emphasis than the intellectual.[4]

Like its more formal counterparts, however, household education found its purpose, significance, and direction by looking to the roles children would play as adults. Girls and boys might master their ABCs together and might proceed jointly to catechism, primer, and Bible, but the remainder of their education was separate and distinct. Girls were trained in housewifery, boys in a variety of occupations. And while character formation was considered critical for both—the code of disciplined behavior looked to the imperative of the earnest performance of duties, to temperance of the passions, and to pious benevolence—girls were shaped as biblical helpmeets, boys as future citizens of the world.

It was a perspective that held fast. In 1819, not long after her marriage, Caroline Howard Gilman responded to the concerns of her sister, Anna Maria Howard White, that the latter's daughter, Lucy, was "running wild for want of culture." Do not be troubled "for her mind, for a year or two," wrote Gilman. "A dull intellect is not forwarded by too early study, and a bright one catches at a leap, at ten years of age, what you would labor to implant— in all the preceding." The aphorism was tailored to the principle of an education based on gender, as was Gilman's concluding comment: "If Lucy can learn the pleasure of contentment—and obedience, never fear for her mind now." To come to understand and accept her lot, she suggested, would "teach her application—when the season for mental instruction arises." The seasoning of the female was for more than one age.[5]

With the exception of those born earliest, particularly Catharine Maria Sedgwick and Caroline Howard Gilman, the literary domestics benefited from the increase and broadening of educational opportunities spurred and legitimated by an ideology which emerged from the Revolution and was actualized in institutional practices. Beginning in the late eighteenth century, learning, whether formal or informal, was invested with more significance than ever. Already perceived as the basic means of socialization, education was now seen as integral and crucial to the survival of the newly independent nation. The republic, it was said, could be maintained and sustained only if its people were schooled in the responsibilities of citizenship and prepared to meet their central obligations through devotion to society rather than self.[6]

Virtue was defined most broadly as a selflessness in which individual desires and interests were secondary to the welfare of the body politic. It was made the linchpin for social and political institutions, and its continual exercise was required for their survival. Only if citizens were instilled with appropriate values and their behavior made exemplary would the Revolution be consummated and a lasting basis for the republic established. Academic content and institutional practices were subjects that continued to stimulate debate, but there was a consensus that education should be directed toward insuring the success of the republican experiment, thereby rendering it as a model for the rest of the world.[7]

Supported by a rapidly expanding population willing to fund instruction for its youth, educational institutions proliferated from the last decades of the eighteenth century onward. Public education was neither static nor uniform in character throughout the young republic, but variations in support, quality, and systems notwithstanding, schooling became more readily available, enrollments multiplied, and girls received nominally the same opportunities in primary schooling. The institutional expansion so visible in public education could also be seen in schools dependent upon private support. Daughters of more privileged families not only could continue their education, but were able to choose from the rapidly increasing number of academies that dotted the landscape. Modeled on the adventure schools which had preceded them, the earliest academies leavened the emphasis upon social accomplishments with more instruction in the subjects being taught in male academies. Some academies even opened their doors to both sexes. The tendency to broaden female education became more pronounced with the emergence of female seminaries such as those established by Emma Willard, Catharine Beecher, and Mary Lyon. Young women enrolled in these and similar institutions received an education comparable to that offered their male counterparts. The curricula were as complete, the demands as great, and the learning as substantive.[8]

But the theoretical broadening of female minds made possible as well the steeping of female consciousness in a well of paradox, conflict, and ambiguity. If an educated citizenry was crucial to the welfare and survival of the republic, who, after all, was a fully endowed citizen? A woman was a legal citizen, but whatever else a politically active republican citizen might be, that individual was certainly not a woman. Gender continued to be the distinguishing factor in the education of the sexes, and the ultimate purpose of a female's training was not fundamentally altered. A woman's needs, interests, and abilities were presumed different, and her schooling continued to prepare her for and direct her toward a role in the home. Republican ideology's stress upon the education of its citizenry was perhaps nowhere more ambiguous than in the importance it placed upon the theoretically political and critical role that woman was to play as wife and mother within the household. Schooled in virtue, the Christian helpmeet was to meet her responsibility to the republic by being the exemplar and teacher of virtue to husband and sons. Without participating politically herself the wife was expected to be a salutary influence upon her politically active husband and to train her sons in political virtue. In sum, lives denied political participation were said to be fully endowed with political purpose. Linking the private woman of the home to the public world of politics was an unprecedented idea in American society that appeared to bestow greater significance upon woman's traditional role and sphere. But it was a paradoxical significance. New and more still implied old and less, so that the gulf between male participation and a semblance of female influence remained wide. Placed in a new role that was more politically symbolic than politically substantive, the woman remained more a symbol of virtue than a fount of wisdom. But the seedbed of contradiction and conflict had been newly stirred.[9]

An equally pressing question for the nineteenth century, particularly in the early decades, was who the leaders of the new republic and its communities were to be. As a result of the political and social changes inaugurated by the Revolution the colonial gentry had vanished and the authoritative institutions of colonial society had been diluted and dissolved. Sources of power and influence had been dispersed among a number of functional elites who participated in a moral, political, and philosophical debate concerning the contemporary state and future of the society. The literary domestics were the daughters of, and most of them became wives of, males who were representatives of those new elites. The daughters of the elite, too, were prepared for the roles of wife and mother within the home, not for positions of public leadership. They were destined to be the wives of leaders and the mothers of future prominent figures.

Female academies offered the cumulative and final academic experience, rather than preparation for the more advanced learning awaiting males in colleges. It was a clear signal directly related to the contrasting roles to be played by men and women as adults. The male's role would be public and his choice of occupation multiple, while the female's would be private and her occupation singularly domestic. The curricula of the academies and seminaries attended by young women dictated the same. Regardless of the rigor or depth in their academic offerings, these institutions' basic mission and intent were to instill a sense of female being and place that was unmistakably social and domestic. It is true that female academies and seminaries provided training for one apparent alternative. Their graduates could, and did in large numbers, become teachers of children. But there was a strong sense that women employed as teachers were serving as surrogate mothers. Except for the very few who remained unmarried, their experience was frequently seen as training for actual motherhood. In the last quarter of the nineteenth century, more than twenty years after she had established herself as a popular author, Mary Virginia Terhune wrote regarding women and the "profession of teaching" that "it is the nature of a being of the mother-sex to gather together and into her care, to brood over and to instruct creatures younger and feebler than herself." Why, said Terhune, for a woman to be a teacher of children constituted the "most satisfactory substitute for a family of her very own."[10]

The more informal education provided in the home, which had played so critical a role in colonial America, continued to be important, particularly in more privileged families. Intellectual stimulation and more advanced education were provided many of the literary domestics in their households. Subject to parental discretion and the stability of family fortunes and circumstances, tutors were frequently employed for personal, private instruction. Even in the absence of tutors, parental example and encouragement and individual motivation made sustained study possible. But like their foremothers, the literary domestics mastered their ABCs and their domestic skills together, and once again, intellectual stimulation that had a tenuous relationship to the overriding social admonition to be wives and mothers contributed to a confused, frequently conflicted sense of the female as a thinking being. With neither college nor a public career in the offing and without objectives beyond immediate studies, the joys of intellectual awakening were difficult to sustain. The eagerness to learn was blunted by deprivation, dampened and diluted by self-doubt. At times intellectual curiosity and excitement foundered in frustration and were undermined and distorted by a concern for questions of legitimacy. It was inevitable that there was on the part of the literary domestics a realization that the development of female minds was not regarded by society as a wholly serious enterprise. Nor were the lure of self-fulfillment and the promise of becoming the cultured wives of gentlemen and tutors to gentlemen's children sufficient to ward off a sense of malaise and disillusionment.

The experiences of the literary domestics born in the last decade of the eighteenth century trace the various strands woven through the ambiguous education of a culturally advantaged daughter. They also exposed the inherent tensions generated by an education that contained contradictory implications for a woman's self-identity. Catharine Maria Sedgwick, born in 1789 and the first of the twelve to enter the literary marketplace, was sixty-three when she recounted her early educational experiences for her grandniece, Alice Minot, in 1853. The memoir is at times detailed in its description of her schooling, but bewildered and sometimes exasperated in tone. "My dear Alice," she began, "I wish I could give you a true picture and a vivid one of my *fragmentary* childhood." What Sedgwick meant was that she has received a fragmentary *education*, and the reminiscences reflect that, in content and style. Segments of Sedgwick's schooling are scattered through the narrative, but, like her education itself, they do not form an integrated or consistent whole. And while Sedgwick did not and would not have said so herself, she also wrote from a fragmented perspective.[11]

Sedgwick's formal schooling had taken place at the turn of the century. But, she quickly noted, learning then had been practically nonexistent, particularly when compared to what she characterized as "the thoughtful, careful (whether judicious or injudicious) education of the present day." Significantly, she did not discuss education in terms of gender either at the turn of the century or six decades later. Her omission, however, simply pointed to the fact that she had been trained since childhood to believe that woman's place was in the home. But Sedgwick could not forgo condemning the formal schooling she did receive. The impression had been made. The impact had been felt. In her own words, that education had been "next to none."[12]

As a young child, eager and bright, Sedgwick might have expected better. "I was reared," she said, "in an atmosphere of high intelligence." For the still fresh, undeveloped, curious mind there was stimulation and the tantalizing promise of unending, unlimited exploration. Reading, whether on her own or listening to a member of the family, was the educational staple of her young life and, as was the case with other culturally advantaged daughters, it would remain the basic ingredient of her educational regimen. It was chiefly in this respect that the family's status and, more importantly, its aspirations to continue as a custodian of culture made possible an environment conducive to the development of the mind. Whether the child was female or male, the opportunity was there, and Sedgwick for one grasped it eagerly. "Love of reading" instilled from earliest childhood was, she wrote Alice, "to me 'education.'" She first developed it from her father's habit of reading to the family. For example, she remembered listening at age eight to passages from Shakespeare and Cervantes. At eleven she was reading constantly on her own, "chiefly novels." (That was also the year she saw her first play, *Macbeth*, in New York City.) At twelve, she recalled, Rollin's *Ancient History* was her fare. Sedgwick not only read constantly, she was constantly urged to do so. A month before Sedgwick's thirteenth birthday, her sister, Frances Watson, advised her to be diligent in reading. "It will be a great advantage to you to read," said Frances, "with the motive of forming and communicating opinions of what you read." When she was sixteen her father wrote to her, "I hope my love you will find it in your power to devote your mornings to reading—there are few who can make such improvements by it and it would be lamented if this precious time should be lost."[13]

Sedgwick, then, had little education in the "common sense," but there were what she described as "peculiar circumstances in my condition that in some degree supplied these great deficiencies." They *were* peculiar circumstances. She was basically untutored, undirected, and on her own, but as the result of living in a cultured household, "there was much chance seed dropped in the fresh furrow and some of it was good seed—and some of it I may say fell on good ground." Sedgwick's metaphor illuminates the fundamental character of her education and its paradoxical nature. Arbitrary, unpredictable, or unstructured as her education was, in such a familial atmosphere there was at the same time a lingering suggestion that cultural enrichment was her birthright. She came to maturity in a home in which learning was valued and the transmission of culture made a responsibility.[14]

Sedgwick did attend the district school in her native Stockbridge, Massachusetts. Her family also sought other opportunities for their child; indeed, if there was "any other school a little more select or better chanced I went to that." For example, when Sedgwick was eight her mother wrote to her father, who was away tending to his political affairs, that Catharine "has got permission to spend a few weeks with [a family friend in Bennington, Vermont] as our school here is worse than none." (The difference between Catharine's and her brothers' education was also made explicit in the same letter. Pamela reported that one brother was making "considerable advances" in Virgil, while the other was trying to locate "a Virgil.") Whatever school she managed to attend, Sedgwick recalled proudly her "intense ambition" to be at the top of her class and "generally being there." But it was difficult to put too much stock in that accomplishment because, as she observed, "Our minds were not weakened by too much study." Her schooling was similar to that offered in many institutions, a curriculum restricted to reading, writing, geography, some grammar, and a smattering of arithmetic. Sedgwick noted wryly that that less than rigorous early training taught her, among other skills, to cipher "in a slovenly way" and to "parse glibly."[15]

Having exhausted the possibilities in rural Stockbridge and its environs, Sedgwick's family enrolled her in a series of adventure schools in New York City, Boston, and Albany. But here, too, Sedgwick found the challenges slight, and if she had not yet developed doubts as to whether her society valued females for their minds or sought to develop their intellectual potential, such doubts may have begun to emerge then. Why, she noted with a mixture of levity and bitterness, as early as the age of eleven she went to New York City "and had the very best teaching of an eminent professor of dancing!—and had a French master who came three times a week." In 1804, four years after her introduction to French, Sedgwick wrote to each of her parents describing in similar language her progress at an academy in Boston. But her tone at that time was slightly different. In November she wrote Pamela to say that she was "very well contented and pleased" with her situation at Mrs. Payne's, and that she was pleased as well with her "French master," who, she said, was "a very excellent one I assure you." Nearly two months later the fifteen-year-old Sedgwick answered Theodore's query about "how my French progresses, upon this I can answer you with a good conscience." In fact, she said, "I hardly find time to attend to anything else; I am very fond of it and it is *my opinion* that I come on very well." But if language study was a way to hone the intellect, like other social accomplishments it was not the stuff to impart a sense of ambition—and in retrospect Sedgwick implied as much to Alice. A letter that Pamela wrote that same year of 1804 suggested as much as well. Despite her increasingly severe bouts with mental illness, Pamela was still able to demonstrate her concern that daughter Catharine receive the proper nurture while at Mrs. Payne's. "With respect to [Catharine's] school," Pamela wrote to her friend Sarah Tucker, as well as to "her dress" and "the elegance and description of society she is to acquire," Catharine "will wish to consult at all times your opinion." That was the stuff that delivered the proper message about the future of a socially elite daughter.[16]

Concerning the great lesson in Sedgwick's more informal education, the home enlarged upon the message of the classroom. Not surprisingly, the lesson hardly fueled the desire to excell intellectually or to seek honors for one's efforts. But it was a lesson that Sedgwick learned well without fully comprehending its significance and without realizing that therein lay the true meaning of her "peculiar circumstances." Her first instruction in what might be characterized as training for a female life, or at least the earliest instance Sedgwick related to Alice, came at the age of seven. It involved the marriage of Sedgwick's sister Eliza, supposedly the glorious moment in her sister's life, and Sedgwick would remember it with unintentional irony as "the first tragedy of my life." Instead of regarding the marriage as a happy occasion, Sedgwick was left with "the impression that a wedding was rather a sundering than a forming of ties." The problem was that Eliza had been like a mother as well as a sister to Catharine, so closely had she governed her and cared for her. Grief-stricken that she was losing her sister forever, Sedgwick had cried at the wedding and had to be taken away. Later the bridegroom, Thaddeus Pomeroy, came to her and, seeking to soothe her, whispered, " 'Your sister may stay with you this summer.' " Sedgwick never forgot her reaction: "*May*! How my whole being revolted at the word—He had the power to bind or loose my sister!" In spite of her rebellious feelings, however, the lesson was implanted: the female person was subject to male hegemony and the female destiny was bound by the domestic sphere.[17]

That, of course, was a lesson learned by many a woman in nineteenth-century America. Gender remained the determinant regardless of status. That was the condition that rendered one's circumstances peculiar. The special privilege of being reared in a family of position and uncommon intelligence became for a female a misleading advantage. "My father had uncommon mental vigor," Sedgwick emphasized, and "so had my brothers—their daily habits and pursuits and pleasures were intellectual—and I naturally imbibed from them a kindred taste." But it was a taste that once acquired, Sedgwick would have little opportunity to develop. Decades later she would still be oblivious to the fact that the intellectual atmosphere she so proudly described to her grandniece was male-focused. There was stimulation for both females and males, but all the promise was male. Perhaps the chief topic of conversation in the family was politics and, said Sedgwick, "I heard my father's conversation with his political friends in the spontaneous expression of domestic privacy." It was the sort of conversation she would hear often. But unlike her four brothers, all of whom became lawyers with varying political interests, the female Sedgwick was not invited to follow her father's public path. Instead, despite her own early interest in politics, she would have to look to "my sisters [who] were just at that period of life when eyes are dazzled with their own glowing future," as helpmeet to a husband.[18]

The turn of the screw in a gentry daughter's "peculiar circumstances" lay in the inculcation of values and attitudes. As much as the intellect might be valued and its qualities encouraged, the development of character was still considered primary. Not only were parents to stand as spiritual and moral models, but they were expected to shape the behavior of their children. This emphasis, however, had a very different twist for a male than for a female, turning in the direction of the world beyond the home for the former, simply turning within for the latter.

Like other leaders of the young republic, Theodore Sedgwick considered devotion and service to one's country critical to the survival of the nation. And nowhere were his convictions more clearly or forcefully articulated than in his own household. Along with her brothers,the young Catharine learned another lesson, but only later would she see that its implications were very different for her. Referring to her father's political career, she recalled, "I received the impression then . . . that the Federal party loved their country and were devoted to it as virtuous parents are to their children—It was to my father what selfish men's private affairs are to them, of deep and everpresent interest." The daughter also came to understand that those involved in public service should eschew personal ambition and gain. Theirs had to be a disinterested act that carried with it the obligation to uphold high standards of conduct. "It was not the success of men or the acquisition of office," her father maintained, "but the maintenance of principle on which as it appeared to them the sound health and true life of their country depended." The uncritical awe with which Sedgwick regarded her father and the degree to which he inspired her suggest that she was certainly as dutiful a student as her brothers. And yet the father's example as an active and influential statesman bore little relationship to any future role the daughter could play. The rhetoric about her importance to the republic notwithstanding, her service would be restricted, secondary, and invisible.[19]

In the novel aptly titled *Home*, Sedgwick revealed that she had learned the lesson and accepted its implications as well. Presented through her spokesman, William Barclay, her description of the family's role is a rationalization for the necessity of woman's adaptation to a limited function within a restricted sphere. Character, says William, is to be developed in children by the family, " 'by the careful use of all the means we possess to train these young creatures, by giving them sound minds in sound bodies; by making them feel the dignity of well-informed minds, pure hearts, and refined manners. And for this we need no college education or foreign masters. Home is the best school—the parent the best teacher.' " There was thus an unintended irony in Sedgwick's expressing her belief to Alice "that the people who surround us in our childhood, whose atmosphere enfolds us as it were, have more to do with the formation of our characters than all our didactic and preceptive education." Certainly that was the case for Sedgwick, the culturally privileged daughter. Her father was the great intellectual influence in her life. But by awakening his daughter's curiosity and anticipation he made it inevitable that she would later experience a sense of intense deprivation. Sedgwick told her grandniece that "my school life was a waste. My home life my only education." But a fundamental lesson in her home life was that there would be little school life and no public life.[20]

The sad, tentative, almost bewildered reflections of the woman of sixty years plus leave a lasting impression. Sedgwick proudly proclaimed to Alice that she thought that she had been a favorite of her peers because she had possessed more ability than most of them, that she had "had more than the rest the means of gratifying" her schoolmates. Yet at the same time she confessed that perhaps she had been too ambitious, too eager for recognition, had suffered from "an excessive love of Approbation."[21]

In her first novel, *A New England Tale*, published in 1822 when she was thirty-two, Sedgwick had timidly set forth what was undoubtedly just a glimpse of her dream of what might have been, of the most and best she could bring herself to fantasy. Characterizing the work as "an humble effort to add something to the scanty stock of native American literature" and as an attempt to present contemporary "sketches of the character and manners of our own country," she apologized if in the process of production the tale had "acquired anything of a peculiar or local cast." If such were the case, she noted, it "should be chiefly attributed to the habits of the writer's education, and that kind of accident which seems to control the efforts of those who have not been the subjects of strict intellectual discipline, and have not sufficiently premeditated their own designs." Sedgwick probably indulged herself in a private moment of recognition, one properly devoid of unseemly ambition, when she portrayed the yearly ritual at a new "public, or as they are called, the town-schools." Noting that the institution reflected a "higher and more expensive order," she described the honors accorded the best students on a particular day. On the one hand, it is a day "during which the young men and boys were to display those powers that they were developing for the pulpit, and the bar, and the political harangue." So far as this exercise is concerned, the "young ladies were with obvious and singular propriety excluded from any part." But females were eligible to compete for prizes in arithmetic, grammar, geography, history, and philosophy, and young Jane Elton, perhaps a projected particle of Sedgwick, receives all, "one after another, in obedience to the award of the examiners." Thus is the "deserving heroine crowned with honours, which she merited so well, and bore so meekly."[22]

Yet another honor was possible. Females could also compete for the annual prize in composition, with the winning contribution to be read by its author before a gathering of the town at the meetinghouse. The decision is made to heighten "curiosity and surprise" by withholding the name of the winner until the moment when "the withdrawing of the curtain disclosed the secret." At the opening of the curtain Jane Elton, of course, is discovered on stage, "seated on the throne, looking like the 'meek usurper,' reluctant to receive the greatness that was thrust upon her." Dressed simply in black, she presents herself with "so embarrassed an air" and reads "in a low and faltering voice, that certainly lent no grace, but the grace of modesty, to the composition." And the subject of her composition? It is "gratitude."[23]

To say the least, Sedgwick was conflicted about herself as an intellectual being. That conflict could be attributed to her society's arbitrary concept of woman's mind and its uses. Cultural training was considered appropriate for a female, but only so much and only for purposes of preparing the female for a private, domestic role. Sedgwick took to it, and didn't. In retrospect, Sedgwick understood that she had possessed strong intellectual aspirations, while feeling that perhaps she had been too eager to develop and express them. And yet she also understood that those aspirations had been thwarted, and she regarded that denial with a critical eye. Despite the fact that she had received more education that most of her contemporaries, she had been given "no regular instruction," she told her grandniece. She saw her training for what it was, superficial and random: "no one dictated my studies or overlooked my progress." And she never ceased to feel or forget the destructive effect of that neglect. "I have all my life," she said, "felt the want of more systematic teaching." Sedgwick did not directly indict the distinctions in roles and spheres, but she did censure one of their consequences: the demeaning and relative neglect of a woman's mind. Hers was a mind that knew it was undernourished.[24]

The scattered observations of Caroline Howard Gilman, born five years after Sedgwick and the other pioneer among the literary domestics, recall the haphazard education of Sedgwick. They recall as well Sedgwick's fragmented perspective. From the same vantage of the 1850s, Gilman characterized the early years of her education at the turn of the century as "the dark age." Other circumstances, including gender, played their part as well. Born in Boston six years before the end of the eighteenth century, Gilman had a childhood that was peripatetic almost from birth. Her father died before she was three, and her mother left Boston to retire to the country with her six children. The boys were enrolled in an academy in Woburn and received there and later at other institutions whatever educational advantages Boston and its environs had to offer. The girls remained with their mother, who proceeded to move from town to town, "changing her residence," Gilman noted, "almost annually, until I was nearly ten." Her mother then died, and Gilman went to live with an older, married sister.[25]

As for what Gilman described as her "mind-birth," there was an education of sorts, but the informal variety was random and the more formal "was exceedingly irregular, a perpetual passing from school to school, from my earliest memory." Her schooling had begun at least as early as age eight, when she attended a private "female seminary." How many different institutions Gilman attended and during what period of years she did not say. But in autobiographical reminiscences written when she was approximately sixty years old she did remember that she had spent time drawing in school and, specifically, that she had stitched the " 'Babes in the Wood' on white satin, in floss silk." Foreign language and exercise were combined when Gilman walked four miles to Boston to attend private classes in French. Gilman herself was primarily responsible for her more informal education. At age eight she was taken with her family to visit their neighbor and friend Elbridge Gerry, then governor of Massachusetts and later vice-president of the United States. There she stumbled upon a volume of Salomon Gessner's religious poem, *The Death of Abel*, and read it eagerly and surreptitiously. The next year she was reading Shakespeare and Pope. By age ten she was writing poetry, and at fifteen she taught herself to play the English guitar.[26]

As uneven and undirected as her education was, it strongly influenced the young Gilman's sense of self. She recalled more as a factual observation than as negative commentary how her sensibility had been molded and directed toward a traditional female future. During the years in which she was writing poetry, playing the guitar, and taking French lessons, she remembered that a "dear friend" in school "was kind enough to work out all my sums for me." The consequence, wrote the elder Gilman blithely, was that "so far as arithmetic is concerned, I have been subject to perpetual mortifications ever since, and shudder to this day when any one asks me how much is seven times nine." In equally unconcerned fashion, Gilman also noted that a teacher who introduced her to Latin was "more ambitious for me than I was for myself." She did comment, at least, that exposure to Latin was then unusual for a girl. Lastly, Gilman studied Watt's *Logic*, but only she said, "to gratify a friend." She was a conscientious student, "but on what an ungenial soil it fell! I think, to this day, that science is the dryest of intellectual chips." Gilman's perspective on her capacities and interests was not idiosyncratic; it reflected the influence of a society that segmented knowledge and directed learning toward the role children would play as adults.[27]

While such an education might serve the needs of a society that assigned roles on the basis of gender, its impact upon the individual was problematic. Gilman's autobiographical recollections suggest that she sensed a void in herself but, having adapted to an assigned condition and place, having gone in the directions that were open to her, she could do nothing but awkwardly skirt it. She did not and could not obliterate her sense of that void, but neither could she fully grasp its significance or deal with it except in oblique, incomplete fashion. When at age eighty-one a literary admirer requested Gilman's autograph, she penned her name and then made "my last— probably *the last*—attempt at versification from my worn out pen." Gilman's poem celebrated an occasion remembered from childhood during attendance as a young girl at the school of "the Misses Mason, three maiden ladies" in Boston. And what was the occasion? It was, said Gilman, "when the honor of opening the Dancing School ball with William Hill was conferred on me."[28]

Gilman's first novel, which she published in 1834 at the age of forty, was the semiautobiographical *Recollections of a Housekeeper*. Issuing the volume under the pseudonym "Clarissa Packard," Gilman played with onomastic as well as substantive allusions. Her first-person narrator immediately informs the reader that her maiden name was Clarissa Gray. The symmetry of Clarissa Gray and Caroline Gilman implied a connection between creator and character. The same might be said about Clarissa's experiences throughout the novel. Like her creator, Clarissa was born in Boston in the eighteenth century. She recalls in familiar language that she was "educated with the few facilities at the time afforded for the young." Webster's spelling book is mentioned as part of her sparse fare, along with Morse's *Geography*, which contained no maps and thereby left her "in glorious uncertainty with regard to the position even of my own country." In a departure from what Gilman would later indicate in her literal auto- biography, Clarissa Gray also tells us that her ciphering book was "my pride, and my mother's too," suggesting a would-that-it-had-been-so-for-me attitude on the part of Gilman, or perhaps that it should be so for her young female readers. Shakespeare and Pope, again read at the age of nine, are mentioned. There is also reference to a daily walk of four miles, in this instance to a town school where Clarissa has her only year of "*solid education*." In addition, Clarissa numbers among her accomplishments (which "are soon told") knitting work, childish efforts at writing poetry, learning music upon a harpsichord, and even the requisite dancing lessons, much like those that Gilman would later, as it were, immortalize in verse.[29]

Reflecting Gilman's attitude toward her own smattering of education, Clarissa implicitly regrets and condemns hers. But in two instances Gilman unwittingly betrays the fact that Clarissa's sense of female place conditioned her developing sense of herself as a thinking being. Clarissa comments that, although her family could afford the "luxuries of life," such luxuries were by no means allowed to interfere with "my education for usefulness." That meant *female* usefulness, for much of her time was spent learning the skills required to maintain a home. While apprenticing with her mother there are minor disasters, of course, but, in an analogy revealing that she had learned well that each gender has its place, she states that beginners always make mistakes, for example "the lawyer who blunders in *his* maiden speech," "the doctor who kills *his* first patient," and "the preacher who soothes *his* first hearers to sleep" (emphasis mine). Clarissa exudes pride in *her* developing skills, as does her mother. Years later, when her future husband introduces himself to the mother, Clarissa recalls that the latter made certain that the suitor understood that Clarissa "could skewer a goose, roll puff paste, complete a shirt, and make a list carpet, as well as I played on the spinet and worked tent stitch." Indicative of changing times, Clarissa objected to her mother's boasting only when she added that her daughter could also "spin a little." To this Clarissa protested "against anything so old-fashioned."[30]

It is clear in the early stages of the marriage that Edward, her husband, has learned his place as well. He is said to be fast "becoming an ambitious lawyer." His determination and clarity of intellect stand him in good stead, for the "strongest efforts of his mind were directed to eminence in his profession." Besides being ambitious, Edward is caring and concerned about his wife, and despite the fact that he must toil over his law books at night as well as during the day, he tucks his Blackstone and Coke under his arm and joins his wife during the evenings. But if he is with her physically, he leaves her alone intellectually. "He read and read," says Clarissa, "while I silently pursued my sewing . . . . " The result, at least for Clarissa, is a "domestic trial." "My jealousy . . . of books" is exacerbated by her guilty recognition that Edward toils "for my subsistence."[31]

Although the crisis has arisen from the fact that while Edward's mind is engaged, Clarissa's is idle, the problem as interpreted by Clarissa is that the books are to blame. She is not jealous of either Edward's books or his career per se, but she is upset that they deprive her of him. Thus once Clarissa's feelings are made known to Edward, the apparent problem is easily overcome. Books "calculated to interest while they elevated my literary taste" are brought home and read to her by a solicitous husband. Edward goes so far as to inform Clarissa "in simple terms" about an occasional legal case, requests her opinion, and, "by sounding the depth and power of my intellect," discovers that "under his guidance there were occasions when even my advice might avail him." (Suggested here, albeit inadvertently, is his surprise that she has an intellect.) Henceforth all is well in the household. Now and again Edward shares *his* life of the mind with Clarissa and she has her husband's companionship. True, her mind is engaged, but there is no doubt that it is engaged gratuitously, with what are properly and naturally male matters. It is equally true that Clarissa is living vicariously. She begins "to be ambitious for him," is pleased with the applause and recognition he receives, and is particularly gratified because "his thoughts were mine before they were the world's."[32]

The perspective already apparent in *Recollections of a Housekeeper* was made explicit in another forum in 1838, four years after the publication of the novel. Gilman was also the editor of the *Southern Rose*, a literary magazine, and it was there that she printed the prospectus for a newly established seminary, the Georgia Female College in Macon. In the prospectus the head of the school, the Reverend George F. Pierce, detailed the course of study. It was to include the "whole course of English Letters and Science," vocal and instrumental music, drawing, and painting, together with Latin, Greek, French, Spanish, and Italian. This curriculum notwithstanding, the Reverend Pierce made it clear that a particularly significant offering would be "a system of Domestic Economy." This was the means by which young ladies would learn what would undoubtedly prove most valuable. They would "be enabled and required to prepare, and keep in good order, all their own clothing, thereby avoiding milliner's bills while at school, and at the same time preparing themselves creditably to do this work for themselves and families, in future life." In short, the Georgia Female College would offer a course of studies "practical and moral, as well as literary." The language and the order of priorities were familiar. Like many others involved in founding female academies and seminaries in antebellum America, Pierce had intertwined the technical, attitudinal, and intellectual, and clearly the last was subordinate. Just as clearly, his primary objective was social rather than intellectual. The college's graduates, he declared proudly, would be able to become "the comfort and pride" of their future gentlemen husbands.[33]

If the Georgia Female College curriculum offered more than what Gilman had received, its intent was the same as the course of study that Gilman had been subject to. Taken together, they detailed the training provided the young elite female of that time and foreshadowed the constraints under which the adult woman would pursue intellectual endeavors and maintain a semblance of intellectual identity. Merely by printing the prospectus in her magazine, one product of that training, namely Gilman, indicated her compliance and approval. But she removed any doubts in the same issue with her praise for yet another secondary school for females, the Brownwood Collegiate Institute for the Education of Young Ladies in Columbus, Georgia. The curriculum was listed, and approving (and revealing) commentary was appended. This list was even more promising than that of the Georgia Female College; besides the mandatory texts on music, drawing, and painting, it included others covering the subjects of grammar, arithmetic, geography, classics, history, natural philosophy, chemistry, astronomy, botany, algebra, Greek, Latin, and French. With her own deprivation in mind, perhaps, Gilman appeared to throw down the gauntlet to male intellectual hegemony with her opening observation: "Read it and ponder—ye haughty specimens of the masculine gender, and tremble at the prospect that your dominion over the realms of science and literature is to be divided and shared by the 'weaker members.' " However, the initial bolt of her words quickly bent into the familiar downward curve in which intellectual desire and ambition gravitated to social expectations and possibilities. "But read it," Gilman continued, "and rejoice, all ye lovers of domestic peace and improvement at the thought that ye are to have intelligent companions for life, who will adorn and dignify your homes . . . ."[34]

Gilman's promise of cultural enrichment for the daughter of an elite family recalls again Sedgwick's (and Gilman's) "peculiar circumstances." The social status of the literary domestics had made possible an education generally superior to that of their peers, female or male. That education had been undirected and the knowledge acquired random, but integral to their learning was the sense that cultural acquisition was their right and the transmission of culture their responsibility. The curricula of both the institutions publicized in the *Southern Rose* promised a more sustained and coherent education than Sedgwick and Gilman had received, while it maintained the claims concerning culture. Ultimately, however, it was gender that had rendered their circumstances peculiar. Neither Gilman nor Sedgwick understood fully its significance in shaping education for them and those who would follow. Gilman lauded institutional offerings that were equal to those provided males, but, with no irony intended, she subsumed intellectuality under female destiny. The schools that Gilman found so laudable did exactly the same. The female child was to be prepared for her place in the world. She was to learn her role and learn to be contented with it. And to male readers Gilman offered the bouquet of the educated woman "who will know how to appreciate your own advancement in intellectual excellence, and give to your children those happy lights and impulses which will secure the best interest of the coming generations."[35]

In a letter written by Gilman only a few months after her marriage in December 1819, the new bride enthused to her sister Anna Maria White, "Can you doubt . . . that I enter fully into the spirit of housekeeping?" That her sister might, indeed, be dubious was an allusion to what apparently had been the content of an earlier letter written by the still unmarried Gilman. And yet, she said, there had been "no change in the general current of my ideas." Rather, "I only find them falling, when they are called upon, naturally and easily to a lower channel." What that lower channel might be had already been indicated. But lest her sister still doubt her sentiments, Gilman eagerly told her, "I have great pleasure in superintending our house, and Mr. Gilman is so easily satisfied with my usual routine, and so sensible of any extra effort on my part, that I have a delightful stimulus to my duty." To be sensible of duty was predictable when the woman received an overriding stimulus.[36]

4

Rights of the Mind,
Duties to the Sphere

Long after Harriet Beecher Stowe and Sara Parton had embarked upon their vocations of wifehood and motherhood, Stowe wrote to Parton's third husband, James Parton, "I believe you have claim on a certain naughty girl once called Sara Willis in whom I still retain an interest." Ask her, said Stowe, "if she remembers curling her hair with leaves from her geometry?" Perhaps Sara had "long been penitent," offered Stowe, "*perhaps*—but, ah me! when I read Fanny Fern's articles I detect sparks of the old witchcraft, and say . . . That's Sara Willis, *I* know!" Stowe was referring to an incident during Parton's tenure as a student at the seminary in Hartford, Connecticut, established by Stowe's sister, Catharine Beecher, where Stowe herself had been both student and teacher.[1]

The incident had been memorialized, as it were, by Parton at age seventeen. For the seminary's "Exhibition Day" in 1829 she had been asked to write a composition to be read before a gathering of the school. Nearly a quarter of a century before Parton would give a thought to becoming a published writer, she flavored her essay with the wit that would later become her trademark. She chose for her subject "Suggestions on Arithmetic." As might be expected, the composition was written tongue-in-cheek, as mathematics was not her favorite subject. Parton began her essay with the observation that she had been a "persecuted girl" ever since her parents had sent her to school with the object "to curb her imagination, demolish her airy castles, in short, to convert her into a plain, sober, matter-of-fact damsel, without a thought beyond her Murray's Grammar, or Daboll's Arithmetic." Shortly after her arrival at "H. F. S."—that is, at Hartford Female Seminary—and after, appropriately, she had first "been somewhat domesticated," she was given "a dose of arithmetic . . . the repetition of which with a proper mixture of angles, triangles, and parallelograms, was expected eventually to effect my cure." Despite stiff resistance the cure took, wrote Parton, and "I became perfectly passive in the hands of my tormentors."

74

Thus every morning and evening found her "busily conning a new arithmetic which had been manufactured since my arrival . . . with the benevolent intention of making an end of me." The sum total, as Parton might have put it, was predictable, and thought and word soon equaled the product. The essay proceeded to give a series of illustrative examples. Upon encountering "a poor wretch evidently intoxicated" Parton had the thought that "that man has overcome three scruples, to say the least, for three scruples make one dram." And when on the Sabbath a churchgoer lamented to her, " 'And how shall we unite these several denominations in one?' " she responded, " 'Why, reduce them to a common denominator.' "

Although resistance was not dead, reminders of the "dreaded examination day" kept the would-be rebel in line, to the degree that on the morning of the examination, when she arose to "make my toilet," she discovered that, "to my great consternation, my hair, instead of forming itself as usual into flaxen circles, very deliberately erected itself into triangles, angles, and parallelograms all over my head." An immediate investigation disclosed that "I had curled it with a leaf of my geometry." Thinking, Parton wrote with choice, if unintended irony, that "my outward man must needs be sacrificed," that is, that nothing could be done, the dutiful pupil started for school to take her examination. Unfortunately, on the way to school, "reckoning, as I went, the rods, inches, and barleycorns over which I was passing," she encountered "a young gentleman whose company, before the days of Euclid and Daboll, was not very disagreeable to me, and whom report had long since tied to my apron strings." When the young gentleman "protested his warm interest," she responded, " 'Interest . . . . What per cent, sir?' " Stupified, the young gentleman mumbled, " 'Madam, at any rate do not trifle with my feelings.' " To which she replied, " 'At any rate, did you say? Then I take six per cent; that is the easiest to calculate.' " After finding herself suddenly deserted, she continued on to school, where she took her seat ready to recite. But at the very moment when the first question was addressed to her, "the whole drift of my friend's conversation at once flashed upon my mind," and she was rendered mute. Thus did she flunk both examinations. "From that day to this I have never opened an arithmetic," wrote Parton, and never given a thought to the subject "without passing my heaviest maledictions on the whole race, from Pike, Daboll and Colburn to our improved patent Brainrack."[2]

The joke, of course, was on Parton herself, just as Stowe unintentionally indicated when she later wrote to her, "*You* a grandmother, Sara! *Can* I conceive it! The girl with a head of light crepe curls, with a jaunty little bonnet tipped on one side and laughing, bright blue eyes—writing always good compositions and fighting off your arithmetic lessons?" Parton's granddaughter Ethel Parton wrote in an unpublished biography of her grandmother of being told many tales of "Yellowbird" or "Sal Volatile," as Sara Parton was supposedly called when she attended Beecher's seminary.

Ethel also reported that the seminary "placed the development of character first and intellectual attainments second" and "professed a third aim—the proper preparation of young ladies to enter society." It was the "custom of the school," wrote Ethel, "for each teacher to have a certain number of the pupils assigned to her with a view to the development of their characters, and Sara was one of Miss Beecher's own charges." Ethel quoted Catharine Beecher as saying that " 'a prime virtue' " to be taught the female students was " 'modesty.' "[3]

According to her husband James, as a child Sara (b. 1811) had been surrounded by newspapers and books in her household and had had the good fortune to be reared by parents who were determined that their children receive the best education possible. For Sara that meant attendance at Beecher's seminary and, in addition, the Emerson Ladies Seminary of Saugus, Massachusetts, and a school in Derry, New Hampshire, headed by Zilpah Grant, who would later establish the Ipswich Female Seminary with Mary Lyon. Her formal education completed, Sara, as far as her husband knew, then experienced "a few years of the usual life of a young lady at home." Sara's brother, Nathaniel Willis, meanwhile went on to Boston Latin, followed by Yale. As Sara would indicate later in her autobiographical novel, *Ruth Hall*, a young female quickly learned what role society expected her to play and in what fashion society regarded her. In Madame Moreau's female seminary, Ruth Hall's peers are perplexed by her evident interest in "stupid books" when "all the world knew that it was quite unnecessary for a pretty woman to be clever."[4]

For most of the literary domestics who followed Catharine Maria Sedgwick and Caroline Howard Gilman the pattern would be repeated. Always primarily social in purpose, their education was limited and frequently haphazard. Maria McIntosh (b. 1803), for example, was taught by her mother. Her only exposure to formal education was at an academy in Sunbury, in Georgia's Liberty County, where she reportedly had an elderly Oxford tutor who was a preacher as well as a teacher. E.D.E.N. Southworth (b. 1819) recalled her early years in Maryland and Washington, D.C., as ones spent in "solitude, reveries, and mischief" until at age thirteen she went to school for the first time at a female academy established by her mother and stepfather, Joshua Henshaw, the former secretary to Daniel Webster. It was then that Southworth "first discovered that she possessed some mental power," a discovery that was apparently a surprise to all concerned. From that point on she read "every book of every sort that she could lay her hands on."[5]

Most of Maria Cummins's (b. 1827) studies were directed by her father, but she was sent to the Young Ladies School established in Lenox, Massachusetts, by Catharine Maria Sedgwick's sister-in-law Elizabeth Sedgwick. And Augusta Evans Wilson (b. 1835) was tutored primarily by her mother, who thought, Wilson told a newspaper reporter, that the " 'best way to educate a girl is to let her browse in a well selected library.' " In short, Wilson in large measure had had to be self-motivated as well as self-taught. Until the bankruptcy of his mercantile firm led Wilson's father to move elsewhere in search of financial rebirth, Wilson had access to the libraries of wealthy relatives in Columbus, Georgia, in addition to her own family's. A lifelong acquaintance of Wilson's, the writer T. C. De Leon, stated in his biographical reminiscences appended to Wilson's novel *Devota* "She was from her childhood one of the closest students of books and not of people that I ever chanced to know. She was born in the library and she grew up in it." Not surprisingly, several of Wilson's fictional protagonists, including Beulah Benton in *Beulah* and Edna Earl in *St. Elmo*, "grew up" alone in libraries. Wilson did briefly attend a female seminary until ill health and the family's financial misfortunes forced her to return to the guidance of her mother and her own efforts.[6]

Access to all of the possible advantages of a female education, combined with individual curiosity and eagerness, aptitude and self-discipline, still did not alter the intellectually ambiguous circumstances of a culturally advantaged female. If anything, it had the potential to compound the ambiguity. The more education these women received, the harder they worked, and the more intellectually ambitious they were, the greater could be their sense of limitation and deprivation, of pointlessness and deep conflict. Eager to learn but increasingly aware that they faced a future restricted to the private sphere and a role as the enlightened, but subordinate companion to a husband and mother to children, these women could not ignore the underlying question of whether they should be educated or, more accurately, whether they should educate themselves. And the question of whether a woman should be an intellectual was inevitably accompanied by others, such as whether she could be, and whether she was not in fact different from or inferior to man. Those questions, conditioned by doubts, uncertainties, and confusions, floated in the minds of the literary domestics. The only answer, which was not an answer at all, was the paradoxical one that woman was and was not an intellectual figure. The self-perception developed that woman was a distinctive intellectual being, necessarily a different species from man.[7]

These perplexing questions and deeply ambivalent responses are illustrated in the educational experiences of three of the literary domestics. Born decades and regions apart and raised in varying circumstances, their experiences nonetheless were strikingly similar. Through their schooling, whether formal or informal, and through the equally significant example, encouragement, and guidance of their fathers, Harriet Beecher Stowe (b. 1811), Susan Warner (b. 1819), and Mary Virginia Terhune (b. 1830) received as much education as a woman could have reasonably expected in their time. All three took advantage of their opportunities. All three were intellectually ambitious, and all three were dedicated to their studies. But for all three, their society's perspective on gender conditioned their sense of themselves just as certainly as it determined their place. The issue was not so much education as the context in which they acquired it.[8]

Lyman Beecher's inadequate income and his ambitions had led him from a first pastorate in rural, isolated East Hampton, Long Island, to a second in the more settled and culturally stimulating Litchfield, Connecticut, and in 1826 similar motivations led him to the Hanover Church in Boston. When he asked his Litchfield congregation to release him from his duties so he could go to Boston, he told them from the pulpit that so far as the nurture and training of his children were concerned, "I never expected or desired to give them anything but their own minds and faculties, properly cultivated and prepared for active usefulness." However, Lyman went on, he had learned that such a gift cost money, more money than his past and present ministerial salary could bear. Lyman was not being ingenuous, he was being persuasive. What was also clear from Lyman's words was that the real expenses for the education of his children stemmed from the training of his sons, not his daughters. His income had been barely adequate, he said, until the "public education of my sons commenced." He even had been able to fund the education of one son by selling some inherited property and taking in boarders. But now, he informed his congregation, "In my attempt to educate a second son I am brought to a stand."[9]

Continuing to exercise his considerable powers of persuasion and negotiation, the evangelist Lyman wrote in a similar vein to the Hanover Church committee assigned to recruit him. He assured them that "in respect to the education of my sons" he did not consider it the congregation's obligation "to furnish for me the means of giving a public education to them all." He had no aversion to their becoming farmers or mechanics. But he did not have the "means" to make them agriculturalists either, and they did not have the "turn of mind" to be artisans. No, as it happened God had been disposed "to bless them with intellect, and most of them, I hope, with piety, and all of them with the love of study." How could anyone deny, then, that it was his duty to do everything possible to offer his sons an education *and* to "give them to Jesus"? In short, Lyman *was* asking the Hanover Church to provide that education for his sons. And he knew how to ask.[10]

What went unmentioned, of course, was that Lyman had a daughter, Catharine, who had come of age in Litchfield, who at least equaled his sons in intelligence, and who, like them, was dedicated to study, although admittedly she may not have been pious in exactly the way Lyman would have preferred. He had another daughter, Harriet, age fifteen at the time he was called to Boston, who also had clearly demonstrated her mental prowess and pious proclivities. But that was just the point. An education such as the one Lyman desired for his sons was no more a prime consideration or expectation for a female than was a public career. He certainly considered the intellectual training of his daughters important, but the main questions for a female were if and when and whom she would marry. Lyman's expectations and concerns were not idiosyncratic; they reflected the norm. And his wife Roxana had shared them. On her deathbed she expressed her wish that her sons become ministers of Christ. Her appeal was granted; all five of them did. Notably, Roxana did not mention her three daughters. Perhaps she did not consider it necessary, because she envisioned domesticity as their only possibility.[11]

Like her mother, Harriet had to juggle uneasily her desire to be with what she was supposed to be. She became reluctantly familiar with the circumstances under which a woman could pursue intellectual endeavors. As a child she was precocious and eager, and there were abundant stimuli. Following her mother's death in September 1816, when Harriet was five, she spent most of the year in the culturally rich environment of her maternal grandparents at Nutplains, Connecticut. That winter she and her brother Henry had their first taste of formal schooling at Ma'am Kilbourne's primary school for boys and girls. She was also surrounded by aunts, an uncle, and a grandmother who, well read themselves, read to her constantly and helped her develop her own skills in that regard. It was at Nutplains that she heard her first poetry, the ballads of Scott and Burns, and the plays of Shakespeare. There was also the prose of Dr. Johnson, a favorite of her grandmother, and for even " 'graver reading' " Rees's *Cyclopedia*, in which her Uncle George was steeped and in which he desired to immerse Harriet. The Bible, of course, was always there, accompanied in the Foote's household by the Assembly's Catechism of the Episcopal Church. In fact, Stowe's aunt, Harriet Foote, considered the catechism almost as important as Scripture. Foote, the " 'highest of High Church women,' " endeavored to have her niece memorize the catechism as a counter to the teaching of Beecher's Congregationalism. (Not surprisingly, Aunt Harriet lost the first battle for the child's allegiance. But years later, following the death of her father, Stowe would convert to the faith of her aunt.)[12]

Aunt Harriet's teaching extended far beyond Episcopalianism. Not the least of her effort was spent impressing upon Stowe the conviction that " 'little girls were to be taught to move very gently, to speak softly and prettily, to say "yes, ma'am" and "no ma'am," never to tear their clothes, to sew and to knit at regular hours, to go to church on Sunday and make all the responses, and to come home and be catechised.' " To come to know that thimble and needle were to be familiar companions and that regular hours were to be spent sewing was for Stowe to be stamped in the image of her grandmother, with her workbasket nestled among her books, and of her mother. At Nutplains, with its " 'interesting and well-selected library, and a portfolio of fine engravings,' " Stowe's dead mother " 'seemed to live again' " for her. It was there, where she saw her mother's painting and her needle work, that the daughter was just beginning to live.[13]

The next summer Stowe returned to Litchfield and attended a district school where, according to her older sister, Catharine, she was quickly proving herself an able student. She was learning to read " 'very fluently' " and was demonstrating that she had " 'a remarkably retentive memory.' " Evidence cited for the latter included her memorization of twenty-seven hymns and two long chapters in the Bible. For the next decade or more Stowe would be steeped in studies, which meant she was stamped as a culturally advantaged female. The Litchfield years were the formative ones for her, and she would later draw upon her experiences for use in her novels *Oldtown Folks* and *Poganuc People*. The northwestern Connecticut town was the site of Judge Reeve's law school, where, Stowe recalled, the " 'sons of the first families from all parts of the Union, and graduates of the first colleges' " enrolled, and of Sarah Pierce's school for young ladies, which enrolled the female counterparts " 'from the first families in all parts of the nation.' " In *Oldtown Folks* the town of "Cloudland" is based upon Litchfield and the "celebrated" academy of Miss Titcomb recalls that of Miss Pierce. Miss Titcomb's academy differs from its real-life counterpart in that boys as well as girls are admitted. Regarding the "dominant sex" in the school, the "young men" are said to be preparing for college while the "boys" entertain "the same ultimate hope." But Stowe sought to counteract the obvious implication by writing that as in "the generality of country academies, the girls and boys studied side by side, without any other restriction as to the character of their studies than personal preference." One Esther Avery is described as "the leading scholar in Greek and the higher mathematics." Not coincidentally, Esther happens to be the daughter of a minister, Mr. Avery, who, as Stowe confirmed in a letter to George Eliot, was based upon Stowe's own father. Still, it is noted that Miss Titcomb, besides teaching the academic subjects of geography and history—the latter, incidentally, the favorite subject of Sarah Pierce—in addition exercises "a general supervision over the manners, morals, and health of the young ladies" and gives especial attention to female accomplishments. Embroidery is most prominent among these.[14]

By 1819 the eight-year-old Stowe was among the ladies at Sarah Pierce's, and by that time the academy was being strongly influenced by John Brace, Pierce's nephew, who had joined his aunt as a teacher and administrator and who, as Stowe also told George Eliot, appeared in fictional form in *Oldtown Folks* as Jonathan Rossiter. Catharine had attended the school earlier, when Pierce had been its sole teacher and, according to Catharine, when " 'the higher branches' had not entered female schools." At that time the subjects included the " 'accomplishments' " of map drawing, painting, embroidery, and piano, along with history, geography, grammar, arithmetic, and the English classics, particularly poetry.[15]

After Brace's arrival a " 'more extended course' " was introduced into the curriculum. Stowe described Brace as " 'one of the most stimulating and inspiring instructors I ever knew.' " In 1845 she wrote to Sarah Beecher, the widow of her brother George, to recommend Brace for a teaching position, saying, "He is a man of the most general information on *all subjects* that I ever knew." He was particularly expert, she said, in botany, mineralogy, and the natural sciences in general, as well as in philosophy and composition. "I do not think you can find his equal," she concluded. But because Stowe was relatively young when she was at the academy, much of the stimulation and inspiration she felt from Brace was received at a distance. As she put it, " 'Much of the training and inspiration of my early days consisted, not in the things which I was supposed to be studying, but in hearing, while seated unnoticed at my desk, the conversation of Mr. Brace with the older classes,' " conversation and recitation that centered upon William Paley's *Moral Philosophy*, Hugh Blair's *Rhetoric*, and Archibald Alison's *On Taste*. In all innocence, Stowe revealed that gender also determined that stimulation and inspiration were gained indirectly. For example, it was the boys, including brother George, who were sent tramping over the hills to search for rock specimens to add to the mineralogical collections; George then related his adventures to sister Harriet. Stowe later recorded those adventures in *Oldtown Folks*.[16]

While the idealized memory of Roxana Beecher was important to her daughter, the living influence of Lyman Beecher was primary. Not surprisingly, she wanted her father's approbation of her as an intelligent being more than that of anyone else in her life. Stowe earned that approbation as early as age twelve and later described the moment as " 'the proudest of my life.' " The setting was again Miss Pierce's school, and the vehicle a composition she had written under the tutelage of Brace. ("I remember what an early stimulus I received in [composition] particularly under his happy mode of conversing and exciting ideas," she wrote Sarah Beecher.) Stowe had been doing compositions under Brace's guidance since she was nine, and had written her very first essay on the subject of "The Difference between the Natural and the Moral Sublime." Three years later she became eligible to submit compositions for the annual exhibition of the students' efforts, and she then presented an essay addressing the question "Can the Immortality of the soul be proved by the light of nature?" (Lyman's daughter, of course, responded in the negative.) That was a " 'proud distinction' " in itself, but it was only the prelude. The essay was read with her father in attendance, and as soon as the reading was concluded she overheard her father ask who had written the piece and Brace reply " 'Your daughter, sir!' " Stowe never forgot Lyman's response: " 'There was no mistaking father's face when he was pleased, and to have interested *him* was past all juvenile triumphs.' " At Miss Titcomb's in *Oldtown Folks* one of the topics assigned the students is " 'The Difference between the Natural and Moral Sublime.' " They are also asked the question, " 'Can the Benevolence of the Deity be proved by the Light of Nature?' " and it is Esther Avery's composition that takes the negative side.

"It was remarkable," relates the novel's narrator, Horace Holyoke, who was based upon Stowe's husband, Calvin, "that the very best writers, as a general thing, were among the female part of the school." Stowe had her proud and cherished memories.[17]

Had Stowe been a male she undoubtedly would have followed her father's example and embarked upon a ministerial career, just as all seven of her brothers did. Male or female, a child of Lyman Beecher's had to have been well aware of the father's active, public career. From the beginning Lyman was busy preaching for a revival of religion, a task that involved more than saving souls and recruiting church members. As Lyman himself noted, "In those days the ministers were all politicians," by which he meant that he and his fellow Congregationalist clergymen spent considerable time "trying to preserve our institutions and reform the public morals." Struggles to prevent disestablishment were waged and voluntary societies founded. Beecher and his cohorts eventually had to relinquish established Congregationalism, but the societies left in their wake became organizational models for reform in antebellum America. Congregationalists also allied themselves with Federalists to do battle against Jeffersonianism. But the alliance between religion and politics proved unequal to the challenge of an increasingly popular party. Calls to rally against the supposed threat to the republic were not heeded at the polls, and Jeffersonians garnered more and more votes within the bastion of Federalism. Still, the struggles were lively and the rhetoric impassioned, and at least in Litchfield they dominated conversation in the home and beyond.[18]

But as much as father inspired daughter and as proud a witness as Stowe was to Beecher's career, Lyman also indirectly guided her energies and shaped her perceptions along clearly defined channels. This was particularly apparent in the household where, Stowe recalled, evangelist Lyman "was famous for his power of exciting family enthusiasm." For example, she mentioned fishing excursions which she remembered "only as something pertaining to father and the older boys, they being the rewards for good conduct." With the males away the house was unnaturally still, and Stowe had " 'perhaps only a long seam on a sheet to be oversewed as the sole means of beguiling the hours of absence.' " Her excitement was great when they returned with their perch, roach, pickerel, and bullheads, as well as with pockets full of young wintergreen " 'of which a generous portion was bestowed always upon me.' "[19]

There were many chores for which Lyman would rally daughters as well as sons. Cutting, splitting, and storing wood involved everyone, and Lyman once spurred his daughter into a fury of activity with the declaration that he " 'wished Harriet was a boy, she would do more than any of them.' " Not surprisingly, Stowe also believed she had to become a boy to meet the challenge. Before plunging in to prove her mettle and, in effect, deny her sex, she recalled "putting on a little black coat which I thought looked more like the boys, [and] casting needle and thread to the wind." Paring and cutting apples provided a further opportunity for an ingenious Lyman to prod his children into making short work of a long project. He introduced Scott's novels into the seemingly endless process, and father and sons alternated recitation from as many scenes and incidents from the novels as they could remember. Always one to merge education with entertainment, Lyman would also seize upon a point of theology raised by a passage, engage one of his sons in debate, and help him practice for his appointed ministerial career. And what role was there for the daughter? Like her brothers, Stowe was both educated and entertained. Listening to the parts being played by males and observing the training provided, she could not fail to learn that needle and thread rather than a black coat signaled her future. With no trace of irony, novelist Stowe later recounted many of those scenes in *Oldtown Folks*.[20]

Stowe learned well, and she certainly remembered the lessons. In the last novel she wrote, *Poganuc People*, published in 1878 when she was sixty-seven, Stowe drew heavily upon the memories of her childhood. In Poganuc, again alias Litchfield, "the intellectual life of cultivated people" is said to be "intense." Topics of conversation include the latest novels of Scott and the poetry of Byron. Political controversy rivals literature as a concern. Federalists fear the inroads made by Jeffersonians; Congregationalists and Episcopalians eye each other with disdain. Male students apprentice in law offices and young ladies of first families have their reading circles, some partisans of Scott and Byron. Just as Poganuc is a fictional Litchfield, so the *Poganuc People*, especially the young heroine and her family, are modeled upon Harriet and other Beechers. Dolly Cushing's father is a clergyman, a Congregationalist, and a minister in a Connecticut town. And like Stowe, Dolly is shaped by life in the parsonage. It is "a silent influence, every day fashioning the sensitive, imaginative little soul that was growing up in its sphere of loneliness there." Stowe's words tell more than she intends. The "sphere of loneliness" has been created for Dolly in large part because the eldest son is away studying for the ministry; another son is teaching in order to pay his past college expenses; and yet another son is presently in college, a fact that is straining the family's finances. Two sons closer to Dolly's age are said to be "in the Academy." And the one elder daughter? She is married and living in another part of the state. Stowe relates these facts without stating that in this configuration Dolly might read her own future.[21]

Dolly receives a familiar early education. In the summer months, when the "big boys" are in the fields, the girls attend the district school where they are taught knitting and sewing. Dolly is teased by her brothers, "spouting scraps of superior Latin at her to make her stare and wonder at their learning," and she complains to a servant that " 'the boys talk Latin to me and plague me when I want to play with them.' " Although excluded from the mysteries of Latin, the curious and bright Dolly does have unexpected moments of discovery possible in an environment like hers. For example, she rummages through the garret in her house, poring over barrels of sermons, theological treatises, and old pamphlets, and stumbles upon a volume of *Arabian Nights* which delights her. Here Stowe drew directly upon an incident from her own childhood, just as she ascribed to Dolly the same devotion to reading she had developed as a girl. Reading, Stowe says, "was with [Dolly] a passion, and a book once read was read daily; always becoming dearer and dearer, as an old friend." Dolly's environment insures that other discoveries will be made as well. Precocious and intense, and sensitive to her surroundings, Dolly is also attentive to admonitions that "little girls . . . must be silent. Little girls should be seen and not heard." An aunt with a striking resemblance to Harriet Foote tells Dolly to " 'sit up straight and hold your shoulders back—the girls of this generation are getting round shouldered.' "[22]

Although Dolly receives the requisite schooling for a daughter of the cultured, the "good old-fashioned principle" upon which her primary education is based is usefulness, and for a female usefulness begins and essentially ends in the home. Household tasks are to be her life's business. Dolly learns to wash and dry, to pound and sift rock-salt crystals, to grind spices; and to brown coffee. Most importantly, there is "the drill of the long and varied sewing lessons that were deemed indispensable to her complete education," and which Dolly deems "a weariness unto the spirit." Most of these tasks can be performed in the morning before Dolly attends to her secondary, that is her academic, schooling. Not incidentally, Dolly recognizes that it is "only at the price of penances like these, well and truly performed," that her "golden *own* hours of leisure were given." Here the child speaks of hours of play, of idle hours when she feels most on her own. But it is the child's germ of an idea that will become the adult female's conception of life. Later, the novel suddenly concludes with the ending of Dolly's adolescent life and the beginning of her marriage, the latter capsuled in an assurance to the reader that the child who has become a woman "held her place among the matronage of Boston" while her sons "graduated at Harvard."[23]

As for Stowe herself, intellectual engagement continued. Shortly before her thirteenth birthday, Stowe's Litchfield days were interrupted by enrollment in her sister's Hartford Female Seminary. Unlike his sons' schooling, Harriet's education cost Lyman practically nothing. Sister Catharine, of course, waived tuition, and Harriet boarded with a family in Hartford who in turn sent their daughter to live with the Beechers in Litchfield while attending Sarah Pierce's school. Stowe would recall proudly that her two most intimate friends at Catharine's school were the institution's " 'leading scholars.' " They were already reading Virgil by the time Stowe arrived, and she immediately began the study of Latin herself. By the end of the first year her verse translation of Ovid became yet another submission for the school's annual exhibition. It was regarded, she remembered " 'as a very creditable performance.' "[24]

The years in Hartford were stimulating and fulfilling. Stowe's interest in poetry intensified, despite the urgings of Catharine to leave poetry aside and discipline her mind with texts like Joseph Butler's *Analogy of Religion*, which she dutifully did for a time. Richard Baxter's *Saint's Everlasting Rest* was another text she studied; she claimed it " 'affected me more powerfully' " than any other book she read. In 1826 she wrote to her Grandmother Foote, noting that father Lyman had " 'received a call to Boston, and concluded to accept, because he could not support his family in Litchfield.' " For her own part, Stowe was still the diligent student. Latin and arithmetic, she reported, were receiving most of her time, and she hoped to prepare herself soon to assist Catharine. For most of Lyman's Boston years Stowe remained in Hartford, teaching as well as continuing her studies and eventually aiding Catharine, even substituting as supervisor of the school. But for all of Stowe's intellectual involvement in Hartford, a part of her was with Lyman in Boston. Years later she wrote to her brother Charles that while looking over her father's letters from his time in Boston, " 'the most active, glowing, and successful period of his life,' " she recalled that it was a period for her when " 'I was more with him, and associated in companionship of thought and feeling for a longer period, than any other of my experience.' " Boston, as Stowe put it, was in the grip of the Unitarians: " 'Calvinism or orthodoxy was the despised and persecuted form of faith,' " and Unitarianism " 'reigned in its stead.' " But Lyman, in " 'the high noon of his manhood, with flood-tide of his powers,' " was ready and eager to do battle. Seeing herself as his supporter and companion at a distance, Stowe used words which were a paraphrase of the very words she used to describe what she believed her mother's relationship had been with Lyman in Litchfield. Like mother, like daughter, it was the cultured female's state of mind.[25]

Susan Warner's sister and biographer, Anna Warner, described the young Susan in terms that might well have served as an epitaph. As a child, wrote Anna, her sister possessed "a strong temper, an imperious will, a masterful love of power that very ill brooked curbing," and, she added, "a relish for the right of way that might have served a boy." The description may well provide the key to understanding the troubled self-identity of this unusually well-educated woman, for, as Anna commented, "so she always told of herself." Had Warner been a boy there would have been a greater opportunity to indulge that "relish for the right of way." In the children's early years the Warners were a family of means, social and financial. Henry Whiting Warner, Susan and Anna's father, was a very affluent New York lawyer who frequently did business at the state capital in Albany, where his own father had served in the legislature during the first decade of the nineteenth century. As early as age four, in 1823, Susan had accompanied Henry on one of his trips to Albany. Had she been a boy that trip might well have been later described as the earliest influence on yet another Warner male destined for yet another career in law and politics.[26]

Susan would never be able to entertain thoughts of emulating Henry in his chosen career, but nevertheless her father was her mentor, her teacher, advisor, and standard of excellence. She had "only one shrine of perfection," wrote Anna, "and it was for him." Not much is known of Susan's mother, also named Anna. Little is said about the mother in Anna's biography of Susan, and she is barely mentioned in Susan's own journals. Apparently she was a *lady*, from a family of even greater means and higher status than the Warners, and Anna refers to a notebook the mother had kept as a young woman "giving token of gay doings and a very easy life." The implication is that the daughters had greater respect for their father. Whatever the case may have been, their mother died when Susan was ten and Anna two, and unlike Stowe's mother, she does not appear to have left a lasting legacy, at least not an intellectual one.[27]

That domain was Henry's. Educated at Union College, he maintained a "life-long delight in Greek"; was given to expressing his feelings and thoughts in "verse and measure"; was "the most devoted adherent of the old-time beautiful Saxon English"; and was withal "the most ardent lover of books and study." Henry made every effort to pass his cultural passions on to his daughters. Many evenings were spent reading to them poetry, fiction, history, and essays. His choice of authors included Shakespeare, Scott, Dickens, Milton, and Boswell. He was a stern taskmaster, Susan's "drill master" in grammar, history, literature, and geography, and, at times, languages. For the most part language study was also a passion of Susan's, as is indicated by what Anna called her "quick, thorough progress" whatever the language. However, neither Henry's demands nor Susan's desire to please him were sufficient to make her as great a lover of Greek and Latin as was her gentleman father. As an accomplished daughter, French and Italian were more to her liking. But he made an impact, and his daily influence was felt. One evening, for example, he questioned his sixteen-year-old daughter about an essay of Blair's which she was to have read that day. That Henry found her comprehension wanting meant that Susan "felt unpleasantly" for at least the remainder of the day.[28]

Henry also saw to it that Susan received instruction from private tutors both within the home and without, mainly in languages, and in singing and piano, appropriate subjects for a young lady-to-be. Susan's education began at a very early age when the family still lived in affluence in their large New York City townhouse. Both daughters were provided opportunities available only to children of privileged families. Exactly when Susan commenced her daily routine as a child scholar is uncertain, but her personal journals, begun at age twelve, find her studying at full speed. Susan's journals also testify, as Anna noted, to the culturally fertile "atmosphere in which she lived." Nor was Susan unaware of the advantages she enjoyed. On one occasion, at age sixteen, Henry brought home some issues of a journal to which he had begun subscribing, titled, "Illustrations of Modern Sculpture." After an afternoon's absorption in her new treasure, her "splendid thing" as she called it, Susan wrote in her journal, "We are rich in such things," adding, "How are those to be pitied who have no such sources of enjoyment."[29]

But while Susan capitalized upon her cultural opportunities, the tale her journals tell is not simply one of a young mind absorbing influences and information, of a person refining herself and broadening her perspective. Rather, the flurry of activity appears frequently to have been spurred by a need to build a structure in a vacuum, to fill a void with study, to ward off a sense of futility by fostering a sense of purpose that nevertheless remained elusive. The compulsion to do, and thus to wonder what to do, appears continually threatened by the underlying question, why do it? It was a question that went to the heart of the elite daughter's nurture. Certainly there was intellectual stimulation and cultural enrichment, but for what reasons, to what end? If the question was asked, there appeared to be no answer, at least no fully satisfying one; and if it was not asked, it was always implicit.

The testimony of the journals is that the effort to do was continually made. The testimony, too, is that Susan felt a need to record her efforts and that Anna, drawing upon only selected journal entries for her biography, felt compelled to draw attention to them, as if Susan's writing it all down and Anna's focusing upon it would make it so, would allow them both to convince themselves that Susan, a female, could and did have capabilities and aspirations. The image Anna struck of her older sister was of one "with always a book in her hand." No matter what the subject of the book, wrote Anna, "she was never ready to lay it down."[30] To pick and choose from Susan's journals is to find her at twelve and thirteen studying Latin, French, and Italian; reading Plutarch's *Lives*, the Bible, Rollin's *Ancient History*, the philosophy of Hume, and Bunyan's *Pilgrim's Progress*; taking singing and piano and painting lessons. At fifteen, studies begun earlier continued and she delved into geography and botany and read the fiction of Scott. At sixteen, there was more language study; more Scott, including Scott on Napoleon; Pope's *Homer*, Cowper, and Shakespeare; the philosophy of Dugald Stewart; Dante and Tasso; more history; and algebra. And at seventeen and eighteen she was still studying languages, reading the French divine Bossuet, more Hume, Defoe's *Robinson Crusoe*, delighting in Molière, and playing the music she found most appealing, Beethoven, Mozart, Thalberg, and Liszt.

On the surface the journals appear to be a record of accomplishment. They offer evidence of Susan Warner, the individual, trying to extend herself and to explore, by the day, the season, or the year. But a close examination reveals an individual struggling to convince herself, a picture of one fearful of idleness, attempting to hold together the pieces of an existence that refused to coalesce. Driving herself, she simultaneously castigated herself for failing to do her duty; goading herself, she nevertheless felt that motivation remained elusive. And all the while the one constant, that which was given, self-contained, and static, pinned like a cameo to her breast, was her identity as a young, educated female. If the legitimacy of her intellectual being was questionable, if her intellectual efforts seemed mocked by pretense, there was little doubt about what her status as a feminine being connoted and prophesied. Drifting through a day and bemoaning wasted hours, she sewed. At times ineffectual and inefficient in her attempts to structure her studies, she tutored and told stories to children of relatives and friends. Unable to discipline herself and to focus upon her studies, she made toy clothing and furniture. Curious about the world beyond her, but shy, timid, and apprehensive, she periodically retreated into herself like a private being.

At twelve the various refrains are introduced in her journal, to remain and to become familiar, to shroud and undermine accomplishment. Feeling ill, Susan states that she will not be able to attend a lesson the following day, "but," she adds, "I must begin again on Monday." The following day she records that she has "lost three lessons," has in fact had only one lesson the entire week, and laments, "I shall not get through in a year at this rate." What the lessons concern she does not say. Four days later she states that the day before was "spent pretty idly," as she gave considerable time to constructing a doll's cap and generally "did very little which was useful." She did not play the piano for the hour set aside for the purpose and did none of her lessons. And today has been little better, although she did exercise and "sewed some on my muslim." Three more days pass and, exasperated with herself, she writes, "Must I say again that I did nothing worth mentioning yesterday?" Unfortunately, that appears to her to have been the case: certainly she had done nothing "useful." What she did do was what she had done for days past: played on the piano, read some (including Hume), played games, told stories to younger children, missed one lesson and attended another. The subsequent notations and reflections follow the same bent. On one day she reads a little of Leigh Richmond's *Entertaining Knowledge* and three chapters of the Bible, constructs toy sofas and chairs, and concludes, "I find that I have spent a most unprofitable week, and as unprofitable a Sunday. The more shame for me. I am now old enough to do better." And on another day she derides the "lazy thing that I was," noting that in the absence of a lesson she had nevertheless failed to use the free time to study, had instead sewed and painted, and had told stories for "I don't know how long."[31]

At fourteen, fifteen, and sixteen, days rather than years might as well have passed. She continued to judge herself, writing at the end of a day in her journal, "Have not done much useful. This is a common case." Missed lessons or practices were dutifully recorded, along with the requisite explanation of illness or poor planning. Meanwhile she would occupy herself with botany, sew, tell stories, absorb herself in Goldsmith's *History of England*, and spend an evening reading *Ivanhoe* to her Aunt Fanny. After pasting varieties of flowers and leaves into a book as part of her study of botany, she observed that she liked "this business very much," but added, "How long I shall like it is another matter." After returning to New York City following a summer in the country, she faced the fact that "I have studied none since I came home" (although she had read some in *Anacharsis*), and resolved upon a structured plan of study: at nine she would practice on the piano; at ten, Italian; eleven, singing and more piano; twelve, Euclid and Paley; one, singing and piano practice again; and two, French. Skeptical and judgmental as ever, she wrote, "How far I shall follow this plan is doubtful; I hope nevertheless to conform to it in some measure." Three weeks later she was back at it again. She had been home for nearly six weeks, and she scolded herself for having "scarcely done anything worth doing." Impatient with herself as she was, there was little doubt in her mind that "I have no reason to be satisfied with myself ever since I have been home. I have, I hope, started today to do better." What that meant was that she had played the piano for two hours, ironed "two night-gowns," read some more in *Anacharsis* and begun Scott's *Life of Napoleon Bonaparte*, listened to her father read Maria Edgeworth's *Ormond*, and talked with him about Pope's *Homer*.[32]

Anna, perplexed by her own personal observations and memories and by the journal's record of her sister's unabating, sometimes frenetic struggle, would largely attribute that struggle to Susan's temperament, to a case of nerves. "Those stormy outbursts in Ellen Montgomery with which critics found fault," wrote Anna, referring to the heroine of Susan's first novel, *The Wide, Wide World*, "were well known to my sister." That was not to imply, Anna added, that Ellen Montgomery was an autobiographical portrait of Susan. But the two did share a common trait, namely, that "where tempests are possible, gleams and glooms are the natural every day weather." Susan herself would write in her journal that she was always "*sufficiently sombre*" and sometimes too much so. "I have so many 'black ideas,' " she noted. "Nerves," Anna thought, *had* to explain why Susan wrote these and other seemingly strange entries, such as "It is a misfortune to be so timid as I am. In company with strangers I can hardly speak, look, or move, with comfort, comparatively, unless it is at our home." Anna believed it very "strange" that such sentiments were felt by one who went on to become "*very* fond of society, and of strangers." And later Susan would write, "I am a poor hand at conversation in company, that's certain. What will become of me if ever I go into company, I don't know." Yet the bewildered Anna observed that others considered her the " 'best talker' " they had ever heard.[33]

Susan's periodic poor health, or at least the aggravation of it, was largely attributed by Anna to the fact that "the love of books reigned paramount" with her sister. "I can see now," wrote Anna, "how it wrought to be the undermining of her health." As proud as Anna was of her sister's studious bent, she thought that Susan studied too much. Did she think perhaps that it was unnatural for a female to be so intellectually involved? It upset Anna greatly "to see how she read and studied, even in the summer time out of town. Books, always books!" In Anna's estimation, her sister was clearly a troubled person, "wedded," as Anna would remember her at age seventeen, "to those sedentary habits which no authority of hers could control." Most significant both in terms of Anna's perspective and Susan's state of being was Anna's observation that "nerves" and "sickness" joined forces most powerfully in Susan when she pondered "the great question." The question, "never forgotten," was, of course, "of future life and what it held for her." Death and the afterlife were what Anna meant. But there was another "great question," left unstated by either Anna or Susan: what type of male Susan would marry. It was the other "great question" because it was the *only* question of the earthly life, because the answer would determine apparently not the course but the nature of Susan's temporal existence.[34]

As it happened, the unexpected answer to that question did indeed change the course of Susan Warner's life. Until her seventeenth year she continued to struggle on in familiar fashion. In one entry she prayed, "If I live I hope not to be idle." In another she pondered which of the French divines she should read, Bossuet, Bourdaloue, or Fenelon, finally settling on the first. But oh, she fretted, "how easy it is to trifle away whole days in doing nothing, and how hard, to one not accustomed to regular and *useful* employment, to spend one hour in application to something worthwhile." And to think, she added, "I am almost seventeen." Later she noted the passing of Christmas day, during which she had taught the children and translated French for their use, read Cowper and begun Dugald Stewart's *Elements of the Philosophy of the Human Mind*, and practiced the piano. In March she asked herself what "account" she could give of the winter passed. Tasso and Dante had stood on the shelf undisturbed. She had let Italian alone and studied French only for the benefit of the children. Stewart she had put aside, and "I am only in the *third* volume of Cowper." Judging herself instead of her circumstances, she concluded that her "willfulness and indolence" were the problem. She was a failure in the eyes of others and, more importantly, "I know I am not what I might have been." What she did not know was that she was not going to become what had always seemed inevitable.[35]

Susan wrote those words during the spring of 1837, the last spring when, as Anna noted, "abundant means and a city home played their part in her education." Susan's days as a wealthy gentleman's daughter were soon to end, and the promise of a future as a gentleman's wife was soon to disappear. Beginning with the Panic of 1837, Henry Warner was involved in a series of financial disputes that adversely affected the family's material fortunes. In New York City, where his legal affairs were generally conducted, successes turned to reverses in rapid order. Mortgage payments on property held by him were demanded in full and could not be met, and title to land was lost when oral agreements were denied. Straitened circumstances forced the family to move to Constitution Island off West Point and live permanently in a cottage that had been purchased originally as a summer residence. But property on the island soon involved them in extended litigation and became a further financial drain. Much money was spent turning a flooded river meadow that connected the island to the mainland into dry land, for pleasure and profit, but when neighbors destroyed the dikes the investment was lost, and litigation began. What followed in succeeding years were eviction threats and the sale of household belongings to pay debts. The Warners were reduced from affluence to necessary thrift, and eventually to constant anxiety that they would fail to find the daily means to live.[36]

The decline was prolonged, torturous, and, looking back, precipitous. As Anna, eight years Susan's junior, expressed it through her narrator, Grace Howard, in her own thinly disguised autobiographical novel, *Dollars and Cents*, "During my first years, we had enjoyed what some of our ancestors had toiled for." But then the family became "like a child slipping down hill,—afraid to let ourselves go, and catching at every bush to stop our progress." Had the decline in the family's fortunes been sudden, dramatic, and total it might have been less painful, "for even in temporal things, the valley of humiliation is far more pleasant than the side-hill which leads to it." In her biography of Susan, Anna surmised that with the family's affairs "on a steady progress down hill" it must have been even more difficult for Susan, who was "in the bloom of her young womanhood." It was one thing for a genteel daughter to deal with the material loss, with the absence of finery. "But," wrote Anna, "the banishment of silk dresses entailed a much heavier loss; that of intercourse with other people." When her status as a socially advantaged female vanished, along with it went her marital eligibility; there could no longer be thoughts of eligible gentlemen. Neither in Anna's comment nor in Susan's journal entries was there a literal statement of that fact; just as one who is still alive might well avoid acknowledging the obvious fact that for all practical purposes one's life had passed. But as Anna said, "a subtile something in the air startled [Susan's] instincts, not yet in training except by romances, nor at all full grown." Anna also said that she had been told "that our change of fortune . . . touched those particular spring blossoms with 'a most unkindly frost.'" And Susan clearly alluded to it. At twenty, writing in understated fashion, she noted, "Truly the times are changed, since we were in our town house"; recalling when she was sixteen, she said again, "Times have changed since then, and as for me I believe I am changed too." However oblique, it was an acknowledgment she could not have avoided.[37]

In the beginning the changes were physical and social, while her inner and intellectual life appeared to be as before. The connection, of course, had always been misleading. Once removed to Constitution Island on an apparently permanent basis, the Warners more and more had to fend for themselves. The gradual but steady loss of servants, from waiter to coachman to cook, meant they had to abandon silks and laces for self-made calicoes, do their own cooking, make their own butter and grow their own vegetables, cut their own wood, and forget "frisky black ponies" for a rowboat used to go to the mainland for supplies. The family also had to "forget" a social status that had once been theirs. As Susan observed in her journal, "It has been a long time since we were used to seeing many people."[38]

But her education went on. There were more domestic tasks for Susan: more sewing, because of the need to make clothes; dusting, in the absence of a housemaid; bread and butter to make. But her intellectual life had always cast a preternatural light on her daily routine, and she would filter her days by drilling Anna in French and a cousin in music; reading Sévigné and Molière; talking with her father; and writing in her journal. At twenty, she wrote in her journal the question "What to say?" and answered, "I will say everything that comes to mind," which meant recording in French a dry list of the day's events, namely, reading Tasso with Anna, teaching geography to the younger girls, reading more Molière, and listening to her father read more Scott. Did she write well? She wished she knew, but, she wrote, "no one here can tell me." She continued to worry about using her time more effectively. There were more and more physical tasks that had to be performed, however distasteful: "I do not like washing dishes, cleaning furniture, sweeping the floors, or setting the table." Still, she vowed she would continue to find time to learn to write French better, even if it *was* "needful to sew as well," even if it *was* true that "I would rather write or read than sew or work." In mind, hers was still the existence of a leisured and educated female.[39]

There had been a change, of course. Her elite female mentality had been developed, in a larger sense, for a social purpose. And that social purpose was no more. Effect had been severed from cause. But her life of the mind had always existed in limbo, cut off more or less from reality. Books and studies had never been hers either for a career or as an integral part of her existence. Rather, they had been the stuff of fantasy, of an existence without moorings. The family's change in circumstances did impinge upon her, but as she wrote in her journal, "As soon as one reads or writes, what do these things matter? One troubles oneself about them no more, they are no longer worth anything, unless perhaps they make one enjoy one's ease all the more." Thus for a few years a part of her remained almost untouched, disembodied and unaffected in the face of disaster. "I do not know how I can be as gay as I am nowadays," she wrote at twenty, "for it is possible that we are to be ruined,—what people call *ruined*. Perhaps I do not know what ruin means." In many respects, it had not been her business to know anything other than the identity of an educated female looking toward marriage.[40]

" 'Educate them as if they were boys and preparing for college,' " Samuel Pierce Hawes said in 1843 to the man he had engaged as a tutor for his two daughters. The comment was remembered by the younger of the two, Mary Virginia Terhune, who was twelve at the time, and she reported it many years later, in the autobiography she published when she was eighty. She remembered probably because she cherished the comment, because she was proud both that she thought of herself as having been educated as if she had been a boy and that her father had desired to educate her, again, as if she had been a boy. Of course, in point of fact Terhune was being prepared neither for college nor for life as a gentleman; she was expected to become the cultivated wife of a gentleman. Thus both the comment and its recollection point to the paradoxical nurture that fostered yet another ambiguous state of mind in yet another advantaged daughter. Formally educated to the level at which, had she been a male, she would have proceeded to college, Terhune would never forget or, in her own fashion, cease to regret that she was not a male. For a female to be educated as if she were a male was to have it impressed in her consciousness that she was merely a guest in the male realm of intellectuality. It was to know that regardless of her training, she would never be a fully involved participant.[41]

Just as Terhune passed over her mother, who was in her mind less than intellectually adequate, to mythologize her grandmother, so she turned to her father for her actual intellectual inspiration. She was convinced that she had inherited "a strain of physical and mental hardihood" from the father to whom she dedicated her autobiography. Although Terhune uncomfortably acknowledged that her father was not a college graduate and that he was a merchant, she assured the readers of her autobiography that "in intellect he was far above the average businessman." In a letter to Kate Sanborn she noted that his library "was more than respectable," distinguished in particular by a collection of English classics that would have given "strength and dignity to 'complete' modern book-shelves." A transplanted native of Dorchester, Massachusetts, Samuel Hawes achieved a position in society that enabled him to provide his daughter with the education of a gentleman's daughter. After apprenticing in a family friend's Boston mercantile firm, Hawes at sixteen moved with his employer to Richmond, Virginia. Nine years later he was a partner in his own flourishing mercantile house and was engaged to Judith Anna Smith, the daughter of a wealthy Virginia plantation family. Before Terhune was born her parents' social and financial status declined temporarily, and the family moved to the countryside bordering Richmond. There Hawes established himself as a country storekeeper, a calling which, Terhune was careful to emphasize, was at the time as "honorable" as that of city merchant. It was also one in which Hawes "succeeded far beyond his expectations." Social and material status restored, the family returned to Richmond. Although Terhune implied that her family was never inclined to an ostentatious display of wealth, their renewed affluence did enable them to enjoy an "abundance" of delicacies and finery, along with a carriage and horses for the family and a riding horse for each of the daughters. At the same time, Hawes added to his success as businessman by becoming a force in local and state politics, eventually taking his place on the magistrate's bench. Among other distinctions, Terhune related, her father became president of a debating society "in which he was, I think, the only man who was not a college graduate."[42]

Although her mother was the first to teach Terhune and the other Hawes children to read and to write, it was her father who motivated her and *managed* the training of her mind. From early in her life, as if she understood from the beginning that he, the male, was the source of legitimation, it was her father's instruction that counted in her mind. When Terhune was five years old, after she had apparently failed to respond to her mother's attempts to teach her to read, her father took her "upon his knee" to scold her because she had yet to learn what he was certain every other " 'nice' " child in the county knew, namely, her "a,b,c's." While her mother "lay sick up-stairs," father Hawes presented her with a volume of the *New York Reader* and urged her to learn, with the aid of a sixteen-year-old female cousin, to read from its pages. Do " 'not forget what father has been saying' " and apply yourself, Hawes supposedly told his tearful daughter; " 'Think how pleased mother will be' " when she recovers and finds you can read a chapter in the Bible to her. As the family legend went, or as Terhune told it, the truant child was thus transformed into the dutiful student.[43]

With a paucity of public schools in Virginia at the time, Terhune began at age seven to attend a series of private schools with other children "carefully selected from families in our own class." Most of the families were Presbyterian, with a sprinkling of Methodists, and instruction included a heavy dose of "moral and religious precepts." Terhune's first teacher at school was a familiar one, the same cousin, now eighteen and a graduate of a female seminary. She was succeeded the following year by "the meek widow of a Methodist clergyman," whose abilities were scant. "It is doubtful," Terhune commented, "if we learned anything worth relating from her," adding, however, that she was gentle and devout and that at least "nothing evil" was imparted. Terhune was probably expressing the sentiments of her father, who "fully appreciated the deficiencies of the small private schools we had attended."[44]

Hawes also resolved to do something about it. Enrollment in a boarding school, one alternative for monied families, was rejected by a father, thoroughly schooled in the principles of republican motherhood, who, according to his daughter, considered entrusting the "moral and mental training" of his children to someone else at such a "formative age" tantamount to the shirking of the parents' "sacred duty." Actually he meant the female parent's duty, which could not be fulfilled if children boarded away from home, "just when girls and boys are most in need of the mother's love and watchful care of their health and principles." Another alternative was enrollment as a day scholar in the " 'Old-Field School,' " described by Terhune as the forerunner of the coeducational secondary school. Run by a male college graduate, Old-Field School was attended by " 'nice' " girls and "well born" boys alike. It was also where older "lads" were prepared for college. Hawes rejected that choice as well, saying within earshot of his daughter, " 'Too much of an *omnium gatherum* to suit my taste!' " The implication was that since his daughters were not being prepared for college, they might receive insufficient attention.[45]

When Terhune was nine or ten Hawes finally decided to bring a tutor, a male divinity student from Union Theological Seminary in Prince Edward County, directly into their home. Terhune recalled that she was exhilarated by the decision because it meant that she, her older sister Mea, and her younger brother Herbert, "lately inducted into the integuments distinctive of his sex," were now to have "a tutor of our own." In fact that was not exactly the case, as they were to be joined in the "home-class" by the daughters of personal friends "of like mind with the independent thinker," meaning of course her father. But as far as Terhune was concerned the divinity student was to be " 'Our Tutor.' " It is interesting to speculate why this particular tutor held such special, positive significance for her. After all, she had had at least two teachers previously. Perhaps it was because they had been female and now she was to have her first male instructor—moreover, a male of advanced learning. Perhaps she thought that now she would be taught by the genuine article, representing what was legitimately the male intellectual realm. At any rate, before meeting him she thought of her tutor-to-be as "my dream-castle" or the "hero of my dreams." Unfortunately, "Mr. Tayloe," as she would later fictionalize him, instead turned out to be the "Evil Genius" of her childhood, and received due treatment in Terhune's *An Old-Field School-Girl*. Although the "well-born" theological student had distinguished himself at the seminary and was "a gentleman in bearing and speech," Terhune, and apparently the other students, found him to be "a coarse, cruel tyrant" in the classroom.[46]

When the tyrant was replaced by a "handsome Yankee governess" from Massachusetts, there was widespread relief. Now it was the person rather than the credentials that "inspired" Terhune. From the "sweet and sunny," "refined and gentle" governess, Terhune learned for the first time "that hard study might be a joy, and gain of knowledge rapture." What she studied included Vose's *Astronomy*, Comstock's *Natural Philosophy*, and Lyell's *Elements of Geology*. Motivated by the example of the governess, who wrote poetry and kept a diary, Terhune also wrote verse and prose and shared her efforts with her teacher. Much to Terhune's regret and annoyance, her beloved governess was claimed in marriage ten months later by a "matter-of-fact personage" who whisked her off to what Terhune characterized as the "outlandish region" of Cape Neddick on the coast of Maine.[47]

During the same period, when Terhune was nine, ten, and eleven, her home education continued outside the hours of her home school. As Terhune indicated in the 1880s to both Kate Sanborn and Florine Thayer McCray, the latter in an interview for the *Ladies Home Journal*, her father remained the guiding influence and supervised her choice of reading. Familiar items included Rollin's *Ancient History*, a translation of Plutarch's *Lives*, issues of the *Spectator*, Bunyan's *Pilgrim's Progress*, Shakespeare, and the poetry of Cowper and Thomson. Occasionally, particularly on winter nights, Terhune's father "relaxed his objections to light reading" and allowed his daughters to peruse periodicals. That reading, usually done in bed, encompassed *Graham's Magazine, Godey's Lady's Book*, the *New York Mirror*, the *New York Observer*, the *Saturday Evening Post*, and the *Saturday Evening Courier*. One of Terhune's favorite authors in these publications was Caroline Lee Hentz.[48]

Hawes continued to devise further means by which to complete his daughters' education. When the Yankee governess departed and no successor could be located, Terhune recalled that her father "determined upon a bold departure from the beaten path of traditional and conventional usage in the matter of girls' education." Terhune and her sister were to be sent from home to board near Hampden-Sydney College and Union Theological Seminary. The two institutions formed an educational center with an atmosphere not unlike that of an "Old World university town." The environs, the adjacent counties of Prince Edward, Charlotte, and Halifax, were also inhabited by many " 'first families' " of Virginia, including a number of aristocratic Presbyterian plantation owners, each of whom was as well "college-bred and a politician," according to Terhune. Hawes probably decided that his earlier objection to sending his daughters away would not apply, since they would be boarding with "Aunt Rice." Aunt Rice was actually first cousin to Terhune's mother, the daughter of the sister of Terhune's revered grandmother. She was also the daughter of Major James Morton, who had served on Washington's staff in the Revolution, and the widow of the Reverend Doctor John Holt Rice, a founder of Union Theological Seminary and its first president.[49]

As Terhune, now twelve, described it excitedly in a letter to a female cousin, the nine months that she spent at her aunt's home, Rice Hill, was a time of " 'privileges and [a] pleasant situation.' " To say the least, it was apt that Terhune spoke of " 'privileges.' " Although this was not her meaning, the greatest privilege she enjoyed there was that, in a more concentrated, comprehensive fashion than at any previous stage in her young life, she was allowed to observe the male intellectual realm, and she probably fantasied that she would one day be a participant. "Were I required to tell what period of my nonage had most to do with shaping character and coloring my life," she later wrote, "I should reply, without hesitation, 'The nine months passed at Rice Hill.' " Stating that "a new, boundless realm of thought and feeling was opened" to her during those months, Terhune's words both reveal an illusion and express literal truth. Without realizing it, even in retrospect when she was eighty years old, living at the site of the two educational institutions had meant that she was as close as she would ever get to being a male student, while she remained as far as she would always be from achieving that exalted status.[50]

" 'Oh, how I wish you were here,' " Terhune wrote to her cousin, describing how she went to the seminary debating society to hear "the young men preach," or to the college to hear the senior males deliver speeches. Believing herself to be a joyful participant in her newly discovered world, Terhune enjoyed most of all what she called the " 'religious privileges,' " meaning a broad range of what were actually social activities. Each Sunday, of course, the entire community did turn out for "church-going," but during the remainder of the week the bill was filled with "Dining-days" at plantations, along with barbeques, anniversaries, and political gatherings. Yet what Terhune, the would-be participant, observed on all of these occasions were males, young and old, practicing or displaying their public and intellectual skills. At church, where the men and women sat apart, worship, prayers, and sermons—the last "intellectual, no less than spiritual pabulum"—were governed and delivered by men. Speech making, which rendered the social *political*, was the prerogative of men, the leaders of their communities, and was an "art [to be] learned by boys." In those days, wrote Terhune, eloquence from pulpit or podium was "indigenous to the soil" of Virginia. Even during meals at the home of Aunt Rice, who supplied "table-board" to students from the college and seminary, Terhune sat in thrilled and awed silence listening to "the informal, suggestive chat of men eager for knowledge, comparing notes and opinions, and discussing questions of deep import—historical, biological, and theological." In the main, Terhune thought the students a "bright set of fellows" and, of course, gentlemen through and through.[51]

To complete this educational experiment, Terhune's father determined upon a scheme regarded as "eccentric in the extreme" by friends and critics alike. As if with an eye to helping her prepare for a role that in actuality she would never play, Hawes engaged as a tutor Robert Reid Howison, then a college graduate, lawyer, and seminary student, and later author of *History of Virginia* and *The Student's History of the United States*. This was the man Hawes ordered to educate his daughters " 'as if they were boys and preparing for college.' " The schedule found Terhune and her sister meeting with Howison from twelve o'clock till half-past two each day, with independent study before and after. This arrangement was regarded as "the most *outré* of 'Mr Hawes's experiments'" as well as a guaranteed failure— other females of their age and status in the vicinity spent five hours a day in a private classroom. But, claimed Terhune, what the doubters and detractors had not reckoned upon, while the "cool brain" of her father had, was the fidelity of the tutor joined with the conscientiousness of his daughters, who had been trained to implicitly obey their father's instructions.[52]

The experiment was an unadulterated success, so far as Terhune was concerned. Despite her previous experience with the "Evil genius," this male tutor she "loved." "I can talk to him," she wrote her cousin, "better than to any other gentleman here. Would not you like to have such a teacher?" Both before and after the fact, she also revered him, particularly for his "mind so richly stored with classic and modern literature, so keenly alive to all that was worthy in the natural, mental, and spiritual world." And he was patient with her, even when her performance was not up to the mark, whether in French, which she began to learn at that time, or in mathematics, "never my strong point." It was Howison, too, who first introduced her to Scott's novels and poems. For Terhune, then, the nine months at Rice Hill represented an idyll of the mind, as in peculiar fashion she inhabited a kingdom of male intellectuality and learned on the spot, as it were, from her male intellectual emissary. "Never," she wrote, "had learners a happier period of pupilage." The sojourn had to end, of course. Howison completed his theological studies and Terhune and her sister returned home. Nevertheless the daughters' education did continue. For the next year each was given a desk in separate corners of a second-story room in their house. There five days a week from nine to one they repaired to continue their French lessons together or to read and discuss their latest history book. That too Terhune described as an arrangement of her father's that others perceived as unconventional, as one more indication of his strange "'ways'" in the education of his daughters.[53]

But since they were in fact not boys preparing for college, other aspects of the sisters' education were entirely conventional, namely, the domestic aspects. Lessons in that realm had never ceased, and Terhune had *learned* early on, as she wrote later in her life, that "needlework" had been the "confidante of women since Eve." Terhune was eager to stress the intellectual relative to the domestic in discussing her early training, but from her mother's "vivid" recollection of the domestic doings of Terhune's idealized grandmother, Terhune knew her female heritage. Those recollections, along with her grandmother's "wedding-night gown" which Terhune still possessed when *she* was a grandmother, led Terhune "to picture" scenes of her grandmother engaged in the daily tasks of domesticity. Even while she was busy with her intellectual pursuits there were moments in the young female's own life that served to remind her of the intended future. Consider, for example, the young Terhune reading aloud from the pages of the *Spectator* to a mother who " 'sat busy with fine needlework.' " Rice Hill, the setting for Terhune's intellectual blossoming, had its instructive domestic element as well. Aunt Rice, "like other gentlewomen of her time and latitude," was described by Terhune as "well versed" in the English classics, her favorites being Pope, Swift, and Addison, as well as in translations from Greek and Latin, but the image of an intellectual woman was not foremost in Terhune's mind. Rather, what Terhune remembered best was Aunt Rice "always knitting lambswool stockings." The widow of the founder of Union Theological Seminary struck Terhune as a " 'character,' " but the "pronounced individuality"of that character was expressed in the roles of "mistress, housewife, neighbor, and general well-wisher." The seminary was regarded as Aunt Rice's "foster-child" and the students who boarded with her were seen as the recipients of her "maternal interest and affection."[54]

After Rice Hill, Terhune's training for domesticity intensified. Just as Terhune's mother "had inherited from her mother taste and talent for dainty needlework," so Terhune was an early student in that regard and participated in knitting fine white stockings for her father. (Mother and daughter were duly encouraged by Hawes, who like other "gentlemen of the old school refused to wear socks and stockings bought over a counter.") But now her training for the role of "notable housewife" began in earnest. The more advanced techniques of sewing had to be learned. This was the mistress of a household's "own especial task," and Terhune was instructed in the "intricacies of backstitch, fell-seams, overcasting, hem-stitching, herringbone, buttonholes, [and] rolled and flat hems." However, the most important task for a "gentlewoman" who hoped one day to supervise her own home was household management. For the "Virginian matron of *antebellum* days" broom and duster were not the implements, nor were bed making, washing, and ironing clothes the tasks. Those were relegated to the slaves. But, Terhune insisted, supervisory tasks kept a southern gentlewoman as busy as her Yankee sister. The buying and storing of large quantities of provisions for the table had to be organized. Every morning following breakfast Terhune's mother summoned the cook to plan the day's menus, and the two went together to the storeroom to measure exact portions for every dish. From flour to molasses, from hams to a variety of condiments, Terhune's mother directed the choice and the amount for the entire household. In this and other branches of housekeeping Terhune observed and learned and participated more and more. For example, as a little girl she had been allowed to polish the breakfast "teaspoons with a tiny towel." Now, as she witnessed her mother "superintend the washing of breakfast china, glass, and silver," Terhune came to understand that the "handling of 'fragiles' was a fine art." These and other tasks, Terhune learned, were to be part of her daily round, appointed to women "by custom and necessity."[55]

Reared with the understanding that males and females were fitted for "*different* offices and *different* powers," as Maria McIntosh phrased it in *Woman in America*, the literary domestics sought to reconcile intellectual desires and ambitions with social expectations and possibilities.[56] Theirs was a constant struggle to establish their legitimacy as intelligent beings. It was an effort that had mixed results. From mixed origins came mixed identities. It was practically impossible for them to separate the issue of woman's intellectual aspirations from the certainties of woman's social role. It was difficult for them to conceive of themselves as intelligent beings (not to mention defend themselves as such) except in terms of their domestic sphere and destiny. Inevitably, the answers they sought regarding female being as nature were supplied by their knowlege and their society's regard of female being as destiny. In effect, their attempts to achieve intellectual legitimacy were subverted by a perspective that placed them in an inferior, defensive, and nonintellectual posture.

Did females possess intellectual curiosity? Were they intellectually capable? Were they or could they be intelligent? The literary domestics were anxious to answer in the affirmative. In reaction to a social stereotype that suggested otherwise, they *insisted* upon it. From New Englander Sedgwick, the first-born among them, born in 1789, who could have been a mother to most of them, to Southerner Augusta Evans Wilson, the last-born, in 1835, who could have been a daughter to a majority of them, the literary domestics inevitably came to recognize that females were belittled as intellectually inferior to males or, at the very least, that the belief that they were different from males implied that they were suspect as intelligent, articulate beings. Sedgwick was well aware of that fact long before she began to write for publication. Her diary of 1811 records an encounter at a social gathering with "two young men of sense . . . who thought it worth their while to talk to me, as if I had an intellectual character in common with them and could comprehend something beyond the first lesson of infancy." It was an experience that was as unusual as it was pleasant. Sara Parton professed not to be bitter toward men for their slighting of women intellectually. But even though she made "no secret of liking the brethren," she added that at least she would have liked "them near—intellectually and socially." The problem was that females were not "near" men. Instead, they were perceived as different, which meant actually that they were inferior. Mary Virginia Terhune addressed the matter with less equanimity in her first novel, *Alone*, when she made clear that she knew there were men who thought that "woman" and "fool" were synonyms. Augusta Evans Wilson was none too pleased, either, with the inferior intellectual image of women. In 1862, with two novels behind her, she expressed her contempt for what she considered to be society's demeaning characterization of women. " 'To be "feminine," ' " she wrote to her friend Janie Tyler, the granddaughter of

President John Tyler, " 'is scarcely a synonym for weak-minded, idiotic, or frivolous.' "[57]

However, it would be wrong to suggest that the literary domestics directly rebelled against or directly resisted the traditional belittlement of females as thinking beings. Nurtured in effect as other than intellectual beings, they inevitably had doubts about their intellectual capacities. They were brought slowly, but certainly and lastingly, to wonder if indeed they possessed intelligence similar to that of males, if they were not instead inferior, and if they would or could ever be equals. As angry as they were that females were deprived of full rights to a life of the mind, they asserted their claims to those rights in a conflicted, ambiguous, and defensive fashion. Because these women were conditioned to believe that it was their traditional and sacred duty to fulfill domestic obligations, rights of the mind were inevitably preempted by duties to the sphere, and wrath turned inward to stir inner conflict. In the end, they were unable to dismiss totally the dictum that intellectual pursuits for women were unnatural and even posed a threat to femininity. They remained vulnerable as well to the charge that women dedicated to the cultivation of intellect would be drawn from their domestic sphere to a more worldly, male one.

The literary domestics tried hard to find a villain in the piece. They little doubted that many males were hostile to females who purported to be intelligent or to demonstrate their intelligence. They little doubted that there were males who opposed the intellectual advancement of females and even felt threatened by it. Many a woman, Terhune charged in *Eve's Daughters*, suffers "the repression of her intellectual strivings by the arrogant who brook not even the shadow of a partner on the throne of Self." Chronicling the life of Mary Abigail Dodge in 1868, Sara Parton declared that there were males who responded to a "woman with brains," of which she considered Dodge an example, as if she had a disease. Men, she noted, demonstrated a " 'desire to keep clear of a woman like that.' " And in a characteristically brisk polemic, "To Gentlemen," she asked rhetorically, "Has that man a call to be a husband who . . . deprecates for a wife a woman of thought and intellect, lest a marriage with such should peril the seasoning of his favorite pudding, or lest she might presume in any of her opinions to be ought else than his echo?" But though they tried hard to find a villain, the literary domestics' conflicted states of mind made it difficult for them to refrain from incriminating themselves as accomplices. If males desired "to keep clear" of intelligent women, women themselves appeared unable to get clear of a conception of being that guaranteed that the subject of female intelligence would be placed in an ambiguous light.[58]

As in a parable, the literary domestics acted out the contradictory strains of their nurture and training, revealing themselves to be the hybrid products they were, at once puppet and puppeteer. Resistance only confirmed acceptance. Intimidated, confused, and defensive, they sought to rebut the pejorative view of woman's intelligence held by their society, while simultaneously they yielded to their self-doubts regarding woman's intellectual capabilities. Their rebellion was most revealing when in anger they retaliated that women were in fact intellectually superior to men—and generally buttressed their claims with traditional feminine qualities linked to and symbolized by woman's heart. Their angry assertion of female superiority left the powers of logic and reason to men, and claimed for women the sway of emotion, the mystique of intuition, or the sanctity of spiritual wisdom. Socialized to believe it, they were unable to discard the conviction that female and male minds constituted separate and unique qualities, and they portrayed females as naturally more emotive than cognitive. "Each creature in the universe finds itself in that position for which its peculiar organization has fitted it, and discovers in its offices the exact correlatives of its powers," wrote Maria McIntosh in *Woman in America*. The male "creature," she said, was fitted with "his unconceding reason and stern resolve," the female "creature" with "her warm affections and quick irrepressible sympathies." The literary domestics might claim that woman's mind was superior, but not that hers was a logical or analytical superiority.[59]

Augusta Evans Wilson, who said in her letter to Janie Tyler that she rejected " 'the canons of feudal ages' " that found " 'woman's desire for logical certitude' " to be " 'unfeminine,' " was stung by the charge that woman's mind was deficient in rational faculties. But in seeking to combat her own sense of inferiority, Wilson both claimed and rejected those faculties, in essence both claimed the powers of the mind and rejected them. The immediate catalyst for Wilson's letter to Tyler was damning criticism of her novel *Beulah* following its publication in 1859. In the novel Wilson had struggled mightily but failed to resolve her conflicted feelings. The intelligence of the central female character, Beulah Benton, is stressed repeatedly. Beulah is characterized "from her earliest childhood" as intellectually "possessed by an active spirit of inquiry." She has an "ambitious" nature and an "eager thirst for knowledge." She masters "with unusual ease and rapidity" all subjects offered at school and branches out on her own to follow those "footpaths which entice contemplative minds from the beaten track." For her no subject is off limits. History, literature, theology, philosophy and science provide the boundless range of her explorations. For her logical discourse is not intimidating. Imagining herself, at the age of seventeen, to have the nature of a Greek philosopher, she feels impelled "with irresistible force, out into the world of philosophic inquiry." Lest anyone dispute these evidences of her capacities, Beulah's physical characteristics remove all doubts: "The whole countenance betokened that rare combination of mental endowments, that habitual train of deep, concentrated thought, mingled with somewhat of dark passion, which characterizes the eagerly-inquiring mind that struggles to lift itself far above common utilitarian themes."[60]

This is not a woman, surely, who suffers from a sense of intellectual inferiority. What, she asks herself rhetorically, "was her intellect given her for, if not to be thus employed?" Beulah laments, " 'I feel humbled when I hear a woman bemoaning the weakness of her sex, instead of showing that she has a soul and mind of her own, inferior to none.' " Beulah shows it and shows it. She also can conceive of herself as the intellectual equal, even superior, of men. After "years" of thinking of one particular intelligent and educated man as her mentor, as her "infallible guide," she is "troubled by a dawning consciousness of her own superiority." When this same man is later suggested as a potential husband, Beulah scornfully retorts, " 'Think you I could love a man whom I knew to be my inferior?' " Indeed, she emphatically declares, " 'you know little of my nature.' " A more important question is how much *Beulah* (or Wilson) understands that "nature."[61]

Yet as much as Wilson sought to counter her society's prevailing stereotype of woman, she reinforced it. The ordeal that Beulah must undergo is the subversion of her head's tyranny over her true woman's heart. At first she goes to the farthest limit of mistakenly making "her own reason the sole judge" of life. She suffers for this, but does not immediately recognize the error of her ways because the "garlands of rhetoric and glittering logic lay over the pitfalls before her." Her closest friend, Clara Sanders, begs her, " 'Please don't pore over your books so incessantly,' " warns her of the dangers of her chosen course, and foreshadows the happy ending by telling her she " 'will never be a happy woman' " until she finds a man to love who is her intellectual equal. That will never happen until head gives way to heart, but Clara does not doubt that this will happen: " 'Ah, Beulah! with all your stubborn pride, and will, and mental endowments, you have a woman's heart; and crush its impulses as you may, it will yet assert its sway.' " Before the melodramatic moment when "her proud intellect was humbled," and Beulah turns to faith in God and, of course, love for her hero, she is brought to veritable "brain fever." That she should have brought herself to such a state was foreordained in the opening pages of the novel, when she is introduced as a pale and sickly six-year-old orphan in an asylum, pale and sickly because the female head of the asylum surmises, " 'she studies too much.' " Freed at last from her obsession with the mind, Beulah is left with her God and her husband, and led to muse wonderingly how it could have been that " 'I was so proud of my intellect.' " In *Beulah* Wilson on behalf of womanhood may have rejected the head for the heart, yet she desperately wanted the world to know that the woman had a head. Locating the distinguishing character of a woman's being in the range of her feelings rather than in the breadth of her ideas, however, meant claiming rights to the life of the mind while acknowledging that the kingdom of the mind was male.[62]

As children of families committed to educating their children, the literary domestics were culturally advantaged. As females, they were culturally confused. They were lured as children to believe that cultural enrichment was their birthright, but the female experience of intellectual restriction, frustration, and belittlement denied them a secure sense of their intellectual capacities, undermined their intellectual self-respect, and withheld intellectual self-confidence. Like little Rosa Lee in Mary Jane Holmes's novel *Meadow Brook*, they would go hesitantly before their male-dominated society seeking acceptance and recognition as intelligent beings. When Rosa Lee applies for a position at her district school, just as Holmes her creator did, both at the ripe age of thirteen, she must present herself to a committee of nine elderly male school inspectors to demonstrate her competence. As might be expected, Rosa's performance astonishes the members of the committee, with the result that, as Rosa tells it, " 'The Nine' were taken by surprise, and instantly three pair of eyes with glasses and six pair without glasses were brought to bear upon me." The committee of nine are surprised that one so young can perform so well: Rosa was prejudged because of her youth. But there is more than a hint that the factor of gender also governs their reaction. They are surprised that a female can perform so well: Rosa was prejudged because of her sex. She has to meet a double burden of proof. As it happens, Rosa Lee does pass the examination. There is apparently no significance to the fact that, two-to-one, the male examiners are without glasses. But in her novel, Holmes could beg the issue.[63]

In their private and their published prose, the literary domestics revealed an overanxious need to tout female intelligence and demonstrate their own. They also pridefully proclaimed the degree of education they had received. Born in varying respects to an elite and educated to a far greater degree than less socially and materially advantaged females and males, they were proud of their cultural inheritance and proud to attest to it. But there was also in their prose a parallel disenchantment stemming from the fact that as females they were denied the educational opportunities open to their male peers. Intellectually stimulated and engaged, they were in turn frustrated and demoralized by the restrictions imposed upon female education. Just as they sought to refute prevailing notions of female intellectual inferiority, so they decried the limits on female education. Here too, however, their protests were undermined by society's and their own sense of female vocation and female place.

Wilson's *Beulah* (1859) was followed, one other novel intervening, by *St. Elmo* (1866), which became her greatest best-seller and which was fired by the same coals of anxiety. Once again the central figure of the novel, Edna Earl, is a female of the highest intelligence. Wilson went to painful extremes to remove any doubts on that matter. Edna's first tutor, the Reverend Allan Hammond, is said to be "astonished and delighted . . . by the rapidity of [Edna's] progress and the vigor and originality of her restless intellect."

Impressed by Edna's "active intellect," Allan induces her to visit his parsonage library "as assiduously as did Horace, Valgius, and Virgil the gardens on the Esquiline where Maecenas held his literary assize." Apparently unconcerned that her female mind might be incapable of logical or rational exercises, Allan does not hesitate to introduce Edna to a wide range of subjects and to teach her "the application of those great principles that underlie modern science and crop out in ever-varying phenomena and empirical classifications." Natural philosophy, chemistry, geology, astronomy, and the law all fall under her purview.[64]

When Edna expresses an "unconquerable desire" to read the Talmud and the clergyman begins to teach her Hebrew, she is joined in her studies by a young lawyer, "a gentleman of wealth and high social position," who also desires to study under Allan. Knowing that this young gentleman is reputed to be highly intelligent, Edna is unable to "resist the temptation to measure her intellect with his, and soon threatened to outrun him in the Talmud race." Naturally, the young gentleman falls in love with Edna and eventually proposes to her. Much to his and almost everyone else's surprise, she refuses him. Only her tutor knows the reason why, and he kindly explains the problem to the young man. " 'You will never be Edna's husband,' " he tells him, " 'because intellectually she is your superior.' " And why should that matter? Because, says Allan, she " 'will not marry one to whose mind her own does not bow in reverence.' " If she did so, she would be " 'miserable.' " Happiness would come for Edna only if she were " 'ruled by an intellect to which she looks up admiringly.' " Claiming to know her " 'nature' " better than anyone's, Allan doubts if she will ever marry any man. If she proves him wrong and does marry, he says, it will only be " 'because she has learned to love, almost against her will, some strong, vigorous thinker, some man whose will and intellect masters hers, who compels her heart's homage, and without whose society she cannot persuade herself to live.' " Clearly, the realm of the heart is woman's, the mind man's, and woman must pay homage to that fact.[65]

In the war of the heart and mind, Edna's tutor is in fact concerned about her. " 'She is all intellect at present,' " he says, and gives " 'her brain no relaxation.' " And he fears that the time will come " 'when her fine mind and pure, warm heart will be arrayed against each other, will battle desperately, and one or the other must be subordinated.' " Not surprisingly, Allan's apprehensions are groundless, for the outcome is inevitable. Having touted Edna's intellect and proclaimed it superior to a man's, Wilson, again twisting and turning about-face, trades brains for feelings and bargains away Edna's head for her heart. When Allan informs Edna about the resistance and hostility she will encounter in her efforts to educate herself, the heroine responds, " 'I do not quite understand why ladies have not as good a right to be learned and wise as gentlemen.' " But what rights does Edna claim? Certainly not recognition as the intellectual equal of males. Later she says bluntly, " 'Neither do I claim nor admit the equality of the sexes, whom God created with distinctive intellectual characteristics, which never can be merged or destroyed without outraging the decrees of nature, and sapping the foundations of all domestic harmony.' " Then what "right to be learned and wise as gentlemen" does she claim? Actually, no such right at all. Without a doubt, says Edna, " 'woman has an unquestionable right to improve her mind, *ad infinitum*,' " but only " 'provided she does not barter womanly delicacy and refinement for mere knowledge.' " If a woman's " 'heart is properly governed,' " if in effect her heart does the governing, Edna declares, she will increase her knowledge and thereby " 'her usefulness to her family and her race.' " But for a woman "usefulness" apparently requires no mind at all, and Wilson unwittingly reaches the ultimate in contradiction and absurdity. " 'Surely,' " says Edna, " 'utter ignorance is infinitely preferable to erudite unwomanliness.' " Edna speaks her mind, even if she does not know her mind. What she knows is her place.[66]

Seeking recognition and self-respect as intelligent beings, and the rights to the life of the mind, the literary domestics betrayed their own sense of intellectual inferiority and disclaimed a life of the mind beyond what they already possessed. At times they exposed inadvertently their compromised perspective, through language that compromised intended meaning. "The problem of education is seriously complicated by the peculiarities of womanhood," wrote Harriet Beecher Stowe in *Oldtown Folks*. In more ways than she knew, Stowe had indeed realized the nature of the problem. "If we suppose two souls, exactly alike, sent into bodies," she continued, "the one of man, the other of woman, that mere fact alone alters the whole mental and moral history of the two." The problem for Stowe was that she believed that male and female souls, while alike, nevertheless possessed male and female minds that were unalike. In her novel *The Pearl of Orr's Island*, Stowe contrasted the more intelligent Mara Lincoln with her male counterpart, Moses Pennel. For example, in childhood Mara, although she is three years younger than Moses, reads whatever he reads "with a far more precocious insight." In fact, writes Stowe, "all her outward senses are finer and more acute than his, and finer and more delicate all the attributes of her mind." Though Stowe's language suggests sensibility rather than simply feeling, we are drawn to conclude that it is feeling rather than thought that she is talking about. And we are confirmed in our conclusion when in the next sentence she says, "Those who contend against giving woman the same education as men do it on the ground that it would make the woman unfeminine, as if Nature had done her work so slightly that it could be so easily unraveled and knit over." Even Stowe's metaphor betrays her perspective. With her mind clouded by her conditioning, Stowe's effort to ameliorate the intellectual condition of women in her society is self-defeating: "There is a masculine and a feminine element in all knowledge, and a man and a woman put to the same study extract only what their nature fits them to see." Intimidated and defensive, Stowe justifies her call for greater educational opportunities for women by denying them a priori the fruits of those opportunities.[67]

The education, whether formal or informal, of the literary domestics spun about them a cocoon from which they could emerge only by a ruse, in disguise, and at their psychological peril. Ruse and disguise deceived the self as well as society, which testified to the personal female peril. "We want original, planning minds," Stowe wrote Georgiana May in reference to the students she and her sister, Catharine, hoped to recruit for their "young ladies' school" in Cincinnati, "and you do not know how few there are among females, and how few we can command of those that exist." "Few men are great," wrote Mary Virginia Terhune in 1887, musing to herself, then added, "and fewer women." In Susan Warner's *Queechy*, one male character says that he is certain that " 'domestic life is the true training for the female mind,' " adding, " 'One woman will learn more wisdom from the child on her breast than another will learn from ten thousand volumes.' " Another male character who in this context is clearly Warner's spokesman rushes to the defense of womanhood, saying that as the woman's " 'sphere is at home,' " her intellectual resources at home must be " 'exhaustless,' " precisely because it is that which " 'she cannot go abroad to seek.' " Terhune said to Sarah K. Bolton in 1888 that she believed that it was entirely possible " 'to make Home the centre of thought and duty' " for women. But that was already the case, and that was the problem.[68]

Part II

THE NOTICE OF THE WORLD

5

Secret Writers

It was ironic that the nineteenth-century transformation of the traditionally male worlds of commerce and gentlemanly letters resulted in an institutionalization of the nation's cultural and intellectual life and gave these women the apparent opportunity to move beyond their traditional sphere by becoming popular, commercially successful writers of novels, stories, and miscellaneous prose. But the very success of the literary domestics made them displaced people in part. Unable in their own minds to leave the home, they were in many significant respects placed beyond the home, beyond female boundaries. In a strikingly ambiguous position, they had difficulty coping. Inevitably, they experienced a continuing crisis of identity. Their conflicted and contradictory responses to their experiences and their need to rationalize them in domestic terms underlined the fact that they were women of the home who simultaneously came to assume the male roles of public figure, economic provider, and creator of culture. They became hybrids, a new breed or, again, literary domestics.

That any of these nineteenth-century women came to have this semblance of male status was a strange development indeed. Women were isolated from and generally denied participation in their country's public life. They were not statesmen or politicians, judges or legislators, entrepreneurs or merchants, or in any way simply prominent, public citizens. Instead, they were nurtured as private, domestic beings, conditioned to live as private individuals and directed to accept woman's domestic role. Unlike a male, a female's person was to be shielded from public scrutiny. Neither her ego nor her intellect was cultivated for future public vocation. After all, her proper sphere was the home. She was to stand in the background, out of the way. Even her exercise of moral, social, or personal influence was to be indirect, subtle, and symbolic. Her voice was to be soft, subdued, and soothing. In essence, hers was to remain an invisible presence.

And yet these women wrote their books. They felt out of place, awkward, and apologetic, and they disparaged and even dismissed their literary careers.[1] Nevertheless, careers they had. This duality of being in fact defined the very essence of the hybrid strains of nurture and experience that had made them literary domestics. As the descendants in varying degrees of an American colonial elite and as the daughters of families who in effect represented or sought to represent the early nineteenth-century remnants of that elite in an increasingly egalitarian democracy, they were heirs to and beneficiaries of a social and cultural heritage. But as much as they had reaped culturally from their families' social aspirations and standing, they had also been taught the significance of gender. Social status gave and gender took away.

That these women became popular writers was as unplanned and as unforeseen as it could have been. It was in that respect as much of an "accident" as a bewildered Catharine Maria Sedgwick sensed it to be. And yet there had been *preparation*. Their education was more than sufficient to enable them to become writers. Their apprenticeship, if such it can be called, began when literature—poetry, history, and, in particular, a growing body of fiction—was read to them and when they read alone. It was an inadvertent, unstructured, and unconscious apprenticeship, the only type there could have been for a woman. Theirs were reading families, even families of "mad book-lovers," as Mary Virginia Terhune labeled hers.[2] From Sedgwick, constantly prompted to read, to Augusta Evans Wilson, set adrift to roam the libraries of her relatives, reading was a staple of both their formal and informal educations. And from Fielding to Scott to the English female novelists who had begun appearing in the late eighteenth and early nineteenth centuries, including Maria Edgeworth, Frances Burney, and Amelia Opie, to others of both sexes who followed, including Dickens, Thackeray, and Charlotte Brontë, fiction was a beguiling interest for the literary domestics.

Although the literary domestics had been counseled to steep themselves in a variety of reading, it was no idle matter for anyone, male or female, to read imaginative literature in the early decades of the nineteenth century. From classical antiquity onward in Western civilization, the muses of artistic fancy and fantasy had been seen as both sources of spiritual and moral inspiration and corrupters of human character and social behavior. American divines, moralists, and educators did not fundamentally alter that tradition. The Puritans deemed literary fancy and fantasy wayward and immoral influences. When Cotton Mather wrote in 1726, "I cannot wish you a soul that shall be wholly unpoetical," he nonetheless railed against "muses that are no better than harlots." Muses, he warned darkly, had a "tendency to incite and to foment impure *flames*." Not given to subtle suggestion, Mather lectured that it was better for impure literature to be "thrown into the *fire* than to be laid before the *eye*" and allowed to "cast coals into your bosom." And it was not merely a question of "impurities." Let all be aware that "the *Powers of Darkness* have a library among us," and while poets, the "most *Numerous* as well as the most *Venomous* Authors," were the worst offenders, "*Romances* and *Novels* and *Fictions*" were likewise tainted and did veritably "belong to the *Catalogue* of this cursed Library." In sum, Mather assured his flock, the whole evil lot had "a tendency to overthrow all Piety."[3]

At the time Mather made this wholesale condemnation, few works of literature that could be classified as novels had appeared in English. Cervantes's *Don Quixote* had been translated in 1612, and Bunyan's allegorical narrative *The Pilgrim's Progress* had appeared in 1678. Daniel Defoe published *Robinson Crusoe* in 1719 and *Moll Flanders* in 1722. But the significant flowering of the English novel only began with Richardson's *Pamela*, issued in 1740. Nevertheless, there was little doubt that *anything* fictitious was suspect in Mather's eyes. And well it should have been, given Puritan convictions about human psychology. New England Puritans believed that in the healthy individual the faculties of imagination and will functioned harmoniously under the reign of a governing reason. But if the imagination, unrestricted by reason, was allowed to stimulate the passions or affections, the individual was lost. And literary fancy and fantasy were considered more likely to unleash the imagination than any other potential catalyst. Mather's immediate concern was the threat to a male's reason, but given the Puritan belief that females were inherently weaker in that faculty and thus all the more vulnerable, he might well have expressed even greater alarm about their reading imaginative literature.[4]

When the novel emerged as a major literary form, it received a verbal flogging on literary, educational, and moral grounds. The late eighteenth-century poet and Connecticut Wit John Trumbull was typically skeptical about the literary upstart. Trumbull was concerned about the novel's moral impact, but most of all he deplored its violation of received aesthetic principles. "Novelists are reduced," he wrote in 1779, "to make brick without straw." Novels were devoid of recognized literary standards and awash in the "ridiculous," he said, and "improbable meetings, impossible bravery, and unaccountable accidents make up the whole circle of the modern Novelist's invention." A few decades later New Divinity theologian and Yale president Timothy Dwight made the same point with the blunt statement that rather than "houses, inhabited by mere men, women, and children," readers of novels were presented "with a succession of splendid palaces, and gloomy castles inhabited by tenants, half human and half angelic, or haunted by downright fiends." At the very least, the consequences were unfortunate: fiction, he declared, "demands nothing, but the luscious indulgence of fancy."[5]

Scottish Common Sense philosophers who were influential on this side of the Atlantic from the Revolution onward also looked askance at any literature that might tempt or distract the reader. Princeton theologian Samuel Miller, whose allegiance to Thomas Reid and Dugald Stewart was unwavering, wrote at the turn of the century, "Fictitious narrative, as a medium of instruction or entertainment has been employed from the earliest ages of which we have any knowledge." But he condemned novels not only for their immorality but for their tendency "to fill the mind with unreal and delusive pictures of life," and thus "in the end, to beguile it from sober duty, and to cheat it of substantial enjoyment." Those who like Miller became disciples of the Scottish Common Sense philosophers posited an ability on the part of human beings to distinguish between right and wrong, but they assumed as well that this was a characteristic to be cultivated, not challenged. Novels, if they were to have any redeeming value, had to mirror the everyday realities of life while simultaneously managing to provide spiritual uplift, emphasize social virtues, and induce allegiance to existing institutions. It was Miller's opinion that at least 999 of every 1,000 novels failed miserably in the task. In general, he said, "there is no species of reading which promiscuously pursued, has a more direct tendency to discourage the acquisition of solid learning, to fill the mind with vain, unnatural, and delusive ideas, and to deprave the moral taste."[6]

An unsigned essay titled "On Novels and Novel Reading" published in the *Mirror of Taste and Dramatic Censor* nine years after Miller had issued his reckoning in 1802 improved the odds for the poor, unsuspecting reader, but the call was basically the same. Echoing Common Sense strictures about leading the reader down wayward paths, this author considered nineteen in twenty novels "positively mischievous." It mattered little if a novel managed to present a "true picture of life"; mere observation of one's own life could accomplish that. And if a novel put forth "an untrue picture of life," the effect and damage were obvious: "it imparts false and exaggerated notions which are sure to corrupt the heart" and in addition "it tends to fill young minds with fancies and expectations which can never, in the natural course of things, be gratified or accomplished." Better not only to "waste no time upon, but to form no taste for" novels, which for the most part were devoid of "higher purposes than those of mere amusement." The truly pious, the author said, know that life is "a state of trial and labour," and education itself should replicate the processes of trial and labor. It was disastrous, then, to promote or allow "a fondness for works of fiction, which delight the fancy, while they hold out treacherous, delusive hopes, and presume to be vehicles of instruction, without, in the smallest degree, taxing the mind."[7]

Novels inevitably invited scrutiny in early nineteenth-century America. Only decades earlier, the leaders of the Revolutionary generation had called upon their fellow citizens to build a free society whose civic and cultural renown would be unrivaled in the world. Having determined upon the republican experiment, those who presumed to lead the nation rested their hopes for America's survival and future greatness upon the republican citizenry's dutiful exercise of virtue. But in the late eighteenth and early nineteenth centuries many worried as well about the impulses of an increasingly egalitarian and materialistic democracy. That worry was tinged with fear as they surveyed an atomized people that appeared less and less inclined to defer to the judgment of its supposed betters. Visions of social and cultural greatness were frequently clouded by anxious speculations on the most effective means by which to shape and control the morality and taste of the public. Were "this species of writing," wrote Samuel Miller, referring again to the novel, "confined to the enlightened and virtuous," that would be one thing. But what concerned him most was "the character and tendency of that heterogeneous mass [of readers] which is daily accumulating from every quarter" of American society. Harvard moral philosopher Andrews Norton wrote in 1807, "In this land, where the spirit of democracy is everywhere diffused, we are exposed, as it were, to a poisonous atmosphere, which blasts everything beautiful in nature and corrodes everything elegant in art." Two years earlier Norton had urged that a literary elite set standards in art for the less educated.[8]

Theoretically, the degree to which fiction, everybody's medium, was judged to teach all who perused its pages their duty and motivate them to perform it for the good of society determined whether it was fit educational fare for sons and daughters of the republic. A differentiation was made, however, between the potential impact upon females and upon males. Of the "*Scribbles* of Madmen" Cotton Mather had warned, "My son, *Touch them not, Taste them not, handle them not*; Thou wilt *perish* in the *using* of them." But the rise in the number and popularity of novels during the early decades of the republic led many commentators to express their fears, albeit in slightly less doomsday tones, for the sensibilities and souls of *my daughter* as well. The author of "On Novels and Novel Reading" sighed nostalgically for "the time when the number of novels being so few they were quickly exhausted," that is, quickly dispensed with, and "history, excellent poetry, and the lighter ethics afforded the customary relaxation to our females in their leisure hours." But now "our females" were too often exposed to "the recital of some incident, piteous and unnatural as weakness and sensibility, degenerated into distraction, can make it, taken from some fulsome novel."[9]

Noah Webster had noted in 1790 that "Belles Letters learning seems to correspond with the dispositions of most females." Believing that this inclination should be cultivated, he declared that "we expect the most delicate sentiments from the pens of that sex, which is possessed of the finest feelings"; in fact, it was his recommendation that females be exposed as much as possible to "writers upon human life and manners." But he was referring to literature comparable to what appeared in the pages of the *Spectator* and perhaps a few of the most notable histories. Novels were an entirely different matter. The best that could be said of them was that "some of them are useful, many of them pernicious, and most of them trifling." So far as Webster was concerned, the problem was twofold. Novels were judged to have literary and philosophical value only if they explored and portrayed all sides of human nature, including the darker sides. But youth, "especially females," should not be exposed to the "vicious" currents of humanity. Conversely, if novels were written in simple, childlike terms in order solely "to paint the social virtues," that rendered them at best "the toys of youth" or "the rattle boxes of sixteen." Nevertheless, all things considered, it was better if there were only novels of the latter variety, that is, "innocent play things"—which were, the obvious implication was, more palatable for female consumption.[10]

Webster and Thomas Jefferson would come to differ sharply on practically everything else, but they did agree not only that education was critical in preparing children for their roles as adults, but that distinctions were to be drawn between male and female academic regimens. In 1771 Jefferson responded to a request for reading appropriate for a gentleman with lists of volumes on various subjects. The longest list pertained to the "Fine Arts" and included the novels of Smollett, Richardson, and Fielding, as well as Sterne's *Tristram Shandy*. In his accompanying letter he also explained his choices. Anyone who pondered the subject at all, he suggested, could not help but come to the conclusion that "the entertainments of fiction are useful as well as pleasant." That was not to say that he was opposed to the pleasures to be derived from the reading of fiction. But, he observed wryly, there would always be the "reverend sage" who could be counted upon to inquire, "Wherein is its utility?" To which Jefferson responded that "everything is useful which contributes to fix us in the principles and practice of virtue." Contrary to what Webster would write twenty years later, Jefferson believed that in regard to literature "everything" meant exactly that. Illustrations of vice, if well done and well written, could prove just as salutary as illustrations of virtue: "when we see or read of any atrocious deed, we are disgusted with its deformity and conceive an abhorrence of vice." Whether we are stirred to admire virtue or abhor vice, he insisted, "every emotion of this kind is an exercise of our virtuous dispositions," and both produce "a habit of thinking and acting virtuously."[11]

Nearly five decades later Jefferson prepared a list for a gentleman's lady that was decidedly different in at least one respect. Praising the learning that had been provided his daughters as "solid," Jefferson made clear that theirs had been an education which "had enable[d] them, when becoming mothers, to educate their own daughters and even," he allowed, "to direct the course for sons should their fathers be lost, be incapable, or inattentive." He considered that reading had been integral to that education, and in 1818 with the aid of one of his daughters he compiled a list of volumes thought to provide a proper core for a female's education. He did recommend in particular "Pope, Dryden, Thomson, Shakespeare, and the French Moliere,

Racine [and] the Corneilles." The *Spectator* also appeared on the list, as did the *Tatler* and *Guardian*. Jefferson apparently believed as well that any predilection for "Belles Letters learning" should be balanced by the study of other subjects. *Histoire Natural de Buffon* (which Jefferson himself had pointedly criticized in his *Notes on the State of Virginia*) was recommended, along with Stephen Pike's *Arithmetic* and John Pinkerton's *Geography*.[12]

Nevertheless, none of the eighteenth-century male novelists were cited, and in their stead female novelists such as Maria Edgeworth were recommended. Of course Maria Edgeworth's novels had not yet been published when the earlier list was composed, but it is doubtful that Jefferson's list for gentlemen would have included novelists whose fiction was primarily concerned with the domestic experiences of women. That was literature for ladies, not gentlemen. In any case, there was no doubt that it was Jefferson's conviction that the world of literature, like so much else, should be divided on the basis of gender. Having defended novels as improving as well as amusing for gentlemen, Jefferson lamented "a great obstacle to good education" of young ladies. This pernicious barrier was none other than the "inordinate passion prevalent for novels, and the time lost in that reading which should be instructively employed." The potential consequences were disturbing, to say the least. Too great a fondness for fiction made for "a bloated imagination, sickly judgment, and disgust towards all the real business of life." Jefferson would not have been happy to be likened to Cotton Mather, but the similarity in both tone and substance is obvious. From Mather's infernal library that inflamed the bosom in the early eighteenth century to Jefferson's fiction that bloated the imagination and sickened the judgment a hundred years later was a short journey indeed. That journey had been facilitated by the perceived vulgarization of American culture as well as by the premises of Scottish Common Sense philosophy. Jefferson, of course, would have readily acknowledged his debt to Reid and Stewart, and, like Webster, he rejected any literature that might delude females and turn them from their duties. It appeared that fiction, if imbibed too much by too many ladies, might do exactly that.[13]

Although the verbal onslaught that had begun in the eighteenth-century against novels as messengers of the devil and promoters of obsessive delusions abated in the nineteenth century, fiction did not suddenly receive a clean bill of health. A growing number of novels were written, published, and bought, but as late as 1834 the *North American Magazine* was issuing strictures about literary fancy and fantasy. Even if novels were not overtly immoral, the *Magazine* was certain that "nudity itself is less wanton than unhallowed passion, thinly veiled." And when Satan was subtle, one had to be even more on guard: "The unspoken thought, the indefinite suggestions of Sterne, have tempted to more irretrievable sin than ever did the audacious panders of Fielding and Smollet." Yet although fulminations similar to those of Mather were atypical by the third and fourth decades of the nineteenth century, the lowly status of novels was still being recalled for contemporary readers, even by the literary domestics who wrote them. In Parton's 1855 novel *Ruth Hall*, Ruth's mother-in-law says to Ruth that she hopes " 'you don't read novels and such trash.' " Whether Parton was recollecting what had been the prevailing sentiment of her childhood in the second and third decades of the century or reflecting contemporary prejudices is not important. By recording that perspective in her own novel she effectively did both. And the dictate that literature must be intellectually substantive and morally and spiritually instructive continued to hold sway. Caroline Howard Gilman highlighted that fact in describing Ruth Raymond's attitude toward reading in her 1840 novel *Love's Progress*. Ruth does not, "like some girls, rush to romances as a novelty, for her parents had allowed her for several years to read one alternately with a solid book." As a result of her parents' tolerance, "the great mass of [Ruth's] thoughts were on the latter, which lay long in her hands, while the novels were hurried through for the narrative." And as for the novels "those works of fancy [were] selected only where authorship claimed literary respect."[14]

Mary Jane Holmes, born in 1825, was said to have developed a fondness for fiction when young. But in part it was a fondness apparently founded in defiance. Holmes even pretended to fan Mather's flames. In her semiauto-biographical novel *Meadow Brook* Holmes's young narrator-heroine, Rosa Lee, wryly relates how Rosa's grandmother, who has a powerful "aversion to everything savouring of fiction," discovers a copy of *Tom Jones* in a trunk full of rubbish: "This my grandmother cautiously took from the trunk with the *tongs* and threw into the fire." Not surprisingly, the grandmother's preemptory act also inflamed Rosa—with an overwhelming desire to read the unholy tale "on the first occasion which presented itself." Once having gleaned its pages, Rosa says, tongue in cheek, she could see "that my grandmother was right in disposing of the volume as she did." If fiction continued to have a questionable status, the suggestion was that the questions were best answered in the reading.[15]

Indeed, those concerned with the issue did not judge all fiction to be lacking in instructive value. Seeking, like those who had gone before, to educate and thereby to implant a sense of virtue in their children, they were concerned that fiction offered little but frivolous entertainment. But entertained themselves by fiction, they rationalized the entertainment offered by some fiction as useful for the enlightenment of the educated and the to-be-educated. An education designed to prepare daughters to be cultured wives and virtuous mothers meant an education that, relatively unstructured and frequently unsupervised, made possible the reading of fiction considered high in quality and appropriate in message. And the daughters' own forays into their families' libraries, their undirected, random reading, led them to pore

over fiction that offered only harmless amusement. Such latitude could have
an unforeseen result. It is true that the enrichment of female minds was a
socially more than intellectually inspired education, for beings implicitly
regarded as other than intellectual. But even that sort of education could
stimulate the curiosity and imagination, could encourage fanciful thought. A
certain sense of destiny did not necessarily prevent idle, wistful dreaming, in
fact often fostered it.

When the Reverend E. P. Parker recounted Harriet Beecher Stowe's
early years for *Eminent Women of the Age*, published in 1869, he was
obviously relying upon the "Beecher biographies," which had appeared six
years earlier, and he wrote that "the novel, in those days, was regarded, by
all pious people at least, as an unclean thing." What Parker failed to
mention, but could have gleaned from the Beecher-Foote family volumes,
was that the young Harriet had had the example recalled and set before her of
her Episcopalian-reared mother, Roxana Foote, eagerly reading during her
late eighteenth-century girlhood. Seated at her spinning wheel, Roxana
turned the pages of contemporary novels such as Frances Burney's *Evelina*,
first published in England in 1778, while she spun her wool and flax. Stowe
recalled that in her own youth, which encompassed the second and third
decades of the nineteenth century, " 'novel writing stood at so low an ebb
that most serious-minded people regarded novel reading as an evil.' " And
for a time there was not a novel to be found in the home dominated by the
evangelical Lyman Beecher and still infused with some dictates of Puritanism. But this did not deter daughter Harriet from searching, albeit with
" 'despairing and hungry glances,' " her father's library for some small tidbit
of fictional lore. Nor did her search go entirely unrewarded, for amidst the
preacher's " 'grim sentinels,' " including " 'Calls, Appeals, Sermons, Essays, Reviews, Replies, and Rejoinders,' " she managed to uncover a
" 'delicious morsel of a Don Quixote that had once been a book.' " Recalled
Stowe, " 'The turning up of such a fragment seemed like the rising of an
enchanted island out of an ocean of mud.' "[16]

As it happened, neither did Lyman Beecher remain stuck in the mud. " 'I
have always disapproved of novels as trash,' " Stowe reported her father as
having said, but even Lyman, once he read them, found " 'real genius and
real culture' " in the novels of Scott. " 'Great was the light and joy,' " Stowe
recalled, when her father announced " '*ex cathedra*' " to one of his sons,
" 'George, you may read Scott's novels.' " Harriet joined George and her
other brothers and devoured Sir Walter, reading through *Ivanhoe* seven
times one summer. Not that Lyman thereafter let poor fiction alone. He later
preached a funeral sermon on the theme " 'The name of the just is as
brightness, but the memory of the wicked shall rot,' " and designated Sterne
as deserving the latter fate, consigning him to " 'oblivion' " for his impurities.
But even if fiction's status remained questionable in the Beecher household,
it was nevertheless being read.[17]

Susan Warner also lived under the yoke of paternal restrictions regarding exposure to the temptations of demon fiction. Henry Warner worried that novel reading might prove to be poor discipline for his young daughter's eager, inquiring mind and encourage idle dreaming. And he himself possessed an idiosyncratic taste manifested, for example, in his "inborn distaste for all French novels." Nevertheless, his own obvious attraction to fiction was too much to resist and he was also concerned that too much restriction might impair the development of his daughter's mind. As Anna Warner described it, referring to a time when Susan was twelve, "Naturally my father was unwilling to have her read many stories: such dreaming was not good." But, Anna added, in order to "furnish safe fuel for the imagination fires," he began the practice of reading to his daughters in the evenings from works of poetry, history, drama, and fiction, a practice that continued for many years, even after his daughters were reading on their own. Obviously, Cotton Mather would have objected, not only to the practice but to Anna's insolent misuse of his more than metaphorical vision.[18]

In the early years Scott was a familiar choice in the Warner household, but there were other authors and literary forms as well, including Dickens, Milton, Shakespeare, Boswell, and Maria Edgeworth. Years later, when Susan was at least twenty-five and her father was still standing guard, even a French novel, *The Wandering Jew* by Eugène Sue, found its way through Henry's porous defenses. Enticed by what he read, in particular by "some marvelously fine descriptions, historical and other," he decided that Susan should read it too, but only certain passages. He therefore adopted the method of marking chapters and passages that were deemed permissible fare for his not-so-youthful daughter, forbidding her to go beyond the boundaries. Having originally been tempted by her father, Warner read novels, but not without trepidation and slight anguish. At age fifteen, Susan had noted with glee in her journal that "I am at length allowed to read Scott's novels!"— adding, "Under great restrictions however." On this occasion the restriction was temporal rather than substantive. Warner could read fiction for only one hour a day, an hour she was careful to save until bedtime so that during the day she would never have to regret that her precious sixty minutes were already gone.[19]

As the years of her youth passed, Warner dotted her journals with references to novels read and, given Henry's lingering presence, being read to her. Behind "shut windows" she read Scott's *The Betrothed*; aboard a ship, Amelia Opie's *Simple Tales*, purchased for her by Henry; and on a stage bound for Canaan, New York, Johann Rudolf Wyss's *The Swiss Family Robinson*. Back at home she listened to her father read Maria Edgeworth's *Ormond* and read *Belinda* herself. With relish and guilt Susan read and listened and wavered, her enthusiasm dampened, but not extinguished, by a critical judgment not unlike her father's and a conscience continually stirred afresh by her father, who knew the dangers well from his own repeated indulgences. At sixteen Warner, driving and castigating herself as always, wrote, "I ought to exert myself," but "I think far too little on what I *ought* to do; it is always what I *like* to do." One thing she liked but thought she *oughtn't* was fiction. "One thing I ought never to do," she said, forthwith hedging, "at least for some time," is "to read novels." Why? Because, Warner said guiltily, "I know they have done me mischief enough already." The same mixture of confession and self-admonition appeared again in her journal the next year: "I think I shall keep clear of novels for one while at least." And the same motivating factors were afoot. Novels were to be spurned, first, because "I get punished for it when I meddle with them;" and, it followed, second, because "I am sure they are about as bad for me as anything I need wish to have." As late as age twenty, following a series of evenings spent listening to Henry read Scott's *Rob Roy*, Warner wrote, "I do not too well like these novels." And why? Because "they make me think of nothing else." That she found "vexatious." As Henry might have told Susan, had he been of a mind to, the problem, dear daughter, is that we do like them too well.[20]

In 1889, when she was fifty-eight, Mary Virginia Terhune listed in a letter a number of novels that she declared to be her "favorite works of fiction." The authors whose works she cited were Charlotte Brontë, Eliot, "Mrs. Craik" (Dinah Mulock Craik), Dickens, and Thackeray. There were not one among the novels listed, she claimed, "which I have not read at least four times." That same year Terhune made clear who among these authors was her favorite. Writing to an editor of the *Critic*, a weekly literary magazine and review that had come into existence eight years before, Terhune stated that she was "mightily stirred up" by an article appearing in the journal's current issue that "dishonors the memory of a pure, noble Woman," namely Charlotte Brontë. What concerned Terhune was that the author of the article professed, indeed "almost assert[ed]," that he had proof that Brontë had been in love with a former teacher and had based her portrayal of Paul Emmanuel in *Villette* on him. The man in question was one M. Heger, and the dishonor lay in the fact that he was a married man. Apparently intending to put the lie to this "sly stab" at Brontë's memory, Terhune requested space for a rebuttal. "Since my early girlhood," Terhune wrote, "Brontë has been more to me than any other writer, living or dead," adding that she could not begin to describe the feeling I have cherished for years for this lonely daughter of the Yorkshire parsonage."[21]

Terhune's passionate response to what she considered a smear upon the moral character of Brontë was undoubtedly sincere, and the linkage of passion and morality with fiction was nothing new for her either. Terhune had begun reading novels in 1843 when she was twelve, directly at the instigation of her beloved tutor from Union Theological Seminary, indirectly as the result of one of her father's "experiments" in female education, of course. Up to that time in her life, she wrote, "novel-reading had been a questionable delight in which I hardly dared indulge freely." It was a familiar situation; her father, Samuel Pierce Hawes, had "grave scruples as to the wisdom of allowing young people to devour fiction." A little taste was one thing, but reading an entire novel Hawes likened to "a dinner of mince-pie and sweetmeats, breeding mental and moral indigestion." Nevertheless, although her father's scruples may have been grave ones, they were not absolute, evidenced in his giving Terhune's tutor complete license to determine her reading. Thus when the tutor advised a tasting of, what else, the novels of Scott, Terhune "fell upon them with joyful surprise that kindled into rapture as I became familiar with the Wizard and his work." *The Heart of Midlothian, Marmion, The Lay of the Last Minstrel, Peveril of the Peak,* and *Waverley* were all quickly digested.[22]

That the arbiters of the literary domestics' nurture and education pondered apprehensively the dangerous power of imaginative tales to foster idle dreams in the minds of young females was one of the many ironies that abounded in their lives. Female education pursued for no other apparent purpose than the enrichment of a female's life and the enhancement of life within the home underlined that female lives were devoid of realistic, substantive intellectual promise or ends. To promote in that context an intellectual education, no matter how lacking it may have been in structure, substance, or rigor, was invariably to stimulate idle dreams, in effect dreams of indulgence.

But while the pundits of female education and the parents of daughters may have concerned themselves with the power of tales to spur deleterious dreams, to stir the imagination, they probably never conceived of the possibility that tales heard or read in intellectual limbo might spur the dreamer, in turn, to create her own tales, to spin thoughts rather than wool and flax. Nevertheless, an unplanned, unlikely apprenticeship could proceed in unobserved, unlikely fashion. For a so-called idle female, the idylls of youth could foster in secret a dream of substance or a simple dream of being. The publisher J. C. Derby related that Mary Jane Holmes told him of her belief that she had been "born to be a writer of romance; or, like Topsy, she *growed* to be one." If she had not been born to write, the growing apparently began at an early age. "As far back as she can remember," wrote Derby, "she was holding converse with people unseen, yet real to her." Holmes wrote to Derby that she could "scarcely remember a time when a story of some kind was not buzzing in my brain and I commenced very early to put my thought to paper." Holmes made her recollections of childhood a part of the fictional youth of Rosa Lee in *Meadow Brook,* the same Rosa Lee whose grandmother gingerly cast *Tom Jones* into the fire. At age nine Rosa speaks of hours spent "alone" in the "deep shadow" of woods, watching "white feather clouds" glimmering above, while sitting and "musing, I scarcely knew of what." Rosa's thoughts and Holmes's language and imagery are dreamlike. "Strange fancies filled my brain," says Rosa, "and oftentimes, as

I sat there in the hazy light of an autumnal afternoon, there came and talked with me myriads of little people, unseen, it is true, but still real to me, who knew and called them all by name."[23]

Rosa's musings are youthful but peculiarly female. Earlier Rosa says she had discovered "accidentally" one day in school that she "possessed a talent for rhyming," and much to the displeasure of her teacher she had proceeded to fill "my slate with verses, instead of proving on it that four times twenty were eighty, and that eighty, divided by twenty equalled four." The suggestion is that the female finds airy verse more appealing that practical multiplication. That same day, continues Rosa, "on a mossy bank, beneath a wide-spreading grapevine with the running brook at my feet, I felt the first longings for fame, though I did not thus designate it then." Despite the fact that *Meadow Brook* was Holmes's fifth novel, the implicit connection between idle rhyming and a yearning for fame does not suggest in the novel a desire to be a famous writer. Rather, it connotes a more basic desire to be. Even when Rosa says that "I only knew that I wanted a *name* which should live when I was gone," adding significantly, "a name of which my mother should be proud," Rosa appears motivated primarily by a desire or need to rescue her female being from limbo.[24]

In solitude, frequently in nature, and always in reverie, the unlikely and unplanned apprenticeship flickered in a fanciful state of unreality that nevertheless embodied real if unnamed desire and feeling. Caroline Howard Gilman recalled wandering as a child of ten or so through the wilds of what is now the Mount Auburn Cemetery in Cambridge, Massachusetts, and the sixty-year-old woman wondered if it was then that she had begun to develop "whatever I may possess of the poetical temperament." E.D.E.N. Southworth remembered solitary moments when as early as age six, " 'very much—*let alone*,' " she meandered throughout her grandparents' estate in St. Mary's County, Maryland, looking into attics, cellars, and cocklofts, and loitering " 'with the old negroes in the kitchen, listening with open ears and mind to ghost stories, old legends, and tales of the time.' " When Southworth wrote her first short story many years later she utilized one of the legends she had heard as a child. Harriet Beecher Stowe claimed that from her earliest childhood she had a " '*passion* for writing.' " Her passion had expressed itself earliest in printed " 'meditations and reflections,' " albeit " 'before I learned to write,' " and afterward she " 'scribbled incessantly' " at Sarah Pierce's school, much to Pierce's disapproval. In her seventies, Stowe wrote of her early " 'dream to be a poet,' " and of the period after she had commenced the study of Latin at her sister Catharine's Hartford Female Seminary and began at age twelve her drama in verse and " 'filled blank book after blank book with this drama.' " She also remembered that Catharine had " 'pounced down upon me, and said that I must not waste my time writing poetry.' " For a female the dream of writing was idle indeed, necessarily apart from serious thoughts concerning an expected future.[25]

Caroline Lee Hentz, who supposedly had written poetry, a drama, and even a novel by age twelve, probably drew upon her own childhood when she began *Ernest Linwood* with the aforementioned incident of Gabriella Lynn, also twelve, being ridiculed by her teacher for writing poetry and warned by her mother against indulging "too much in the dreams of the imagination." Keep writing poetry, says Gabriella's mother, but write it for yourself and me, and do not attempt to make too much of it. A male admirer of Gabriella's expresses the same message when the still youthful heroine tells him that she has given up writing poetry " 'as one of the follies of my childhood, one of the dreams of my youth.' " Continue your education, he urges Gabriella, continue " 'to read, write poetry, ramble about the woods and commune with nature, as you so love to do, and not think of assuming the duties of woman, while you are yet nothing but a child.' " Oh, he anguishes, if only " 'I could make you stop *thinking* for one year.' " But if Gabriella is encouraged by both her mother and her male friend to continue to dream, albeit without taking the dream seriously, she is also told by a female guardian and mentor when she must leave aside her idle dreams, and why:

"There is a period in every girl's life, my dear Gabriella, when she is in danger of becoming a vain and idle dreamer, when the amusements of childhood have ceased to interest, and the shadow of woman's destiny involves the pleasures of youth. The mind is occupied with vague imaginings, the heart with restless cravings for unknown blessings. With your vivid imagination and deep sensibility, your love of reverie and abstraction, there is great danger of your yielding unconsciously to habits the more fatal in their influence, because apparently as innocent as they are insidious and pernicious. A life of active industry and usefulness is the only safeguard from temptation and sin."

There was no doubt, of course, that a " 'life of active industry and usefulness' " entailed one thing, and one thing only, for a female.[26]

Youthful dreams in peculiar circumstances aside, the literary domestics did not envision their reading and reverie as an apprenticeship or expect and plan to become professional, published writers. For a female, idle dreams were one thing, a planned professional career quite another. That is suggested in part by the literary domestics' ages when their first volumes of fiction appeared. Nine of the twelve were thirty years old or more. Three of those nine did not publish volumes until they were close to or beyond forty, and two others issued only one volume in their thirties, waiting until their forties and fifties, respectively, before another appeared. Significantly, the only three of the twelve to publish volumes in their twenties—Maria Cummins, Mary Virginia Terhune, and Augusta Evans Wilson—were the last of the group to publish, in the 1850s. The example had been set for them. They had the advantage and the motivation, perhaps, of knowing that others had gone before.

Regardless of the age at which a woman began her professional career, regardless of whether others had preceeded her, for her and her society the act of national, commercial publication was steeped in significance. To enter the public realm was for the woman to enter a new realm of being. It was in fact a testing of the limits imposed upon a woman's life, and it suggested the will or the desire on the woman's part to test or resist those limits. It suggested a new assertion of a woman's being, for, simply stated, to be a published writer was to have a visible influence, a public role beyond the home. It was to leave woman's private domestic sphere for man's, to meddle in the public affairs of men. Paradoxically, familiar circumstances and attitudes facilitated the private becoming public. No doubt it helped that they could write behind closed doors in the privacy and secrecy of their homes. It helped, too, that they could write behind the shield of anonymity or a pseudonym. That provided a meaningful cover for women. At the very least, anonymity contributed to a sense of psychological security, and offered a partial, tenuous hold on social propriety. The literary domestics could write and, as it were, attempt to hide the deed. Psychologically as well as physically they could make the gesture of writing behind closed doors. They could write hesitantly for the world and try to stay at home. The invisible figure, apprenticed unknowingly and in all innocence, could become the secret writer.

By the end of the eighteenth century there were glimmers through the veil: the anonymous American *lady* author appeared. Lyle Wright's bibliography, *American Fiction*, cites thirty-two works of fiction by American women during the half century previous to 1820. All thirty-two appeared from 1793 onward, and the overwhelming majority were published anonymously. If one eliminates the seven novels of the British writer Susanna Rowson, thereby reducing the number to twenty-five, the figures are even more striking. Three of the works were by, respectively, Mrs. Caroline Matilda Thayer, Mrs. P. O. Manville, and a Mrs. Patterson, whose effort amounted to twenty-seven pages. Two by Ann Eliza Bleecker appeared posthumously, ten and fourteen years after her death, rendering them effectively anonymous. All of the remaining twenty were anonymous publications. It was a time when no one imagined that the emergence of a national publishing industry was only a few years in the future; when, as was the tradition, most or all of these publications were probably financed by the author or author's relatives rather than by the printer or bookseller; when publication was local, noticed only by a few, and sales were small; when, in short, the lady author barely ruffled the quiet, dignified calm of her domestic anonymity with her single, mostly unnoticed fictional appearance. Nevertheless, as one goes down the list of publications and sees once every few years the appearance of "By a Lady," "By a Lady of Philadelphia," or "By an American Lady," one can imagine the hesitant, timid, and apprehensive character of their acts. It is to detect their own reaction to the dictum that a woman was not supposed to be a published writer.[27]

The literary domestics provide evidence that the dictum remained in force. Ten of the twelve literary domestics resorted to anonymity, at least in the initial stages of their careers. Sedgwick, again the pioneer among them, wrote anonymously throughout her career, with only a few exceptions. Thirteen years after she began publishing in 1822, "Miss Sedgwick" appeared on the cover of *Tales and Sketches*. For fourteen years after that Sedgwick again wrote anonymously, until an edition of her collected works bore her name on the title page. And no author's name appeared on her last novel, *Married or Single?*, published in 1857. Of the last three writers to appear in print, in the 1850s, Cummins wrote all of her four novels anonymously before her death at thirty-nine; Terhune wrote under the pseudonym of "Marion Harland" throughout a career that lasted sixty-odd years, into the twentieth century; and Wilson published her first and third novels, among a total of nine, anonymously.[28]

Between Sedgwick and those who came last, Gilman resorted to the pseudonym of "Mrs. Clarissa Packard" in her first novel; McIntosh published for six years before using her name; and Parton and Warner began and continued to write under the pseudonyms of "Fanny Fern" and "Elizabeth Wetherell," respectively. Generally, Southworth and Stowe did write under their own names, but at the very least Southworth's first story appeared anonymously. Stowe also contributed anonymous pieces to periodicals, including, for example, the *New York Ledger*. There are as well indications that before *Uncle Tom's Cabin* made her not only a public but a controversial figure, Stowe on occasion disguised her identity. For example, when one of her first essays appeared in the *Western Magazine*, Stowe wrote a friend, "It is ascribed to Catharine, or I don't know that I should have let it go. I have no notion of appearing *in propia persona*." Later in her career Stowe occasionally used the pseudonym "Christopher Crowfield." Only Hentz and Holmes apparently used their real names throughout their careers, and they expressed apprehension indirectly about that fact. Like several of the other literary domestics, both Hentz and Holmes wrote novels that include female characters who are secret writers. Neither, as far as can be determined, adopted pseudonyms or wrote anonymously, but clearly for both there were thoughts within of secret female writers, within the person and within the text.[29]

While it is true that the literary domestics who published anonymously were practicing a well-worn tradition, one that went back at least to the pre-Revolutionary British aristocracy, for them gender was far more significant in this regard than social status. When eighteenth-century gentlemen had demonstrated the learning of their letters for their peers in polite society, they generally wrote anonymously, because it was considered vulgar to appear in one's own name before an inferior public. But for these women the psychological and social implications of maintaining anonymity went far beyond the desire to maintain a façade of gentility. Consider the case of

Susan Warner. In the quiet bosom of her family she listened to stories, she read stories, and more, she spun and told her own. At twelve, she noted in her journal that after dinner she had "begun to tell stories" to her younger sister and cousins, and two days later, again after dinner, that she had "told stories." At fifteen and sixteen she writes of having "talked stories" and of spending the day "talking stories." Later her sister Anna wrote that at fifteen Susan had a "lively imagination" that gave her the "most deep-seated, far-reaching love of stories; she could make one out of anything." Anna marveled, "What comical young novels of her writing I have yet!" Many of those "Novels," added Anna, were written even earlier than most of her journals, which were begun when she was twelve.[30]

But the flights of fancy, the stories spun before the hearth tell only half the tale. The "lively imagination" and the pleasure in its cultivation were obviously there, but they belonged to a private, domestic woman. Intertwined, a desire to create and an identity as other than a creator fostered a conflict that would plague these women throughout their lives. Indeed, it created a divided self that would never be totally reconciled. One entry recorded in Warner's journal in 1839 provides a glimpse of the hermetic journalist who would become a literary domestic. Warner made the entry shortly after she had turned twenty, eight years after she had begun her journal but eleven years before her first novel appeared. It was like a whisper behind a closed door: "I have never liked to read those journals where people speak freely of their most private sentiments and most secret thoughts. Nevertheless, perhaps I would be willing to write in that fashion if I was very sure nobody would ever see it; and it is even possible that I may do it, at all risks, but not just now." Warner was not contemplating writing for publication; she was wondering if she should—or would—ever express herself openly in her own private, secret journal. When, a decade later, she decided to "come out . . . before the world," as she phrased it in a letter, it is not surprising that she came out as "Elizabeth Wetherell." It was a way perhaps to insure somehow that "nobody would ever see" what she wrote. It was a way to risk it. She could "do it" and deny it.[31]

Obviously, all of the literary domestics risked it. But while anonymity served as a means by which a social dictum and its reflection in self-image could be partially skirted, it also constituted obeisance to that dictum. Something was asserted, but something was yet imposed, and the tale of the private domestic woman emerging on a public stage told a story of what was and was not possible. There was resistance in the writing, but there was by no means total liberation: the woman surfaced as a published writer, but she surfaced in disguise. The writer was a woman, but the published work was not ascribed to her. These women had not stepped beyond the doors of their homes; only their works had, and anonymously at that. In fact, although the literary domestics' struggles to become published writers cloaked a struggle to extend and to assert greater control over the manner of their being, by becoming *secret* writers they demonstrated that their social conditioning was powerful enough to cripple their efforts, if not to prevent them. A secret is a type of denial, and by becoming secret writers they were labeling themselves; to be secret writers was in a sense to state that they were not writers at all. It was to testify to an implicit recognition of wrongdoing, of guilt, perhaps of shame. Even more, it symbolized the invisibility of woman, the nonbeing of woman, the restriction of woman. It was ironic that these published writers simultaneously testified to their existence and resisted invisibility and nonbeing, and limitation as well. And it was ironic that to be a secret writer was also to announce that resistance, to call attention to it. To screen themselves, their being, in public, was inadvertently to dramatize in public the private subjugation of their lives.

The disjunction of the private woman in the public world initiated a process of self- and social revelation, a process of self- and social discovery. For the literary domestics the revelation was not intentional, nor was discovery total. The use of pseudonyms or the choice of anonymity, in and out of texts, symbolizes this peculiar phenomenon. The paradox of literary domesticity was that secret writers were not so secret. Inadvertently, the literary domestics were revealing more than they realized or intended. As published writers they in effect shared their secrets with thousands. At the very least, it was almost inevitable that the name of a best-selling author would become known to the public. For these writers, anonymity related more to a state of mind than a state of reality. To choose to write under a pseudonym was more symptomatic than practical, as all of the writers who chose that form of publication discovered.

The immediate publishing success of Maria Cummins's *The Lamplighter* in 1854 prompted the windmills of journalism to fan speculation as to the identity of the anonymous author. "The author of The Lamplighter, whoever he or she may be," said the *Daily Herald* of Newburyport, Massachusetts, "has struck a note which will find a response in the public heart." The *Boston Gazette* wrote, "We are not informed who may be the author of 'the Lamplighter,' but we know it is one who understands how to make the chords of the human heart vibrate with every touch." Whether thanks to rumor, word-of-mouth, or detective work, the net closed around Cummins. "It is the production of a lady," affirmed the *Commonwealth* of Boston. "Rumor gives the authorship of this work to a lady, a former resident of Salem," said the *Worcester Palladium*, correctly. And another publication noted, "It is said to be written by a lady of this neighborhood, but her name has not been announced."[32]

Friends made their guesses as well. The "great question in the literary circles of this city," wrote Asahel Huntington to Cummins, is "who is the author of 'The Lamplighter.' " A former teacher, said Huntington, was "pluming herself on the honor of being the early teacher of the great future authoress." Huntington was "quite prepared to believe you to be the author," and concluded with "I can keep a *secret*. Will you communicate one if you please." Either Cummins complied or Huntington confirmed her authorship independently. After reading the novel, Huntington announced to Cummins three weeks later, "I am ready now most heartily to join in the universal chorus of praise, which [*The Lamplighter*] is receiving from the public." Strangers were also eager to make contact, in a variety of ways. John P. Jewett, Cummins's publisher, wrote her to say that a mother had written with the information that she had named her baby Gertrude Flint, after the orphaned heroine of the novel. Jewett added that he had been "importuned by Gentlemen from various sections of the country to give them an introduction to you." Naturally, said Jewett, "I have positively refused all such applications, deeming it not only improper but decidedly annoying"; he said he had informed them that "it was not part of the contract between you and me that I should introduce, or you should be introduced." Inevitably, speculation in the wider world turned into knowledge. "It is rumored in literary circles," said the *Boston Transcript*, "that the authoress of the new volume which has met with so wide a sale, is the daughter of Hon. David Cummings [sic], widely known as a Judge of the Court of Common Pleas of this Commonwealth." And the *New-York Daily Tribune* proudly announced that the author of *The Lamplighter* was indeed "Miss Cummings [sic], a young lady in the vicinity of Boston, whose name we believe now comes before the public as an author for the first time."[33]

But precisely because the fact of publication did not mean that a woman ceased to be a private domestic being, the literary domestics failed to grasp beforehand, and were thus unprepared for, the consequences of their acts and the impact upon themselves. At the very least, they did not anticipate the immediacy and extent of the notice they received in the literary marketplace. However, once the dream of indulgence became more than a dream they quickly discovered some unavoidable consequences, and they reacted predictably. In documenting lives of nonbeing, in making the invisible visible, and in asserting the will to do so without fully comprehending that fact, the literary domestics set the deep conflict of innocents in bold relief.

In the spring of 1822 Harry Sedgwick informed his brother-in-law William Minot that he was writing "expressly for the purpose of communicating to you and Mrs. Minot a secret which ought not to be longer held." The secret was that his sister had "written a tale," and more, that she had been persuaded "with great difficulty" to have it published. Since agreeing to that course of action, Harry wrote, she had been "filled with terror and alarm," and he had no doubt that she "sincerely regrets that she has been persuaded to appear before the public." After commenting a bit upon the tale's contents and its publishing prospects, he concluded with the following message: "What I have now told you is of course a profound secret—We all concur in thinking that a lady should be veiled in her first appearance before the public."[34]

The lady in question was of course Catharine Maria Sedgwick, and the tale was *A New England Tale*, her first novel. The event was serious indeed. With the date of publication imminent, the author suspected that a momentous change was about to take place in her life. "I have a *perfect horror* at appearing in print," she admitted to her brother Theodore, "and feel as you have seen me when I have been trying to make up my mind to have a tooth out." That was no jest; during her lifetime Sedgwick had to have all of her teeth extracted. Jest or not, it did not hide her deep anxiety. After the novel, which was issued anonymously, actually appeared, Sedgwick recognized that her life had changed dramatically and, in her opinion, for the worse. "I am more anxious than I can express to you to remain unknown," she confided to a friend, "but that, I fear, is impossible now." As she phrased it, the problem was that by publishing, anonymously or not, she was "obtruding myself upon the notice of the world." For the private Sedgwick it was a problem that defied resolution and could not be left behind. Five years later, while laboring over her third novel, she wrote to her brother Charles that "to be the subject of public inquest is not agreeable to a woman of any womanly feeling." Just how profoundly disagreeable public notice was for Sedgwick had been revealed a few years before when, stung not by public criticism but by an editor's praise, she wrote to Harry with telling impact: "Do pray do something about it—I did hope my name could never be printed except on my tomb," and, she added, as "for that I shan't care so long as I am safe below." It would be after the fact, of course, as unchangeable as the fact of her deep conflict.[35]

In 1854, when Mary Virginia Terhune was twenty-four, her first novel, appropriately titled *Alone*, and privately financed by her father, became an unexpected best-seller, thirty-two years after Sedgwick's first novel had appeared. Terhune had actually begun writing *Alone* at age sixteen, in secret of course: "In that book I lived and moved, and had my inmost being for that year. I spoke to nobody of what I was doing. The shrinking from confiding to my nearest and dearest what I was writing, was reluctance unfeigned and unconquerable in the case of this, my best beloved brain-child." Terhune was not motivated to rewrite the novel until the age of twenty-two, when she read some pages from the six-year-old manuscript to her siblings. Their favorable response, she said, constituted the " 'Open Sesame' of my literary life." She began rewriting the novel the very next day. On 28 January 1854, shortly before *Alone* appeared, Terhune wrote to her friend Virginia Eppes Dance the startling news that "*it has gone out of my hands!*" Publication was imminent and she was " 'fidgety,' " to say the least.[36]

With the publication of *Alone* Terhune committed herself to writing, committed herself as much as she would ever be able to. But long before that, long before she herself recognized that the process was underway, she had begun taking tentative steps, as she put it using that familiar phrase, to go "out in the world." At ten or eleven, during the reign of her tyrannical "Evil

Genius" tutor, while the " 'big girls' " were writing school compositions, Terhune compiled and kept hidden in a trunk beneath her clothing a burgeoning collection—a "shabby, corpulent portfolio," as she called it—of rhymes, tales, and sketches. To no one, not her tutor, her schoolmates, or her family, did she confide her secret. "Never a syllable had I lisped to one of them" of its existence, she wrote. But under the sympathetic hand of her poetry-writing Yankee governess, Terhune was encouraged at twelve to remove her youthful pieces from their hiding place, to bring them "out of limbo," as she put it, to show them "by timid degrees" to her benevolent mentor. The governess praised Terhune's writing, but not lavishly, suggested topics, and offered guidance about their treatment. Terhune remembered the period and the person gratefully and wrote about both in the language of literary domesticity: "Intellect and heart throve under her genial influence as frost-hindered buds under May sunshine." However, it was not as if the twelve-year-old henceforth launched herself on a career; the secretive literary neophyte did not exactly go public. At thirteen, for example, Terhune wrote a story in ten parts that was "laid away in the fat portfolio nobody except myself ever opened." She did make a bold decision at fourteen to begin sending a few essays to daily and weekly papers, but they were always submitted "under the shelter of a *nom de plume*."[37]

At sixteen Terhune wrote a story titled "Marrying Through Prudential Motives," rewrote it at eighteen, and using the initials of her forenames, Mary Virginia, submitted it to *Godey's Lady's Book* under the pseudonym of " 'Mary Vale'—a veiled suggestion of my real name." Supposedly mislaid by the editor, the article was not issued until four years later, and a further two years passed before Terhune discovered that it had been published. Prior to that, when she was nineteen, the inevitable happended; a few friends discovered that Terhune was the author of a series of articles on religion which had appeared under the name of "Robert Remer," another of her early pseudonyms. The disclosure prompted her to write to a friend, "My surprise was only equalled by my mortification and wounded feeling." "Believe me," she implored her friend, "it is no laughing matter with me; I cannot, I do not expect others to understand the feelings which induce me to keep this secret, but you may perhaps think they are weighty, when I tell you, that I would rather anything else that my bosom guards in silence should have been proclaimed." In spite of this slight exposure, she continued to guard her "secret."[38]

Terhune made her final choice of incognito when at age twenty-three she drew upon the initials of her first and last names before marriage, Mary Hawes, and "Marion Harland" appeared as the author of a temperance story entitled "Kate Harper" that was published in the *Southern Era*. Terhune had submitted the story "without intimating to any one" that she had committed such an "audacious" act. When "Kate Harper" actually appeared she was away from home and immediately wrote to her father confessing her authorship, while stipulating that "the secret should be kept among ourselves." While "Marion Harland" constituted a "hint of my name," it was a hint "so covert that it was not guessed at by readers in general"; Terhune was not yet prepared to go any further than that. She was willing to allow her father to inform the editor of the *Southern Era* as to her identity in order to collect payment for her story, and she continued for two years to submit tales and poems to the weekly. But she also preserved "my incognito" and would continue to do so throughout a career that spanned more than half a century.[39]

In the last decade of the nineteenth century, after forty years as a national best-selling author under the name of "Marion Harland," Terhune replied to a letter inquiring about her use of a pseudonym. "My reason for choosing a 'pen name' at all," explained the sixty-two-year-old woman, "was the desire of a young writer to screen her personality from even her intimate friends." It was also the need of a young woman to screen the nature of her act from, and lessen its impact upon, herself. Publishing anonymously symbolized a conflict that was as deep as it was dimly and poorly understood. Recalling the occasion of having submitted her story, "Kate Harper," Terhune noted that it was "with a hazy idea of, in some degree, preserving my identity to myself" that she had introduced "Marion Harland" to the public. The appearance of "Marion Harland" in print expressed a need, and hid the privately identified woman from the public world.[40]

Of course, Terhune did become identified before the world, in a literal sense at least. And although she continued to use her pseudonym throughout her career, she abetted the process of discovery somewhat. During the second half of the nineteenth century, as the list of women engaged in public activities lengthened, a number of volumes appeared providing biographical information and describing the activities of many of them. Women involved in reform movements such as abolition, temperance, and women's rights, founders of educational institutions, physicians, and ministers were included, in addition to those engaged in literary endeavors, and, as various prefaces indicate, the women themselves provided some of the material. Sketches of Terhune appeared in several such biographical collections, including *Women of the South Distinguished in Literature* (1865), *Our Famous Women* (1886), and *Successful Women* (1888). The ultimate in biographical revelation, of course, occurred when Terhune published her autobiography in 1910, albeit as "Marion Harland." But Terhune as private being did not cease to exist. For example, when Kate Sanborn asked her for information to be included in *Our Famous Women*, Terhune did write Sanborn a letter that provided commentary on her education and literary career as well as on the subject of domesticity, but she began her letter by saying, "I confess that my sentiments on the subject of a biographical notice may be summed up in the needy knife-grinder's exclamation, 'Story! Lord bless me sir! I have none!' None that would interest the public." There had been much joy and some grief in her life, Terhune said, but "with this the world has nothing to do."[41]

The preface to *Our Famous Women* claimed that the collection had been compiled in response to a perceived need on the part of many women for a sense of their peers' reactions to changes in their society. "Causes both economical and moral have tended to break up old habits of life and thought," it said, with the result that "new demands" had been made upon women's "capacity and conscience, which experience has not yet taught them to satisfy." Accordingly, the preface continued, it seemed appropriate to tell "the simple story of what a few women have done" so as to provide "inspiration and incentive to the many women who long to do." Apparently, however, it had not been a simple matter to gather information from a number of the women chosen for inclusion (Harriet Beecher Stowe, along with Terhune, also appeared in the volume) because "with the natural modesty of worth, these ladies shrank from needless publicity, and at first hesitated to allow the use of their names." But the lever of persuasion was found when the publishers assured their subjects that their object was not "to gratify a vulgar curiousity," nor were they interested in information related to "private joys and sorrows." Rather, they wished in part to tell the story of these women's "labors, discouragements, and successes" and thereby "kindle new hopes and ambitions in unknown hearts." Faced with that expressed intention, the preface claimed, the women in question decided it would be "churlish to refuse."[42]

The editors of comparable volumes encountered similar problems, and they were not always successsful in persuading their previously anonymous authors to step into the limelight. Julia Deane Freeman, the editor of *Women of the South*—who, ironically, published her volume under the pseudonym of "Mary Forrest"—was unable to include all of her chosen subjects, as there were those, she noted in her preface, "whose *incognito* I could not presume to invade." It was her hope, said "Mary Forrest," that their work "will yet ... be given to the world with the name of the author." John S. Hart experienced the same frustration in his attempt to inform the reading public about the women behind the books. Noting in his preface to *The Female Prose Writers of America* that women were not readily disposed to provide information about themselves, Hart admitted that he had encountered "much difficulty" preparing the collection of sketches. "Few things," he said, "are more intangible and elusive than the biography of persons still living." (Readers of today would note the irony that when Hart referred to "persons" he meant women.) Anxious to emphasize that his volume contained "an unusual amount of authentic information," Hart nevertheless admitted that his information had been "difficult to obtain" and that his sketches were only "as full and minute as circumstances would justify, or as the writers themselves would allow."[43]

The sketches would have been more detailed and complete had

respondents like Caroline Howard Gilman been more forthcoming. Hart was particularly pleased to note that he was presenting for the first time biographical information on Gilman, whom he described as a long-established favorite of the public. But his presentation was incomplete. Gilman responded to his request for details about her life by observing, "It seems to me, and I suppose at first thought, it seems to all a vain and awkward egotism to sit down and inform the world who you are." On the basis of that opinion she had made her decision not to tell all: "I have purposely confined myself to my earlier recollections, believing that my writings will be the best exponents of my views and experiences." Despite herself, Gilman was telling more than she knew, exposing the deep vein of conflict that dominated her sense of herself as a published writer. "Is there not some inconsistency in this shyness about autobiography?" she asked, as if, in contradictory fashion, seeking to put the question to the very public that she avoided. After all, she wrote, alluding to the autobiographical temper of her fiction, she had "opened my heart to the public for a series of years," numbering twenty-plus. She had written under pseudonyms, but "all the pulses of life and hatred and sorrow" of her life had been "so transparently unveiled, that the throbs may be almost counted." So "why should I" or other authors "feel embarrassed in responding to this request?" she asked. Given that this private woman could not answer her question, it is remarkable that she could pose it so starkly.[44]

Susan Warner was even less cooperative with Hart. Unlike Gilman, she declined to have anything published about her. The reading public wanted to know " 'Who is Elizabeth Wetherell?' " Hart wrote, but that inquiry had resulted "so far in no disclosure beyond the fact that she is the author of the 'Wide, Wide World,'—and nothing more." In short, he concluded, "the authorship of these volumes is a secret and likely to be so kept for some time." Actually, Hart already knew who "Elizabeth Wetherell" was, and he had asked Warner more than once if he could let the public know. Somehow, he had discovered Warner's identity a year earlier and had written to ask permission to print that information in *Sartain's Union Magazine*. She had refused him, and had let him know that she was upset that he possessed such knowledge: "I had no mind in the first place to have my real name known at all," she wrote Hart, "and though that is now beyond my control, I do certainly wish never to see it in print." The published writer was consistent at least in attempting to prevent publication of her name. Shortly after she had finished writing *The Wide, Wide World* in 1850, but prior to its publication, she had responded to Lydia Sigourney's offer of a fifty-dollar prize for the best essay on "Female Patriotism" to be published in *The Ladies' Wreath*. After Warner won the competition and after *The Wide, Wide World* had had its initial publishing success, Warner wrote in her journal that her publisher had told her that "people have written to know my name,—Mrs. Sigourney among them." Warner had already had a dialogue with herself in her journal, noting that Sigourney had written that "she wishes to know me," and affirming to herself that "I humbly beg leave to decline and keep my incognito." As Warner's sister Anna, who was also a writer, phrased it, "We had both wished to keep our names in hiding." Symbolically, the two sisters had reached back to two other invisible females—that is, to their grand-mothers—and borrowed their names: "I was going before the world as 'Amy Lothrop,' " Anna related, "while for a long time my sister was known chiefly as 'Elizabeth Wetherell.' "[45]

It is not surprising, then, that Warner responded to Hart's request to print her name in *Sartain's Union Magazine* by informing him that regarding public acclaim, "I desire that Miss Wetherell take it all,—not I." Thus did "Miss Wetherell take it all" as well in Hart's first volume on female writers, issued in 1852. But three years later Hart published another edition. By that time Warner's second novel had appeared and, as Hart noted, its immediate publishing success was greater than that of *The Wide, Wide World*. Hart could not resist telling the world Warner's true identity, with or without her permission. "The real name of 'Elizabeth Wetherell' is Susan Warner," he wrote. But, he added, as if to apologize for his transgression, "as she continues to use her *nom de plume* in all her publications, it has seemed but meet to do the same in writing of her." Thus Hart used Warner's pseudonym in his sketch on her; at the beginning of the sketch "Elizabeth Wetherell" was printed in large letters, with "Susan Warner" bracketed below in smaller type. It is likely that Warner had not given her permission for the disclosure. As it happened, in *Queechy*, which had appeared three years before, the female protagonist, Fleda Ringgan, is also a secret writer. After having submitted to a magazine what she describes as " 'some of my scribblings,' " Fleda tells her cousin Hugh what she has done. He is pleased but surprised, and asks, " 'Did you sign with your own name?' " Fleda is even more incredulous that Hugh would ask such a question than he was that she would submit her work for publication. " 'My own name!' " she exclaims in disbelief, adding in mocking tones, " 'Yes, and desired it to be printed in large capitals.' " " 'What are you thinking of?' " she says. Asking his forgiveness, she tells him that she has used his name for a pseudonym.[46]

Being private domestic females, the literary domestics did not find it easy to grapple with unexpected public notice, and resisted a public status that had never before befallen American women. The difficulty they experienced was more than that of attempting to separate the private from the public: they had unexpectedly been placed in the male role of public figure, a role that had not been and was not supposed to be part of the female experience. Being a published writer forced them, as Warner had expressed it in words so often used by the literary domestics as to constitute their fearful epitaph, to "come out . . . before the world." Perhaps none of the writers bared her conflict more than Sara Parton did. Parton always wrote under the pseudonym "Fanny Fern." Her daughter, Ellen, referred in a letter to her mother's "life long dread of *publicity*—which," said Ellen, "we *all* share." In part, Ellen felt that Parton's dread had been fueled by uncomplimentary "stories" that Parton's second husband, from whom she was divorced, had "fabricated" about her. But, said Ellen, Parton "always said the public had a right to know an author as such, and should seek to know nothing of the woman."[47]

That was certainly the sentiment that Parton had imparted to the perpetually inquisitive John S. Hart. Hart had included Parton in his 1855 edition but, in contrast to his exposure of Warner, he had maintained Parton's incognito. "We would be glad to give the true name of this authoress," he wrote in truthful words. "But she prefers still to maintain her *incognito*, and a proper deference to the obligations of courtesy (which are as binding in literary as in social life) forbids our doing what would otherwise be an equal gratification to our readers and ourselves." Why Hart was treating "Fanny Fern" differently from "Elizabeth Wetherell" he did not say. But he did add, "With regard to the personal history of FANNY FERN, we feel a similar restraint." Thus, he concluded, he would only relate what "may be referred to without the slightest violation of propriety."[48]

That same year Parton's sense of propriety was violated. Her highly autobiographical novel *Ruth Hall* had just been published, and a review in *Harper's Monthly Magazine* declared, "It has sold universally; and that profoundly interesting question whether Ruth Hall is Fanny Fern has been debated from the Penobscot to the Mississippi." The *New Bedford Mercury* commented on the fact that the contents of *Ruth Hall* were indeed autobiographical—and Parton immediately wrote a letter to the editor disputing the statement. In the same letter she also vehemently denied that a forthcoming biography of "Fanny Fern" was to be issued with "her own guaranty." She wanted to make clear that "the work referred to will *not* 'appear under my own guaranty,' " that she had "never authorized it," and that she also had "never been consulted with regard to it." That was undoubtedly so, given the fact that the biography was critical of Parton. But as she wrote in the letter, she was "and have always been, opposed to any such work (my life having been a humble one, in no way of any interest or concern to the public) and that for any sketch of Fanny Fern which has yet appeared, I am not responsible."[49]

The private Parton continued to grapple with her alien status as public writer. Fourteen years later, in 1869, "Fanny Fern" herself contributed to yet another biographical collection, *Eminent Women of the Age*, a sketch of "Gail Hamilton," a pseudonym for another female writer, Mary Abigail Dodge. The absurdity of one zealously private female pressing into print another equally private female was so apparent as to take on the trappings of farce, however unintentionally. "I consider no crime more radically heinous than the violation of privacy," Hamilton-Dodge wrote to Fern-Parton in response to the latter's request for information. "You must have suffered from it too severely yourself to be surprised at any abhorrence of it on my part." Indeed, Parton considered publication of information about her person comparable to being "laid on the gridiron." What was more, a sketch of "Fanny Fern," identified as Sara Payson Willis Parton, appeared in the same volume. "Who is to serve me up," Parton wrote to Dodge, "the gods only know." Not that Parton cooperated in her grilling. Yet a third pseudonymous author, "Grace Greenwood," whose real name was Sara Jane Lippincott, contributed the sketch of Parton and explained that she had "written this article with little more personal knowledge of Mrs. Parton than I have been able to obtain from brief biographical sketches, and the recollections and impressions of friends." That same year, apparently before *Eminent Women of the Age* appeared and probably for the purpose of being forewarned, Parton's husband James wrote to Lippincott asking for a copy of the sketch. Lippincott complied with the request and also said, "I have done my best for Mrs. Parton—but that I fear is not much—I worked in the dark comparatively. I did not know her—in fact, knew no one who did know her well." But perhaps Greenwood-Lippincott succeeded better than she knew, even with secondhand information. She wrote of Parton's prose, "Her own fortunes, loves, and hates live again in her creations,—her heroines are her doubles." When the private woman stepped upon the public stage, a double exposure was inevitable.[50]

6

No Happy Woman Writes

"'God forbid,'" answers the female writer Ruth Hall when her little daughter Nettie asks, "'When I get to be a woman shall I write books, mamma?'" Ruth Hall is a thinly disguised version of Sara Parton in Parton's thinly disguised autobiographical novel *Ruth Hall*. The novel itself is perhaps the most fully and directly autobiographical piece of writing amid the welter of literal and figurative allusions to their own lives in the literary domestics' quasi-fiction. "'God forbid,'" Ruth repeats, adding, "'No happy woman ever writes.'" While sitting in a chair, musing and remembering, Ruth turns the pages of her recently published first book. Like Parton's initial book, *Fern Leaves From Fanny's Portfolio*, issued in 1854, Ruth's is a collection of sketches previously published in newspapers and magazines. Both collections, the real and the fictional, were produced directly as the result of the mother's need for money. Like Parton's, Ruth Hall's first marriage had ended suddenly with the premature death of her husband, Harry. Ruth had quickly discovered that her husband had left her and their two children without financial support and she subsequently had been refused all but nominal aid from his as well as her own parents; this had also been Parton's experience. Contrary to the traditional demands placed upon women, Ruth Hall, like her creator, was forced to earn a living in order to support herself and her children. With the death of her husband the wife had to attempt to perform what she and her society regarded as the man's task. Implicit in Ruth's response to her daughter, then, is the premise "'No happy woman ever writes'" *for a living*.[1]

With her youngest child in her lap, Ruth looks over her book. It is indeed "Ruth's book!" and she speculates that only a few of its readers will "know how much of her own heart's history was there laid bare." She remembers why, how, and under what circumstances every piece was written: "Each had its own little history. Each would serve, in after-days, for a land-mark to some thorny path of by-gone trouble." The first and foremost trouble was material need. With the "proceeds" from one article, "little shoeless feet were covered"; with the income of another article or two, "a little medicine, or a warmer shawl was bought." Still others recall the physical difficulties of composition; one sketch was "composed while walking wearily to or from the offices where she was employed." Ruth's collections and Parton's language are totally colored by the sense of a woman wrongfully and unexpectedly burdened with a man's job, with male responsibilities, while simultaneously having to perform female duties. And always there was the reminder of *why*, of the prime motivation of writing for a living, as yet another article "was written with little Nettie sleeping in her lap."[2]

The struggles and humiliations experienced by Ruth Hall were the same as those endured by Sara Parton. Faced with the new and unexpected demand that she be her family's economic provider, and after failing in her attempts to start a school, to obtain a teaching appointment, and to support herself as a seamstress, Ruth, possessing the requisite ability and education (that is, having been exposed to "peculiar circumstances") and recognizing the opportunity, turned to writing for a living. But for Ruth, as for Parton, it was a profession chosen only from necessity, only because it was available to her, and only because she was able to grasp the opportunity. Parton chose the pseudonym of "Fanny Fern"; Ruth chooses "Floy" as her *nom de plume*. To emphasize to her daughter that "'no happy woman ever writes,'" Ruth reminds her that it was the death of Nettie's father, the family's original, legitimate economic provider, that brought her mother to her career; as Ruth phrases it, "'From Harry's grave sprang "Floy."'"[3]

Neither "Floy" nor "Fanny Fern" was supposed to have happened. The image of someone springing live from someone else's grave does not suggest an anticipated, planned event. The nurture and training of a female were not designed to produce a professional, financially successful writer. It is true that the peculiar circumstances of these women provided them sufficient education to enable them to write, and they were able to benefit from the opportunity presented by the new commercial publishing industry. However, the education these women received was not intended to prepare them for either a career or financial independence. Measured by the dominant prescription governing all female lives in the nineteenth century—and for that matter, before and after as well, from the colonial period into the twentieth century—a "happy woman" was supposed to be the woman who married, had children, managed a household, and was materially supported by her husband.

"Floy," like "Fanny Fern," was a family's economic provider. Broadly speaking, a woman acting as an independent economic figure was an incongruity, and as a matter of fact the literary domestic has in that respect been a practically invisible figure to historians. The literary domestics' previous designation as "sentimentalists" stamped them as leisured ladies who lay idle in a well of bathos out of which, somehow, books appeared, rather than as females who wrote and published books. The image has been that of the lady whose effusions poured on to page after page, rather than that of the woman who worked, produced a product, negotiated in the literary marketplace, and received money for her labor. Women were not supposed to be economic providers, any more than they were supposed to be statesmen or clergymen, and these women have not been regarded as such. But, besides entering a public realm dominated by males and becoming part of an identifiable profession, these female writers gained an opportunity to produce more income from their own labor than had ever before been possible for a member of their sex. That is, of course, to underline the issue that these women were, and any women would have been, unlikely actors in the public economic realm, almost entirely a male realm.

Since she had not been reared for such things, it should hardly be surprising that Harriet Beecher Stowe, for example, clearly found it a novelty when her early tales and sketches brought her money. In 1838, long before her husband Calvin would tell her that "money matters are entirely in your hands," she wrote to one of her sisters to inform her that she had received forty dollars for a "piece." That alone was a remarkable event but, reported Harriet, "Mr. Stowe says he shall leave me to use [it] for my personal gratification," and that was a ludicrous idea—"as if a wife and mother had any gratification apart from her family interests." Stowe was speaking from an ingrained female consciousness that predated her by a couple of centuries in America. For the adult female before and during the nineteenth century marriage was a nearly universal experience, and the white "working mother" as the twentieth century understands that term was a most unusual figure. To paraphrase Mary Virginia Terhune, the social dictum that the household was the center of duties as well as thought for women was not unique to the nineteenth century. And in this case, at least, the social dictum also described social reality. As wife, mother, and mistress in the bosom of a household, female being was enveloped, governed, and consumed by what Stowe designated "family interests."[4]

To look for "distinguished" women in the marketplace in seventeenth-, eighteenth-, or nineteenth-century America is, with isolated exceptions, to look in vain. Males were the political, religious, and cultural leaders of society, who made the economic decisions in the public sphere that affected the affairs of colony, company, community, and nation. Males were the economic managers; they were the primary economic producers beyond the household; and they controlled the distribution of material resources. There could not have been a clearer, sharper distinction in the gender-determined economic spheres of influence or power, in activity or responsibility. Males performed and ruled in the public sphere; females were subordinate, dependent, and centered in the private sphere.

That is not to say that females were excluded from economic functions or responsibilities. It is to say, first and foremost, that the female economic role was only part of a total matrix of being. Her economic functions and responsibilities were primarily family- and home-identified and family- and homebound, in significantly different fashion than for a male. While it is true that most of what males produced materially was directed toward the use, support, and well-being of their families, nevertheless males were expected to have a profession or occupation whether or not there was a family to be maintained. That is to say, too, that apart from identifying himself or being identified by his community as a husband or a father, a male could have the independent identity of a magistrate, a merchant, a doctor, or a farmer. The closest a female could come to such a separate identity, separate from being a wife, mother, and mistress of a household, was to be the wife of a merchant or a minister or a farmer, the mother of his children, and the mistress of his household. And while most males in an agricultural society worked in or near the home, they at least had the theoretical option of employment beyond the home in a variety of capacities, and they initiated and maintained most of whatever links there were with the world beyond the home.

The female vocation, then, was domesticity, in colonial as well as in independent America. Daughters were trained for domesticity, and for the most part they received their training in households, mostly their own, sometimes in others'. Just as females did not look outside the household for economic identity or responsibilities, so within it economic tasks were only part of the larger role of housewifery. Materially productive functions were not perceived as separate from family need or welfare, and they did not constitute the central identity for women. Rather they were encompassed by the overall identity of domesticity. Even the choice of tasks to be performed was limited, and for the most part the tasks were distinguished on the basis of gender. Most females performed a set of common tasks, and these were tasks predominantly performed by females. Their primary responsibilities included cooking, cleaning, care of children, and general household management. Women also performed more readily identifiable economic functions—more readily identifiable, probably because they involved products that could be sold as well as consumed by the family—such as food preservation and cloth production. It is true that in the absence of males, whether due to a scarcity of male labor, sickness or death, divorce or abandonment, travel or war, or a variety of other factors, individual women did manage farms and run taverns and shops. And it is true that some wives worked alongside their husbands in farms and businesses. But even then official sanction by society for a more highly valued economic position was not forthcoming, certainly not permanently. Those functions were performed by females *in place of or in the absence* of males, or *helping* males, which is simply to say that nevertheless they were male functions. Such cases also reinforced the notion of women as helpmates, as secondary, supportive, or, at best, substitute workers. Those exceptions to the rule made no fundamental alteration in either the female or the male economic status in society.[5]

Until recently it has been claimed that female economic status was fundamentally altered from the early nineteenth century onward. This interpretation rests upon the interrelated premises that gender determined identity and roles for both sexes to a greater extent than had been the case in colonial America, that women's role as economically productive members of the household declined in significance, and that their status diminished proportionally. According to this thesis, women's economic contribution lessened with the introduction of new machine technology and the removal of household production to the factory; simultaneously, men's economic opportunities and their place of occupation were increasingly separated from the household. Economic contribution and higher status then came to be equated with a male marketplace beyond the home, while economic dependence and subordinate status were ascribed to women left behind in the home. Stripped of importance as economic figures, women are presumed to have suffered a loss of social and self-esteem and to have tried to compensate by exalting and more closely identifying with wifely and motherly functions.

This is a suspect and unlikely scenario. It is difficult to believe that women suffered a loss of status as the result of the loss of specific economic functions, when the overall function of domesticity itself, of which those functions constituted only a part, had not engendered high social or personal status for women in the first place. Moreover, the most recent examinations of the evidence have challenged the scenario. For example, it had been claimed that roles in colonial America had not been sharply distinguished on the basis of gender, that women's contributions had been perceived as relatively equal to those of men, and that consequently women had displayed a strong sense of self-esteem. The latest research on eighteenth-century women reaches virtually opposite conclusions, and demonstrates that women were keenly aware of their dependent and inferior social position. Recent analysis also does not suggest anything but complete identification with the home on the part of women. Female lives characterized by little diversity or choice were circumscribed by the four walls of the home. Women's lives were experienced within the household and their concerns centered on the household, where they were subordinate to husbands who controlled the finances and exercised ultimate authority more generally. Secondary figures within the home and isolated from the world without, women also voiced discontent with housewifery. Their tasks, especially if compared with those of their husbands, seemed boring and monotonous, the demands upon their time too consuming for the development of other interests. Theirs were necessary duties more than experiences that brought fulfillment and self-esteem. The portrait that emerges is of a female who was indeed housebound, mentally and physically.[6]

Studies of nineteenth-century women undertaken recently have also raised questions about the supposed decline in female economic roles and status. Research indicates that some women, at least, actually gained economic opportunities rather than lost them. The extraordinary success of the literary domestics is but one example; the more visible and numerically more significant female teachers provide a second example. The republicanism that made an educated citizenry a requisite fueled the expansion of universal education regardless of gender. Women might not be fully endowed citizens, but they could become republican wives and mothers. Moreover, the increase in primary and, particularly, secondary education for males and females represented an opportunity for women that seemingly took them beyond the home and made them financially independent. More and more teachers were needed in the first half of the nineteenth century, in part because there was an insufficient supply of male teachers, and increasing numbers of women entered the classroom. But again, the cloak of domesticity was not discarded, nor was the separation of spheres altered. Instead, the vocation of teaching represented de facto preparation for the role of motherhood in the household. Proponents of the movement to train women to become teachers commonly looked upon the female instructor as a surrogate mother. And the large majority of teachers, who were generally young and single, eventually married and left the classroom for the home.[7]

But whether women gained or lost, of greater significance is the fact that already established perspectives on gender and the persistence of traditional values regarding female nature, duties, and sphere affected women's lives and shaped female identity in ways that enveloped economic developments in the nineteenth century. In retrospect, conceptions of gender simultaneously altered and buttressed the status of women. As much as the condition of women changed it remained the same. Such was the case with what was still considered women's work. "Family interests" continued to be the focus of a female's existence. In the nineteenth century nine out of ten women married, and for the large majority of them the household remained the locus of occupation. By far the greater part of what had been women's traditional work, namely, cooking, cleaning, washing, care of children, and household management, continued to be their responsibility. Contrary to what some historians have asserted, women also continued to participate in household economic production even as tasks changed, were lost or replaced. The historians' claims that women's economic role declined in the nineteenth century has been primarily based upon the premise that household manufacture reached its height in the second decade of the century and then plummeted to negligibility in the second quarter. But recent research has shown that while women's role in household production did decline in terms of agriculture and textiles, other manufacturing replaced it, and women in the home continued to play their part as adjuncts of the factory system. In fact, opportunities for women, particularly rural women, may have increased as improvements in transportation enabled women to play a more specialized and market-oriented role in the manufacture of products as diverse as cigars, butter, brooms, cheese, and brushes.[8]

In or out of the home, women's work was determined more by traditional values concerning female nature and role than by the transformation of the economy. Throughout the nineteenth century the majority of women who were employed outside their own homes worked as servants in the homes of others. The development of machine technology and the emergence of the factory system did produce further opportunities for female employment, but assumptions about female nature, capacities, and responsibilities governed women workers to a great extent.[9]

Generally, female factory workers were, like female teachers, paid less than men, and in the tradition of their colonial forebears they were assigned less skilled tasks. Colonial women, in the processing of raw materials or in the production of finished goods, had performed their manufacturing functions by hand and had engaged in work that was less skilled, more monotonous, more easily interruptible, and relatively safe. Essentially it was work that was compatible with the performance of primary household tasks, particularly the care of children. Whether or not women in the nineteenth century took their children into the factories, they were assigned work that for the most part had the same characteristics as the preindustrial labor of colonial women. The more skilled, more demanding, more hazardous machine-operated functions were generally assigned to men. In fact, preliminary research indicates that machine technology bypassed many women's tasks in manufacturing, with the result that the nature of women's work in the factory, mill, or shop remained essentially the same in 1900 as it had been in 1800. Considerations rooted in gender also affected the behavior of women. Married or single, the large majority were motivated to leave the home only because the financial demands of their families made it necessary. Once in the marketplace, they sought work close to their homes, at establishments where their husbands and fathers worked, and chose positions and tasks that enabled them to continue to meet their responsibilities within the household. Many of them were young and single, and as soon as they married they returned to the household. In the end, then, whether women left the home to work or not, the home went with them, and they went back to the home.[10]

That the literary domestics were popular, highly successful writers obviously made them economic oddities of their time for a variety of reasons. For example, they not only practiced a profession that reached far beyond their homes, but produced significant income for a number of parties in addition to their families, including most directly publishers, booksellers, and printers. They were among the forerunners of a new profession in a new American industry. And, of course, simply by being paid published writers they were (and would be today) part of a very small minority, male and female. Nevertheless, the very fact that the literary domestics were aware that "Floy" was an oddity, and that as players on the historical stage they reacted to their anomalous status in defensive, ambiguous, conflicted fashion, thereby further betraying their sense of deviance, demonstrates that they were recipients of a common female legacy and conditioned to fulfill a common female destiny. In that critical respect, the literary domestics were not oddities at all. For them, as for their foremothers, contemporaries, and descendants, the context in which a female performed any economic role was more important than the role itself. The issue of an economic role for a woman was primarily governed, encompassed, and interpreted in relation to a private, domestic identity.

Because the literary domestics produced substantial income from their pens, a social accomplishment was transformed into an economically productive task. In fact, the need for money played an important role in nine and possibly more of the twelve literary domestics' careers. As Parton phrased it in another volume of her sketches, *Fresh Leaves*, published after both *Fern Leaves* and *Ruth Hall*, the personal and familial material "necessities" of these literary domestics "forced them out from the blessed shelter of the home circle." Parton's words provide a clue to how the very identity that was enveloped by "family interests" and that barred these women from the role of family provider simultaneously and paradoxically justified their endeavors to fulfill that role.[11]

The need for income launched the professional careers of some of the literary domestics, careers that might otherwise never have been. In the absence of financial need, four of these twelve writers might never have written for publication. Like Parton, Maria McIntosh, E.D.E.N. Southworth, and Susan Warner began writing for publication only after their families or they, as single individuals, were in need of money. Material needs fundamentally altered and enlarged the literary careers of others. For two of them, Harriet Beecher Stowe and Caroline Lee Hentz, financial exigencies related to the inadequate income and ill-health of their husbands were determining factors in dramatically expanding and altering their careers. The less than ample income of Caroline Howard Gilman's husband and adverse economic conditions spurred the Gilmans' hopes that they might be able to count upon supplementary income from Caroline's literary enterprises. The degree to which the material needs of their families played a role in the careers of Augusta Evans Wilson and Mary Virginia Terhune is not totally clear. But Wilson definitely provided significant support for her parents' family and contributed to her own livelihood, while Terhune made important and timely additions to her husband's income. For all of these women a variety of factors made their literary income necessary, important income: the sickness and death of fathers and husbands, divorce and separation, financial disaster, or simply inadequate supply of funds. These were socially elite women, but the socially elite were not necessarily people of wealth. And even for those that were, affluence was not necessarily permanent.

A number of these women became the sole or primary providers for their families, while others supplied important supplemental income. That meant that, for whatever reason, no man in their family was fully meeting that male responsibility. To varying degrees, then, the literary domestics were women of the home who for family reasons had to assume responsibilities beyond their traditional female sphere. Social background dictated the career, a newly commercialized gentleman's industry gave them the opportunity, and simple economic need led these private domestic women to assume what E.D.E.N. Southworth would call the "double burden" of man and woman.[12] It was a condition of their lives that made them distinctly uncomfortable. Even to make money, needed or not, was to jostle their female consciousness with male preoccupations. They were quick to rationalize their income on the basis that they and their families needed the support. To justify their pursuit of literary income simply as the right of any individual was neither easy nor likely for them. To think that they could have done so, or done so without grave misgivings, would be to remove them from their historical context. They assumed a responsibility beyond their sphere, but they justified it in terms of the traditional perspective of that sphere. Because they were women from elite families their circumstances might have been peculiar, and yet as American women of the nineteenth century their responses were representative.

Those women who had to resort to self-support and who achieved financial independence were anomalous figures in the eyes of their society. But they existed because male support sometimes disappeared, and replacements were not necessarily forthcoming. Downward mobility was not an uncommon experience in the nineteenth century. Born in 1803 and 1819 respectively, neither Maria McIntosh nor Susan Warner married, and over time the financial support from their fathers diminished and eventually disappeared. If, as McIntosh implied, woman as a publicly self-supporting figure was "contradicted alike by sacred and profane history," McIntosh herself became a living contradiction. "Different spheres of action" were accorded to man and woman as part of "the fulfillment of God's design in the formation, the preservation, and the perfection of human society," she wrote in 1850, but the paid publication of these very words suggested that the design had unraveled.[13]

Signs of a misbegotten design appeared early in McIntosh's life. She was born in Sunbury, Liberty County, Georgia, a health resort for neighboring planters, and witnessed its decline in her youth. When McIntosh was three her father, the Revolutionary War brigadier general and wealthy planter Lachlan McIntosh, died and management of the family mansion and estate passed into the hands of her mother and others. After she nursed her mother through a long terminal illness, the responsibility became hers, at age twenty.

For fourteen years McIntosh's subsistence came from her inheritance. In 1835 she sold the family property and moved to New York City, where she invested all of her money in securities. Two years later she was bankrupt, having lost everything in the financial crisis of 1837. For several years McIntosh was supported by friends, a married sister, and a half-brother. In 1841, at the age of thirty-eight, she began to provide for herself when *Blind Alice*, the first volume of "Aunt Kitty's Tales," was published, two years after it had been completed. Nearly two decades later a letter McIntosh wrote to Maria Cummins dated 1 October 1857 indicates that McIntosh, still dependent upon her pen, was somewhat apologetic about her role as a businesswoman. "You are aware," she wrote Cummins, that her publisher, John P. Jewett, "makes his payments in paper at four months." He had last paid her in July, she said, and now she was anxiously awaiting another payment, "as enabling me to meet some debts here—but I just only hope, work and be patient." McIntosh added, "If I were only not in debt, I should care for nothing—but that others should lose by me—that I should be compelled to fail in my obligations troubles me a little." Apparently, McIntosh was not at all certain that she could depend upon Jewett to meet his quarterly payment, but she was placing no blame: "I have nothing but sympathy" for him, she assured Cummins.[14] McIntosh's benevolence toward Jewett may well have been justified. He may well have been on time with his payments and otherwise fair and just in his transactions with her. But her positive response may also have been that of a woman who was indeed performing a "different office," different, that is, from that which her society thought proper for her to perform, that for which she had been nurtured. Thus rather than expecting payment for work performed, perhaps McIntosh felt gratitude for any help delivered or favor done. That at least was the clearly expressed attitude of a number of the literary domestics toward their publishers, regardless of the fact that they had earned what they received.

On 13 July 1851, six months after Susan Warner's first novel, *The Wide, Wide World*, was published, Catharine Maria Sedgwick wrote to her niece, Kate Sedgwick Minot, to sing its praises. "Its simplicity and truth to nature are remarkable," she enthused. She felt that the novel made "you turn back to your childhood when everyone was good or bad—when you loved or hated without analyzing character or dissecting nature." Sedgwick asked her niece if she knew that Susan Warner was the author of the novel, and if she remembered how Sedgwick had "vainly labored" to make Kate and Warner friends in their childhood. Her effort had failed, she reminded Kate, because "you were repulsed by her reserve and her frightful long long neck." Sedgwick herself had been "intimately acquainted" with Warner's mother, "a very superior person." And while there was no denying that Warner's father was "a man of considerable talent," neither could it be disputed that he was "a bigot and everywhere crotchical [*sic*]." As if to illustrate her point, Sedgwick added that Henry Warner had "speculated himself into and out of a handsome property and I am told their poverty was the impulse that led her to write."[15]

Had Susan Warner read Sedgwick's letter, she would have found much in it to ponder, much to make her blush, much to deny and affirm. In all likelihood she would have blushed with pleasure at Sedgwick's praise of her novel, and then, remembering, blushed again in guilt. Shortly before the novel's publication Warner had spent three weeks on Staten Island at the home of her publisher, George Putnam, correcting proofs of *The Wide, Wide World*—and reading two of Sedgwick's novels, *Redwood* and *Clarence*. "Dismally poor," she had written home to her sister Anna; "*inexpressible*," she wrote home again, expressing herself very clearly.[16] Warner would not have contradicted Sedgwick's allusion to her reticence, but she probably would have been wounded by her ugly-duckling caricature. She might have been intrigued with the idea that her mother, who had died when Warner was still very young, was "superior." The reference to her beloved father's "talent" would have pleased her; that to his flawed character would have angered her.

But as for the rumor regarding the *raison d'être* for Warner's literary career, Warner would have confirmed it. She was thirty-one when the novel was published. She had not married. Her father's once healthy financial fortunes had suffered severe reversals, and the family—Henry, his daughters Susan and Anna, and their Aunt Fanny—desperately needed money. Susan had written *The Wide, Wide World* for money, and she and Anna wrote many more novels for exactly the same reason. As Susan's journals and Anna's biography of her reveal, the family's financial affairs declined dramatically from the eighteenth year of Susan's life onward. Henry continued to provide for the family for nearly a decade; thereafter his daughters became contributors, and after ill health and age incapacitated Henry they became the family's sole support.

The same Panic of 1837 that had engulfed Maria McIntosh precipitated the decline in the Warner's fortunes. It was then that Susan, the well-born daughter, had pondered the fact that the family might be "*ruined*," confessing, "Perhaps I do not know what ruin means." To that stage in her young life there had not been much reason for her to have known about such matters. But not many days after that journal entry she wrote: "There are almost no pleasures in this world that are not either preceeded or followed by pain. My dear father went to town tonight; his affairs give him trouble enough. I do not know what is to become of us." And a few days later she revealed that she was learning quickly what "ruin" meant: "Father is in town. Alas, he carries a heavy burden, and we cannot help him. He bears up passably well, but truly there are times when he feels it only too much. Far from us, alone in the midst of a multitude; between the chagrins and the sorrows that are in his path, sometimes he thinks he shall die; so he told us the other day." Actually, Henry lived for almost forty more years, but these were extremely hard times for the Warners, "years of many privations," as Anna called them. "In town" was New York City, where Henry struggled with his previously lucrative legal affairs. Susan recorded the journal entries on Constitution Island, where the family had begun to live year round as a means of saving money. Existence there imposed a particular hardship on Susan, for their life was quickly "shorn of almost everything girls are supposed to want."[17]

For almost a decade the business of maintaining the family remained "his affairs"—that is, Henry's—and he continued to produce the sole income. The three women made their traditional female contribution by doing without and doing more and more for themselves. However, during the winter of 1846, one spent on the island "for economy's sake," a winter when "very little money came in . . . from any source," the sisters began the move that would transform them into businesspeople. First Anna invented "'a game of Natural History,'" complete with a book to tell about animals and a set of hand-painted cards to illustrate them, a game to be produced and sold commercially. Then, as Anna related it, Aunt Fanny said one day, "'Sue, I believe if you would try, you could write a story.'" Anna was uncertain if her aunt had said specifically that Susan could write a tale "'that would sell,'" but, said Anna, "that was what she meant."[18]

It no doubt was what she meant, because by the middle 1840s even women in the home were well aware that there was a substantial literary marketplace. In Warner's *Queechy*, when Fleda Ringgan is asked by her cousin Hugh (he from whom she appropriated her pseudonym) if the magazine is going to pay for her "'scribblings,'" Fleda's response is unequivocal. "'I am sure if they don't they shall have no more—that is my only possible inducement to let them be printed. For my own pleasure, I would far rather not.'" Anna's account notwithstanding, it is possible that the idea of writing occurred first to Susan. As early as the fall of 1839 Susan wrote in her journal, "I do not write often enough to profit by it. I am not ignorant that much is wanting to make me write well. I fear I shall not do it in a long time. But I will persist; that is the way to succeed." And in another entry recorded the winter of the same year she observed, "I should like to write a little, but I am not as lively at night as I am in the morning. There is no remedy for that. Often it is not possible for me to write before afternoon, and perhaps not then." Seven years later Aunt Fanny provided the catalyst. Warner began *The Wide, Wide World* in 1846 and finished it by the end of the summer of 1849.[19]

The novel was not accepted for publication until a year later and did not appear in print until December of 1850. Even then, however, there was not a happily-ever-after ending to the Warner family story. In the spring of 1849 the Warners had been forced to sell many of their household belongings in order to pay what Anna called an "unjust debt." Let go were Susan's Chickering piano, a Domenichino print, rare books, and all but "stray bits of furniture"; a Gilbert Stuart portrait of George Washington was saved and later bequeathed to West Point, where it hangs today. When the novel was accepted a year later there was "great joy" in the household, but no immediate sense of great relief: "how little we counted upon anything, in those days," said Anna. There was no way, of course, that the Warners could have anticipated the extraordinary success of the novel. At any rate, anticipation did not pay bills, so the two sisters did not simply wait upon the result. When the news came both had "gone to writing again." Susan had already begun her second novel, *Queechy*.[20]

In fact, hard times continued until well after publication of *The Wide, Wide World*. While writing her second novel and waiting for the proofs of her first, Susan recorded in her journal, "I have been all but thinking of a governess's place—anything but living on nothing, or on borrowed money." That idea was rejected because it would break up "our home circle," take time away from writing, and possibly have an "unhappy effect upon one's mind and character." While correcting proofs, Susan noted, they were burning tallow candles as the "oil-can" was at the grocers and "no money existing to fetch it thence full." In addition, they were borrowing money: there were unpaid debts; Henry needed clothes "immediately," Susan and Anna "proximately." They had floated a bond on their island property, and the title to the property had gone into the hands of a receiver; with the quarter's rent well overdue they were presented with an eviction notice. Fortunately, Henry was at home when the notice was presented and managed to forestall that threat.[21]

What they were living on was a lot of anxiety, a little bit of hope, and some money that had begun to come in from the sale of Anna's "Natural History" game. As Susan related later, income from the latter was all that kept them from total "want" during that period. Publication of Susan's novel was still a month away, and the family was reduced to literally banking on her winning the fifty dollars for her essay on patriotism in the competition sponsored by Lydia Sigourney. If she did not win they had no idea where they were going to get the money for "winter hats and cloaks, etc., etc." Nor added Susan, did they know "yet either in the least where we shall, if we live, spend the winter." And wherever they spent the winter, there was still "no oil that will burn." Meanwhile, she noted, "I am writing, writing; have no idea of how much worth." Two weeks later she learned that she had won the contest; patriotism had paid fifty dollars.[22]

Finally the novel was published, and after a delay it sold. Susan Warner was launched on an unexpected career as a literary domestic with an unanticipated success, "'such success,'" publisher Putnam wrote, "'as convicts *me* (I am bound to confess) of sad want of faith and good judgment.'" In gentlemanly fashion, Putnam was even willing to brave comment on the possibilities of Susan's supporting herself by a literary career. Earlier that spring of 1851, Susan had written to Putnam inquiring, as paraphrased by Anna, if there was "hope she might thenceforth live by the pen?—or should she betake herself to needle and thread?" As a gentleman of the nineteenth century, Putnam knew what subjects to sidestep: "'I should not dare to offer even suggestions, touching the difference between pens and needles.'" But as a businessman he would say that "'it is fair to say that many have chosen the pen with less warrant and encouragement.'" A woman had her place, but after all, business was business, and the success of Susan's first novel indicated that there would continue to be a place for her in the literary marketplace.[23]

The Warner sisters did go on to earn their family's living by the pen. Henry's law practice never recovered; age, ill-health, and changing legal practices guaranteed that. He had once supported them, and he had even been the one who found a publisher for *The Wide, Wide World*. But within a year after its publication, the daughters assumed the role of "breadwinners to the family." If they did not make "fabulous sums" from their writing, they did make "a good deal." That meant food, clothing, and a full "oil-can," as well as secure title to their home on Constitution Island, but it did not mean the comfort or status of their childhood days. There were still many debts to pay, there was much ground to recover and the process took many years. Hard times continued and financial crises arose anew. In 1857 the threat of foreclosure on their island property took practically all the money they had, and they were nearly as destitute as in the prepublication "Natural History" days. "So we worked," Anna wrote. "Big books, little books; now and then an article for some paper or magazine." That same year Susan wrote publisher James T. Fields to inquire about the possibilities of offering a collection of poetry for schoolchildren. Another publisher, Appleton, she said, had been interested, but only "'in a year from now,' one of them said to me." This was unacceptable to Susan: "I can't wait so long—that is, I cannot if anybody else will do it;—I can't afford to wait, and I am afraid, too." If Fields was not interested, did he know of a publisher who might be? she asked. Meanwhile the Warners made their own clothes, kept their expenses minimal, and supplemented their literary income by grading papers and writing lessons for a local school. As a series of consecutive journal entries by Susan in the 1860s testified, they continued to produce income from their writing. "We are very poor just at the present time," she lamented one day, and recorded the next, "Work, work, and get off all the last of the copy and the preface"; again a few months later, "Feel I must work, and ought to be brave. Must be economical too, to make our funds last till we can get another book out." As Anna had observed at the onset of their "breadwinner" days, they had been forced to learn how "to save, not to spend"; later they even had to learn to manage all the "business matters" of the island. They had learned and assumed a new role.[24]

The downturn in her father's financial fortunes, along with the resultant alteration in her family's social standing, was probably a prime reason Susan Warner remained single. The same may have been the case with Maria McIntosh. Whatever their reasons, financial disaster led both of them to become self-supporting, Warner in her thirties and McIntosh in her forties, both by the pen. Both ended up with only one half of E.D.E.N. Southworth's "double burden," and the wrong half at that. In contrast, Southworth and Sara Parton eventually assumed the full, dual burden. Both began by taking the traditional path, marrying and having children. But after Parton's first marriage ended with the death of her husband and her second with a divorce, and after Southworth's marriage failed, both became the sole providers for themselves and their children. Parton's first volume of sketches appeared when she was forty-two. Southworth's first novel, *Retribution*, was published when she was thirty. From that point on, both lived by the pen.

Both Parton and Southworth took pride in their successful performance of their dual functions. It might be said that their pride symbolized the opportunity they, along with the other literary domestics, had been given to broaden their female sphere. In that respect their pride indicated a possible alteration in female identity and status. However, it was a pride born less of an opportunity productively pursued than of a female's successful perform- ance of a man's function in the absence of a male. It was the pride of women who had ventured beyond their sphere without losing their primary identity as private, domestic females.

Although Parton became the sole supporter of herself and her two children, the road that led her there had not been mapped out beforehand. The biographer James Parton, Sara's third husband, whom she married well after she became financially independent, wondered after her death why she had waited so long in her time of need to turn to her pen for income. After all, he recalled in a volume he published in honor of her memory, young Sara had written "bright, pretty pieces" for her father's *Youth's Companion*. Actually Sara had even corrected proof for her father's publication as early as age twelve, as she herself later recounted. But that was more like an extra pair of hands on the family farm than on-the-job training; little on-the-spot Sara had made her contribution to "family interests."[25]

James Parton has been called the leading biographer of his age, but as historian and social commentator he had a blind spot. His criticism of the nurture of women like his wife revealed that he had right under his own nose the knowledge to answer his question. But it was knowledge he did not fully understand. "It is only in the United States," complained the British-born James, "and in a few circles of Great Britain, perhaps, that educated women can get to the age of thirty-six [Sara's age at the end of her second marriage], *wholly* unversed in . . . knowledge of the world." Raised to marry and expecting to be supported by their husbands, James scoffed, they end by knowing "nothing of [their husbands'] business." In fact, "they know nothing of any business." That was exactly the point, of course. Sara had not been reared to know anything about a husband's business, and although her education and her precociousness had enabled her to write a few pieces and correct proof for her father's juvenile publication at an early age, that was a far cry from being a professional writer. Between one and the other, no connection had been originally envisioned, by either her family or herself. Parton's granddaughter Ethel claimed that during grandmother Sara's attendance at Catharine Beecher's seminary in Hartford, Sara's compositions had gained her notice beyond the educational institution. A local newspaper editor frequently asked Sara if he could print excerpts from her compositions when he had space to fill in his paper. Wrote Ethel, "Helping out an editor was what any good-natured Willis would naturally do." That was to suggest the existence of a heritage that was gender-blind—which was not exactly the case. Indirectly, Sara Parton said as much herself in *Ruth Hall*, echoing the wonderment of James Parton and indicating the source of Ethel Partons' tale. When in the midst of her struggles to earn a living the idea of writing occurs to Ruth Hall, she remembers that some of her schoolgirl compositions had been reprinted in "a paper" and muses, "How very odd it had never occurred to her before." Yet for women of her time it was not odd, not at all.[26]

Sara Parton began as she was supposed to begin: following her schooling and a few years of what James Parton called the normal life of a "young lady," she married a Boston banker, Charles Eldredge, in 1837. With one significant exception, *Ruth Hall* generally tells it all. From that point in her life until and including the publication of her first volume of sketches in 1854, everything and everyone in Parton's life is paralleled almost exactly. Nine years of idyllic marriage follow for Ruth, who is described as an exemplary housewife and a happy mother—"a *mother*! Joy to thee, Ruth!" The idyll is marred only by the death of one child—as also happened to Parton. But it is terminated by the death of Ruth's husband Harry. It is an inopportune moment for Harry to die; a beneficent banker, he has made too many ill-advised loans to friends and acquaintances and leaves Ruth and two daughters without financial support. Following Harry's death the young wife supports herself and her children, first inadequately as a seamstress and at last successfully as a writer under the pseudonym "Floy." In between there are abortive attempts to obtain a teaching appointment and to start a school for young girls.[27]

Throughout, little aid and no comfort are offered by hostile parents-in-law, an unbeloved father, and a nasty brother. The only comfort comes from the memory of a beloved but dead mother. The cast of characters, likewise drawn from Parton's real life, is also relatively complete. The most prominent fictional disguises are those of Parton's parents-in-law, Hezekiah and Mary Eldredge, who are Mr. and Mrs. Zekiel Hall in the novel; and Nathaniel Willis, Jr., Parton's poet-editor-publisher brother, who is featured as the poet-editor-publisher Hyancinth Ellet.[28] In-laws and brother get their knocks in the novel in return for the ill-treatment Parton felt they dealt her in real life. Indeed, their characterizations can only be called an act of revenge, however true to life the portrayals may have been. In contrast, Oliver Dyer, editor and publisher of the weekly *Musical World and Times* and later an associate of Mason Brothers, which published *Ruth Hall*, gets his due as Ruth Hall's savior-publisher, John Walter. In addition, several minor figures from Parton's life also receive mention, including an unsympathetic landlady. Even James Parton, a minor figure at that stage in her life, appears in the guise of the writer Horace Gates.

Most importantly, of course, there is Parton herself as Ruth Hall. The novel *Ruth Hall* is Parton's justification for her deviant female life writ large. Parton's pride in her eventual achievement of financial independence and successful support of herself and two children was in many respects a bitter pride. Upon completion of her schooling, Ruth's father advises her to get married or, failing that (and in her society that would indeed be a failure), to teach school. Immediately after Ruth marries Harry Hall, her mother-in-law reminds her that the duty of wives is to be "keepers at home."[29] Reinforcement with a twist takes place after Harry's death when Ruth initially turns to her society and to both sides of the family for sympathy and support. There is little or no place in society for a woman without a husband: she is an unwanted blot on the social scheme. Woman is supposed to become the dependent wife of a husband. Failing that, she becomes simply an unwanted, helpless dependent.

Aware of Ruth's predicament, aware that she lacks the training necessary to support herself, Ruth's father-in-law, a prosperous physician (like Parton's father-in-law), tells his wife that Ruth " 'has been a spoiled baby long enough; she will find earning her living a different thing from sitting with her hands folded, with Harry chained to her feet.' " " 'I wash *my* hands of her,' " he informs Ruth's father, who is just as anxious to evade responsibility. The father's reaction is summed up when he responds to Zekiel: " 'I don't know why I should be called upon. Ruth went out of my family, and went into yours, and there she was when her trouble began.' " The only help, if such it can be called, is the in-laws' offer to care for Ruth's eldest daughter, provided the mother agrees to give them total control of the child's upbringing. Ruth first refuses, then reluctantly assents. Under the terms of the agreement, which is the same as the one Parton herself made with her in-laws, upon their deaths their property would go to Parton's daughters only if the eldest had remained with them until that time. The enmity between Parton and her in-laws was intense, to say the least: the mother-in-law, Mary Eldredge, not only omitted Parton from her will but further stipulated that a portrait of her deceased son, Charles, be given to someone other than Parton.[30]

Just as Parton had done, Ruth Hall first attempts to support herself by traditional means, mainly as a seamstress. Some of her customers include former social acquaintances who condescend to allow her to sew for them while refusing to continue to associate with her. " 'If Ruth Hall,' " one says, " 'has got down hill so far as this, I can't keep up her acquaintance.' " In all respects, Ruth's new, altered role as a "suppliant for public favor" leaves her with a "feeling of utter desolation." When her income from sewing proves inadequate and her attempts to find a teaching position and to start a school fail, Ruth finally turns to writing. Her radical departure from traditional female ways encounters traditional barriers. As a woman, Ruth is of course a "novice in business-matters." As a genteel woman she finds it "very disagreeable applying to the small papers." Editors fail to treat her with "that respectful courtesy due to a dignified woman," and she recoils from their "free and easy tone." Eventually, however, "Floy" appears in print. The *Standard* is the first to accept one of her articles. The pay is small and is withheld until the day of publication. Later the *Pilgrim* joins the *Standard* in publishing her pieces, but neither publication pays her well. According to James Parton, the *Mother's Assistant* published Parton's first fictional sketch, paid her fifty cents, and made her wait until publication to receive payment. But the real-life counterparts of the *Standard* and the *Pilgrim* were probably the *Olive Branch* and the *True Flag*. Early in Parton's career she made weekly contributions to both Boston papers and received a combined total of six dollars a week.[31]

Her literary career launched, Parton's perspective on woman's role nevertheless remained fundamentally the same. The convictions and experiences of Parton's alter ego, Ruth Hall, corroborate that. Motivation is clear. At the outset, when Ruth's first efforts to publish her sketches fare poorly, she wonders, "Would a brighter morrow *ever* come?" And then, in answer, "Ruth thought of her children, and said again with a strong heart—*it will*." For Ruth it is difficult to be a literary domestic, to be both a mother to Nettie and Katy and a professional writer. The bulk of Ruth's "writing must be done at night, when Nettie's little prattling voice was hushed, and her innumerable little wants forgotten in sleep." Nevertheless, it is precisely because of the "wants" of Nettie and Katy that she must write on: "Scratch—scratch—scratch, went Ruth's pen; the dim lamp flickering in the night breeze, while the deep breathing of the little sleepers was the watchword, *On*! to her throbbing brow and weary fingers." After "Floy's" first pieces have been accepted and Ruth's prospects brighten for gaining additional income from her pen, she explains to an editor the reason for her sudden laughter and tears by saying, " 'It is because it will be bread for my children.' "[32]

Initially the fame of "Floy" outpaces her income, and her situation worsens before it gets better. But that serves only to make Ruth redouble her efforts. Katy is now living with her paternal grandparents, Ruth's in-laws, but has been promised that she will return home when Ruth can afford to care for her, and "mama *never* broke her promise—*never*." Daughter and mother do what they can: Katy prays to God every night "to help her mother to earn money, that she might soon go home again"; as for the mother, " 'Floy' scribbled on, thinking only of bread for her children, laughing and crying behind her mask." The more she writes behind her mask, the nearer she moves to the "port of independence."[33]

With the reprinting of her sketches in various newspapers, "Floy's" fame grows quickly, and the journey to the port of independence is quickly traveled. The fictional version of Oliver Dyer, John Walter, is the first to come to her rescue. Having read a number of her pieces, John is both sympathetic to what he suspects to be her plight and well aware that her commercial prospects are bright. Sitting in the office of his own newspaper, the *Household Messenger*, after reading her latest article, John says to himself, " 'A bitter life experience she has had too; she did not draw upon her imagination for this article. Like the very first production of her pen that I read, it is a wail from her inmost soul; so are many of her pieces.' "[34]

Speculating that she is underpaid, John writes to "Floy" stating that he might be able to pay her more than she is currently receiving and that he would like to obtain her exclusive services for his paper. It would be an arrangement that would prove mutually beneficial, John suggests, adding that he writes to her for " 'partly business and partly friendly reasons.' " Ruth is overjoyed with his offer and his letter: "how sweet it would be," she imagines, "to have him for a brother." Her decision to respond is made immediately, except that she hesitates, thinking " 'No, not to a stranger!' " But putting aside all doubts, she writes him a long letter, "a sweet, sisterly letter," as if he were a brother who has been away "ever since before Harry's death." She tells him about her struggles and reveals her real name—for contract purposes, of course. The two exchange letters, John addressing her now as " 'Dear Sister Ruth,' " and a contract finally arrives in the mail offering more money for one-eighth the amount of writing. It is a contract that Ruth considers "brief, plain and easily understood, *even by a woman*, as the men say," and she is pleased with the negotiation, not the least by her own handling of it, reflecting at one stage, " 'This bumping round the world has at least sharpened my wits!' "[35]

That is not to say that contact with the world has dulled Ruth's maternal feelings. When the editor of the *Pilgrim* rebukes her for having accepted John's higher offer, despite the fact that the *Pilgrim* had given "Floy" her earlier opportunity, Ruth defends herself by responding, " 'I considered it my duty to avail myself of that increase of salary. My circumstances have been exceedingly straitened. I have two little ones dependent on my exertions, and *their* future, as well as my own, to look to.' " Although Ruth's maternal feelings give birth to business wit, she cannot forgo pleading female inexperience and calling upon John Walter's male expertise in financial matters. When a publishing house offers to collect "Floy's" articles into a volume and pay her "so much on a copy, or $800 for the copyright," Ruth is uncertain what to do. With daughters Katy and Nettie in mind, the $800 is a temptation, but considering "Floy's" popularity and the potential for sales, payment in royalties appears the better route. The decision is made to accept royalties. Forthwith, she questions her decision and turns to John for advice: I need a " 'head wiser than mine' " in business, says Ruth, " 'I am a novice in such matters.' " John confirms Ruth's original decision and applauds her substitute for experience, " 'strong common-sense.' "[36]

Through correspondence, Oliver Dyer solicited Parton's, that is, "Fanny Fern's," exclusive services for his *Musical World and Times*; discovered the author's true identity; and offered double the amount of money for half the literary production required by the *Olive Branch* and the *True Flag*. Parton accepted the offer and then, when the two Boston papers increased their offers in an attempt to retain her, was advised by Dyer to continue writing for all three publications. Dyer also advised Parton in her negotiations with J. C. Derby regarding Derby and Miller's publication of Parton's first volume of sketches. Derby gave Parton the same choice of either payment for copyright or royalties, although sources vary as to what his exact terms were. Derby claimed he offered Parton $1,000 for the copyright, while James Parton put the figure at $600. (The discrepancy is intriguing, in light of the halfway figure of $800 offered "Floy" in *Ruth Hall*.) Both Derby and James Parton quoted the same figure of ten cents a copy in royalties and confirmed that Sara accepted that form of payment, and thereby made $8,000 for the 80,000 copies sold within a year.[37]

When John Walter writes Ruth Hall to tell her that her book, appropriately titled *Life Sketches*, is selling faster than the publisher can supply copies, Ruth is not merely proud; she is a proud mother. Her "mother's heart" has provided her with the determination to succeed. Financially secure, she decides to leave her unnamed city of unhappy memories and "make her a new home. Home? Her heart leaped!—comforts for Nettie and Katy,—clothes—food,—earned by her own hands!" After Parton's literary career was well underway, she moved from Boston to New York City, where she bought a new home. She negotiated lucrative contracts for additional volumes of sketches and for two novels. And not least, she pushed Robert Bonner into upping his ante for her in his *New York Ledger*. There is little doubt that Parton became a hard bargainer in her own right. Her experiences with publishers, in particular, made that necessary. As she wrote to Harriet Beecher Stowe late in her career, it was her opinion that publishers were "publishing wolves." Bonner, of course, was the exception. "I wish they were all like Bonner of the Ledger," she told Stowe, "who sent me the other day a check for five hundred (over the liberal pay I get every week) as an expression of his good will, and it is not the first time he has remembered me in this way." But Bonner's example did not alter her negotiating stance. Years later, she responded to a request from the *Galaxy*

that she supply the literary monthly with a series of articles by stating that
she would be happy to do so, "*but* I cannot spend the necessary time and
labor on them for the sum you proposed." And what was the editor's reaction
to that she asked straightforwardly: "Would you like me to try my hand, and
at what rate of compensation?" The hard edge was tempered by bitter
experience. The woman in distress had been sneered at and refused aid by
those to whom she had automatically looked for support. Bitter pride was the
residue when a woman of traditional mind was forced to become an
independent, self-supporting economic provider.[38]

Determination to maintain her independence and to protect her earnings
for those dependent upon her also remained. Sara married James Parton,
eleven years her junior, on 5 January 1856. On the day of their marriage they
signed an agreement. It stated that she had property in the form of
investments, copyrights, and contracts, and that she could if she wished "at
any time hereafter . . . confer benefits out of her said property" to her
children. The agreement further stated that the "property and Estate of said
Sara and the income thereof should be enjoyed by her and be managed and
applied for her benefit and under her direction and by her Trustees as fully
and absolutely as if she were a feme sole." The designated trustee was Oliver
Dyer. Later, Sara's will left her property to her younger daughter, Ellen, and
to her granddaughter, Grace Ethel Thomson, the child of Sara's older
daughter, who had died previously. James Parton and Robert Bonner were
the executors.[39]

Four months after their marriage, the Partons moved into the Brooklyn
house purchased with Sara's earnings. Sara wrote an essay to commemorate
the event. Titled "My Old Ink-Stand and I; or, The First Article in the New
House," the article began, "Well, old Ink-stand, what do you think of this?
Haven't we got well through the woods, hey?" Parton's dialogue with her
inkstand goes on to allude to past troubles and present triumphs. Hadn't the
inkstand "vowed" to stand by her and "haven't you *done* it, old Ink-stand?"
Implicitly, the question was posed: Parton had achieved financial independence with her literary labors, as symbolized by the house, but now that she
was married again, would she stop writing? There was a clear answer: "Turn
my back on *you*, old Ink-stand! Not I." She explains that once she and her
children had been "thrown aside" by others. But their abandonment of the
struggling mother and "their sneers" had served only to motivate Parton to
succeed on her own: "the title deed, and insurance policy, of this brand-new
pretty house" were proof of that. And just as her pen, and her "Ink-stand,"
had been the instruments of that success, so they would continue to enable
her, married or not, to go it alone: "Haven't you agreed to do it, long years to
come?" Parton did not renounce her literary career. Just as she had never
freely chosen it, so she felt compelled to continue it. Despite the fact that she
suffered from cancer during the last five years of her life, she wrote until her
death. Toward the end she dictated her columns for the *Ledger* to her
husband, James Parton.[40]

In the same volume of sketches that included the essay on the "Ink-

Stand," Parton as "Fanny Fern" asked rhetorically, "Literary fame! alas— what is it to a *loving* woman's heart, save that it lifts her out of the miry pit of poverty and toil?" That question suggests the existence of a dual identity, a joining together of alien spheres. E.D.E.N. Southworth said as much in writing that it was in the "darkest days of my *woman's* life, that my *author's* life commenced." The emphasis was Southworth's, and what she meant was that her woman's life had run afoul. Like an increasing number of young women in the early nineteenth century, Southworth found employment as a teacher in the interval between the end of her own schooling and marriage. She began teaching at age fifteen in 1834 while living in Washington, D.C., and continued to do so until she married in 1840. Within the year she and her husband, Frederick Hamilton Southworth, moved to Prairie du Chien, Wisconsin, where Southworth again held a teaching position. Whether her husband was employed in Wisconsin or not is unknown, but there are indications that at the very least he did not have steady employment. For example, in 1844 Southworth and her husband returned to Washington and lived in her grandmother's house along with Southworth's mother and her mother's second husband, Joshua Henshaw. The Southworths also had a son, Richmond, and Southworth was pregnant with her daughter Lottie. As Southworth told Lottie fifty years later, Henshaw almost immediately forced them to leave the house, apparently because Southworth's husband was unemployed and expected the grandmother to provide support. "It was *then* that S. [Southworth's husband] finally abandoned us and went to Brazil," wrote Southworth to Lottie. He "had no mind for supporting wife or children," she said.[41]

Although Southworth never directly or specifically described what had happened between her and her husband, she was anything but reticent about her subsequent struggle to support herself and her two children. From explanatory notes to readers accompanying installments of her fiction in magazines like the *Saturday Evening Post*, to sketches in biographical collections, to letters she wrote to her daughter and granddaughter near the end of her life, Southworth claimed for herself the leading role in a tale of a woman burdened and consumed by anxiety and ill-health in her effort to meet the responsibilities of being both father and mother. After her husband left her on her own with two children to support, Southworth later wrote in a sketch for John S. Hart, she was "broken in spirit, health, and purse—a widow in fate but not in fact—with my babes looking up to me for a support I could not give them." Southworth was not totally without help. She told Lottie that an "old midwife" had assisted at her birth and that Lottie had been cared for by a twelve-year-old black girl named Mandy Taylor. "I would walk up and down the city trying to get work and come home failing and despairing," she wrote in one letter to Lottie. And in another she told her that "I had only little baby fingers wandering over my bosom and I so starved, that I had not milk enough"; "I had not a shoe on my foot, except an old pair of india rubbers," "no cradle for my baby, no rocking chair to rock her."[42]

Southworth did find ways to support them, however meagerly at first. She returned to teaching as an assistant in a public school in the fourth district of Washington and remained there for three or four years at an annual salary of $250. That income was supplemented by Southworth's work as a copyist for the federal land office. By the end of the 1840s she was head of the fourth district's primary school, had eighty students to supervise, and utilized the first floor of her home for the classroom. Southworth's promotion, however, did not bring self-sufficiency; her salary, she said, was "inadequate to our comfortable support."[43]

During this period Southworth's career as a writer slowly developed as well. Her first story appeared in the *Baltimore Saturday Visitor* in 1846 and more were printed in the abolitionist paper the *National Era* the following year. She would write later that at the time she was "a poor, obscure young public school teacher, out of favor with my friends and neighbors on account of my writing for an abolition paper." She was also unknown as a writer except to the readers of the *Era*. But in 1849 her first novel, *Retribution*, was serialized in the pages of the *Era* and then published in book form the same year by Harper. The years of extreme poverty and obscurity, of desperation and despair, were coming to a close. "Oh, Lottie," she wrote later, "if the Lord had not given me the gift of writing what would have become of me or you?—worse than widowed as I was—worse than fatherless as you were?"[44]

Following the successful publication of *Retribution*, Southworth's position began to improve. As she related it to Hart's readers, she saw the publication as her deliverance, amounting to the rescue of one who "had been poor, ill, forsaken, slandered, *killed* by sorrow, privation, toil, and friendliness [friendlessness?]." It was a tale of deliverance that Southworth never ceased telling. In addition to Lottie and to the readers of Hart's volume, others who read her tale of woe and rescue ranged from those who perused her fiction, to those who read the *Saturday Evening Post* during the 1850s, all the way to those who happened to catch her interview with the *Washington Post* in 1894, five years before her death at the age of seventy-nine. While nursing her sickly son, Richmond, "keeping school and keeping house," Southworth said, she began *Retribution*, because "it was absolutely necessary to do something else to increase our income." Although she had not intended it to be as long as it turned out, the novel grew from installment to installment, and "number after number" appeared in the pages of the *Era*. Southworth wrote before school hours and after, "sometimes long into the night," when Richmond was sleeping or at least did not require her care. Thus did the "school-keeping, the house-keeping, the nursing, and the novelette" proceed until Southworth's own health deteriorated. "I did my best," she wrote, "by my house, my school, my sick child, and my publisher," but, she admitted, her best was not good enough. Richmond suffered and complained, school officials found fault, and her editor at the *Era* "would reject whole pages of that manuscript which was written amid grief, and pain, and toil that he knew nothing of." (Southworth made certain to note that all the passages he deleted were restored in the book version.) She continued to struggle "when I only wished for death and for rest." Alluding to the privation and hardship of those years in her novel *The Curse of Clifton*, Southworth claimed, "There are many poor women, in every city, who have not work enough to earn their necessary food and fuel. . . . Yes, hundreds who die annually of innutrition [*sic*]." She challenged those who might be skeptical, insisting, "I know it. For I have lived among them, and seen for myself, and not another."[45]

Finally, however, all seemed to change for the better, and she was "born as it were into a new life." Her novel, written in installments for the *Era*, was accepted and published by Harper. When positive reviews followed, Southworth felt that she had "found independence, sympathy, friendship, and honour, and an occupation in which I could delight." It had been a long struggle, and then it had ended "very suddenly, as after a terrible storm, a sun burst." Although the publishing market opened wide for Southworth following the success of *Retribution* and remained open to her fiction for forty years, her struggle apparently was not over. For a number of years afterward the *National Era* continued to serialize her fiction, and that same year of 1849 she began a relationship with the *Saturday Evening Post* that would last for eight years, until she agreed to write exclusively for Robert Bonner's *New York Ledger*. Just as *Retribution* had seen publication in two forms, her novels and stories were published as books following their serialization in periodicals. Her prolific pen and her success in publishing what she wrote enabled Southworth to stop teaching and concentrate totally on her writing. But anxiety, overwork, ill-health, and even a need for income continued to dog her, continued as a part of her tale. And she never forgot, or let others forget, that she was a woman who had been forced to pay her own way, forced to materially provide for herself and others. "My own dear sainted father never forsook me," Southworth told Lottie, referring to the fact that her father had died when she was a child. "God took him to heaven—But the others—the stepfather—the husband—all I should have looked to in childhood and youth,—in womanhood and wifehood and in motherhood— what were they to me?" That was both her plight and the rationalization for her literary career.[46]

In the years after *Retribution* made her literary career possible, Southworth's most difficult period was the time prior to the contract with Bonner's *Ledger*. Her health remained poor. This was also the time of Southworth's running battle with the *Post*, and editor Henry Peterson was sharply criticizing her style, her excessive length, and occasionally her tardiness, in direct correspondence with her and even in unsigned notices in the *Post*. Southworth, for her part, saw herself as a naive woman, relatively helpless, exploited, and adrift in a man's world of business. That is the image she later imparted to Bonner. Before he came along, she wrote him, she had thought she might possess "some genius in popular writing." But at the same time she had "not one bit of business tact," and her pen became "the prey of whoever moved to seize it." Having seized it, the unnamed parties did not do right by her: "I was dying from the combined effect of over work and under pay, of anxiety, and of actual privation." When Bonner signed her for the *Ledger*, she told him, "[you] changed my life." After that, "Every improved circumstance around me, every comfort in my home, every attainment of my children speak of your kindness and liberality."[47]

Southworth, the woman, would continue to look to Bonner, the man, to fend for her in the world of literary economics. Later, when she was experiencing difficulty in dealing with her publisher, T. B. Peterson, she asked Bonner for help. Bonner replied by sending her a sample draft of a note she might send to Peterson. Southworth was delighted with it. You must have felt Peterson's "insolence to a woman," she wrote Bonner, "as if it had been aimed at you, yourself." The note's thrust was "as *strong* as a knight's lance and as fine as a lady's needle," and she had little doubt that it would "penetrate even that brute's thick skin." Southworth liked the note so much that she decided to copy it word for word and send it under her own signature.[48]

From 1857 onward Bonner was more than Southworth's publisher, as far as she was concerned; he was her savior. And Bonner was indeed generous to her. He provided her with a secure outlet and salary for her fiction; he repeatedly raised her salary; and on more than one occasion at her request he guaranteed the salary in the event of incapacitating illness. Bonner even helped her son find employment when he reached the age of twenty-one. Southworth always expressed her gratitude, and in the strongest terms. Following Bonner's efforts on behalf of her son in 1867, she wrote, "Indeed under Divine Providence you have been the foundation of all our prosperity." That had been the case since he had first entered her life. After that, "I was able to live easily on my income and to enlarge my cottage and educate my children and furnish my rooms and help my parents—all through your liberality." Had Bonner not come along, she was certain the worst would have transpired: "I do believe that *anxiety* added to hard mental work would have put me in my grave before my children were grown." Again and again over the years, Southworth wrote, Bonner provided, and the writer thanked her publisher in similar tones, sometimes in the same words. "Your letter crowned the day," she wrote later in 1867; on "Christmas Morning" 1868, "I received your kind note yesterday, . . . and I thank you from the depths of my heart"; and 29 March 1887, "Your kind letter came today to give me new life and inspiration. . . . You have been 'a tower of strength' to me for thirty years."[49]

Bonner and Southworth did, of course, have a "business" relationship, and Southworth did bargain with him over the years. But for this woman of the home, business could never be conducted "as usual." Her gratitude to Bonner for his generosity was genuine, but her prompt acknowledgments and reminders of his liberality were also effective tools of bargaining. Even before Bonner she had demonstrated that in her new role she had learned some of the traditional tactics. In 1852 she assured Abraham Hart, whose firm was to publish the following year her collection of tales, *Old Neighborhoods*, that the success of her latest novel, *The Curse of Clifton*, undoubtedly would provide him with "an excellent notice" which he could "use in advertisement" to promote the collection. And she also was capable of acting independently of Bonner. Her note to him in December 1873 thanking him for his Christmas gift of $300 expressed her gratitude in typical fashion, but then she proudly informed him that the $8,000 which she had saved and invested in U.S. bonds was now paying $400 a year in interest.[50]

Southworth had her none-too-subtle suggestions for Bonner as well. In 1876 when she sent him the first installment of what was to become *Married in Rage*, she commented that she could not see how anyone who read "the first two pages, could help going on with it," and pointed out that the first scene was definitely "a fine subject for illustration—provocative of curiosity and enquiry." Angered by what she considered an attempt in 1887 to plagiarize *The Hidden Hand*, first published in 1859, the nearly seventy-year-old Southworth forthwith wrote Bonner that "we are helpless to prevent this outrage . . . unless you publish 'The Hidden Hand' in cheap pocket book form, immediately." But there was never much doubt as to the perspective of the person who was doing the bargaining, when the accompanying justification was, implicitly or explicitly, her family's material needs. After Southworth had negotiated a new salary agreement with Bonner in 1833, she wrote, "Heaven knows it was not for myself alone that I wanted to write on the same terms as lately; but for those whom it is my duty to take care of." Her son Richmond became a doctor and married, but neurological disorders rendered him an invalid for most of his life, and son and wife lived with Southworth during the last decades of her life. She also noted that ever since 1876 she had been forced to take care of her sister's "large family."[51]

The nature of Southworth's burden and the nature of her regard for the burden were always clear. A stretch of illness in 1875 prompted a request to Bonner that he grant her "a rest of three months or *less*, without loss of income." There was "no one in the wide world" to whom she could turn, she said, "if I cannot appeal to you." When Bonner predictably and generously acceded to her request, she thanked him profusely—"I think you have saved my life . . . " Had he not responded favorably, Southworth assured him yet again, "anxiety—added to mental and physical prostration" would have proved overwhelming. Stated simply, she was "a woman with the lifelong double burden of man and woman laid upon me." Southworth had "been at work ever since I was fifteen years old," she told Bonner in 1881, "school teaching, copying for the land office, school teaching and writing for the press—up to this day, and I hope, God willing, to work to the end of my earthly life." In her 1894 interview with the *Washington Post*, probably her last, she mentioned that she had written seventy-three books, "almost one for each year of my life"; she was seventy-five. "I shall not write any more books," she told the *Post*. But, she added, "Haven't I done enough?"[52]

7

Buying My Time

"I am compelled to turn my brains to gold and to sell them to the highest bidder," wrote Caroline Lee Hentz to her publisher Abraham Hart on 13 November 1851. The next spring Harriet Beecher Stowe informed Gamaliel Bailey of the *National Era*, "I like every mother of family cannot afford to be literary except by *buying my time* from other duties." There had been major changes in the existences of both of these wives and mothers. In particular, financial need had expanded their literary careers and transformed their lives. Hentz was thirty-three when her first novel was published in 1833. Thirteen years elapsed before a second appeared in 1846. A few years later the incapacitating illness of her husband, the multitalented Nicholas Marcellus Hentz, made her a full-time writer and the sole economic provider for the family. Story by story, Stowe came to realize that she could meet some of her family's material needs through her writing. A volume of fictional sketches appeared in 1843 when she was thirty-two. Her next volume did not appear until nine years later, when *Uncle Tom's Cabin* burst upon the political as well as the literary horizon. Calvin Stowe's always inadequate income, his ill-health and eventual retirement, and the unexpected success of the antislavery novel placed Harriet in the position of primary supporter of the family, and motivated her to produce ten novels and volumes of stories and miscellaneous prose over the next quarter of a century.[1]

After the Hentzs were married in 1824, "rolling stone" Nicholas led them to seven different towns and seven educational institutions.[2] After four years at the University of North Carolina in Chapel Hill, where Nicholas held the position of Professor of Modern Languages and Belle Lettres, the Hentzs established, supervised, and taught in academies and seminaries in Covington, Kentucky, and Cincinnati, Ohio, then in the Alabama towns of Florence, Tuskegee, and Tuscaloosa, and finally in Columbus, Georgia. It is not clear how soon Hentz became deeply involved in the operation of the

164

schools. She gave birth to five children, one of whom died at age two, in the first nine years of their marriage, and having supposedly begun writing as early as age twelve, she produced some plays and short stories during the early days of her marriage and published her first novel, *Lovell's Folly* in 1833. But at least by the time of their stay in Florence, Alabama, where the family remained for nine years, from 1834 to 1842, the longest of their stays anywhere, she was assisting her husband in teaching and in disciplinary and supervisory activities; significantly, she had primary responsibility for the care of their boarding students. And she was sufficiently involved, as well as exasperated, to write in her diary in 1836: "It requires more than the patience of a Job, the wisdom of a Solomon, the meekness of a Moses, or the adaptive power of a St. Paul—to be sufficient for the duties of our profession."[3] It was appropriate that she characterized it as "our profession," but it is clear that she considered herself to be helping Nicholas in *his* profession.

Hentz was also doing some occasional writing during this period, but she does not seem to have considered it a source of income. Apparently, however, her duties at their seminaries were beginning to give her a sense of contributing to the material welfare of the family. The travails of a worldly occupation led to an age-old human reaction in the female Hentz: "school again—Alternate coaxing and scolding, counsel and reproof—frowns and smiles—oh! what a life it is—oh woe is me—this weary world!" The inevitable addition to that familiar complaint had a slight twist: "I am often tempted to say—Yet man is doomed to earn his subsistence by the sweat of the brow and the fire of his brain and why not woman also?" Why not, indeed, she might have added a decade later in 1846, when they were establishing another school in Tuskegee, Alabama, and a major outlay of funds was required. She wrote at that time to a friend that in view of their expenditure of "a great deal of ready money" it was fortunate and "very apropos at this time" that she had been able to buy "all our parlor furniture with the money I got from my *stories*." The money came from selling her stories to magazines, and more came in later that year when Hentz published her second novel, *Aunt Patty's Scrap-Bag*.[4]

But in that very same year diary entries by their son, Charles, now nineteen and studying medicine at Harvard, testified that the family was still supported primarily by income generated from the Hentzs' school, and that Nicholas was still head of the household in terms of financial matters. In July, Charles wrote in his diary that he had received word of a decline in enrollment at his parents' seminary, and less than a month later more news of a predictable nature followed. Because the family's finances were precarious there might not be sufficient funds to enable Charles to continue his studies: "Pa writes that he will find it difficult to send more than a part of the money next fall." Anxious to ease matters for his parents, Charles contemplated leaving school and working for a year. But two weeks later there was a reprieve. "I was joyfully surprised," he wrote, to receive a letter "containing very good news—Pa's money matters have been so arranged that he will find no trouble in sending me to the Lectures—I am most grateful to hear it." Charles recalled later that this was a difficult period for his mother, that she had "a most laborious life of it" in Tuskegee: "She had to fill all the duties of housekeeper for a large household of boarders; and fulfill her laborious duties as teacher." He marveled that she had also found time to continue her writing. But despite his mother's major contribution of labor, the management and control of the financial fruits of that labor remained "Pa's."[5]

Only a few years later, however, the situation changed completely, and Nicholas ceased to be even nominally the head of the household. Always an intense, nervous, restless personality, he became more and more the neurasthenic. His eccentric behavior, which included the habit of suddenly dropping to his knees at unpredictable moments and assuming a prayerful pose, became more pronounced, and eventually he experienced what his doctor son Charles called a "general breaking down of the nervous system." Nicholas's periods of serious illness apparently began in 1849, a year after the family had moved to Columbus, Georgia, to establish yet another school. By the end of 1849 he had already begun a series of visits to his married children in Florida, undertaken for the "restoration of his health"; these visits would increase in frequency and duration. Caroline assumed total control of the school in his absence, and apparently after a while maintained that control even with Nicholas at home. He was becoming increasingly subject to severe "mental depression." In September 1850 Charles noted in his diary that his father was looking better but felt "no better." "Alas," Charles mused somberly, "would to God he were rescued from his suffering and melancholy."[6]

Early in 1851, after Caroline had begun to provide the entire support for herself and Nicholas, she turned exclusively to writing as a means of income. In a series of letters to one of her publishers, Abraham Hart, Hentz tried to legitimate her attempts to get more money for her fiction not on the basis that she was a professional writer and therefore had a right to do so, but that she needed money to support her family. Hentz, for example, said to Hart that she wanted to explain why she desired more money for *Rena, or the Snowbird*, "so you may not think me dictated by mercenary motives." The reason was simple: her husband was sick. Were he able to fulfill his role as family provider, Hentz wrote, "I would think it a privilege to write for the mere pleasure and further reputation that I might acquire." But because her husband could not meet his responsibility to his family, she had to: "On me alone rests its support—Urged by this sacred duty I now write, not for *mere* pleasure or reputation, however dear the last may be." *Rena* appeared in 1851 under the imprint of Hart's firm.[7]

Toward the end of 1851, Hentz was bargaining with Hart again, this time about compensation for *Marcus Warland; or, The Long Moss Spring*. But

she had extra leverage now. She had shown the novel to another publisher
and received a higher bid than Hart had offered. Before signing a contract she
wrote to Hart to tell him about the other offer, hoping that he might raise his.
Using exactly the same phrase, she eagerly assured him again that "I am not
actuated by mercenary motives." Her husband still suffered from ill-health,
she said, and thus she was indeed compelled to turn her "brains to gold" and
market them for her family. Hart was not moved, and apparently claimed
that she had already agreed to his offer and therefore had no right to solicit a
higher bid from another publisher. Hentz responded by reiterating her
justification for her actions; "For two years my husband has been a suffering
invalid," she wrote, and as a consequence "the whole support of the family
devolves upon me, as well as the task of ministering to his suffering day to
day." Given that circumstance, she asked, "is it strange that I should try to
obtain the highest value for my productions?" At any rate, she concluded,
how much was Hart willing to pay? Apparently enough; *Marcus Warland*
was published by A. Hart in 1852.[8]

It might be argued that Hentz was using her husband's illness as a ruse,
that her plea of poverty was merely a pretext for jacking up her price. But that
seems unlikely. Nicholas was seriously ill for the last decade of his life, and
she did have to support them. As early as 1851 it appeared that Nicholas
would never again be capable of contributing anything himself. Charles
recalled visiting his parents that year, when "Mother was devoting herself
entirely to writing and nursing father, who was a most miserable invalid."
Charles had been unprepared for the dramatic change in his father, "so
haggard and wasted, with long white beard and unshorn white locks."
Momentarily Charles broke down completely: "I threw myself on his bed,
and threw my arms around him, and sobbed as I never did in my life before."
Nicholas was a "wretched hypochondriac," wrote Charles, and he sometimes spent "whole days in a state of unutterable wretchedness."[9]

As has already been noted, Hentz had published only two novels in the
two decades previous to her husband's illness. After he became incapacitated, she produced fifteen volumes of fiction, both novels and stories, in less
than half as much time. The change in her family's financial circumstances
motivated the increase in her literary production and drastically altered her
life. Most significantly, it led her to adopt the traditional male role of
economic provider. She was able to rationalize her act on the basis of family
need, but it was a rationalization she needed. It was also a rationalization
that her society understood.

After a while the entire family shared in supporting and caring for
Nicholas. He stayed in various parts of Florida with his married children,
while Caroline divided her time between visiting him and staying in
Columbus, Georgia, by herself and in Florida with her son Charles. She sent
money for Nicholas's keep, wrote to thank her daughter Julia for looking
after him, and urged another son, Thaddeus, to supply his father with snuff

just as Charles, now a physician, supplied him with morphine. Meanwhile, Caroline kept writing, negotiating, and publishing. One novel in particular that she maneuvered through the publishing process was *The Planter's Northern Bride*, written in reaction to *Uncle Tom's Cabin*. A transplanted northerner who had imbibed her adopted region's sympathies, Hentz acknowledged Stowe's talent but, she wrote Abraham Hart, she could not "conceive how a woman could write such a work." The truth of the matter, Hentz said, is that "slavery, as she describes it, is an entirely new institution to us." Hentz thought she might write a refutation. Did Hart happen to know how much Stowe was being paid for the work? And suppose she did write her refutation, "what particular phase of the subject" did Hart think she should focus upon? Was there "no danger of a surfeit?" Hentz might also have had in mind the $200 prize she had received that year from the people in Columbus for *Marcus Warland*, a novel published in 1852 that also had a southern flavor.[10]

By the end of 1852 Hentz was writing her new novel. It was about the "struggle between love and prejudice," she wrote Hart, with love triumphing and the truth being told about southern institutions. Alluding to the widespread response to *Uncle Tom's Cabin*, Hentz stressed that "there shall be no *Cabin* in it, most assuredly—The public have had enough for one century." *The Planter's Northern Bride* was finished and ready for publication in 1854, but there were delays. When the delays continued, Hentz nudged Hart: "I am really getting quite impatient," she wrote. And she finally expressed resignation: "Do you know, that the book has been delayed so long, I feel as if its interest were lost, and look for its appearance with much less sanguine hopes, than I did months ago?" What Hentz did not know, and what was probably causing the delay, was that a change in her publisher's management was underway due to Abraham Hart's retirement. But the novel finally did appear that year.[11]

The year before the author of the novel to which Hentz responded wrote to Eliza Cabot Follen about what "an agreeable surprise" it had been when she received $10,000 from the antislavery novel's first nine months of sales alone. After all, said Harriet Beecher Stowe, she had married "a man rich in Greek and Hebrew and Latin and Arabic, and alas, rich in nothing else"; having always been poor and expecting to remain so, "the idea of making anything by a book, which I wrote just because I could not help it never occurred to me." Stowe was not being exactly truthful, however, and in fact contradicted herself in the same letter. Although the novel's popularity and her remuneration were a surprise, Stowe was already well aware that she could garner income from her writing, however small the amount. And she revealed as well that whatever the amount of earnings derived from her writing in the past, it had always gone to meet the needs of her family.

Stowe, the mother of seven children, five of them born in the first seven years of marriage, was correct in stating that "the nursery and the kitchen were my principle fields of labor." But it did not take Stowe long to discover that "when a new carpet, or a mattress, was going to be needed," she could make the purchase with a publication. Her efforts became imperative when financial stability was threatened and the "family accounts . . . wouldn't add up—then I used to say to my faithful friend and factotum, Anna . . . 'Now if you will keep the babies and attend to the things in the house for one day I'll write a piece, and then we shall be out of the scrape.' " That, Stowe said, was how "I became an authoress." What she was actually saying was that she had begun as a sometime author while still a full-time wife and mother. Husband Calvin's income as a teacher-scholar-clergyman always seemed inadequate and the material needs of the family more than he could fully meet. Recognizing that she could contribute income through her writing, Stowe became more and more a writer, while remaining a full-time mother.[12]

Stowe struck the traditional pose in a letter to Sara Parton, claiming that she was in essence nothing but a woman who was out of her element in the world of business. "[A] snuffling yankee businessman," she wrote, "takes me in hook and line and does pretty much as he pleases with me." There seemed no other way but to let a lawyer "do the talking for me and make my contracts." That was her observation in the 1860s, but both before and after that time she was very much her own active businessperson. Prior to the unexpected financial windfall from *Uncle Tom's Cabin*, Stowe's literary income may have been only a supplement to her family's income, but when you needed, say, a *"feather bed"* and when your husband "had only a large library of books, and a great deal of learning," well, you were likely to track down every available penny. That is exactly what Stowe did in 1840 after she received payment for some of her very first sketches, which had appeared in annual gift books issued before the Christmas holidays. Writing to her publishers, Carey and Hart, she noted that the "terms of compensation" had been $2 per page for one article, which had run forty-three pages, $1.50 a page for another, which had been thirty-nine or forty pages. (She could not remember how long the second article had been.) Carey and Hart had paid her $100 when, even giving them the benefit of doubt, the "sum due me" was $144.50.[13]

After *Uncle Tom's Cabin* the sums got bigger, and Stowe bargained for those as well. And her literary income became first the major and then the sole support for the family. It made a difference that she had married a man who not only made little money but also constantly worried about the material well-being of his family. "My love you do wrong to worry so much about temporal matters—you really *do wrong*," Stowe wrote to Calvin in 1844. "Every letter of yours contains such unbelieving doubts 'who will take care of us and keep us out of debt?' " Begging him not to worry, she assured him that God would care for them and, anyway, she added, "I'll engage to bring things right in the spring." When Calvin later resigned his teaching position at Bowdoin College in order to accept another at Andover Theological Seminary, Stowe questioned his motives. "I trust under God my dear husband that pecuniary advantages *are not* the weight in the scale— Satan tempts you on this head with inordinate anxiety about your family." She wanted him to "do right—naught else weighs a feather." Calvin also had little inclination to manage money. As early as 1853 Calvin informed his wife that responsibility for management of the family's resources was entirely hers. Having relieved himself of that obligation, Calvin had no qualms about transferring to her the additional duty of supporting the family. Later that year he reminded Harriet to "think of your responsibilities, an old man and six children." He could have added that she was also obliged to contribute to the support of her father Lyman and his third wife. Little wonder that when Stowe was negotiating for the serialization of her next novel, *Dred: A Tale of the Dismal Swamp*, in the *National Era*, she would remind editor Gamaliel Bailey that as a "mother of family" she could not afford to be literary except by "*buying my time*."[14]

Stowe's earnings became even more critical from the 1860s onward. Calvin retired from teaching in 1864 and suffered from periods of ill-health until his death more than two decades later. With the exception of Georgiana, all four of the children who survived to adulthood continued to rely upon their mother for support. The twins, Hattie and Eliza, remained unmarried and lived at home; Fred, who became an alcoholic, required institutionalization and then support during his unsuccessful attempts at rehabilitation; and Charley, who entered the ministry, needed substantial aid after beginning his career. Stowe did not question the legitimacy of the demands that the members of her family made upon her. But the strain had been great enough before, and now it grew.

In 1850, before her family had become so dependent upon her literary earnings, she had told Calvin, "You must not expect very much writing of me for it drinks up all my strength to care for and provide for all this family—to try to cure the faults of all—harmonize all." And later the next year she admitted that "I can earn two hundred dollars by writing," but, she complained, "I don't want to feel that I *must* and when weary with teaching children, tending baby, buying provisions, settling bills, cutting out clothes still I feel I must write a piece for some paper." In 1860, when her writing had become a major source of support, she pleaded with Calvin "to *try* to be considerate and consider how great a burden I stagger under." And a few years later she wrote to her daughters, Hattie and Eliza, that she hoped they understood "how heavy is the weight which lies upon me," and hastened to inform them that she was providing daily income from her writing and also attempting to arrange the family's finances in order to secure "a higher income from our property so that we may have a solid and certain basis of two *thousand* a year to go on." Those were wearying challenges, and pray she did not become ill, for "if my health fails all will fail." Obviously she too had become anxious about temporal matters.[15]

Stowe had more projects underway than it seemed she could handle, and while they all represented prospects for remuneration, there never seemed to be enough money. And thus there was always not-so-subtle bargaining to be done. In a series of letters to her editor and publisher, James T. Fields of the *Atlantic Monthly* and Ticknor and Fields, she reported that a story was going well, "but the fact is I am constantly tempted to swerve aside from it for the need of a hundred or two dollars here and there that I could make by stopping to write this or that article." She asked that he check his accounts to see if anything were owed her, adding, "It worries me to think how quickly I could earn a thousand dollars . . . ." Stowe began to send Fields a series of pieces for publication in the *Atlantic Monthly*. Having requested a hundred dollars for each piece, she mentioned the "spicy sprightly writing" they required, which she said was good because it kept her "from thinking of things that make me dizzy and blind and fill my eyes with tears so that I can't see the paper." When they were to be published in book form in 1864 as *House and Home Papers*, she urged that the volume be issued in time for the Christmas season and expressed irritation when her suggestion was ignored. The next year she said to Fields that she was "quite sure we lost a sale of at least a thousand" by not having the volume out in time for the Christmas market, "and my part was done before October," she reminded him. To the publisher James R. Osgood, for whom she was completing a volume of stories, she wrote to ask if she could use one of them for an upcoming issue of a magazine. The problem was that she was also involved in writing a serial for the *Christian Union* and did not have time to write "anything else," but she needed the $200 that had been offered.[16]

Through the end of the 1860s and into the 1870s the pace held. A letter to the twins in 1869 bemoaned the fact that she had been ill. As *"all* the income that supports the family comes from my ability to labor at my pen," she found it particularly frustrating to be suffering from poor health when she was "beset with offers" for her fiction: "Mr. Ford who has sent me 300 for two stories in the South's Companion wants me to promise him another for the same sum. The Western Home sent a cheque for 100 and begs for an article—In short you see that my health just now is gold for my family." Earlier that year she had bargained with Fields about payment for *Oldtown Folks* and then had prompted Osgood, who had joined publishing forces with Fields, to be certain to send a review copy to the *Banner of Light*: "That paper commands an immense circulation and influence and a notice of the 'spiritualistic features' of the book in it would ensure a sale of many copies." And she had already conceived the plot for what would become *Pink and White Tyranny*. She wrote Edward Everett Hale, whose *Old and New* was going to serialize the novel, that she agreed to his offer of $150 for each

installment, but as she was "under necessity this spring of writing for
immediate income," she needed to have promise of payment "on receipt of
manuscript" before she could start writing. Granted that, she would "begin
immediately." As the need for money seemed unending to Stowe, so too did
the pressure entailed in managing that money appear unrelenting. For the
woman who was a substitute manager for economic affairs that proved at
times an exasperating state of affairs. While away in the late 1870s visiting
and helping her daughter Georgiana, who was expecting a baby, she let her
irritation show. Wondering why Calvin had forwarded a bill to her, she wrote
to ask, "Why cannot you when I am gone attend to such things and not send
them here to me?" After all, she said, "It is *your* house—which you hold and
I have no claim on or right in and so my dear Sir please pay the bills of it and
look to the cares." She had made her point.[17]

Stowe's obligations extended beyond her husband and those children who
continued to share a home with her. Hoping that her son Fred's stay in an
institution would end his alcoholism, she willingly bore the expenses. When
that failed, she proceeded to arrange various positions for her son. By
investing $10,000 in Florida's Laurel Grove Plantation, she insured that
Fred would be made overseer of the thousand acres devoted to the
production of cotton. But she could not guarantee the cure of her son's
alcoholism, and his drunkenness remained habitual. Her last, equally
unsuccessful effort on his behalf involved an arrangement whereby Fred
helped in the management of her own orange groves in Mandarin, Florida. In
the late 1870s and early 1880s Stowe also helped her son Charley and his
wife Susy establish themselves in Charley's first parsonage in Presque Isle,
Maine. When Charley considered moving for financial reasons, she offered
to send them "$500, rather than have you make any change—or try any
other place—I will back you up." Even after Charley had taken another
position in Saco, Maine, Stowe advised them that "you can count on $300 a
year from me a sum I calculate equal to houserent and fuel." And later she
gave them the $7,000 necessary for the purchase of a parsonage after they
had settled permanently near Stowe's own home in Hartford,
Connecticut.[18]

For Stowe, the "mother of family," financial interests meant one thing.
When Houghton Mifflin, the publishing descendant of Ticknor and Fields,
brought Stowe back into the fold after she had left them for four of her novels,
Stowe kept at them to pay her quarterly or yearly accounts. Once in 1885,
for example, she informed them that she had not yet received her fall
payment. "My husband's long illness brings heavy expenses," she wrote,
"and a little money would be appreciated now." It was a natural reason to
ask to be paid. Stowe had said it a half century before: "as if a wife and
mother had any gratification apart from her family interests."[19]

The long, front-page obituary of Augusta Evans Wilson which appeared in the *Mobile Register* on 10 May 1909 lauded the writer who had made Mobile, Alabama, her home and spoke of her ability to turn "white paper into piles of greenbacks."[20] It was ironic that this image was used to describe Wilson, who was an ardent, inflexible promoter of woman's traditional role as wife and mother within the home, and without a doubt Wilson would have considered the reference to her money-making distasteful and undignified. But then a lack of "greenbacks" due to financial disaster and circumstances that were, if not distasteful and undignified, certainly unpleasant due to war and sickness, governed Wilson's early years. In fact, the adversities faced by Wilson's family probably delayed marriage for her and contributed to her becoming a writer.

Poverty and an uprooted existence became the norm of the family's life a few years after Wilson's birth and continued for the first two decades of her life. Her father, Matt Ryan Evans, left his father's South Carolina plantation and moved to Columbus, Georgia, where he and his brother established the mercantile firm of M. R. Evans and Company and acquired considerable land as well. At first he apparently also made considerable money and was welcomed into the upper echelons of Columbus society. Evans married Sarah Skrine Howard, the daughter of a wealthy planter, began building a large mansion, and before it was completed Augusta Evans was born. The year was 1835. In the early 1840s unwise business decisions exacerbated by a depression led to the bankruptcy of the firm, the loss of the mansion, and impoverishment. The family journeyed to a succession of towns in Alabama, through Texas, and back to Alabama in search of employment and new beginnings. Mobile was the last stop, and there in 1849 a fire destroyed the family's rented house and most of their belongings. By 1850 there were eight children and, because of a decline in their father's health, an uncertain income with which to support them. Eighteen hundred and fifty was also the year that Wilson, age fifteen, began writing *Inez*, her first novel, which was not published until 1855. Wilson reportedly hoped that her parents' respect for literature would overcome any objections they had to her acceptance of money for her endeavors. Their need for that money might have helped as well.

Inez did not sell well, but *Beulah*, published four years later, did. With money from its sales, Wilson purchased a home the family had been renting and registered the deed in her father's name. The arch-Rebel Wilson was caught up short with her next novel, *Macaria; or, Altars of Sacrifice*, by the war with the hated North, or, according to Wilson, with hated New England, "that *Synagogue of Satan*."[21] Wilson thought she had a good contract in February 1863 when she signed with West and Johnston of Richmond, but the war and its course guaranteed that little money was made from the southern edition of a novel that contained an impassioned defense of the South. Thanks mostly to J. C. Derby, the northern edition of *Macaria* left Wilson and her family with some much-needed money. The close of the Civil War found the family in a state of poverty again, Wilson's father in poor health, and her brother Howard suffering from typhoid fever and a war wound that left an arm and shoulder paralyzed.

The extraordinary commercial success of *St. Elmo*, published in 1866, ensured its author's popularity and undoubtedly ended financial worries for her family. A year before she published her next novel, *Vashti; or, "Till Death Do Us Part,"* she married the wealthy Lorenzo Madison Wilson in 1868. She was thirty-three, and he was sixty. No longer burdened with any financial concerns, and with a husband to care for in traditional housewifely fashion, Wilson allowed her literary production to fall considerably. She had written four novels in thirteen years, two in the last four years before her marriage, but she wrote only four more in the last forty-one years of her life. *A Speckled Bird* and *Devota*, her last two novels, were written after her husband died, and in the last seven years of her life.

As if it were well known to the citizens of Mobile, the *Register* claimed in its obituary that Wilson the wife put her pen down when her husband came home each day; before marriage she had written from the middle of the afternoon to late evening. Other evidence also supports the *Register*'s claim and its implications. Both *Beulah* and *St. Elmo* allude to elements of Wilson's biography and foreshadow her marital commitment. Both Beulah Benton and Edna Earl, heroines, respectively, of the two novels, are impoverished orphans who attempt to support themselves initially by teaching and then primarily by writing. As Beulah tells an incredulous magazine editor who had not expected to pay her, " 'I am poor, sir, and write to aid me in maintaining myself.' " It is as if there is no choice in the matter. " 'Unluckily,' " she adds, " 'I belong to the numerous class who have to look away from home for remuneration.' "[22] Both Beulah and Edna stop writing and, as it were, look back to the home when they marry.

Apparently irked by opinions to the contrary, Mary Virginia Terhune wrote to an editor in 1889 that dressmaking was a trade that could be "thoroughly learned and carried on" by a woman "not as a *pis aller*, but as a man would conduct his business." Terhune also asked why women could not be chemists, florists, fruit raisers, fancy cooks, beekeepers or poultry fanciers. "I know I could make a living in any one of these ways, except the chemistry," her letter concluded. Those comments, plus the fact that the specific reason for the letter was to ask when her manuscript was due and how much she was going to be paid for it, would seem to indicate that this woman, a prolific and best-selling writer for half a century, was unabashedly propounding woman's right to work and to have a career just like a man. And yet Terhune was as domestically self-identified as any of her cohorts. Her actual views can be seen from a closer examination of the letter. For her "man" and "business" were clearly and naturally linked, as in "business is a man's activity," and all the jobs she proposed for women were to her mind just as clearly and naturally linked to a female's traditional sphere.[23]

In an autobiography filling nearly five hundred pages Terhune's long career received short shift. Terhune wrote and published her first novel two years prior to her marriage. Her second novel was also published shortly before her marriage. The unexpected success of the first novel, which launched her career, receives due treatment in her autobiography. But as if to suggest that she thought it improper to discuss such endeavors once she was married, less is said of her second novel, and relatively little about the remainder of an extraordinarily successful career that spanned more than five decades. However, after approximately three hundred and fifty pages there are two references to her career that are revealing. Noting that in 1861 she had three books in the hands of a failing publisher, all of which were " 'good sellers' " and from which she had anticipated her semiannual remittance of "fat royalties," Terhune added, "I had come to look upon royalties as my husband regarded his salary, as a sure and certain source of revenue." Indicative of her success is the fact that it had taken Terhune only seven years to come to that expectation. She also commented that until that time "we had never known the pinch of financial 'difficulties.' " But now there *was* a difficulty: her husband, the clergyman Edward Payson Terhune, was suffering from ill-health and needed extended time away from the pulpit. Fortunately, in lieu of Terhune's royalties her husband's congregation in Newark, New Jersey, produced the necessary funds.[24]

The second reference revealed that of all Terhune's many successful books, including more than twenty-five novels, *Common Sense in the Household* was the one in which she took greatest pride. That should not be surprising, because this book more than any of her others made home and career literally one: *Common Sense in the Household* became Terhune's biggest best-seller of all by dispensing recipes and miscellaneous domestic prescriptions. Terhune did not stop writing novels, but *Common Sense in the Household* brought Terhune into the household advice market.

A series of letters from Terhune to Albert Bigelow Paine, editor and author, regarding a "girls' serial" that Terhune was to do, probably for *Youth and Home*, also captures the literary domestic in full garb, bargaining in familiar fashion. The letters find Terhune in her late sixties and early seventies, but she was not an idle old woman. Would Paine please make up his mind, Terhune not too gently asked? "My hands are *full* of work," Terhune wrote, and she wanted a yes or no: "My time is too valuable to be spent upon possibilities." If she were asked to do the project, it would get done. Proof of that could be seen in the fact that "my list of orders is always full." At the moment, she informed Paine, she had just finished one book, was correcting proofs of another, and a third was ready to go for Scribner's fall trade. Besides that, she was preparing to go abroad to gather material for a series of popular biographies which, she emphasized, had been "ordered" by a publisher. (Interestingly, the series, which began to appear a few years later, focused on the "hearthstones" of writers.) Paine should be able to understand that she needed to "know definitely what you would like to have me do for you." Three days later Terhune was spelling out the contract, including how many chapters she would write (twelve), how many dollars per thousand words (fifteen), and how many dollars per installment (forty). Twelve days later Terhune specified how she desired payment for the chapters: "It would be quite convenient to receive payment for them weekly, say, beginning with November 1, as you suggest."[25]

After the first of November Terhune was in London, as she had said she would be, doing the research for the biographies, when she received word of Paine's resignation from the editorship of the magazine. Terhune immediately wrote Paine. She was sorry he had resigned. She was also very concerned about payment for the manuscript of the serial. It had been completed and it was in the hands of the magazine, but it had not been published, and she had not been paid. "I can ill afford to lose this money just now," Terhune told Paine. She did not want to press "Mr. Batcheller," apparently the publisher of the magazine, if he meant to pay, "but I know his ways of old, and suspect something crooked." What the gentleman should understand, she added, with the obvious expectation that Paine pass it on, was that having accepted her manuscript "he has bound himself for the amount due me even if he has not published a line." Presumably matters were settled amicably; at least Terhune's friendship with Paine was preserved. Four years later she wrote Paine to congratulate him on a book he had completed. Terhune, at seventy, at the beginning of the twentieth century, was as busy as ever and viewing herself in the same way. She was busy reading and drafting replies to a thousand letters that had all been received in the last ten days. She had just written a daily article. She had spent a day in New York City. And she had "done everything else that devolves upon the mother of a family."[26]

As has already been mentioned, Caroline Howard Gilman's relatively early venture into the national literary marketplace was hurt financially by poor contracts and especially by the Panic of 1837. Nevertheless, the Gilman family looked to income from her books to help them with their material needs and, to a certain extent, relied upon that income. That was the case even with Gilman's literary paper, the *Rose-Bud*, begun in 1832 and called the *Southern Rose* from 1835 on. But if the income garnered—or anticipated—came from her pen, the money was considered his, that is, husband Samuel's. Most revealing in that respect is a letter Samuel wrote to his sister, Louisa Gilman Loring. In the letter he refers to the impact of the Panic of 1837, noting that he and Caroline had expected more income from the *Southern Rose* than had been forthcoming. But what is most striking in the language of the letter is the automatic, unconscious shift in personal pronouns: "The disasters of the last two or three years in Charleston and over the country have taken from us the revenue which we had reason to expect from the Rose, and which induced me to venture on the purchase of my house." And just as the expected income from her literary efforts led him to buy his house, so did his resultant debts necessitate that they struggle to make ends meet, so that Samuel had to again reverse his pronouns: "This leaves me encumbered a longer time with the debt than I had anticipated, and compels us to restrain anything superfluous." At least, however, Samuel regarded his house as theirs to enjoy—"our house is so extremely comfortable that it overbalances the other inconveniences."[27]

Samuel's perspective on family economics was shared by Caroline. Hard times continued into the 1840s, and Caroline wrote to her sister, Harriet Fay, "I cannot say much about our economy just now—we pinched so intolerably for several years, that we take pretty easily to a few luxuries." For two summers, she said, she "would not buy an ice cream," and "I have never used linen in the hottest day of summer." As for Samuel, he did not buy a book "for four years." But Samuel had other problems, too. It had been two years since they had visited Harriet, said Caroline, and "Mr. Gilman then owed $7000, now he owes $2000 and owns the Island House beside." Caroline hoped that better times were coming for Samuel: "In two years if his life is spared, he will not owe a cent." No doubt there was a good chance of that, particularly if Caroline's books sold better.[28]

Most of the literary domestics made a lot of money. In that sense they were financially successful professionals. They bargained with publishers and editors over the shaping of contracts, the selling of books, and the establishment of prices and payments. By that definition they were businesspeople. But their society had not expected that they, as women, would become economic providers or businesspeople, and as a result the literary domestics did not in their own minds become legitimate economic providers or businesspeople. Instead, they remained fundamentally private domestic women. Whether they needed the money or not, a burgeoning, increasingly profitable publishing industry had unexpectedly swept them up. Whether they were single or married, a number of them supported themselves and their families with their literary income. But they often had a sense that something had gone wrong; that they were forced to do it; that they were deviants, anomalies, merely substitutes for males. Basically unrecognized by or unacceptable to their society as economic providers, they had difficulty recognizing or accepting it themselves. In many ways they did it and denied it.

In 1830, eight years after Catharine Maria Sedgwick had begun her career, after she had written four novels, after she had earned a significant income, she would "confess" to a bank that she had no occupation. It was a confession that made her feel "inferior," she admitted. Six more years and four more novels later Sedgwick would scoff at her brother Charles's reference to her ability to make money, saying, "With characteristic confidence in another's ability and success you put me up to making money out of my poor brains." "This," she assured him, "is a dream." Sedgwick did make money but, ironically, did it as if it were a dream, as if it were unreal. To a great extent her brothers, her conduits to the marketplace, managed her literary business and interceded for her. Harry was her first representative in the 1820s, until he began to go blind; he subsequently suffered mental illness and was institutionalized. Robert, Charles, and Theodore took turns afterward. But Sedgwick was at the very least a silent partner and sometimes a direct participant in her business affairs. Sounding very much like Harriet Beecher Stowe when she bargained with the same firm, Sedgwick wrote Carey and Hart regarding her contributions to their "annuals" that as they had paid her less than anyone else for her previous pieces she had decided to "take the liberty" to name her price, namely, eighty dollars for the particular story in question. And if they considered that too much, she said, "allow me to add that this is considerably less than I receive from the Token for an equal amount of writing." That same year, 1836, Charles was conducting business for her with Harper concerning her novel *The Poor Rich Man, and the Rich Poor Man*, but Sedgwick told him what the nature of the business would be. "I *want* you," she wrote, "to come to some conclusion with Harper." Speak to them or write to them, she said, but make contact. Seller and merchandiser alike, she said that Charles should urge upon Harper the policy of informing their correspondents in the towns of New England that her novel was meant for "popular consumption" so that they would put it up for sale "at once." In the meantime, she added, Charles should contact another party to see if he would take fifty copies of the novel to sell on commission.[29]

But Sedgwick, one of the literary domestics who was not in need of money, was unable to think of herself as an economic provider or businessperson. Rather, as one of those literary domestics who was without a husband and children of her own, Sedgwick was forever seeking to create the family she did not have by making all about her constitute her family life. There was a sense of that even in her business dealings. When negotiating in 1857 with Harper about her last novel, significantly titled *Married or Single?*, she emphasized that she felt theirs to be a personal rather than a strictly business relationship. She certainly did not "subscribe to the old selfish and sordid adage that there is 'no friendship in trade.' " It also gave her pleasure, she wrote, to think that "*you* will feel a personal interest in my success." A year later, in urging Harper to purchase the plates of *Redwood, Clarence*, and *The New England Tale* so that all of her works would be in the hands of one publishing house, she admonished Harper that they "should" do this as they had "so long been my publishers." It was a matter that should be decided quickly, she declared, adding that her nephews Ellery and Theodore Sedgwick would represent her on the issue.[30]

In her journals, which she did not intend to be read until she died, an 1828 entry includes reference to Sedgwick's opinion that her "fortune" was not large enough to enable her to maintain an "independent establishment." It is possible that Sedgwick meant that she alone did not have the income to live as she was accustomed to living. It is more likely, however, that this woman who had already proven herself a commercial success as a writer was actually revealing her inability to imagine living by herself, on her own. That would have been a bold move, tantamount to living a male existence. The same journal entry dwelt primarily on her unhappy state as a woman alone, a spinster in others' houses, namely, those of her brothers. A quarter of a century later, again in her journal, she recalled her desire to build and maintain a home of her own. She had not done so, she wrote, because she had been at first "chiefly deterred" by her limited means. "But I might have done it," she admitted, able now to see at least partially the fact and acknowledge it. Had she been able to think in those terms and act accordingly she might have been able to concentrate successfully upon establishing and supporting a home of her own, "and the little income that has gone like dew might have told in one channel." In her sixties now, she wrote, "It is past." But although it was past, Sedgwick had an "opinion" about it. She suspected that "no single woman living in the household of others [had] been happier" than she had been. Nevertheless, she advised every unmarried woman who could, by whatever means, to "secure an independent home," indeed, "to have it." In doing so a woman could "avoid dangers and irritations and perchance save heartaches—that the world never knows or suspects." What Sedgwick's private journal entry suggested was that to live like a man—independently by one's own means—you had to think like a man, and not like a private domestic woman. Sedgwick had had the opportunity to live in economic independence. But women did not work for a living, they worked for the family; and she had no independent family of her own.[31]

8

A Man's Clothing

In 1874, two years before the nation's centennial, Caroline Howard Gilman, eighty years of age herself, recounted the events surrounding her first publication in a letter to one of her daughters. The year had been 1810, fully a quarter of a century before Gilman the novelist presented herself to the American public as "Clarissa Packard." The publication, Gilman told her daughter, was "a poor poem, written by a poorly educated girl of sixteen." She had composed it at a time when "no lady writers were known with us." Someone in her family had sent the poem to a Boston newspaper without her knowledge. The poem was published, and "when I heard of it," said Gilman, "I cried half the night with a kind of shame." At the age of sixty, in some autobiographical notes that would comprise the sketch submitted to John S. Hart's *Female Prose Writers of America*, Gilman also recalled that she had "wept bitterly" at the poem's appearance and had been "alarmed." Why? It was, she wrote, "as if I had been detected in man's apparel."[1]

That was one elderly woman's recollection of the first public appearance of one literary domestic. As striking as her words are, what may not be readily apparent is that at one and the same time the act is confirmed and well-nigh denied. The speaker admits the deed and, retroactively, practically effaces the record; she in effect nullifies her history and thus herself, as if she were prophetically preparing the way for the historical treatment she and her kind would receive for the next century. Yes, she says, she had written the poem. But she had been ill-prepared for the task and the result had been wanting. That she had written the poem at all was surprising, for she had not been aware of any precedents of female authorship, of any tradition to draw her, a female, to that path. If someone else had not submitted the anonymous poem, it might never have seen print; it would probably have remained an invisible act by an invisible figure, the work of a private domestic woman forever a secret writer. The poem was published, but even so, she recalled the fact more as an accessory to it than as its perpetrator. What she remembered

180

was on one occasion a sense of shame, on another, alarm. What had struck her was the illegitimacy of the act and thus of herself, the sense of wrongdoing, of guilt that she had betrayed her femininity and committed a male act. Absent was pride of accomplishment. Practically unthinkable was the development of a new image of self in a new realm of being.

For a sixteen-year-old girl in the early years of the nineteenth century to accept and claim for herself recognition as the creator of a single youthful poem had the potential to be a revolutionary act. It was to project the female as a creator of culture, and that represented the boldest and most presumptuous act of all on a female's part. With the broadest of implications, it was indeed to select for herself "man's apparel." By the time Gilman referred to her inappropriate trappings, the word "culture" had undergone a process of extension. From its original use as a noun of process referring specifically to husbandry, it had broadened from the sixteenth century onward to include among its definitions the cultivation and training of the human mind, until by the nineteenth century it had become as well an independent noun denoting the achievements of a civilization. The history of the idea of culture to the mid-twentieth century has been characterized as a record of the intellectual and emotional responses of human beings to experience and change. But for the literary domestics that history had constituted a record of man's responses, not woman's. The documents of civilization, whether scholarly, political, artistic, economic, or scientific, represented predominantly male achievements.[2]

For a woman to apply her knowledge to acting as a creator of culture was to presume to encroach upon a traditionally male realm. That was not a presumption the literary domestics could manifest openly. True, as the daughters of elite families they had been exposed to and stimulated by culture, and they were eager to *cultivate* their own faculties in this regard. Pleased by the quality of writing in a letter from Louisa Gilman, her future sister-in-law, the nineteen-year-old Caroline Howard wrote her in 1813 to say, "Why girl, you have led me a perfect race of sentiment. The lady that I thought was chiefly excellent in a good jest and wild frolic, has surprised me with delightful composition and matured ideas. Cultivate this talent, I beg Louisa." On a day in 1803 when the thirteen-year-old Catharine Maria Sedgwick was relatively sanguine about the mixture of social accomplishments and more intellectually substantive subjects she was learning at an adventure school in Albany, she wrote her mother to say that she was "more pleased with my School" than she had been at first because "we are getting on very fast in our Studies." Sedgwick was still having to cope with the mixture but she knew the division of labor she sought. "I have begun another piece of embroidery," she wrote, this time a "landscape" which she thought had "a very cultivated and rather a romantic appearance." Nevertheless, she added, "I shall not devote much time to it as I think my Geography and writing is of much greater importance." But desire was not accompanied by choice, and without choice there could be little control of priority of being. The literary domestics were associated with and acquired culture, but they did so in limited, artificial, at times arbitrary fashion. And whatever the constraints, the circumstances governing their involvement with culture were inevitably ambiguous. With a presumed destiny that was private, not public, and a role that called for the support of others, women could become receptors of culture. Already acquainted with its artifacts, they could be companion to husband and instructor to children. But to go beyond that, to envision themselves as contributors to culture, was problematical for those who, in a sense, looked to a culturally invisible past. As Virginia Woolf phrased it more than half a century later, "We think back through our mothers if we are women." In the world of accumulated culture there was practically no female imprint, let alone a female intellectual "room of one's own."[3]

In 1878 Gilman wrote to a Mrs. Slade, the editor of a magazine entitled *Good Times*, to ask if she wished to republish some of Gilman's "verses" that had appeared thirty years before in the *Ladies Almanac*, edited and published by Gilman from 1836 to 1840. Gilman took the opportunity to compliment Mrs. Slade on previous issues of her magazine and to ask if "young people enter into your ideas and act upon them?" Recalling the "dark ages" of her youth, she observed, "Now in my eighty-fourth year, when I think of the few intellectual resources of my girlhood, it seems to me, in contrast, all this culture should breed mental giants in later days." Perhaps Gilman had in mind the earlier days when, though no longer just a girl, she had been unable to bring herself to claim that high male throne of creator of culture and truly make it the female's own. In 1834 Gilman's literary magazine, then titled the *Southern Rose-Bud*, added the subtitle "Devoted to the Culture of the Imagination, the Understanding, and the Heart." But that same year in her magazine, an unconscious sleight of mind led Gilman to regard a female literary colleague from the former mother country as more male than female. Writing in the *Rose-Bud*'s pages Gilman inadvertently transformed the British writer Mrs. William Fletcher into a Mr. She began with a reference to Fletcher's background that called forth the image of the literary domestics' own peculiar circumstances. Fletcher was self-taught, wrote Gilman, but her talents had "rendered her independent of her family." In fact, Gilman went on, Fletcher's "uncommon native talents and masculine understanding had raised her to an elevation in society." It was as if any woman who had transformed her life so as to become independent of the family ipso facto had become something other than a female, that something other being a male. Following the bent of her understanding, Gilman, the female who had once felt "detected in man's apparel," concluded with an observation to the effect that Fletcher's "appearance partook of the masculine character of her mind."[4]

A literary domestic, however, could not become the male that Gilman had rendered Fletcher. When John S. Hart asked Susan Warner to disclose her real name to the real world, it was very much in character for Warner to refuse. It was incumbent upon her to respond that "it would be premature that one who has just made a beginning should set herself in a collection of literary worthies among old and tried names." To refuse on the basis that she had written only one novel was merely a pretext; how could Warner allow herself to be set alongside "literary worthies" when the genuinely "old and tried names" were all male? It mattered little that Hart was compiling a collection of female writers. When Warner wondered in her secret journal whether or not she would "do it, at all risks," that is, merely express herself in her journal, and decided "not just now," one can question if "now" ever became a reality for Warner, if she in her own mind made even that first step.[5]

One of the "literary worthies" with whom Warner refused to compare herself sent his congratulations when Mary Virginia Terhune's first novel, *Alone*, entered its sixth edition. Terhune's delight notwithstanding, her response to Henry Wadsworth Longfellow's letter betrayed a perspective similar to Warner's. Clearly Terhune was on the road to " 'Fame,' " Longfellow wrote, and she must " 'feel as does the traveller in the Tyrol who sees, at a turn in the rocky pass, a finger-post with the inscription—"To Rome." ' " Only take care, he added, not to be " 'molested by the bandits who sometimes infest that route.' " Nothing, Terhune admitted, could have brought her "keener and more exquisite pleasure" than to receive a favorable sign from a man whom she regarded as one of the nobles of culture. But Longfellow's warning was both belated and gratuitous. Terhune had already been compromised, if not " 'molested.' " The burden of her female identity had already forestalled dreams of a flight to fame, and for the homebound there could be no fantasy of reaching Rome. No, regardless of desire, not "for one mad hour," Terhune said, was she able to allow herself to imagine that she "could ever gain the right to stand for one beatific moment on a level with the immortals whom I worshipped." Even in the moment of her "petty triumph" the woman knew her limitations. When a friend hinted that she might be underestimating her potential, reminding her that " 'yet you occupy an important niche,' " Terhune would have none of it. " 'I know my place,' " she had responded. " 'But the niche is small, and it is not high up. All that I can hope is to fill it worthily, such as it is.' " Her place could not be that of a lord of creation.[6]

To be a creator of culture was not a likely or an acceptable way for women to state that they had being, either to themselves or to their society. To think of themselves as legitimate creators of culture would have required a leap of vision that could only have drawn upon a confidence and a faith in their own ability and power to create and shape their own lives. To recognize themselves or to claim recognition as creators of their society's culture would also have been to knowingly signal a transgression of appointed spheres and an abandonment of duties they felt obligated to fulfill. Instead, branded by their society with a sense of intellectual inferiority and guilty that as writers they might be betraying the limits of their prescribed female sphere for man's, they became creators of culture without the presumption of that state of being.

It is no accident that the lives and the pages of the literary domestics, their private and their public lives and pages, were filled with secret writers and secret writing. Secrets and secreting abound. Harry Sedgwick decides to reveal the secret that his sister, Catharine, has written a novel. The preadolescent Mary Virginia Terhune secretly adds to her collection of verse and prose and hides it in a trunk beneath her clothes. Secrets are revealed after the fact and secrets are foreshadowed, back and forth across the nearly imperceptible boundary dividing the fictional from the real. When Beulah Benton in Augusta Evans Wilson's novel *Beulah* enters an editor's office to initiate the process that will put her in print as the pseudonymous "Delta," she is "closely veiled." After the disruption of the Civil War, years after the publication of *Beulah*, the Rebel Wilson returned to the New York offices of her publisher, J. C. Derby, so heavily veiled that at first she went unrecognized by Derby. It would appear to have been no accident that Wilson had described Beulah's state of mind as the heroine entered an editor's office thus: "she could not forebear smiling at the novelty of her position, and the audacity of the attempt she was about to make." Beulah Benton may have smiled, but she smiled behind the veil.[7]

In their efforts to extend their lives and to express their beings as creators of culture, to extend and express beyond what was acceptable for their sex, there was little smiling at all on the part of the literary domestics. It was a difficult, painful, and always ambiguous effort. Perhaps the most striking act of secrecy and deception on the part of the literary domestics was the concealment even from themselves of the fact that they were creators of culture. They represented themselves to self and society as nothing more or less than private domestic women, as women of the home. The desire to be more was intense, but no other design had been foreordained, and it was difficult if not impossible to envision being anything more.

Almost immediately following the marriage of Harriet and Calvin Stowe in 1836 and years before Harriet became established as a writer, Calvin, an educator and clergyman, was sent abroad by Ohio's legislature, which had commissioned him to report upon Europe's common schools. Harriet was clearly envious. "My dear," she wrote Calvin after he had left, "I wish I were a man in your place; if I wouldn't have a grand time!" But Harriet was not a man and, whatever her wishes, the opportunity was not to be hers. As Mary

Scudder says in Stowe's novel, *The Minister's Wooing*, " 'You men can have everything, ambition, wealth, power; a thousand ways are open to you: women have nothing but their heart; and when that is gone, all is gone.' " The "heart" was the badge of woman's being as wife and mother in the home, and that was the only badge of identity woman was supposed to have.[8]

Stowe certainly had difficulty envisioning any other identity for herself. In 1850, after Stowe had begun to be recognized as a published writer, Sarah Josepha Hale asked her for biographical materials for inclusion in a collection that would later be published under the title *Woman's Record*. The volume was intended, Hale said in her letter to this wife and mother, to be a compilation of reports on " 'distinguished women.' " Stowe was taken aback: "distinguished women" seemed a contradiction in terms. At least it was an alien concept to Stowe, "wholly innocent as I am of any pretensions" to such a status. Hale's request was incongruous to this private domestic woman of modest self-regard. Rather than recognizing that as a published writer she had in that respect left her cloistered setting, Stowe responded as if Hale's request were a case of mistaken identity. Unselfconsciously, Stowe revealed her own self-image when she wrote to Hale that she had read the request "to my tribe of little folks assembled around the evening centre table to let them know what an unexpected honour had befallen their Mama." And Hale's suggestion that a "daguerreotype" of Stowe be inserted in the volume, well, that was an idea that was "especially . . . quite droll." Stowe did admit to Hale that in a moment of fantasy she had "diverted myself somewhat with figuring the astonishment of the children should the well known visage of their mother loom out of the pages of a book before their astonished eyes." But, no, Stowe's letter to Hale concluded, having reflecting in "sober sadness" upon the true character of her life, it was clear that it had been so "uneventful and uninteresting" that "I do not see how anything can be done for me in the way of a sketch." After all, her being and life had been simply "retired and domestic." Any public testimony to the contrary, any recognition of her as a distinguished personage would have been astonishing to her.[9]

Stowe's response all but denied that she was even a writer. Given my female experience, my familial nurture, she seemed to be saying to Hale, how could I possibly be the "distinguished" person your letter assumes me to be? Insofar as Stowe was a historian of her own life, her commentary had validity. When *Woman's Record* finally appeared in 1853, Stowe was not included. Indirectly, Hale's preface to the volume provided a historical explanation. "Within the last fifty years," Hale wrote, "more books have been written by women and about women than all that had been issued during the preceding five thousand and eight hundred years." Indicating more specifically what had been the case for America, Hale added, "Far the greater portion of works concerning the female sex has been published within the last twenty years." To be more precise still, Hale might have gone on to say that the record of the last twenty years was obviously not sufficient to have undone that of the previous five thousand and eight hundred. At least for Stowe it had not been sufficient.[10]

But if there was an inability to imagine oneself as other than a woman of the home, there yet remained desire and discontent. Stimulated in part by a genuine desire—or a dream—to extend one's being beyond a prescribed and confining range, resentment was fueled by a darker foreboding that the mode of existence itself was potentially destructive. Perhaps the most powerful expression from any of the literary domestics of an explosive resistance to the limits set upon female being that nevertheless implied the internalization of those constraints is found in a series of letters written by Mary Virginia Terhune to her close friend, Virginia Eppes Dance. In 1848 she had written from Richmond, Virginia, to Dance in the outlying countryside saying, "You speak of 'the blues' and beg for advice." Only eighteen herself, Terhune nonetheless felt knowledgeable about the problems of womanhood and sufficiently confident to offer advice: "I am convinced that the true cause of your malady is want of exercise, not of body but of mind and heart." Dance's "youthful mind," Terhune said in earnest innocence, needed "excitement," although she was not referring to youthful excitement. In the first place, she continued, "you must not be content with merely treading in the path trodden by others"—as if Dance could choose to tread anywhere else. "I appeal to you," Terhune asked her, begging the issue, "if the unvarying routine of your ordinary occupation does not weary and disgust you." If it did not, Terhune clearly thought it should; she stated with a note of conviction suggesting she knew firsthand whereof she spoke that one had a "craving for something nobler," for "something more lofty."[11]

Three years later, in 1851, as if weary herself and no longer able to tolerate her sense of disgust, Terhune wrote to Dance again, this time to relate the excitement *she* craved. Terhune was little more than a month away from her twenty-first birthday, three years from the publication of *Alone*, and four years from marriage. But though she was still a young woman, unmarried, and though she had not yet launched her alter identity, "Marion Harland," the following passage from her letter captures the language, tone, perspective,and complex ambiguity of literary domesticity, and suggests the roots of that paradoxical phenomenon. "A man, darling," she wrote to Dance, "goes into the broad world to battle, stimulated by the presence and influence of his fellows, his every action has a witness and is censured or approved—while woman finds her warfare *within*—Oh the battles agonizing and terrible that are fought within that penetralia! the victories, unheralded save by angels who have seen and sympathized—and the defeats after which she tries, still uncomplaining, perhaps smiling to the last." Terhune is clearly envious of the fact that man can go into the "broad world to battle," envious and resentful that she cannot. She is not, at least to Dance, "uncomplaining." She too would like the broader plain of endeavor, the greater opportunities, the promise and possibility of different and expanded challenges. She too, her outburst implies, would welcome access to a wider world ready to define and mark her action, to impart to her work an added sense of depth, resonance, and measurement, to give to her a greater sense of accomplishment.[12]

What woman suffers in being barred from man's world and being restricted to woman's world "within," Terhune suggests, is not only a denial of ambition but a deprivation and threatened devastation of her spirit. Within herself, within that secret "penetralia," woman is isolated. Alone, she is deprived of the stimulation of worldly others. She is denied psychological and emotional reinforcement and support. Even if woman's work is significant, even if there are "victories," it is significance that is unrecognized and victories that are unheralded. Such a lack of acclaim contributes to a sense that society regards her life and her work as without importance or value. The likely effect of this demeaning of woman is a stunting of woman's sense of self, of self-worth.

Ironically, however, the most telling denial implicit in Terhune's words is perhaps that which she denies herself. Despite the anger and envy, the frustration, discontent, and disillusion, Terhune basically does not and cannot reject the premise that woman's life is "within." That is the given of the female life, the given nature of it. She protests her condition, but she simultaneously speaks from and exhibits that condition. " 'What could ail her?' " Terhune says the world asks, and Terhune rhetorically asks herself the same question, having already supplied the answer. It is that though she protests the limits of her lot, she must accept them as well. Terhune's words are those of a woman who, charged with a powerful desire to be and to do, struggles to relate that desire to her society's and her own conception of woman's nature and sphere. She acknowledges and accepts the fact that society does not invite woman into the "broad world to battle." That is the way it is. Man has his sphere and woman hers. Woman's fate is inextricably tied to the fortunes of the sphere of domesticity and there is no rallying cry for woman to leave that sphere. There is only the inevitability of having to confront "warfare within."

When Terhune left her sphere, it was as if she wished she had not. Obviously she felt she should not yet feared that she had. It was as if she neither could bear nor considered it proper for her, a woman, to have her actions witnessed. Her sense of "mortification and wounded feeling" at age nineteen when she was revealed to be "Robert Remer," the author of a series of published articles, recalls Caroline Howard Gilman's alarm and shame. Terhune had engaged in secret writing from an early age, and like Gilman she had earlier memories of discomfort directly associated with writing. At age fifty-two Terhune told Kate Sanborn that she had been embarrassed forty years earlier to admit that she had written a simple school composition. It was a feeling that never left her. "To this day," she said to Sanborn, "I shrink from saying 'I wrote that,' and talk, except with intimate friends, of my books is indefinably and inexpressibly painful to me." Terhune also wrote of the day that she took the manuscript of her first novel, *Alone*, to its publisher, Adolphus Morris, in Richmond, Virginia. Presenting herself and her manuscript to the male Morris had been nothing less than an agonizing confrontation for the private female Terhune. She had been forced to tell him, face to face, that she had written a book, and furthermore, she had been forced to admit that she had written before. Reading Terhune's account of the incident, one senses one is reading a fearful confession of sin. "It was positive *pain*," Terhune stressed, "to tell him that I had been writing under diverse signatures for the press since I was fourteen." Her confession was complete when she "owned with blushes that scorched my hair" to her previous publications. When *Alone* was published, she would write again to her female friend Dance not to announce that she, the female Terhune, had gone "into the broad world to battle," but to say, "You will read it and like it if only because I wrote it." It was a moment, perhaps, to indulge in dreams and express ambitions, but that was not possible for Terhune. "My own fears," she confided to Dance, "are the drawback to sanguine expectation."[13]

These culturally privileged women vacillated and struggled in confusion to resolve their ambivalence regarding woman's powers and place. To be preoccupied with the subject betokened doubt about the first and discontent with the latter. In her essay significantly titled "The Sex of the Soul," published the year of her death, 1856, twenty-three years after her first novel had been published, Caroline Lee Hentz boldly set forth her subject. "The question respecting the relative intellectual powers of men and women," she stated, "is one which has been often agitated, but never fully resolved." And resolution would not be forthcoming, she added, until the order of society was changed and "*both* sexes are subject to the same mental discipline." There has never been a nation, she claimed, in which women "trans-cend[ed] or equall[ed] the masculine sex in intellectual vigor." Such equality has never been allowed and such equality can never exist, she continued in telling and familiar language, where "the first rules impressed on the female mind are those which bind it to a more limited and peculiar sphere." From early childhood, the male is taught that he is to be "lord of creation" and that he is to rule and command "by the powers of a godlike mind." His mind is involved with "high pursuits" and "noble aims" and his life is one of continual challenge. In contrast, the female is taught "from the cradle of infancy to the bridal altar" that, in effect, "her frame [is] immortal rather than her mind, her body imperishable instead of her soul." Instead of being assigned worthy tasks and being expected to meet significant challenges, the female "is even told to hold down the aspirations of her intellect." With such a history, Hentz concluded, it is impossible to measure or compare the potential intellect of the two sexes. But there is one principle of which she is certain: "Mind, we verily believe, is of no sex."[14]

However, that is not the conclusion of Hentz's essay. Despite her particular emphasis and the apparent certainty of her words, Hentz could not conclude on that note. She was not able to. After criticizing the demeaning notion that females are intellectually inferior, and after implicitly demanding equal treatment and opportunity, she reverts to saying that, of course, "we would not alter the course marked out by Him, who directs the planets in their brilliant paths, and preserves the eternal harmony of the spheres." Hentz is not talking about celestial spheres: it is the spheres of the sexes she would not and cannot disturb, particularly the female's. After all, she asks, "Were woman to leave her own, for man's more sun-like sphere, what account can she render to her own neglected duties, to her own deserted orbit?" Once again, place awaits, destiny calls, and the woman is eclipsed.[15]

To a degree, the literary domestics were able to overcome inner restraints and outer circumstances. After all, they did become published, commercially successful writers. But theirs were not simple cases of daring and rebellion. As writers they were more defensive than they were aggressive. This is nowhere more clearly illustrated than in their responses to male animus. As these women discovered, male hostility to their attempts to enter the broad world to battle as creators of culture was inevitable. They wrote of their discovery, identified and delineated it in their prose. But in the throes of their crisis of identity, their defense of the position of the literary woman was undermined by their primary self-identification as private domestic women.

Sara Parton, as much a rebel as any of these women, was also as handicapped as any of them by her basic identity. This is demonstrated, for example, in a fictional sketch in which she attempted to rebut those who looked askance at women as writers. The critical attitude in Parton's story, "A Practical Blue-Stocking," is voiced by Harry Seldon, the friend of one James Lee, whose wife, Emma Lee, is engaged in literary activity. " 'I understand he has the misfortune to have a blue-stocking for a wife,' " says Harry, " 'and whenever I have thought of going there, a vision with inky fingers, frowzled hair, rumpled dress, and slip-shod shoes has come between me and my friend—not to mention thoughts of a disorderly house, smoky puddings, and dirty-faced children.' " Clearly a woman who writes is not a woman at all; at best she is a woman who fails her true calling. Harry concludes, " 'Defend me from a wife who spends her time dabbling in ink, and writing for the papers.' " Persuaded to visit the home of the Lees, Harry is disabused of his false notions. To his surprise, he discovers that the woman who writes is neither inky nor disheveled. The tastefully garbed and carefully combed Emma manages a home that is a model of order and cleanliness, and cares for children who are loved and secure. Harry also discovers that Emma is a writer only because her financially distressed husband needs money. The familiar justification of the literary woman as family provider is buttressed by a portrayal of Emma Lee as a paragon of traditional femininity.[16]

"Bluestocking," an eighteenth-century British term, came to be applied pejoratively to a woman who had intellectual or literary ambitions—unnatural pretensions, as the society of the literary domestics saw it. The literary domestics were aware that "female writer" was considered a contradiction in terms, that such a being was seen as unnatural, such a woman as unfeminine. Sara Parton was not the only one to reject the brand of the bluestocking while revealing its inner mark. Not surprisingly, Augusta Evans Wilson was the most aggressive and conflicted in attempting to rub out the spot of blue. In Wilson's novel *St. Elmo*, the widow Ellen Murray engages the Reverend Allan Hammond as tutor to the orphaned Edna Earl, who has already displayed a "restless intellect." But " 'for heaven's sake,' " the widow admonishes the clergyman, " 'do not make her a blue-stocking.' " When Allan asks Ellen if she has ever met a bluestocking in the flesh, Ellen answers that fortunately she has not. " 'You consider yourself lucky, then,' " asks Allan, " 'in not having known De Staël, Hannah More, Charlotte Brontë, and Mrs. Browning?' " But they " 'were truly great geniuses,' " protests Ellen; it is not " 'genius in women' " that she rejects. That genius that you so admire, Allan says to her, might never have been exhibited if those women had been denied the opportunity to develop it. And genius or not, if women are going to be " 'strangled with an offensive sobriquet,' " so might whatever ability they have be strangled; they might as well have " 'millstones tied about their necks.' "[17]

Edna Earl, who has been listening to the exchange, then asks Allan about the meaning of "bluestocking," to which the sympathetic reverend replies:

> "A 'bluestocking,' my dear is generally supposed to be a lady, neither young, pleasant, nor pretty (and in most instances unmarried;) who is unamiable, ungraceful, and untidy; ignorant of all domestic accomplishments and truly feminine acquirements, and ambitious of appearing very learned; a woman whose fingers are more frequently adorned with inkspots than thimble; who holds housekeeping in detestation, and talks loudly about politics, science, and whose hair is never smooth and whose ruffles are never fluted."

Supposedly the caricature does not intimidate Edna. From the beginning of the novel she is characterized as a female "obstinately wedded to the unpardonable heresy that, in the nineteenth century, it was a woman's privilege to be . . . learned." From the outset it has been her objective to obtain an education that will enable her to teach. It becomes her ambition to write.[18]

Like Beulah Benton in Wilson's earlier novel, Edna Earl embarks upon her "daring scheme of authorship." And like Beulah, Edna at first decides to "conceal the matter" and pursue her literary ambitions "in secret." Her "timidity and a haunting dread of the failure of the experiment" give her no other choice. Eventually, however, just as she had encountered in her efforts to obtain an education the obstacle of a compromised member of her sex in the person of Ellen Murray, so she must face male condescension and hostility toward her literary ambitions. She confronts it directly in the person of Douglass Manning, a prominent figure in the literary world and the editor of a national magazine for which Edna desires to write. Douglass places little confidence in female intellect and judges Edna's projected first novel as " 'beyond your capacity—no woman could successfully handle it.' " Perhaps, he suggests, she should attempt something " 'better suited to your feminine ability.' " For example, he asks condescendingly, might she not write " 'sketches of homelife' " or a " 'pretty ballad that sounds sweet and soothing when sung over a cradle' "? Douglass may be Edna's most withering detractor, but he is not her only one. She hears constantly from those around her that her ambitions are unnatural for a woman, certain to end in failure, and, not least, guaranteed to incur the wrath of man. Even her wise old friend, the Reverend Hammond, tells her that " 'men detest female competitors in the Olympian game of literature.' " Poor Edna wonders if "all women were browbeaten for aspiring to literary honors."[19]

Browbeaten or not, Edna will not be dissuaded from her goal, and she eventually reaches it—or at least seems to. In reality she is as compromised as her benefactor, Ellen Murray, or, more to the point, as her creator, Wilson. The first sign that something is amiss with Edna comes when the author relates that the heroine's moment of literary acclaim coincides with her being threatened by a serious *heart* condition perhaps attributable to and certainly exacerbated by her literary labors. She rejects her doctor's order that she cease writing, telling him that this is impossible, as her work is essential to her life. But in both the lives and the prose of the literary domestics, this is a familiar sign. Intellectual activity is a most unnatural activity for women, putting a particular strain on the female constitution.[20]

The second sign that Wilson's design is a compromised one is seen in the relationship Edna forms with her major detractor, the editor-critic Douglass. Edna may find Douglass's counsel distasteful but she cannot avoid paying tribute to his male intellect and, in effect, demeaning her own. In spite of their original difference of opinion, a relationship between the two develops, and their contrary natures, intellectual and otherwise, are emphasized. Douglass may be intrigued with the expansion of Edna's mind, but it is her growing reverence for him that is most appealing. On her part, Edna pays a "deferential homage" to his "dispassionate judgment," and learns to rely upon his "strong, clear mind." Approvingly, and revealingly, Wilson notes the interaction of their disparate natures. The common premise that women were intuitive and overly idealistic and men empirical and practical is echoed in Wilson's declaration that Edna's "intense and dreamy idealism" was countered by Douglass's "positivism," and her "fervid and beautiful enthusiasm surged and chafed and broke over this man's stern, flinty realism."[21]

Inevitably, Douglass proposes marriage. It is a proposal that Edna considers. Not only does he meet her exacting moral and intellectual standards, she also believes that it would be a dazzling honor to become the wife of the "noblest ornament of the profession." After all, Wilson states, without fear of contradiction, what more could "a mere woman" desire than to "rule the destiny of that strong man, whose intellect was so influential in the world"? She means, rule his heart; a woman could not presume to rule his intellect. Wilson is not being sardonic. For once she means literally what she says. Edna Earl does not marry Douglass Manning, but only because she does not love him. After more than five hundred pages devoted in part to her struggle to succeed as a writer, the novel ends with Edna's ceasing to write altogether and accepting her rightful position as a woman in marriage. Intent upon enshrining Edna as a literary figure, Wilson nevertheless cannot forgo placing the heroine where she belongs: in the home. *St. Elmo* is a tale that inadvertently juxtaposes a woman's unnatural literary ambition and her true domestic destiny. The first is pursued only to be left aside at the last moment for the second. It need only be added that from the moment of Edna's decision to marry, her heart condition miraculously disappears. In body and soul she has remained a true woman.[22]

Terhune's "warfare within" surfaced on more than one occasion in her fiction. Her novel *Phemie's Temptation*, in particular, includes her most explicit treatment of woman as bluestocking. It satirizes male intellectual subjugation of women as motivated by men's fear of female intelligence. But it also reveals most glaringly Terhune's insecurity, doubts, and sense of illegitimacy as a creator of culture. Phemie Rowland, a young unmarried woman who is the central figure in the novel, is scorned for her obvious intelligence. It is the opinion of her brother-in-law, Seth Mandell, that " 'she has altogether too much will and head for a woman.' " In fact, he believes that " 'her sentiments and language border upon incendiarism.' " But, he adds smugly, if she has " 'some absurd ideas about learned women and intellectual affinities,' " she will " 'drop them' " when she learns more about the realities of her world. Seth is partly right. Although Phemie does not "drop" her ambitions or totally shed her belief in her capabilities, she does modify the one and camouflage the other, and still she pays dearly for being intelligent. But of course the price she pays as a fictional character was predetermined by the compromised bargaining position of her creator.[23]

Phemie's price is a disastrous marriage to a publisher, Robert Hart, who is her intellectual inferior. The unmarried Phemie Rowland is said to have a "genuine love of learning." But because of youthful innocence and a mind that "thirsted" after stimulating companionship, she is attracted to and deceived by the apparently cultured, charming, gentlemanly Robert. She fails to recognize Robert for the vainglorious, insecure, and shallow man that he is. Phemie's closest friend, Ruth Darcy, a strong advocate of women's rights, does try to prevent the marriage by confronting Robert with the

"truth" of the matter. " 'You are not Phemie Rowland's peer in intellect,' "
Ruth tells Robert, and as " 'superiority on the part of a wife is an
unpardonable sin, unforgivable by the husband,' " she warns him that " 'if
she should outshine you, you will hate her.' " In spite of Ruth's highly
favorable evaluation of Phemie's intellectual powers, there are limits to what
even Ruth can foresee regarding a future role for Phemie. For example,
rather than envision major achievements for Phemie in her own right, she
speculates that if Phemie is fortunate she might become " 'a true helpmate to
a great scholar, or a man who had it in him to achieve eminence in any
department of letters.' " Robert is stung by Ruth's comments and detests her
for her humiliating appraisal of his intellect. But Robert is deceived himself
by his own condescending and demeaning attitude toward females in general.
He is attracted by Phemie's beauty and surprised that a woman so attractive
is also intelligent. Robert, however, has little difficulty in envisioning a
beautiful and intelligent woman as a pleasing possession and an ornamental
prize for his own display.[24]

The marriage takes place, and disaster ensues. As Terhune observes
contemptuously, the fault lies with her heroine, now Phemie *Hart*, not with
her husband. Phemie as wife fails "to belittle herself" to the level Robert has
decided is "the maximum of intellectual altitude in the woman who was to
call him lord." Phemie's most grievous misstep is to become a secret writer.
Before her marriage to Robert, Phemie's father had suffered financial
reversals, and his dutiful daughter had helped meet the family's expenses by
earning money as a teacher, clerk, and author of a text on chemistry. Now
married and on a year's honeymoon in Europe, she secretly accepts a
position as a foreign correspondent for a newspaper. Here too the motivation
is helping others, this time paying for the special education of a blind brother.
Thinking that all the while he has been financing the brother's education,
Robert is appalled upon their return home to learn of her independent action.
Once Phemie's secret is exposed, the marriage is doomed.[25]

When Robert learns that Phemie has also written a book and arranged
through a third party to have it issued anonymously by his own publishing
house, he is completely undone. She must have known, he tells her, that her
" 'clandestine operation' " would bring him nothing but " 'pain and mortification.' " Not only has she had the gall to assert her " 'sovereignty,' " but her
worst sin has been to threaten him intellectually: " 'In the pride of intellect,
which is your besetting sin, you have learned to look down upon your
husband as a being of a lower sphere.' " She should have been like " 'most
women,' " he says, and sought " 'no happier and higher lot' " than giving him
a happy home. Instead, he charges, by writing a book, and a successful book
at that, " 'you have unsexed yourself.' " She has presumed to become a lord
of creation. It is Robert, of course, who has been unsexed and unhinged by
Phemie's becoming a bluestocking. Poor Robert espies proof of Phemie's
blueness in the critics' references to the ' " "enlarged views' " ' and the

' " 'breadth and vigor of thought' " ' to be found in her book, and not the least
by the fact that " 'strong-minded females and radicals' " apparently delight in
those views and thoughts.[26]

Already threatened, Robert fears that worse is yet to come. He reminds
his wife that once the " 'anonymous novelist' " becomes known, he will have
to suffer the awful indignity of their becoming identified as " 'Mrs. Hart *and
husband.*' " That may appeal to you, Robert rails at Phemie, but think of
what it will mean to me—no less than " 'my loss of manliness' "; just imagine
that I will have to sun myself " 'in the reflection of your fame.' " Terhune
sets body to language: "In his exasperation at the picture he had drawn he
resigned his pipe altogether and stood up, rearing his fine figure to its full
height, stamping the left boot-heel, then the right, upon the velvet rug, and
plucking, in an irritated way, at his beard, assertive of physical manliness [as]
if his intellectual supremacy *were* menaced by his subordinate's audacity."
Beside himself, Robert feverishly paces the room and, having "assumed yet
another eminently masculine attitude," turns to Phemie to exclaim, unneces-
sarily, that regarding " 'literary women,' "—" 'I detest the class.' "[27]

Terhune would appear to have done in her man and finished off the myth
of the male as sole lord of creation, and patriarchal marriage to boot. Phemie
has apparently asserted her independent powers of mind. But Terhune was
unable to make any such unambiguous claim for woman. Robert abdicates,
but Phemie seizes no thrones. The fault does not lie in Phemie's being a
"strong-minded wom[a]n;" it is in Robert's being a weak-minded man. Had I
known, says the surprised Phemie, " 'that you would be displeased with me
for attempting authorship, I would never have penned a line.' " Phemie
ceases to write and the marriage limps along—limps along, because despite
Phemie's capitulation the damage has been done. The wife has been
"unwomanly" enough to threaten the husband's male ego. But Terhune
quickly assures the reader that Phemie is not unwomanly at all. Her identity
as the author of a successful novel is "discovered," but she is also found to be
" 'not a bit of a blue.' " If she is a brilliant conversationalist, she is also a
beautiful, charming hostess. In fact, from the opening pages of the novel
Terhune finds it necessary to excuse Phemie's intelligence with her beauty.
Unfortunately, Robert can no longer bring himself to excuse her intelligence.
He still seeks to regard himself as the "owner of this glorious accessory," to
claim his wife as his "property." But the balance of beauty and brains has
been to his mind tipped for the worse. As Terhune phrases it, "that homage
paid to Phemie's beauty, manners, and dress was acceptable to her lord, as
praise of her intellectual gifts was distasteful."[28]

After two years of growing disenchantment, the wounded Robert finds in
the failure of his publishing firm a pretext for skulking away. As he writes
accusingly to Phemie in a note he leaves behind, " 'The world will say that I
have fled the country because I dared not face my furious creditors. *You* will
know that the fear of their wrath is but a minor thong in the whip that has

driven me into exile.' " Robert would appear to have been routed from the cultural arena and Phemie, now unencumbered by wifely obligations, can apparently resume her career as an author. In fact, Phemie does begin to write again, but she does so from necessity, not choice. Unknown to her husband at the time of his chosen exile, she is pregnant. Without a husband to support her and with a child due in a few months, Phemie Hart is devastated by Robert's abandonment of her. But the female heart knows its duty. The birth of a daughter awakens her from her despair; she now has "something for which to plan and work." She must write to support herself and, above all, her child. The daughter becomes a symbol of hope, and a vehicle for hope as well. Phemie believes Robert will one day return. She hopes the child will insure that their reunion is a permanent one: " 'I have hoped until I believe, that when he has once looked into his baby's eyes, he cannot leave us again.' " Phemie's literary career, then, is a necessary but unwanted and unnatural obligation.[29]

The extent to which Phemie's literary occupation constitutes an unnatural sphere of activity becomes all too obvious. It is one thing if she, the wife, must perform the husband's duty and support what is left of her family. It is quite another if her literary tasks interfere with motherly care and devotion, with the infant daughter's needs. At first Phemie attempts to be a full-time mother, but she finds that this makes her a part-time writer and therefore an insufficient provider. It goes without saying that the contradictory demands adversely affect her health. Reluctantly, the decision is made to write more and care for the child less. If it is "a hard lesson for baby," it is worse for the mother: "Morning after morning she bent over her accounts or copying, pity and grief tugging at her heart-strings in one mighty strain of maternal anguish, as the angry scream, and anon, the piteous wail of the neglected child pierced her ears." Being a writer does interfere with being a mother, and there is little doubt as to which ideally should have priority in Terhune's view. The only solace for the woman who must be a writer by day is that she can be a mother at night. Being maternal at night is the sole recompense of the daily "violence she had done her own feelings in carrying out the discipline prescribed by Duty and Necessity." Being a mother, if only at night, enables her to endure her predicament. Deprived of her husband, the child is the one " 'well-spring' " in an otherwise "bleak waste" for the "lonely and toiling woman." The daughter, in fact, even learns to do *her* duty by learning to occupy herself and play by herself, "whispering her baby prattle all the while, lest she should disturb the writer." Needless to say, Terhune's is not a ringing but a wringing manifesto for the female creator of culture.[30]

The truth is that Phemie is forced to go on writing. After five years Robert does return, but not for long. He has never forgiven Phemie for her original sin. During his long exile he has become dissolute and unemployable, and now he cannot forgive Phemie for having to support him, especially from her literary earnings: "It galled him to see her obliged to do it now." Nor does the baby make a difference; Robert is alternately indifferent and disdainful toward his daughter. This constitutes the greatest "disappointment of [Phemie's] cherished hope that their infant was to be the instrument of the father's regeneration." Robert is even disposed to ill-treatment of his daughter, and Phemie's disappointment turns to rejection. This time Robert does not abandon Phemie: she sends him packing. Yet Phemie's final act of will is not a triumphant one. The novel is devoid of triumph. Instead, Terhune suggests that the reader forgive and sympathize, forgive Phemie and sympathize with her plight. "Phemie was neither a perfect woman," Terhune tells us, nor, obviously, was she "a model wife." Phemie's final decision to banish her husband from their home may have been "a sin against God and man," but do not forget, writes Terhune, that "she did not go unpunished." That is to say, among other things, that Phemie's literary career has a future.[31]

Appropriately, the final word is spoken by Seth Mandell's "mouth-piece," that is, by his wife, Phemie's sister Emily. Emily has always prided herself on being a true domestic woman. In light of Phemie's intelligence, she had forecast her failure:

> "It is the invariable mistake of literary women to think that they can leave the work of their households to servants, while they cultivate their higher talents. A woman should not marry unless she can make up her mind to sacrifice all thought of pursuing the bent of her own mind and taste—to conform herself to her husband's notions in everything; to study his interests in every imaginable way; to consider nothing menial that can add to his comfort; to live in and for him alone. He has a right to demand this. If more of our sex—especially the stronger-minded portion of it—rightly understood this cardinal principle of the married state, we should hear less of the unhappy lives of learned ladies."

Just as Seth criticized Phemie for possessing " 'too much . . . head for a woman,' " so does Emily. Reflecting upon Phemie's final state of domestic disaster, Emily expresses gratitude that she herself " 'never had any temptation to become [a] strong-minded wom[a]n.' " It is fitting then that Terhune chose to title her novel *Phemie's Temptation* rather than, for example, "Phemie's Desire." Desires may or may not be sanctioned by God, or man. Temptations almost never are.[32]

The degree to which the literary domestics were capable of recognizing their very genuine desires to broaden and control their lives and, in turn, finding the courage and means to express satisfactorily those desires was problematical at best. It was a formidable task, one guaranteed to induce conflict for the individual, to direct desires and energies down one channel when social pressure and conditioning pointed and impelled the individual to another. In that regard, male guardians of the kingdom of culture did not necessarily welcome women into the revered realm. Sara Parton discovered that fact in the most extreme way possible when she sought aid from her brother, Nathaniel Parker Willis. Willis was certainly in a position to help her. Even before he had graduated from Yale, Willis was recognized in some circles as a leading American poet. His first volume of poetry was published in 1827, the year of his graduation. Subsequently he wrote and published poetry, drama, fiction, and miscellaneous prose. He also continued the tradition of his male forebears by becoming an editor and journalist. It was Willis's editorship of the *Home Journal* and his status in the literary world generally that led Parton to ask him if he would be interested in issuing some of her sketches or, failing that, if he would suggest other publishers where she might submit her pieces. Willis responded with blunt rejection and wholesale condemnation. "You overstrain the pathetic," he replied to Parton, "and your humor sinks into dreadful vulgarity sometimes." In short, he found Parton's writing repugnant, and concluded, "I am sorry that any Editor knows that a sister of mine wrote some of these which you sent me." Willis had the reputation of helping young writers get started and, as previously noted, he was not above "puffing" other writers regardless of merit or selling himself in obsequious fashion. Nevertheless, he did not see fit to help, puff, or sell his sister.[33]

But Sara Parton got her revenge in *Ruth Hall*. When the idea of writing for a living occurs to Ruth Hall, her first thought is to turn to her brother, Hyacinth Ellet, "the prosperous editor of the Irving Magazine." Convinced that she can write as well as some of the contributors Hyacinth employs and has "praised with no niggardly pen," she feels certain as well that he will agree to publish her. Barring that, she thinks, "he surely would be brotherly enough to point out to her some one of the many avenues so accessible to a man of extensive newspaperial and literary acquaintance." As was the case with her creator, Ruth is surely wrong. Hyacinth Ellet's response echoes that of Nathaniel Willis. One can envision Sara Parton with pen and paper eyeing Nathaniel's letter, contemplating how to change the prose without altering the spirit: "I have looked over the pieces you sent me, Ruth," Hyacinth writes. "It is very evident that writing never can be *your* forte; you have no talent that way." It is possible that "some inferior newspapers" might employ you, he adds snidely, but be assured that your articles "never will be heard of out of your own little provincial city." No, he has all the contributors he requires and has no literary acquaintances who could possibly be interested. Better, he concludes, that she seek "some *unobtrusive* employment." After finishing the letter and again having "glanced at her children," Ruth vows to press on—unaided by Hyacinth.[34]

Parton also pressed on with her character assassination of her brother. He is described by one character as " 'a conceited jackanapes, who divides his time between writing rhymes and inventing new ties for his cravat.' "

Another, a former female friend of Ruth's and a social snob herself, seeks to justify her and Hyacinth's estrangement from Ruth in the latter's fallen state by commenting, " 'Hyacinth has just married a rich, fashionable wife, and of course he cannot lose caste by associating with Ruth now; you cannot blame him.' " Parton's bitter fictional portrayal of her brother may or may not have been a just one, but Nathaniel Willis apparently was socially ambitious and more than a bit of a literary dandy. Oliver Wendell Holmes, for one, characterized Willis as something of an " 'anticipation of Oscar Wilde.' " On the occasion of his funeral in 1867, a journalist wrote of Willis in a fashion that recalled Parton's: "A man of no settled convictions, of no depth of character, a gilded butterfly of society, whose only elysium was to bask in the evanescent sunshine of social favor, he became at last a crushed and broken thing, his powdered plumage soiled and battered."[35]

There were exceptions to the rule of male indifference or hostility, of course. The literary careers of E.D.E.N. Southworth and Sara Parton might never have expanded to the extent that they did had it not been for the fortuitous intervention of Robert Bonner and his *New York Ledger*. Early on, before Harriet Beecher Stowe's writing could even be called a career, husband Calvin had some encouraging words for her. "You must be a *literary woman*," he wrote her in 1842 from Cincinnati while she was visiting relatives in Hartford and arranging the publication of her first collection of stories. "It is so written in the book of fate." She should plan accordingly, he said, look to her health, and "brush up your mind." Calvin even suggested that she use the name "Harriet Beecher Stowe" for publication. It was "a name euphonious, flowing and full of meaning," he said, quite correctly. Just as Caroline Lee Hentz entered the most productive phase of her career she was fortunate to have what amounted to a literary adviser in the person of a Doctor Wildman. In fact, according to what Hentz wrote an acquaintance in 1851, it was Wildman who first urged her to cease teaching and devote her full energies to writing. "He said '*he* would stand by me'—and not to fear any consequences," Hentz wrote to a Mrs. Stafford. "He comes and I read to him chapter by chapter as I write, and [he] cheers and animates me by his praise." Wildman was indeed the exception, however. "Now my dear Mrs. Stafford," said Hentz, "you know that we much more frequently find a female friend, combining the qualities we admire than a male, but when we do meet one of these rare jewels, we ought to prize them." Wildman was a rare jewel because he was a male friend. He was a prized friend because as a male he was one of the elect. In recognition of and in gratitude for Wildman's encouragement and support, said Hentz to Stafford, "I have dedicated my 'Rena or the Snowbird' to him as you will see." And so she did.[36]

Not surprisingly, aid and comfort from men was much more likely to come from relatives, the case of Nathaniel Willis notwithstanding. Regardless of ambiguous or unusual circumstances, it was crucial, valued support.

In his hour of financial crisis, it was Henry Warner who tramped the streets of New York City with his daughter Susan's first novel. After seeing to it that his daughter, the future Mary Virginia Terhune, was educated as if she were a male preparing for college, Samuel Pierce Hawes went a significant step further and arranged for her to meet the Richmond bookseller Adolphus Morris, and more, financed the publication of her first novel through Morris. That was to say to his daughter substantively as well as symbolically that even if Mary Virginia was not male, she was a writer. Hawes did not stop there. He had read *Alone* in manuscript and he read it again when it was published. As Terhune recalled, it was for her a significant rereading. Her father began reading the novel late one afternoon and stayed up until the early morning hours finishing it. At breakfast the following day he put his arm around his expectant, anxious daughter and announced, " 'I was right about that book.' " That was supposedly all he said, but for Terhune it was enough. As she wrote later, "I never had—I shall never have—another reader like him." Terhune's father remained her supporter and apparently her primary reader. He took her first and second novels to New York City and arranged for reissue of the one and publication of the other. Hawes not only continued to read her subsequent novels, he also discussed characters and plots with her, with intensity and interest. "It was," his daughter wrote, "strange— phenomenal—when one considers the light weight of the literature under advisement and the mental calibre of the man." Whether or not Terhune was correct in her judgment of the literature or the man, it was entirely in character for the female to thus pronounce upon the literature and the man.[37]

Regardless of the support received, however, social dictates and ingrained personal tenets of behavior held sway more than they were circumvented. Catharine Maria Sedgwick received more complete and sustained male support throughout her career than any of the other literary domestics. Her politician-statesman-jurist father Theodore Sedgwick encouraged the intellectual development of his daughter, and her four brothers, Henry Dwight, Theodore, Jr., Robert, and Charles, persuaded, cajoled, and induced Catharine to become and to remain a writer. Henry Dwight, known as Harry, *husbanded* her literary affairs for nearly ten years as critic, agent, and manager, until blindness threatened and, finally, mental illness struck him down. To a lesser extent Theodore, Robert, and Charles encouraged and supported her from book to book and publication to publication. Thus Sedgwick enjoyed what was tantamount to a literary escort almost to the end of her literary journey. But in that creative sojourn Sedgwick, the private and domestic woman, was a bewildered, timid, and reluctant passenger. It is fair to say that without her fraternal escort she probably would never have undertaken the journey. She began a literary career as if she were biding her time while waiting for the legitimate domestic career she was never to have, and to an extent she regarded her literary endeavors as a pale substitute for what she believed should be the calling of a true woman.[38] Not surprisingly, then, the woman who became a creator of culture was never able to regard herself as one.

Theodore Sedgwick, mentor to a daughter who could admire him but could never hope to follow in his footsteps, wrote to the nine-year-old Catharine in 1799, "There is not in America a little girl of your age who can write a better letter than you can, and you cannot give any one else so much pleasure, by writing as myself." He read her letters over and over again in his private chamber, he told her, and although sometimes they made him cry and sometimes laugh, "both give me equal pleasure." In retrospect, Theodore's letter to Catharine appears as a harbinger. He died almost a decade before his daughter's literary career began, but his sons fulfilled his legacy by championing Catharine's intellectual potential.[39]

It was Theodore's second son, Harry, who became Sedgwick's most ardent supporter and devotee. In 1812, a year before their father's death and ten years before *A New England Tale* was written, Harry wrote a remarkable letter to his sister. The sentiments expressed were exceptional in their time, suggesting that Harry, then in the full enjoyment of his physical and mental health, was an exceptional individual. He began by telling Sedgwick that he had found "a delightful scrap of yours on the sacred character of a *pastor*," and intended to insert it in Boston's *Weekly Messenger*. He wanted to do that, he said, so that she might "enjoy the novel pleasure of seeing yourself in print." (Only later would Harry fully realize that for his sister, appearing in print was not a matter of light enjoyment.) He told her that he desired to "claim for 'my fair countrywomen' the need of their genius; how triumphantly shall I prove their precocity of intellect!" By claiming his sister's genius, he hoped to prove it to her. Lightheartedly, Harry went on to tell "my dear sister and dearest muse" that by "appointment of the superior powers" he had been granted the opportunity to "guide the public taste and direct the public mind." What he meant was that he had been asked to edit the pages of the *Weekly Messenger* every third week. As one of his first official acts, he would print Sedgwick's "scrap." Now, he went on to say, "unlike the Turk, I *can* bear a sister near the throne." Relishing the moment, he sought with continued jest to gently encourage his sister: "I proffer to you the fairest portion of my dominion—nay the royal palace—the imperial Seat itelf. You shall reign sole empress of the *Poet's Corner*." But as he and his brothers courted Sedgwick for culture's world, they found her a reluctant bride.[40]

Theodore, Jr., also did his best to prompt and persuade the would-be author in her first effort. Although the brothers were successful in getting Sedgwick to write the tale, they were not able to dispel the teller's sense of inadequacy. While she was engaged in turning what had begun as a religious tract into a novel, she wrote to a friend, "My dear brother Theodore makes a most extravagant estimate of my powers. It is one thing to write a spurt of a letter, and another to write a book." *A New England Tale* was completed and published, but Sedgwick remained of like mind. In the spring of 1822, shortly before the novel's publication, she wrote Theodore in a joint letter from her and Harry to say that she did not at all like launching her book "without the passport of your approbation." It would "grieve" her beyond description, she said, to publish anything that might displease him, "particularly since my attempting anything was in consequence of the impulse of your advice and wishes."[41]

Harry, meanwhile, wrote his brother-in-law William Minot to tell the "secret," to tout the literary abilities of his sister-client, and to express openly his concern about her lack of confidence. The tale was "very beautiful," he thought, "but not equal to her capacities." The problem was that Sedgwick might not continue writing and fulfill those capacities "unless she is encouraged by her success this time." Hesitating slightly lest the suggestion be thought improper, he nonetheless boldly asked if Mrs. Minot would consider reviewing the novel in the *North American Review*. On 6 May, the day before the novel's publication, Harry wrote again to Minot to sound the same theme with a slight variation. He was "anxious," he said, to know the Minots' opinion of the novel, and he insisted they tell him "the truth, the whole truth, and nothing but the truth." In case they had forgotten what *he* thought, he repeated that he was confident that his sister could do better, but he worried that unless the novel was "well-received" she might not attempt to do better. That same day brother Theodore was doing his best to bolster the confidence of the leading character. Having read the first 130 pages of the novel, he wrote "Dear Kate" to tell her, "It exceeds all my expectations, fond and flattering as they were." He had never doubted the result, he said, but having seen it confirmed, his heart was filled with "pride and pleasure." All he desired now was to be able in person to "greet the architect of this exquisitely beautiful fabric." Meanwhile, Harry had written the Minots again to express his pleasure at their positive response to the novel. "You will pardon my solicitude upon the subject," he added, "when you consider that I had considerable agency in inducing Catharine to suffer it to be printed."[42]

The "architect" herself, of course, remained invincibly humble. In a series of letters written to Susan Higginson Channing shortly after *A New England Tale* was published, she busily apologized for book and author. "I claim nothing for it on the score of literary merit," she said of the novel in one letter, and in another disclaimed "any pretension as an author." After all, "my production is a very small affair anyway," she added, as if to settle the matter. By this time Harry had already written to inform her about the novel's surprisingly successful sale and to prompt her to press onward. This was not the time to be apprehensive: "Have done with these womanish fears," he admonished her. Buoyed as he was by the "certain prospect of your future eminence," he thought she should be planning her next novel. Harry had some advice on that topic as well. Perhaps, he suggested, she should consider "writing in disconnected masses, which you can afterward weave together." In that way, he thought, she could net her "bright ideas" on the fly and mount them later. Whether or not Harry truly fancied himself a literary critic, he obviously was concerned that if Sedgwick stopped writing at the moment she might not write on the morrow.[43]

By September of that year Sedgwick was back at work. Harry was back in the mails telling Minot that not much should be expected until the onset of winter, as his sister was being plagued by interruptions. Nevertheless, he was confident. "I think she will do something grand this time," he wrote. The cycle repeated itelf; Sedgwick's brothers took turns encouraging her, Sedgwick warned them and others not to expect much, and, with another book completed, dispensed the increasingly familiar disclaimers. By June of 1824 Sedgwick had finished *Redwood* and was preparing it for the publisher. To Theodore she wrote that she was "in a more quiet state of mind than you would expect" regarding the novel. She had done what her brothers and friends had urged her to do and "done it as well as I could." But, she added, "I am not ambitious," and if only all would be content with the "humble" recognition she deserved, then she would be "quite tranquil."[44]

When the novel appeared in July, Robert wrote to tell Sedgwick, that wherever he went he received "compliments, felicitations, and even homage for the honor I have come to, by my relation to the author of Redwood." Harry wrote Minot again to say that all concerned were "highly delighted" with the novel's success, all that is except his sister. "The author," he added, "seems to care least about it." But that did not deter Harry from assiduously managing her affairs and defending her reputation. Harry complained to Minot about a negative review of *Redwood* that had appeared "in your literary Gazette." In light of all the "praise" the novel had received, an unfavorable review could be tolerated, he said. But what he found objectionable was the reviewer's insinuation that, given the style of *Redwood*, it appeared that a man had written it. That, said Harry, "is unfounded."[45]

Harry and his brothers' ambitions for their sister both pressured her to write and pressured her. Sedgwick was pleased by their interest in and support for her literary efforts. She was also fearful that she would disappoint them. Their interest and support notwithstanding, she possessed little confidence in her own creative abilities. The peculiar circumstances of her education had done little for her in that respect. By June of 1825 she was in the midst of her struggle to write what would become *Hope Leslie*. As usual, Harry was closely attendant upon her efforts and Sedgwick reacted to the intensity of his gaze: "you *must* moderate your expectations—or you will be sadly disappointed." She was lacking, she said, in the "power of gratifying them" simply because she did not have either the "necessary material or talent." Even if she possessed the requisite ability, which she obviously doubted, he should not overlook the fact that "my education has been too defective, and my knowledge too circumscribed, to permit the expectation that I can do anything better or half as well as I have done." Sedgwick's professed lack of ambition thinly disguised her sense of inadequacy and her dread of failure. By belittling her creative efforts she betrayed her inability to assert the legitimacy of those efforts. The desire and the talent were there, the conviction was not.[46]

Writing to Charles in January of 1827, Sedgwick informed him that she had progressed beyond 150 pages with *Hope Leslie*, "but I shall never finish it," she added, "at least to my satisfaction." That summer she noted in her journal that she was very aware that "what distinction I have attained is greatly owing to the paucity of our literature." No, there could be little justification for "self-complacency" on her part, she wrote, and with gathering momentum she finished spinning her cocoon. Not only could she take little credit for a God-given "talent" that was "not my own," but she had to accept blame for not having improved it by "industry and careful cultivation."The truth of the matter was that she had "more cause to mourn over what I have not done than to exult in what I have done—more cause for humility than for pride." Thus did Sedgwick conclude her journal entry, roping an ego that had long since been corralled.[47]

Sedgwick's evaluation of her literary standing represented as much the dominance of her sense of inferior regard as it did a triumph of personal honesty. It reflected the inability of the private domestic woman to claim a rightful place in the male cultural firmament. She was not beneath caring about her literary efforts, but she could not rise above the traditional woman's station to which she had been born. When a reader of *Hope Leslie* wrote to her commenting about the novel, Sedgwick, rather than assume the role of the author that she was, defaulted. "Literary occupation is rather a pastime than a profession with me," she confessed, and then, in apparent contradiction, severely criticized the reader's observations. In a way, she was correct to default. Neither then nor later could she unequivocally commit herself to a career as a writer.[48]

Now Harry was no longer able to press Sedgwick to regard her literary endeavors (and herself) more seriously. The successful publication of *Hope Leslie* had been shadowed by the pall of Harry's mental illness. Shortly after the novel's appearance, Charles apologized for his failure to send congratulations. He had no doubts that the success of the novel would give pride and pleasure to all in the family. But at the moment, he added, "to talk of anything, to think of anything but what can be done for our Harry seems as incongruous as to dance on the grave of the dead." And of course Sedgwick's concern was not for her career, but for her beloved brother. "To see a mind once so powerful, so effective, so luminous, darkened, disordered, a broken instrument—to see him stared at by the vulgar, the laugh of children—oh," she wrote, "it is too much." Small as it was, she found some consolation in her belief that his love was "an inextinguishable light; it shines through the darkness." For Sedgwick, however, Harry's illness meant as well the loss of crucial support for what had already been a supposedly perfunctory endeavor, a "pastime" rather than a "profession."[49]

It was necessary for Sedgwick to continue "my humble literary labors" without Harry's aid and encouragement. In 1829 he voluntarily entered a Boston mental asylum. As Sedgwick wrote an acquaintance, "a powerful excitement overcame his reason." She thought his "derangement" was only partial, meaning that it had not "touched his affections or affected his temper." *Clarence*, Sedgwick's fourth novel, appeared a year later. While readying the novel for publication she wrote to Charles to complain in familiar fashion that she was not satisfied with it. More importantly, she confided that "I miss excessively, more than words can tell, the light and repose of dear Harry's criticisms." She had depended upon him during her literary career as on no one else, particularly because she had been able to rely upon his criticisms not being "severe." To balance that, she now had "more experience," "more self-confidence," and consequently "vastly less fear or care about the result." Not surprisingly, Sedgwick had not achieved the degree of equanimity she claimed. Unable to believe in or proclaim her literary achievement, she was no less apprehensive about her literary fortunes. Again and again she professed a serenity of soul only to betray inner tremors. At times her words, in turmoil, tumbled one upon the other. With *Clarence* in press, she wrote to Susan Higginson Channing to say, "I am now hardened enough to talk of my works (oh! how the word and all its relations have made my blood tingle) with perfect nonchalance." What she intended to say was overwritten by what she said. What she wrote to Channing three months later following the release of *Clarence* was more direct. She was "delighted," she owned, with Channing's favorable response to the novel. For a literary domestic good news on that score was soothing: "I shall never get the calm nerves of a regular-bred author, and I quake and tremble on every fresh appearance."[50]

In between the dates of her two letters to Susan Higginson Channing, Sedgwick recorded in her journal that she had sent the last proofs of the novel to the publisher. In almost exactly the same words she had used in her journal in the summer of 1827, she castigated herself for having failed to "improve" her God-given talent. And then she admitted and, perhaps for the first time, recorded the hope she held: "I honestly confess that I earnestly desire and hope for success and expect it." Expectations notwithstanding, however, the woman prayed to God to make her "humble" and not bitter toward the world should she be disappointed. On 12 June, the day after the novel appeared before the public, she sent a copy to Lydia Maria Child. "I am just now heartsick about it," she wrote to Child. She had not as yet heard "a single opinion" and her courage was "drooping." Eleven days later she heard from Susan Higginson Channing. That same month Charles wrote in mock horror to beg her not to write another novel or "my family will be ruined." The problem was that everyone in his family was locked away in his or her room absorbed with *Clarence*.[51]

Sedgwick continued to write despite the death of Harry in 1831. "My life is now passed under a deep desolate shadow," she wrote the day before his death. Harry more than anyone had sponsored this literary domestic, and now he was dying, "he whose web of life from my cradle has been interwoven with mine, so that it seems to me they cannot be parted without shattering the whole texture." Shortly after his death she wrote to Louisa Minot, William's wife, to say, "I mourn the separation . . . I feel as if part of me were dead." A year later she noted the anniversary of his death, recollecting that "day of anguish," and penning as a type of testimonial, "My dear Harry, my heart has been faithful to your memory." Whether or not she intended the allusion, she had kept the faith in large part by continuing to write.[52]

Beginning in 1835 Sedgwick published a spurt of works, including *The Linwoods*, *Home*, and *Tales and Sketches* in that year alone; *The Poor Rich Man, and the Rich Poor Man* in 1836; *Live and Let Live* in 1837; and *Means and Ends* in 1839. Harry was gone, but she still had Charles, Robert, and Theodore to support her and, increasingly, their offspring, as well as a number of acquaintances. And the struggle went on for a while in the same manner. In 1835, having nearly completed *The Linwoods*, she wrote to thank Louisa Minot for her encouragement. "I need it just now," she said, "for when I am on the verge of that irretrievable descent into the printer's hands I always feel utterly despondent." With all but a few alterations remaining to be done, she wrote to Charles's daughter, Catharine Maria, or Kate, only fourteen but already a regular correspondent, to say, "The conclusion now hangs heavy." It was clear why. The day before, her publisher, Harper, had asked her if " 'the book was heavy.' " As Sedgwick explained the term, one that a later generation would take as its own more than a century afterward, "heavy" in publishing parlance suggested the "amount of matter" in a book. To say the least, Harper's question weighed heavily upon Sedgwick's spirit: "I felt as if he were a bird of ill-omen uttering a prophecy." He had touched the insecure author and she had responded as she always had. "I feel at times utterly disheartened and *dismayed* about the thing," she wrote Kate. She asked Kate to keep her confidence. It had been her experience, she said, that whenever her expectations fell and she communicated as much to her friends, their expectations rose. For some reason they doubted her "sincerity."[53]

Sedgwick's literary productivity decreased radically after the early 1840s. She continued to produce short tales and miscellaneous pieces, but her next and, it turned out, last novel did not appear until 1857. In part she wrote less because she was getting older. Sedgwick was now in the second half century of her life. But she probably also wrote less because she was losing the support that had always been most crucial to her. All four of her brothers died before she did. Following Harry, Theodore died in 1839 and

Robert in 1841. Only Charles remained; his death occurred in 1856. It was fitting that Sedgwick finished and published her last novel after all her brothers had died. It was perhaps a final expression of gratitude for the confidence and support that had enabled her to write at all. The novel was titled *Married or Single?* Struggling to finish the book, she once again thanked Louisa Minot for her support, noting, "How few are left of those that made success dear to me!" And when she wrote to Kate in April 1857 to relate her final trial, there was an echo to the letter. She had "a miserable feeling of incompetence" for the task, and there were times, she said, when her "old desire of success" took over. The result was that she became "worried and anxious and utterly discouraged." Nevertheless, she was well and she was working hard. But "oh—dear Kate . . . when I think of all those whose hearts beat for me and more than mine at the publication of my early books." They were now "all gone," and when that thought occurred, her strength left her and "I *stop*."[54]

There remained a final coincidence that symbolized a last fulfillment of the legacy: Sedgwick's niece Kate married William Minot, Jr., the son of the William Minot to whom Harry had written more than thirty years before to reveal his sister's "secret." Shortly after the two-volume edition of *Married or Single?* was published, Minot, Jr., apparently wrote Sedgwick to communicate his favorable response. She replied by telling him that "your last letter was a greater blessing than you could have anticipated." It was not that she could "now personally care much for success or failure." But deprived of the "help and sympathy" that had always been hers before, she had been "bent with fear that there was some mistake." And even that did not stand as Sedgwick's last word. The very same day she wrote to Minot's wife, Kate, to say that she had arrived home exhausted late one evening to find the published volumes. In such a condition she "did not bear well the shock of seeing my books—really out—and at everyone's mercy." At age sixty-seven, the private woman of the home still found it a trial to be a literary domestic.[55]

As Sedgwick's life demonstrated, the desire of a woman to extend the limits of her prescribed sphere was blunted by her own deep inner restraints as much as by the disapproval of the society responsible for embedding those restraints. The desire could not be expressed forthrightly and instead turned inward, to be fused with what every woman was supposed to desire. Through the persona of Rosa Lee, the narrator and central character of her semiautobiographical novel *Meadow Brook*, Mary Jane Holmes, in as detached a fashion as any literary domestic, appears to toy good-humoredly with what were the twin focuses of her life: a vocation beyond the home, specifically both teaching and writing, and the female calling within the home, marriage. Paralleling Holmes's life, which began in Massachusetts and included a few years in Kentucky, the novel is set in both the North and South and is narrated primarily through the first-person voice of Rosa, who informs us that she is writing the tale while she tells it. Occasionally, and unaccountably, the voice changes to the third person, as if not only to mock the dual control of Rosa as narrator-writer but also to give the lie to the supposed detachment, and thus control, of the once-removed creator, Mary Jane Holmes herself. "Lie" may be stating the case too strongly, but one cannot forgo at least questioning Holmes's detachment.

Early in the novel Rosa jests with herself about the subject of marriage when, at fourteen years of age, she is confronted with "my first lesson in lovesickness" as she is smitten with a Doctor Clayton. Rosa dreams of becoming the good doctor's wife, but although he is attracted to her, he has ambitions for a more socially and financially advantageous alliance. Hopelessly lovesick, Rosa nevertheless mocks her malady as "a kind of disease which is seldom dangerous, but, like the toothache, very disagreeable while it lasts." For a period of weeks "I pined away," Rosa admits, but she can now see that her reaction was "wholly foolish and ridiculous." After all, if she had become the wife of Dr. Clayton instead of remaining Rosa Lee, "this book would undoubtedly never have been written." (The double entendre is the stock in trade, so to speak, of the literary domestics and this instance of it is most precious.) Rosa appears to have clearly chosen commitment to writing over commitment to being a wife. Had she married Dr. Clayton in place of writing a book,

> I should probably have been engaged in washing, dressing, scolding, and cuffing three or four little Claytons, or in the still more laudable employment of darning the *socks* and mending the *trousers* (a thing, by the way, which I can't do) of said little Claytons [sic] sire; who, by this time, would, perhaps, have ceased to call me "his Rose," bestowing upon me the less euphonious title of "she," or "my woman."

Almost immediately, however, one is led to question the authenticity of Rosa's and Holmes's irreverence regarding marriage and the intensity of her literary ambition. Allusion is made to the English writer Hannah More's "disappointment" in a relationship and her subsequent career as an author. From More's model Rosa takes "courage": "if I could not have the doctor I could at least write for the newspapers, and some day I might perhaps be able to make a *book*. This, I thought, would amply atone for the loss." Rosa has transformed her commitment to writing from her first choice of career to a substitute, a replacement for her true first preference, to wit, marriage to the good doctor.[56]

Later in the novel Rosa once again calls into question the blessedness of spinsterhood compared to the bliss of the marital state. By now Dr. Clayton has married and a new eligible bachelor, the cultured and wealthy Richard Delafield, steps forth. Rosa's desire to be a bride remains; only the identity of the potential groom has changed. Before Rosa's love is requited, however, she is forced to undergo yet another disappointment. Not realizing initially that Richard is indeed eligible, Rosa is led to believe that he is married. As a result, she says, "I made up my mind to be an 'old maid,'" and more, "with calm resignation I thought how much good I would do in the world, and how I would honor the sisterhood!" What exactly she will do and what resultant tribute she will bring to single women are both vague, although the implication is that as a teacher or a writer she will attempt by her example to unsully the name of spinsterhood. Nevertheless, when she discovers that Richard is actually unmarried, it appears that neither good deeds will be required nor tributes forthcoming; Rosa receives "comfort" from her newly acquired knowledge and "the state of single-blessedness appeared to me far less attractive" than before.[57]

Unfortunately, Rosa Lee's tribulations are not at an end. Thinking that her affection is unreturned, that Richard has no eye for her, Rosa again—for two paragraphs—affects a desire for the single state and ruminates upon a bridesmaid's career: "I should never marry—*that* was a settled point—I should teach school all my days, and by the time I was twenty-five (it seemed a great way off then) I should have a school of my own, 'Lee Seminary' I would call it." Apparently, however, hope for the single woman will respring eternal. The possibility that Richard might be smitten with Rosa is raised when he awkwardly hesitates to put his arm around her, a prospect that entices Rosa and threatens yet again her plans for a career beyond domesticity: "I was perfectly willing," thinks the eager Rosa, "to sit there with his arm around me! It might have dispelled all ideas of 'Lee Seminary' of which I was to be Principal!" This cavalier dismissal of the pedagogical profession that Rosa had embarked upon at age thirteen, as had Holmes, contradicts the solemn and inspired proclamations that appeared before the novel was fifty pages along:

> Of the many thousand individuals destined to become the purchasers of a copy of this work, a majority have undoubtedly been, or are still teachers, and of these many will remember the time when they fancied that to be invested with the dignity of a teacher was to secure the greatest amount of happiness which earth can bestow. Almost from my earliest remembrance it had been the one great subject which engrossed my thoughts, and frequently, when strolling down the shady hill-side which led to our schoolhouse, have I fancied myself the teacher. . . .

Now it appears that, for Rosa at least, an imagined embrace is far more engrossing than pedagogical dreams. It remains only for Holmes to complete the cycle and cease her cavalier treatment of woman's true destiny.[58]

Although the novel reaches its inevitable end, one last twist is in store for poor Rosa, when the good Dr. Clayton makes another appearance. A widower now, Dr. Clayton rediscovers his old ardor for Rosa and proposes marriage. Thinking that her love for Richard will never be returned, Rosa at first accepts. The night before the ceremony, however, she comes to her senses, recognizing that a marriage without love would be without blessedness: " 'I will not do this great wickedness and sin against both God and man.' " Such an outburst is not surprising. But in a novel replete with jest and good humor, the unadulterated zeal of Rosa's exclamation removes any doubt as to the nature of Holmes's convictions regarding marriage. In the end marriage is not a subject for comedy.[59]

At long last Rosa does of course marry Richard Delafield. What then is to be said for Rosa, who at age nine first expressed her "longings for fame," who as the child poet spoke of wanting "a *name* which should live when I was gone," a "name of which my mother should be proud"? What can be said is what Rosa says following the marriage, says with no sense of irony but with pride and happiness: "I began to realize that I was no longer Rosa Lee but *Mrs. Richard Delafield.*" Thus does Rosa—and Holmes—inadvertently mock the earlier expression of a desire for being, by disappearing into the being of another.[60]

And, finally, what of Rosa the writer? Having writ marriage large, Rosa can jest again about authorship. For Rosa it is "a subject over which I grow pale and 'nervous.' " Ironically again, *this* jest we take seriously, this sign of Holmes's failure of nerve, of her inability to promote herself as a serious writer. From the outset the reader knows that the book was written; thus it is no surprise to hear that "after many wakeful nights and restless days, after sick headaches, nervous headaches, and all kind of headaches, the plan was marked out for a story." The plan is to make herself the "heroine" of her novel and "give to the world as much of my history as I thought proper." Should she fail in the execution, says Rosa, begging the issue, she will at least be comforted by the assurance that there will be "people stupid enough to buy my book and possibly to like it, just because little Rosa Lee, who used to climb fences and hunt hen's eggs with them in her childish days, had written it." The unintended implication is that both the desire to write and the writing itself are childish. Inevitably Rosa refers to her writing of the book as "my secret," and describes the moment when "the secret was out, and with many blushes I plead guilty, and producing my manuscript, watched Richard while he read it." It is only fitting that Richard, solicitous of Rosa's health and concerned that she might be exhausted by the effort, asserts control over his wife who is a writer. Should the reader come across stylistic infelicities or flaws in the novel, says Rosa, "you may know it was there that Richard took my pen from my hand, or hid the inkstand." Rosa is not complaining, and neither is Holmes.[61]

To the reader who had written to ask why she had chosen to adopt a " 'pen-name,' " Mary Virginia Terhune had stated that she had little doubt that had her first manuscript been returned " 'with thanks' " then " 'Marion Harland' would never have been heard of more." It had been audacious enough for the secret writer simply to make an initial appearance before the world, and she might easily have been induced to withdraw. Actually *Alone*, Terhune's first novel, had been returned, and but for the intervention of her father the author probably would have retreated into her cocoon. E.D.E.N. Southworth admitted to the same inclination, writing in her preface to *The Haunted Homestead* that had her first story been rejected she would not have continued writing. And why should that not have been the case? As Harriet Beecher Stowe said, how could the "retired and domestic" woman presume? And what could she claim for that which she did produce? Certainly very little. As creators of culture the literary domestics were imbued with humility and were wont to deprecate their efforts, which remained in their own eyes "my little books" (Wilson), "my simple tales" (Terhune), "my little enterprises" (Gilman), "my humble literary labors" (Sedgwick). Sara Parton, as feisty as any of them, might have been expected to unceremoniously seize the honor. But Parton would say of her first novel, *Ruth Hall*, "I do not dignify it by the name of 'A novel.' " Rather, she wrote, she was "aware that it is entirely at variance with all set rules for novel-writing." For that reason she labeled her book a "primitive mode of calling." What that calling suggested was the effort to depict a simple truth to life. Sara "never fired a shot at random in the air," wrote her third husband, the biographer James Parton, adding that, "Something real invariably suggested the subject."[62]

To claim little was the familiar mode. "I try to be very natural," Mary Jane Holmes wrote to the publisher J. C. Derby, "and describe human nature as I have seen it." Terhune claimed to be at a loss to explain the wide appeal of her works: "Why they sold I frankly confess myself unable to decide," she said, although she was willing to offer as explanation that they "deal naturally with every-day life." Southworth insisted to the reporter for the *Washington Post*, "Everyone of my books was based upon the incidents in life that I saw, even the most improbable of them." And speaking of her prose works, Caroline Howard Gilman admitted to John S. Hart, "My ambition has never been to write a novel." Of the novels that she had written, Gilman said that anyone could see that "the story is a mere hinge for facts." Of her poetry, she told Hart, "I have never thought of myself as a poet, only a versifier." Obviously, for the woman to think of herself at all in relation to the palace of culture was to think less of herself. For the most part the literary domestics rejected the idea that they might be or could be creators. Wondering what to write in French in her secret journal, the youthful Susan Warner had decided forthwith to "write whatever comes into my head." In terms of their literary assessments of their own published works, the literary domestics rarely claimed a much more developed aesthetic.[63]

On occasion there was a glimmer of greater ambition. Sedgwick boasted little and, for example, was reluctant to claim more than that *Clarence* had "something to do with every day and present life." As for her dissatisfaction with anything that she wrote, it was, she believed, "the misfortune of a familiarity with fine works carrying your tastes so far ahead of your capacity." But in her preface to *Redwood* she did admit that "whenever the course of our narrative has thrown opportunities to our way, we have attempted some sketches of the character and manners of the people of this country." Even so, to her mind those opportunities could not amount to much. As she had said to brother Harry, she was hampered by "defective" education and "circumscribed" knowledge, and in her very first effort, *A New England Tale*, she had not been able to do more than describe "characters and scenes with which I was familiar." The suggestion was that she had soon "exhausted all that observation and experience that infuses life into a performance of this nature." Gilman stated that *Recollections of a Southern Matron* was "penned in the same spirit and with the same object, as the 'New England Housekeeper'—to present as exact a picture as possible of local habits and manners." The disclaimer fused with the claim when without guile Gilman eagerly assured her readers, "Every part except 'love passages' is founded in events of actual occurrence."[64]

Sedgwick actually wrote a remarkable story about (as its title, "Cacoethes Scribendi," indicates) a woman's incurable passion for writing (or did she mean scribbling?). In fact, the story is also about the passion's cure. The story was included in her 1835 collection, *Tales and Sketches*, on whose title page "by Miss Sedgwick" appeared; she returned to anonymity subsequently. Everything about the story has a "to be or not to be," an "is and is not" character. It is a story of fantasy that speaks of social reality. It is a striking story struck in seventeen short pages. The setting is a secluded village near the " 'literary emporium' " of Boston. It is remarkable only in that it is "duller even than common villages." The most significant cause of the village's dullness is what makes it in fact a remarkable setting. All of the eligible young men emigrate: "Literally, there was not a single young gentleman in the village." Moreover, "a peculiar fatality hung over this devoted place": whenever death struck, husbands were the victims. As a result, every woman in the village is either "a widow or maiden."[65]

Nevertheless, the village of single women is marked by a singular state of "health and cheerfulness," for all is not as it appears. Rather than being overcome by "the gloomy perspective of dreary singleness," the maidens and mothers are content, because they are confident that the maidens are "sure to be mated." "As soon as they found themselves *getting along*," Sedgwick tells us, the young men "loyally returned to lay their fortunes at the feet of the companions of their childhood." In addition, although it is true that there is not one eligible male in the village proper, there is on the outskirts a young man named Ralph Hepburn who is, naturally, a truly remarkable young man. He is physically blessed in all respects and is "full of good humour, kindheartedness, spirit, and intelligence." Ralph is also multitalented. He writes poetry, he sketches, and he sings, plays, and composes music. For good measure, he also manages in perfect order the farm that has been in his family for four generations. Not surprisingly, Ralph's prospects are "thorougly canvassed" by all of the "mothers, aunts, daughters, and nieces" of the village. Nevertheless, Ralph, "perhaps from sheer good heartedness," is reluctant to give to just one woman "the heart that diffused rays of sunshine through the whole village."[66]

The story is Ralph's, but is not. The story belongs to the widow Mrs. Courland and her daughter Alice—or it does not belong to them at all. Mrs. Courland is Ralph's aunt, and thus Ralph and Alice are cousins. Alice is the only daughter of Mrs. Courland, the only sister of five brothers, the only niece of three single aunts, the only granddaughter of a grandmother, and the only cousin of the village's "only beau," Ralph (there is no mention of Ralph's being a cousin to the five brothers). Although Alice is remarkable in her own way—"no girl of seventeen was ever more disinterested, unassuming, unostentatious, and unspoiled"—she and Ralph are only on "terms of cousinly affection," just as Ralph is simply the "kindest of nephews" to Mrs. Courland.[67]

It is when an incurable passion for writing strikes the village that the balance is altered, only not in the manner one might suspect. The passion strikes Mrs. Courland. She had in the past developed "literary taste" from her days in Boston, and has also had "literary ambition." Now she reads the *North American Review* from cover to cover and fancies only conversation that concerns books. But a narrow income and the demands of her children, most notably those of her five boys, have prevented her from "indulging her literary inclinatons; for Mrs. Courland, like all New England women, had been taught to consider domestic duties as the first temporal duties of her sex." It is when Ralph returns from Boston with two annuals that Mrs. Courland is beset. The annuals are actually a gift for Alice, and it is Alice who first reads them and is enthralled by a story of two "faithful lovers" that ends in marriage. " 'It ends beautifully,' " says Alice. " 'I hate love stories that don't end in marriage.' " However, it is the "fate" of Mrs. Courland that the annuals are "destined to fix," or so it would seem. She has been aware of "the native productions with which the press is daily teeming," and has even "felt some obscure intimations, within her secret soul, that she might herself become an author." And when she opens one of the annuals and discovers that she knows the authors whose names the publisher has attached to the previously "anonymous pieces," she is stunned: "If by a sudden gift of second sight, she had seen them enthroned as kings and queens, she could not have been more astonished." Mrs. Courland devours the annual: "All the art and magic of authorship was made level to her comprehension, and when she closed the book, she *felt a call* to become an author . . . as if it had been in truth, a divinity stirring within her." That evening she writes her first piece and in the morning presents it to her family and a few friends, "*her* public." Only Alice fails to applaud and to encourage her to publish it, because "she feared failure, and feared notoriety still more." Undaunted, Mrs. Courland submits her piece and it is published.[68]

The passion engulfs her like an incurable disease. She writes and writes and publishes and publishes. The disease also spreads, for Mrs. Courland, partly because she is mindful of the "pecuniary" advantages and mostly because she is desirous that others should share her calling, induces her three single sisters, the three aunts, to write as well. All are qualified, one in botany, one in education, and one (more than the others) in the "Solemn Hours" of spinsterhood, and all write and publish accordingly. The grandmother is urged to write also, but she refuses, saying her penmanship is poor and she never learned to spell, "no girls did in my time." Ralph, too, refuses, much to Mrs. Courland's regret, for she is convinced that Ralph can do anything. But "good sense and filial duty" restrain him, as they have in the past whenever Mrs. Courland has urged him to fulfill "the hankerings after distinction that are innate in every human breast."[69]

Alice is the last to resist the passion, that is, the disease. She is " 'gifted,' " says her mother, " 'well educated, well informed,' " and " 'everything necessary to be an author.' " But she is adamant in her refusal, for "she would as soon have stood in a pillory as appeared in print." Nevertheless, Alice is consumed by another form of this plague of writing, and she is "destined to be the victim of this cacoethes scribendi" in one form or another. If she will not write, then Mrs. Courland will write about her. Actually, Mrs. Courland writes about everyone and everything in the village. She now responds to every person and every event on two levels. Even regarding calamities in the village, including deaths and funerals, "she wept as a woman, and exulted as an author." Therefore, her own daughter's life can become her subject. In the past, men were authors and women simply wept, but, says Sedgwick, "times have changed. The lean sheaf is devouring the full one. A new class of sufferers has arisen, and there is nothing more touching in all the memoirs Mr. D'Israeli [Benjamin Disraeli] has collected, than the trials of poor Alice, tragicomic though they were." Thus Alice's private life becomes a *"public life."* Mrs. Courland's only regret is that Alice has "no lover whom she might introduce among her dramatis personae." She does think of Ralph as a possibility, but knowing that Alice would not like to be linked with him in print, the mother resists the temptation, for she has not been able to totally merge "the woman in the author."[70]

Everything else about Alice is written, however, and everybody, including the three aunts, joins in the writing. In fact, Alice becomes such a prominent figure in the village that she, ironically, becomes known as a "blue stocking." Therefore it seems to Mrs. Courland that Alice might as well become a writer herself. When Alice still refuses to take the step her mother accuses her of being afraid to actually be a bluestocking, and asks Ralph if that is not the sign of a "weakness" in her. " 'It would be a pity, aunt,' " says Ralph, " 'to put blue stockings on such pretty feet as Alice's.' " For the first time since the onset of the plague, Alice not only smiles, she blushes. That blush and smile signal the denouement.[71]

Mrs. Courland and her three sisters resort to one last stratagem to make Alice an author. They submit an old school composition of Alice's for publication and it is accepted. They are well aware of Alice's determination not to be an author. "But they fancied it was the mere timidity of an unfledged bird; and that when, by their innocent artifice, she found that her pinions could soar in a literary atmosphere, she would realize the sweet fluttering sensations they had experienced at their first flight." Then, Ralph appears to succumb to the passion, and immediately sits down at Mrs. Courland's desk to write *his* piece. As he writes, Alice's published composition arrives and mother and aunts excitedly show it to her. The gentle and modest Alice explodes: "She burst into tears of irresistible vexation, and threw the book into the blazing fire." The awkward moment is dispelled when Ralph rises from the desk and gives Mrs. Courland what he has written. It is only a single sentence, and in a poor hand. Mrs. Courland reads and rereads the sentence and, says Sedgwick, "She forgot her literary aspirations for Ralph and Alice—forgot she was herself an author—forgot everything but the mother." She rises and embraces Ralph and Alice as husband-and-wife-to-be—for what Ralph has written is his proposal of marriage. All that remains is for the village to celebrate the marriage, for Alice to become the "happy mistress" of Ralph's farm, and for mother and aunts to relinquish, "without a sigh, the hope of ever seeing her an Author." Thus did Sedgwick write, more than in any other of her fictions, about all of her selves.[72]

" 'I want a wife,' " says a man to a woman in Sara Parton's fictional sketch, "A Chapter on Literary Women," " 'I don't want a literary woman.' " Literary women, he sneers, are nothing but " 'nondescript monsters; nothing feminine about them. They are as ambitious as Lucifer; else, why do they write?' " Women write, answers the woman, " 'because they can't help it. . . . There is that in such a soul that will not be pent up—that must find voice and expression; a heaven-kindled spark, that is unquenchable; an earnest, soaring spirit, whose wings cannot be earth-clipped.' " While it is true, the woman reluctantly admits, that there are " 'vain and ambitious female writers,' " there are nonetheless women who remain deserving of " 'the holy names of wife and mother.' " For all of these women, the name was literary domestic, which they could not help being because they were earth-clipped.[73]

Part III

WARFARE WITHIN

9

The Crisis of Domesticity:
A Crisis of Being

The curious aside of three to four paragraphs suddenly appears well into Caroline Lee Hentz's last novel, *Ernest Linwood*. The flow of the narrative is in fact abruptly interrupted by a few detached offbeats. Hentz's words are given necessarily to the central female character of the novel, Gabriella Lynn, because Gabriella is also the narrator of the novel, the teller of her own tale. But Hentz's words break away from the character of Gabriella, just as the steady beat of the narrative is broken: "If I do not pass more rapidly over these early scenes, I shall never finish my book." Book? Gabriella is writing a book? This book? Yes, she is writing a book, but then again she is not. "Book!—am I writing a book? No, indeed! This is only a record of my heart's life, written at random and carelessly thrown aside, sheet after sheet, sibylline leaves from the great book of fate. The wind may blow them away, a spark may consume them. I may myself commit them to the flames. I am tempted to do so at this moment."[1]

The *moment* is suspended, out of context. From earlier pages we know that Gabriella has been ridiculed by her male teacher, whom she likens to an "Olympian king-god," for writing poetry, for having "diverge[d] from the beaten track." We know that she has become a secret writer of poetry and keeps a secret portfolio of poetry, although we have been told this only in passing. So a writer of a sort has been mentioned briefly in the book or novel. But even the image of that secret so-called writer recalled from the opening pages of the book is of a little girl, frightened and mortified, running from her classroom, running from Olympus, until she reaches a "by-path" in the woods that leads to her home and her mother. True, the thoughts of the little girl and the words of the narrator—the latter being the little girl writ older and thus the thoughts and words as one—tell us that when the little girl, Gabriella, reached the path in the woods, "The moment I turned into that path, I was supreme. It was *mine*. The public road, the thoroughfare leading through the heart of the town, belonged to the world." If there was a suggestion of hidden desire foreshadowing the secret writer, nevertheless the lasting impression was that the desire, rather than being nurtured, wilted in the woods. Wilted, because we were also told the following about the incident in the classroom:

> Perhaps some may think I am swelling small things into great; but incidents and actions are to be judged by their results, by their influence in the formation of character, and the hues they reflect on futurity. Had I received encouragement, instead of rebuke, praise instead of ridicule . . . I might have sang as well as loved. . . .

Presumably, then, Gabriella did not grow to sing, or write, and instead grew only to love, that is, to become a wife and mother and remain in woman's "beaten path" of domesticity. Until the sudden and suspended moment many pages later there has not been any reference whatsoever to the fact that Gabriella is either writing or has written the book that she is narrating. There has been no other reference in the novel thus far to the fact that she is or has been a writer for the world to read. There has been no preparation for the sudden momentary aside to that effect.[2]

But in that moment Hentz—nominally Gabriella—tells us that she once dreamed of a literary career, "once thought it a glorious thing to be an author." She had had fantasies, she says, of what it might be like to have "thousands" read her words, even more "to speak, and to believe that unborn millions would hear the music of those echoing words." She once dreamed, in other words, of what it would be like to be a creator of culture, to have power and influence, "to possess the wand of the enchanter, the ring of the genii, the magic key to the temple of temples, the pass-word to the universe of mind." But this writer of a book who has not written a book, has never written a book, paradoxically no longer dreams of being an author. Although, she says, she "once had such visions as these," she has them no longer, for "they are passed."[3]

In enigmatic language we are told why they have passed, with the implication that she possesses grave, hidden knowledge of the literary life, although the experience is not claimed directly. Why should she dream of writing, she asks, when to write is "to hear the dreary echo of one's voice return through the desert waste"? Why should she enter the exalted realm of culture, "enter the temple and find nothing but ruins and desolation"? Why should she write, spurred by the most moral of motivations, "lay a sacrifice on the altar, and see no fire from heaven descend in token of acceptance"? Indeed, why should she "stand the priestess of the lonely shrine, uttering oracles to the unheeding wind"? She does not literally claim to have been an author read by thousands, destined to be read by millions, but she asks, "Is not such too often the doom of those who have looked to fame as their heritage, believing genius their dower?" For herself, she no longer dreams. She will not entertain such a fate: "Heaven save me from such a destiny."

"Better the daily task," she says, "the measured duty, the chained-down spirit, the girdled heart."[4]

As abruptly as the aside began, it ends, and the flow of the narrative begins again; that is, the fictional character, Gabriella narrates in context again. Her narration picks up where it left off without skipping a beat, as if there had never been an interruption, and for a while, at least, Caroline Lee Hentz, the once-removed author, has apparently ceased obtruding upon the place of her character. As if unable to prevent herself, she has usurped the place of her narrator, delivered her curious messages out of the context of the novel, and once again relinquished the tale to her fictional persona. But by obtruding herself upon the pages of her novel, by momentarily usurping for a few paragraphs the place of her fictional narrator, Hentz has left her messages, her "oracles." And just as the ambiguous messages can be linked with the entire novel and, not incidentally, with the larger context of Hentz's personal life, so they must be placed in the even broader context of literary domesticity if one is to interpret their several meanings. What we have is yet another involuntary signature of a literary domestic. In yet another form, as if in a separate note placed between the covers of the bound volume, placed separately but left permanently, the woman writer has inadvertently suggested that something is amiss, that her experience has been somehow different from that of a male creator of culture. If she is a "priestess," hers is a throne without power. Hers is a voice without influence. But she is more than just a witness to an uncontrolled fate.

In the beginning, Henry Dwight Sedgwick had beckoned to his sister Catharine to enter the male palace of culture and there to take the imperial seat. "You shall reign sole empress," he had said in 1812, "of the *Poet's Corner.*" It was as if he had been appointed a spokesman more than a decade before the emergence of the American publishing industry and had been told to inform women of the coming opportunity to traverse the traditional boundaries of their lives and occupy and control a center stage in society. But he had said "empress" and not "emperor," and even if, as is likely, he had not meant more than was implicit in traditional discourse, it was a significant distinction, for it foretold the character of the reign of the literary domestics for the next half century and beyond.

As much as the literary domestics admired the male palace of culture and looked upward to Olympus, they admired it from afar, and from below, for they could not imagine that this or any of society's bastions of power were theirs to rule. As much as they secretly aspired to wear the emperor's clothes they balked at doing so, for fear that they would be ill-fitting. Women of inferior self- and social regard could not presume to leave their lowly sphere for the higher spheres of men. They could not bring their humble domestic selves to approach, let alone to enter, those revered gates. Their all but literal denial that they were artists was a confession that they truly were unable to envision themselves as emperors. In that respect the opportunity presented was illusory, and paradoxically, while the literary domestics ranked as best-selling authors in the literary marketplace throughout much of the nineteenth century, they never left the cloistered corridors of their domestic consciousness. Their published prose made them public figures, but their identities remained private and domestic. Regardless of their apparent success in a world beyond the home, they could not help but be bound and committed to woman's realm.

While writing *The Wide, Wide World*, Susan Warner admitted in a letter to her sister that she questioned just "how profitable this kind of musing is,—where memory furnishes material which imagination takes." For the literary domestics, the questions are: What were the boundaries and configurations of their imaginations? What material did mind and memory offer? And to what muse could and did these women look for motivation and direction? What was possible? In many ways they could not help but inform us of the answers. The literary domestic was an empress, not an emperor, and the empress had to wear her own clothes. The light and the shadows of fiction and reality were necessarily imposed upon each other. The boundary separating their fictional prose from the reality of their private domestic lives was problematical at best. Even in their wildest flights of fancy there was a symbolic if not always a self-evident or literal truth. When Robert Bonner told E.D.E.N. Southworth in 1878 that he had received letters from readers of the *New York Ledger* complaining that her fiction contained too many "unimportant details," Southworth could not hide her irritation, replying that there were a "half million readers who *being satisfied, say nothing*" but that those who did complain probably did so because "they are in a hurry to get to the secret mystery of the plot." Had Southworth been fully cognizant of the fact she might have said that the true "secret mystery" was in the "unimportant details," in the domestic details, at any rate, for the literary domestics made woman's destiny the core of their fiction and in large part wrote their fantasies as they dreamed and lived them. Southworth said as much ten years later when Bonner wrote her again on the same matter and she responded that "it is utterly impossible for me to write in any other way than my own." Southworth spoke more truth than she knew. The prose of the literary domestics defined them and meant more to them than they could say, and at times they could not help but say it and show it.[5]

The writer was a woman, and the mask of the writer revealed rather than hid the face of the woman. The two were one, inseparable. Secret female writers could not help but expose secretive women; indeed, there are signs that they sensed they were revealing themselves. Revelation often came fast on the heels of denial. In the introduction to *Eve's Daughters*, "Marion Harland" marvels that "my book is written!" "After the first page," she says, "I could not stay heart or pen," thereby telling us that her "heart" directs her "pen"; that is, Mary Virginia Hawes Terhune tells us, the woman writer who chose the initials of her first name and unmarried surname in order to formulate her lifelong pseudonym. Speaking of her life's prose, Caroline Howard Gilman, once writing as "Mrs. Clarissa Gray Packard, " at other times anonymously, and at others under her own name, says that for years she had "opened my heart to the public," with the result that the "throbs" of her heart had been "transparently unveiled"—this from the woman writer who caught herself in the inconsistency of writing about her life while refusing to say more for public print. And "Fanny Fern," that is, Sara Parton, at a time when only the few whom she wanted to know were aware of her true identity, had written an autobiographical novel, *Ruth Hall*, wherein Ruth Hall, herself a pseudonymous author by the name of "Floy," says of her book *Life Sketches* that only a few of her readers will know the extent to which "her own heart's history was there laid bare."[6]

There was no question that literary domesticity was an office enveloped in a mystique and trappings and characterized by a perspective and a language different from those of a male creator of culture. The heart was the symbol of woman, of woman's traditional being, of woman's involuntary life, of woman's nurturing, caring for, and living for others. The heart's record was the woman's revealed record of her life of domesticity, the only life she could have. In her mind the woman is not the emperor of culture. She is, by default, the empress of heart. And just as the woman is only nominally a writer, her tale is only superficially imaginary. What she relates is not a literal transcription of her domestic life but its inner truth. It is not so much the actual content, but the tone, the temper, the character of that life. No special talent is claimed. The woman cannot be a creator of culture because she has no choice of being; her destiny is not hers to shape or control. Secret aspirations notwithstanding, she cannot be a maker of books because her mind is made over by a life of domesticity. The circle of domestic concerns was a closed, absorbing, and consuming one for these women, and although literary careers obviously extended the boundaries of their lives, the focus of their beings revolved around and fastened them to a common and conventional ground. They became popular writers, but the inner compass of their lives held them to a familiar course. By a process peculiar to themselves they could only involuntarily and in ironic fashion impose themselves upon the alien male role of published writer. Unable to separate themselves from domestic callings governed by the interests and behavior of others, the domestic and the literary became one, or rather the domestic absorbed the literary and the private woman of the home intruded upon the pages of a public literature.[7]

In effect, the literary domestics exposed their own tale simply by being literary domestics. The absorption of the literary by the domestic was testimony to the restrictive character of their lives, of the limitations of their beings, of what they could imagine in life. They could write only about the heart's record of domesticity because that was all that they knew. It was their only subject because that was the only subject of their lives. The tale of literary domesticity, of secret writers and secret histories of the heart, apparently innocent and innocently told, inevitably revealed the secret tale of the denial and control of the heart, of the fundamental denial and control of woman's being. Secret writers inadvertently revealed the secret subjugation of female lives, told of the dependence of female minds and female beings. The compromised struggle of the woman to be a writer reflected the compromised struggle of the woman. Rather than an extension of female lives, literary careers extended the plane of woman's domestic struggle. Finding themselves in a new role, the literary domestics nevertheless could not discard a traditional identity, and literary domesticity represented a new, public telling of old, private tales.

In a sense Caroline Lee Hentz has no choice but to tell the "record of my heart's life" in *Ernest Linwood*. Hentz, viz. Gabriella, is not the creator of an imaginary tale, and her struggle, her obsession strictly speaking, has not been that of a creator of culture. She implies that she has experienced the life of a writer while simultaneously denying that she has in fact experienced it, because she is actually telling about the woman's struggle of domesticity. Hers is a crisis of domesticity, which in essence constitutes the woman's crisis of life. She does not write about having entered the "temple" of culture because she is actually speaking of the temple of domesticity, a temple she has never left. And because she is telling or writing of life within that temple she does in fact hear her "dreary echo" reverberating within those walls—she has found "ruins and desolation" within, and she has made a "sacrifice" of her being that has not been acknowledged. Indeed, within that temple of domesticity she is and has been "the priestess of a lonely shrine," and she utters the "oracles," issues the "sibylline leaves" of what she believes to have been the woman's heart's record since antiquity, the record of "the daily task, the measured duty, the chained-down spirit, the girdled heart." Rather than a willed creation, her life has been consumed by the woman's "great book of fate."

Hentz's oracles become increasingly clear, at least to us. The degree to which the literary domestic understood her own wisdom is always open to question. Writing from within, consumed from within, she is not a detached authority. But her oracles become clearer with each added intrusion, as she cannot help but continue to intrude upon her tale. "What am I writing?" Hentz suddenly asks—and asks herself—approximately a hundred pages later, again interrupting the flow of her, nominally Gabriella's narrative. At times, she claims, she has to "throw down the pen" and exclaim to herself in exasperation, " 'It is all folly, all verbiage.' " It is not easy to look within oneself and know what one sees. She believes that what she has to relate is important. " 'There is a history within worth perusing,' " she says to herself, " 'but I cannot bring it forth to light.' " She turns " 'page after page with the fingers of thought,' " thinking in relation to those words from within that " 'it seems an easy thing to make a transcript of these for the outward world.' " But she senses that it is not easy at all. "Easy! it requires the recording angel's pen to register the history of the human heart." What she means to say is that it is the "recording angel's pen" that is required, not that of the lord of creation, because she is writing the history of the *woman*'s heart. Her destiny has been to love, not to sing. The "critic," she acknowledges, may say that it is an easy thing; " 'only follow nature, and you cannot err,' " he says, follow nature to record that "small portion" the writer wishes to relate. But, she responds, the writer is a woman, and "that portion be of love." It is a portion which the lord of creation, the "cold philosopher," disdains as fit only for "romantic maids and moonstruck boys." But for woman "love is the great motive principle of nature, the burning sun of the social system." In the view of the literary domestic, those who would "praise a writer for omitting love from the page which purports to be a record of life" would praise God for creating a "sunless" world.[8]

Hentz has loved, and to an extent is writing of the love of "romantic maids," but it is a love that must lead to the love sanctified by God, that is, marital love. Just at the heart's record is a record of the woman's life of domesticity, so the record of the true woman's love is that of marital love, the love of her "social system." "Woe to her," writes Hentz, "who, forgetting this heavenly union, bathes her heart in the earthly stream, without seeking the living spring whence it flows; who worships the fire-ray that falls upon the altar, without giving glory to him from whom it descended." Woe to the woman who does not recognize and pursue a higher love. The second intrusion of Hentz's is ending, but not before it has become clearer that the "altar" of the priestess is the marital altar and not that of Apollo. Again, this is not a book but a record of the heart's life, a testimonial to the woman's mind and heart made over by a life of domesticity. Because she faltered before a dream of literary majesty, hers became a domestic dream, and the dream denied was that of the wife and mother in a state of marital bliss. The grave, hidden knowledge she possesses, her heart's record to relate, is that of the "girdled heart." The priestess is tempted to commit her record to the "flames" because her tale is of the crisis of domesticity, the woman's crisis of life.[9]

The third intrusion provides the third clue to the secret writer's secret history of the heart. At this stage of the novel, Gabriella has decided to marry the man for whom the novel is named, Ernest Linwood. The courtship is concluded and, writes Hentz, or says Gabriella, "I have now arrived at a period of my life, at which the novelist would pause,—believing the history of woman ceases to interest as soon as an accepted lover and consenting friends appear ready to usher the heroine into the temple of Hymen." Hymen, of course, was the Greek god of marriage, and there can be no further doubt which temple encloses Hentz. Nor can there be any doubt which temple encloses the secret of woman's life. Says the author-narrator, "There is a *life within life*, which is never revealed till it is intertwined with another's." To write of the dream of domesticity is automatically to write of the reality of domesticity. As a woman she must tell or write about the life that shrouds the dream. For the woman, "In the depth of the heart there is a lower deep, which is never sounded save by the hand that wears the *wedding-ring*. There is a talisman in its golden circle, more powerful than those worn by the genii of the East."[10] She is not a creator of culture but a woman of the home, of the marital circle, of the circle of domesticity. In writing about the controlled fate of woman, the domination of her being, Hentz embodies her own thwarted marital dream.[11]

Hentz's intrusions, relative to the rest of the novel, are merely the most overt expressions of the fact that the entire novel is an embodiment of the domestic absorbing the literary, of the actual record of a woman's life coalescing with the imaginary parts of the novel. On 20 February 1836, at Locust Dell outside Florence, Alabama, twelve years after her marriage to Nicholas Marcellus Hentz, and before his illness led to her becoming a full-time writer, Hentz received a copy of a Philadelphia newspaper that contained a poem of hers titled (ironically) "Reubens and the Unknown Artist." At the time, she noted in her diary that "I find there is one link that still binds me to the great world." But what governed her in her private world and in effect separated her from the wide world was something else. Two months later she wrote in the same diary, "I have concentrated all the feelings that were once diffused in a measure over the world—in one object and placed all of my earthly happiness there." There could be little else of significance in her life when "I have anchored all my hopes on one goal—and my heart is filled with constant fear lest the anchor will fail." Hentz was talking about her marriage, not a literary career.[12]

In writing about what she recorded as the crisis of the moment in her life, Hentz was also illustrating generally the nature of the woman's crisis of life or being. From the beginning, all of the woman's hopes and fears were anchored to a life of domesticity, to a life as wife and mother in the home. From the beginning, the female will to express her being, to shape her life, was directed to a life of domesticity. In that sense, the confrontation of her will and her certain destiny guaranteed for woman an ongoing crisis of life, an ongoing crisis of domesticity. Governed and absorbed by the needs, demands, and actions of others, the particular manifestation of that crisis— the shape of the crisis of the moment—was necessarily related to and dependent upon the lives or beings of others. As it happened, Hentz's crisis of the moment was an ongoing one as well.

The key to his wife's hopes and fears, Nicholas Marcellus Hentz became as well the catalyst for Hentz's personal crisis of domesticity. Charles, the Hentzs' son who became a physician, described his father in an unpublished autobiography and in a series of diaries as possessing "a very affectionate, kind disposition." But Nicholas was also, Charles said, "one of the most nervous, jealous, suspicious characters that ever lived." And just as later in life Nicholas became more and more the victim of periods of "mental depression" and was rendered a "miserable invalid" to such an extent that his wife had to become the family's sole provider, it was Charles's belief that "from the beginning of their married life, my mother's happiness was constantly crossed and most bitterly tried by his most unreasoning and unhappy jealousy of disposition." His mother could not attend any social gathering, he claimed, or later mention in his father's presence "the polite attention of any gentleman without undergoing afterward a stormy ordeal." It did not help matters, said Charles, that his mother possessed "one of the most lovely, sunny dispositions that ever existed," that she was "charming in person and conversation," and that she was therefore "always a centre of attraction wherever she went." The stir created by her person "inevitably, always excited my poor dear father's jealous temperament to frenzy." Charles's characterization of his parents' relationship was based at least partly upon his own observations. "My earliest recollections," he wrote, "are associated with scenes of this kind, to which I was often a bewildered and frightened listener." By no means lacking in sympathy toward his "poor dear father," Charles noted that Nicholas himself was aware of his problem: "he sometimes, especially in later years of his life, spoke of his infirmity and spoke of it as a disease."[13]

In her novel Hentz modeled the character of Ernest Linwood upon her husband. For Gabriella's "heart's record," for the history of her "girdled heart," Hentz drew heavily upon her own "great book of fate." The marital web that had ensnared Hentz was transparently recorded in the pages of Gabriella's book. As the narrator of her life, Gabriella tells of her early knowledge of woman's certain destiny. Her mother Rosalie, near death, says to her, " 'If you live to years of womanhood, and your heart awakens to love,—as, alas, for woman's destiny it will,—then read my life and sad experience, and be warned by my example." Rosalie is referring to the secret manuscript of *her* life that she has written for Gabriella's eyes only, and left for her daughter to read after her death. Thus does the former " 'prodigy,' " Rosalie, " 'the *dream-girl*,' " the reader of " 'impassioned romance[s],' " who wrote that her girlhood was a period when " 'my heart was slumbering, and my soul unconscious of life's great aim,' " speak and write and warn of what must be the aim of another dream-girl's life. The prophecy is as unerring as the warning is unavailing. By the time Gabriella reads her mother's manuscript, appropriately titled "My Mother's History" and sanctified by Gabriella as "my mother's *heart*, for so the manuscript seemed to me," her own woman's heart has long since awakened. The first time a young man tells her that she is "beautiful" she is ensnared: "for one moment a triumphant consciousness swelled my bosom, a new revelation beamed on my understanding,—the consciousness of woman's hitherto unknown power,—the revelation of woman's destiny." But her heart has been "warned" as well, for in her moment of triumph she glimpses defeat: on cue, before she has even met him, she glances at a portrait of Ernest Linwood and reads in his face "either a history of past disappointment, or a prophecy of future suffering."[14]

Hopes and fears, romantic dreams and grim realities alternately capture and imprison Gabriella throughout the entirety of the novel. Following her mother's death, Gabriella is informally adopted by the cultured and wealthy Mrs. Linwood, Ernest's mother, and brought to live in the widow's splendid but foreboding mansion, Grandison Place. Both the home and the person of Mrs. Linwood conjure up dreams and nightmares in the consciousness of Gabriella. It is Mrs. Linwood who speaks from both experience and prophecy and who tells Gabriella that she knew beforehand that the heroine would come to love Ernest: " 'It is your destiny,' " she informs her. But she also tells Gabriella that her " 'dream of love' " has to end in a " 'day of awakening.' " Woman's dreams of marital bliss must be cast aside, Mrs. Linwood admonishes, because " 'God never intended their realization in this world.' " Just prior to her marriage to Ernest, Gabriella reads the manuscript of her mother's heart's history. Naturally, the particular history also tells the universal destiny. Having feared otherwise, Gabriella learns that the union of her parents was sanctified in marriage. She swoons in gratitude, repeating to herself the words of her mother's text, " 'friend—lover—husband,' " and exclaims, " 'God of my mother, forgive my dark misgivings.' " But she learns as well that her father, perhaps a bigamist and perhaps now dead, may have abandoned her mother and left her to die from the proverbial broken heart. In the tale within a tale, there is a "*life within life;*" in the "golden circle" of the "*wedding-ring*" there is indeed a "lower deep." Overcome, this time in grief, Gabriella literally falls on her mother's grave, wondering, "Why should I wish to live?"[15]

She will "wish to live" in order to endure her own circle of matrimony. When Ernest first encounters Gabriella in a lighted glen, she is immediately conscious of "a shadow passed over the sunshine." From that moment light and shadow provide a running metaphor for "future suffering." Like Nicholas Marcellus Hentz, the French emigré, scientist, linguist, and educator, Ernest Linwood is cultured, erudite, and accomplished. Like Nicholas, Ernest is also at the mercy of a possessive, jealous temperament and, like Nicholas, he knows it. Early in their courtship he warns Gabriella, " 'I am naturally suspicious and distrustful.' " There is also a suggested but hidden warning when Ernest declares his love and asks Gabriella to marry him. At first she hesitates, telling him that her mother's past may have disgraced her name and suggesting that he read the " 'history of my parentage.' " Ernest, however, dismisses her qualms. " 'What do I care for the past?' " he says. It is their future together that concerns him, and his words suggest that such a future should concern her as well. " 'Talk not of a clouded name. Will not mine absorb it?' " he asks rhetorically. " 'I ask for nothing but your love,—your exclusive, boundless love,—a love that will be ready to sacrifice everything but innocence and integrity for me,—that will cling to me in woe as in weal, in shame as in honor, in death as in life. Such is the love I give, and such I ask in return.' " And forthwith he demands more than asks, " 'Is it mine? . . . Is this love mine?' " Gabriella narrates that the answer as demanded is forthcoming. Gabriella is totally his. Gabriella also foreshadows what else is forthcoming: "Let woman tremble rather than exult, when she is the object of a passion so intense. The devotion of her whole being cannot satisfy its inordinate demands." She adds, "Not then was this warning suggested. To be wildly, passionately loved, was my heart's secret prayer. . . . Such was the dream of my girlhood."[16]

Mrs. Linwood adds her more direct warning, and before Gabriella is married her girlhood dreams are transformed into the tempered hopes of womanhood. Echoing Charles Hentz's description of his father, Mrs. Linwood tells Gabriella that Ernest is " 'just, generous, and honorable,' " but that " 'he has qualities fatal to the peace of those who love him,—fatal to his own happiness; suspicion haunts him like a dark shadow,—jealousy, like a serpent, lies coiled in his heart.' " Even before their marriage, Gabriella sees evidence of Ernest's distrust, of his jealousy, whereupon she and Mrs. Linwood have yet another exchange of confidences. The elder dispenses wisdom and the younger takes it to heart. Worried that Gabriella's passionate love for Ernest will prove a fatal catalyst, that she " 'will love him too well for your *own* peace,—too well for *his* good,' " Mrs. Linwood admonishes her that " 'it is not by the exhibition of idolatrous affection, that a wife secures a husband's happiness. It is by patient *continuance* in well-doing that she works out the salvation of her wedded peace.' " When the " 'young girl' " marries a man she believes to be the model of perfection, and " 'after marriage' " discovers his faults, the woman must yet keep to her " 'wedded vows' " and " 'fold over her woman's heart the wings of an angel. She must look up to God, and be silent.' " In short, she must bow down " 'in the spirit of gentleness and Christian love' "—even when the husband's " 'cold, inscrutable glance, the chilled and altered manner, the suspicion that walketh in darkness' " tries the " 'strength of woman's love.' " Gabriella indeed takes Mrs. Linwood's meaning, if not her warning, takes it entirely. " 'You have roused me to nobler views, and given existence a nobler aim,' " she responds. " 'I blush for my selfishness. I will henceforth think less of being happy myself, than of making others happy; less of *happiness* than *duty*; and every sacrifice that principle requires shall be made light, as well as holy by love.' " Gabriella is finally ready for marriage, even if she cannot be prepared for this marriage.[17]

In 1830 Nicholas Hentz wrote an apologetic, pleading letter to Caroline. His apology was for scenes past; his plea was for forgiveness and understanding in light of the intensity of his attachment to her. "I am a cross-grained one, but I am sure you don't know how I love you all," he said. What he meant was that he was certain that she did not realize how he loved *her*. "Oh—*home*," he said, "that word makes all the chords of my heart vibrate," adding, "and *you* are home." If only she could know, he wrote, "how much I can love, and how much I do love, you might perhaps understand better, some of my ways." In *Ernest Linwood* Ernest offers similar apologies, similarly worded, and pleads for forgiveness and understanding on the part of Gabriella after the inevitable scenes that follow their marriage. He cannot bear even the thought of another male paying her the least attention, and when attention is shown or he suspects the slightest interest, jealous rage rules the day, rules him and rules Gabriella. Incident and eruption follow one another, all leading to Ernest's apologies. "'Gabriella, I am a wretch,— deserving your hatred and indignation,'" he moans on one occasion. "'I have insulted your innocence, by suspicions I should blush to admit.'" But what he really wants to say is, "'Love, too strong for reason, converts me at times into a madman. I do not ask you to forgive me; but if you could conceive of the agonies I endure, you would pity me, were I your direst foe.'" And later, after still another wild scene, Ernest apologizes and pleads with her again, saying, "'O, Gabriella! you can have no conception of what I suffer, while I writhe in the tempter's grasp.'"[18]

Although Gabriella is always in effect guiltless, she is wary of Ernest and not always completely open with him, which stirs his suspicions and fuels his rage. Remembering Mrs. Linwood's admonition "'You have no right to complain [and must] endure all,'" she resolves to forbear. And she embraces the brief intervals of calm and repose, thinking them happiness. "Never had I been so supremely happy, as since my reconciliation with Ernest," she muses on one occasion. "Never have I loved him so entirely, or felt such confidence in my future happiness." But self-deception is necessary to withstand pain. For there is pain. "'Let me be loved,'" she pleads once to no one in particular, and later pleads with Ernest to "'save me,—my husband, save yourself from a doom so dreadful... if I were only *trusted*, only *believed*.'" And there is even rebellion, protest. "My happiness was the first desire of his heart," she says of Ernest, "the first aim of his life; but I must be made happy in *his* way, and by his means." His touch is "gentle, warm, heart-thrilling," but it is as well "the hand of Procrustes; and though he covered the iron bed with the flowers of love, the spirit sometimes writhed under the coercion it endured." But despite the pain, and despite the rebellion, she must always resolve to endure and to submit, and she always does both. To one woman who has earlier described her as "'the model wife of the nineteenth century,'" but who eventually expresses indignation at Ernest's unchanging behavior and wonderment at her endurance, submission, and forgiveness, Gabriella responds by saying, "'He is my husband; and I love him in spite of his wayward humors, with all the romance of girlish passion, and all the tenderness of wedded love.'"[19]

Like the heroine she created, Hentz saw her ardor and devotion severely tested. Certainly the most dramatic as well as the greatest challenge occurred in the middle of the 1830s. What Nicholas would describe later in life as his "disease" had reached an acute stage during the family's residence in Cincinnati, Ohio. Having gone there to teach in a female seminary, he and Caroline also became actively involved in the city's social and literary life, in particular Daniel Drake's circle, to which Harriet Beecher Stowe also belonged. Charles Hentz would later recall that his mother was "a much admired member of the circle." That fact coupled with "father's unfortunate temperament was the cause of many an unhappy scene between them."[20]

A most unfortunate and unhappy incident in the summer of 1834 led to what Charles called a "fearful culmination," the resolution of which was the Hentzs' permanent departure from Cincinnati. The cause was a familiar one, in substance if not degree. According to Charles, "a gentleman who was a prominent member of this literary circle, by the name of Col. King (I believe) carried his admiration of Mother too far." Specifically, Colonel King sent a note to Hentz that she obviously found disconcerting. Rather than simply returning it without an answer, Hentz was apparently planning a secret reply censuring the man's conduct. Her proposed clandestine action was prompted, said Charles, by "her dread of the effect a disclosure of the matter would have upon father." Hentz's efforts, however, were unavailing because, as Charles recalled, Nicholas

> suspected something wrong and laid a trap for mother—he took his gun and pretended that he was going across the river—; he returned after a short absence—and stealthily entered his room; where she was bending over his desk, writing to this gentleman—; preparing to return his importunate note— Father seized upon this in a paroxysm of passion—; sent for Col. K. and a most turbulent, dreadful scene ensued—Mother fortunately found means to send for Dr. Drake instantly—; the good doctor came immediately, whilst father was upbraiding poor mother, and attacking Col. K.—; he slapped him in the face, and I suppose behaved like a maniac—. . . .

The "dreadful scene" precipitated an equally "dreadful emergency." The end of the Hentzs' marriage appeared imminent, but the intervention of Dr. Drake prevented the rupture. Instead, the school was immediately closed, and almost as immediately the family departed Cincinnati. From there the Hentzs journeyed to Florence, Alabama, in June of 1834. It was a journey, Charles remembered, that produced "a sad scene between mother and father," in which a "weeping" Hentz and her husband considered separation. "Young as I was," said Charles, "it affected me profoundly." Again, it was in Florence that Hentz wrote in her diary of her "hopes and fears," hopes anchored in her life of domesticity, fears generated by her particular crisis of domesticity.[21]

The note in *Ernest Linwood* comes not from an admirer of Gabriella's but from her father, who has appeared on the scene from out of nowhere.

Motivated by the same fear of an intensely jealous husband, Gabriella decides to conceal the note and a later meeting with her father, and she too is caught in the deception. Ernest's wrath and scorn know no limits. The wife who has already been less than open with him is now, he thinks, compounding her betrayal with falsehood: " 'Do you expect me to believe that that bold libertine who made you the object of his unrepressed admiration was your father?' " Eventually, however, Ernest does believe Gabriella and follows the already familiar pattern, pleading for her forgiveness. The stage, then, is set for the cycle to begin once more, as indeed it does, climaxing with an episode in which Ernest not only wields a gun but fires it and shoots a man. Concerned that readers might be skeptical, might "say such scenes never occurred in the actual experiences of wedded life," Gabriella, or Hentz, declares unequivocally "that I am drawing the sketch as faithfully as the artist, who transfers the living form to the canvas."[22]

By the end of the novel, after fantasy has had its day, after multiple deviations of plot and subplots too numerous to mention, calm and resignation are achieved. As Gabriella the narrator, now one with Gabriella the character, phrases it, "We love each other as fondly, but less idolatrously." Both husband and wife are chastened, and for both the fires have cooled. There is a child, of course, named Rosalie after Gabriella's dead mother, and, says Gabriella, "Its fairy fingers are leading us gently on in the paths of domestic harmony and peace." As for the "history" of Rosalie the mother, her name has been posthumously cleared, for her husband, Gabriella's presumed-to-be-dead father, has not only been found, but the dual charges of bigamy and abandonment have been proved erroneous. Mysteries, misunderstandings, and mistaken identities were at fault and all has been cleared, including his name and his character. The father cannot have his wife in happy life but he has her in blissful memory, just as Gabriella and Ernest are "anchored at last in a more blissful haven."[23]

Hentz may not have written her novel "at random," but in a sense she "recorded" it without choice, for the issue of Gabriella's "record of my heart's life" dominated Hentz's own life. The incident in Cincinnati symbolized the issue of her life. On Sunday morning, 7 February 1836, in Florence, Alabama, while listening to the singing of birds, Hentz recalled a previous Sunday morning shortly after they had settled in Florence. She remembered hearing "the first notes of the bluebird," she wrote in her diary, "but it had *then* no music to my ears." Rather, "the chords of my heart rung to discordant sounds. Let me be grateful to my Maker that it is now tuned to greater harmony."[24]

But the degree to which harmony ruled within Hentz is questionable. The arrival two weeks later of the Philadelphia newspaper containing her poem served only to remind Hentz of her forced isolation. And there were too many unpleasant memories, memories that would not go away because they were linked tightly to the present. Two days after the poem arrived she recalled having attended years before a Washington Birthday Ball in Boston. Now, she wrote, she found herself "in this secluded spot, convinced of the emptiness of all those glittering vanities." Was she any happier now? "No!— far less so—Had I always valued the blessing allotted me in the domestic circle as I now do, I might still have mingled with a world I no longer love too well." Two more weeks passed and she noted, "My spirit is gloomy and the night cloud is on my soul." The note-passing, gun-toting episode in Cincinnati was still plaguing her: "Must the consequences of one trans-gression follow us through the pilgrimage of life?" The memory remained a part of her present daily life of domesticity: "Must we carry to the altar of duty our purified and still burning affections, and meet there but cold approval and toleration—Yes! all is unavailing but Heaven will guide the path of the erring!" Obviously, memory and guilt were still hers, in part because Nicholas would not forget, either. Even death (the death of "Col. K"?) had no effect. "I dared to hope, " she wrote, "that resentment would die over the coldness and darkness of the tomb." But the crisis of her life had predated Cincinnati and it would last beyond the present. One night less than a week later, after nursing one of her sick children until two o'clock in the morning, she continued to document her obsession: "Oh! how the visions of the past dim and awful floated round me, as I sat by the fading embers, in the loneliness of the midnight hour." She knew what she feared: "That past, I fear, which will ever more give color to the future."[25]

A month and a half later Hentz wrote about anchoring all of her hopes and fears in her marriage. She had no other choice. She had done so long before. Her circumstances were merely made more vivid in the present. Even a "very complimentary" letter from one of her readers asking to correspond with her failed to touch Hentz. "Such things," she wrote, "do not affect me now—I do believe there is a radical change in me." Her hopes remained centered on one thing. On 26 May she noted in her diary that Nicholas had given her "a pair of beautiful little flower vases." He had written " 'Remember me' " on them, and she recorded, "I value the gift as highly as any that was made in the days of courtship." And her fears remained centered on one thing as well. Five days later, after they had received an invitation to dine with neighbors, she confessed, "There is nothing I dread the sight of, so much as an invitation to a party." When this invitation arrived it seemed to her "as if a ghost presented itself to my view, and I must say *Avaunt*." Later that summer, after attending a lecture, she reflected on events since she had last heard the speaker three years before in Springfield, Ohio. "Oh, that it were as in time past," she wrote, and her words were those that would be echoed in *Ernest Linwood* almost twenty years in the future: "Save me—Oh! Thou who hast created me, from this nightmare of the soul—this— gnawing of the heart." What she prayed for was the calm stillness of domestic tranquility. "Let me not be impious to wish that I had never been born," she wrote. "I pray but for indifference—Let principle remain—but let feeling be taken away." The longing seemed to be for that same quiet haven. It was the best she could hope for.[26]

While in Florence, Alabama, Hentz also wrote to Elizabeth Peabody claiming that the relationship with Nicholas had been "a romantic match" from the outset, and that "the romance has not worn off." That was a different twist, for the need, apparently, on that day or in this letter, was to express hopes rather than to give way to fears, to dream rather than to despair. "I do not think," she continued, "I ever appreciated his excellent qualities of the head and heart half as much as I do now." Cincinnati did not go unmentioned. Instead, it was remembered from a different perspective. "While in Cincinnati, in a constant round of exciting visits, in the midst of all the fascinations of society," she acknowledged, "I did not feel so entirely my dependence on him for happiness." The separation from society was not unnoticed, but she spoke of the romance of solitude rather than the imprisonment of isolation, saying, "Here where there is so much less to interest me abroad, I have reason to lift up my heart in gratitude to heaven, who has blessed me with a companion who becomes every day more dear to my affections." And then there was the ultimate irony when she enthused, "Does not this prove that the most romantic and sudden attachments are not the most fleeting?" If her married life did not prove that love was eternal, obviously Hentz hoped that her letter would.[27]

How many more crises within the crisis occurred in the last two decades of Hentz's life with Nicholas is unknown. But apparently his "nervous, jealous, suspicious" nature was rendered dormant only after he became a complete invalid in the late 1840s. On 5 March 1851, early in the period during which Hentz would produce out of necessity the bulk of her literature, she wrote to a Mrs. Stafford discussing both her husband's illness and her relationship with her friend and literary advisor Dr. Wildman. "I will say to you frankly," she confided to Mrs. Stafford, "just as I would speak if I were sitting by your side, in that dear chamber of yours and holding your hand in mine, that the restless feelings which, you know, prevented Mr. H from enjoying my *male* friends, seem to have subsided during his illness." Caroline continued, "He seems so distressed on my account, that the support of the family has fallen on me, that he rejoices in anything that contributes to my happiness, from whatever source it flows."[28] Hentz had been forced to turn her "brains to gold," but at least her heart had found a haven. *Ernest Linwood* was published by three different houses in 1856. It was issued first by Boston's J. P. Jewett and by New York's Sheldon, Blakeman. Both published a second edition that same year, along with Cleveland's Proctor and Worthington. In all of these cases the title was simply *Ernest Linwood*. Thirteen years later, in 1869, thirteen years after Hentz's death, T. B. Peterson of Philadelphia reissued the novel under the title, *Ernest Linwood: or, The Inner Life of the Author*.

The mind was made over. Essentially, the life was without choice. For a woman nurtured for a predetermined life of domesticity, marriage entailed both an immanent and a lasting crisis of being. Immanent, because the "moment" of marriage promised the lasting resolution of her life, the absorption of her being. Lasting, because within each "moment" of her marriage there lay the seeming potential of the immanent fulfillment of her life's dreams or, willy-nilly, the realization of her life's worst fears. Everything, in short, was at stake. "Marriage is such a momentous affair," Mary Virginia Terhune explicitly told her female readers in *Eve's Daughters*, "such a portentous All to us that we tremble at the remotest menace of peril which may wreck hope and heart." In choosing "the partner of your heart, your home, your life," the woman must take care, she said, because "the reality is a beautiful, yet an awful thing. It is putting your life out of your own keeping."[29]

Shortly before her own marriage to the clergyman Edward Payson Terhune, before putting her life beyond her keeping, Terhune had her own expectations and a sense of what she was supposed to think, feel, and say. She had as well her own apprehensions, and she could not prevent herself from expressing them. Twenty-five years of age in 1856, Terhune wrote a letter to her friend Virginia Eppes Dance, a letter she included in the autobiography published half a century later, in 1910, when she was eighty. What is interesting is the part of the original letter that Terhune chose to omit from her autobiography. Each version unwittingly projects Terhune at one and the same time as sociologist and personal specimen of her life. The sociologist charted the patented course of her past to her present life. The person remembered a pleasurable past, acknowledged a joyful present, looked sanguinely to a hopeful future. But she appeared to tremble at the absence of volition. Given past and present, she seemed to be saying to "dear Eppes," it was difficult to comprehend that not only was there to be a "change" in her life, but that that change would surely come in "one little fortnight." "Here, in the home of my girlhood," she wrote, "where all else is unaltered, and I seem welded, as it were, into the household chain, I cannot believe that my place is so soon to be vacant." The juxtaposition of a set past and present and a set future pressed "Brain and heart" alike with "crowding thoughts and emotions that I wonder how I preserve a composed manner."[30]

And yet having read only the version of the letter presented in Terhune's autobiography, one might wonder at her obvious discomposure, wonder why she had written to Dance, "The past, with its tender and hallowed memories, the present, with a wealth of calm, real happiness; the bright, although vague, future, alike strive to unchain my mind." But the aged woman had edited out the young woman's apprehensions, perhaps in an attempt to present a more joyful image. The original letter went on. "Never,—I say it gladly, thankfully," she had insisted to Dance, "never for one instant since my betrothal, have I doubted the wisdom of my choice, or contemplated this lifelong union except with happy hope." Nevertheless, she forthwith contradicted herself: "Yet there are times when the sense of the importance of such a trust as the happiness of another, and that one the best-loved, makes me tremble." There had been doubts, indeed fears had crowded hopes, and Terhune admitted, "There are many and solemn thoughts that come to me in hours of solitary reflection." What about her own "deficiencies," she wondered, that she was now imagining for the first time? What if she ended by "impairing her husband's usefulness" or "clouding his life with disappointment"? She had no answers, she said, and "when those fears assail me" she looked to God to give her strength.[31]

A year later the married Terhune wrote again to Dance, this time in response to news of her friend's engagement and impending marriage. Of Dance's "new estate," Terhune said, "I have many and bright hopes for you." These hopes, she assured Dance, were founded on knowledge of the character of the bride-to-be as well as upon "him whom God has given you as your other and stronger self." She went on, "You have a mate worthy of you—one whom you love and who loves you." And after all, "what more does the woman's heart crave?" Dance had chosen wisely, she said, and "happiness" such as Dance had never known, she insisted, "must be the result." It was the woman's predicament. The dream of happiness was necessarily the dream of a happy marriage, and the fear was of anything less, for there could be no other dreams.[32]

It was difficult to jest or even write with equanimity about woman's one and only destiny. On 6 January 1836 Harriet Beecher, soon to be Stowe, wrote to Georgiana May to say, "Well, my dear G., about half an hour more and your old friend, companion, schoolmate, sister, etc., will cease to be Hatty Beecher, and change to nobody knows who." As Georgiana was also engaged and due "to encounter a similar fate," did she wish, asked Harriet, "to know how you shall feel?" Not for a moment, obviously, did Harriet consider the fact that her confidante might feel any differently when her time came, and neither was she willing to forgo relating those feelings. "I have been dreading and dreading the time," she said, wondering how she was going to be able to cope with the coming "overwhelming crisis." But now "it has come, and I feel *nothing at all*." What she felt was well-nigh more than she could bear; if she felt nothing at all it was because she was nearly numb. The letter took weeks to write. Maintaining a brave front, the letter continued in a similar vein following the date of marriage. "And now, my dear, perhaps the wonder to you, as to me, is how this momentous crisis in the life of such a wisp of nerve as myself has been transacted so quietly." Repeating herself, she said, "My dear, it is a wonder to myself." But the crisis had not been "transacted" for all time. She claimed to be "tranquil, quiet, and happy," but she also admitted, "I look *only* on the present, and leave the future with Him who has hitherto been so kind to me." The letter was finally completed. "Dear Georgy," wrote the married woman, "naughty girl that I am, it is a month that I have let the above lie by." And why had the "naughty girl" been so delinquent? Simply, she said, "because I got into a strain of emotion in it that I dreaded to return to." She would return to it no more, she claimed.[33]

Within a woman's certain destiny her hopes and fears waited upon the discretionary powers of a man. A life within a life was to be largely shaped and determined by the husband, invested with authority over his wife. While on a visit to Boston in the winter of 1849, Susan Warner, thirty and unmarried, wrote home to tell her Aunt Fanny that she had engaged in a conversation involving both sexes—while Warner herself was knitting—that had touched upon "*obedience* whether due from wives to husbands." Warner had affirmed the principle. E.D.E.N. Southworth informed her readers in her collection of short stories, *The Wife's Victory, and Other Nouvellettes*, that "The Wife's Victory" and its sequel, "The Married Shrew," had been written "to illustrate that distinct principle of Christian ethics and social philosophy, indicated by the text of Scripture selected as [their] motto." Southworth's choice of Scripture, Ephesians 5:23–24, left no doubt about the principle illustrated: "The husband is head of the wife, even as Christ is head of the Church; Therefore, as the Church is subject to Christ, so let the wives be to their own husbands in everything." The ancient sentence was accepted in the present. " 'I am "antiquated in my tenets," ' " affirms Grace Wynne in Terhune's *Moss-Side*, " ' "content to live forever in my husband's shadow; to own him as authority for doctrine; dictator of action; liege of my person, possessions, and will." ' " She is " 'Guilty!' " she says passionately, and asserts that " 'every loving wife' " should say the same. " 'What is this modern clamor about "obedience" in the marriage relation?' " Gertrude Dean asks testily in Sara Parton's novel *Rose Clark*. " 'How easy to "obey" when the heart cannot yield enough to the loved one,' " she says, leaving no doubt that her heart was girdled, that is, chained, adding that the " 'chain cannot fret when it hangs so lightly! I never heard the clanking of mine.' "[34]

Ears that could not hear were blocked by fears that would not be stilled, before the fact or after the realization. In Hentz's *Marcus Warland* the southerner Florence Delavel rejects a suitor's proposal of marriage. " 'Let me follow my own volitions, for at least three or four years to come,' " she says, seeking a stay of sentence, " 'let my mind soar unfettered to the heights where I wish to stand.' " The autonomy that Florence desires so passionately is contrasted to the dependency and subordination inherent in the imperial law of woman's destiny. Pleading with her suitor, Marcus Warland, she acknowledges that " 'I have always dreaded the idea of love . . . because I know, if I once yielded to its power, I should become far more of a vassal than any slave on this broad plantation.' " But Florence acknowledges as well that the time will likely come when she " 'may be tempted to wear those bonds, which, though covered with roses and seemingly light as air, must be stronger than steel, and heavier than iron.' " And that time does come, when in the final pages of the novel she yields her fantasy of autonomy to marital love and submits to her husband.[35]

Florence Delavel's hesitations were based not only upon her desire for an autonomy impossible in marriage, but also on her concern that the woman's great and only destiny was dependent upon the discretionary powers of another. " 'There is something terrible,' " Florence tells Marcus, " 'in the thought of giving one's happiness so completely in another's power, to hang trembling, palpitating on the frail dependence of another's truth and constancy.' " Exacerbating an already deep concern, there was also fear of being subject to the arbitrary ambitions and fancies of human beings. Catharine Maria Sedgwick's Sarah Herbert Silborn in *Married or Single?* knows " 'that God instituted marriage, to produce in that relationship, as in all others, the highest happiness and the purest virtue.' " But she knows as well that many marriages are riddled with " 'fearful disorders and imperfections.' " Marriages were, after all, rooted in and subject to " 'the passions, the prejudices, the ignorance, and the weaknesses of men and women.' " Marriages, too, were tainted from the outset if both women and men failed to choose their mates wisely and maturely. Instead, says Sarah, " 'Ambition, greed, govern; an accident, an overpowering vanity, a whim, a fancy, sets the seal on life!' "[36]

That a woman had to try to get married at all costs could mean that to avoid paying one price she would pay another. In Terhune's *Charybdis*, Constance Romaine, twenty-seven years old and still supported by her brother, experiences increasing pressure to find a husband and thereby shift her dependency to more socially desirable shoulders. Her only proposal comes from the elderly, crass, and dictatorial Elnathan Withers. Expressing irritation at Constance's hesitation during a conversation with his wife, her brother outlines alternatives considered even less attractive: " 'In the event of my death or failure in business she would be driven to the humiliating resource of taking in sewing for a livelihood, or to seek the more degrading position of a salesperson in a store.' " Acting as his emissary, the brother's wife confronts Constance directly and urges her to consider the critical factors in her decision. " 'Either you like him well enough to marry him,' " she says, " 'or you do not.' " What she means is that, like him or not, Constance had better marry him. " 'Your situation will be bettered by an alliance with him; or it will not.' " She means that even if the choice is dismal, there actually is no choice. Constance marries the elderly Elnathan and, Terhune tells her readers, "She marched at his chariot wheel, a slave in queenly attire, whose dreams were no more of freedom, to whom love meant remorse, and marriage pollution, the more hopeless and hateful that the law and Gospel pronounced it honorable in all."[37]

But even if woman's worst fear materialized and her great and only destiny became her great and only disaster, divorce could not be accepted as a solution. To countenance divorce was to open Pandora's box, to trigger countless unimaginable fears. In *We and Our Neighbors*, Harriet Beecher Stowe expressed dismay "that a large proportion of marriages have been contracted without any advised or rational effort," but she was even more disconcerted by the "wail, and woe, and struggle to undo marriage bonds, in our day." No doubt Stowe's fears were heightened by the fact that legislation governing divorce in the United States had become less restrictive since the end of the eighteenth century. In a majority of states, the grounds upon which one could sue for divorce were defined as liberally in 1860 as they were a century later, in several of the states even more liberally. Generally, the statutes were less restrictive in the United States than in other Western countries, and in fact during the nineteenth century, Americans apparently obtained more divorces than were granted in all of Europe. Statistics are incomplete for the nineteenth century, but they do indicate that there was a steadily increasing incidence of divorce throughout the period, with a dramatic increase after the Civil War. Stowe, for her part, was amazed, as she indicated in *Pink and White Tyranny*, that those who professed concern and interest in the condition of women were "so short-sighted and reckless as to clamor for an easy dissolution of the marriage contract." Were they so blind that they did not see that "this is a liberty which, once granted, would always tell against the weaker sex?" Were they seriously in favor, for example, of "having every woman turned out helpless, when the man who has married her, and made her a mother, discovers that she has not the power to interest him and to help his higher spiritual development?" The demons that lay in wait to destroy woman's hopes and make a reality of her fears came in all disguises.[38]

Reinforcing this openly pragmatic opposition to divorce was an equally weighty objection based upon principle. Stated succinctly, it was that the seal on woman's destiny had been affixed by the hand of God. Marriage was a sacred and therefore a lasting vow. In Augusta Evans Wilson's aptly titled *Vashti; or, "Until Death Do Us Part*," Vashti Carlyle is mistreated, deceived, and betrayed by her husband, but Vashti will not consider divorce. " 'I could not recognize the validity of divorces, for human hands could not unlink God's fetters, and man's laws had no power to free either of us from the bonds we had voluntarily assumed in the invoked presence of Jehovah.' " Scorning divorce as " 'sacrilegious triffling,' " Vashti instead chooses separation. The wife in E.D.E.N. Southworth's short story "Sybil Brotherton; or, The Temptation" is similarly deceived and mistreated by her husband. When he deserts her shortly after the birth of their first child, Sybil refuses to bow before her husband's threat to dishonor her unless she grants him a divorce. After the apparent death of her husband, Sybil's promising relationship with her pastor gives her hope that she will finally achieve "the acme of human happiness." Shortly before their wedding, however, she discovers that her husband is actually alive, and the promise of a happy marriage is transformed into a cruel "temptation." She turns to the Bible *"with an earnest desire to find that which she sought—*Christian permission to free herself," but finds nothing.[39]

Southworth also expressed alarm in *The Deserted Wife* about the fact that in "no other civilized country in the world is marriage contracted, or dissolved, with such culpable levity as in our own." As noted, Southworth was contracted in marriage to Frederick Southworth in 1840 and was deserted by him several years later when she was pregnant with her second child. Nonetheless, she never considered divorce. In fact, she refused to consider it an option, even when Robert Bonner apparently induced Senator James Dixon of Connecticut to submit a bill to Congress that would have made a legal dissolution possible. Entitled "A Bill for the Relief of Emma Southworth," the proposed statute was designed to give the courts of Southworth's residence, the District of Columbia, the power to grant divorces. When in 1895 Southworth's granddaughter, Rose Lawrence, informed her seventy-six-year-old grandmother that she intended to seek a divorce, Southworth tried to dissuade her. In marriage, she wrote, there are three parties; the husband, the wife, and the "heavenly Father who in his Divine Wisdom and Goodness first instituted marriage." Thus, she told her granddaughter, marriage is a "Divine institution and he or she who annuls it by divorce commits sacrilege." It would be far better, said Southworth, "to suffer much—to suffer anything, than to bring reproach upon God's Divine institution of Holy Matrimony." If husband and wife could not live together "without distress and even *danger*" they should separate and live apart, but they should not divorce. "*I* suffered much," said Southworth proudly, "rather than resort to divorce." She told Rose of the bill that had been submitted to Congress. It had passed, "much to my regret," she said. "I never availed myself of it."[40]

If practical reasons merged with principle to render a marital union permanent and divorce impossible, then perhaps a woman could allay concern, avoid the risks, by renouncing marriage itself. Marriage, however, was considered imperative and the solitary life was rejected. To be a spinster was not to be just an invisible woman, it was to be less than a woman. "We must give our girls in marriage," wrote Southworth to her daughter Lottie about Lottie's daughters, one of whom was the aforementioned Rose, "or else have a home full of fretful old maids." When Beulah Benton in Augusta Evans Wilson's novel *Beulah* is faced with what she fears will be the permanent departure of Guy Hartwell, she begs him not to leave. " 'My heart dies within me,' " moans Beulah at the thought of what her fate would be. Following his departure, Beulah, the fictional woman-writer, is not so coincidentally motivated to complete a "sketch . . . designed to prove that woman's happiness was not necessarily dependent on marriage. That a single life might be more useful, more tranquil, more unselfish." Having written the last word of her article, Beulah, in tears, drops her head on her desk. Wrote Wilson, "Oh, 'Verily the heart knoweth its own bitterness.'" Beulah, of course, does marry Guy at the end of the novel and is thus rescued from having to disprove her article, rescued from the bitter nonentity of spinsterhood.[41]

It was not written in statute, Scripture, or the pages of a woman's "great book of fate" that she could remain single. It was not imprinted on the consciousness of the literary domestics, either. "I am inclined to think there is more individuality in single than in married women," wrote Catharine Maria Sedgwick in her journal in the late 1830s. "Their position is singular and forced. There is something peculiar in their history." Despite its air of impersonality, Sedgwick's observation stemmed from the singular roots of her own peculiar history. More than any of the other unmarried literary domestics—Maria Cummins, Maria McIntosh, and Susan Warner—Sedgwick felt compelled (that is, forced) to justify and rationalize to herself in a private journal and to the world in her public prose the status and being of the unmarried woman. But she could not avoid subverting her own defense of the single woman since, single herself, she felt herself to be less than a woman. Conditioned to believe that the marital state was woman's natural condition, she could not help but believe that spinsterhood was in turn a forced, an unnatural state of being.[42]

In essence, Sedgwick's life was dominated by the same hopes and fears. Her heart's record was also the history of the girdled heart. For her, too, life was a crisis of domesticity, the woman's crisis of being. The woman-writer charged that it was deplorable that the spinster was considered a pitiable, at times laughable, anomaly in nineteenth-century American society. In her preface to *Married or Single?* Sedgwick wrote in reference to "the moral of our story," "We have given (we confess, after some disposition to rebel), the most practical proof of our allegiance to the ancient laws of romance, by making our hero and heroine man and wife duly and truly." She should not, therefore, "be suspected of irreverence to the great law of Nature." Having said that, however, she added, "But we raise our voice with all our might against the miserable cant that matrimony is essential to the feebler sex—that a woman's single life must be useless or undignified—that she is but an adjunct of man—in her best estate a helm merely to guide the nobler vessel." Rather, said Sedgwick concerning the unmarried woman, "we believe that she has an independent power to shape her own course, and to force her separate sovereign way." Nevertheless, in defending the single woman Sedgwick was actually motivated not so much by a desire to claim for woman the right to a sovereign destiny, but by her dread of failing in woman's sole allotted destiny.[43]

In the text of the novel itself, Grace Herbert's sister Eleanor makes clear Sedgwick's true sentiments. Distraught that Grace is close to entering what she fears will be a disastrous marriage, Eleanor complains to her husband Frank, who is unopposed to the marriage, about the prevailing conviction that women must get married at any cost, that otherwise they will be considered less than women. The first lesson the mother teaches her daughters, Eleanor says, is " 'that an "old maid" is an impersonation of whimsicalities, at best to be pitied, and that her condition is, at all risks, to be avoided.' " " 'Vulgar men,' " she also tells her husband, speak of single women " 'with scorn or pity,' " adding that " 'you, Frank, are reconciled to such marriages as my sister's will be, because—"she must be married!" ' " Do not, she pleads with him, " 'go on in the common rut and multiply these miserable matings (not unions), by saying "women must be married." ' " But in attempting to alter her husband's attitude, Eleanor betrays her own: " 'If a woman misses her highest destiny, if she cannot fold her heart in the bonds of conjugal affection, fortified by congenial education, taste, and disposition, if she cannot vitalize her union with a religious sentiment, then for pity's sake, dear Frank, counsel her to try "that other fate." ' " What Eleanor dreads is that her sister will suffer the fate of the " 'mismated wife and incompetent mother, condemned to stagnation instead of progress, and finding the last only and miserable consolation in the resignation to an indissoluble tie!' " But as to the question of woman's highest destiny, the married Eleanor knows the answer.[44]

Married or Single?, Sedgwick's last novel, represented merely a last exposure of secret lifelong domestic hopes and fears. In *Means and Ends*, basically a manual of education for female adolescents, Sedgwick advised "my young countrywomen" to educate themselves in order to have "an independent pursuit, something to occupy your time and interest your affections; then marriage will not be essential to your usefulness, respectability, or happiness." But she also stated unequivocally her undeviating allegiance to the dictum that "God has appointed marriage" for woman, that woman was "designed" for marriage, and that marriage was "the great circumstance" of woman's life. In her short tale "Old Maids," a female character laments the fact that " 'old maid' " conjures up the image of " 'a faded, bony, wrinkled, skinny, jaundiced, personage,' " whose mind has " 'dwindled' " and " 'who has outlived her natural affections.' " It is dread of spinsterhood, she says, that motivates many a woman to marry and results in her being " 'yoked in the most intimate relation of life, and *for life*, to a person to whom [she has] clung to save [her] from shipwreck, but whom [she] would not select to pass an evening with.' " Of such " 'misery there can be no "end, measure, limit, bound." ' " Nevertheless, after Sedgwick presented a series of cameos illustrating the productive, honorable, and satisfying lives of single women, she brought forth another spokeswoman to utter the familiar bottom line. The unmarried women is again defended but, says the spokeswoman, " 'it is safer for most of us to secure all the helps to our virtues that attend a favorable position.' " And what might the most "favorable position" be ? For women there can be no doubt that " 'married life is the destiny Heaven has allotted to us, and therefore best fitted to awaken all our powers, to exercise all our virtues, and call forth all our sympathies.' " For women, then, powers, virtues, and sympathies are linked to one higher destiny.[45]

Sedgwick never married and thereby assured for herself the status of a statistical oddity in the nineteenth century. But the ideal she shared—and was hostage to—with other women of her generation and of generations before and after was to become the compleat wife and mother in her own dream home. It was the great issue of the life of this woman who was a writer. In 1842, at age fifty-two, she wrote to the British essayist Anna Jameson to comment upon certain opinions that William Ellery Channing had expressed on the subject of marriage. "I was surprised at a declaration of Dr. Channing to me," she said, "that as far as his observation had extended he believed that in most cases the majority of women would have been happier to have remained single. This opinion I think proceeded from the horror of the subjugation of one mind to another." Sedgwick may have been surprised to hear a man speak of a "horror" that she herself shared, but she was probably also confused and perplexed to hear at the same time the conviction expressed that a majority of women might have led more satisfying lives had they remained unmarried. Channing had undoubtedly touched the core of her inner conflict regarding woman's great and certain destiny. Hers was a deep and lasting ambivalence. Hers was a mind and being subservient to and obsessed with a destiny she could neither totally embrace nor totally reject. At age forty-four, in the journal which she did not allow to be read during her lifetime, Sedgwick herself wondered if her "constitutional timidity" had been responsible for "keeping me single." By that she meant that perhaps she had hesitated for fear that what was possible could never approximate the ideal she envisioned in man or marriage. Nevertheless, she immediately qualified herself by adding that had she had the opportunity to marry a man she "truly loved," she doubted that timidity would have prevailed. Apparently, however, those who sought her did not engender that commitment, while those "I could have conjured into *beau ideal*" sought elsewhere.[46]

Sedgwick's choice of spinsterhood, if choice it can be called for a woman who considered her existence "singular and forced," was influenced by her observation of marriages she considered unsatisfactory. In 1847 she wrote to her niece and namesake, Kate Sedgwick Minot, to say, "So many I have loved have made shipwreck of happiness in marriage or have found it a dreary joyless condition where affection has died of starvation, so many have been blighted by incurable and bitter sorrows." Sedgwick found evidence close to home, in the marriages of her two sisters, Frances and Eliza. As she confided in 1853 to Kate's daughter Alice, she found the marriage of Frances to be "not a congenial one—she endured much heroically." And her other sister Eliza "had, I think, a rather hard life of it—indifferent health and the painful drudgery of bearing and nurturing twelve children." During the same period Sedgwick turned again to her journal to conjecture further about ideality and reality. Had the readers of her public prose been able to read her private journal they would have recognized a familiar story. It was the "duty of women," she thought, especially of those like herself, "those who are clothed with the authority," to dispense with "the spectre of old maidism— the spectre that terrifies so many girls into hasty and ill appointed marriages." But if Sedgwick spoke and wrote with a sense of authority, her words were issued as oracles. "I certainly think a marriage the happiest condition of human life," she wrote. And yet just as she believed that the marital state promised most, so had she questioned the promise itself: "it is the high opinion of its capabilities which has—perhaps kept me from adventuring in it."[47]

Sedgwick had also begun life, as she phrased it, as "the primary object of affection to many." Most important in that respect were her four brothers, who provided care, comfort, and affection throughout her adult life, building a protective wall of familial concern and intimacy around her. Walled in, Sedgwick was thereby deterred from seeking to build her own walls of domesticity. At age sixty she commented in a letter to Anna Barker Ward, "Engagements seem every day affairs, but when they come to our friends we realize that they are the great event of life." While it might be wiser, she suggested, to avoid the risks of marriage, "*safer* to escape the chances," nonetheless "it is happier to take the risks and so it *is* the subject of congratulations."[48]

But Sedgwick herself, conflicted and ambivalent to the core, sought more or less to avoid the risks by remaining with her brothers in her own marriage of circumstances. In a way she acknowledged that fact in a letter written when she was fifty-two that noted, "The affection that others give to husbands and children I have given to my brothers." She knew that hers was an unusual circumstance. "Few understand," she wrote, "the dependence and intensity of my love for them." That dependence and intensity reached their fullest development in her relationships with Robert and Charles. In fact, it is no exaggeration to state that during two separate periods that bridged most of her adult life, Robert and Charles served as surrogate husbands and their offspring as surrogate children. Over the years Sedgwick's journals and letters are replete with references to the depth of those two relationships. Typical are her ardent declarations at age twenty-three in 1813 to Robert that "I do love you, with a love surpassing that of an ordinary woman," and at age thirty-nine in 1829 to Charles that "I know nothing of love—of memory—of hope—of which you are not an essential part." Sedgwick's bond with Robert was fundamentally altered by his marriage in 1822; her link to Charles was not severed until he died in 1856, during her sixty-seventh year.[49]

That Sedgwick was motivated to form with Robert and Charles what were for her sacred unions beyond the sacred altars of matrimony suggests that the purity and autonomy of her dream of ideal matrimony were not sufficient. Perhaps she steered, or drifted, clear of legal marital union for fear of encountering a dreary familiarity, but the airy intimacy of her dream was not sufficiently alluring or fulfilling. She needed at least to imitate a matrimonial role in a play of imagination. However, there too Sedgwick found the substitute relationships wanting, because inevitably she found herself placed in the background of her brothers' affections. Before Robert married, Sedgwick had written to him to say that when he did give "to another a higher place," she prayed that his devotion to a wife would not detract from his love for her: "You may love another better—you must not love me less." Her demand notwithstanding, after Robert became engaged Sedgwick immediately recognized that "we cannot walk together so close as we have done."[50]

Charles was already married when Sedgwick turned to him as a replacement for Robert. She was fortunate that Charles's wife Elizabeth was generous in her willingness to share husband and children. Sedgwick became totally devoted to Charles and she did not have to concern herself with losing him to another. But that was only to say that from the outset she had implicitly accepted a secondary place in his affections. That was the permanent flaw in what became for Sedgwick her lasting circumstance. She came to realize increasingly the compromised nature of her life, that for one who had begun life first in the affections of many it was "difficult . . . to come by degrees to be first to none, and still to have no substitutes." Unmarried in fact, Sedgwick was married in mind to a destiny as a private domestic woman. But she wandered betwixt and between. Unwilling or unable to commit herself to legal matrimony, she nevertheless sought substitutes, only to find them wanting.[51]

It was in the midst of that state of affairs that Sedgwick began her literary career. It was probably no coincidence that Sedgwick began writing when Robert became engaged in 1821. A year later, shortly after *A New England Tale* appeared, Sedgwick told Susan Higginson Channing that she had begun what had first been a religious tract "because I wanted some pursuit, and felt spiritless and sad." Later in the summer of 1822, Robert, now married, complained to his sister that she no longer spoke in "that language of the heart, by which you are accustomed so faithfully to interpret its emotions." Nearly another year passed before Sedgwick felt sufficiently detached to admit to him that her reticence had been part of an attempt to make his presence and professions of affection "less necessary" to her. Clearly as part of her effort at detachment Sedgwick had directed her "language of the heart" to a new object. She had become the apprehensive and reluctant author.[52]

Six years later, in the winter of 1828, after she had written and published three novels and more, Sedgwick wrote to her sister Frances to say that she had accomplished "very little" of late. A "paralysis" had enveloped her, she said, and "I have lost my energy of purpose—my interest in life—at least so I feel at times." The past filled her with "sad thoughts" and the "future does not excite me." With the arrival of spring she turned to her journal again to confide and to repeat that during the entire winter she had experienced "a sort of mental paralysis." Sedgwick also "feared the disease extended to my affections." It did not appear that the onset of spring promised a change:

> I will not say, with the ungracious poet, that I turn from what Spring brings to what she cannot bring, but alas! I find there is no longer that capacity for swelling, springing, brightening joy that I once felt. Memory has settled her shadowy curtain over too much of the space of thought, and Hope, that once to my imagination tempted me with her arch, and laughing, and promising face, to snatch away the veil with which she but half hid the future—Hope now seems to turn from me; and if I now and then catch some glimpses of her averted face, she looks so serious, so admonitory, that I almost believe that her sister Experience, with an eye of apprehension, and lips that never smile, has taken her place. All is not right with me, I know.

There were a number of reasons why all was not right with Sedgwick's life. Primarily the fault lay in her "solitary condition," her "unnatural state" she called it. It was in this journal entry that she bemoaned being "first to none." She had begun life first to many but now at thirty-eight, having long since left the spring of her life, she acknowledged that "others have taken my place, naturally and of right, I allow it." And yet although she did remain important to others, she was second in their affections and could not deny that second best meant living without the "best sources of earthly happiness." In the familial embrace of all of her brothers she had an "agreeable home." Her brothers and her sisters were all affectionate and generous toward her, and "their children all love me." By now Sedgwick had become especially close to Charles's daughter Kate, "my adopted child." But that good fortune was a pale substitute for a family of her own. All that happiness, she wrote, "is no equivalent for those blessings which Providence has placed first, and ordained that they should be purchased at the dearest sacrifice." While she lived, what she recorded was meant for her eyes only. She did not set it down "in a spirit of repining." But she thought it best to be honest. In the future, after her death, it might "benefit some one of all my tribe." In the meantime, she would look to the afterlife, hoping to diminish the temporal.[53]

In May of 1830, after having completed her fourth novel, *Clarence*, Sedgwick acknowledged in her journal that it had been "an employment and sometimes a solace to me through months of various experiences." In spite of her family's continued support and the absorption in her literary career, depression on Sedgwick's part about her failure to engage in what she considered her primary calling, namely a domestic one, remained her prevailing state of being. Literary achievement could not unequivocally fill the domestic void. That June, touched by anxiety over the fate of her latest novel, she hinted darkly in her journal at events of deeper concern. There had been "lights and shadows" in her life of late, she wrote, "but I have no courage to tell the *real storm*." Later in the summer she wrote again that the season had "*not* been a happy one," and hinted again at causes "unknown and that will be untold" which had contributed to a "depression of spirit." She was probably unhappy about the "blunders" committed in *Clarence*, and she was certainly grief-stricken about Harry, who had entered a Boston mental asylum only a year before. But whatever the specific causes may have been, her depression stemmed primarily from her "condition of inferiority and dependence." "I hanker after the independence and interests and power of communication of a home of my own," she wrote. It was being "*second best*" that brought on her "paralysis of mind and heart." Deprived of woman's role as wife and mother in her own home, she was desperate for "something exciting to keep alive my powers." If intimidation, fear, and anxiety and feelings of inadequacy and illegitimacy in the face of over-whelming challenge, all of which engulfed Sedgwick in her literary career, were the stuff of excitement then she had indeed experienced a stimulation of her powers. But in the woman's mind that was to exercise false power, without a legitimate base. It amounted to being granted an extension of power minus its true source. "Ah it is a world of shadows," she wrote in her journal in 1832, "and I seem to myself the most fleeting among them." She could not transfer the desire.[54]

Sedgwick maintained her substitute lives, which meant, as she had phrased it in 1828, that she continued "craving such returns as have no substitutes." With Charles nearest, she continued to look to her brothers and their families for what she desired most. But as she reiterated in her journal in 1833, her "craving to be first" was destined to remain unfulfilled "when circumstances have placed me in all my relations in the position of second best." Sedgwick regarded the combination of her substitute lives as constituting little more than the diluted life of a woman who desired but had no home of her own, and it was a life that had dissolved only to spread a like tone. Shortly after her niece Kate's birth in 1821, Charles, delighted by the fact that the infant looked like her aunt, possessing features similar to those of "the very person of all others first and last I should wish her to resemble," wrote to Sedgwick to say that his strongest desire was that his infant daughter "do credit to her name." On her part, Sedgwick was devoted to all of her brothers' and sisters' children, her surrogate children, but Kate was for her "the first object and stood alone in the relationship she has bourne." As she wrote many years later in 1856, the year Charles died, Kate "had been the child of my supreme love."[55]

Her first love, Robert, died in 1841. She had remained close to him, if not as close as she had once been. Fittingly, she nursed him during his last days. Fittingly, too, her role and Robert's were exchanged in the end, with him needing the care and support he had previously provided her. "Reversing what was our natural relation," she told Anna Jameson, "we were descending the hill he leaning on me so that to every other feeling was added that most tender one that comes from nursing, supporting, watching." Sedgwick also cared for Charles during the six months previous to his death. The day after he died she wrote of her sense of desolation, her sorrow, in a letter to his daughter, her adopted daughter Kate. She had been with Kate's father at the time of his death, and now she felt that "it is all done—my work is all done—with all the sweet and loving and kind faces around me the house is—oh how vacant—how cold—the love of my life is gone." Her grief, her sense of loss, were complete. One week later she wrote again to Kate, saying, "I can never speak—I hardly dare think of what this loss is to me."[56]

In February 1835, while struggling with *The Linwoods*, Sedgwick had written to Kate, fourteen at the time, to tell her of the pain she was enduring while laboring over another of her children, namely, the book. Having apparently shown portions of the uncompleted manuscript to friends, Sedgwick was indeed pleased that she had received a favorable response. "Was there ever a mother who had a child," she asked rhetorically, "that she expected would be floated by the world and scarcely tolerated by her best friends and suddenly finds the clouds of her fears vanishing and her trembling child basking in the sunshine of favor"? For Sedgwick, what her literary career amounted to depended upon her perspective. As "a mother who had a child" she had always cared about her books, as she believed a mother should care about her children. As an author of books Sedgwick had cared as well, but in an entirely different manner. She believed she could or should have been a true mother. In truth, however, her literary career had stood more as a reflection of her inner self than apart from it. Sedgwick could even write (as she did at the end of that year in her journal) that "my books have been a pleasant occupation and excitement in my life." And if that was not the entire truth, if frequently the occupation had been a daunting one and the excitement unnerving, the substitute life had relieved her "from the danger of ennui and blue devils that are most apt to infect a single person." And although she might have objected to the description as too grand to apply to her "humble literary labors," the single person had given birth to a literature. Still, the private domestic woman would insist that her books constituted "no portion of my happiness." That, she said, she derived "from the dearest relations of life." She had to think it so.[57]

For the literary domestics, the struggle of the writer revealed the struggle of the woman. The domestic absorbed the literary because domesticity provided the matter and the metaphor for their lives. To claim her literary inheritance Sara Parton had looked to her mother, an eighteenth-century woman, asserting that had the mother been reared in the daughter's era, she would have been a writer of repute. Nevertheless, daughter Parton, the nineteenth-century writer, exhibited foremost a domestic commitment. When Parton's married daughter Grace died, leaving a six-week-old child, Parton informally adopted the girl and raised her, although this, she said, "involved a sacrifice of much literary work, or its unsatisfactory uncompleteness." But Parton could not see that she had a choice, and she could not regret her action. "*She* is my poem," Parton said of her granddaughter Ethel, or Effie as she was called. She did not always speak in sober tones concerning her sense of obligation. At times she revealed a characteristic wryness, as when she closed a letter to Robert Bonner saying, "If this is written so badly that you can't read it, know that while writing it I have talked to my cook about dinner, and washed Effie's face and hands, and mended a hole in her stocking. . . . Don't you wish you were a woman?" But her commitment was clear. Parton was a writer who remained wedded to her domestic calling.[58]

In response to the charge that the woman who engaged in intellectual pursuits was abandoning her domestic duties, Parton declared, "The idea is losing ground that a woman's mentality perils puddings and shirtbuttons." That, of course, was a twist in the usual order of peril, and in Parton's new order there was no peril. There had been "too many shining, tasteful houses and well-ordered tables presided over by cultivated women," she claimed, for that "old-fogyism" to have credence. Parton had moved to new ground without being able to vacate the old. She defended the writer Mary Abigail Dodge as a "living, breathing, brilliant refutation of the absurd notion that a woman with brains must necessarily be ignorant of, or disdain, the everyday domestic virtues." Cultivated or not, the woman remained domestically cultured. With or without brains, the woman was domestic, which meant that she was dominated by the life around her. With or without brains a woman had to attend to puddings and shirtbuttons.[59]

The tales of others had aided Harriet Beecher Stowe in forming her recollection of her mother as one of those "widely sympathetic natures, in whom all around seemed to find comfort and repose." Regarding herself, daughter Stowe reflected in an undated private memorandum that she had spent all of her time rearing children and supporting and seeing to the needs of a family that had received "all my life and strength and almost my separate consciousness." It was a wonder that Stowe could speak of having a separate consciousness. Early in her career, in 1848, she wrote to her friend Georgiana May of its domestic hues, dark and light. Referring to a recent illness, she said that she had "felt no disposition to write." Nor had a return to good health altered her literary affairs: "I have been so loaded and burdened with cares," she said, "as to drain me dry of all capacity of thought, feeling, memory, or emotion." Those were somber thoughts. Did a brighter perspective change matters? In the following sentence of the same letter, Stowe flip-flopped. She was now thirty-seven years old, she noted, and she liked the idea that she would grow old with "six children and cares endless." She wished May could see her, she said with pride, "with my flock all around me. They sum up my cares, and were they gone I should ask myself, What now remains to be done? They are my work, over which I fear and tremble." Two decades later, when she had temporarily set aside her literary work, Stowe explained to her publisher's wife, Annie Fields, that she had "not been able to write a word, except to my own children." The meaning was not epistolary: the metaphor was domestic. One should understand, Stowe said, that the varying needs of her children required that she "write chapters which would otherwise go into my novel."[60]

For the woman the literary role was an extension of her domestic role. In familiar fashion Catharine Maria Sedgwick, as a woman of the home, indeed, even as an unmarried woman, ministered to the needs of those around her. She was, said one of her nieces, "the confidante and adviser of everybody who came near her." Expressions of gratitude from those whom she served, in turn, were tantamount to constant reminders and reinforcements of her role. "You are now engaged in the best of all employments," her brother Robert wrote her in 1813, when she was twenty-three, "conferring happiness on those who love you and whom you love." Twenty years later her brother, Charles, told her of "the power you have over others," enthusing that she could "turn darkness into light—and perplexity into peace, if not joy." As pleasing as those and many similar commendations may have been for a woman of the home, they barely disguised an implicit declaration of what was woman's proper role and manner of being. The woman was praised for fulfilling what was her proper role in her proper sphere. The "best of all possible employments" was the only employment for women. In the end, the declaration was an injunction, a ruling on what was allowed and, by implication, what was not to be granted. As was implicitly clear in a letter Sedgwick received in 1837 from her sister-in-law Jane Sedgwick, widow of Harry, Sedgwick's literary role was regarded as secondary to her domestic role, and the latter provided the underpinnings of the former. Having received a supportive note from Sedgwick, Jane wrote to say, "Never did so precious a morsel fall from your pen as your last letter!" Sedgwick had received abundant gifts from God, Jane told her, but none were as important as "the power of your sympathy." It was her supreme gift, enthused Jane, adding that she would not exchange Sedgwick's letter "for all Redwood, Clarence, Hope Leslie, and the rest of those very precious books." That was the seal on the dictum that whatever Sedgwick did as a writer, she was more or less foreordained to be a literary domestic.[61]

In discussing her personal experience of literary domesticity, Mary Virginia Terhune answered a question about how as a fully committed wife and mother she could do justice to her writing by saying, "Domestic duties have never hampered me." Rather than regarded as a hindrance, obligations of service to others in the home were to be habitually performed because they were primary duties. Rather than interrupt the domestic daily round, literary affairs were absorbed all around and transformed. Prior to taking their equisite husbands, both of Augusta Evans Wilson's fictional women writers, Beulah Benton and Edna Earl, speak in Wilson's language of literary domesticity. " 'Books are, to me,' " says Beulah, " 'what family, and friends, and society, are to other people.' " Edna imagines that her work is to her 'what I suppose dear relatives must be to other women.'"[62]

Even the process of literary creation itself could be transformed in the mind into a cycle of conception, birth, and nurture, as when the publisher J. C. Derby related Stowe's saying, "Creating a story is like bearing a child, and it leaves me in as weak and helpless a state as when my baby was born." The metaphor was not an uncommon one even for men in the nineteenth century, but for these women the metaphor for life was more domestic than literary. On Terhune's part, if she could not be a creator of culture she could be a mother of prose. On one occasion the published writer Terhune said of herself in an interview, "I think two-thirds of me is 'mother' "; on another she said what was probably closer to the truth, namely, that she was a " 'good three-halves mother.' " While Terhune questioned, derided, and dismissed the artistic merit of her literary efforts, in stark contrast she could speak proudly and lovingly of herself as the "mother" of her literary works and of a particular book as a "bantling" or a "brainchild," or of her works collectively as her "brainchildren." Caroline Howard Gilman denied that she was a novelist and said, "My only pride is in my books for children." And the mother could add confidently, "I know that I have learned the way to youthful hearts." Sedgwick understood her publisher's query in trade terms as to how "heavy" her nearly completed novel, *The Linwoods*, was, but the following day her mind also had made otherwise of the matter and the meaning when, struggling to complete the novel, she had related to Kate that 'the conclusion now hangs heavy." Sedgwick was a woman who would have a child. As a writer she was "a mother who had a child."[63]

10

The Great Question
of Moral Life

Five years before the outbreak of the Civil War, Harriet Beecher Stowe
wrote a column for the New York weekly newspaper, the *Independent*.
Famous by then as the author of *Uncle Tom's Cabin*, she took as her subject
the effect upon the nation's literature of the "great contest of principle which
is now going on in this country between freedom and slavery." It was a
controversy, she wrote, that had generated the "most brilliant displays of
forensic eloquence in the senate-chamber, of sacred enthusiasm in the pulpit,
of earnest and manly vehemence in the lecture-room." The fervent and
idealistic Stowe claimed, "It is teaching our whole nation to think, feel, and
reason." That, of course, was debatable, as was her assertion that only a few
years before "a book devoted to this subject could scarce find a publisher
who dared issue it." Actually, an antislavery press had been active since the
1830s. But there had been a change. The "contest of principle" had
generated broad interest, and "now," Stowe wrote, in words that called to
mind the impact of the growth of the American publishing industry, "every
publisher and every press pours out anti-slavery books of every form and
description, lectures, novels, tracts, biographies." The vision was of a nation
deep in the throes of a morality play. Parenthetically, she noted, regarding
the novel in particular, its concentration on "the great question of moral life"
was becoming "one of the features of the age." No doubt recalling the days of
her childhood when Lyman Beecher had alternately imposed and lifted his
own ban on the reading of fiction by his children, she commented that
previously "the only object of fictitious writing was to amuse." But now, she
said straightforwardly, a novel was "understood to be a parable—a story told
in illustration of a truth or fact."[1]

Had Stowe been of a mind to and had she fully comprehended the
stirrings of her own "heart," she might just as appropriately have chosen for
her column's discourse the historic effect upon the nation and its literature of
the great conflict of principle that embroiled the woman's mind and heart.

The battle lines had been drawn before the fact, and with little or no choice in the matter the literary domestics were absorbed in a fundamental struggle all and only within the bounds of domesticity for self- and social esteem and for individual and social lives of influence and value. The parable of literary domesticity, its own story revealed in illustration of its own peculiar truth, involved both a frustrated quest and conflicted findings. Aligned with the private sphere and foresworn to the performance of duties in that sphere, the literary domestics' quest was circumscribed, compromised, and intensified. Burdened with a lowly self-image and faced with what they considered society's devaluation of woman's person, sphere, and role, they paradoxically had as their task the redemption of lives that had yet to be lived. Theirs was an inherent handicap. With little choice in life, they looked anxiously to their only mode of life for happiness, fulfillment, and significance. Because domesticity offered the woman what was essentially her only opportunity, because it promised all she could be and embodied everything that was at stake, she fantasied as well as grasped for a peculiar success. Hers was an intense confrontation with a single destiny. Hers was a life premised upon a principle of crisis.

The parable of literary domesticity revealed ambiguous and contradictory truths. Just as the literary domestics felt compelled to look within the circle of domestic concerns for satisfaction, for all joys, and for ultimate purpose, so was it inevitable that they found within themselves the stirrings of discontent, the sum of fears, and the basis for disillusionment. Their eagerness to glorify woman in the name of her mandated ethic of life, selfless service to others, warred with their apprehension that woman's condition was actually demoralizing and debilitating. Their desire to envision the wife and mother as a strong, independent, and commanding figure in service to the family reflected their anguish that woman's was a dependent and frequently vulnerable status. To question and assess the quality of woman's duties was to question and assess the character of woman's life of domesticity, and that was to call into question the life's role they were bound to accept. Conditioned by the very circumstances they daily judged, they in effect were led daily to judge themselves as well. For them the destiny of the quotidian was to be alternately immersed in and beset by opposing waves of near-saintly pride and profound doubt as to their personal worthiness and the ultimate value of their domestic lives.[2]

For the literary domestics themselves revelation was not, as has been stated, wholly intentional and self-discovery was not total. Theirs was not a premeditated plan or deliberate effort to expose their condition. They sought an understanding, not an exposé. But they did not consciously control the scenario. Since it was the underlying obsession of their inner lives it was inevitable that their struggle surfaced in their public prose, just as it dominated their private thoughts. That too was one of the historic features of the age. And had the mind not been clouded by the anguish of the heart,

Stowe might just as well have brought her judgment consciously and clearly to bear upon the effect of that struggle on the private woman, as well as upon its social significance. After all, there was a secret alliance, sometimes acknowledged, among those who exhibited similar responses because they shared similar circumstances. Only the woman, they felt, could tell the true story of the woman's life of domesticity. But an obsession suggests an absence of self-awareness and of self-control. The woman's immersion in her own peculiar history made ultimate self- and social knowledge elusive and the foreboding nature of the life to be understood forestalled personal resolution. To criticize or perhaps condemn the life was to criticize or condemn the self. The parable of literary domesticity suggested the existence of a moral warfare within that was difficult for them either to ignore or to acknowledge, and told a moral tale that was difficult for them to resolve or rationalize. For these women who were writers that was their own ultimate secret revealed in plain view.[3]

In a letter written to George Eliot in April of 1869, Stowe told her, "What strikes me most in your writings is your *morale*." She explained, "You appear to have a peculiar insight into the workings of the moral faculties." Stowe was actually identifying in Eliot what she felt to be the stirrings of a kindred soul. Woman to woman, she was attributing to Eliot a sensibility that Stowe found recognizable. Without elaborating, she told Eliot that she appeared to understand "religious development" in a manner similar to Goethe, although, said Stowe, Eliot's was clearly an "*English*" manner. More importantly, however, it was also clear to Stowe that Eliot was "as thoroughly woman" as she was English. There were times when she read her fiction "supposing you man," Stowe said, only to arrive at "contrary conclusions from internal evidence." Internal evidence provided the telling signs and indicated the true source for the telling assessment of the woman's life. "No my sister," Stowe wrote solemnly, "there are things about us no *man* can know and consequently no man can write." It followed necessarily, Stowe said to Eliot, that "being woman your religion must be different from man's." Nevertheless, although the profession of a "religion" implied a previous conversion it did not necessarily indicate the existence of a redeeming and successful practice.[4]

"What could ail her?" Mary Virginia Terhune had said that the world asked of woman. But in her letter to her friend Virginia Eppes Dance she was also asking implicitly, "What can ail me?" The effort was to interpret the self to the self and to forge a satisfactory perspective on the life led. What was demanded was a process of self-discovery, and implicit was the sense that in light of her singular outer circumstances only the woman could fathom for herself the code of her inner being. In Susan Warner's *Queechy* a gathering of relatives and friends expresses mystification as to the meaning of a poem written by "Hugh" that has recently appeared in a magazine called *Excelsior*. Unbeknownst to the group, "Hugh" of course is the secret pseudonym of the novel's central female character, Fleda Ringgan, who happens to be present during the reading. It is given to Guy Carleton, who will become Fleda's husband by the end of the novel and who suspects the author's true identity, to supply the appropriate general commentary. " 'There is a peculiarity of mental development or training,' " he observes enigmatically, " 'which must fail of pleasing many minds because of their wanting the corresponding key of nature or experience.' " Adding to the mystery, he also says, " 'Some literature has a hidden freemasonry of its own.' "[5]

The struggle was made by the woman writer to know herself, to arrive at a plausible understanding of her existence. "Is it not possible that even woman's fitful moods are not without a governing principle?" asked Maria McIntosh in her novel, appropriately titled *Woman an Enigma; or, Life and Its Revealings*. And might not "this principle be detected," she suggested, "by noting her varying aspects, and the influences under which they have been exhibited?" Since there were questions, there must be answers, so, wrote McIntosh, let us remove from woman "fold by fold, the wrappings with which conventional forms have concealed her heart too often even from herself, let us lay bare its sources of thought and feeling." However, the questions were: What did and could the woman know of herself? And what could she knowingly write of her life? The answers depended upon what there was to be known. "Fitful moods" indicated a troubled "heart," and the effort of the woman to dislodge hidden thoughts and feelings branded her and fueled her war within.[6]

To a young heart the prescription seemed simple enough. In 1813 the eighteen-year-old Caroline Howard had written to the younger Louisa Gilman, sister of the man she would marry six years hence, to say, "If you are distressed, unburdening your thoughts on paper, will compose your mind and promote reflection; which to an innocent heart is almost invariably a relief." If, on the other hand, Louisa was "happy," said Caroline, then she should "let the sportive children of your fancy, run from their retreat in your brain, and their little playful sports will beguile harmlessly many an hour." Whatever the nature of one's thoughts, she concluded, first, "we may derive benefit, in planting them more clearly in our own minds;" and second, "undoubtedly, in unfolding by writing the germ of any idea, we more plainly see its properties, and more understandingly apply them." The cultivation of the heart by the mind appeared a controlled process with predictable results.[7]

Almost three decades later, in the early 1840s, Caroline Howard Gilman informed her younger sister Harriet Fay that she had found her latest letter to be "one of the most delightful you ever wrote." But, she mused, "it seems strange that while I am failing so completely with my pen, you should be so bright." The problem, she confessed, was that at the moment "I have something amounting to aversion to the whole writing process." In an aside

she asked if her sister had read "Mrs. Adams Letters." They still interested
her "a good deal," Gilman said, but "books have not engaged me as they
once did." Actually, books, particularly her own, had come to engage her too
much. Thirteen days later her condition had not improved. Although "my
pen is not as busy as formerly," she told her sister, "my heart is quite as
open," but it was her "hope," she said, that the "feverish disgust I have felt at
writing is wearing away." Apparently the burden of her thoughts weighed
heavily on her heart and distress dampened fancy. Certainly the mind was
not composed and the heart was neither relieved nor beguiled. Writing, said
Gilman, instead "seemed to be almost a disease." Reflection obviously was
not benefiting the heart, and application had come to a halt.[8]

It was both curious and ironic that for the woman a book could be
construed as sign and symptom of a disease. But for these women writers the
notion was not an unlikely one. For the literary domestics, troubled minds
hinted at the malady of the heart. "Simple" tales of singular lives were the
products of existences lived with involuntary and unsettling intensity.
Plumbing the self heightened warfare within and made resolution all the more
elusive. In that same year of 1869 Stowe had confirmed in another of her
letters to George Eliot that she had drawn heavily upon her own and her
family's history for her latest novel, *Oldtown Folks*. It was an admission
easily verified. In recognizable fashion Stowe utilized the setting of Natick,
Massachusetts, the boyhood home of her husband Calvin and the "Oldtown"
of the novel, as well as that of Litchfield, Connecticut, which as noted is
appropriately dubbed Cloudland. She also based her fictional personages
upon figures from the Beecher-Stowe family saga too numerous to mention.
To indicate a few examples: Stowe herself told George Eliot that she had
drawn upon the characters of "my Aunt Harriet [Foote] who taught me the
church catechism" for Debby Kittery; of "my dear many sided father,"
Lyman Beecher, for Dr. Avery; and of "my son—my silent blue-eyed
golden-haired boy" (her son Harry, who had drowned in the Connecticut
River while a student at Dartmouth) for Harry Percival. Although she set the
novel in the period from 1787 to 1793, many of the incidents in the story
were based upon the experiences of members of her family that actually
occurred decades later, and Stowe carved as well from her own, her
husband's and her father's childhood reminiscences which stretched the
mind of the book from earlier in the eighteenth century to the first decades of
the nineteenth century. The contours of that intellectual plane were largely
shaped by Stowe's admirable effort to trace historically the faces of latter-
day Puritanism, with especial reference to its Edwardsian manifestation, the
multifaceted religious controversies of the early nineteenth century in which
her father was so deeply involved, and the romantic Christianity elaborated
by her brother, Henry Ward Beecher, and eventually adopted by Stowe
herself.[9]

But if the recounting of eighteenth- and nineteenth-century New England theology determined the intellectual milieu of the book, the mind at work was of course that of the book's author, the nineteenth-century woman Stowe. And the mind at work in *Oldtown Folks* betrayed a familiar, troubled psychology. One revealing sympton appears when Horace Holyoke, the narrator of the tale and the character based upon Calvin Stowe, comments upon Esther Avery, who appears to have been drawn by Stowe with both herself and her sister Catharine Beecher in her heart's mind. Horace describes Esther against the background of New England religious history, but it is woman's history that emerges from the background. Esther, Horace relates, was "one of those intense, silent, repressed women that have been a frequent outgrowth of New England society." Her malady, he suggests, was not unique to her particular female person, for "moral traits, like physical ones, often intensify themselves in course of descent, so that the child of a long line of pious ancestry may sometimes suffer from too fine a moral fibre, and become a victim to a species of morbid *spiritual ideality*." That Esther is from a long line of female ancestry as well, that she suffers from a taut female fiber, and that she has become a victim to a female species of internalized and intensified ideality are also evident, for having described the religious malady Horace then observes the female afflicted. Esther, he says, appeared "less like a warm, breathing, impulsive woman, less like ordinary flesh and blood, than some half spiritual organization, every particle of which was a thought."[10]

Esther was a product of the times, that is, the late eighteenth century, when "life was so retired and so cut off from the outward sources of excitement" that for women "*thinking* grew to be a disease." But if Horace's commentary is intended to be applied to a limited chronology, the line of reasoning implicitly if inadvertently extends to a broader chronology, namely, that of the woman. Theology, says Horace, was the dominant subject of thought in the late eighteenth century "and woman's nature has never been consulted in theology." The theological system of St. Augustine was especially compelling to individuals at the time, and thus while all were analyzing Augustine, "it was the women who found it hardest to tolerate or to assimilate it, and many a delicate and sensitive nature was utterly wrecked in the struggle." More and more Stowe's subject of theology in the late eighteenth century appears a pretext for a simultaneous indirect commentary on the woman's predicament. Not only has woman never been consulted in theological matters, it is implied, she has never been consulted in the basic organization and direction of her life. It is and has been the woman's great struggle, Stowe's words suggest, to tolerate and assimilate a life not freely chosen in the face of a destiny imposed. And it remains a struggle that is consuming, fragmenting, and torturous.[11]

In fact, Stowe suddenly sets religion aside and the war becomes Esther's alone, or the warfare within of woman alone. Through the narrator, Horace, and by utilizing the persona of Esther, Stowe appears to approach an understanding of herself, the literary domestic. The process described parallels the making of a literary domestic. Esther embodied, says Horace, what Plato had thought would be the ideal "human thinker and philosopher," the "MAN-WOMAN," or the "human being who unites perfectly the nature of the two sexes." The nature created is the consequence of a familiar history of nurture and training. On the one hand, says Horace of Esther, "from a long line of reasoning, thinking, intellectual ancestry she had inherited all the strong logical faculties, and the tastes and inclinations for purely intellectual modes of viewing things, which are supposed to be more particularly the characteristic of man." On the other hand, "from a line of saintly and tender women, half refined to angel in their nature, she had inherited exquisite moral perceptions, and all that flattering host of tremulous, half-spiritual, half-sensuous intuitions that lie in the borderland between the pure intellect and the animal nature." But Stowe verges upon rather than reaches understanding. Plato's envisioned union was not so perfect for Esther; in fact, it was her "misfortune." Esther had the man's taste for life but she could not taste life like a man. The mind received signals from the heart only to relay them inward again, and her lot was to suffer "the internal strife of a divided nature." It was Esther's misfortune, observes Horace, that "her heart was always rebelling against the conclusions of her head. She was constantly being forced by one half of her nature to movements, inquiries, and reasonings which brought only torture to the other half."[12]

In the introduction to *Eve's Daughters*, published in 1882, Mary Virginia Terhune noted that when she had been asked two years before to write a "series of popular articles upon the 'Physical and Mental Education of Women,' " she had reread Dr. Edward H. Clarke's *Sex in Education*, issued seven years earlier. In his influential study, the doctor from Harvard Medical School had argued that women did have the mental potential necessary for higher education. While reading this favorable evaluation Terhune may have nodded and recalled that her father had held similar convictions decades before Clarke. It is certain, however, that she did not assent to Clarke's main contention: that exercise of the female intellect caused serious damage to the female body. Indeed, young women supposedly risked their very lives in the enterprise. With barely concealed sarcasm, Terhune concluded: " 'They have Moses and the prophets. Let them hear them.' " Turning her back on wise men and pointedly dedicating her own volume "TO MY SISTERS, the Wives, Mothers, and Daughters of America," Terhune suggested that the volume's significance lay in the fact that "women can say things to women which we would not bear from men,—things which men do not *know*." As there was among women a "Guild of Sentiment" from which men were barred, she claimed, so there was a "Guild of Suffering known in its fullness of bitterness only to the initiated." But that was to allude inadvertently to a dual membership, and it was to overlook the fact that the "freemasonry" of one "guild" might call into question that of the other.[13]

"The drawback to a woman's advocacy of any cause," Terhune wrote, in an effort to elicit the nature of *her* cause, is that "her idealistic sympathetic, *maternal* nature makes her a partisan." Said the literary domestic, "Her subject becomes her bantling." But the woman's certain destiny juxtaposed against her singular history spawned a dual partisanship, and the question was whether and how she could acknowledge even to herself what she could hardly bear to know. The question was whether prescribed sentiment could survive discontent, let alone suffering, or whether resolution and thus deliverance was possible when the head sought to overrule the heart and the heart rebelled against the conclusions of the head. The question was whether the "bantling" could be other than ill-formed.[14]

"It is an uncommon event to meet a woman," Terhune continued in *Eve's Daughters*, who when pressed would deny "that at some period of her life, she had not wished she had been a boy." Nevertheless, she asserted, the vast majority of the "best thinkers and workers of our sex would aver more freely that they would not exchange places with their brothers." On the contrary, they were not "ashamed of their place in the world." Conscious of their high responsibility, they did not "crave another field of action which is, after all," Terhune insisted, "really no wider or higher." Terhune proceeded to lecture the current generation of mothers among her readers and she forthwith contradicted herself: "The sooner and more thoroughly your child's mind is disabused of the low-caste contempt of her womanhood," she wrote, "the happier for her, the more promising for the next generation." Inadvertently, Terhune had betrayed her presumption that the present generation of mothers as well as their daughters held womanhood in extremely low regard. There was probably, as well, a lingering "odium" that tainted Terhune herself. But indirect revelation was the order of the day, because Terhune's consideration was directed to the past and the future, and in her concern with the future she sought a reevaluation of the past. As soon as the female child could "understand stories of heroic and valorous deeds," the literary domestic suggested, the mother could "tell her what Woman has done for humanity and what she may do in the future."[15]

The intent was to communicate a tale of the holy habit of the woman's life. Stowe's Eva Van Arsdel Henderson, in *We and Our Neighbors*, asks, " 'In this great fuss about the men's sphere and the women's, isn't the women's ordinary work just as important and great in its way?' " The same question was posed in Maria McIntosh's *Woman in America*, a book that had as its subtitle *Her Work and Her Reward*. Declaring that every "object in creation finds itself in that position for which its peculiar organization has fitted it, and discovers in its offices the exact correlatives of its powers," McIntosh made the objective of her study (and the reason for its subtitle) the discovery of "the work designed for [woman] here, and the reward which awaits its performance." Inadvertently, McIntosh also pointed to the struggle inherent in the effort to shed a favorable light upon a familiar figure commonly regarded in the background. Woman's grand role, she stated, was to be a " 'help-meet' in the labors, the trials, and sufferings of mortality." The biblical helpmeet, of course, was the woman relegated to a supportive, secondary, and dependent position.[16]

The literary domestics enveloped their hopeful re-vision in a domestic dream of celebration. It was a dream that enclosed them, and at times the aura of the dream blurred and the rush to celebrate obscured an otherwise transparent urgency born of doubt and disillusionment. As in a fairy tale, they imagined their sphere, their land, their *home*-land, within a dreamland. They looked upon home life as if it were a rarely glimpsed, untouched, beloved paradise, a paradise that was a fantasy all their own. In 1822, the year *A New England Tale* appeared, Sedgwick, who had no home of her own, enthused in a letter to Susan Higginson Channing that "there is no equivalent to me for the pleasures of home, the voices and the smiles of brothers and sisters, and the caresses of children." More than three decades later, Stowe urgently communicated her support for the aims of a recently issued periodical. Writing to the editor, she declared that there was no higher objective than "to exalt and beautify home and common life, to render ordinary existence beautiful." Terhune evoked in her 1910 autobiography "the spirit of Home, sweet, radiant, and indescribable," just as she had rhapsodized in her 1865 collection of stories, *Husbands and Homes*, about "Home! wife! peace! Sweet synonyms that sum up the rapturous emotions of many a satisfied heart." Home was theorized, willed, and sanctified by McIntosh in *Woman in America* as "the sanctuary of true and warm affections, the nursery of pure and high thoughts." Sedgwick chose *Home* for the title of her quasi-novel, and in that book called it "a word, that to my mind expresses every motive and aid to virtue, and indicates almost every source of happiness."[17]

In retrospect, Stowe mused that her mother's childhood home in Nutplains, Connecticut, Stowe's own childhood home away from home, had been "a vision of Eden." An original source, a place of her beginnings, Stowe's Eden was like a dreamland, a setting yearned for and nostalgically recalled. Sunbury, Georgia, was another Eden, at least in the mind of McIntosh, who claimed that her birthplace evoked a similar response in "the hearts of those who grew up in its shades." Theirs was a collective "memory of its loveliness," she said, which still existed "as a bond of union" among those "hearts" who sought to remember. Akin to utopia, it was like *no* place, from which, McIntosh's words implied, "no distance can wholly sever" the heart from the memory. The mind could retain an image even if time and circumstance had altered a place. McIntosh's childhood Sunbury had become, she admitted, a "desolate ruin." Alternatively, the mind could create the image even if Eden had perhaps never existed. When Stowe returned to Nutplains as an adult, she was "surprised to find that the hills around were so bleak and the land so barren; that the little stream near by had so few charms to uninitiated eyes." A magical place for the initiated, "home" wrote Sedgwick in *Hope Leslie*, was nevertheless a place that could "never be transferred; never repeated in the experience of an individual."[18]

The promise of romantic love made Eden all the more alluring. After all, it was a woman's destiny to love, and her dream was of a love fully returned. Nonetheless, dreams of romantic love spawned a literature of courtship that in the majority of instances stopped short of the marital altar. As if to bequeath to their younger readers nothing but their own dreams, the literary domestics depicted an intimate and blissful attachment that bloomed between female and male on the pathway to marriage. Gay, gossamery, loving relationships were woven into episodes of courtship, and youthful heroine after youthful heroine stood in a leafy, flower-dotted glen and, preparatory to the prized proposal, eagerly received paeans from a lover kneeling at her feet. Page upon page was devoted to dialogue in which fiancée and fiancé pledged undying affection. The dialogue once concluded and the betrothal decided, the tale ended abruptly. It was as if it had to be. As a young woman is told by her uncle in Augusta Evans Wilson's novel *At the Mercy of Tiberius*, while " 'there is no heaven on earth' " there is the illusion of it in " 'the season of courtship and betrothal.' " That " 'wonderful light,' " he muses, " 'shines only once full upon us, but the memory of it streams all along the succeeding journey; follows us up the arid heights, throws its mellow afterglow on the darkening road, as we go swiftly down the slippery hill of life.' " It beckons to us, he says, " 'as hope's happy prophecy, this sparkling prologue, and we never dream that it is the sweetest and best of the drama that follows.' "[19]

Moments of courtship were obviously conducive to the fancies of romantic love, but the promise of that love was necessarily linked to the promise of marriage, and for the woman that was a promise that had to be kept. Idealized love was handmaiden to the promise of the appointed place. Love's moments were not to be indulged solely for love's sake. "Know and maintain for yourself," Terhune admonished her youthful readers in *Eve's Daughters*, "that life has nobler aims than the fascination, for vanity's sake, of so many gallants per season." Occasionally, the words of the literary domestics traced beribboned love letters of marriage in which the childlike domestic dream of love, happiness, and contentment extended beyond the marital altar. In those instances their idealization of the bond of love between the sexes revealed a wish that wife and husband be united in bliss forever, a desire to assure themselves as well as their readers that the true tale of a wife and husband's devotion was an unending love lyric. In E.D.E.N. Southworth's *Her Mother's Secret,* Odalite and Leonidas Force enjoy "a real, poetic, romantic, sentimental love match of the oldest fashioned pattern. He thought that he had found in her the very pearl, or rose or star of womanhood. . . . She thought she had discovered in him the man of men." In a phrase, "Each would have suffered or died to save the other a single pang." But despite the moments of playtime in fantasy, the dream of romantic marital bliss was tucked away in the literary domestics' consciousness and in their prose like a toy in the attic, not totally discarded or rejected, but reluctantly parted with, perhaps a sign it had no place in the everyday reality of their mature lives.[20]

In fact, as often as marital love bloomed in the fantasies of the literary domestics, fears of the dark shades of sexual passion in and out of marriage loomed in their consciousness. Talk had to be of love because the woman was destined to love, that is, she was destined to marry, but that made the woman dependent on love, subject to the whim of love, helpless before the fate of love. In the eyes of God and man the young female was required to present herself at the marital bed with her chastity intact. But there was the disturbing thought that the linkage of love and marriage in the collective mind of young womanhood rendered women vulnerable to male sexual manipulation and exploitation. In pursuit of love's fancies the young female could become a puppet on a string, dangling as a sexual object irrelevant to the sacred ties of marriage. The example of youthful Jessie Manning in Sedgwick's *Married or Single?* conveyed the message that an illicit seduction destroyed a requisite innocence, or worse, a female life. "Wisdom!" Sedgwick declared. "She had none of it beyond the instinct of a pure nature—never, perhaps, . . . had a human being lived in this world, with less acquaintance with it than [she]." A seamstress employed by the wealthy mother of Horace Copley, Jessie is seduced by Horace and abandoned by him at pregnancy; her child dies at birth and she succumbs to consumption. Seduced or not, at the very least the disillusioned lover lost innocence. Terhune's Jessie Kirk in *Jessamine* is deprived of both her innocence and her marital prospects. The would-be seducer, Orrin Wyllys, subverts Jessie's relationship with her fiancé through false innuendo and lures her into a romantic dalliance with him. That Orrin is stopped short of actual seduction matters not at all. " 'I was a happy trustful child when you crossed my path,' " Jessie tells him. But now, says the no-longer-innocent maiden with no dreams of love, " 'I am a hard, bitter suspicious woman—and the change is your work.' "[21]

In the fictional fare of the literary domestics the classic villain not only violates society's behavioral code through the most obvious acts of lawlessness, he acts the role of the wanton seducer and thereby betrays the woman's ideal of romantic love. In Maria Cummins's aptly titled *Haunted Hearts*, Captain Josselyn is a most vivid example of the most villainous. Disguised as a British naval officer, Josselyn enters a small New Jersey town, resides at the local inn, and proceeds to ingratiate himself with the natives. What follows is a series of heinous acts, including robbery and murder, but the worst is seduction. Josselyn, whose true vocation is piracy, is eventually captured, brought to trial for crimes other than seduction, and is in the end confronted outside the jailhouse by an angry crowd, and by the woman he has seduced, along with their child. The climactic, histrionic confrontation confirms the fact that seduction of the female innocent has been the worst of Josselyn's sins. The full-blown description includes everything from Josselyn's "fiendish laugh" and his "hissing" at the child to the moment when, with the gathered crowd looking on, he raises his foot to kick the mother, "and—the indignant crowd gave a simultaneous yell of expostulation—but he did it—he kicked her!" The sexual vulnerability and exploitation of woman mocked the ideal of romantic love by rendering her a sexual pawn, outside the bounds of holy matrimony. To exploit woman as a sexual toy independent of marriage was to toy with the system of her life.[22]

What mocked as much if not more was society's double standard of sexuality, a standard that in essence granted men the sexual freedom to deprive women of their required sexual chastity. In Harriet Beecher Stowe's *We and Our Neighbors*, Maggie McArtney is, indeed, a "fallen" woman, but she wonders why she should be the sole recipient of society's wrath, why she should be "treated as if she were the very offscouring of the earth"— particularly when the man who seduced her is "moving in the best society, caressed, flattered, married to a good, pious, lovely woman, and carrying all the honors of life." Maggie asks, "Why was it such a sin for her, and no sin for him? Why could he repent and be forgiven, and why must she never be forgiven?" The discriminatory imposition of such a rigid standard constituted a thinly veiled reminder that, unlike man, woman was barred from pursuing or enjoying "all the honors of life" save one, and a single violation of that standard made likely a denial of even that "honor."[23]

"Ah!" wrote Sara Parton of the "fallen" woman's plight in *Fern Leaves From Fanny's Portfolio*, "pass her by on the other side; speak no word of encouragement to her . . . . Leave no door of escape open, close your homes and your hearts." When "homes and hearts" were closed to the woman, there was nowhere else to go and no other life to lead. Writing to her niece Kate in 1853, Sedgwick described one such "fallen" woman and damned the double standard. The woman in question was from Boston, she said, and after her single illegitimate liason, "she was expelled from society," despite the fact that she was "ever after a most exemplary little woman." Sedgwick recalled that "she was never in a house except those of her immediate family," and she added, "it was considered a high price of virtue in them to let her lie on the ground." It was intolerable, Sedgwick declared, that "in men the *permitted* grossness in thought, word and deed can't be spoken of!" But what was worse was that "a poor girl, ignorant of her nature, with opportunity thrust upon her, and love blinding her is the victim thro' life of a single offense." Bursting with indignation, but betraying an underlying sadness, perhaps despair, Sedgwick ended by saying, "It is a perpetual punishment with no hope of pardon—a rack from which the death penalty is the only escape." Ruined for marriage, the woman was ruined for life.[24]

Once man and woman were married, male infidelity, an ultimate betrayal of the ultimate romance, threatened to rewrite the love letters of domestic bliss. Among all of the "actual sorrows of wedded life," wrote Mary Virginia Terhune in *Eve's Daughters*, "marital infidelity is a sin and a woe, *sui generis*." As if it were unimaginable that the woman herself could destroy her dream of true love, the sin spoken of is man's, the woe woman's. It is also a misery that women endure in silence. "Yes!" insisted Terhune, "because they must!" And because they must, "it has driven more to madness, to suicide, to desperate destruction of their own souls than all other goads combined." As older woman to younger, Terhune wrote, "I wish I could assure you with truth, loving young wife, that the crime is rare."[25]

Throughout her life E.D.E.N. Southworth overflowed with information about her struggles to support herself and her two children with her pen following her separation from her husband, Frederick Hamilton Southworth. But Southworth would never directly or specifically reveal what had happened between the two of them. She did acknowledge that he had abandoned her and had gone to Brazil, and the not-so-secret writer littered her path with clues regarding what had happened prior to his exodus. They were clues strong enough to beg a particular interpretation. Southworth made it explicitly clear that her days would never be spent nostalgically recalling the rhapsody of marital love. For John S. Hart's 1855 edition of *The Female Prose Writers of America*, she wrote, "Let me pass over in silence the stormy and disastrous days of my wretched girlhood and womanhood." By "womanhood" Southworth meant marriagehood, as was later made evident in "An Autobiography of the Author" that was appended to the 1860 publication of a collection of her stories. For that glimpse, the same essay was used that had been written for Hart, except that Southworth or an editor changed the voice from the first to the third person and the already quoted passage to "Let us pass in silence over the disastrous days of Emma's fatal marriage."[26]

In a sense Southworth did maintain her silence and keep her secret regarding those days, but she never forgot them. The memory was a memory that mocked, as she could not leave behind even her story of a broken love. For example, she wrote to her daughter Lottie a half century later, on 19 January 1894, and recalled the day of Lottie's birth, "that 7th of May 1844 that brought me a little angel from the heart of the Heavenly Father to heal and comfort my poor broken heart!" It was during "those sad days," she said, "when I used to go the post-office in hopes of getting a letter from Brazil and day after day, and week, come home crushed and disappointed." Then, she told Lottie, "I would press you close, close to my breast, close to my aching heart and you seemed like a balsam that drew out all the pain."[27]

Apparently, however, other than acknowledging the fact that her husband, Lottie's father, had abandoned her, the seventy-five-year-old woman had yet to tell her own daughter about the specific causes of the pain. Five months later, in June of 1894, she wrote again to Lottie, again recounting those past tribulations, and said, "Some day I will tell you all about it." And once again, a year later, she wrote to Lottie, "There! There! It is a half century ago but seems as if it were but yesterday." The subject of the letter was the same. And she repeated, "oh! I have never told you all about those days. But I will when I see you and Rose again." (Rose, of course, was Lottie's daughter, Southworth's granddaughter; as previously noted, Rose had recently separated from her husband.) "The dear Heavenly Father made it all up to me," Southworth continued, "and I ought to forgive and forget." But she said with emphasis, "*I do forgive but I cannot forget.*" It is questionable whether Southworth ever told Lottie or Rose any more regarding her husband, just as it is not questionable whether she ever forgot what there was to tell.[28]

But in the fashion of a literary domestic, Southworth may have been telling her story to the world throughout her career. From the beginning her fiction contained variations on the theme of a woman sexually betrayed and abandoned, of marital infidelity and desertion. And there were Southworthian hints that the theme might have been hers. Written a few years after her husband left her and published serially in the *National Era* during 1849, Southworth's first novel, *Retribution*, subtitled *Or, The Vale of Shadows, A Tale of Passion*, concentrates on the theme of sexual infidelity. In her autobiographical sketch Southworth claimed that she had begun *Retribution* after considering "several subjects of a profoundly moral and philosophical nature upon which the very trials and sufferings of my own life had led me to reflect, and from among them selected that of *moral retribution.*" And in her preface to the novel she told the "reader," "The story, as a whole, is not *unfounded* in fact .... "[29]

The novel itself focuses upon the marriage of Hester Gray and her subsequent betrayal by her husband, Ernest Dent, who seeks a sexual relationship with Hester's closest friend, Juliette Summers. Hester never becomes privy to the affairs of another's heart, but, always one to muse, she thinks to herself, " 'Love married to veneration is ecstasy—love divorced from veneration is anguish.' " Believing that said ecstasy is hers and unaware of the anguish that might be hers, Hester remains blissfully ignorant right up to her death from consumption. Having described the death of Hester, "the loving, but unloved; the gentle yet oppressed; the confiding, though deceived," Southworth interjects herself again to tell her "reader," "The people with whose history I have been trying to amuse you, really 'lived, and moved, and had their being;' really loved, and sinned, and suffered, in this veritable world of ours." With Hester "*out of the way,*" Ernest and Juliette marry, but their relationship is marred by fits of jealousy, mistrust, and guilt, and inevitably ends in disaster for both. Not one to let the reader miss the moral, Southworth closes the novel by saying, "I have tried to show you how from the sin, domestic infidelity and treachery, sprung inevitable the punishment, domestic distrust and wretchedness." When the sin of Ernest and Juliette is exposed for the reader, Hester's retribution, and perhaps Southworth's, is made complete.[30]

But Southworth remained a handmaiden to the theme of the broken chain of love. Published only a year later, Southworth's second novel, *The Deserted Wife*, centered upon the same theme of sexual betrayal combined with that of abandonment. And the literary domestic was not done. Married in fact for only four years, Southworth considered herself a wronged woman, which is to say that in her own mind she had been denied, through no fault of her own, woman's only true identity. In a sense it can be said that she rejected the recourse of divorce that a United States senator's bill would have allowed her because she considered the bill irrelevant and the issue of her legal marital status moot. Legislation could neither replace nor retrieve what she had lost forever, and married in name only, she spent nearly the last fifty years of her life writing of wronged women.

Sara Parton also confronted the issue of marital infidelity and desertion, but with an ironic twist. Before her first marriage in 1837 to the Boston banker Charles Eldredge, she received a letter of love from Eldredge that, in the language of love, promised everything. "I love thee with a passionate earnestness," he began, "a depth and strength of affection that language may not paint and thought scarce imagine!" Nevertheless, by the aid of his language he asked her to imagine all she could. "Imagine," he said, "what rapture would possess me when we are once fairly embarked on the boundless ocean of love, with no limit to enjoyment and no restraint but the will." "Imagine," he went on, "imagine me then fully thine by bridal as well as troth, and then paint if thou canst the rapture that follows." But she could not, he said, "thou canst not," because "imagination hath no spell where with to conjure up so bright a dream." From all indications, Parton's nine years as Charles's wife were largely nine years of happiness. Parton certainly remembered them as such. However, in a perverse way that too became a memory to be mocked. Following Eldredge's unexpected death in 1846, and after Parton struggled for three years to support herself and two children, all of which was faithfully remembered in *Ruth Hall*, Parton entered a second marriage in 1849 with Samuel P. Farrington, a Boston merchant. If in her first marriage Parton had been able to "conjure up a dream," she found in her second that reality imposed a nightmare. Goaded in part, probably, by Parton's cherished memory of her first husband and by her sexual unresponsiveness, Farrington apparently sought an end to what he may have conceived as his nightmare, and an end to the marriage. He charged Parton with desertion and, aided by his brother, spread false rumors of her sexual infidelities. The marital misalliance ended in separation after two years, followed by separate divorces after two more.[31]

In perverse fashion, the entire episode illustrated the truth that for the woman love and marriage were inextricably linked, that the woman was not so much dependent upon love as she was wedded to a station in life. By piecing together miscellaneous documents from Parton's personal papers the story can be read. Many years later, in a letter written in 1899, Parton's daughter Ellen stated that Farrington "was a very common man, but [Parton] supposed him to be a good man." This supposition was based in part on the fact that Farrington was a member of Boston's Park Street Church—he was, wrote Ellen, "active in its prayer meetings." Parton married Farrington, claimed the daughter, "solely to provide a home for her children," adding, "but not until all her efforts to do so by her needle had failed—for it was not till later years that she attempted to support herself and them by her pen." Although Parton had a place in mind, rather than love in her heart, she "did not deceive [Farrington] as to her inability to love him," Ellen asserted, "but supposed she could render an equivalent in her care of his home and two motherless children, for he was a widower." But this bargain was not made in heaven. "It was all a terrible mistake," said Ellen, "he became jealous of her appearance, and even of her love for her dead husband, and raged that he could not obliterate his memory." The sorry episode ended, said the daughter, by Farrington's "trying to fabricate matter for a divorce from her. Later she got a divorce from him, and heard that he did also, in another state on the plea of desertion."[32]

Parton herself kept a variety of materials in an envelope marked by her hand "Farrington Papers, To be opened only in case of my death. My daughter Grace will understand the duplicity of S. F.'s letters." The documents enclosed indicate that Ellen's description of the relationship was not simply the biased recollection of a loyal daughter. For example, Farrington's brother Thomas wrote, in a document dated 28 January 1851 and entitled "To Whom it May Concern, or For Mrs. S. P. Farrington," that "I deny ever having used the following words in regard to Mrs. S. P. Farrington, my brother's wife 'that Mrs. S. P. Farrington at other houses had received visitors who remained all night, and supposed she did at Marlboro.' " Thomas Farrington also stated that "I deny ever having uttered such words or anything like them and if I ever have uttered words injurious to her character I extremely regret it, and Mrs. Farrington may rest assured that she will have no reason to complain for the future of my remarks I may make in regard to her." A notice that Samuel Farrington inserted in the *Boston Daily Bee*, dated 25 February 1851, states "I hereby forbid all persons harboring or trusting my wife, Sarah [*sic*] P. Farrington, on my account from this date, having made suitable provision for her support." Farrington's divorce was granted on 7 September 1853 in Cook County, Illinois, on the grounds of desertion, and Parton also kept a copy of the decree, which states that "the said defendant has without any reasonable cause deserted and absented herself from the said complainant for the space of two years and upwards before the filing of said bill." Parton had no desire to contest the divorce. As her granddaughter Ethel wrote later, it was granted "to her great relief and satisfaction." The entire "miserable episode," wrote Ethel, "was to her a kind of nightmare. She could never bear to recall it."[33]

The 1899 letter from Parton's daughter Ellen was written in response to an inquiry regarding Parton's marital history. "Dear Sir," the letter began, "Relying upon your promise of secrecy, which I know as a gentleman you will keep, I will answer your first question—My mother *did* marry again in Boston a few years after my father's death . . . ." In response to other questions, Ellen said she had no idea if Parton's second husband was related to "Mrs. Stowe"; regarding his name, she responded that "his name is immaterial as you will not mention him or the marriage either in person or on paper." Ellen's words suggest that Parton in one respect may have attempted to remove from the public record while she lived any evidence that there had been a second marriage. If so, she succeeded to an extent: a number of biographical references published in the nineteenth century mention only Parton's first and third marriages, as if the second had never occurred. Parton also omitted the episode from *Ruth Hall*, while recreating, as has been noted, every other known event in her life from that period. It was an episode that Parton definitely wanted to forget and wished she could efface. "All this is very painful to me," wrote Ellen, "and my mother never spoke of it, or thought it concerned others," although, she noted, her mother "never withheld the knowledge" of it from those close to her. That was not exactly the truth. Following Parton's death, correspondence between Ellen and James Parton (who, incidentally, were later married), suggests that Farrington attempted to gain money from Parton's estate and may even have resorted to blackmail, threatening disclosure of the marriage. Uppermost in James's mind, at least, was that the secret be kept from granddaughter Ethel—"She must *never* know of these things." As it happened, "never" lasted only a decade after Parton died. Ethel then learned of that period in her grandmother's life, and Parton's daughter Ellen admitted to her gentleman inquirer that efforts to insure secrecy notwithstanding, "the stories that man fabricated about her are still heard in echo, I believe," adding that they had contributed to her mother's abhorrence of publicity.[34]

Contradictory as always, Parton, the woman who wrote behind the veil of "Fanny Fern," may herself have contributed to the echoes, for she later drew upon her memory and her sealed documents to portray the second marriage and its aftermath exactly and faithfully, at least from her own perspective, in her only other novel, *Rose Clark*. As if she could not avoid it, Parton/Fern appeared to be forever caught in double, if delayed, exposure. In *Rose Clark*, Gertrude Dean, second fiddle to Rose in the novel, plays the part. Like her creator and her fictional counterpart, Ruth Hall, Gertrude also enjoys a love song of a first marriage. " 'Never was a wife blessed with a truer heart to rest upon,' " she says, " 'never was a wife nearer forgetting that happiness is but the exception in this world of change.' " But after a number of years her husband dies unexpectedly, leaving her with a child, and for a while she too struggles to support the two of them. As she tells Rose, " 'I found the world what all find it who need it. Why weary you with a repetition of its repulses— of my humiliations, and struggles, and vigils? Years of privation and suffering passed over my head.' " The message has a familiar ring, of course, and after a while she marries a widower with two children.[35]

At first, Gertrude relates to Rose, she hesitated when John Stahle proposed to her. " 'My heart recoiled at the thought,' " she says, " 'for my husband was ever before me.' " She desired a home for her child, but she did not love Stahle and she told him so: " 'I told him that the marriage must not be consummated—that my heart was in my husband's grave—that I could not love him as I saw he desired, and that our union under such circumstances could never be a happy one.' " Stahle protested, saying that even if he could only have her " 'friendship' " in marriage, that would be sufficient for him. Nonetheless, he tricked her by planting an announcement in a newspaper that they had already been married, and in her confusion Gertrude agreed to the marriage. Then a more fundamental deception was exposed. Thinking she had married " 'a conscientious *Christian*,' " Gertrude found instead that " 'he was a hypocrite, and a gross sensualist. That it was passion, not love, which he felt for me, and that marriage was only the stepping-stone to an else impossible gratification.' " In short, the marriage unraveled when Gertrude proved sexually unresponsive. Separation followed, and with the aid of his brother Stahle sought to place the onus on Gertrude by circulating rumors that she had refused to join him in another city and that she had been unfaithful to him. The rumors of her infidelity were particularly galling to her and, because in the eyes of society she had violated the woman's standard of fidelity, mortifying. " 'Men stared insolently at me in the street,' " she recalls, and " 'women cast self-righteous scornful glances.' "[36]

True to the letter, Stahle's divorce based upon desertion was granted. As Gertrude tells her brother, " 'I have a copy of the divorce papers in my possession, and the only allegation there preferred is, that I did not accept Stahle's invitation to join him.' " Gertrude, unlike Ruth Hall and Sara Parton, chooses painting rather than writing as a means of supporting herself. And she gets her revenge. Expecting Gertrude to " 'just fold her hands, and let the first man who offered to find her in clothes,' " Stahle is chagrined when he learns years later that she has achieved eminence as a painter. " 'She was good-looking,' " he tells an acquaintance, " 'and it was what I reckoned on to sustain the rumors I took care to circulate about her before I left; but what does she do but shut herself up, work night and day, and give the lie to every

one of them.' " As for Stahle, his successful business career suffers a decline
and he ends as a clerk in a grocery store. One can only surmise what
happened to his real-life counterpart.[37]

When Sara Parton, as "Fanny Fern," contributed a biographical sketch of
Mary Abigail Dodge, or "Gail Hamilton," to *Eminent Women of the Age*,
she noted that her subject had once commented that wives needed to be told
by their husbands that they were loved. "Our author has probably heard
husbands reply to this," wrote Parton, " 'Why, *that* is of course understood;
it is childish to wish or expect such a thing put into words.' " Whether it was
a matter of " 'childishness' " or not, said Parton, "if it makes a wife happier,
is it wise, or best, for a husband to overlook that fact?" But Parton had no
questions about one matter: "sure I am," she said, that "many a wife loses all
heart for her monotonous round of duties for the want of it." Besides, she
added, "when men the world over have promulgated the fact that women are
but 'grown-up children,' where's the harm of being 'childish?' " Implicit in
Parton's flippancy, however, was the idea of the monotony of woman's duties
fostering the love fancies of the young maiden, and of the harm done when
women remained forever childish. Whether the dream of love made the
woman happier or not, it would be wiser and better to make else of love and
thereby make more of the woman's life.[38]

The literary domestics trucked heavily in love stories, in love attained as
well as denied, in the allure and danger of the passions. But they sought to
remind themselves and they continually reminded their readers of a higher,
truer love. "What love is," wrote Maria McIntosh in *Woman an Enigma*, is
"not the sport of an exuberant fancy, not the wild tumult of passion,"
although, she acknowledged, perhaps mindful of her own tendency, that to
such had love's "pure name . . . been too often applied." Rather, love was
"the deep, earnest emotion with which a spirit devotes itself to another spirit,
seeks its happiness and rejoices in its excellence, willingly surrendering to
these the attainment of its own personal desires." Responding simultaneously to their own self-doubts and to a society they felt devalued
them, the literary domestics sought to affix a seal of purpose and significance
to their designated lives. At the center of the familial circle of mutual needs,
desires, and dependencies, they could conceive no other or higher standard
for their lives than selfless devotion and service to those in the home. The
necessary measure of their lives, it was the singular ethic for a single destiny.
"Such a love—and no other deserves the name," said McIntosh, "elevates
and purifies the heart into which it enters and, instead of the absorbing
influence which passion exercises, it extends its view of its own obligations,
and strengthens it for their performance."[39]

The literary domestics were forever signing their pictures in the name of the morality of love. In the preface to her novel *Pink and White Tyranny* Harriet Beecher Stowe hastened to inform her audience that hers was "a story with a moral." As if concerned that her intent might nevertheless elude obtuse readers, she took them by the hand and explained her less than subtle approach. She had decided, she wrote, to adopt "the plan of the painter who wrote under his pictures, 'This is a bear' and 'This is a turtledove.' " Those who might still worry lest they miss the moral were assured that "we shall tell you in the proper time succinctly just what the moral is." In the reading of it there was no missing the moral, but true to her word, Stowe left nothing to chance. Late in the novel she turned and addressed her audience: "Love, my dear ladies, is self-sacrifice; it is a life out of self and in another. Its very essence is the preferring of the comfort, the ease, the wishes of another to one's own, for the love we bear them. Love is giving, not receiving." Stowe had signed her picture.[40]

Like a combination of catechism and rally, the literary domestics recounted lessons learned as if by rote to tutor womankind, and they sounded and sought to elicit praise of womankind. The spur to catechism and rally was the ever-present, underlying attempt beneath and beyond their prose to quell inner tremors of doubt regarding the *raison d'être* of the woman's life. Women's hearts, claimed Augusta Evans Wilson in a letter to Rachel Lyons Heustis, "are enshrined for holier idols than the world can erect; they must have either Love or Duty. The fortunate and happiest women have both." The fortunate and happiest had both by making love duty and duty love. The desire, the need, and the effort were to persuade themselves and their kind and to alert mankind that woman's obligations were of the highest order. In the name of the woman of the home, they expressed and professed woman's need to feel useful, to believe that she could shape a life of significance and live a life of demonstrated accomplishment. " 'I am waiting for the drumbeat of duty,' " says Beryl Brentano in Wilson's *At the Mercy of Tiberius*, " 'and my march may begin at any moment.' "[41]

To transform destiny into duty was to transform and spiritualize the person. "What a change had the discipline of life wrought in Isabella's character!" wrote Catharine Maria Sedgwick of Isabella Linwood in *The Linwoods*. There had been no change in the qualities of the person as such, for they were "still the same; the same energy of purpose; the same earnestness in action, the same strength of feeling." What had changed was that those qualities were now "flowing in the right channel," that is, they now had "a moral aim"; they were now "governed by that religious sense of *duty*, which is to the spirit in this perilous voyage of life what the compass is to the mariner." Actually, the direction of the woman's journey of life was known; it was the spirit of the voyage that remained in question. "A happy temperament," Sedgwick wrote in that tale of wrecked voyages, *Married or Single?*, "may sustain one through a healthful and occupied youth, but nothing less than a religious spirit can meet the strain when cares, and toil, and change—that come to all—come." If that were not so, Sedgwick asked, "Why do so many married and unmarried women waste, and fret, and fritter away life, instead of seeing that each cross, trial, and blessing is a rung of that ladder which is set for them to mount to heaven! Let them pray and strive for the spirit that makes life duty, and duty life." Printed on the title page of Augusta Evans Wilson's novel *Macaria; or, Altars of Sacrifice* were the words, "We have all to be laid upon an altar; we have all, as it were, to be subjected to the action of fire." For the woman of the home that was as much an expression of need as it was a call to duty.[42]

Fulfillment of duty and consciousness of usefulness were equated with happiness and were subsumed under selfless service. Utilizing their prose to promote and inculcate the ethic, the literary domestics presented their younger heroines in the female's initial stages of instruction. Augusta Moray, the heroine of McIntosh's pointedly titled *Two Pictures; or, What We Think of Ourselves, and What the World Thinks of Us*, is predicably admonished by her minister to " 'Get away from yourself—let your sympathies and work be no longer for yourself . . . but for the needy and sorrowing wherever you find them.' " Maria Cummins's Mabel Vaughan, in the novel of the same name, is informed by the headmistress of her female academy that the " 'great lesson of love' " is more important than any of the formal subjects taught at the school: " 'Learn above all things,' " the headmistress says sternly, " 'to beware of self-love, and cultivate to the utmost a universal charity.' " The lesson is to be "learned patiently, truly, and with the whole heart, not carelessly scanned, or foolishly toyed with, but diligently received into the soul, and planted there forever." That lesson had been so fully learned by E.D.E.N. Southworth's Catherine Kavanaugh in *The Curse of Clifton* that she "lived only for the good of others," having "grown to believe that there was no individual happiness for herself except in the service of others."[43]

It was the woman's life that had to be redeemed, and the literary domestics' at times strident message to their reading public was that having learned well the supreme ethic of selfless service, women could not help but lead lives of supreme value. As Terhune's Ida Ross phrases it in *Alone*, " 'The more we have to love, the better we feel, the better we are.' " Of the day that Ruth Raymond, in Gilman's aptly titled *Love's Progress*, realizes her life's duty it is said, "That day had unfolded a fresh leaf in her heart's history; it was no longer an impaled butterfly that moved her sympathy; a new *love* stirred her affections, the love of suffering fellow creatures."[44]

If home was Eden, if no ordinary, workaday home was envisioned, no merely mortal woman could stand at its door. And in serving others, the more than mortal woman became more than a "help-meet." She became the controlling force in her circle. She became like Southworth's Vivia Laglorieuse in *Vivia* "ever the medium of animating, sustaining, or redeeming life to all within her sphere." When active self-sacrifice was made a duty, the performance of duty transformed the woman into a force for control, influence, and power. Fleda Ringgan in Susan Warner's *Queechy* is no less that the central, controlling force in her sphere. Obviously full of " 'character!' " she is " 'happy in doing her duty,' " " 'admirable at managing people,' " in short, the " 'moving spirit of the household.' " The most compelling testimony to woman's superiority is her boundless capacity for devotion to others. The pages of Sedgwick's *Home* present an animated prototype of the domestic woman dressed in perfectionist robes. She is the conductor orchestrating the morality of home economics:

> What sense she has manifested, what beautiful order and neatness in her domestic economy, and in a higher moral economy, how she excells all others. How she sees and foresees, provides against all wants, avoids irritation and jealousies, economizes happiness, saving those little odds and ends that others waste. How she employs the faculties of all, brings the virtue of each into operation, and if she cannot cure, shelters faults. She shows each in the best light, and is herself the light that shines on all—the sun of her *home*.

Sedgwick's wife and mother is the dominating figure responsible for establishing the standards of behavior, seeing that others adhere to those standards—and in the process making everyone supremely happy about it.[45]

In the Edenic home the dream was at the very least a partnership of love between husband and wife. Rather than a ruling husband, the ethic of love's selfless service was to rule the man as well as his wife. The humanized wife and husband were wedded in mutual respect and perfect harmony. Stowe sought to assure the readers of *We and Our Neighbors* that the true tale of a wife and husband's union was one of an intense, benevolent partnership. "Intimate friendship—what the French call *camaraderie*," she stated, was "the healthiest and best cement." In the introduction to *My Wife and I*, Stowe described the marital relationship in religious terms, as "the oldest and most venerable form of Christian union on record." Her chosen title, "MY WIFE AND I," she stressed, was to be construed as the "sign and symbol of more than any earthly partnership or union," as instead "something sacred as religion, indissoluble as the soul, endless as eternity—the symbol chosen by Almighty Love to represent his redeeming, eternal union with the soul of man." Although the partnership was to be made in the spirit of the hereafter, it was nevertheless to be an earthly one of mutual love defined as reciprocal devotion and service. Writing to her twin daughters Hattie and Eliza in 1859, Stowe explained the purpose of the domestic, albeit sacred, arrangement. "God, in conducting us into this love," she told them, "knows we cannot step

272

to his height at one step, and so he has ordered our human relations so that we shall learn this great lesson a little at a time." To a woman "he sends some one man" but to the man as well he sends "some one woman for whose sake all things seem to become possible." Together, she declared, they might attempt to "rise to the great height of loving to spend and be spent for others as he does."[46]

Ironically, however, the figure that frequently intrudes upon and disrupts the idealized balance of mutual respect and benevolence is the paradoxical one of the loving woman in service to others who is simultaneously glorified as a superior, strong, commanding figure directing and controlling all in her sphere, including the traditional head-of-household, the male. That figure is only partially obscured in Caroline Lee Hentz's novel *Robert Graham*. Ostensibly, Hentz was attempting to present a cameo of Linda and Roland Lee, wife and husband, mother and father of a child, seated cosily beside each other before the hearth in their tranquil home. It is a fitting touch that Hentz, the literary domestic, puts a book in Roland's hand. At the moment, however, as if compelled by a superior force, he is more interested in "perusing a fairer page in the face of Linda." Unaware that their young son Walton has entered the room, he is drawn to Linda's face and wonders why it is illumined by a "radiant smile," why her arms are outstretched, why she has glanced at him "as if directing his attention." In part, his questions are answered when he hears the "cherub voice of infancy," when he sees their son, "her own darling Walton." After the "beautiful young mother" embraces Walton and kisses him on his "soft, round cheeks [and] baby brow," Linda presents her son to her husband, to enable Roland to admire their child's "infantine loveliness and grace." What is made possible is also demanded, and Roland of course acquiesces, "so as to satisfy her fond, exacting maternal pride." Still, he obviously admires—as he must—"the lovely, graceful mother more." This domestic dream is completed, Linda is satisfied and fulfilled, as Roland embraces her and Walton, the mother and her child, his heart swelling "with love and gratitude too deep for utterance."[47]

Hentz seems to be the soft singer of domestic blissfulness, her dream-sketch full of sentimentality, an exaltation of the home. The home is the Garden of Eden, an oasis of harmony, affection, and virtue, with no tension and nary an instance of conflict disturbing the tranquil setting, with no anger and certainly no hostility marring the joy and contentment shared by every member of the family. Linda is goodness and beauty, the feminization of everlasting virtue. In Roland's embrace of both mother and child is the symbolic fulfillment of his role, the promise that not only will he continue to woo his beloved mate and worship her long after they have stood at the altar, he will also provide for the family's security and comfort. And Walton is, and will be, loved and nurtured in virtue by Linda, loved and materially provided for by Roland, and in fulfillment of the American family's primary obligation, properly raised.

The underlying tone, however, is not contentment but yearning. Although Roland is not the ruler of this Garden of Eden, neither is he an idle or purposeless figure. Although he is understated, he is planted in the scene, as it were, to pay homage to Linda. The cultivation is of a different sort. Walton is effectively Linda's child, not hers and Roland's. The dream-sketch is Linda's, not the family's, as Linda reaches for her child, directs her husband's gaze, and practically wills the final embrace. Hentz, the literary domestic, presented "a fairer page in the face of Linda" by way of compelling tribute to the domestic woman.

In the prose of literary domesticity the male Roland Lee does not stand alone in his worshipful admiration of ideal womanhood. The domestic dream has its male chorus of female-worshippers. And the male in awe of woman, the male who praises her and who is inspired by her, is a male who acknowledges her superiority. Of course, in a prose captivated by courtship most male admirers are single suitors rather than entrenched husbands. Typically, the prospective husband attributes a hybrid combination of qualities to his beloved intended, a woman who is virtuous, of course, but who at the same time represents a peculiarly potent, energetic strain of traditional, retired femininity. In *Poganuc People*, Stowe's Dolly Cushing receives just such a curious accolade from her suitor, Alfred Dunbar, who says, " 'She impresses me as having, behind an air of softness and timidity, a very positive and decided character.' " That character, that " 'sort of reserved force,' " is apparent in Dolly's defense of " 'everything high and noble.' " The central heroine of Parton's *Rose Clark* impresses a male admirer as " 'so pure, so childlike, so trusting and yet so strong, so immovable in what she considers right' "; and the female paradigm of Warner's *Daisy* is told by her suitor that she is " 'strong as a giant, and gentle as a snowflake.' " As McIntosh phrases it in *The Lofty and the Lowly*, with help from Wordsworth's couplet, each woman in the eyes of the dream man is " 'A perfect woman, nobly planned' " and planning to head for the home; but each is also planning " 'to warn, to comfort and command' " in the home.[48]

The man who reaches the dream home is prepared for his task. In the dream home the woman's influence is not to be denied by any male; even more, the male is to be acquiescent. " 'You can mold me at your will,' " a suitor promises his intended bride in Mary J. Holmes's *Hugh Worthington*. Stowe's *My Wife and I; or, Harry Henderson's History* articulates the effect of that molding, which is both unofficial and undeniable. Commenting upon the relationship between his mother and father, Harry Henderson describes his mother's influence—read iron command—over his father as a "spiritual and invisible" one, as that of the "soul over the body." The power of the soul, or of his mother, is a "subtle and vital power which constantly gains control and holds every inch that it gains" over the "visible, forceful, obtrusive, self-assertive body," or his yielding father. Gradually but surely, says Harry, his mother became his father's "leader and guide," and his father began to exhibit "new and finer traits of tenderness and a spirituality [that] pervaded his character and his teachings." Harry has observed what his father readily acknowledges to his son that she " 'made me by her influence.' "[49]

The ideal man made by literary domesticity was made in the image of the ideal woman. The transformation constituted the feminization of the male, for the heroes, at least in most respects, exhibit the qualities of heroines. In fact, Holmes's Irving Stanley in *Hugh Worthington*, said to be "kind and gentle as a woman," is "laughed at by his own sex, as too gentle, too feminine in disposition." But, writes Holmes, "those who knew him best loved him most, and loved him, too, just because he was not so stern, so harsh, so overbearing as men are wont to be." The feminized male was the ideal male partly because he did not manifest those qualities that the supposed traditional male was thought to want, and to be wont to exhibit. In *Two Pictures*, McIntosh wrote in her preface concerning the fictional character of Hugh Moray that there were those "who may recognize in the child-hearted Commodore Moray . . . a feeble portraiture" of one whom they knew and of whom it could be said, " 'None knew *him* but to love *him*.' " McIntosh's attribution of female and, therefore, exemplary qualities to an admired male character, real or fictional, was an act of love in which all the literary domestics joined. In this instance Moray, and presumably whomever he was based upon, demonstrated among other qualities a "generous consideration for others" and a "more than womanly tenderness."[50]

Qualities were also joined to actions, actions on behalf of womanhood and domestic life. The ideal, feminized male is also fully capable of discerning the graduated obligations entailed in his love of womankind. Hentz's Russell Rovington of *Lovell's Folly* realizes that before he can marry, he must first see to the needs of his mother and sisters. His primary obligation is to protect them from the threat posed by a $20,000 debt incurred by his late father. If necessary, he is ready to deny himself the affection of the heroine, to renounce marriage itself. In short, he is "the devoted son, the affectionate brother, merging every selfish consideration in the all-governing principle of filial and fraternal affection." Not so indirectly, the male hero feminized represented another way to excite interest in the fortunes of heroines.[51]

Yet as Harriet Beecher Stowe also affirmed in her 1859 letter to her twin daughters, there was in Eden an even greater love, an even more "unselfish" love that stemmed "from this love of man and woman," and that was a "parent's love [which] is all giving." When Sedgwick's niece Kate became pregnant in the early spring of 1844, Sedgwick went a step further, stating that not only was parental love of a higher order than the love between wife and husband, but the former promised to have a necessary salutary effect upon the latter. Children, she wrote her niece, constituted the "greatest good in life" not least because they "secure loving married people from the desperate selfishness that is apt to grow out of their very love when it is pent up in such a narrow channel and passed one self to another." But if the call was to both parents to lead this ultimate life among lives of active selflessness, the calling was nevertheless preeminently the woman's. Following the birth of Kate's child later that year, Sedgwick wrote to congratulate her, stating again that Kate had "received the *best* gift that God gives to his creatures." She also warned Kate again, saying, "I trust my dear child" that the future "will find you guarding against that mere extension of self love with which some parents love their children." What Sedgwick hoped was that Kate would find in her newborn child a "newspring of love," that she would receive a renewed "impulse of activity of devotion" to those in her immediate circle, that is, that Kate would recognize a new "opportunity of doing good." Motherhood constituted woman's most challenging involvement because it demanded that she give the most. Gilman was unconsciously redundant when in *Recollections of a Housekeeper* she asked through her alter ego, Clarissa Packard, if the total care and cultivation of a child was not "occupation enough for a young mother." At age sixty-nine in 1863, long after Gilman's most demanding days of motherhood had passed, she acknowledged to her daughter Eliza that "still the mother-want will come." From this act of giving the most, the woman claimed the most.[52]

The claim was both implicit and explicit. It was implicit in the simplest, most basic of first duties. Sara Parton's "A Mother's Soliloquy" delineates the mother's charge, fully accepted: " 'I am the centre of [the child's] little world; its very life depends upon my faithful care.' " The language is saccharine, the tone maudlin, but the point is made: " 'It is my sweet duty to deck those dimpled limbs—to poise that tiny, trembling foot. Yet Stay,—my duty ends not here! A soul looks forth from those blue eyes—an undying spirit, that shall plume its wing for ceaseless flight guided by my erring hand.' " In Parton's *Ruth Hall*, long before Ruth Hall becomes the writer "Floy," happiness is unrestrained when Ruth gives birth to her first child, which brings her "another outlet for thy womanly heart"; she possesses "a mirror" from which her total being shall be "reflected back"; and she has most of all "a fair page on which thou, God-commissioned, mayst write what thou wilt; a heart that will throb back to thine, love for love."[53]

The claim was made explicit in the most grandiloquent terms. Terhune hoped in "A Christmas Talk with Mothers" that women would recognize the "grandeur of the work assigned to them." Mothers were, wrote Terhune, "the architects of the nation's fortunes; the sculptors, whose fair or foul handiwork is to outlast their age, to outlive Time, to remain through all Eternity." Implicit or explicit, this claim, more than any other, constituted a defense and justification of the woman's life. Men had their functions and women had theirs, said Terhune in *Eve's Daughters*, but women could not and should not forget, she wrote, "that part of it which men *can not* perform, to wit, the bearing, the nursing, and the rearing of those who are to carry on the work of the species in years to come." By assuming control of first duties, the woman projected for herself lasting power and glory.[54]

The woman's dream of the glory of domesticity amounted to a transformation of desire into what was imagined to be the only dream possible. The literary domestics' urgent, compelling mission was to envision the woman in the manner of Southworth's aptly named Mrs. Hardcastle in *The Discarded Daughter* as in "the full bloom of perfectly developed vital beauty" directly as the result of the fact that "marriage and maternity had been to her healthful, sanguine, and joyous organization, what it should be to all women, a continuous accession of new life, health, and happiness." It was not by accident, however, that the woman's dream frequently hovered out of context or lacked dramatic moorings in the public pages of the literary domestics because the real drama was not literary, but personal. In 1821 Charles Sedgwick wrote his sister to ask, "Are you writing a novel that you want a sketch of Nelson's mansion, or are you leagued with Cooper in setting off the dark shades of real life against the bright creation of a poet's fancy?" Like his brother, Henry Dwight, before him, Charles was being whimsical, but his question was a question to be asked in earnest as well. At the time, his sister Catharine was not only beginning her first novel, she was also beginning her career—and she was beginning both without realizing it. That was an appropriate opening to Sedgwick's career, as well as to the saga of literary domesticity. When Caroline Howard Gilman was working in 1838 on the story of Ruth Raymond, later to be titled *Love's Progress*, she wrote to her sister Harriet Fay, "It is a curious thing in my narratives, that when I sit down to write a chapter I have no more idea of the result than my readers." That did not strike her as the correct way to proceed. "It cannot be the right way I am certain," she said, "and I wish I could discipline myself into a regular story." But what manner of control was possible when the dream of the way it was supposed to be was spawned by forebodings of the way it was to be?[55]

In an undated letter to her publisher, James T. Fields, regarding her latest unspecified work, Harriet Beecher Stowe recoiled at the deadlines contained in the contract. "I am so constituted that it is absolutely fatal to me to agree to have any literary work done at certain dates," she said. Uncharacteristically for a literary domestic, she claimed to be "bound by the laws of art." She explained that "sermons essays lines of distinguished people I can write to order," but, she continued, "at times and seasons a story *comes*—grown like a flower—sometimes will and sometimes won't like a pretty woman." When the "spirits" cooperated, she said, "I can write." And when they did not, "When they grin, flout, make faces and otherwise maltreat me I can only wait humbly at their gates, watch at the post of their doors." But even when the muses beckoned, when as women of the home the literary domestics turned inward, turned back upon themselves, the "dark shades of real life" bedeviled the "bright creations" of their fancies. That was inevitable when their tale was of dreams born of reality. It was foreordained when the woman was bound by the laws of her destiny.[56]

To resort to dreams to rationalize secret truths was tantamount to openly telling the truth. To tell of dreams denied was to tell of the secret knowledge of a personal reality. "Ah! could we lay bare the secret history of many a wife's heart," wrote Sara Parton as "Fanny Fern" in her telltale novel, *Ruth Hall*, "what martyrs would be found, over whose uncomplaining lips the grave sets its unbroken seal of silence." When the woman became a writer it was difficult not to break the "seal of silence." When the mind was made over it was difficult to separate dreams from reality. "She ventured too much upon those she loved and trusted," wrote Anna Warner of her sister Susan, recalling the late 1850s, when the two unmarried women were struggling to write books and pay bills. "As in the old time," wrote Anna, remembering Susan's early penchant for telling tales, "she broke her heart over the peccadilloes of imaginary heroes and heroines"—and "now, when she put the same faultless standard for people of real flesh and blood, and they came short, the pain was great. Always setting her dear true heart upon something that slipped aside and fell to atoms. And then the head ached, and the hands hung down." When the life she had to live proved either unavailable or unbearable, it was not surprising that what Maria McIntosh called in *Two Pictures* "the burdened heart and bitter consciousness of the woman" surfaced, in whatever guise. Just as the woman could create her dream, she could give it the lie, as Terhune did in saying in *Ruby's Husband*, "I am writing hard things and heavy to be borne by the young with whom hope is reality, and thoughts of love dearer than promise of life, wealth, and honor." That was so, continued the literary domestic, because "he who sketches from nature must, perforce, oftentimes fulfill the thankless task of iconoclast."[57]

To project the woman of the home as a strong, commanding, independent figure, to tout the selflessly serving woman as a powerful figure of influence and control was to beg the issue and betray an underlying conviction that the opposite was the case. The insistent, urgent presentation of woman as the glorified, ultimate practitioner of the ethic of selfless service stood instead as a transparent shield overlaying an always dependent and vulnerable figure. For herself or for some unspecified source, Southworth compiled a series of what she labeled "Mental Photographs." Included under the heading "your favorite" were her selections of color, flower, and tree, the hour of the day and the season of the year, painters, poets, and musicians. Under "What is your idea of happiness" she wrote "power, beauty, united circle." Under "What is your idea of misery" she penciled "the opposite of the above." Her favorite "Style of Beauty" was "Intellectual and Queenly." And in answer to, "If not yourself who would you rather be," she stated, "A Queen Regnant."[58]

In the consciousness of literary domesticity there was a vision of power and a lament of powerlessness. A fantasy of strength, control, and autonomy was engendered by the pall of burdens, subordination, and dependence. To the editor of a magazine Terhune charged that "women's work is nine times out of ten, a 'pot-boiler,'—a hook on which she hangs until a husband appears to catch her from below. Then she lets go with both hands." That was to say, as Terhune did in "Nobody to Blame," that "every wife is dependent, no matter what may be her fortune or strength of character." And what of her partner in love turned worshipful admirer? Even " 'good husbands,' " she wrote, would rarely "esteem it a lasting shame to themselves, if their wives had ever the least occasion to look back longingly to lost liberty, or to speculate secretly, whether wifehood—after all that has been said and written to dignify it—be anything more than honorable and licensed beggary." The conflict between head and heart engendered graver reflections. In *Caper-Sauce*, Sara Parton sought in one essay to blame husbands for their wives' bondage. Husbands, she said, "are very fond of the results that the 'family slave' brings about, in the shape of good food and well-mended clothes." And in another essay she responded to a lecture on woman's domestic duties by complaining, "I heard not one syllable from him upon the home duty devolving on the *father* and *the husband*." Not a word had she heard, wrote Parton, as she supplied her own, on what was "binding" on the man: "As if that *could* be 'home,' in any true sense, where *both* did not know and practice these duties." It was foremost the woman's mandate to make love duty and duty love, but, asked Parton in *Ginger-Snaps*, "is the self-sacrifice and self-abnegation all to be on one side? Is the 'weaker' always to be the stronger in this regard?" Having written on the subject herself, Harriet Beecher Stowe noted in *My Wife and I* that "in our days we have heard much said of the importance of training women to be wives." Nevertheless, she asked, "Is there not something to be said on the importance of training men to be husbands?"[59]

In *Recollections of a Southern Matron*, Caroline Howard Gilman timidly offered an explanation for the husband's failure to respond to his wife's needs. Suggesting that men did not understand "the moral and physical structure" of women, she noted that they "wound through ignorance and are surprised at having offended." Stowe was less timid in *The Pearl of Orr's Island*. "Men understand women only from the outside," she wrote, "and judge them with about as much real comprehension as an eagle might judge a canary-bird." The problem was that man was not of womankind. "The difficulty of real understanding," said Stowe, "intensifies in proportion as the man is distinctively manly, and the woman womanly." And Parton's anger was ever ready. "*They* don't dream," she said of men in *Ginger-Snaps*, "unless in very exceptionable cases, how a wife longs sometimes to have a husband testify his pleasure at her invariable good cheer in some other way than by gobbling it up, till he is as torpid as an anaconda."[60]

And the shadows were long indeed when love's sacred duties overwhelmed the woman. In *Recollections of a Housekeeper*, Gilman emphasized that woman conscientiously strives to fulfill her domestic duties, yet "cares eat away at her heart." The demands made were unceasing; each "day presses on her with new toils, the night comes, and they are unfulfilled; she lies down in weariness, and rises with uncertainty." "Many a woman," wrote Gilman, "breaks and sinks beneath the wear and tear of the frame and affections." Men were irritated by women's tears, noted Terhune in *Husbands and Homes*, but "let us rather be thankful for this flow, when sleepless nights, and days of fatigue, and solitude ... have racked and strained muscle and nerve, turned our daily bread into ashes, blunted our perceptions to all that was once beautiful to the sight, pleasant to the ear, stimulative to the intellect." Maria McIntosh sounded her notes of distress in *Woman in America*, keening for woman's afflictions: "Work—work—work, till heart and hand fail, till the cloud gather on her once sunny brow, and her cheeks grow pale, and friendly consumption come to give rest from her labors in the grave, or the throbbing brain and overanxious heart overpower the reason, and a lunatic asylum receive one more miserable inmate." McIntosh even resorted to citing an officer's report for the Retreat of the Insane in Hartford, Connecticut, drawing attention to its claim that many young women sought refuge in "lunatic" hospitals, unable or unwilling to do battle any longer with their domestic circumstances, what with "child-bearing, nursing, and the accumulation of household duties and drudgery." In one strike McIntosh had indicted the entire sweep of woman's destiny, by in effect linking the love fancies of the young and the joys of motherhood to a report on the mentally diseased.[61]

It was a report that Southworth would have read with interest, and lowered her head. Young women, she said in *The Deserted Wife*, were neither physically nor emotionally prepared for the burdens of marriage. In becoming wives they risked "wasting of health and life; the failing of beauty, decline of grace, and loss of attractions." If anyone doubted her, wrote the woman whose mother had married at age fifteen and who had herself married at age twenty, they need only mark "the vexations, [the] nervous irritability so common in young mothers, so destructive to domestic harmony and happiness." Suggesting that one must "ponder" a subject in order to acquire "knowledge," Parton asked in *Caper-Sauce*, "What is then to be the mental status of that mother who has a perpetual *baby* in her arms, and only time to 'ponder' that baby, so weary is her body with its 'ponder'-osity?" Rhetorical questions were a favorite literary device of Parton's. Previously, she had asked in *Ginger-Snaps*, "What of the ten or twelve, even healthy children, 'who come,' one after another, into the weary arms of a really good woman, who yet never knows the meaning of the word *rest* till the coffin lid shuts her in from all earthly care and pain?" Subtlety was not Parton's favorite approach.[62]

In 1899, Mary Virginia Terhune, the woman who almost twenty years before, in *Eve's Daughters*, had stated that a woman encountered difficulty in being an advocate because her idealistic, sympathetic, and above all, maternal nature made her a partisan, wrote an editor with a thought in mind. She wanted, she said, to write a piece entitled "The Woman with the Suds." If the title was unclear, Terhune's explanation was not: "It will be a plea for the class who make up three fourths of the women lunatics in N. E. insane asylums—the women whose intellects and finer tastes never have a chance." If the editor desired the essay, said Terhune, she would prepare it for him. But "whether you wish it or not, the article will be written." Of that the editor could have been left with little doubt. "The 'suds' are a-foam within me," she wrote, "the soapy steam is in my mental nostrils, and I must get it out." For Terhune the guilds of sentiment and suffering had obviously joined forces. Head and heart were in turmoil.[63]

The vise of woman's circumstances pressed and predicated the nature of the moral inquiry of her life. To seek the joys of life within the boundaries of her singular destiny was to confront the governing maladies of her life. To be dependent on the success of a single destiny was to be overwhelmed by sacred duties. Having identified with woman's destiny, Harriet Beecher Stowe continually measured herself in terms of duties performed. A sense of achievement, however, was well-nigh impossible. Instead, sacrifice of self proved debilitating. And Stowe's allegiance to selflessness notwithstanding, that very ethic ran counter to her desire for personal autonomy. At times Stowe did maintain a relatively satisfying life as a wife and mother, but veins of discord and despair were evident not only in her open admission concerning the heavy burden associated with the rearing of her children but also in her relationship with her husband Calvin. In 1844, having retreated from her home for a short visit to her brother Henry Ward Beecher, she wrote to Calvin to say that her brother's home embodied the "calm, placid quiet retreat I have been longing for." Temporarily extricated from her woman's circumstances, she had been able to reflect. Calvin himself had been away from home and, said Stowe, "you have no idea of the commotion that I have lived in since you left." The endless litany of household duties to be performed and children to be cared for echoed through her letters. Always there was "the cleaning—the children's clothes, and the baby." That the psychological burden had grown was equally apparent in her anguished dirge that everything in her home "often seemed to press on my mind all at once. Sometimes it [seemed] as if anxious thought [had] become a disease with me from which I could not be free." Whether Calvin was a sympathetic listener is open to question.[64]

In other significant respects Stowe's relationship with her husband was marred by strain and doubt. In part the friction between the two was rooted in disparate needs and different conceptions of their relationship. Calvin's personal demands came into conflict with Stowe's own desire for sexual and emotional autonomy, and she found it necessary to deny her husband. Calvin had been left a childless widower little more than a year before his marriage to Stowe and he looked to her to provide an end to his desperate loneliness, satisfy his sexual and emotional needs, and give him the children denied him in his first marriage. Stowe did not eschew intimacy but Calvin's demands were so intense and unremitting that her own autonomy was continually threatened. Writing to her prior to their marriage, Calvin foretold the immensity of those demands: "I will react upon all you have given me thus far, I will keep asking for more as long as I live (the fountain of that which I want is in you inexhaustible)." The problem, of course, was that Stowe's reserves were not inexhaustible. To try to meet Calvin's physical demands meant not only disregarding the need to protect her health but also denying her desire to control her reproductive function. To attempt to fulfill Calvin's emotional demands involved the risk of setting her own self adrift in the turbulence of Calvin's continually vacillating temperament. The problem, too, was that Calvin found it practically impossible to curb his demands. They were apart during nearly a third of the first fifteen years of their marriage, and their correspondence tells a story of a relationship continually beset by crisis. Faced off like soldiers in combat, they struggled to maintain both their positions and their marriage.[65]

Calvin's letters harp upon his sexual needs. He repeatedly lamented that "my arms and bosom are hungry, hungry even to starvation." He recalled the times that he had "lain on the same pillow with you, your face pressed to mine, and our bare bosoms together," and practically cursed the celibacy enforced by their separations. His desire to "just step into your bedroom . . . and take that place in your arms to which I alone of all men in the world ever had a right or ever received admission" nearly drove him into a frenzy. A devoted but markedly more restrained Stowe did not respond with the same passion. Determined to control the number and spacing of her children, Stowe saw their separations from a different perspective. Certainly she was sincere in writing that "I have thought of you with much love lately—a deep tender love—and I long to see you again." But she was also aware that the most effective method for controlling fertility, abstinence, was inherent in separation.[66]

In their unabating sexual tug-of-war, neither Stowe nor Calvin emerged unscathed, or victorious. Stowe's struggle to control her fertility was only partially successful: she gave birth to seven children and suffered at least two miscarriages. And her decision to try the water cure in Brattleboro, Vermont, in the mid-1840s reflected a growing invalidism fed from manifold sources, physical and psychological. She no doubt sought to rest a body exhausted by at least two miscarriages, drained and worn by family chores. Her journey away also promised a retreat from the tension engendered by psychological as well as by sexual conflict, and by the demands associated with bearing and rearing children. And it offered the opportunity to contemplate, in relative repose, unfulfilled ideals. Most certainly Stowe would have agreed with her husband that their conflicting needs were "bringing us both to the grave by the most lingering and painful process." Recalling that Stowe had been "so feeble and the prospect of permanent paralysis [had been] so threatening" during the winter prior to her departure for Vermont, Calvin admitted that he was resigned to their separation. Nevertheless, he informed her that he himself had fallen into a species of invalidism, had been in "a sad state physically and mentally" that winter. But the cure he proposed for himself meant the end of their separation and promised a recurrence of Stowe's invalidism: "If your health were so far restored that you could take me again to your *bed and board*, that would be the surest and safest, and indeed the only infallible way." In the end, they could not help each other. One's needs clashed with the other's; one's cure brought the other's illness.[67]

Inevitably the separation had a different effect upon each of them. Stowe had sought the water cure only after her condition had worsened. She could therefore regard absence from husband and children not as abandonment but as separation necessary for her eventual restoration to them. She could rationalize that she was continuing to serve them, rather then herself. Her psychological conflicts resolved, the water cure meant relief from the burdens of domesticity, a supportive atmosphere that was predominantly female, and physicians sympathetic to her maladies. It also brought a welcome respite from Calvin's demands. The separation intensified rather than assuaged Calvin's sexual longings, and it reintroduced loneliness. Brimming with anger and frustration, he recounted the one week that he had spent with her in Vermont. Their separation had made him all the more eager to see her, yet he still had to deny himself during this interlude. He had enjoyed their visit, had been satisfied to "see that you do love me after all." But that satisfaction had been severely limited by the "mean business of sleeping in another bed, another room, and even another house, and being with you as if you were a withered up old maid sister instead of the wife of my bosom." He concluded that "of all contemptible things the most unutterably intolerable is *having the love of marriage and denying the power thereof*."[68]

Other letters indicate that Calvin almost preferred separation to practicing abstinence when with his wife. In one letter written after Stowe had been away for ten months, he told her that "much as I suffer from your absence, I should suffer still more from your presence, unless you can be in a better condition than you have been for a year past." Why would the presence of someone to whom he was deeply devoted bring pain and frustration? Calvin bluntly reminded his wife, "It is now a full year since your last miscarriage, and you well know what has been the state of things both in regard to yourself and me ever since." A few months later he had changed his mind and stated emphatically, "I want you to come home." Why the reversal? What would he expect on her return? A sentence or two later he revealed his hope that her return would bring an end to his celibacy: "It is almost in fact eighteen months since I have had a wife to sleep with me. It is enough to kill any man, especially such a man as I am." Stowe did return shortly. She wrote to Calvin that she was "better but not well." As Calvin would relate to his mother, she compared herself to "a broken pitcher that has been boiled in milk, that needs very careful handling, or it will come to pieces again." Inevitably, the conflict between the two continued. Calvin no doubt continued to lament any restrictions on their sexual relationship. And Stowe, her devotion to her sons and daughters notwithstanding, must have had some misgivings about the two children whose births were crowded into the end of her childbearing years.[69]

Written a few days before their eleventh wedding anniversary in 1847, a letter of Stowe's to Calvin is indicative of her marital experiences, symbolic of her hopes and disappointments. Recognizing that she was "a very different being" at the outset of their marriage, she recalled her total desire "to live in love, absorbing passionate devotion to one person." The first time she and Calvin were separated was her "first trial." Comfort came with the prospect of motherhood: "No creature ever so longed to see the face of a little one or had such a heart full of love to bestow." That experience, however, proved to be agonizing: "Here came in trial again sickness, pain, constant discouragement—wearing wasting days and nights . . . ." In all of Stowe's marital experiences there had been much disappointment, much agony. She noted retrospectively that her and Calvin's very different characters made "painful friction inevitable." After eleven years the damage had been done, and the cost was tallied in Stowe's admission that "I do not love and never can love with the blind and unwise love with which I married." Stowe's love had been blind because it had known little of human inadequacy, unwise because it had asked too much. Had she the choice to make again she would choose the same, but she would love "far more wisely." Hers was the comment of a mature, chastened individual who had come to recognize the disparate needs and experiences brought to the marriage by each of them. But her attitude toward motherhood suggested greater regret. She had wished for much, yet felt she had received little. "Ah, how little comfort I had in being a mother," she wrote. "How all that I proposed met and crossed and my way ever hedged up!" In despair, she was even brought to thank God for teaching her that "I should make no family be my chief good and portion." But that was only a line in a letter sent out in a dark moment of self-recognition that there could be no other way.[70]

Shortly after the publication of *Oldtown Folks* in 1869, Stowe had responded to George Eliot's comments concerning the "success of the book." Implicit in Stowe's words was the suggestion that success for a woman was different than for a man. "Is it not true," she asked, "that what we authors want is not praise so much as sympathy?" That was to focus on the quandary of the person rather than the quality of the book; regarding the latter as a genus, the woman said, "A book is *a hand* stretched forth in the dark passage of life to see if there is another hand to meet it." The book was a symbolic hand stretched forth not only for sympathy but for deliverance. Later that summer Stowe extended a sympathetic hand to Eliot for what Stowe regarded as a familiar predicament for the woman. The image was one of intense commitment in debilitating circumstances. "I have been as you are," she said, "the one on whom many depend, a fountain from whom many draw and hence come deathly exhaustions." In 1872 she wrote again to explain her silence of a few years. "I have never answered," she said, "because two years of constant and severe work have made it impossible to give a drop to anything beyond the needs of the home." The words of Stowe's letters, borrowed from the pressing consciousness of her own circumstances, composed an acknowledgment of her own "dark passage" of life.[71]

11

Preachers of the Fictional Page

In her journal of 1836 Catharine Maria Sedgwick noted with more than idle interest the rationale for fiction presented by the British literary critic and moral philosopher Sir James Mackintosh in the posthumously published *Memoirs of the Life of the Right Honorable Sir James Mackintosh.* Sedgwick recorded Mackintosh's comment that " 'Fictitious narrative . . . was one of the grand instruments employed in the moral education of mankind, because it is only delightful when it interests, and to interest is to excite sympathy for the heroes of fiction—that is, in other words to teach men the habit of feeling for others.' " It is not surprising that Mackintosh's statement struck a vein of truth for Sedgwick. Her consciousness could faithfully receive from his words the call to fulfill the principle of selfless service. The "habit of feeling for others" could be readily identified as hers in service to others. And for the woman who had become a writer it could be reassuring indeed to regard the instrument of "fictitious narrative" as hers to utilize in the practice of her guiding principle and in the redemption of her woman's life. Sedgwick dutifully transcribed some additional observations of Mackintosh's regarding Coleridge, to the effect that it was impossible " 'to give a stronger example of a man whose talents are beneath his understanding, and who trusts to his ingenuity to atone for his ignorance.' " Coleridge was the subject, but Sedgwick might very well have applied the words to herself, particularly those of the very next sentence she recorded: " 'Talents are, in my sense, habitual powers of execution.' "[1]

For the woman to conceive of the literary habit as no more than a translation of the domestic habit represented the familiar adaptive act of doing and denying. Rather than suggesting a new path and purpose for Sedgwick's literary career, already into its fourteenth year in 1836, Mackintosh's words spoke implicitly to what had been the case from the beginning. The woman had been able to transgress traditional boundaries and enter the world beyond the home by denying to herself and to the world that she had committed any transgression at all. For the woman who could not turn away from sacred duties, who could not discard her domestic habit, to be a literary domestic involved a fantasy of being that enabled the woman of the home to extend her being in the world without betraying the vows of her destiny.

In 1822 Sedgwick dedicated *A New England Tale* to Maria Edgeworth, who had regarded her fictional tales as devoted to the domestic "education of the heart." The dedication to Edgeworth, Sedgwick wrote, stood "as a slight expression of the writer's sense of [Edgeworth's] Eminent Service in the Great Cause of Human Virtue and Improvement." When Sedgwick sought in 1826 to counsel her brother Theodore on the perils of authorship, she claimed that despite having to grapple with multitudinous fears in connection with publication, there had been for her "always one sustaining thought—one impassable barrier between despondency and despair," and that was first and foremost "the consciousness of a moral purpose." That was the preeminent conviction regarding one's book, "the feeling that if it was a 'rickety child,' it was a good child." And that was the sustaining conviction that honored her as a mother of morality and rendered her a mother of prose. "Your book," she wrote to Theodore without betraying a shred of doubt, "I am sure will never give you a pang after it is fairly out." "It will do good, confer happiness and reflect honor on its parent." The scenario as she envisioned it was, perhaps, more hers than his.[2]

Following the publication of *Hope Leslie* a year later, Sedgwick turned aside from any dreams of renown and instead looked to God "for Thy approbation," and prayed that *Hope Leslie* might "go forth with Thy blessing and produce some good moral feeling!" To attempt to produce "good moral feeling" in others was something for which the private domestic woman could strive. The only fame that she could enjoy with unadulterated pleasure was achievement in that endeavor. "I am not just now at all in love with novel-writing," Sedgwick wrote Lydia Maria Child in 1830, but she added, in words foreshadowing Mackintosh's, "when I look to the romances of others I think that a romance may be made a fortunate vehicle for the highest communications of one mind to another." When Charles wrote her in praise of *Home* after its publication in 1836 she was sincerely gratified. "The success of that little book," she reported, "has been a great pleasure to me, because it strengthens my hope of doing some good to my fellow creatures." Without that hope and that success there could be little else. "To work from ever so good a motive without success," she added, "is not inspiriting." While it was true that commercial success might be necessary in order to reap moral riches, the possible lack of one did not prevent her wishing for or living off the other. Typically, she forecast in 1837 that *Live and Let Live* would not match the publishing successes of her previous books. Neverthe-less, she could still write in her journal that "I hope it will do some good."[3]

The literary domestics could enter man's world because they had not left behind woman's work. In the manner of the woman of the home, they as writers exemplified the "habit of feeling for others" by writing for the good of humanity. That constituted a rationalization of their literary careers. But it was justification in the name of woman. Eulogizing Sara Parton in the pages of the *New York Ledger* following her death in 1872, Robert Bonner stated unequivocally that the "fixed purpose" of her life had been "to accomplish some good," and he cited the contents of a letter to that effect. "I really *do* desire to do *some good* with what influence I have," Parton had written Bonner, adding, "If I know myself, that is my *first* wish." Any evidence that she might have accomplished her wish, Parton claimed, constituted her reward; she wrote to Bonner in the beginning of 1868 that the countless letters she received testifying to the "good" she had done were her "best and sweetest reward." It was a *woman's* reward. It had been Maria Cummins's reward, claimed the Reverend Nathaniel Hall in his eulogy at her funeral. Hers had been "a simple gladness," he said, "less that she had gained the public's applause than that she had touched, to issues humane and philanthropic, the public's heart." It was Susan Warner's reward. As she had written to John S. Hart, she could not work for "mere personal fame." What Warner *could* work for was suggested in her reaction to praise. "Certainly it is most pleasant to me," Warner responded to one of her readers, "to know that anything I have written has been of any use and comfort to anyone." It was pleasant, and reassuring, for the woman to think that she was fulfilling her duty in life.[4]

Augusta Evans Wilson knew her woman's duty. She knew the lesson she wished to impart. "I am inexpressibly gratified that you esteem *St. Elmo*," she wrote to her literary friend J. L. M. Curry in 1867, after the novel had appeared, having interpreted Curry's favorable response as a sign that "I may be the humble instrument of doing some good." Wilson had attributed the same sentiments in similar language to Edna Earl, her fictional counterpart in *St. Elmo*. It was Edna's hope to "enoble human motives or elevate aspirations" through her writing and thereby to make men, women, and children "happier, or wiser, or better." Edna is ridiculed for her didactic intentions by the magazine editor Douglass Manning, who regards them as extraordinary, even absurd, and certainly contradictory to what the public desires. Novels should amuse, says Douglass, not moralize. Undaunted, Edna still wants to succeed as a writer, still wants her books to sell, because "the fondest hope of Edna's heart was to be useful in 'her day and generation'—to be an instrument of some good to her race." She hoped for literary popularity, says Edna, " 'not as an end, but as a means to an end—usefulness to my fellow creatures.' "[5]

The stance taken by Mary Virginia Terhune's Phemie Hart in *Phemie's Temptation* is identical. On her honeymoon in Europe, Phemie feels useless and guilty because of the " 'superabundance of leisure' " she possesses and the pleasant life she and her husband are leading. She therefore resolves to write. It is a resolution that will lead quickly to the unraveling of her marriage, but, says the unsuspecting Phemie, " 'I longed to do my full work in the world, instead of living for my selfish gratification.' " Having " 'yearn[ed] over the weary-hearted, the poor in spirit, and the afflicted of my kind,' " she determined that " 'I dared not keep silence.' " As Terhune phrased it later in the novel, Phemie writes because she has an "earnest desire to do good."[6]

In part, the literary domestics' profession of moral intention for their literary efforts represented an acceptable substitute for a cultural presumption they could not claim. At first glance it was, again, an habitual declaration, simple and innocent enough, even fainthearted. Mary J. Holmes boasted little when she averred, "I mean always to write a good, pure, natural story, such as mothers are willing their daughters should read and such as will do good instead of harm." And Caroline Howard Gilman could not have sounded less like an aspirant to literary celebrity or more like the unassuming, self-effacing literary domestic when she wrote in 1838 to her sister Harriet Fay, "I may as well be writing as making shirts, better too if I can help give a moral covering to naked human frailty." Gilman's metaphor makes the metamorphosis of shirtmaker to word producer appear but a natural, uneventful, and practically insignificant transition.[7]

But the thread that bound the stitching of cloth to the weaving of metaphor cloaked the humble in public with righteous garments. Theirs was a habit of more than faithful followers, one that embodied more than the translation of a traditional, habitual act. For the literary domestics to conceive of themselves as (recalling the words of Sir James Mackintosh) "instruments in the moral education of mankind," to regard themselves as chosen "to teach men the habit of feeling for others," was to presume not only a moral posture but a public posture of moral superiority and leadership as well. For the private and humble that was a presumption of a paradoxical order. The literary domestics proclaimed selfless service to be the primary standard of behavior for all human beings, male and female. But they perceived women who were more dependent in the home than were independent men in the world, as necessarily more aware of the mutual dependence and needs of all human beings. Selfless service, they avowed, governed the moral beings of women more than men. Women constituted their own moral elite. The claim was to be nothing more than a woman, but the attempt was to claim more for the woman. To an extent the claim harbored the right to accuse and judge man and his society for leaving woman to fulfill sacred duties alone. In that respect, the literary domestics sought more than tribute—they sought retribution. By embracing humanity through the new national network of print, the female writer appeared before her society as an emblem of the woman visibly selfless, visibly martyred, and visibly superior.

As a historical tableau it was a drama of perverse irony. The assertion of superiority stemmed from a condition of inferiority. The cameo presented was uniquely the literary domestics' own. Compromised, they were galvanized, and the self-effacing stood poised in the home in judgment before the world. Secret writers in a society that deemed notoriety unwomanly, they could not bring themselves straightforwardly to seek acclaim. "Our first essential resurrection," wrote E.D.E.N. Southworth alongside an autograph that was her own, "must be from the grave of self." But the self would not be still, and the impulse was to assert a superior order of being for inferior women. They struck the most timid of poses, but the banner of moral righteousness stood waving in the background. In the manner of the domestic woman's service to her family, they wrote for the family of humanity. Exemplifying what they proclaimed to be the moral superiority of the domestic woman, they attested to their moral intentions and affixed to their works the seal of virtue. Compelled to rationalize their literary roles as extensions of woman's domestic role, they claimed honor for themselves and made woman's sacrifice a charge against man. They did not seek "to excite sympathy for the heroes" of life so much as they sought to solicit sympathy for the heroines in the home.[8]

The meek and lowly made separation from the world a saintly condition, and that was to identify for themselves their own holy order. Women want approval from men, says Alma Cutting in Augusta Evans Wilson's *At the Mercy of Tiberius*, but she adds, " 'We don't mistake chaff for wheat, and the purest, sweetest, noblest and holiest friendship in life is that of a true, good woman.' " That was to imply the existence of a woman's religion. "I do not believe that men can ever feel so pure an enthusiasm for women as we can feel for one another," wrote Sedgwick in her journal in 1834, adding, "Ours is nearest to the love of angels." That was also to recognize a like love of the mutually afflicted. "It is the women who hold the faith in the world," wrote the beleagured Stowe to her clergyman brother Henry Ward Beecher, by which she meant, and charged, that it was the "mothers and wives who suffer and must suffer to the end of time to bear the sins of the beloved in their own bodies."[9]

In part the biblical helpmeet sought to sanctify her domestic temple by looking beyond the world, and not surprisingly she looked to the benevolent, merciful, anthropomorphic God of nineteenth-century Protestantism for divine sanction in the world. Once the Enlightenment had altered the conception of the universe to enlarge human capacity and render God more sympathetic, evangelical and rational Protestants alike posited a relationship between human beings and God that stood in contrast to that envisioned by a Calvinism of earlier centuries. The omnipotent God of Calvin, who stood in judgment over sinful human beings, determined their fate, and elected few among many, had already been tempered by the Puritans and was further displaced by nineteenth-century Protestants in favor of a loving if still demanding God. All individuals were still admonished to seek the blessing of God, but all individuals were offered the possibility of salvation. The search for grace was fraught with more significance, in that the individual had greater responsibility to engage in that search and demonstrate commitment toward others. A grave responsibility, however, implied a glorious possibility and, increasingly, a social responsibility. More and more, the call to Christians joined the sacred to the social.[10]

"I do not know that the course of *unitarianism* as such makes very rapid progress," Sedgwick, a Unitarian herself, wrote to one acquaintance in 1829, "but liberal opinions—sure pioneers—are fast gaining ground." She continued, "The clouds of Calvinism that so long hung one dark uniform canopy over New England are everywhere breaking away, and as you well know in some of its happiest portions have quite rolled off and revealed a pure, serene heaven to be explored by the enquiring eye of faith." By the "clouds of Calvinism" Sedgwick actually meant what she regarded as the pall of Puritanism but, even so, she was undoubtedly in an unusual state of euphoria the day she wrote that letter. Only the year before her misnamed shroud of Puritanism had denied to her mind's eye as pure a vision of heaven. In March of 1828 she had written to the Swiss historian Leonard Sismondi about his reaction to her characterization of New England Puritans in *Hope Leslie*. She had meant to treat them with "filial reverence," she wrote Sismondi, and if he thought that she had erred in that respect she desired to "redeem a fault" rather than "degrade them in your estimation." Acknowledging that the inadequacies she had attributed to them were "the vices of their age," she also credited them with a virtue unusual for their century. The Puritans, she declared, exhibited "a most generous and self-devoting zeal to the cause of liberty," at least to the limits of their understanding and capability. However, Sedgwick refused to mince words about her region's imposing ancestors: "Their bigotry, their superstition, and, above all, their intolerance, were too apparent on the page of history to be forgotten." In Sedgwick's historical scheme, past and present, the clouds of Calvinism were dark indeed, and if they had constituted a more ominous presence in colonial times they yet wanted dispersing in the young republic. In her words, the seventeenth-century Puritans were "in the thraldom of Judaic superstition, and adhered steadfastly, as unhappily a majority of their descendents do, to Calvin's gloomy interpretation of Scripture, even now the popular dogma in our enlightened country."[11]

Nevertheless, whether Sedgwick's letter of 1828 or that of 1829 presented the more accurate report on the state of Protestantism in her time, the mere fact and nature of her literary disquisitions suggested change. The message of Calvinist theology was, if not completely cast aside, certainly moderated throughout the nineteenth century. Born two decades after Sedgwick, Sara Parton, who deviated from her origins, demonstrated that the change was more and more in evidence. At her birth Parton had been named

Grata Payson, after the mother of the Portland, Maine, congregational minister Edward Payson, whose sermons had influenced Parton's father, Nathaniel Willis. An intransigent Edwardsian, Payson envisioned for his congregation a righteous and stern God who stood in judgment over sorely lacking human beings. Apparently, Payson himself participated in that judgment; his sermons painted human character in such a dark light that his parishioners were heard to greet each other as "Brother Devil" after one of their minister's perorations. Willis himself had been dismissed as publisher of the Portland *Eastern Argus* in part because he pursued religious issues with overriding zeal. He had gone thence to Boston where in 1816 he had founded the *Recorder*, a religious newspaper.[12]

It is probable that Willis was somewhat perturbed by the development of his daughter's religious enthusiasms or lack thereof. Daughter Sara was remembered by Harriet Beecher Stowe during the former's days at Catharine Beecher's Hartford Seminary as a "bright, laughing witch, half saint, half sinner, poor sister Katie's best-loved pupil, her torment and her joy." That Parton worried, if not tormented, "sister Katie" (that is, Catharine Beecher) is suggested by a letter that Catharine wrote in 1829 to Parton's parents, Nathaniel and Hannah Willis. After rendering a less than favorable report on Parton's "economical" habits—"she is very thoughtless about her expenses—I have done as well as I could do for her—and yet her bills are larger than either you or I expected probably"—Beecher equivocated on her spiritual state. "I do not feel much confidence in Sara's *piety*," she wrote. "But I *do* think that a religious influence has greatly improved her character." She thought Sara was "very lovely," she said, "and tho' her faults are not all eradicated, and tho' I still fear the world has the *first* place, yet I think religion occupies much of her thoughts." That, of course, begged the issue as to the nature of Sara's religious "thoughts."[13]

An essay of Parton's titled "Notes on Preachers and Preaching," written in 1869, revealed that forty years later daughter Sara's mind was still more on the world than on heaven. What she demanded from her clergyman above all was more concern with humanity's trials and proportionally less with an intricate and demanding theology that focused upon God. "I don't believe in a person's eyes being so fixed on heaven," she said, "that he goes blundering over everybody's corns on the way there. If that's his Christianity, the sooner he gets tripped up the better." (It is difficult to imagine one of Cotton Mather's parishioners, male or female, writing thus of him.) "Oh, if clergymen would only study their fellow men more," she went on, and spend less time trying "to unravel some double-twisted theological knot, which, if pulled out straight, would never carry one drop of balm to a suffering fellow-being, or teach him how to bear bravely and patiently the trials, under which soul and body are ready to faint." Parton did acknowledge that in her day there was more sympathy and encouragement emanating from the pulpit than disquisitions on God's wrathful judgment of human failing. "But, oh!" she wrote, perhaps with Jonathan Edwards and Deacon Willis, if not Mather, in mind, "why *will* clergymen persist in *scaring* people to heaven?" Was, she asked, " 'God is Love' blotted from out" the pages of the Bible?[14]

Parton's expression may have been her own but her scriptural interpretation was not. "God is Love" was successfully found by many Protestants in their Bibles more and more in the nineteenth century and it was discovered on their lips as well. Harriet Beecher Stowe, after a struggle, distanced herself from her father Lyman Beecher's strain of latter-day Puritanism, and Beecher himself had moved some distance from his forebears. Long after Stowe had joined the more liberal Episcopal Church, her family church of the maternal side, she wrote in 1883 to her sister Isabella Beecher Hooker to note that "you said you wished there was some name for God that expressed all human affection—Father, lover, Friend." There was such a name, said Stowe: "You have it in St. John in the words God is *Love—Love*—Essential Love covers and expresses all." E.D.E.N. Southworth, baptized in her father's Roman Catholicism but reared in her mother's Episcopal faith, drew the same connection between God's love and human love. Using the same language in *The Discarded Daughter*, she described the relationship between Alice Chester and Alice's minister, Milton Sinclair: "When loving each other most, they loved God most. The soul incapable of love, is still more incapable of religion—nay, love often elevates the irreligious into the worshipper. Love can redeem any soul; it was LOVE that gave itself for *all* souls! Love is religion—for 'God is Love.' " One's commitment to God was expressed in love of others, and in loving others came knowledge of God. Stowe told her twin daughters Hattie and Eliza in 1859 that they would never know God "*till* you love someone as I do you—you have educated me quite as much as I you—you have taught me the love of God—by awakening such in me."[15]

For many nineteenth-century Protestants, piety involved more than an inner conviction and passive devotion. If the involvement was private and personal, the commitment was social. One served God by lovingly and actively serving others. Henry Warner, a Presbyterian, wrote to his wife Anna in 1822 that he was pleased to hear that an acquaintance of theirs was "a professor of Christianity." Certainly, he said, the "absence of this is an almost infallible indication that everything else is wanting." Nevertheless, "profession," he reminded her, "is a thing which must be permitted to stand low upon the scale of *evidences*." After his daughters Susan and Anna had joined the Mercer Street Presbyterian Church in New York City, the first sermon they heard concerned the perennial subject " 'What must I do to be saved?' " The answer they learned was one that Susan, always one to bring herself up short on any path, would repeat and elaborate upon over the years in her journal. "I wish to note that I give myself today to my Savior to 'follow him fully,' " she wrote on one occasion. The Lord had given her "abundant cause to love and trust him" and it was her duty to "bring forth much fruit to his glory while I live—I do wish that."[16]

The converted were to display their love of God, their Christianity, through selfless interaction with others. Messengers of God's love, their mission was to be accomplished through the performance of good deeds on behalf of others. When Mary Virginia Terhune heard that her friend Virginia Eppes Dance had experienced conversion and joined the Presbyterian Church in Virginia she wrote to express her joy. " 'God is good oh! how good!' " she said, adding the reminder, "God has appointed unto each one his work." "Let us be diligent," Terhune said to her friend, "in the performance of ours." In *Em's Husband* Southworth explicitly made the connection developed by nineteenth-century Protestantism between faith, love, and works. The occasion is provided when Emolyn Palmer, the heroine of the novel, hears a blind preacher explicate the Christian's duty to manifest piety more in outward behavior than in spiritual, internal communion. Emolyn listens intently and hears: "How Faith without Love was cold, and either, or both, without works, dead. How Faith and Love must go forth in good uses, must go forth, through brain, heart, and hand, in good thoughts, good feelings, and good deeds to all." The message to all in the predominantly Protestant republic was to display their faith in good works, to commit themselves to benevolence, and to convert others and purify the society. Responsible for their own individual fate, Americans were as well responsible for the salvation of their society. "Trust in the Lord/And do good," wrote Stowe on many of her autographs. The Methodist Augusta Evans Wilson presented the same dictum in a letter to her friend, Rachel Lyons Heustis. "The earth," Wilson declared, "is merely a vast vineyard in which the Father has laid out *work* for all of us . . . ."[17]

Like any clergyman doing the bidding of God, the literary domestics sanctioned their literary interventions as work dictated by God which thereby transformed mere humble efforts into righteous proclamations. In reply to reformer Dorothea Dix's praise of *The Wide, Wide World*, Susan Warner rejected any credit for herself: "I do not deserve your commendations,—not in anywise. You say 'God bless me' for what I have done,—nay but I say 'Thank him for it,' and I wash my hands of all desert in the matter." As if to answer any who might have doubted Susan's words, Anna Warner later wrote in her biography of her sister that *The Wide, Wide World* had indeed been "written in closest reliance upon God: for thoughts, for power, and for words." Maria Cummins also ascribed all of her efforts to heaven, stating in a letter, "If I have ever done anything worth doing, it has been through the motives and spirit" of God. And in an oft-repeated declaration, Harriet Beecher Stowe went so far as to exclaim that God Himself had penned *Uncle Tom's Cabin*. After E.D.E.N. Southworth had been told by a Professor Powers that he had first read a novel of hers when his father, a

Baptist minister, gave him *The Deserted Wife*, Southworth reported the conversation in a letter to her daughter Lottie. "He asked me if it was not a source of great comfort to me," wrote Southworth, "to reflect on the many books I had written and the many youth I had taught and hearts I had comforted, etc. etc." Ever anxious to disavow even the semblance of vanity, Southworth related her response: "I told him I thought more of my failures in fidelity to the gift and the Giver than I did of success," It was a humble way to acknowledge success.[18]

With intent or not, the literary domestics characterized themselves as preachers of the fictional page. The implicit ordination was professed in varying fashions. "No one can feel as I do the imperfection of the labor I achieve," Sedgwick wrote characteristically to clergyman William Ellery Channing in 1837. Nevertheless, there was work to be done. "With the great physical world to be subdued here to the wants of the human family," she said, "there is an immense moral field opening demanding laborers of every class and of every kind and degree of talent." And, said Sedgwick to Channing as one clergyperson to another, "Neither pride nor humility should withhold us from the work to which we are clearly 'sent.' " When Stowe promised her readers that she would deliver the explicit moral in *Pink and White Tyranny* she promised also to "send you off edified as if you had been hearing a sermon." Mary Virginia Terhune was confident that she understood the true significance of her first published novel, *Alone*. "Seriously," she wrote to Virginia Eppes Dance, "I have much pending upon this venture. The success of the book may be the opening of the path I cannot but feel that Providence has marked out for me." And Caroline Lee Hentz confided to an acquaintance of hers that her "vocation," that is, her literary career, was obviously the one "for which God endowed me." Clearly the humble had been called, and humility had not deterred the literary domestics from exuding pride in their calling.[19]

The ordination was by God's leave on behalf of woman. It was an ordination in the cause of women generally. "Is not woman's mission truly a mission of love?" asked Maria Cummins in *Mabel Vaughan*. "And can she fail to fulfill all its duties nobly, and find all its trials lightened and relieved when she has once taken to heart that lesson, once fortified herself with that spirit so beautifully exemplified in Him whose life on earth was a glorious manifestation of love made perfect?" Woman might not be literally divine, but she could emulate Christ's character to a degree that certainly made her superior to the merely mortal male. Resorting to their own holy "fictitious narratives," the literary domestics rendered woman's hearth more sanctified than man's pulpit. Stowe did more than liken the home to the church in *The Minister's Wooing*, more than compare woman's role to the clergyman's. Home, she said, was the "appointed sphere for woman, more holy than cloister, more saintly and pure than church and altar. . . . Priestess, wife and mother there she ministers daily in holy works of household peace." Holy preachers of God's love, the literary domestics preached as well for woman's exalted calling. "I believe it is possible," Mary Virginia Terhune was reported as saying, "to elevate household 'drudgery' into a Mission," and she claimed in her autobiography that she had begun learning in the earliest days of her marriage "to regard housewifery as a profession that dignifies her who follows it, and contributes, more than any other calling, to the mental, moral, and spiritual sanity of the human race." She had received her "call to this ministry," she wrote, in that rural Virginia "cottage parsonage," Charlotte Court-House, where she had first followed her clergyman husband in 1856.[20]

Isolated in the home, the woman claimed a holy retreat. "The world is on one side, and we on another—with our Lord," wrote Susan Warner on Constitution Island off West Point, New York, during the 1870s, in the last entry she made in her private journal. But embattled in the home, the woman still looked to judge man's world. The literary domestics demeaned their literary efforts and themselves by limning them as the humble efforts of humble creatures. True to their socialization, they subscribed to the dictum that bound woman to the private, secondary, domestic sphere and denied her the world beyond the home. But as the daughters of elite, cultured families, as private women who became publicly successful authors, they also broke those fetters by fostering a domestic brand of noblesse oblige that was decidedly their own.[21]

As God's instruments they had adorned themselves with the mantle of righteousness in the effort to nurture, teach, and save souls in the name of the Lord. And simply as the daughters and wives of those who deemed themselves members of a saving elite, they had learned to attach a spiritual commitment to a social superiority that presumed responsibility for the welfare of society. Not surprisingly, then, the literary domestics joined their male counterparts in activities of benevolence and reform that bound together the sacred and the secular. Mary Virginia Terhune, for example, taught Bible classes, superintended the infant department of a Sunday School, and performed the miscellaneous functions required of the wife of a Presbyterian clergyman in parishes from Virginia to Newark, New Jersey; to Springfield, Massachusetts; to Brooklyn, New York. But Terhune also broadened her activities as president of the Women's Christian Association in Newark and directed that organization in raising funds and finding positions for the poor, including providing employment as seamstresses for three hundred women one winter. While in Brooklyn Terhune also managed a training school for nurses.

In Brockport, New York, where her husband was a vestryman of St. Luke's Episcopal Church, Mary J. Holmes helped to found a temperance club and as late as 1893, when she was sixty-eight, participated in organizing soup kitchens for the unemployed during the depression of that year. Catharine Maria Sedgwick supported efforts to alleviate conditions in New York City's tenements and in 1848 became the first director of that city's Women's Prison Association, which was engaged in reforming jails that held women. She was also connected with the Isaac T. Hopper Home, which conducted Bible classes, provided room and board, and found employment for women released from prison. Looking to the souls of humanity readily constituted for these women a linkage of spiritual concern to a social preoccupation with the welfare of humanity. Caroline Howard Gilman, who claimed that the "religious feeling was always powerful within me," was also proud to state that she had been among the "few" to establish the Sabbath School and Benevolent Society at Watertown, Massachusetts. She also was instrumental in establishing a benevolent society in Charleston, South Carolina. "I have endeavored, under all circumstances, wherever my lot has fallen," wrote Gilman, "to carry on the work of social love."[22]

Social affiliation, then, contributed to the literary domestics' conviction that they must "do" for humanity and to their professed intentions to "do good." At first glance, the production and presentation of pure, humble tales for the healthy nourishment of fellow Americans appeared to be nothing more than the genteel woman's counterpart, albeit in a radically new manner, to her gentlemanly brethren's worldly performance of duties. Mirrored, of course, was the presumption of a social and cultural elite that they not only *could* exercise leadership within the context of deferential relationships but that they *should* also prescribe and pass judgment upon the civil, social, and moral behavior of their contemporaries in an increasingly mobile and fluid society. With the Revolution, the virtual monopoly of power and visibility enjoyed by the colonial elite disappeared, along with the class itself, but their nineteenth-century intellectual and social descendants still assumed it to be their duty to shape and inculcate standards of behavior for the benefit of the general populace.

Theirs, however, was not simply another manifestation of traditional noblesse oblige. Stripped of the socially accepted colonial distinctions of status and hierarchy, the presumption of superiority that legitimated acting on behalf of others was edged by a concern bordering on fear in the face of rapid social, economic, and political change. The attempt to influence, discipline, and restrain a newly democratized society reflected as well a basic recoil against popular power, a defensive action by those with diminished authority and control, and an antipathy toward a society increasingly under the sway of values of a different order. The obligation to serve and better humanity came to have a deeply ambivalent meaning in American society. And with the success of republicanism perceived to be in the balance, ambivalence was transformed into heightened anxiety about the fate of the nation. Supposedly dependent upon a pious, enlightened, and politically informed populace, the republic appeared to be threatened by leveling forces that challenged traditional authority, by an egalitarianism that called deference into question, and by an individualism that mocked the concept of a society bound together by an organic hierarchy.

Those still aligned with the values of an earlier era did express genuine support for the republican ideology of liberty and natural rights, of equality and freedom of opportunity, but they simultaneously harbored a profound skepticism about the materialistic, individualistic impulses of the young nation and shared a deep distrust toward their perceived social inferiors. The great anticipation of popular democracy and the promise ascribed to it were hedged throughout the nineteenth century by questions regarding who was to lead and what were to be the guiding values of the republic. For many who sought to retain leadership the presumption of social superiority had to be reconciled with the fact of a declining exercise of power, of a necessary sharing with and perhaps loss of power to social inferiors. They had to face as well a forcible challenge to the values that had legitimated the power held by the eighteenth-century elite. Deference, hierarchy, and gentlemanly leadership all appeared to be yielding before an egalitarianism that exalted the common man and fueled an increasingly powerful individualism and materialism.[23]

In her "Notebook of Memories of Her life" that she wrote for her grandniece Alice in 1853, Catharine Maria Sedgwick recalled that hers had been a prominent Federalist family. Theodore Sedgwick, among all of the males of the families of the literary domestics, represented the most direct linkage to the elite leadership of the Revolutionary generation. When he had ruled as patriarch of his family in the last decades of the eighteenth and early years of the nineteenth centuries, the Sedgwicks did not hold the name of Jefferson in a particularly favorable light. More revealing, daughter Catharine often heard the masses labeled Jacobins, sansculottes, in her home circle, and she claimed that her father had been "born too soon to relish the freedom of democracy." In a pointed anecdote, she related that she had "seen his brow lower when a free and easy mechanic came to the *front* door!"[24]

The supposed affront to Theodore Sedgwick was a portent of changes that would be political as well as social in character. Informing Alice that "the federalists believed that all sound principles—truth, justice, and patriotism, were identified with the upper classes," Sedgwick nonetheless designated them "sincere republicans." But, she noted paradoxically, "I think they began to fear a Republic could only continue to exist in utopia." The Federalists' opponents, the "democrats," were credited by daughter Catharine with "much native sagacity" as well as confidence in their ability to govern, "some from conceit—some from just conviction," but she also made clear that they had "less education—intellectual and moral—than their opponents" and "little refinement." In conjunction with the fact that they also had an "intense desire to grasp the power and place that had been denied to them and a determination to work out the theories of the government," their relatively unlettered and unpolished character had not been regarded as a fortunate circumstance. From the perspective of Federalists like Theodore Sedgwick the battle had been joined between the lower orders and those who considered power and authority their prerogative.[25]

Lest Alice think that her great-aunt was speaking, in the middle of the nineteenth century, of her current convictions and biases, Sedgwick added, "All this, my dear Alice, is an afterthought with me." Implicitly contrasting her adulthood with her earlier years, she suggested that maturity had brought a more democratic bent of mind: "Then I entered fully and with the faith and ignorance of childhood into the prejudices of the time—I tho't every democrat was dishonest, grasping and vulgar."[26]

Twelve years later Sedgwick wrote to the journalist and biographer James Parton, husband of Sara, to recall the same combination of republican sentiment aligned with antidemocratic condescension. The catalyst for her letter was the publication of Parton's biography of Aaron Burr, and she chose the occasion of complimenting the author to speak again of her father's Federalist party. The shift in the balance of her comments indicated that if she had developed a more democratic cast than her father, her devotion to the principle of elite leadership had shifted more by degrees than in kind. "That party," she wrote Parton in tones that betrayed the intensity of her convictions, was "the *purest*—the most disinterested, and I believe as enlightened as any that ever existed." While it could not be denied that the Federalists had made "the fatal mistake of distrusting the people," nevertheless neither could it be denied that "they were *true* to them in the highest sense." If as an elite they considered themselves superior to the people, theirs was a principled, responsible sense of superiority. She knew this to be true, Sedgwick insisted, because as a child she had "listened devoutly" to their conversations in her home at Stockbridge, Massachusetts. Inadvertently calling forth the image of a bygone era when political life had constituted to a much greater extent the private preserve of gentlemen, Sedgwick remembered that those had been gatherings "held in the intimacy of ripened friendship—in the faith of unwavering and reciprocal confidence between my father, Governor Jay and the other prominent men of the Federal party."[27]

The colonial gentry was no more, and the influence and leadership of the like-minded in the early decades of the nineteenth century and beyond were tenuous and increasingly under challenge. But nostalgia for a social hierarchy of the past and the relatively unquestioned deference accorded the eighteenth-century gentleman combined with a persistent belief in the need for the redeeming influence and superior leadership of an elite. When Sedgwick, her father's daughter, wrote in her 1835 novel, *The Linwoods* that an American colonial society distinguished by an "artificial code" had been replaced in the wake of the Revolution by a society "graduated by nature's

aristocracy (nature alone sets a seal to her patents of universal authority),"
she was reiterating an eighteenth-century perspective for the benefit of an
unheeding Jacksonian America. Noting in her preface that she had set the
novel in the context of Revolutionary America, Sedgwick said she had done
so "to exhibit the feeling of the times" for the consideration of the present
era. Her aim was necessarily limited, of course; she had avoided "historic
events and war details," for she was "aware that no effort at 'a swashing and
a martial outside' would conceal the weak and unskilled woman." Nevertheless if she was able to give to her "younger readers" only a "slight"
impression of that period she hoped thereby to "deepen their gratitude to the
patriot-fathers" and "increase their fidelity to the free institutions transmitted to them." The desire was not to dampen the republican spirit, but to
define it properly and give it a correct hue.[28]

In 1821, two years after she had married the Harvard-trained Unitarian
clergyman Samuel Gilman and accompanied him to the South's first
Unitarian church, Caroline Howard Gilman wrote to her sister Harriet Fay
to clarify the character of the Gilmans' life in Charleston, South Carolina.
She was concerned that her sister had received erroneous "reports" that
might have led her to "form wrong notions of our style of living and standing
in Society." In the first place, she said, her husband's congregation ranked
"about where Mr. Lowell's does in Boston." That was to say that it was
"highly respectable," of course, but just as certainly it was also to say that
neither the Gilmans nor the congregation were part of the "fashions and
aristocracy" of Charleston. Had they been of a mind to join that set it might
not have been possible, anyway, as "Episcopacy takes the lead" here, said
Gilman, and there was without question "a light feeling of contempt" for all
who stemmed from the Congregationalists, including Unitarians. Perhaps if
they had arrived in Charleston in "carriage and four and taken a smart
house" they might very well "have been courted," particularly in light of the
"letters which Mr. Gilman brought." But, she said, with an air of superiority,
almost smugness, the Gilmans' "humble style of living made us forgotten" by
the so-called fashionable, and the warm reception of the congregation "made
us forget them." The truth was, Gilman assured her sister, "our situation is
precisely that, which is calculated to afford most happiness." Had they
become embroiled in the life of the "gay and fashionable" they might have
caused "much jealousy" and, more importantly, they might have "neglected
some of the duties which now render Mr. Gilman so eminently useful."
Putting the matter in proper perspective, Gilman concluded by saying that
"we associate with just enough fashion to keep us animated in society, just
enough mental cultivation to preserve literary taste, just enough riches and
display not to regret that we are limited, and receive just enough attention to
make us satisfied with our influence." With obvious pride Gilman had set
forth an implicit code of values and described a cultivated and refined life of
restraint, discipline, and usefulness.[29]

As a genteel clergyman's family, the Gilmans embodied an appropriate symbol of historical change and continuity. In the colonial era the clergy had allied themselves with the gentry and had elicited their support in the cultivation of a spiritual and moral tone. In turn, the colonial gentry had acknowledged the critical importance of religion in fostering responsible and ethical behavior. The forces unleashed by the Revolution brought to an end the gentry's dominance, and in the succeeding decades of the early nineteenth century the clergy, concerned that their influence was diminishing as well, became uncertain about their role and identity in a democratic society in flux. The response varied from individual to individual, of course, but generally the clergy became all the more concerned with the promotion of morality, and many as well became involved in the benevolent and reform efforts that Gilman proudly described as "the work of social love." They came to see themselves as the nation's guardians of virtue, and in that emerging identity they found a role that was political as well as moral. Although the Gilmans, freshly transplanted in the 1820s from Massachusetts to Charleston, a southern center of fashion and culture, were in a special circumstance, their presumption that they had an obligation to play a social and moral role was prevalent among the clergy. Presumption, however, did not necessarily insure actual fulfillment of the obligation. Nonetheless, as Gilman indicated it was an effort that clergyman Samuel as well as his wife had undertaken and made central to their lives. That they did so despite the isolation, vulnerability, and alienation they felt indicated the predicament of many with similar aspirations in the egalitarian democracy.

Their adherence to republican principles notwithstanding, those who were more comfortable with earlier values yet still sought to exercise leadership looked upon the democratic trends of the new nation with mixed emotions. The egalitarian ethos of democracy in conjunction with the economic growth and industrial development of an emerging American capitalism engendered social changes marked by an increasingly dominant individualism, a raucous and volatile politics, a pervasive materialism, and an intense ambition for upward mobility. Many of the emerging practices and governing mores of nineteenth-century society did not accord well with earlier ideals and concepts of character. For the gentry-minded, ambition appeared to subsume principle, prospects for individual gain took precedence over serving the public interest. And the cast of the emerging leadership, especially in politics, remained suspect. The gentleman yielded before the opportunist; the candidate's basic political principles, if indeed he had any, became less important than his charismatic personality; and the electoral contests increasingly resembled displays of hoopla in which those who could revile opponents while flattering voters emerged triumphant. In the eyes of those who looked askance at these trends, the politics of expediency, not principle, reigned supreme, and shrewd, coarse politicians, not statesmen, were the beneficiaries.[30]

When Susan Warner's father Henry went to Albany, New York, in the 1820s to conduct his legal affairs he was filled with contempt for what he considered the low life in that center of political activity. His arrival occurred in an era in New York state politics that has since been noted by historians for its opportunism, demagoguery, and political intrigue. Henry's own father had served in New York's state legislature in the early years of the century but there was little likelihood that the son would follow in his father's footsteps. His letters to Susan's mother, Anna, were filled with disdain for what he undoubtedly judged to be the vulgarity of a more common sort. He made little effort to conceal his feelings of revulsion. "So here I am, my dear Anna," he wrote in June of 1821, "on the pinnacle of Capitol Hill and within a door or two of the capitol itself," which he described as a "place of debate and folly, a place which raises no sentiment of awe, even of respect, as I behold it, but rather excites association of disgust, and contempt and shame. Such is the character of our Legislature!" Another letter at the beginning of the next year spoke of cardplaying and other "amusements" of the lawyers and legislators in his company, activities that "afforded a *reasonable and fit*" fare for their ilk, he sneered. "What a contrast to the pleasures of our peaceful and happy home!" he wrote longingly.[31]

That fall found his perspective unchanged, if anything more harshly critical. He wrote from Albany again to say that he was "not and never shall be, a lover of the society of mere men of the world." After being subjected for an hour to their "senseless babble," he wrote his wife, "it is an unspeakable relief to retire to my chamber and converse with you." It was probably a state of exasperation rather than reflections upon principle that motivated Henry Warner, still ensconced in Albany in the fall of 1822, to write to his wife, "Nothing can be more just than your view of the folly of marrying for money. . . . " No, he insisted, "Nothing upon earth can compensate for the want of personal worth in a life-companion." In his legal dealings for money in Albany's pit of politics he clearly found his worldly companions unable to satisfactorily compensate him for their lack of character.[32]

At midcentury Maria McIntosh, the daughter of wealthy and socially prominent Georgians, asked fretfully in *Woman in America* what it was about Americans and their way of life that appeared to elicit "ridicule from foreigners." Was it the "simplicity of our political organization" or, referring to Zachary Taylor, could it be the "plainness of our citizen-president" and his "unceremonious reception which, as the representative of a republican people," he provided visiting dignitaries? Or was it perhaps our "less liberally endowed" academies and colleges, or could it be the "want of splendid architectural adornments" in American cities? It was none of these or other similar characteristics of American life, she concluded, for if visitors from foreign lands possessed a "faculty of vision" they were able to see, in one respect, "that beautiful consistency of practice and principle which all men honor"—alluding to democratic simplicity in contrast to European aristocratic grandeur. In still other respects, she said, they would marvel that "so much has been done" in two centuries of labor, coming so close to, if not equaling, two thousands years of labor abroad.[33]

However, McIntosh asserted, "their respect for us vanishes" when they look "to our social life, to its feverish ambition, its mean jealousies, its ostentatious displays, its fretful sensitiveness, its strange contrasts, its want of all harmony and beauty, of all repose and dignity." If McIntosh appeared to contradict herself, it was because the implicit subject of her discourse was the need for a code of gentility to govern and guide the bustling democracy, the need for exemplars of that code, a republican elite, to hold greater sway over the democratic masses. What foreigners most often observed, she thought, was a hodgepodge of "uneducated laborers," a "heterogeneous mixture of enterprising industry and despairing indolence," and a variety of "vice and misery" exhibited by immigrants arriving yearly from Europe. This, in the eyes of foreign observers, said McIntosh, made "up the sum of what they denominate American society." But what they did not encounter for the most part, she noted, was a less visible way of life and its less visible representatives.[34]

Nevertheless, the hidden life of which she spoke was in McIntosh's idealization the "true American life, the life in which labor and refinement walk hand in hand." Its representatives, she said, possessed "a thorough understanding of themselves and their position," and they constituted "a class, intelligent, educated, and often even highly accomplished." Alluding inadvertently, perhaps, to a period fifty years or more in the past, McIntosh claimed that these were individuals who had "set before them an ideal nobler than any yet attained on earth." And they were a group, she added, placing her context perhaps more in the present, that was "working out that ideal in the quietness of spirits dwelling in too high a region to be disturbed by the capricious winds and currents of fashion." If the suggestion was that this more noble way of life did not constitute what was most obvious about mid-nineteenth-century American life or that those who epitomized it were not the most visible leaders of the contemporary American spheres of power and influence, it was also McIntosh's belief that such a manner of being should provide the true measure for all American lives and that its exemplars should guide and set standards for all Americans. The reactions of foreigners to the American scene constituted for McIntosh evidence for that observation.[35]

But if McIntosh looked to the past for an idealized code of conduct by which to evaluate the present, the present visible life she judged was a male world. In the very same volume in which she swore allegiance to woman's private domestic sphere, she announced her intention to seek a position of "elevation" from which "to awaken the attention of her countrywomen" to all that was impeding their social progress. And for the female to cast a jaundiced eye at the nineteenth century's ballyhoo of individualism, of material progress and abundance, was to pass judgment on a male celebration. "The rapid variations of fortune resulting from commercial enterprise," observed McIntosh, "have a tendency to engender feverish dreams and wild speculations." But those were "dreams" and "speculations" spawned by *male* "enterprise." Economic individualism seemed nothing more than base, destructive, and heedless selfishness. Economic opportunity did not appear to have fostered a concomitant sense of social responsibility. Accumulation of goods and elevation of personal status seemed to be the ultimate goal of Americans. Upward mobility depended upon performance in the marketplace and, McIntosh thought, there were "few comparatively who hold themselves aloof from mercantile speculation in some of its forms." But those "few" included womankind, which had no choice but to remain "aloof."[36]

In the eyes of those like McIntosh, far too many subscribed to a new ruling code that equated virtue with wealth and the ostentatious display of wealth with talent's achievement. The fear was that the mania for wealth would undermine spiritual and moral values, that a nation gripped by uncertainty in the midst of change and growth would continue to reel helplessly before forces that threatened, in the words of McIntosh, "to press out of sight all that is noblest among us." Like many, McIntosh put her faith in education, hoping that it would instill in the youth of America "the principles of true Christian civilization" and teach them that "no extrinsic advantages of wealth or station will atone for the want of those personal qualities that command respect." It was hoped that education would implant the belief that the only life to be pursued in the young republic was "a life of usefulness, of true refinement, and of wise philanthropy." And, like many, McIntosh hoped that in addition to a "thorough public instruction" the country would look to "the more enduring influence of its homes, to become the source of blessing to the world." But for the literary domestic to look to the home as a source of influence was to give the message a twist of her own. For the woman to look to the home was to indict man and the values of his society in the name of a female moral elite. It was to censure a world beyond domesticity and a pursuit beyond women.[37]

In her fictitious narrative of 1866, *St. Elmo*, Augusta Evans Wilson delivered her social sermon through her fictitious woman writer Edna Earl. In the novel Edna Earl becomes spokeswoman for women of all ages in nineteenth-century America. Through her fiction and through her essays in a national magazine, she has come to be regarded by her sex as their leader, as their teacher and confidant. Edna proclaims the need for a reformation of American society. Everywhere she looks in her "study" of the country she espies "social leprosy." She is alarmed that "lofty idealism seemed trodden down," repulsed by the "altars of mammon." Statesmen appear "almost extinct" in America, and revered political ideals are reviled by "howling demagogues and fanatics." Edna fears most of all a growing moral decadence, a social license that threatens the nation's moral fiber.[38]

Edna's call is directed primarily at the "wives, mothers, and daughters" of her country, urging them to claim and act upon their roles as moral guardians and reformers of their nation. Her belief is that "the intelligent, refined, modest Christian women of the United States [are] the real custodians of national purity, and the sole agents who could successfully arrest the tide of demoralization breaking over the land." Her message is heeded, as evidenced not only by, ironically, the commercial success of her publications, but by the daily "letters . . . from all regions of the country" she receives testifying to the fact that she rests secure "in the warm hearts of her noble countrywomen." A source of particular pride to Edna is the allegiance paid her by young women; "To these her womanly heart [turns] yearningly; and she accepts their affectionate confidence as an indication of her proper circle of useful labor." For the woman who is a writer, who in mind has never left the home, this is the claim in the name of woman of a superior order of morality. Comparable to the reign of gentry-minded brethren, literary domesticity was an anxious reign of justification. But it was more than an unpretentious carbon copy of their male counterparts' presumptive practice of prescribing for and governing the behavior of contemporaries. The literary domestics' desire was to be more than social functionaries of gentlemen's lives, more than lady dispensers of piety and benevolence. Their desire was simply to justify the lives of the lowly and claim superior moral influence over those who ruled them.[39]

The desire was nurtured in the woman who stayed at home and from there attempted to influence her man in the world. The ideal male was a man of the world, his world. He was marked at birth for the world, prepared from the outset to assume his place as a leading citizen, nurtured and trained to perform his civic, social, and moral duties. For the literary domestic the ideal male was *her* male, whether in her home or in his world. In 1833, thirteen years after her marriage, Caroline Howard Gilman enthused about her husband in a letter to her sister-in-law, Lousia Gilman Loring. "Oh, Louisa!" she exclaimed, "let you and I always be ready like good wives and sisters, to hear the praises of our husbands!" Whether or not Gilman was accustomed to hearing the praises of her clergyman husband Samuel, she wanted to praise him. Samuel was "all in the maturity of life," she said, by which she meant approvingly that he exhibited "no weariness in doing good—prudent in society and cheerful, animated and devoted in the pulpit." In the home, he met "every requisite for home that can gladden the hearts of his wife and children." But he met her standards in the world as well—"the trait that most delights me is his zeal as a Christian minister." The proud wife spoke of Samuel as an approving mother might of her well-trained, dutiful son: "No languor is allowed to steal into his religious services. He commits to memory with singular perseverance which you know," she added, as if speaking from her own memory of the labor, "is a gratuitous labor and [he] writes with a freshness of a first sermon."[40]

Thirty years later Gilman the mother approved the man her daughter Eliza was to have for a husband. The young man was apparently rich in cultural attributes, and it was Gilman's pleasure that the intended bridegroom share his wealth of character with her daughter. "I congratulate you that you are to be married to a worthy man," she wrote to Eliza. He was worthy because his worth would be of value to Eliza, "a help for your heart and conscience, an intellectual companion, to share and enlarge the aspirations of your mind, and a 'musical' friend to harmonize with the Mozarts and Beethovens of this and a better world." Harriet Beecher Stowe found her daughter Hattie's intended to be ideal in character. Writing about him to Eunice Beecher, wife of her brother Henry Ward Beecher, Stowe obviously found him ideal for cultivation as well. He had a "good solid mind," she thought, "steady and judicious." His education had been "very fair," evidenced by the fact that he possessed "a good talent as a writer—and as a speaker I should think he might be rather above the average." There was room for improvement, but he seemed to be a man who would "grow and ripen from year to year." Room for improvement meant there was work to be done: "there has seemed to me to be in him some of that crudeness which sometimes is seen in a man of large nature that takes time to *fill up* all round." That very likely meant that Hattie would have to take the time to fill him up, but it would probably prove an enjoyable task, since, Stowe continued, his "social nature" was "very genial and kindly." Of particular importance, his "moral tone" was "high and militant" and he appeared willing "to begin at the bottom of the ladder and work his way upward." No doubt Hattie would be there with him at every rung, because the "best thing of all—and what must be decisive," Stowe concluded, "is that Hatty loves him."[41]

The male needed to be worked on, and the work to be done was the female's. When Sedgwick's niece Kate gave birth to her fourth son in 1859 Sedgwick wrote to congratulate her and to say that contrary to what Kate might think, having four sons was a blessing because they offered her a greater opportunity to exercise influence and provide guidance. "Womenkind," said Sedgwick, "get on without much supervision to a tolerable degree of virtue or safety." As confirmation of that fact she noted that "women even among the savage races are not utterly depraved." In contrast, it is "the masculine nature that grows rank without pruning or training." Therefore, said Sedgwick, "I think your four boys are not a doom but a high calling." In Augusta Evans Wilson's *At the Mercy of Tiberius*, a dying Ellice Brentano asks daughter Beryl to look after son Bertie. " 'His conscience, of course, is not sensitive like yours,' " mother tells daughter, " 'because you know, a boy's moral nature is totally different from a girl's and like most of his sex, Bertie has no religious instincts sending him always in the right direction.' "

There can be no doubt that Beryl must guide Bertie, for " 'women generally have to supply conscientious scruples for man and you can take care of your brother, if you will.' " Of course Beryl does.[42]

The ideal man of the world exhibited that familiar sense of superiority that displayed itself in socially responsible behavior. He was to possess as well strong qualities of character, noble ambition, and good intentions. The epitome of gentlemanly republicanism, he was the very type to temper the emerging egalitarian thrust of nineteenth-century America, to define and shape the principles of a young, eager, and perhaps heedless democracy. In her journal of 1837, Sedgwick noted that she had "always been fond of a sort of character-drawing reverie." But while others "build castles in the air," wrote Sedgwick, "I fill them with tenants." At the moment, she was filling her journal with reveries about a political exile whom she had recently met. An Italian who had been imprisoned after he sought a separate state for Lombardy in the early 1820s, Federico Confalonieri had been jailed for twelve years before his sentence for life was commuted to exile and he came to the United States. Here was a man, Sedgwick thought, who was most "*distinguished*," who had "sacrificed most to the cause," but who had "endured with most dignity and gentleness." Most importantly, he had shown himself to be "a man that circumstances can subdue, but whose spirit, like angelic spirits, makes all circumstances subservient to his progress." Sedgwick was totally enthralled with Confalonieri. "I have never seen any man who has so realized to me my beau ideal," she wrote: he was a man who made real not only "the dreams of my youth" but also "the *sane* portraits of my maturity." He may also have been a man who recalled to her her Federalist father. She had "imagined" such a man before, she continued, but never until now had she seen one who seemed to have "the tone of high breeding which, in spite of our democratic theories and principles, we associate with the old aristocracy, blended with that humility, respect, and tenderness for his kind which marks the Christian philosopher of the present day." Withal, this "beau ideal" was probably Sedgwick's conception of the perfect leader for democratic America—of "perfectly earnest and sincere" convictions, he also inspired "as unwavering a faith" as possible in his followers.[43]

On occasion the literary domestics manned their castles with appropriate leaders of the world. Rather than pursue his own social or material advancement, Maria McIntosh's Robert Grahame, in *The Lofty and the Lowly*, harkens to " 'Duty! The Right! The True!' " Robert asks himself, " 'Is not this the only substantial good in the whole of creation? Is not the pursuit of any other object like chasing a shadow?' " In Mary J. Holmes's *Cousin Maude*, James De Vere is also characterized as "indeed a noble-hearted man." He is as well "generous, kind and self-denying," and finds his "chief pleasure in doing others good." Caroline Lee Hentz'e Roland Lee, the husband of wife Linda's domestic dream, naturally chooses to devote himself to overseeing the public welfare. He is representative of the "noble class of men who, by the union of physical and intellectual power, assume command over inferior minds, and make them subservient to practical good." Men like Roland, men "who, without reserving themselves for great occasions to reap whole harvests of renown, go on steadfastly in the path of right," are in fact "the bone and sinew, the strength and reliance of the land." To be righteous without renown had a feminine ring to it. But that was not surprising in a man who was to do a woman's bidding. It was even more appropriate for a man made over in a woman's image.[44]

More often, however, the man of the world was a ship eager for launching, but lacking a captain, sail, and port of destiny. " 'If I may look forward to the day when I shall be to you friend, brother, guardian, lover, all in one,' " says Richard Clyde, the first to propose to Gabriella Lynn in Hentz's *Ernest Linwood*, sounding like he is a steady hand preparing to assume the helm, then " 'I shall have such a motive for excellence, such a spring to ambition, that I will show the world the pattern of a man, such as they never saw before.' " Clearly the captain needs some wind for his sails. In Stowe's *The Minister's Wooing*, James Marvyn tells his fiancée Mary Scudder, prior to his departure on a long voyage, " 'It is only in your presence, Mary, that I feel that I am bad and low and shallow and mean, because you represent to me a sphere higher and holier than any in which I have ever moved, and stir up a sort of sighing and longing in my heart to come towards it.' " Apparently, however, Mary's presence is a spiritual one and therefore transportable, for when James has been faced with temptations in the past, he assures Mary, " 'your image has stood between me and low, gross, vice.' "[45]

Nor does it necessarily matter if the male's wooing is rejected. Once inspired and shown the way he can, even if reluctantly, move onward. In *The Linwoods* Sedgwick puts words in the mouth of her suitor similar to those of Stowe's when the temporarily spurned Eliot Lee says to Isabella Linwood, " 'I must now part from you forever; but wherever I go your image will attend me.' " If Isabella will not attend him in the home, says Eliot, her image will in the world—" 'it shall defend me from temptation, incite me to high resolves, pure thoughts, and good deeds.' " Whether the plot is simple or complex beyond recall, and whatever the basis for the rejection, the message is clear, and often repeated. At one stage in Hentz's incredibly convoluted *Eoline*, Eoline Glenmore tells Horace Cleveland that their mutual attraction must be for naught, as she has previously pledged herself to the terminally ill St. Leon and must comfort him until his death. When St. Leon miraculously recovers, Eoline informs Horace that she must maintain her pledge and sever their relationship—but not before she speaks words to guide and to exhort, to reveal to Horace his duty: " 'You will go out into the world and be a wrestler for its honors and win its laurels of fame. And I shall hear of you and be proud.' " Others may have more base objectives, but " 'let the selfish live for their own happiness,' " she says to him. " 'Let us live for something noble, Horace,—the happiness of others.' "[46]

Those males fortunate enough to join a woman in her home are also better prepared to live a worthy life in the world. In Susan Warner's *Queechy*, the wealthy and privileged Guy Carleton is said to be "an uncommonly fine example of what nature alone can do for a man." But Warner adds, "A character of nature's building is at best a very ragged affair, without religion's finishing hand;—at the utmost a fine ruin—no more." What he needs is a religious mentor, that is, a woman's "finishing hand." By the end of the novel Guy is fully aware that the touch he needs is Fleda Ringgan's. " 'She is right and I am wrong,' " says Guy. " 'She is by far the nobler creature—worth many such as I.' " If he cannot be her equal, he can at least " 'be something other than I am!' " Aided by an " 'all wise Governor' " and, by novel's end, his bride Fleda, Guy decides to dedicate his life and wealth to the benefit of the poor and uneducated. Maria McIntosh's Euston Hastings is not as easy a convert for Evelyn Beresford in *Charms and Counter-Charms*. Equally wealthy and privileged, Euston is also intent upon a life of selfish and illicit pleasure, a fact that is discovered by Evelyn only after their marriage. But eventually he is transformed by his wife's influence, to the point that he stands in awe of her " 'firmness of principle.' " Evelyn is, of course, a model that he can never hope to match, but, he tells her, " 'it is to those qualities that I would desire to ally myself through my whole existence.' " The woman remains in her home and the man goes into his world, by her leave, in her image. When Augusta Evans Wilson's Beulah Benton finally marries Guy Hartwell in the closing pages of *Beulah*, the rapid transformation of his character is a foregone conclusion: "His wife was his idol; day by day, his love for her seemed more completely to revolutionize his nature. His cynicism melted insensibly away; his lips forgot their iron compression: now and then his long forgotten laugh rang through the house." The cynical and misanthropic Guy having been made over in woman's image in a few pages, the final sentence of the novel proclaims, "May God aid the wife in her holy work of love." The woman stays at home to receive the world's and man's tribute.[47]

Thinking as private domestic women that they could not enter the wide world, the literary domestics thought to make woman's private domestic world wider, and the thought was that woman would shape society by influencing and controlling man. The man living in the world by woman's ethics testified to the higher moral and spiritual sphere of the woman's life in the home. Woman was restricted to the home and tied to an inferior status, but the literary domestics claimed superiority for her and imagined a reformation of society in her name. To make a woman's sacrifice of being a force for good was to make the sacrifice significant.

But the fantasy of power was the creation of the powerless. Those who had to make a success of their only destiny were plagued by underlying fears of helplessness. The impulse to envision themselves as morally superior and as beings of a higher and separate sphere was a response of those who felt excluded from and denied a place in the world. They sought to judge a world that could not be theirs. The vision of saintliness was the lament of those without influence who served a world that did not serve them.

When the literary domestics looked at nineteenth-century America, they were repulsed by a society they perceived as dominated by individualism and materialism. In part, they shared the perceptions and values of their social and cultural milieu. But they also saw a way of life that ignored and dismissed them on the basis of gender and in effect mocked the woman's prescribed manner of being. Harriet Beecher Stowe's *The Pearl of Orr's Island* is nominally the romantic tale of Mara Lincoln and Moses Pennel, but the tale of romance cloaks a social parable. Sixteen years of age and infatuated with the thirteen-year-old Mara, Moses does not in actuality love her at all. His is a self-love. His feeling for her is intense, but it is self-centered and borders on the destructive. He is "egocentric, exacting, tyrannical, and capricious." Reflecting on both Moses and Mara, Stowe commented, "Nothing so much shows what a human being is in moral advancement as the quality of his love." Naturally, it is the quality of Mara's love that is superior. Mara's devotion to Moses is "maternal and care-taking." Instinctively, she assumes responsibility for his development, and his faults sting her "with a kind of guilty pain, as if they were her own."[48]

Young adulthood brings little change. Still selfish and egocentric, Moses possesses "more desire to be loved than power of loving." Oblivious to the needs of others, adverse to serving others, Moses's dream is not for "somebody to be devoted to, but for somebody who should be devoted to him." Typical of "many young men in America," his ambitions are fixed on "wealth and worldly success," and he scorns religion, viewing it as a deterrent to his "future schemes." Mara does become the means by which his reformation is secured, but not until she is near death. " 'I have seen how true and loving in thought and word and deed you have been,' " he tells the dying Mara, " 'and I have been doing nothing but take.' " He also reveals to her that he has had in the past a " 'sacred presentiment . . . that my spiritual life, if ever I had any, would come through you.' " On the last day of her life, Moses comprehends finally the "real spiritual beauty and significance of Mara's life." With her death, Moses achieves his moral awakening and feels "a new and stronger power of loving." Nevertheless, Stowe has another underlying message. Before dying, Mara has the last word. She expresses love for Moses, encourages him, and imparts her hope and belief that even with her gone he will live a useful, Christian existence. But she does not forgo telling Moses of her disappointment in him, and says that reformed or not, he can never become her equal. " 'I have felt in all that was deepest and dearest to me, I was alone,' " she informs him, adding with finality, " 'You do not come near to me nor touch me where I feel most deeply.' " But that was to say that the woman did not "touch" the man, that she was not a force in his life. By herself, as a morally superior being, her holy role was not in this world. In a sense, she is morally pure by default.[49]

Morally pure, however, did not mean unscathed. To be ineffectual in man's world did not mean to be untouched by it. To judge man and the ways of his world had the ring of an accusation. When Rolf Rossitur in Susan Warner's *Queechy* is faced with the loss of his wealth and privileged status he simply withdraws and crumbles, leaving his family to cope on its own. Rolf does halfheartedly attempt to deal with his family's greatly straitened circumstances by moving wife and children to a farm—but subsequently refuses to involve himself in its management. His transformation and failure are total, as are the effects on his family. "Once manly, frank, busy, happy and making his family so," writes Warner, "now reserved, gloomy, irritable, unfaithful to his duty and selfishly throwing down the burden they must take up, but were far less able to bear." Forced to labor long hours and ridden with anxiety, Rolf's wife is totally debilitated, and the judgment is, "All be his fault—that made it so hard to bear." What also has to be borne is that the son is destroyed as well. Already frail, he is forced to work at a sawmill in order to support the family and meets a premature death, for his spirit and strength have been "left to wear themselves out under trials his father had shrunk from and other trials his father had made."[50]

If the seldom seen moral man of literary domesticity worships the woman as a holy being and the home as a divine refuge from the profane world, even that worship is sometimes only rhetorical. Sedgwick's Henry Redwood of *Redwood* is introduced as a sensitive, patient, compassionate man burdened with an unfortunate past. What is stressed, however, is that Henry's past might have been different had he been capable of acting upon his moral convictions. "It had been Mr. Redwood's destiny through life," observes Sedgwick, "to feel right and to act wrong—to see and to feel, deeply feel, the beauty of virtue but to resign himself to the convenience or expediency of wrong." Henry's catalogue of sins, both overt and covert, is lengthy. He marries his first wife secretly because her sin is to be impoverished. His fear is that disclosure will result in loss of his inheritance. Abandoning his young and pregnant bride for a sojourn in Europe with his father, he learns of her death while away. Unaware that a child has been born, he refuses to acknowledge his marriage, and thereby renders his daughter from the union illegitimate. Marrying a second time, Henry chooses his shallow but wealthy cousin. Upon her death, he abandons their daughter to the care of a frivolous grandmother. To say the least, Sedgwick's tale is murky—and yet predictably clear. Henry recognizes his failings. He knows he has been derelict in the performance of his duties. But his moral awareness has not prevented him from defiling the supposedly sacred atmosphere of two households.

Speaking of his second marriage, Sedgwick has Henry dutifully make his speech: " 'I have dispossessed this temple of the divinity for which it was formed, I have destroyed the innocent—contaminated the pure—and my child—my only child—the immortal creature whose destiny was entrusted to me, I have permitted to be nursed in folly, and devoted to the world without a moral principle or influence.' " For Sedgwick, Henry judges himself and says it all.[51]

Rather than do woman's bidding, Augusta Evans Wilson's Maurice Carlyle and E.D.E.N. Southworth's Harold Middleton involve unwitting wives in their monetary schemes. Both Maurice and Harold are consumed by their desire for wealth and position and both marry simply to acquire money. Neither wife is willing to consider divorce, and both Wilson's Vashti, of *Vashti; or, "Until Death Do Us Part,"* and Southworth's Sybil, of "Sybil Brotherton; or, The Temptation," are left to face lives in desecrated homes. After Vashti discovers Maurice's intentions and flees him within hours of their wedding, Maurice adopts the desperate tactic of attempting to have her declared insane, in hopes that her wealth will then accrue to him. Her home destroyed, it matters little to Vashti that his scheme fails. Harold is frustrated because Sybil has in fact no money. Angered by his discovery, Harold abuses her physically as well as verbally, deserts her for days at a time, and finally abandons her, but not before leaving her with a child and in poverty.

Surprisingly, neither tale can compete with Caroline Lee Hentz's *Rena; or, The Snowbird* in deed, melodrama, or moral recriminations. In his single-minded quest for power and position, Herbert Lindsay leaves a trail strewn with betrayed women and domestic shells. Herbert seduces and abandons one woman, fathering a child he refuses to acknowledge; abandons another woman at the altar in order to marry still another, wealthier woman; and pursues a career in politics to the neglect of his wife and son. After the fact, Herbert confesses. Writing to Debby Wright, the woman he abandoned at the altar, he says, " 'I feel all the injuries I have inflicted,' " and more, " 'I feel the curse of your unmerited forgiveness.' " In a perverse twist, Herbert asks Debby to make amends for him by caring for his illegitimate daughter as well as his neglected wife. Herbert's lament, a final grievous thought for his wife, strikes the mournful note that echoes through the prose of literary domesticity: " 'I have chilled her by coldness, bruised her by harshness—yet she loves me still, Oh! woman, woman! great and marvelous is thy love! Ill-requited, wronged and suffering woman! surely there must be a heaven for thee, if not for transgressing men!' " Having relegated woman to saintly places, Herbert writes to his son Sherwood of the world, warning him of the dangers of ambition, hoping that the son will learn from the sins of the father. " 'If you believe there is any happiness to be found, *seek it*,' " he writes, " 'but not in the high places of the earth. Let my name be a Pharos, warning you of the shoals of ambition.' " He concludes with the familiar tribute to, if not a higher being, certainly one who is separate from his world, saying, " 'I tell you, Sherwood—the heart of a woman is a sacred thing.' " Earthly power is man's, but the hope is that he not exercise it. Which is to say to man, as Herbert says to Sherwood, " 'Trample on everything else if you will, but spare the heart of woman.' " Failing that, woman must condemn man fittingly, Herbert's last act is to commit suicide.[52]

When in the name of woman the literary domestics posed as moral and social critics of ambitious man and his materialistic society, they were calling into question male economic practices and pursuits upon which they themselves were dependent. It was men, not women, who were expected to be the money-brokers of society. And in the eyes of society money was men's to control, to dispense to their dependents. As Sara Parton commented in her biographical essay for *Eminent Women of the Age*, "I myself have heard a man ask a wife who had borne him twelve children, and who was an economical, painstaking thrifty house-keeper, 'What she *did* with the *last* dollar he gave her?' " What was loaned, not given, could be recalled. It was more common for the woman to provide title to property than to claim title. After Caroline Lee Hentz visited a new bride in her Alabama neighborhood she wrote in her diary of 1836 that the woman was "not handsome—not even pretty,—nor witty," but, she observed, "her father has four or five hundred negroes and that makes her lovely, in this southern land."[53]

Rather than claim title to property, the woman readily sought access to man's, in the South as well as the North. Through her narrator Harry Henderson in *My Wife and I*, Stowe commented pointedly, "The world has been busy for some centuries in shutting and locking every door through which a woman could step into wealth, except the door of marriage." Man's ways were not woman's. "All vigor and energy, such as men put forth to get this golden key of life, is condemned and scorned as unfeminine." As for the woman of the "upper classes, who undertakes to get wealth by honest exertion and independent industry," she "loses caste, and is condemned by a thousand voices as an oddity and a deranged person." But of the woman "gifted with beauty, who sells it to buy wealth" Stowe wrote, "That way of getting money is not called unwomanly." Wrote Mary J. Holmes in *Millbank*, "Could we but look into the hearts of those around us, how many a one should we find which, with not a particle of love and oftentimes of respect, sells itself for money and that alone."[54]

For the woman to view the wider world in the manner of moral and social critic was to recognize forces from which neither she nor her smaller world could escape. To be dependent upon man and his society was to be captive, and susceptible to man and the values of his society. From their familial, domestic perspective the literary domestics looked beyond the home and saw a general subversion of values to which they held allegiance, but they also saw the pursuits of a society that were threatening and damaging to their own intimate, singular existence. Seeking to project the home as moral beacon to the world, they shuddered before the dimming of its light. In her introduction to *The Deserted Wife*, E.D.E.N. Southworth, who was habitually preoccupied with unhappy wives and husbands, argued that "the primary cause of unhappy marriage is a *defective moral and physical education*." The failure of society to teach its children "PRUDENCE" in the home, she said, could be seen in the life of society in "rash and culpable mercantile speculation, ending in insolvency," and in the life of the home in "hasty, inconsiderate marriages, ending in bankruptcy of heart, home and happiness." The failure of society to teach its children "FIDELITY" in the home led to "irregularity and unfaithfulness in business, embezzlement of funds, etc." in the life of society, and to "broken marriage faith and deserted families" in the life of the home.[55]

To an extent the literary domestics regarded the nineteenth century's apocalyptic forces of individualism and materialism as not only alien to woman's own consciousness but as emanating from social elements that were not their own. As the daughters of those who could trace their cultural roots to European beginnings they, like their gentlemen counterparts, derided the nouveau riche who aped the fashionable life of aristocratic Europe. When she was living in New York City in 1821, Sedgwick wrote to her sister Frances that she was without difficulty resisting the feverish "temptations" of that city's social life. "I am, it is true, in a city where fashion maintains her empire," said Sedgwick, "and has her willing and unwilling subjects, but if I was with you in your house, or with Charles in his blessed retreat I would not be much more independent of fashion than I am now." Actually, she said, with an air of gentle if genteel condescension, "we have nothing to do with the fashionable gaities of the City. Our visiting is all of a familiar and domestic kind." Forty years later Mary Virginia Terhune positioned her social self less gently, but no less distinctly, when in her novel *Husks* she castigated fashionable society in which "bestial idolatry has risen to a pitch of fanaticism" in "vile caricatures of foreign courts, foreign manners, and foreign vices." Equally revolted, and typically outspoken, Sara Parton noted in her essay, "A Glance at a Chameleon Subject," the presence of "harlequin costumes," women "strutting like peacocks," and "carriages, with their liveried servants"—all this, Parton said indignantly, "in our republican streets."[56]

But if there were social distinctions to be made, there were apprehensions rooted in gender that could not be hidden. In a world that corrupted the home, woman was, alas, not uncorruptible herself. As Americans appeared to look away from a virtuous, republican heritage and ahead to the gods of social advancement and material progress, the literary domestics feared failure in their quest for a good name for woman. " 'As long as one class is distinguished by education and refined manners, and another is marked by ignorance and vulgarity,' " says Willie Sullivan in Maria Cummins's *The Lamplighter*, " 'there should, and there must, in the nature of things, be a dividing line between the two, which neither, perhaps, would desire to overstep.' " But, he adds, " 'I have seen more ignorance, more ill-breeding, more meanness, and more immorality in the so-called aristocracy of our country, than I should have believed possible would be tolerated there.' " And what is worse, he says, is the " 'effect of an uninterrupted pursuit of pleasure upon the sensibilities, the tempers, and the domestic affections of women.' "[57]

In the woman of fashion the literary domestics found a historical artifact that stood as damning evidence of woman's uncontrolled fate. A product of circumstances she did not control, she testified to woman's helpless dependency. Without question the woman of fashion was to be abhorred. " 'Married belles and married beaux are not harmless, nor should they be tolerated in really good society,' " admonishes Irene Huntington in Augusta Evans Wilson's *Macaria*. But it was the female of the social duo who was the greater offender. Says Irene, " 'Women who so far forget their duties to their homes and husbands, and the respect due to public opinion, as to habitually seek for happiness in the mad whirl of so-called fashionable life, ignoring household obligations, should be driven from well-bred, refined circles, to hide their degradation at the firesides they have disgraced.' " The woman of fashion was to be condemned because she gave the lie to the moral justification of the woman's being. She symbolized the materialism of an age but she also provided unholy evidence that regardless of social status, women were narcissistic and pampered and led lives that were idle, unproductive, and without redeeming value. The awful thought was that they were the playthings of men.[58]

Anxious to laud woman's name and exalt her life, the literary domestics vehemently censured those who disgraced and dishonored the name and works of woman. In judging the man's world they criticized their own for being kept by man. In Caroline Lee Hentz's *Lovell's Folly*, Florence Fairchild, garbed in the "flimsy veil of artificial refinement," is judged lacking in the "moral perception of those finer shades which constitute the beauty of sensibility." Sedgwick's Matilda Preston, in "Second Thoughts Best," is criticized for her "intense love of admiration," and for spending too much time attending to her physical appearance. In Stowe's *Pink and White Tyranny*, Lillie Ellis's "unconfessed yet only motive for appearing in church [is] the display of herself and the winning of admiration." And Terhune castigated Lucy Hunt in *Husks* for spending her time in church "speculating upon the probable cost of Miss Hauton's Parisian hat, or coveting Mrs. Beau Monde's sable cloak." In "To the Ladies: A Call to Be a Wife," Sara Parton asked of she who "flirts with every man she meets, and reserves her frowns for the home fireside" and of she who "thinks more of her silk dress than her children," how she could presume to think she had "a call to be a wife." Those women who betrayed their sex, wrote Parton in "Rag-Tag and Bob-Tail Fashions," were "defiling womanhood, and . . . bringing it into derision and contempt." Contained in the judgment was a plea, because the literary domestic wanted woman "to *be* something, to *do* something higher and nobler . . . " But that "something" had to be and to be done in a home that waited upon man.[59]

In *Beulah*, Augusta Evans Wilson looked upon worldly women and lamented. "Oh, woman! woman! when will you sever the fetters which fashion, wealth, and worldliness have bound about you, and prove yourselves worthy of the noble mission for which you were created?" The mission was to stay by home and hearth and keep burning a holy light to guide man in the world; how much longer, Wilson wondered, would "heartless, soulless wives, mothers, daughters, and sisters" instead dance "mothlike, round the consuming flame of fashion"? The threat was that women, "by neglecting their duties, and deserting their sphere, [would] drive their husbands, sons and brothers, out into the world, reckless and depraved, with callous hearts, irrevocably laid on the altars of mammon." The call was for divine inspiration, and the story to tell was of a glorious past: "God help the women of America! Grant them the true womanly instincts which, in the dawn of our republic, made 'home' the Eden, the acme of all human hopes and joys." In the name of a past, and of a present to be rewritten, the hope was for a different future.[60]

12

A Right Regard for Womanhood:
A Word or Two on All Sides

On 19 July 1848, in the small town of Seneca Falls, New York, Elizabeth Cady Stanton read the amended version of the Declaration of Independence issued by the first women's rights convention. Following the precedent of 1776, this female portion of humanity, also seeking a change in the affairs of the earth, thought it proper to speak to the subject of motivation. Echoing the male patriots of the Revolution, the convention's "Declaration of Sentiments" stated that only a long-suffering people could possess sufficient cause to urge momentous changes in society. But, it claimed, the cause of this people was more than justified. Basically, the charge was that the self-evident truth of the equality of "all men and women" had been betrayed by American society; that the "inalienable rights" with which women were endowed by their Creator had been violated; and that the various political bodies of the United States had exercised their powers without the "consent" of and to the detriment of women. Literally speaking, the opening words of the document were somewhat illogical. Generally, the American people, men and women, had not recognized the equality of women as a self-evident truth and had not regarded women as having been granted by their Creator the same inalienable rights accorded men. Clearly, too, the male governing bodies of the nation had not deemed it a requirement that they govern with the consent of women. Officially, neither truths nor rights nor powers had been violated, because they had never been sanctioned. The words of the document that followed made this logically clear.[1]

The history of the matter, the declaration said, was certainly evident. Women had indeed been long-suffering: "The history of mankind is a history of repeated injuries and usurpations on the part of man toward woman, having in direct object the establishment of an absolute tyranny over her." Listed among the many rights denied women in the nineteenth-century American democracy were those of suffrage, of equal opportunity for education, of control of property brought to marriage and of wages once

316

married, and of equal rights in divorce and custody of children. The tyranny of man over woman was testified to, read the statement, by man's comprehensive attempt to destroy woman's "confidence in her own powers, to lessen her self-respect, and to make her willing to lead a dependent and abject life." All rights denied were forthwith claimed in the name of the long-standing assault committed against woman's being. In short, continued the "Declaration of Sentiments," because "women do feel themselves aggrieved, oppressed, and fraudulently deprived of their most sacred rights, we insist that they have immediate admission to all the rights and privileges which belong to them as citizens of the United States."[2]

The woman's movement for an equality of being and for the full rights of citizenship in the American republic did not begin or end in Seneca Falls, and neither at that first women's rights convention of 1848 nor afterward was there unanimity in approach or sentiment. The previous half century had witnessed manifold evidences of a struggle in various guises to change the character and status of woman's life. Some were more apparent than others. The more positive conception of human nature fostered by the Enlightenment and the political ideals of the Revolution had contributed to the concept of republican motherhood which bespoke a symbolic political influence for the woman in the home. Nineteenth-century Protestantism's call to join the sacred to the social had led in the name of God, and in the spirit of the woman of the home, to women's involvement beyond the home in a variety of benevolent and moral reform societies formed early in the century. Voluntary associations organized to increase religious influence, to aid the poor, to eliminate prostitution, to stamp out drunkenness, and to rid antebellum America of slavery more and more engaged women in public efforts to influence and shape American life, often directly and, it can be argued, always indirectly on their own behalf. The abolitionist movement of the 1830s, particularly the Garrisonian wing, with its emphasis on the absolute moral equality of all human beings, had planted in the consciousness of a number of female abolitionists, including some at Seneca Falls, the principle that women were essentially human and only secondarily female. The principle embodied the most fundamental challenge possible to common perceptions of woman's person and place.[3]

Without a doubt, however, the overwhelming number of women struggled knowingly and unknowingly, by and with themselves, in the solitude of their homes. Unwittingly in many respects, the literary domestics brought that struggle onto the public stage. Six of the literary domestics had entered upon their quasi-professional careers before that summer of 1848, and six followed during the subsequent decade. Most of the twelve had been secret writers of a sort well before 1848, and for the remainder of the century and a bit beyond a number continued to do battle in their own fashion. In fact, the literary domestics played a major part in the nineteenth century's dialogue regarding the being and status of women in America. Looking backward and forward, they made it manifestly clear that the struggle was a personal as well as a social one. The consciousness of the literary domestics enclosed a battleground upon which opposing forces warred in a confrontation with both selves and society. When Harriet Beecher Stowe wrote Edward Everett Hale in 1869 to negotiate the terms governing the serialization of her novel *Pink and White Tyranny* in the magazine titled, ironically, *Old and New*, she told the Boston Unitarian clergyman, philanthropist, and popular author that her "design" was "to show the domestic oppression practiced by a gentle pretty pink and white doll on a strong minded generous gentleman who has married her in a fit of poetical romance because she looks pretty." Her novel, said Stowe, would represent "in a quiet way an offset to a class of writing which I am sorry to see which represents men as in most cases oppressors and women as sufferers in domestic life." That was the "plan" of her book, she said, "and being to some extent a woman's rights woman, as I am to some extent something of almost everything that goes, I shall have a right to say a word or two on the other side." Stowe spoke more truth than she realized, for the literary domestic, in conflict within herself, did indeed stand on all sides of the "woman" issue.[4]

That the literary domestics desired change is undeniable. Writing to her friend the British essayist Anna Jameson in 1845, Catharine Maria Sedgwick commented that "there is much agitation on the subject of women's rights." She noted that Margaret Fuller's *Woman in the Nineteenth Century*, which had recently appeared, was "as plain spoken as the Pentateuch on subjects which women have never spoken before," with the result that all was astir. "The men are shocked and disgusted," she said, "and the women rather scared and uncertain what to say, or whether to speak at all." Sedgwick herself regarded Fuller as "a woman of learning and much thought," but she also believed that Fuller sometimes mistook "diversity for originality and untried noveltie for great and newly discovered truth." Noting that there were nonetheless "right and admirable suggestions to men and women" in Fuller's book, she added approvingly, "the cause of Eve's daughters is making progress here." Specifically, she pointed to laws that were being enacted "in many of the States in their favor—Rhode Island gives them a certain portion of the husband's property and puts it beyond the reach of his creditors and our Massachusetts legislators have recently secured to a married woman her inheritance and earnings."[5]

A year later Sedgwick was still more optimistic, in fact overly sanguine in her appraisal. Writing to Jameson again, she claimed, "The basis of women's rights is beginning to be understood and acknowledged." She repeated her observation that "several of the states have made favorable laws" in regard to women and claimed that "the independent existence of a married woman is secured," by which she meant that "her rights to her earnings and her inheritance" are secured. That was "nearly all" woman wanted, said Sedgwick, and gave "the impulse to a better education" than women had ever received. Any education that made woman "capable of a greater diversity of employments and of the management of property," thought Sedgwick, would "give her a higher estimate with the mass of men than she has ever yet enjoyed—for this is what they understand." The blend of inferiority and condescension in Sedgwick's observation was a precious example of the woman's trademark.[6]

A right regard for womanhood and the opportunity for woman to sustain herself economically did appear to be justifiable goals to the literary domestics. Connecticut, wrote Stowe to George Eliot in 1869, was in the midst of repealing *"the whole of the old unjust English marriage property laws as regards women,"* with the object to *"set them free."* In one essay in *Ginger-Snaps*, published in 1870, Sara Parton warned men that they "will have to choose their words in addressing 'women folks' " because a woman could now "earn her own living independent of marriage,—that often hardest and most non-paying and most thankless road" to subsistence. No longer, said Parton, would the woman be compelled "to face the alternatives of serfdom or starvation." Rather, when she married—and who could doubt that she desired to?—she could do so "for love and companionship, and for cooperation in all high and noble aims and purposes, not for bread and meat and clothes." Even "The Old Maid of the Period," asserted Parton in another essay in the same volume, "feels well and independent in conse-quence, and holds up her head with the best, and asks no favors," and, she wrote, " *'Woman's Rights'* has done it." The battle was engaged, and there was more than sufficient cause. In a third essay titled "Woman's Millen-nium" Parton complained about the inequitable treatment accorded women in the courts, particularly in divorce cases. "Compliments, and flattery, and gifts we can all have" until we grow old, wrote Parton, "but *justice*, messieurs! ah! that's quite another thing. Female eyes have grown dim looking for *that*, all through the ages."[7]

The basic question was how to seek deliverance from wrongs without betraying the woman's revered sense of self. How could a woman be equal to yet different from a man? Phrased another way, how could she become fully equal without ceasing to be truly womanly? The dilemma was how to claim equal rights of being without violating the *woman's* claim to being. "I hold to woman's rights to the extent that a woman's own native name never ought to die out and be merged in the name of any man whatever," wrote Stowe to Parton in the 1860s. The literal reference had symbolic meaning. As writers the literary domestics had entered a wider sphere of being they did not feel was legitimately theirs, and when they looked to other literary women they, in essence, looked back to find the woman.[8]

After having read a tribute in the *North American Review* to Lydia Maria Child in the 1830s, Caroline Howard Gilman wrote to her sister-in-law Louisa Gilman Loring that Child "deserves all praise and is the American Mrs. Jameson." Actually, said Gilman, Child was "better" than Anna

Jameson because "I do not believe she will ever lose her feminine modesty, as I think the latter has done in the Loves of the Poets." In 1840 Sedgwick found in Jameson what Gilman had sought. Sedgwick approved of Jameson's use of her "gifts," she wrote to her, "as you have used them in the cause of the oppressed, the wronged, working in all those circles that widen into that of general humanity." Sedgwick also approved of the manner of Jameson's usage, not least in regard to Jameson's efforts on behalf of women, when compared to other champions of women's rights: "I believe your incidental explanations of the condition of women and the hand that from your high elevation you stretch out to them, invariably is of more avail than a professed and noisy championship." Those who had become public figures were apprehensive about their womanly selves. Looking at themselves, they could not forget a given sense of self. In her autobiography, Mary Virginia Terhune remembered meeting Maria Cummins and four years later Augusta Evans Wilson. On the separate occasions of making their separate acquaintances, recalled Terhune, both were already popular authors, and "both were quietly refined in manner and speech, and incredibly unspoiled by the flood of popular favor that had taken each by surprise." In a manner of speaking, both were for Terhune credible women.[9]

The literary domestics were awed by, and regarded with a mixture of trepidation and admiration, the woman who would appear on man's public platform, but they were reassured whenever they espied womanly qualities. In the early 1840s, after Susan Warner had heard Catharine Beecher deliver an address on the subject of sending female teachers to the West, she wrote to her sister Anna "Whatever anticipations might have been formed of somewhat bold, unbecoming, unwomanly in the exhibition, they were not fulfilled." Rather, noted Warner, "Miss Beecher made a most agreeable impression upon me." It was all to the good that Beecher's address had been "well written and very interesting" and, significantly, had been for the "most part read by her brother." However, what was as important to Warner was the fact that Beecher's "deportment was very modest, delicate, and proper." Beecher, wrote Warner approvingly, "is I daresay an admirable woman." Lucy Stone visited Sedgwick in 1849, and after she had left Sedgwick wrote to her niece Kate to describe "the female impersonator of reform." Stone was well prepared for the task before her, being a "person of rare gifts with a good New England education for ground work, and a collegiate course at the Oberlyn [sic] Institute of four years where," said an amused Segwick, "the eleven girls—good 'grecians' found out that Paul . . . was a women's rights man!—where they ascertained that he only forbade them to *gabble*, not talk in the churches." Out in the world Stone was on the march, but in Sedgwick's eyes she was a woman on the march; besides possessing "grace," she also had about her an "entire self-forgetfulness and divine calmness that fit her to speak in the great cause she has undertaken." The suggestion was that because Stone was, in Sedgwick's estimation, entirely self-effacing she must be divinely confident.[10]

The battle with society necessarily entailed warfare with self. The question remained the same, but with an additional twist. The woman who saw herself as different from man desired equality, but did the difference she presumed cripple her in the struggle for equality? In the *New York Ledger* in 1859, Parton indicated her willingness to attend a woman's rights convention despite her antipathy to personal notice. The nature of the declaration was not without import. The desire for justice did not necessarily bring the wherewithal to demand it. The preference was to be accorded justice, rather than to have to command it. In Parton's 1855 novel *Ruth Hall*, Ruth says that if men only understood that the " 'suffering' " inflicted upon woman forced her to " 'either weep in silence over such injustice, or do violence to her womanly nature by a public contention for her rights, such outrages would be much less frequent.' " If she were a man, she says, " 'it would be so sweet to use my powers to defend the defenseless.' " The desire was to exercise power like a man; the fear was that she would be found a defenseless woman. When she had recently had the opportunity to listen to the " 'eloquent' " Lucy Stone, says Ruth, " 'it really did appear to me that those Bloomers of hers had a mission!' " Nevertheless, she adds, " 'I could never put them on.' " The women who sought the equal rights of a free and independent individual found it difficult to envision her restricted and dependent self acting freely and independently on her own individual behalf.[11]

When Robert Bonner came to the aid of E.D.E.N. Southworth in her difficulties with T. B. Peterson, her primary book publisher, Southworth expressed her gratitude in part by writing to Bonner, "If all men were as prompt and spirited in defending the women dependent upon them, as you are, then we should not hear so much fuss about women's rights." That was to speak to an order of spheres. It was one matter for the woman to protest against the wrongs committed against her in her own sphere; it was quite another matter to seek the ultimate right of exercising the powers of man's sphere. If men were women's true and proper champions, said Southworth, "we should all be very glad to leave our rights in the hands of our *brave big brothers*." Rather than assault big brother, it was preferable, and more natural, to encourage and seek his blessing. The woman who was embattled was more likely to look to her traditional protector. As Hester Grey says in Southworth's *Retribution*, " 'Talk of woman's rights; woman's rights live in the instincts of her protector—man.' " Southworth's *Ishmael; or, In the Depths* and its sequel, *Self-Raised; or, From the Depths*, provide the fullest and most striking illustration of the literary domestics' ideal male in the world defending woman's rights. Originally serialized in the pages of the *New York Ledger* in 1863 and 1864 under the title, "Self-Made, or Out of the Depths," and printed again in the *Ledger* in 1874, the novel was published in book form in 1876. The tale of Ishmael Worth, truly the literary domestics' woman's man, is no more revealing than the story concerning its writing and publication. Southworth, the self-described woman of the "double-burden," the mother who resorted to the man's literary trade to support herself and her children, regarded the story of Ishmael in a special light. Shortly before its original publication in the *Ledger*, Southworth wrote to Robert Bonner, "This story is different in character to any that I have written before"; therefore, she cautioned, Bonner should look upon it as an "experiment." Previously, said this woman of elite Maryland lineage, she had tried to write in a style "catered for what I believed to be the popular taste," but in the tale of Ishmael she had been more conscious of "a higher aim—popular good."[12]

The "character" of the tale, she believed, required that she be "deliberate in developing it," and she "feared that such deliberation might be dangerous to its popularity." She was torn between her desire to develop it in "harmonious proportions" and "my fear of wearying my readers." Always concerned to maintain her source of income, which obviously meant maintaining her literary popularity, Southworth emphasized in her letter to Bonner that "this story, I repeat is an experiment." If Bonner thought it was a dangerous experiment, one that risked her popularity, "I can easily return to my old style," she said, especially "if this should not please the millions."[13]

The portrait of Ishmael was dear to Southworth's heart. "I never was so much in love with any hero, that I ever wrote of," she confided to Bonner in another letter, "as I am with Ishmael and that is the truth." She did not say that "in vanity," she insisted, adding, and revealing more than she knew, "I am only the transparent glass through which my hero is shown as through a window." Still, she could not help but risk saying, "I do not think in all literature that Ishmael has his equal—there!" And yet she could only risk so much, adding again, "Don't tell anybody I said it for they will be sure to misunderstand me and set it all down to personal vanity." If the truth were known, she said with unintended irony, "if they only knew how little credit I take to myself, they would exonerate me from the charge." In part, however, Southworth did not intend to be misunderstood. She would express the hope that her tale of a paragon of a female protector would be inspirational for all young people in the latter half of the nineteenth century. It was also her hope that she would thereby gain a greater financial return for the story of Ishmael. Shortly before the two-volume publication of the novel in 1876, she wrote to Bonner in response to his wish to buy the copyright to the volumes. She would accept his financial terms, she told him, except for the fact that "the work of 'self-made' is dearer to my soul than all my collected works." Unable to say directly to Bonner that she hoped that he would purchase the novel at a "dearer" price, she said instead of "this best work of my heart and hand and brain" that she had written it "not only for money, for fame, but for *humanity*." If Bonner had been of a mind to dispute her claim, Southworth would not have allowed it. "Indeed," she said, "I know that the last motive was the strongest inspiration." As the year was 1876, she also knew that she wished "to publish it this centennial year, as it is eminently a National work." Obviously, she thought that this might make it eminently salable as well, and thus make the copyright more valuable to Bonner.[14]

In the concluding sentence to the preface of the first volume, Southworth offered her hero Ishmael as a "guiding-star to the youth of every land, to show them that there is no depth of human misery from which they may not, by virtue, energy, and perseverance, rise to earthly honors as well as eternal glory." If Southworth appeared to be pumping for national sales, as well as likening herself to Horatio Alger, whose rags-to-riches tales for boys were enjoying notable popularity, her formula nevertheless differed in two respects. Although Ishmael Worth is initially unaware of it in the story, he eventually discovers that his origins are impeccably genteel. The character of Ishmael Worth also was not entirely a creation of Southworth's imagination, but apparently based upon William Wirt, attorney general of the United States under James Monroe. Wirt was linked to Ishmael by the *Ledger* when it stated in 1864 that the fictional Worth had been based on a real-life person who was "an accomplished gentleman, a learned jurist, [and] an eloquent advocate" as well as an attorney general. And in 1877 the *Ledger* identified Wirt by name in response to a query from a reader.[15]

More importantly, however, Ishamel's moral qualities, his uncompromising righteousness, and his perseverance are displayed in the novel in acts of selflessness extending to everyone within reach, but especially to women. A pitiful and apparently illegitimate orphan who rises to become an eminent, highly respected lawyer bent upon promoting the public good, Ishmael utilizes his legal talents primarily on behalf of women. At the outset, Ishmael's position is said to be the most ignominious and difficult one imaginable for a white male in nineteenth-century America. There is little doubt, wrote Southworth, that the ordinary mortal would have been doomed: "Our Ishmael had neither father, mother, name, nor place in the world . . . he had nothing—nothing but the eye of the Almighty Father regarding him." Nonetheless, Ishmael develops into a conscientious, dutiful, ambitious youth whose models include Revolutionary heroes such as George Washington and Patrick Henry. He eagerly pores over a history of the young nation, and this book and the Bible become the "first media of his inspiration" and provide him with "his idols, his models, and his exemplars." But if his heroes are male, his life, beginning with his determination to exonerate his deceased mother, is dedicated to protecting, promoting, and revering the name of womanhood. In as histrionic a scene as any in the literary domestics' prose, the young illegitimate Ishmael literally stands upon the grave of his mother (the text includes a drawing depicting the very moment) and solemnly swears that he will strive to bring glory to her maiden name: " 'Oh! poor, young, wronged mother! and broken hearted mother! sleep in peace; for your son lives to vindicate you. Yes, if he has been spared, it was for this purpose—to honor, to vindicate, to avenge you!' " Ishmael is eventually united with his very much alive father, but as a symbol of his determination to meet his commitment to his mother, he refuses to assume the father's distinguished name.[16]

It only remains for Ishmael to devote his life as a lawyer to defending wronged women in court and to seeking to amend laws that discriminate against them. Ishmael has male ambitions, but he pursues female gains. Southworth constructs an obvious case against a husband who has deserted his wife for nine years and is now trying to force a reunion with her by claiming custody of their three children. Ishmael, who has been asked to accept the husband's suit, admits that the law is on the father's side. But he protests that the law is supposed to be a minister of justice rather than injustice, and declares that " 'it appears to me that justice and mercy are on the mother's side.' " He refuses the husband's case and offers the wife counsel without charge. Arguing the case, Ishmael not only defends the mother, he also is counsel for womanhood to the world. Wrote Southworth, "He spoke noble words in behalf not only of his client, but of woman— woman—loving, feeble, and oppressed from the beginning of time . . . " Thus was the case of the oppressed presented to the perceived oppressors.[17]

The desired equality of being was elusive and difficult to pursue, was hindered and thwarted by profound, contradictory, ambivalent impulses from within as well as pressures from without. The private woman's system of checks and balances was veiled, but it was as restrictive and perhaps as punitive as that imposed by a public, male world. Catharine Maria Sedgwick asked in *The Linwoods*, "If our young ladies were to give a portion of the time and interest they expend on dress, gossip, and light reading, to the comprehension of the constitution of their country, and its political institutions, would they be less interesting companions, less qualified mothers, or less amiable women?" Sedgwick did not deny the risk: " 'there are dangers in a woman's adventuring beyond her customary path.' " Nevertheless, she wrote, "better the chance of shipwreck on a voyage of high purpose, than expend life in paddling hither and thither on a shallow stream, to no purpose at all." But to achieve greater control of one's own being one had to participate in controlling the world, and before that could transpire it was necessary for the woman to develop not only a higher but a different estimate of self. It was necessary to reenvision a sense of place in order to undo an inferior sense of self. In 1812, at age twenty-two, Sedgwick wrote to her father Theodore, a man who had been a leader of his nation and who was then one year from his death, to say, "I have regarded your life to find some rules of action to apply to my own, but," she informed him sadly, "I have relinquished the scrutiny with the same feeling of disappointment that the humble architect of the cottage would turn from the survey of a lofty palace, in which he had almost absurdly hoped to find a model for his little dwelling." What she had found in surveying her father's political career, and found absurd as a yardstick for her future, was "a life dignified by usefulness, of which it has been the object and the delight to do good, and the happiness to do it in an extended sphere."[18]

Seventy years later, Mary Virginia Terhune in *Eve's Daughters* recalled the moment and the manner in which it had been impressed upon her youthful consciousness exactly where the boundaries of woman's sphere lay. Her father Samuel, the deviser of unconventional methods for his daughters' education, was again her primary teacher, albeit in this vein along entirely conventional lines. As Terhune revealed in her autobiography a century after Sedgwick's letter to her father, she knew as a child that her father, the male, was the "master," without a doubt "head of the house." He was also master of affairs beyond the home, the family's only citizen in the world. Noting proudly that her father was respected in his community for "his intelligence, probity, courtesy, and energy," Terhune recognized implicitly that as "his place in society and church was assured," so only could be his family's. Her father was also deeply involved in the political affairs of his community and his state and, indirectly through the latter, in the politics of his nation. Terhune remembered that she grew "used to political wrangling from my youth up." She became accustomed as well to discussing political issues with her father, and it was in that context that this particular lesson was imparted. In *Eve's Daughters* she related the events of a morning during the campaign of 1840 when she, then ten, and the staunchly Whig Hawes were horseback riding, and daughter questioned father about the policies of the "old line Whig party." Apparently pleased with the acuity of her insight, father Samuel became animated, then smiled and sighed, and said, " 'Ah, my daughter! if you had been born a boy you would be invaluable to me!' " Remembering that she had been "crushed," Terhune wrote, "There is a pain at my heart in the telling that renews the real grief of the moment." However difficult the lesson, she learned from her grief. As she related in her autobiography, when Polk defeated Clay for the presidency in 1844 it was her father who was crushed. On that occasion the "woman-child" played her proper role, and her "whole soul went out in longing to comfort the defeated demigod." The "demigod" was Clay, but Terhune might just as well have been referring to her father, her hero from a sphere that was barred to her.[19]

The march to an equality of being had subterranean routes. "*Different* offices and *different* powers" is what Maria McIntosh attributed to men and women in *Woman in America*, "leaving to others the vain question of equality or inequality." And yet she herself had addressed that question only two paragraphs before by attaching to women a "political inequality, ordained in Paradise, when God said to the woman, 'He shall rule over thee,' and which has ever existed, in every tribe, and nation, and people of earth's countless multitudes." But McIntosh was not done. Turning a page, she claimed that "while all the outward machinery of government, the body, the thews and sinews of society, are man's, woman, if true to her own not less important or less sacred mission, controls its vital principle." Pages later she more or less repeated herself, saying that while man was better fitted to govern the body politic, "woman is by nature equally fitted to preside over its inner spirit, over the homes from which the social as distinguished from the political life must be derived." And still later in her book she told her female readers that if they performed their "holy work" in the home nobly, they would "have done more real good to your country, more to insure the continuance of institutions depending on the intelligence and virtue of her people, than all the demagogues who ever harangued in or out of Congress." That claim, of course, whether implicit or explicit, harbored a frustrated, resentful outcry. The lowly would not discard their humble garments, but to an extent, at least, they found those garments ill-fitting. There can be little doubt that the badge of inferiority pierced their hearts.[20]

It was evident, wrote Sedgwick in *Means and Ends*, that "men and women are destined to different departments of duty." She could not believe, she said, that "it was ever intended that women should lead armies, harangue in halls of legislation, bustle up to the ballot-boxes, or sit on judicial tribunals." Where, then, lay the great result of women's lives? Having placed woman away in the home, away from man's world for an apparent eternity, Sedgwick looked to the woman in the home for lasting influence over man's world: "By an unobtrusive and unseen process, are the characters of men formed, at home, by the mother, the first teacher. There the moral basis is fixed." Restricted and resigned to small earthly affairs, the woman must claim ultimate worldly effects. The marital system was woman's order of life, and it enclosed, wrote Sedgwick in *Married or Single?*, " 'the central point, whence all the relations of life radiate, and the source of all political and social virtue.' " Marriage, wrote Southworth in *The Mother-in-Law*, "is the most sacred tie on earth. . . . The peace of families, the social welfare of the whole community, depend upon its being held so." The woman might be the mute, deferential supporter of man's political affairs, but she was, nevertheless, envisioned as the political mother superior of a utopian order. Augusta Evans Wilson wrote in *St. Elmo* "that the borders of the feminine realm could not be enlarged, without rendering the throne unsteady, and subverting God's law of order. Woman reigned by divine right only at home." But the woman did reign at home, and she reigned by divine right. By that fact and by that right the borders of the feminine realm enclosed lives beyond.[21]

Denied a role in the historical body politic and unable to envision equality in her present world, the woman claimed superiority in a millennium to come. But it was a claim that masked a fearful, plaintive plea. The introductory note to the 1899 edition of Harriet Beecher Stowe's *My Wife and I; or, Harry Henderson's History* asserted that Stowe "sheltered herself behind the masculine fiction of Harry Henderson." But Henderson's "masculine fiction" is replete with what amount to defensive eulogies on behalf of the feminine tale. The narrator of his own history, Harry has as much or more to tell of the history of the women he has known. Regarding his mother, he relates more than the fact of her iron command and redeeming influence in terms of his father. In particular, Henderson utilizes the character of his mother to comment upon the relationship—actually, on the lack of a relationship—between domestic women and the political state and to speculate upon the ideal political state. Given what he perceives to have been the saintly control his mother exerted over her family, Harry wonders "whether the politics of the ideal state in a millennial community should not be one equally pervaded by mother-influences." The "Woman question of the day," he believes, is, "Shall MOTHERHOOD ever be felt in the public administration of the affairs of state?" Harry's question is in fact rhetorical, for he has his own answer. To him the state is actually an aggregate of families, and while the state has been ruled by " 'conscript fathers' " it has not been ruled by " 'conscript mothers.' " And yet, he asks, "is not a mother's influence needed in acts that relate to the interests of collected families as much as in individual ones?"[22]

Originally published in 1871, *My Wife and I* delivers not only Harry Henderson's answer for history but also Stowe's evaluation of the state of political affairs in the United States, with woman on the sidelines. As Harry speaks, one can imagine Stowe writing with her mother in mind:

> The state, at this very day, needs an influence like what I remember our mother's to have been, in our great, vigorous, growing family,—an influence quiet, calm, warming, purifying, uniting—it needs a womanly economy and thrift in husbanding and applying its material resources—it needs a divining power, by which different sections and different races can be interpreted to each other, and blended together in love—it needs an educating power, by which its immature children may be trained in virtue—it needs a loving and redeeming power, by which its erring and criminal children may be borne with, purified and led back to virtue.

Is, then, Stowe recommending that women enter the legislature, sit on the judicial tribunal, or rule the ship of state? Not exactly: "Yet, while I thus muse," Harry pauses, "I remember that such women as my mother are those to whom in an especial manner all noise and publicity and unrestful conflict are peculiarly distasteful." (Henderson's remembrance recalls, again, Stowe's reminiscences of her mother in the "Beecher biographies.") "My mother," Harry continues, "had that delicacy of fibre that made any kind of public exercise of her powers an impossibility." Henderson does not claim that that trait is an exclusively "feminine characteristic"; some male poets and philosophers have exhibited it, he says. But whom does he name specifically? Jesus of Nazareth, of course. And of whom does he speak generally? He speaks of women, "women of this brooding, quiet, deeply spiritual nature," women who "cannot attend caucuses, or pull political wires, or mingle in the strife of political life," women who nevertheless, he insists, "are yet the most needed force to be for the good of the State." And, finally, whose need is in fact being addressed? "I am persuaded that *it is not till this class of women feel as vital and personal responsibility for the good of the State as they have hitherto felt for that of the family, that we shall gain the final elements of a perfect society.*" Henderson's plea is in the end on behalf of woman.[23]

It is the ultimate form of doing and denying, and the act is envisioned in a manner peculiar to a literary domestic. In a letter of 1856 Wilson asked, "Should not Excelsior be the watchword and motto of the true artist?" It was certainly Wilson's watchword and motto, and spoke to her intent. "To reform the world implies being above it, does it not?" she asked again. "O!" Wilson enthused, "Art should elevate, should refine, should sanctify the heart." The woman who was not a citizen might yet be the mother of a millennial society. Sedgwick expressed her surprise to Louisa Minot in 1836 that *The Poor Rich Man, and the Rich Poor Man* had been "received with far more favor than I expected." It was "an honor," she said, "I did not expect on this side of the grave." In the future she intended to write more "books of this description which suit the mass of readers—In this country we must do everything for the majority." To "do more for the majority" suggested something different for a woman than for a man. Writing in 1859 to the "Committee on Libraries for the Ward Schools of New York," Sedgwick noted that her books "for young people" had originally been used in the public schools, but since the reorganization of the schools she wondered what had happened to them: "It would gratify me beyond pecuniary benefit to know that they contributed, tho' it might be in small measure, to the moral education of the young people who are to be the controllers of the destiny of our country." It was Sedgwick's present wish to contribute to society, and for a woman to dream of contributing entailed dreaming of a future society.[24]

Mary Virginia Terhune wrung out an anguished portrayal of a woman writer named Isabel Oakley in her second novel, *The Hidden Path*, published in 1855. The fictional female writer mirrors her creator. Isabel is not even the central female character of the novel, but if her moments are brief they are full of tension and conflict, as writer and woman are inextricably linked in the mind and emotions of Isabel. In torturous fashion Isable eschews any pretensions as a writer by representing herself as a mere woman of the home. But at one and the same time the rationalization of the writer is the message of the woman. The limitation of self is tied to an evaluation of self. The borders of domesticity define as well as enclose the identity of Isabel. They both limit resistance and define limitation.

The nineteen-year-old Isabel has already embarked upon her literary career when she tells Frank Lyle, the man who will eventually become her husband, what supposedly motivated her to become a writer. She sounds like an individual of bold desire and unchecked ego. Her literary ambitions bespeak messianic purpose. She would be empress to the world. Spurred by a troubled awareness of " 'the misery, the self-love, the ignorance of everything that makes man most happy, that prevail in the world,' " she saw that " 'I had my mission.' " And she perceived her mission as a writer as an expansion of the mission of the selflessly serving woman, " 'to give—not merely to those in my limited sphere of my personal influence, but to the toiling, suffering masses whom my pen could touch.' " Armed " 'with the authority of an inspired command,' " says Isabel, she felt compelled to make her pen " 'my sceptre.' " Somewhere, she says, " 'an earth-wearied soul is sinking beneath her load.' "[25]

The vague grandiosity and apparently unstemmed fervor of the rhetoric of the empress derives directly from the inner turmoil of the self-effacing woman. The words obscure her true meaning, just as her *nom de plume* cloaks her true name, but the mission of the writer is really to express the agony of the woman. It is to address man's ignorance of everything that makes woman unhappy. It is a message Isabel reports because, intended or not, she cannot help but express it. The misery of the world she names is as much her own as womanhood's. And it is the misery of the self-effacing woman that makes her simultaneously the self-righteous empress. Like the slow development of a photograph's negative, the more Isabel speaks the clearer her meaning becomes. More and more her inner turmoil exposes her rhetoric. Self-conscious, uneasy, and full of doubt in her role as a writer, she finds it necessary to demur and say, " 'I am a woman, weak and dependent.' " But she is stirred to add that she is " 'not ashamed to avow it.' " The prevalent, destructive self-love of the world is embodied more by ruling man's actions than by those of dependent woman, and is counter-pointed by the selflessness of woman, woman who serves others more than herself in deed and of necessity. Isabel cannot pretend to be " 'what some miserably misguided fanatics call "superior to my sex." ' " Nevertheless, she says, " 'When true to ourselves and to those whom God has entrusted to us to love and cherish, "the sex" has no superior—not even in boasted man!' " Isabel cannot deny that "boasted man" occupies the superior office in society. She cannot but acknowledge that " 'his is the higher sphere.' " Even so, she insists, " 'he can do no more in it than we can in ours—work for his Creator and his kind, according to the measure of his strength.' " And as for the woman who has become a writer: " 'To me it is appointed to do,' " says Isabel, proclaiming her mission again, " 'to some—O! my soul sickens in blasphemous despondency, sometimes to think how many—to suffer!' "[26]

Isabel discovers, however, that in choosing the pen for her scepter she has taken upon herself an additional cross to bear. By rationalizing and declaiming to herself and before society that her role as writer is merely an extension of the traditional role of woman, she is thereby enabled to write. But she has also thereby invited the opprobrium of her society, broadened her horizon of self-doubt, and touched chords of guilt. As the printed page has become a new medium to express the old troubles of woman, so has the literary woman become a new embodiment of the troubled woman herself. Rather than on the page to the world, Isabel tells her tale in person to her brother, Maurice, a year older and a seminary student at Princeton.

> "O, brother! When you saw me enter the path which should have been forever barred to woman, you must have known the evils, the mortifications, the woe I was tempting. Why, why did you not dissuade me—drive me back! But no! you and all whose opinion I obeyed as law and truth, blessed me, as though I had not been rushing on to the ruin of my happiness. . . . Had you intimated that I was separating myself from the delicate and good of my sex; establishing myself without the pale of the privileges accorded as the due of their modesty and helplessness; setting myself as a target for envy and malice and contemptuous pity—above all, excluding myself from that which you knew was as my very life—the affection of my kind—how thankfully would I have remained in the obscurity of my home!"

Having extended the base of her misery, Isabel has obscured for herself the origins of her misery. She is fearful that as an author she has " 'transgressed the bounds providence has marked for us,' " that she is guilty as charged. But Maurice tells her that the fault lies not in her and her deviance but in the ruler of both the private and the public sphere, that is, in man himself. " 'We men,' " he tells her, who regard ourselves as " 'enlightened Anglo-Saxons of the nineteenth century,' " are actually " 'as veritable tyrants to woman as were the feudal lords of the Middle Ages.' " His catalogue of the sins of men against women reads like a gentleman's primer for the nurture and education of the gentlewoman: " 'We cultivate her mind, and forbid her to use it; unlock to her the store-houses of learning, and suggest that she secrete what she bears away; recommend to her to live a mean parasite, rather than brave patrician scorn by earning a livelihood by manual or intellectual labor.' " The tragedy, says Maurice, is that " 'we are training up a generation of ornamental dunces—mentally and physically weak—to be the mothers and guides of the future guardians of our Republic and Religion.' "[27]

Although Terhune can name the sins of man and the sufferings of woman, she cannot suggest that woman turn the tables and become emperor, tyrant, or lord. Maurice, still Terhune's vehicle, describes a position that is as obvious as it is deeply conflicted: " 'When I reflect upon this monstrous injustice, my condemnation is less harsh of those misguided traitors to their sex, who rush into an opposite, and as fatal an extreme, and batter at the doors of our churches, medical colleges and court-houses.' " Woman is not to take man's place in the world or even take an equal place beside him. Rather, she is to remain in place, and be accorded her due instead of rendered a dunce. Terhune defends her fictional literary domestic as Maurice describes her. " 'Women like you, my dear sister, do more in one year to effect your emancipation, than these unfeminine ranters will in a century.' " Behind the empress is, after all, simply the selfless woman whose record of service to all around her should be accorded its proper recognition. " 'The time is certainly coming,' " Maurice assures Isabel, " 'when the glittering diadem of the authoress will not blind men to the loving eyes beneath it; when, through the sacerdotal robe in which your worshippers have arrayed you, shall be perceptible, the rise and fall, regular and healthful, of the woman's heart.' " In his vision of " 'utopia,' " he concludes, the sister will be friendly companion to brother, the wife will be adviser to husband, and the mother will be teacher to children, most especially to daughters. By pursuing her mission, he says in encouragement, " 'you may hasten the dawning of that Millennium.' "[28]

In 1901, when she was seventy-one, Terhune began writing syndicated columns on a variety of "women's affairs" for the Philadelphia *North American*, and continued to do so until 1910. From 1911 to 1917 her columns emanated from the Chicago *Tribune*. In her autobiography, published in 1910, she reported a friend's comment that " 'it is not Literature' " and her own response, " 'No, but it is *Influence*, and that of the best kind.' " A year later, Terhune wrote to a friend to ask "if you have seen my Christmas sermon in The Tribune today." Her "syndicate work," she said, had become "more and more dear to me," adding, in words that she had also used in her autobiography, that it was "not literature" but was "Influence!" She had, she said, "material affection for my Big Family." She concluded the letter by saying, "Thank you for saying that I am beloved! I desire that assurance more than gold, yea, more than much fine gold." In 1903 the woman writer told an interviewer visiting her home that her average mail in response to her column for the *North American* ran to five hundred letters a week. "That makes over twenty thousand letters a year," she declared, proud of all that evidence testifying to her "influence" and to the fact that she was "beloved." "It is like keeping my finger upon the pulse of universal womanhood," she said at the end of the interview, recording her own pulse on stage center.[29]

The desire was to have the beat of the woman's life finally heard. The most controversial demand of the Seneca Falls convention in 1848 was suffrage. It constituted a claim for recognition and power. By the end of the nineteenth century suffrage had become the primary focus and objective of the women's rights movement. In the years before the Civil War the demand for the franchise had been based primarily upon the premise that women should be recognized as individuals, with the same rights and responsibilities as men. However, from the beginning advocates also had argued that spiritually and morally superior women should have the franchise because they thereby would not only be able to protect their special interests associated with domesticity, but they would also have the opportunity to cleanse and purify man's public sphere of activity. In essence, that was to argue that women should have the vote not because they should have the right to function like men, as autonomous individuals, but because they possessed, and could contribute to the public sphere, different capacities and special talents. A rationalization was being offered for allowing women to perform a man's function in the manner of a woman. By the latter part of the century this had become the dominant argument. In either case, women were asking men for the franchise, since only men could vote to give it to them.[30]

There was disagreement among the literary domestics regarding suffrage. But although their declarations on the specific issue differed, their perspectives on womanhood were the same. In *Eve's Daughters*, Terhune descried "the shrill clamor for 'uncontrolled enfranchisement.'" This "hubbub," she wrote, "is folly and beneath the dignity of genuine womanhood." Women are not "rebellious serfs," she said. To cultivate and utilize our "intellectual faculties" is not to "usurp the functions of men"; in fact, she asserted, to do so would be "asinine." The suggestion was that women belonged to a special and exclusive elite of their own and would be only demeaning themselves by joining man's tawdry political club. "'Do I believe that women should vote?'" asked Parton in *Folly As It Flies*, published in 1869. "I am heart and soul with the women-speakers and lecturers, and workers in public and private, who are trying to bring this about." Clearly Parton thought that women were treated like serfs, and certainly she urged them to be rebellious in terms of the franchise, which she regarded as a "lever of power" by which women might be able to "be lifted out of their wretched condition, of low wages and starvation." But in *Caper-Sauce*, published in 1872, she wrote, "It grows clearer to me, every day, . . . why women are not allowed to vote." And what was her growing insight? Simply that if women could vote "there would be little margin then for all this cheating, this pocketing of salaries without an equivalent." She envisioned that the "sidewalks, gutters, [and] streets would be as clean as a parlor floor," and that the "drinking places would be disgorged of husbands, fathers, lovers, and brothers," and, she added for good measure, "also the billiard and gambling saloons."[31]

Obviously, Parton thought that sinning man needed woman's saintly touch. Augusta Evans Wilson, however, worried that if the saints kept political company with the sinners they would risk pollution themselves, and in *St. Elmo* Wilson denigrated the female advocates of suffrage as "'a few unamiable and wretched wives, and as many embittered, disappointed, old maids of New England; whose absurd pretensions and disgraceful conduct can not fail to bring a blush of shame and smile of pity to the face of every truly refined American woman.'" Never one to quibble, Wilson the Rebel without a doubt was thinking more of abolitionist women than of women generally. But equally without a doubt she was thinking purely of womanhood when she went on to write that " 'the day which invests [women] with the elective franchise would be the blackest in the annals of humanity, would ring in the death-knell of modern civilization, of national prosperity, social morality, and domestic happiness! and would consign the race to a night of degradation and horror infinitely more appalling than a return to primeval barbarism.' " For Wilson, needless to say, the destiny of woman was not a subject for equivocation. But neither was it for Harriet Beecher Stowe, who, in contrast, did not fear the consequences of granting women the franchise and did not doubt that women should most assuredly have the vote. "Yes, I do believe in Female Suffrage," she wrote Parton in 1869. "The more I think of it," she said, "the more absurd this whole government of men over women looks." What irked her was "this agreement of Tom, Dick and Harry not to pass the cake plate lest we make ourselves sick with cake," which, she repeated, "seems absurd." The southerner Wilson, and the New Englander Stowe could not have disagreed more on the subject of suffrage and its potential effect upon women. "Dare not trust us with suffrage lest we become unwomanly?" asked Stowe scornfully. "Let them try it. Unsexed?—I should like to see what could make women other than women and more than men." The southerner Wilson and the New Englander Stowe could not have agreed more on the differences between the sexes.[32]

The strong sense of a distinctive self was also tied to a definite sense of place, and a desire for the rights of being had to be resolved with the obligation to perform the duties of the sphere. Terhune penned two homilies on two separate occasions that attested to the woman's responsibilities within the home. "She who neglects to comb her hair and darn her children's socks while she is painting for posterity," she wrote in 1883, "or who accepts an invitation to address a Woman's Suffrage convention that calls her a hundred miles from home while her baby lies ill with the croup, would be as selfish in devotion to her Speciality had her choice lighted on Kensington embroidery or on—preserves!" And in 1887 she affirmed, "Your one-idea man is as truly diseased in perception and in judgment as is the woman who rides her hobby of art, literature, social, religious, or political reform, rough-shod over the wreck of domestic comfort and happiness." Even Parton, who distinguished between "Two Kinds of Women," that is, the obsessive mother and housekeeper and the woman "on the public platform" who neglected domestic duties, declared that if forced to indicate a preference she would choose the woman of the home, because "*her* children have a home at least." Children needed to be fed and clothed and nursed when sick, "and no mother," wrote Parton, until she first saw to these duties "has any right, in my opinion, on the public platform."[33]

In 1872, at the age of seventy-eight, Caroline Howard Gilman wrote a poem entitled "Household Woman" which she dedicated to the Ladies' Sewing Circle of the Unitarian Church in Charleston, South Carolina. Most of the poem testifies to what women can be and can become beyond the home. Beginning with the woman as student, Gilman moves on to acclaim the achievements of women in a variety of fields, noting specifically in footnotes that she had in mind the accomplishments of Harriet Hosmer, sculptor; Maria Mitchell, astronomer; Rosa Bonheur, painter; Fanny Kemble, actress; Elizabeth Blackwell, physician; Dorothea Dix, crusader for the mentally ill; and even Gilman's own daughter, Caroline Howard Gilman Jervey, who, like her mother, became not only a wife and mother but a writer as well. But the last two of the twelve stanzas provide Gilman's final testimony, her last word on the subject. "Yes, honored by the Female name," reads the poem, "Springing elastic into fame!" And yet, wrote Gilman, "amid this varied sphere"—the use of the singular "sphere" is a wonderfully ironic touch and, as always, probably unwitting—the name of the woman of the home was "as dear," to her, "When still her household tasks she plies." She plies them with "cheerful duty," and with "every lowly path well-trod" she "Looks upward, trustingly, to god." The loyalty is to what woman has been in her traditional sphere. She has been restricted and denied, has suffered wrongs, has been exploited and maligned and effaced from the pages of history. And yes, woman can embrace other selves and should be granted the opportunity to perform other tasks. But, affirms, Gilman, the life of woman in the home has not been idle, useless, wasted, or without redeeming value, and Gilman will not turn away from her.[34]

Catharine Maria Sedgwick wrote to Susan Higginson Channing in 1833 that "we have had a droll time getting up a society in our Church." She was probably referring to a benevolent or moral reform society, because she expressed her opinion that "I do not think it is within a woman's prescribed destiny to do any public duty." It was, of course, an issue with which the woman struggled in her own fashion. "We are, some of us, very ridiculous persons in full light," said Sedgwick, as if to suggest that some men were not. And she began to describe the "droll" affair: "After claiming rights and surrendering them, caballing and diplomatizing—no, I will not," she declared, stopping in the middle of a sentence and capping the building crescendo of her thought. "I am betraying the secrets of our order, and we ought, for our own dignity, to be as secret as the Freemasons." But for the woman who was already a writer it was already too late, and, like the literary domestics to come, she would continue to reveal the secrets of her order more or less in the form of a secret code before a mostly uncomprehending world. For the literary domestics to have done otherwise would have been, in terms of their own understanding, to deny their existences. Their secrets would out, and they found their place in history by documenting so-called lives of nonbeing, by making the invisible visible.[35]

The literary domestics' peculiar education gave them minds to use but, they thought, no vocation in the outside world, and in that respect they never became fully professionalized. But despite themselves and in spite of their world, they did after all become creators of culture. Primarily they wrote about private, domestic lives and, in their own fashion, a world beyond. To the extent that their views were skewed, that did not represent a refusal to see or an escape from reality. Instead, it spoke to the nature and the significance of their achievement. Their lives were enveloped by the perspective, the language, the metaphor, and the meaning of domesticity for women. But to say that they were passively submissive to their dependent lives of domesticity is to be contradicted by the voice of their prose, private and public. In the end, in their desire for more, they got and achieved more as literary domestics. They spoke to and about their condition, to and about their hopes and fears, their joy and their torment, and always about their conflict. Foremost, they were tired of being nameless pawns, and if indeed they had to suffer to the end of time they did not want to suffer in silence. They were tired of bearing without due recompense the sins of their not-so-beloved, tired of the toll of their not always beloved domestic lives. Simply, they wrote about the woman's promise and betrayal in the home. They struggled with the issues of their lives, even if they were unable to achieve successful resolution. And their morality play had a vast audience. As best-selling authors they entertained, instructed, and shared grievances as private women on a public stage. They were compromised and crippled as writers, as creators of culture, but they reported that fact. They told their story regardless of their intentions, and in a larger sense that was an ultimate exercise of control and freedom. Their struggle was to place before history the record of woman's being, past and present, without having to reject their own witness.

Epilogue

The landscape of literary domesticity is littered with symbols docile and symbols loose, with the debris of didacticism and unintended irony, with quaint fables and mocking metaphors. The meanings are sometimes obvious and sometimes subterranean, and a number of the latter are stark, compelling, and striking in import. None are more so than the meaning of Crazy Sal. Crazy Sal is dream and crisis compressed into one. She is her own tale. She is a figure that appeared inevitably in the saga of literary domesticity. She is treated in her tale and by her creator sympathetically, even reverentially. She is reminiscent of a type of deranged holy figure. She is saint, martyr, victim, all three. But she is also comical, witty, and satirical. A spirit either displaced from her own being or too much in touch with her own existence, or both, Crazy Sal is a seemingly detached, undigested bit of fictional lore, perhaps because her creator claims she is crazy.

Fittingly, Crazy Sal is not the central character in the novel in which she appears, namely, Mary Jane Holmes's *The English Orphans; or, A Home in the New World*. The novel itself has a little bit of everything of literary domesticity, as well as most of the familiar trappings and excesses of many Victorian novels. Mystery is the order of the day, coincidences abound, and revelations follow. There are many tears and many love songs in the pursuit of love. Deaths occur from starvation, scarlet fever, and consumption. Tales of rags to riches and riches to rags are intertwined, and the rich and fashionable are simultaneously satirized and aped. There are caricatures aplenty, from rakes to ideal men and from frivolous ladies to noble selfless women.

None is more saintly in her selfless service than Mary Howard, Holmes's central character. When we first meet the nine-year-old Mary in the opening pages of the novel she is being teased by a handsome young boy, George Moreland, a few years older, for hiding her face beneath a large sunbonnet. Mary has donned the ungainly bonnet to hide her two extra, overlapping

336

front teeth, which have made her less than comely. Both George and Mary are on a vessel sailing from old England to New England. George, who has been left a large fortune by his father, is going to Boston to live with a wealthy uncle who has been appointed his guardian. Mary is going to America with her family, her parents and a younger sister and brother, where they hope to begin a new life. Times have been difficult for them in England. Mary's mother has been disinherited by her gentry father because she has married her poor music teacher. She has struggled to raise her three children while her husband has struggled to support them. They look to the promise of the new land for better times. While on ship George Moreland becomes dangerously ill with fever, and Mary, infatuated with him in spite of his having been unkind enough to taunt her about her two ugly teeth, stays by his side and nurses him to health. George is grateful for her efforts, of course, and shows his appreciation by giving her a small golden chain with a locket containing his likeness. Upon disembarking in Boston George and Mary say good-bye, apparently forever.

In one respect the remainder of Mary's tale and the central story of the novel are easily told. The family travels from one Massachusetts town to another without much success. Along the way another child, baby Alice, is born, and the father dies unexpectedly. The mother and her four children end up in Chicopee, where the mother and her son die of starvation. Of the three remaining children, one daughter, the prettiest, is adopted by the wealthiest woman in town, a Bostonian who summers in Chicopee. Mary and baby Alice go to the poorhouse, where life is harsh, so harsh that baby Alice also dies. Mary struggles and survives and is eventually adopted by a genteel widow. The widow, a former Bostonian and once affluent as well, has been left with barely enough money to maintain a respectable house and to have Mary as a companion. Mary attends the local district school, excels, becomes a teacher at an unusually young age, earns enough money to attend for one year the Mount Holyoke Seminary of Mary Lyon (the latter makes a cameo appearance), and is enabled to complete her schooling at Mount Holyoke when a mysterious benefactor provides the necessary funding. At the end of the novel she of course marries George Moreland, her childhood love of the high seas. Never having forgotten his angel of mercy, George has from a distance and in disguise followed most of Mary's adventures. A graduate of Yale, wealthy in his own right and a successful merchant as well, George has fallen in love with Mary. And no wonder. No longer an ugly duckling—her two extra teeth were pulled at the poorhouse—Mary has not only become an attractive young woman, she is also educated, accomplished, and full of grace and character. She is the perfect lady for the perfect gentleman. Theirs is a marriage ordained by heaven.

It is of secondary interest that Mary's story parallels somewhat that of her creator, Mary Jane Holmes. Holmes's father also died when she was very young; Holmes taught school beginning at the age of thirteen; and

Holmes married a Yale graduate. But of far more compelling interest is the tale of Crazy Sal. Mary Howard first meets Sally Furbush, or Sal as she is generally called, in the poorhouse, where Sal, an older woman, is an inmate. "Inmate" is the appropriate term, for the poorhouse is inhabited by a variety of mental and physical "destitutes." Some are eccentric, some are deranged, some are mentally feeble, and all are interesting, but none more so than Crazy Sal. Forewarned of the presence of the "goblin Sal," Mary hears her before she sees her: ascending a "dark stairway" she stops before a "dark closet" beneath the "garret stairs" and detects "a sneer and a hiss," followed by "a wild, insane chuckle." Afraid but intrigued, Mary "longed to ask who Sal Furbush was." In a sense, Mary spends the remainder of the novel finding out. At first, sounds continue to precede sights. Mary hears a different-sounding voice from the dark closet saying, " 'Come here, little dear, and see your Aunty.' " And what sounds like yet another voice speaks from the dark closet about other inmates. One inmate, a Mrs. Grundy, is Sal's ever-present foil. Grumpy, stern, and somewhat pretentious, Mrs. Grundy presumes to manage the poorhouse, even though she has no official capacity. She also tangles daily with Crazy Sal, who mocks her and taunts her and creates general havoc, with the usual result that Mrs. Grundy orders Sal locked away in the "dark closet." After one such occasion, Mary again passes by the closet and hears Sal singing the English national anthem and "finishing every verse with 'God save Miss Grundy.' "[1]

When Mary finally gets to meet Crazy Sal what she sees before her is "a little, shrivelled up woman, with wild flashing eyes, and hair hanging loosely over her shoulders." Sal is "shaking her fist in a very threatening manner" and her face is "going through a great variety of changes, being at first perfectly hideous in its expression, and then instantly changing into something equally ridiculous, though not quite so frightful." Terrorized, Mary is put at her ease when Sal takes her by the arm and says, " 'Don't be alarmed, duckey, I shan't hurt you; I'm Sal. Don't you know Sal?' " After first inquiring about Mary's deformed teeth, Sal then asks a question that begins the process of answering whether or not she is simply crazy: " 'Do you know grammar, child?' " Thus are we provided with the first hint to the puzzle of Crazy Sal: she is educated. When Mary responds that she knows a little grammar, Sal is delighted, for now she will have an " 'associate.' " Why, says Sal, " 'the greatest objection I have to the kind of people one meets with here, is that they are so horribly vulgar in their conversation and murder the Queen's English so dreadfully.' "[2]

In a sense Sal is an obsessive " 'grammarian' " because she has been a wife and mother. She provides her own explanation. She imagines that she has been at the poorhouse for a long, long time. " 'Perhaps you don't know,' " she says to Mary, " 'that I lost little Willie, and then Willie's father died too, and left me all alone.' " Their graves, says Sal, " 'are away on the great western prairies, beneath the buckeye trees.' " One night, thinking she heard

" 'Little Willie's voice,' " she lay down on his grave, and when she " 'awoke
my hair had all turned gray and I was in Chicopee, where Willie's father used
to live.' " After a while she was placed in the poorhouse, she says, because
they " 'said I was crazy, but I wasn't.' " Her head was " 'clear as a bell' "
and she knew as much as she ever did, says Sal, " 'only I couldn't tell it,
because, you see, the right words wouldn't come.' " Thus the grammar. But if
Sal is full of sad thoughts and serious words she is also a comic figure. Never
able to forget Mrs. Grundy for long, she suddenly asks Mary how many
genders there are. When Mary, who has been studying Smith's *Grammar*,
responds, " 'Masculine, Feminine, Neuter and Common,' " Sal screams,
" 'O, get out with your *common* gender.' " *Her* grammar speaks of
masculine, feminine, neuter, and " '*Grundy* gender,' " the last belonging
exclusively to " 'the lady below with the cast-iron back and India-rubber
tongue.' "[3]

With the arrival of Mary and baby Alice at the poorhouse, Crazy Sal not
only gains an "associate" but also gets to play mother again. In baby Alice
Sal sees little Willie; the baby " 'looks like Willie,' " she declares, " 'only
not half so handsome.' " When Mary protests that this "Willie" is a girl, Sal
says it is of no consequence, " 'he's Willie to me.' " Alice is Willie to Sal, as
well, when Alice succumbs to the rigors and measly fare of the poorhouse.
When Alice is near death, Sal says of her, " 'Willie's going to find his
mother.' " And when Alice actually dies Sal on her own shuts herself up in
her dark closet, where she is overheard whispering to herself, " 'Yes, little
Willie's dead, and Sally's got *three* in Heaven now.' " Significantly,
however, when the wife of the head of the poorhouse dies, Sal says to Mary,
" 'Weep, oh daughter, and lament, for earth has got one woman less and
Heaven one female more!' " She is the "long-suffering woman" who is
weeping for her kind. Shut up in her dark closet much of the time, generally
against her will, Sal speaks of herself as " 'secluded from the visible world
nearly half the time.' " When she is "crazier than usual," her command of
language is "proportionately greater." She is also secluded from herself
much of the time, and Mary prays for the "poor old crazy woman," asking that
the light of reason might again dawn upon her darkened mind." Sal is never
literally called "Crazy Sal," but that is how she is effectively characterized
all the time.[4]

In fact, even when Sal is visible to the world with a vengeance and, in a
fashion, very much in touch with herself, she is still considered crazed. And
she provides cause. Much of her energy is expended on bedeviling Mrs.
Grundy, but she has additional other-worldly moments. When Mary is
allowed to take Sal to church with her, where they know they will be seen by
all elements of society, high and low, Sal sees to it that she, Sal, is "rigged
out in a somewhat fantastic style." Her dress is an old plum-colored silk. A
gauze handkerchief thrown around her neck is fastened to her belt by a large
yellow bow. Her bonnet is entirely covered by a thick green veil, and even

though the sun is shining she carries with her a large blue umbrella. Sal and Mary strike off for church "attracting more attention, and causing more remarks, than any two who had passed through Chicopee for a long time." On the way to the church Sal stops to remove her shoes and stockings. When Mary asks her what she is doing, Sal says, " 'I guess I know better than to wear out my kid slippers when I've got no Willie's father to buy me any more.' " She will put them back on when they get to the church, she says.[5]

Sal is generally approving of the Sunday sermon, declaring the clergyman is " 'a well-read grammarian, only a trifle too emphatic in his delivery.' " Later, however, she has some additional thoughts on the matter. " 'Miss Howard,' " she says to Mary, " 'I've been thinking what a splendid minister was spoiled when they put dresses on me! Oh how hard I had to hold myself today to keep from extemporizing to the congregation.' " Without a doubt, she is firmly convinced that she could have outpreached the preacher. " 'I reckon there wouldn't have been quite so many nodding as there were,' " she says. Nevertheless, in or out of the church Crazy Sal has her divine moments, and as a result Sunday at the poorhouse is "usually the noisiest day in the week." As Holmes describes it, "Sal Furbush generally took the lead, and mounting the kitchen table, sung camp-meeting hymns as loud as she could scream." In short, Mary finds that "the poor-house with Sal Furbush shut up, and the poor-house with Sal at liberty, were quite different affairs."[6]

But the best and perhaps the worst of it is that Crazy Sal is a writer. " 'An authoress!' " exclaims Mary when Sal tells her, " 'an authoress!' " " 'To be sure I am,' " declares Sal. " 'What's to hinder?' " Given the fact that she was once unusually knowledgeable, she says, added to her command of grammar and her self-described " 'uncommon powers of imagination,' " she was able to " 'produce a work which, but for an unaccountable freak of the publisher, would have rendered my name immortal.' " Unfortunately, the publisher to whom she sent her " 'six hundred pages of foolscap' " rejected it. Says Sal, " 'It was a terrible disappointment, and came near turning my brain.' " But there are other publishing houses, she says, and " 'one of these days I shall astonish mankind.' " True to her intentions, at any rate, Sal begins her next "work" before Mary leaves the poorhouse. Significantly, it is after Alice dies that Sal's "old desire for authorship" returns. Exasperated with trying to teach the other inmates the Queen's English, Sal begins what else but a grammar, which, she announces, will contain "Nine Hundred and Ninety Nine rules for speaking the English language correctly."[7]

Little more is mentioned at that moment about Sal's literary efforts. Nothing is said by Mary, and little is written by Holmes. After all, Sal is crazy, and no further comment is made until the day Mary leaves the poorhouse to join her Boston lady. That morning Mary enters Sal's room and finds her sitting on the floor with all of her clothes strewn around her. She has been looking for something to give Mary " 'to make your young heart happy,' " she tells her, but " 'I can find nothing except the original MS. of my first novel.' " (This is the first time that Sal's work has been referred to as a novel.) " 'I do not need it now,' " says Sal, " 'for I shall make enough out of my grammar.' " Take it, then, she tells Mary, " 'and when you are rich and influential, you'll have no trouble in getting it published,—none at all.' " Strangely enough, Holmes does not have Mary comment on the novel or even look at it, neither at the moment Sal gives it to her nor at any other stage of Holmes's novel. Just as Mary is leaving, Sal, with her eyes looking "very bright," with a "compression about her mouth seldom seen, except just before one of her frenzied attacks," and after bathing her head in water "as if to cool its inward heat," whispers in Mary's ear, " 'If that novel should have an unprecedented run, and of course it will, you would not mind sharing the profits with me, would you?' " Without Willie's father to support her, she must fend for herself.[8]

For the remaining two-thirds of the novel, during Mary's subsequent adventures, Crazy Sal goes practically unmentioned until the very end of the tale. Described as " 'raving crazy' " since Mary's departure, she sends word to ask if Mary has " 'taken the first step towards the publication of my novel.' " On another occasion, she informs Mary that her grammar is progressing and that shortly she intends to write "Harper" and warn him so that he will be able to hire the extra help necessary to publish a work of that kind. She also tells Mary that she has concluded the dedication for the grammar, to wit, " 'To Willie's father, who sleeps on the western prairie, this useful work is tremblingly, tearfully, yet joyfully dedicated by his relict, Sarah.' " It is the first time that the name "Sarah" has been used; it will take to the end of the novel to finally and fully explain the significance of the name.[9]

At novel's end, George betrothes Mary. He has watched her improve in "manners and appearance" and has seen to her education, for he proves to be the mysterious benefactor who enabled her to complete her education at Mount Holyoke Seminary. Having decided to marry her, he also announces his wish that she do no further teaching. The future he paints for her is of "one bright dream of happiness." Mary too has decided not only to accept George but to have Sal live in their dream home with them. The decision is a just one, for it was Sal who helped Mary to survive the poorhouse, who taught her grammar, and who was responsible for seeing that Mary's two ugly teeth were removed—Sal, who had long before lost her own domestic dream. After the marriage ceremony comes a final discovery in a novel long on revelation. As Mary discovers more and more about her life and her past, she finds a past for Sal. Crazy Sal is, after all, literally her Aunt Sarah. Sal is discovered to be the half-sister of Mary's mother, both daughters of the same mother from separate marriages. Thus are both Sal and Mary of the same foremother, linked to what had been the same invisible past.[10]

A final effort is made to deal with the problem of Sal's sanity, or lack of it. The best medical advice in Boston is sought but, writes Holmes, "her case was of so long standing that but little hope was entertained of her entire recovery." Sal does become "less boisterous" and even sometimes appears "perfectly rational for days." Of course, she retains her "taste for literature," and only George can prevent her from sending her now complete grammar to a publisher. It does not matter to her, as George tells her, that she is no longer "obliged to write for a living." For, as Holmes phrases it, "it was not *money* she coveted, but *reputation*,—a name,—to be pointed at as Mrs. Sarah Furbush, Authoress of 'Furbush's Grammer,' &c.,—*this* was her aim!" But George tells her that although she may write for the " 'entertainment' " of family and friends, he will not allow her to send anything to a publisher. There is apparently nothing for Crazy Sal to do, then, but remain at home.[11]

Notes

ABBREVIATIONS USED IN THE NOTES

AAS	American Antiquarian Society Worcester, Mass.
Alderman-UVA	Alderman Library University of Virginia Charlottesville, Va.
Barnard	Barnard College Library Barnard College New York, N.Y.
BPL	Boston Public Library Boston, Mass.
CIA	Constitution Island Association West Point, N.Y.
DAC	Department of Archives and History State of Alabama Montgomery, Ala.
EI	Essex Institute Salem, Mass.
Houghton-Harvard	Houghton Library Harvard University Cambridge, Mass.
HSP	Historical Society of Pennsylvania Philadelphia, Pa.
Huntington	Henry E. Huntington Library San Marino, Calif.
LOC	Library of Congress Washington, D.C.

343

MHS	Massachusetts Historical Society Boston, Mass.
Morgan	Pierpont Morgan Library New York, N.Y.
NL	Newberry Library Chicago, Illinois
NYHS	New-York Historical Society New York, N.Y.

NYPL
  NYPL-Berg
  NYPL-Manuscripts
	New York Public Library
	  Henry W. and Albert A. Berg Collection
	  Manuscripts Division
	New York, N.Y.

Perkins-Duke	William R. Perkins Library Duke University Durham, N.C.
Schlesinger-Radcliffe	Arthur and Elizabeth Schlesinger Library Radcliffe College Cambridge, Mass.
SCHS	South Carolina Historical Society Charleston, S.C.
Smith	Sophia Smith Collection Smith College Northampton, Mass.
South Caroliniana–USC	South Caroliniana Library University of South Carolina Columbia, S.C.
Southern Historical Collection–UNC	Southern Historical Collection University of North Carolina Chapel Hill, N.C.
Sterling-Yale	Sterling Memorial Library Yale University New Haven, Conn.
Stockbridge	Stockbridge Library Association Stockbridge, Mass.
Stowe-Day	Stowe-Day Memorial Library Hartford, Conn.

1. Caroline Howard to Harriet Fay, 19 March 1819, Gilman Family Papers, AAS.
2. I first proposed that these women be known as the literary domestics in my article "The Literary Domestics: Private Woman on a Public Stage," in *Ideas in America's Cultures: From Republic to Mass Society*, ed. Hamilton Cravens (Ames: Iowa State University Press, 1982). As I stated then, I myself used the term "sentimentalist" in previous articles, but increasing skepticism about the term's accuracy and usefulness led me to search for a more appropriate designation. In one of my articles I in fact used "sentimentalists" in my title ("The Sentimentalists: Promise and Betrayal in the Home," *Signs: Journal of Women in Culture and Society* 4 [Spring 1979]:434–46), although as I suggested then it was my belief that these women should be regarded as important vehicles for the study of the experiences and perceptions of nineteenth-century American women, rather than as "objects of neglect, dismissal, and scorn," which has been the case from Hawthorne's oft-repeated outburst that "America is now wholly given over to a damned mob of scribbling women" to Leslie Fiedler's ridicule of "the purely commercial purveyors of domestic sentiments," and beyond. See Hawthorne to William D. Ticknor, January 1855, quoted in Caroline Ticknor, *Hawthorne and His Publisher* (Boston: Houghton Mifflin Co., 1913), pp. 141–42; Fiedler, *Love and Death in the American Novel* (New York: Criterion Books, 1960). Alexander Cowie was one of the first to paint these women as simplistic conformists. Cowie claimed that their fiction "functioned as a sort of benign moral police, whose regulations were principally comprised under the heads of religion and morality"; see "The Vogue of the Domestic Novel, 1850–1870," *South Atlantic Quarterly* 41 (October 1942). But others have followed suit. Henry Nash Smith observed in an article that "popular fiction was designed to soothe the sensibilities of its readers by fulfilling expectation and expressing only received ideas. . . . The best-selling novels of the 1850s thus express an ethos of conformity." In a subsequent volume Smith continued to overlook the fundamental ambivalence of these women toward the values of their society and their status in it. Their novels, he claimed, were written to "relieve the anxieties aroused by rapid upward mobility, especially the fear of failure, and to provide assurance that the universe is managed for man's [*sic*] benefit." And John T. Frederick was not far from Smith in his assessment of the character of their fiction. See Smith, "The Scribbling Woman and the Cosmic Success Story," *Critical Inquiry* 1 (September 1974):47–70; idem, *Democracy and the Novel: Popular Resistance to Classic American Writers* (New York: Oxford University Press, 1978); Frederick, "Hawthorne's Scribbling Women," *New England Quarterly* 48 (June 1975):231–40. The opposite perspective has been taken by Helen Waite Papashvily, who stated that the fiction "encouraged a pattern of feminine behavior so quietly ruthless, so subtly vicious that by comparison the ladies of Seneca appear angels of innocence," and by Dee Garrison, who claimed that "common to all these best-sellers is a rejection of traditional authority, particularly in domestic life, in religious faith, and among class-ordered mankind"; the authors, Garrison said, were "clearly women in revolt." See

Papashvily, *All the Happy Endings: A Study of the Domestic Novel in America, the Women Who Wrote It, the Women Who Read It, in the Nineteenth Century* (New York: Harper and Bros., 1956); Garrison, "Immoral Fiction in the Late Victorian Library," *American Quarterly* 28 (Spring 1976):71–89. Ann Douglas in *The Feminization of American Culture* (New York: Alfred A. Knopf, 1977) has more or less linked óne perspective with the other. She equates sentimentalization with a querulous, domestic feminization and, calling a plague on both houses, casts these women (among others) and their nineteenth-century clerical brethren in the role of villains, blaming both for encouraging a supposed decline from the strength and rigor of Calvinist culture and for paving the way for the subsequent rise of a consumer society. The welter of confusion and contradiction in these perspectives suggests a failure to come to terms with the complexity of the concerns that dominated both the lives and the prose of these women. In *Woman's Fiction: A Guide to Novels by and about Women in America, 1820–1870* (Ithaca: Cornell University Press, 1978), Nina Baym quite rightly seeks to treat these women seriously and calls for a new approach to their fiction. But Baym herself fails to deal adequately with both the women and their published prose in a historical context. Eschewing complexity, she regards the fiction as comprising straightforward "tales about the triumph of the feminine will." Although Baym does not doubt that these women had conflicts in their lives "as human beings generally do," she does "not find their fiction beset by contradictions, defenses, or duplicities." She writes, "Happily, our authors said, the world's hardships provide just the right situation for the development of individual character." Baym even places these women beyond the bounds of conventional domesticity, claiming that they argued that neither husbands nor children were essential to women's identity, nor was marriage an ultimate objective. Within the last decade a growing and impressive body of feminist criticism on women writers has appeared that, nevertheless, continues in too many instances to dismiss the literary domestics on purely aesthetic grounds and neglects to regard them anew in their own social, cultural, historical context. For example, in an otherwise insightful and stimulating article Myra Jehlen is willing in essence to dismiss the "scribbling women" as conformists, as relatively uncomplicated believers in "the natural goodness of middle-class values." See "Archimedes and the Paradox of Feminist Criticism," *Signs: Journal of Women in Culture and Society* 6 (Summer 1981). The literary domestics, no less than other women writers, require what Elaine Showalter has described as "a more flexible and comprehensive model of women's writing which places it in the maximum context of culture." For any study of women's writing and women's culture, it is always essential, as Showalter suggests, "to get at the primary and self-defined nature of female cultural experience." See "Feminist Criticism in the Wilderness," *Critical Inquiry* 8 (Winter 1981). As I have tried to demonstrate in this study, the previously neglected personal papers of these women in conjunction with their published prose and other historical sources, both primary and secondary, provide a valuable means for an exploration of the experiences and the perceptions of reality of nineteenth-century women. They also provide a vehicle not only for affirming the existence of a female past, but for capturing the positive value as well as the negative significance of that past.

3. Stow Persons's perceptive and lucid study *The Decline of American Gentility* (New York: Columbia University Press, 1973) stands as the most significant attempt to identify the male social type to which the literary domestics were linked as daughters and wives. The new American gentry, as Persons designates it, was one of

a number of functional elites to emerge in the early nineteenth century following a post-Revolutionary dispersal of power held by the old colonial gentry. Although Persons has stated that the old gentry class of the antebellum South resisted the disintegration into functional elites, the values expressed by the three women in the study whose origins were southern, namely Maria McIntosh, Mary Virginia Terhune, and Augusta Evans Wilson, and those manifested by the two transplanted southerners, Caroline Howard Gilman and Caroline Lee Hentz, suggest, albeit from a gender perspective, that there were similarities in the social perspectives of northerners and southerners. Given the social, political, economic, and cultural transformations of American society following the Revolution and the continued alterations of the face of the American nation throughout the nineteenth century, historians have not yet been able to adequately describe or gauge in relative terms the various social levels of the democratic republic. And any study addressing this subject will have to bring into consideration and devise a terminology adequate to describe differences in gender.

4. Catharine Maria Sedgwick to Professor Potter, 9 May 1838, NYHS.

5. Ibid.

6. Mary Virginia Terhune quoted in a biographical sketch in Kate Sanborn, *Our Famous Women* (Hartford: A. D. Worthington and Co., 1886), p. 628.

CHAPTER 1. *THE FANNY FERN*

1. *New York Ledger*, 6 Sept. 1873. An undated clipping of this letter as it appeared in the *Ledger* is also found in the Sara Parton Papers, Sophia Smith Collection, Smith. I am indebted to James Parton, a descendant of Sara Parton, for assistance in locating this source.

2. The best sources for Bonner's life and career are the Robert Bonner Papers, NYPL-Manuscripts; the *Ledger* itself; Ralph Admari, "Bonner and 'The Ledger,' " *American Book Collector* 6 (Jan.–June 1935):176–93; and J. C. Derby, *Fifty Years Among Authors, Books and Publishers* (New York: G. W. Carleton and Co., 1884), pp. 200–207.

3. Admari, "Bonner," pp. 184, 190; Derby, *Fifty Years*, p. 207; undated clipping of interview with Bonner, Robert Bonner Papers, NYPL-Manuscripts.

4. Admari, "Bonner," p. 189; Bonner interview; and see also Bonner's correspondence with various writers, Robert Bonner Papers, NYPL-Manuscripts; Derby, *Fifty Years*, p. 203.

5. Bonner interview; Derby, *Fifty Years*, pp. 200–204.

6. Derby, *Fifty Years*, p. 213; James Parton, *Fanny Fern: A Memorial Volume* (New York: G. W. Carleton and Co., 1873), pp. 53–54; Elizabeth Bancroft Schlesinger, "Fanny Fern: Our Grandmothers' Mentor," *New York Historical Society Quarterly* 38 (Oct. 1954):503; Sara Jane Lippincott [Grace Greenwood], "Fanny Fern–Mrs. Parton," in n.a., *Eminent Women of the Age* (Hartford: S. M. Betts and Co., 1869), p. 73.

7. For a more detailed summary of Mason Brothers' campaign, see Susan Geary, "The Domestic Novel as a Commercial Commodity: Making a Best Seller in the 1850s," *Papers of the Bibliographical Society of America* 70 (1976):365–93.

8. *New York Ledger*, 19 May 1855; 9 June 1855; 9 Nov. 1872; Derby, *Fifty Years*, pp. 202–03.

9. This and following commentary is based upon analyses of early nineteenth-century publishing, including William Charvat, *Literary Publishing in America, 1790–1850* (Philadelphia: University of Pennsylvania Press, 1959); Hellmut Lehman-Haupt with Lawrence C. Wroth and Rollo G. Silver, *The Book in America: A History of the Making and Selling of Books in the United States*, 2d ed. (New York: R. R. Bowker Co., 1972); Luke White, Jr., *Henry William Herbert: The American Publishing Scene, 1831–1858* (Newark, N.J.: Carteret Book Club, 1943); John Tebbel, *A History of Book Publishing in the United States: The Creation of an Industry, 1630–1865* (New York: R. R. Bowker Co., 1972); Matthew J. Bruccoli, ed., *The Profession of Authorship in America, 1800–1870: The Papers of William Charvat* (Columbus: Ohio State University Press, 1968); Lyle H. Wright, "A Few Observations on American Fiction, 1851–1875," *Proceedings of the American Antiquarian Society* 65 (20 April 1955–19 Oct. 1955):75–104. Discussion of similar transformations in nineteenth-century English publishing can be found in Richard D. Altick, *The English Common Reader: A Social History of the Mass Reading Public, 1800–1900* (Chicago: University of Chicago Press, 1957). Eighteenth-century developments are surveyed in Ian Watt, *The Rise of the Novel: Studies in Defoe, Richardson and Fielding* (Berkeley: University of California Press, 1967).

10. A good example of this phenomenon is found in White, *Henry William Herbert*, p. 12.

11. Mary Virginia Terhune [Marion Harland], *Phemie's Temptation* (New York: Carleton, 1869), p. 180.

12. Rufus Wilmot Griswold to James T. Fields, 10 July 1843, quoted in Bruccoli, *Profession of Authorship*, pp. 175–76.

13. Sara Parton [Fanny Fern], *Ruth Hall: A Domestic Tale of the Present Time* (New York: Mason Brothers, 1855), pp. 305–7.

14. Nathaniel Parker Willis to James Russell Lowell, 1844, Houghton-Harvard.

15. Nathaniel Parker Willis to James T. Fields, undated, Houghton-Harvard. George Pope Morris, a journalist and a poet as well, began his association with Willis when the two collaborated as foreign correspondents on social affairs for the *New York Mirror*.

16. James D. Hart, *The Popular Book: A History of America's Literary Taste* (New York: Oxford University Press, 1950), p. 67. Using data from the federal census of 1840, Maris Vinovski and Richard Bernard have found that 91.5% of the nation's white population was literate. There was considerable regional variation, however. It has been estimated that one out of every five white southerners was illiterate, compared with one out of ten Americans in western states and one out of thirty-five in middle Atlantic states. See Vinovski and Bernard, "Beyond Catharine Beecher: Female Education in the Antebellum Period," *Signs: Journal of Women in Culture and Society* 3 (Summer 1978):864–65; Carl Degler, "The Two Cultures and the Civil War," in Stanley Coben and Lorman Ratner, eds., *The Development of an American Culture* (Englewood Cliffs, N.J.: Prentice-Hall, 1970), p. 99.

17. Robert E. Spiller et al., eds., *Literary History of the United States*, 3 vols., 3d ed., rev. (New York: Macmillan Co., 1963) 1:236.

18. Tebbel, *History of Book Publishing*, p. 207; White, *Henry William Herbert*, p. 9.

NOTES 349

19. A description of novels published prior to 1820 can be found in Henri Petter, *The Early American Novel* (Columbus: Ohio State University Press, 1971). Susannah Rowson was born in England of English parents in 1762, spent part of her childhood in the colonies, but returned to England and published three novels as well as poetry and criticism before crossing the Atlantic again in 1793.

20. The tale is told in Henry Walcott Boynton, *Annals of American Bookselling, 1638–1850* (New York: John Wiley and Sons, 1932), pp. 161–62. Nearly a century earlier, Samuel Richardson had a similar response to *Pamela*'s unexpected popularity. Despite his knowledge of the literary market, Richardson was surprised at the novel's "strange success" and sold two-thirds of the copyright for twenty pounds. See Watt, *Rise of the Novel*, p. 55.

21. Lyle H. Wright, "A Statistical Survey of American Fiction, 1774–1850," *Huntington Library Quarterly* 11 (1938–39):309; idem, "Propaganda in Early American Fiction," *Papers of the Bibliographical Society of America* 33 (1939):100.

22. Henry Dwight Sedgwick to William Minot, [Spring 1822]; Henry Dwight Sedgwick to Catharine Maria Sedgwick, 25 May 1822, [4 June 1822], Sedgwick Family Papers, Sedgwick IV, MHS.

23. Henry Dwight Sedgwick to C. M. Sedgwick, 24 Aug. 1824, 5 Oct. 1824, ibid.

24. Journal of C. M. Sedgwick, 10 June 1827, Catharine Maria Sedgwick Papers, MHS; Sedgwick to Charles Sedgwick, 21 Nov. 1826, in *Life and Letters of Catharine M. Sedgwick*, Mary E. Dewey, ed. (New York: Harper and Bros., 1872), p. 180; George Haven Putnam, *George Palmer Putnam: A Memoir* (New York: G. P. Putnam's Sons, 1912), p. 22; Sedgwick to Sedgwick, 7 March 1830, Catharine Maria Sedgwick Papers, MHS; Lyle H. Wright, *American Fiction, 1774–1850*, rev. ed. (San Marino, Calif.: Huntington Library Publications, 1948), pp. 252–55; undated document compiled by Sedgwick, Catharine Maria Sedgwick Papers, MHS.

25. *Southern Rose-Bud*, 31 Aug. 1833; Caroline Howard Gilman to Lewis J. Cist, 19 Jan. 1838, Ferdinand J. Dreer Collection, HSP.

26. Caroline Howard Gilman to Harriet Fay, 13 April 1838, reprinted in Mary Scott Saint-Amand, *A Balcony in Charleston* (Richmond: Garrett and Massie, 1941), p. 111; Gilman to Fay, 5 June [1838], 28 June [1838], Gilman Family Papers, AAS.

27. Samuel Gilman to Louisa Gilman Loring, 8 Nov. [1838], Samuel Gilman Papers, South Caroliniana–USC.

28. Caroline Howard Gilman to James Munroe, 8 May 1851, BPL; Gilman to Munroe, 9 Feb. 1852, Houghton-Harvard.

29. Caroline Howard Gilman to Rufus Wilmot Griswold, 9 Dec. 1851, Rufus Wilmot Griswold Papers, BPL; Gilman to nephew, undated, Samuel Gilman Papers, South Caroliniana–USC.

30. Caroline Howard Gilman to nephew, undated, South Caroliniana–USC.

31. John S. Hart, *The Female Prose Writers of America* (Philadelphia: E. H. Butler and Co., 1852), p. 66; *Allibone's Dictionary of Authors*, 3 vols. (Philadelphia: Childs and Peterson, 1859) 1:1172.

32. Mary Virginia Terhune [Marion Harland], *Marion Harland's Autobiography: The Story of a Long Life* (New York: Harper and Bros., 1910), pp. 243–45;

Mary Virginia Terhune to Virginia Eppes Dance, 5 June 1854, Perkins-Duke.

33. Mary Virginia Terhune to Virginia Eppes Dance, 18 Oct. 1855, Perkins-Duke; Florine Thayer McCray, "Marion Harland at Home," *Ladies Home Journal* 4 (August 1887):3; Terhune, *Autobiography*, p. 344. To avoid confusion, I have used the married names of the literary domestics—the names by which they were identified during most of their lives—throughout the text, except in a few instances which should be self-explanatory. (Four of the literary domestics, as noted, did not marry.) Thus in this instance the married name Terhune is used, rather than the unmarried name Hawes, even though Mary Virginia was unmarried at the time.

34. Anna B. Warner, *Life and Letters of Susan Warner* (G. P. Putnam's Sons, 1909), pp. 282–83; Journal of Susan Warner, 7 Nov. 1850, Susan Warner Papers, CIA; Derby, *Fifty Years*, pp. 304–5.

35. Journal of Susan Warner, 22 Feb. 1851, Susan Warner Papers, CIA; Warner, *Life and Letters*, p. 346; Derby, *Fifty Years*, p. 305; Putnam, *George Palmer Putnam*, p. 218; Grace Overmyer, "Hudson River Bluestockings—The Warner Sisters of Constitution Island," *New York History* 40 (April 1959):137; Frank Luther Mott, *Golden Multitudes: The Story of Best Sellers in the United States* (New York: Macmillan Co., 1947), p. 124; Warner Journal, 2 Aug. 1851, Susan Warner Papers, CIA.

36. Warner, *Life and Letters*, pp. 460–61, 491; Putnam, *George Palmer Putnam*, p. 216.

37. White, *Henry William Herbert*, pp. 37–39; Putnam, *George Palmer Putnam*, pp. 171–91, 361–65.

38. *New York Times*, 30 June 1899; *New York Journal*, 30 June 1899; *Washington Star*, 30 June 1899; undated clipping, *Washington Star*, E.D.E.N. Southworth Papers, LOC.

39. Henry Peterson to Southworth, Sept. 1849, E.D.E.N. Southworth Papers, Perkins-Duke; *Saturday Evening Post*, 16 Nov. 1850; 4 Dec. 1852; 20 Sept. 1856.

40. Henry Peterson to Southworth, 26 Dec. 1856, E.D.E.N. Southworth Papers, Perkins-Duke.

41. *Saturday Evening Post*, 11 April 1857. Part of this episode, with no mention of Peterson's letters, is discussed in Regis Louise Boyle, *Mrs. E.D.E.N. Southworth, Novelist* (Washington: Catholic University of America Press, 1937).

42. Robert Bonner to Southworth, 10 Oct. 1856, E.D.E.N. Southworth Papers, Perkins-Duke.

43. Ibid., 22 Oct. 1856.

44. Southworth to Robert Bonner, 18 Feb. 1861, 28 Sept. 1867, 12 Jan. 1869; receipt dated 27 Sept. 1867, ibid.

45. *Washington Star*, 4 June 1904; Southworth to granddaughter Emma, 22 Aug. 1895, E.D.E.N. Southworth Papers, LOC.

46. Derby, *Fifty Years*, pp. 202–3, 209; James Parton, *Fanny Fern*, pp. 52–53; *Eminent Women*, p. 72.

47. Robert Bonner to Sara Parton, 10 Jan. 1868, in Derby, *Fifty Years*, pp. 215–16; *New York Ledger*, 26 Oct. 1872, 2 Nov. 1872, 9 Nov. 1872; Ellen Eldredge to Robert Bonner, 30 Nov. 1873, NYPL-Manuscripts.

48. Sermon preached by Nathaniel Hall, 8 Oct. 1866, copy deposited with Cummins Family Papers; W. W. Clapp, Jr., to Maria Cummins, 16 March 1854; R. B. Fitts to Maria Cummins, 17 March 1854; contracts and broadside, Cummins

Family Papers, EI. The figure of 73,000 is cited in the *Hingham* (Mass.) *Journal*, 15 Dec. 1854; see also Mott, *Golden Multitudes*, p. 125.

49. Derby, *Fifty Years*, pp. 571–74; Tebbel, *History of Book Publishing*, p. 293; *New York Times*, 8 Oct. 1907; Laura C. Holloway, *The Woman's Story* (New York: John B. Alden, 1889), p. 333.

50. Augusta Evans Wilson to West and Johnston, 22 Feb. 1863, Clifton Waller Barrett Library, Alderman-UVA; William Perry Fidler, *Augusta Evans Wilson, 1835–1909* (University: University of Alabama Press, 1951), pp. 44–45, 74; Derby, *Fifty Years*, pp. 392–95.

51. Augusta Evans Wilson to a friend, 20 June 1866, Clifton Waller Barrett Library, Alderman-UVA; Fidler, *Wilson*, pp. 129, 166–67; Derby, *Fifty Years*, p. 397.

52. Harriet Beecher Stowe to Eliza Cabot Follen, 16 Feb. 1853, Follen Miscellany, MHS; Stowe to James T. Fields, undated, James T. Fields Papers, Huntington.

53. "Bookselling: From Appleton's New American Cyclopedia," *American Publishers' Circular and Literary Gazette* 1 (1858):391; "Notes on Books and Booksellers," ibid. 1 (1863):166–67 (the table from the *Boston Post* was reprinted here); Lyle H. Wright, "A Few Observations on American Fiction, 1851–1875," *Proceedings of the American Antiquarian Society* 65 (1955):93, 102; *Nation* 14 (1872):334–35.

54. Dr. Cummings to Catharine Maria Sedgwick, Aug. 1851, in Dewey, *Life and Letters*, p. 221; Journal of Catharine Maria Sedgwick, 11 and 13 Nov. 1835, in Dewey, *Life and Letters*, p. 248; autobiographical sketch, Caroline Howard Gilman Papers, SCHS, reprinted in Hart, *Female Prose Writers*, p. 52; Terhune, *Autobiography*, p. 285; Southworth to Robert Bonner, 24 March 1887, E.D.E.N. Southworth Papers, Perkins-Duke; interview in the *Washington Post*, 2 Dec. 1894; Tebbel, *History of Book Publishing*, p. 240.

55. Boyle, *E.D.E.N. Southworth*, p. 39; Hart, *Popular Book*, p. 119; Derby, *Fifty Years*, p. 397.

CHAPTER 2. FAME NEVER WAS

1. Journal of Susan Warner, 2 Aug. 1851, 30 July 1851, Susan Warner Papers, CIA.

2. Susan Warner to John S. Hart, 17 March 1851, Maurice Family Papers, Southern Historical Collection–UNC.

3. Journal of Catharine Maria Sedgwick, 10 June 1827, July 1827; Sedgwick to Robert Sedgwick, 6 July 1827, Catharine Maria Sedgwick Papers, MHS.

4. Sedgwick journal, 17 Dec. 1835, ibid.

5. Augusta Evans Wilson, *Beulah* (New York: Derby and Jackson, 1859), pp. 397, 401, 403–4.

6. Caroline Lee Hentz, *Ernest Linwood* (Boston: John P. Jewett and Co., 1856), pp. 349–50. The powers and privileges of the colonial gentry and, in particular, the sense of responsibility and tradition along with the aspirations and ambitions held by elite males in the first half of the nineteenth century are analyzed in Stow Persons's *The Decline of American Gentility* (New York: Columbia University Press, 1973).

7. The wide variety of sources for all of the literary domestics and individual members of their families, including the many scattered letters, are cited throughout this study where relevant. The subsequent citations on the families of the literary domestics indicate the general sources relied upon. Primary information for Cummins and her family is limited, but the largest collection of documents can be found at the Essex Institute, Salem, Massachusetts. See also Cummins's obituary in the *Boston Daily Advertiser*, 2 Oct. 1866; *Dictionary of American Biography*, p. 600; and miscellaneous sources cited in *Notable American Women*, p. 416.

8. Information on Warner's family can be found in the Susan Warner Papers, Constitution Island Association, West Point, N.Y. Published sources that were particularly helpful include Anna B. Warner, *Susan Warner* (New York: G. P. Putnam's Sons, 1909); Olivia Phelps Stokes, *Letters and Memories of Susan and Anna Bartlett Warner* (New York: G. P. Putnam's Sons, 1925); Hilma Robinson, *The Warners of Constitution Island* (West Point, N.Y.: Constitution Island Association, n.d.); Grace Overmyer, "Hudson River Bluestockings—The Warner Sisters of Constitution Island," *New York History* 40 (April 1959):137–58. I am also indebted to the late Hilma Robinson for sharing her detailed knowledge of the Warners.

9. The best source for Hentz's family is the Hentz Family Papers, Southern Historical Collection, University of North Carolina. See also Edward Burgess, ed., *The Spiders of the United States: A Collection of the Arachnological Writings of Nicholas Marcellus Hentz* (Boston: Boston Society of Natural History, 1875), esp. the preface, and Collier Cobb, "Nicholas Marcellus Hentz," *Journal of the Elisha Mitchell Scientific Society* 47 (January 1932):47–51

10. Especially important primary sources are the Mary Virginia Terhune Papers, William R. Perkins Library, Duke University and the letters of Terhune in the Clifton Waller Barrett Library, Alderman Library, University of Virginia. See also Mary Virginia Terhune [Marion Harland], *Marion Harland's Autobiography* (New York: Harper and Bros., 1910); there is a biographical appendix on Edward Payson Terhune at the end of the autobiography.

11. The Massachusetts Historical Society has a vast collection of papers of the entire Sedgwick family. Other depositories with important letters of Catharine Maria Sedgwick are Stockbridge Library Association, Stockbridge, Massachusetts, and the Pierpont Morgan Library, New York City. A selection of Sedgwick's correspondence is found in Mary E. Dewey, *Life and Letters of Catharine M. Sedgwick* (New York: Harper and Bros., 1872). Secondary sources include Edward Halsey Foster, *Catharine Maria Sedgwick* (New York: Twayne Publishers, 1974) and Mary Michael Welsh, *Catharine Maria Sedgwick* (Washington: Catholic University of America Press, 1937). The reference to Theodore Sedgwick's boyish gaieties is found in his daughter Catharine's "Notebook of Memories of Her Life Dated 1853," Catharine Maria Sedgwick Papers, MHS. The definitive biography of Theodore Sedgwick is Richard E. Welch, Jr., *Theodore Sedgwick, Federalist: A Political Portrait* (Middletown: Wesleyan University Press, 1965).

12. Many of the papers of the Beecher and Stowe families have been preserved and the primary collections are found at the Stowe-Day Foundation, Hartford; the Arthur and Elizabeth Schlesinger Library on the History of Women in America, Radcliffe College; and Sterling Memorial Library, Yale University. Selections from Harriet Beecher Stowe's correspondence are found in Annie Fields, ed., *Life and*

Letters of Harriet Beecher Stowe (Boston: Houghton Mifflin Co., 1897). Another important source is Charles Beecher, ed., *Autobiography, Correspondence, Etc., of Lyman Beecher, D.D.*, 2 vols. (New York: Harper and Bros., 1864–65). Milton Rugoff's lively and richly detailed study is the definitive biography of the family: *The Beechers: An American Family in the Nineteenth Century* (New York: Harper and Row, 1981). The most informative narrative of Harriet's life remains Forrest Wilson, *Crusader in Crinoline: The Life of Harriet Beecher Stowe* (Philadelphia: J. B. Lippincott, 1941).

13. The most important collection is the Sara Parton Papers, Sophia Smith Collection, Smith College. The James Parton Papers, deposited at Houghton Library, Harvard University, are also very informative. Published sources include Sara Parton's obituary, *New York Ledger*, 9 Nov. 1872; James Parton, *Fanny Fern: A Memorial Volume* (New York: G. W. Carleton and Co., 1873); Milton E. Flower, *James Parton: The Father of Modern Biography* (Durham: Duke University Press, 1951); Henry A. Beers, *Nathaniel Parker Willis* (Boston: Houghton Mifflin Co., 1885); J. C. Derby, *Fifty Years Among Authors, Books and Publishers* (New York: G. W. Carleton and Co., 1884), pp. 200–226. The characterization of the *Eastern Argus* is found in *The History of Portland* (Portland: Maine Historical Society, 1972/1865), p. 600.

14. Two large collections of Southworth's papers are found at the Library of Congress and the William R. Perkins Library, Duke University. See also the autobiographical sketch dated 17 June 1893 to S. T. Pickard, Houghton Library, Harvard University; obituaries in the *New York Times*, 30 June 1899; *New York Journal*, 30 June 1899; *Washington Star*, 30 June 1899; autobiographical sketches in John S. Hart, *The Female Prose Writers of America* (Philadelphia: E. H. Butler and Co., 1855), pp. 211–15; and Southworth's *The Haunted Homestead* (Philadelphia: T. B. Peterson and Bros., 1860), pp. 29–40. A published secondary source is Regis Louise Boyle, *Mrs. E.D.E.N. Southworth, Novelist* (Washington: Catholic University of America Press, 1939).

15. Other than scattered letters, the sources for McIntosh are secondary. They include Hart, *Female Prose Writers*, pp. 63–69; *The Living Female Writers of the South* (Philadelphia: Claxton, Remsen and Haffelfinger, 1872), pp. 223–29; Julia Deane Freeman [Mary Forrest], *Women of the South Distinguished in Literature* (New York: Charles B. Richardson, 1865). See also Harvey H. Jackson's biography of her father titled *Lachlan McIntosh and the Politics of Revolutionary Georgia* (Athens: University of Georgia Press, 1979).

16. The three major collections on Gilman and her family are deposited at the South Carolina Historical Society, Charleston, S.C.; the South Caroliniana Library, University of South Carolina, Columbia; and the American Antiquarian Society, Worcester, Massachusetts. Published sources include Arthur Gilman, *The Gilman Family* (Albany: Joel Munsell, 1869) and Mary Scott Saint-Amand, *A Balcony in Charleston* (Richmond: Garrett and Massie, 1941).

17. A few of Holmes's letters are found in various depositories, but there is no major collection extant. Published sources include obituaries in the *New York Times*, 8 Oct. 1907 and *Nation* 10 Oct. 1907; Derby, *Fifty Years*, pp. 571–74; Laura C. Holloway, *The Woman's Story* (New York: John B. Alden, 1889), pp. 333–34; Frances E. Willard and Mary A. Livermore, eds., *A Woman of the Century*, p. 390. On Daniel Holmes, see *Yale University Obituary Record of*

Graduates, 1918–1919, pp. 836–37.

18. Some of Wilson's letters are deposited at the Alabama Department of Archives and History, Montgomery, Alabama; the Library of Congress; and the Alderman Library, University of Virginia. Other sources are her obituary in the Mobile (Ala.) *Advertiser and Register*, 10 May 1909; William Perry Fidler, *Augusta Evans Wilson* (University: University of Alabama, 1951); Derby, *Fifty Years*, pp. 389–99; Freeman, *Women of the South*, pp. 328–32; *Living Female Writers*, pp. 270–80; *Woman's Story*, pp. 151–53.

19. Maris Vinovski and Richard Bernard have demonstrated that only a tiny percentage of the population attended college in antebellum America. Basing their findings on federal censuses, they show that 0.8% were enrolled in 1840, 0.8% in 1850, and 1.0% in 1860. See Vinvoski and Bernard, "Beyond Catharine Beecher: Female Education in the Antebellum Period," *Signs: Journal of Women in Culture and Society* 3 (Summer 1978):859.

20. See Chapter Nine.

21. Caroline Lee Hentz, *Ernest Linwood* (Boston: John P. Jewett, 1856), pp. 1, 18.

22. Ibid., pp. 18, 29–30.

23. Ibid., pp. 166–67.

24. Ibid.

25. Ibid., p. 167.

26. Augusta Evans Wilson, *Beulah* (New York: Derby and Jackson, 1859), p. 171; Sara Parton quoted in a biographical sketch in Sara Jane Lippincott [Grace Greenwood], "Fanny Fern—Mrs. Parton," *Eminent Women of the Age* (Hartford: S. M. Betts and Co., 1869), p. 67.

27. Mary Virginia Terhune to Kate Sanborn, 3 March 1883, in n. a., *Our Famous Women* (Hartford: A. D. Worthington, 1886), p. 632; Terhune, *Autobiography*, p. 28.

28. Terhune, *Autobiography*, pp. 5–6.

29. Ibid., p. 14. Sandra M. Gilbert and Susan Gubar's provocative study based primarily upon nineteenth-century English women writers touches upon other aspects that relate to my analysis of the literary domestics' "anxiety of authorship," to use their terminology. Their observation that they were "surprised by the coherence of theme and imagery that we encountered in the works of [women] writers who were often geographically, historically, and psychologically distant from each other" points to gender as the decisive factor that cuts across many boundaries. Obviously, my own study supports that thesis, but in a number of respects Gilbert and Gubar's focus on literary theory and criticism suffers from a lack of social, cultural, and historical specificity regarding the writers they discuss. In addition, their perspective on gender is preconceived and overly preoccupied with the negative aspects of women's struggle against oppressive patriarchal culture(s). Their generalizations in that respect lead them to overlook, for example, the efforts of women to *affirm* not only the existence of a female history and a female present, but also the valued elements of their foremothers' history and those of their own lives. A selfless life is not, to use their own words again, "a life that has no story;" it is a life that has many different stories. The *anxieties* of life, at least for the literary domestics, stemmed from manifold sources. There were conflicting efforts to submit to and resist the restraints of patriarchal society, but there were as well endeavors to affirm the significance and value of lives

led while attempting to cope with desires to extend that significance and value. In studying the histories of women in patriarchal society we need to guard against the predilection to view women as entirely man-made and woman-denied. Otherwise we, ironically, will continue to perpetuate the act of denying and thus effacing those histories. See Gilbert and Gubar, *The Madwoman in the Attic: The Woman Writer and the Nineteenth-Century Literary Imagination* (New Haven: Yale University Press, 1979). For a study that explores British women writers from the nineteenth century to the present and that is in my view more valuable for comparative purposes, see Elaine Showalter, *A Literature of Their Own: British Women Novelists From Brontë to Lessing* (Princeton: Princeton University Press, 1977).

30. Augusta Evans Wilson quoted in a biographical sketch in Julia Deane Freeman [Mary Forrest], *Women of the South Distinguished in Literature* (New York: Charles B. Richardson, 1865), p. 332.

31. Mary Virginia Terhune [Marion Harland], *Eve's Daughters; or, Common Sense for Maid, Wife, and Mother* (New York: John R. Anderson and Henry S. Allen, 1882), p. 6; Wilson, *Beulah*, p. 171; Terhune, *Autobiography*, p. 7.

32. Harriet Beecher Stowe to Charles Beecher, undated, in Charles Beecher, ed., *Autobiography, Correspondence, Etc., of Lyman Beecher, D.D.*, 2 vols. (New York: Harper and Bros., 1864–65) 1:301, 315.

33. Ibid. 1:301, 304.

34. Catharine Beecher to Charles Beecher, undated; Roxana Foote to correspondent, quoted in Beecher, *Autobiography* 1:55.

35. Beecher, *Autobiography* 1:61–62. Lyman Beecher's comment refers to the English novelist Frances Burney's *Evelina*, which had the apt subtitle *The History of a Young Lady's Entrance into the World*. Published in 1778, it was Burney's first novel.

36. Roxana Foote to Lyman Beecher, 18 March 1798, 23 Feb. 1799, Stowe-Day. Sara Parton was correct in her aside about fertility at the beginning of the nineteenth century: women then gave birth to approximately eight children. See Wilson H. Grabill, Clyde V. Kiser, and Pascal K. Whelpton, "A Long View," in *The American Family in Social-Historical Perspective* (New York: St. Martin's Press, 1973), pp. 373–96.

37. Roxana Beecher to Harriet Foote, 29 March 1801, Stowe-Day.

38. Ibid., 29 March 1801, 29 April 1801, 8 May 1802.

39. Mary Hubbard to Esther Beecher, January 1806, in Beecher, *Autobiography* 1:140.

40. Beecher, *Autobiography* 1:141; Mary Hubbard to Esther Beecher, 1806, ibid. 1:142. The text referred to is Antoine Lavoisier's *Elements of Chemistry* (1790).

41. Roxana Beecher to Lyman Beecher, 9 March 1810, Stowe-Day; Catharine Beecher to Charles Beecher, undated, in Beecher, *Autobiography* 1:219; Beecher, *Autobiography* 1:282. In both *Oldtown Folks* and *Poganuc People* Harriet Beecher Stowe drew upon the Litchfield of her childhood. See Chapters Four and Five.

42. Roxana Beecher to Esther Beecher, 13 Jan. 1811, in Beecher, *Autobiography* 1:232.

43. Roxana Beecher to Samuel Foote, 6 Nov. 1814; Roxana Beecher to Harriet Foote, [Nov. 1814], Stowe-Day.

44. Harriet Beecher Stowe to Charles Beecher, undated, in Beecher, *Autobiograpy* 1:302.

45. Harriet Beecher Stowe to Charles Beecher, undated; Catharine Beecher to Charles Beecher, undated, ibid. 1:306, 324.

46. Catharine Maria Sedgwick, "Notebook of Memories of Her Life Dated 1853," Catharine Maria Sedgwick Papers, MHS, pp. 1–2.

47. Ibid., pp. 8, 38.

48. Ibid., pp. 37, 42–43.

49. Ibid., p. 53.

50. See Welch's *Theodore Sedgwick* for a detailed and perceptive analysis of Sedgwick's political career.

51. Pamela Sedgwick to Theodore Sedgwick, 22 June 1777; Pamela Sedgwick to Elizabeth Mayhew, [1780], 25 May 1782, 1 June 1783, 6 Feb. 1785, Sedgwick Family Papers, Sedgwick III, MHS.

52. Pamela to Theodore Sedgwick, 31 Jan. 1789, 17 Feb. 1789, ibid.

53. Pamela to Theodore Sedgwick, 12 July 1789, 24 July 1789, 14 Aug. 1789, 23 May 1790, 26 June 1790, ibid.

54. Pamela to Theodore Sedgwick, 23 Oct. 1791, ibid.

55. Pamela to Theodore Sedgwick, 4 Dec. 1791, ibid.

56. Theodore Sedgwick to a friend, 6 Dec. 1791, Theodore Sedgwick to "Dear Sir," 14 Dec. 1791, Pamela to Theodore Sedgwick, 4 March 1792, ibid.

57. Pamela to Theodore Sedgwick, 11 Dec. 1792, 15 Jan. 1798, 10 Jan. 1799, 11 Feb. 1799, ibid.

58. Catharine Maria Sedgwick to Theodore Sedgwick, 1 Feb. 1801, Catharine Maria Sedgwick Papers, MHS.

59. Sedgwick, "Notebook of Memories," pp. 41–42.

60. Ibid., pp. 69–70, 57–58, 35, 80–81; Catharine Maria Sedgwick to Pamela Sedgwick, 29 Nov. 1805, Sedgwick Family Papers, Sedgwick IV, MHS.

CHAPTER 3. THE SEASON OF INSTRUCTION

1. In addition to my own research and that of other scholars cited, the following commentary on American education generally and women's education specifically from the colonial period through the early decades of the nineteenth century is based upon Thomas Woody's *A History of Women's Education in the United States*, 2 vols. (New York: Science Press, 1929), supplemented for the colonial period by Lawrence A. Cremin's *American Education: The Colonial Experience, 1607–1783* (New York: Harper and Row, 1970). However, the perspective on women's education is my own. Obviously, more research needs to be done, and studies currently underway by Barbara Miller Solomon and Anne Firor Scott should prove illuminating. Published more than fifty years ago, Woody's two volumes remain the basic source, but they are more descriptive than analytical. Imaginative in approach and convincing in argument, Cremin's study nevertheless suffers from a failure to distinguish carefully between the education offered females and males. Inadvertently, then, his is basically an analysis of the male experience.

2. Woody, *Women's Education*, pp. 137–53; Cremin, *American Education*, pp. 186, 524.

3. Woody, *Women's Education*, pp. 195–237, 268–300. In his analysis of the southern colonies Cremin also emphasizes the strong rural bias and dispersed population that made the household an especially important agency for education. See *American Education*, pp. 113–37. A detailed description supporting Woody and Cremin is found in Julia Cherry Spruill, *Women's Life and Work in the Southern Colonies* (New York: Russell and Russell, 1969/1938), pp. 185–207. Throughout the rest of this book the original publication date of a volume is given following the virgule (/).

4. Bernard Bailyn was one of the first to define education broadly and to suggest that the family was the primary educational institution in this regard during the colonial period. See his *Education in the Forming of American Society: Needs and Opportunities for Study* (Chapel Hill: University of North Carolina Press, 1960). Cremin demonstrates not only the significance of the family as a sustained and systematic educator, but also the emphasis upon values, designated by him "piety and civility," which formed the core of education.

5. Caroline Howard Gilman to Anna Maria Howard White, 27 March 1819, Caroline Howard Gilman Papers, SCHS. On the continuing role of the home as a central social and cultural institution in the early nineteenth century, see Stow Persons's *The Decline of American Gentility* (New York: Columbia University Press, 1973), esp. pp. 74–79.

6. Linda K. Kerber was one of the first to examine the state of women's education in the early republic, the calls for its improvement, and the rationale upon which they were based. See "Daughters of Columbia: Educating Women for the Republic, 1787–1805," in Stanley Elkins and Eric McKittrick, eds., *The Hofstadter Aegis* (New York: Alfred A. Knopf, 1974), p. 36–59. She elaborated upon this topic in *Women of the Republic: Intellect and Ideology in Revolutionary America* (Chapel Hill: University of North Carolina Press, 1980), pp. 189–231. See also Mary Beth Norton, *Liberty's Daughters: The Revolutionary Experience of American Women, 1750–1800* (Boston: Little, Brown and Co., 1980), pp. 256–94, and Nancy F. Cott, *The Bonds of Womanhood: "Woman's Sphere" in New England, 1780–1835* (New Haven: Yale University Press, 1977), pp. 101–25.

7. Republican ideology and its impact have received close scrutiny from a number of historians recently. See, for example, Gordon S. Wood, *The Creation of the American Republic, 1776–1787* (Chapel Hill: University of North Carolina Press, 1969), as well as Wood's introduction to *The Rising Glory of America, 1760–1820* (New York: George Braziller, 1971), and his essay, "Republicanism as a Revolutionary Ideology" in John R. Howe, ed., *The Role of Ideology in the American Revolution* (New York: Holt, Rinehart and Winston, 1970), pp. 83–91. The contemporary attitude that education was integral to the survival of the republic is discussed in Cremin's *American Education: The National Experience, 1783–1876* (New York: Harper and Row, 1980), part 2.

8. The female seminary movement is described in Woody, *Women's Education*, pp. 329–459. Keith Melder also devotes a chapter to the subject in *Beginnings of Sisterhood: The American Woman's Rights Movement, 1800–1850* (New York: Schocken Books, 1977), pp. 12–29. Beecher's Hartford Female Seminary is perceptively analyzed in Kathryn Kish Sklar, *Catharine Beecher: A Study in American Domesticity* (New York: Norton, 1976/1973), pp. 59–104. Anne Firor Scott explores the career of Emma Willard in "What, Then, Is the American: This

New Woman?" *Journal of American History* 65 (December 1978): 679–703, and Willard's seminary in "That Ever Widening Circle: The Diffusion of Feminist Values from the Troy Female Seminary, 1822–1872," *History of Education Quarterly* 19 (1979):3–27. The latter article is especially cogent in analysis of values concerning women. Characterizing these values as either "traditional" or "feminist," Scott suggests that historians locate nineteenth-century women along a continuum with the contrasting sets of values at each end, rather than simply designating women as either traditionalists or feminists. In this context, the literary domestics, like Emma Willard, were in the middle of the continuum and, not surprisingly, experienced an ambivalence similar to that which Scott ascribes to Willard. Sklar offers a complementary analysis of Mary Lyon in "The Founding of Mount Holyoke College," in Carol Ruth Berkin and Mary Beth Norton, *Women of America: A History* (Boston: Houghton Mifflin Co., 1979), pp. 177–201. See as well Elizabeth Alden Green, *Mary Lyon and the Founding of Mount Holyoke: Opening the Gates* (Hanover: University Press of New England, 1979). I am also indebted to former Dartmouth College student Laura Robertson's insightful honors thesis titled "A Throne of Her Own: Mary Lyon and the Founding of Mount Holyoke College."

9. As early as 1954 Janet Wilson James noted that justifications for female education in the early republic were based upon the moral role women would play as wives and mothers. See "Changing Ideas about Women in the United States, 1776–1825" (Ph. D. diss., Radcliffe College, 1954). The two most important sources are the studies of Linda K. Kerber and Mary Beth Norton. Kerber was the first to locate and define the concept of republican motherhood in the context of late eighteenth-century political theory. See "The Republican Mother: Women and the Enlightenment—An American Perspective," *American Quarterly* 28 (Summer 1976):187–205. In developing the concept further, she has pointed to its inherently paradoxical character in *Women of the Republic*, esp. pp. 269–88. I am also indebted to Kerber for alerting me to the fact that although female citizenship was defined in the passive mode, as I have argued here nevertheless women in the early republic were legal citizens, just as children are citizens today. Norton's analysis in effect parallels Kerber's. Norton does ascribe to republican motherhood an unprecedented significance for women in the political realm, but she characterizes its implications as ambiguous. See *Liberty's Daughters*, esp. pp. 242–55, 295–99. In an alternative interpretation, Joan Hoff Wilson has argued that the Revolution did not fundamentally alter the political consciousness of women. See "The Illusion of Change: Women and the Revolution," in Alfred Young, ed., *The American Revolution: Explorations in the History of American Radicalism* (DeKalb: Northern Illinois University Press, 1976), esp. pp. 414–31.

10. Mary Virginia Terhune [Marion Harland], *Eve's Daughters; or, Common Sense for Maid, Wife and Mother* (New York: John R. Anderson and Henry S. Allen, 1882), pp. 10, 27. Anne Firor Scott's article on the Troy Female Seminary suggests that it was an exception. Not only does Scott argue that Troy instilled what she characterizes as "feminist" values along with those which were more "traditional," she also estimates that a relatively high proportion looked upon their teaching as a serious career. See Scott, "The Ever Widening Circle." The feminization of teaching is strikingly illustrated by the example of antebellum Massachusetts. Maris Vinovski and Richard Bernard have estimated that one in five women in Massa-

chusetts taught school at some time in their lives. See "Beyond Catharine Beecher: Female Education in the Antebellum Period," *Signs: Journal of Women in Culture and Society* 3 (Summer 1978):856–69.

11. Catharine Maria Sedgwick, "Notebook of Memories of Her Life Dated 1853," p. 80, Catharine Maria Sedgwick Papers, MHS.

12. Ibid., p. 80.

13. Ibid., pp. 90, 85, unnumbered, 143, 86; Frances Watson to Sedgwick, 6 Nov. 1802, Sedgwick IV; Theodore Sedgwick to Sedgwick, 23 April 1806, Sedgwick III, Sedgwick Family Papers, MHS.

14. Sedgwick, "Notebook of Memories," pp. 80, 90.

15. Ibid., pp. 81–82; Pamela Sedgwick to Theodore Sedgwick, 9 July 1798, Sedgwick Family Papers, Sedgwick III, MHS.

16. Sedgwick, "Notebook of Memories," p. 82; Sedgwick to Pamela Sedgwick, 11 Nov. 1804; Sedgwick to Theodore Sedgwick, 29 Dec. 1804; Pamela Sedgwick to Sarah Tucker, 17 Oct. 1804, Sedgwick IV, ibid.

17. Sedgwick, "Notebook of Memories," pp. 134, 112, 113.

18. Ibid., pp. 90, 55, 80–81.

19. Ibid., p. 55.

20. Catharine Maria Sedgwick, *Home* (Boston: James Munroe and Co., 1835), p. 42; Sedgwick, "Notebook of Memories," pp. 74, 111.

21. Sedgwick, "Notebook of Memories," p. 88.

22. Catharine Maria Sedgwick, *A New England Tale* (New York: George P. Putnam and Co., 1852/1822), pp. 1–2, 74, 79, 81.

23. Ibid., pp. 81, 84.

24. Sedgwick, "Notebook of Memories," pp. 81, 90.

25. Caroline Howard Gilman, "Autobiographical Sketch," in John S. Hart, ed., *The Female Prose Writers of America* (Philadelphia: E. H. Butler and Co., 1855), pp. 53, 51. An unpublished autobiographical essay from which this sketch was drawn is deposited with the Caroline Howard Gilman Papers, SCHS. See also an unpublished biographical essay in the Samuel Gilman Papers, South Caroliniana–USC.

26. Hart, *Female Writers*, pp. 51–53; Caroline Gilman, preface, *Oracles from the Poets* (New York: Wiley and Putnam, 1844), p. 8.

27. Hart, *Female Writers*, pp. 53–54.

28. Caroline Howard Gilman to J. Batchelder, 24 Sept. 1875, Houghton–Harvard.

29. Caroline Howard Gilman, *Recollections of a Southern Matron and New England Bride* (Philadelphia: John E. Porter and Co., 1867, pp. 317–19. This is a combined edition of two works which were first issued separately. *New England Bride* was originally published as *Recollections of a Housekeeper* in 1834.

30. Ibid., pp. 320–23.

31. Ibid., pp. 344–45.

32. Ibid., p. 347.

33. *Southern Rose*, 22 Dec. 1838. The only complete edition of the periodical is found at the Charleston Public Library, Charleston, S.C.

34. *Southern Rose*, 22 Dec. 1838. In their analysis of female educational experience in antebellum America, Vinovski and Bernard have concluded that the

increase in opportunity notwithstanding, education itself continued to be strongly influenced by premises concerning the role women would play as adults. See "Beyond Catharine Beecher."

35. *Southern Rose*, 22 Dec. 1838.

36. Caroline Howard Gilman to Anna Maria Howard White, 5 Jan. 1820, Caroline Howard Gilman Papers, SCHC.

CHAPTER 4. RIGHTS OF THE MIND, DUTIES TO THE SPHERE

1. Harriet Beecher Stowe to James Parton, undated, Sara Parton Papers, Sophia Smith Collection, Smith.

2. "Suggestions on Arithmetic" (later printed in the *New York Ledger* on 30 Nov. 1872 following Parton's death), Sara Parton Papers, ibid.

3. Harriet Beecher Stowe to Sara Parton, undated, Sara Parton Papers; Ethel Parton, "Fanny Fern: An Informal Biography," manuscript deposited with Sara Parton Papers, Sophia Smith Collection, Smith. Granddaughter Ethel's comments, which were apparently based upon Sara Parton's recollections of Beecher's seminary, roughly parallel the more substantive and insightful analysis in Kathryn Kish Sklar, *Catharine Beecher: A Study in American Domesticity* (New York: Norton, 1976/ 1973), pp. 59–94.

4. James Parton, *Fanny Fern: A Memorial Volume* (New York: G.W. Carleton and Co., 1873), pp. 36–37; further information on Parton's education is found in Ethel Parton, "Fanny Fern." Sara Parton [Fanny Fern], *Ruth Hall: A Domestic Tale of the Present Time* (New York: Mason Bros., 1855), p. 21.

5. Biographical sketch of Maria McIntosh in Julia Keese Colles, *Authors and Writers Associated with Morristown* (Morristown, N.J.: Vogt Bros., 1895), p. 174; autobiographical sketch of E.D.E.N. Southworth in *The Haunted Homestead* (Philadelphia: T. B. Peterson and Bros., 1860), pp. 34–35.

6. Cummins Family Papers, EI; Augusta Evans Wilson quoted in William Perry Fidler, *Augusta Evans Wilson* (University: University of Alabama Press, 1951), p. 21; T. C. De Leon in *Devota* (New York: G. W. Dillingham, 1913/1907), p. 128.

7. In her examination of fifty-one women who constituted the first generation of nineteenth-century feminists, Blanche Hersh has noted that these contemporaries of Stowe, Warner, and Terhune also received an exceptional education relative to other women. Not surprisingly, however, their education reinforced rather than diminished a strong identification with domesticity. See *The Slavery of Sex: Feminist-Abolitionists in America* (Urbana: University of Illinois Press, 1978), esp. pp. 119–56.

8. An educational pattern similar to Stowe's, Warner's, and Terhune's in the distinctions made on the basis of gender is described in Jean Strouse's biography of Alice James, the younger sister of William and Henry James. The singularity of the education provided her notwithstanding, Alice James, born in 1848, was still expected to become accomplished rather than learned, the latter being reserved for her male siblings. Alice James's mental breakdown in the face of the intellectual demands she made upon herself was also more dramatic than the tensions exhibited by the literary domestics, but at least one source of stress, the role that defined women

as other than intellectual, was the same for all of them. See *Alice James: A Biography* (Boston: Houghton Mifflin Co., 1980), esp. pp. 37–59, 117–131.

9. Charles Beecher, ed., *Autobiography, Correspondence, Etc., of Lyman Beecher, D.D.*, 2 vols. (New York: Harper and Bros., 1864–65) 2:39–40.

10. Ibid. 2:45.

11. That the patriarch Lyman was the dominant influence in the lives of all his children is amply demonstrated in Milton Rugoff, *The Beechers: An American Family in the Nineteenth Century* (New York: Harper and Row, 1981). Lyman's impact upon another daughter is persuasively analyzed in Sklar's *Catharine Beecher*. Yet another daughter, Isabella, angrily protested Lyman's discriminatory practices in the education of his children: "At sixteen and a half, just when my brothers began their mental education, mine was finished. . . . Till twenty three, their father, poor minister as he was could send them to College and Seminary all *six*—cost what it might, but never a daughter cost him a hundred dollars a year, after she was sixteen." Isabella Beecher Hooker to Rachel Burton, 25 Jan. 1859, quoted in Anne Throne Margolis, ed., *The Isabella Beecher Hooker Project* (Hartford: Stowe-Day Foundation, 1979), p. 10.

12. Harriet Beecher Stowe to Charles Beecher, undated, in Beecher, *Autobiography* 1:310–19.

13. Stowe to Beecher, undated, ibid. 1:312, 318.

14. Catharine Beecher to unnamed correspondent, undated, Stowe to Beecher, undated, ibid. 1:366, 530; Harriet Beecher Stowe, *Oldtown Folks* (Cambridge: Harvard University Press, 1966/1869), pp. 440–42; Stowe to George Eliot, 25 May [1869], NYPL-Berg.

15. Catharine Beecher to Charles Beecher, undated, in Beecher, *Autobiography* 1:226.

16. Catharine Beecher to Charles Beecher, undated, Stowe to Charles Beecher, undated, ibid. 1:226, 534–35; Stowe to Sarah Beecher, 29 Sept. 1845, Stowe-Day. The texts to which Stowe referred were William Paley's *Moral and Political Philosophy* (1824), Archibald Alison's *Essays on the Nature and Principles of Taste* (1790), and Hugh Blair's *Lectures on Rhetoric*. The last was published in Great Britain under the title *Lectures on Literature and Belles Lettres* in 1783 and issued in this country with the new title in 1830.

17. Stowe to Beecher, undated, in Beecher, *Autobiography* 1:537; Stowe, *Oldtown Folks*, pp. 452–54.

18. Beecher, *Autobiography* 1:268.

19. Stowe to Beecher, undated, ibid. 1:522–24.

20. Ibid., p. 524.

21. Harriet Beecher Stowe, *Poganuc People: Their Loves and Lives* (Boston: Houghton Mifflin Co., 1896/1871), p. 91, 125.

22. Ibid., pp. 106, 9, 83, 121, 89, 243. In the margin of her own copy of *Poganuc People*, Stowe penciled beside a passage describing the aunt, Miss Debby, engaged in conversation with Dolly the words "Aunt Harriet Foote, exact." See Preface, *Poganuc People*, p. ix.

23. Ibid., pp. 145–46, 265.

24. Harriet Beecher Stowe to a son, 1886, in Annie Fields, ed., *Life and Letters of Harriet Beecher Stowe* (Boston: Houghton Mifflin Co., 1897), p. 43.

25. Stowe quoted in Fields, *Life and Letters*, p. 49; Stowe to Grandmother

Foote, 4 March 1826, ibid., p. 52; Stowe to Charles Beecher, undated, in Beecher, *Autobiography*, 2:109–10.

26. Anna B. Warner, *Susan Warner* (New York: G. P. Putnam's Sons, 1909), p. 34.

27. Ibid., pp. 109, 25.

28. Ibid., pp. 19, 60, 178, 91, 112, 131.

29. Ibid., p. 92; Journal of Susan Warner, 26 Oct. 1835, Susan Warner Papers, CIA. I am indebted to the Constitution Island Association, which made these journals available to me; to the Highland Falls Public Library, Highland Falls, N.Y., which provided facilities for research; and especially to Martha Tezak and Hilma Robinson, both of whom graciously aided me.

30. Warner, *Susan Warner*, p. 91.

31. Warner journal, 13, 14, 18, 21, 22, 26 April 1832, Susan Warner Papers, CIA.

32. Warner journal, 25 Oct. 1833, 10 July 1824, 19 Oct. 1835, 9 November 1835, ibid.

33. Warner, *Susan Warner*, pp. 142, 139, 164; Warner journal, 24 July 1834, Susan Warner Papers, CIA.

34. Warner, *Susan Warner*, pp. 120, 162, 119.

35. Journal of Susan Warner, 10 Jan. 1836, Susan Warner Papers, CIA. Anna Warner quotes extensively from a journal that is not deposited with the Susan Warner Papers and has presumably been lost. The remainder of the entries cited in this paragraph are found in Warner, *Susan Warner*, pp. 157, 166, 167–68.

36. Warner, *Susan Warner*, p. 167. Some of the events that left Warner's family in straitened circumstances are detailed in journals that she kept intermittently during these years. Other sources include Warner, *Susan Warner*; Hilma Robinson, *The Warners of Constitution Island* (West Point, N.Y.: Constitution Island Association, n.d.); Grace Overmyer, "Hudson River Bluestockings—The Warner Sisters of Constitution Island," *New York History* 40 (April 1959):137–58.

37. Anna B. Warner [Amy Lothrop], *Dollars and Cents* (New York: George P. Putnam, 1852), pp. 5, 7; Warner, *Susan Warner*, pp. 176–77, 157; Warner journal, 7 Oct. 1839, 14 Nov. 1839, Susan Warner Papers, CIA. George Haven Putnam, suggesting that Anna and Susan wrote *Dollars and Cents* together, called it "an attempt made by the two sisters to produce a book together." There is no suggestion in either Susan's journal or Anna's biography that this was in fact the case. See *George Palmer Putnam* (New York: G.P. Putnam's Sons, 1912), p. 217.

38. Warner, *Susan Warner*, p. 176; Warner journal, 19 Sept. 1839, Susan Warner Papers, CIA. Entries from 19 Sept. through 2 Dec. 1839 are in French: I am indebted to former Dartmouth College student Bernard Sheahan for his translation of these entries.

39. Warner journal, 21 Sept., 24 Oct., 29 Oct. 1839, ibid.

40. Ibid., 5 Nov., 15 Nov. 1839.

41. Mary Virginia Terhune [Marion Harland], *Marion Harland's Autobiography: The Story of a Long Life* (New York: Harper and Bros., 1910), p. 97.

42. Ibid., pp. 42, 3–4, 24, 144.

43. Ibid., pp. 71, 48–49.

44. Ibid., pp. 67, 66, 70. Commentary on female education in Virginia during

Terhune's youth is found in Richard Beale Davis, *Intellectual Life in Jefferson's Virginia, 1790–1830* (Chapel Hill: University of North Carolina Press, 1964), pp. 42–45.

45. Terhune, *Autobiography*, p. 70.

46. Ibid., pp. 70–75.

47. Ibid., pp. 88–89.

48. *Ladies Home Journal* 4 (August 1887):3; Kate Sanborn, "Mary Virginia Terhune," in *Our Famous Women* (Hartford: A.D. Worthington, 1886), pp. 633–34; Terhune, *Autobiography*, p. 84.

49. Terhune, *Autobiography*, pp. 92–93. Hampden-Sydney College and Union Theological Seminary, both of which were prestigious and influential institutions in the early nineteenth century, are described in Davis, *Intellectual Life*, pp. 54–58.

50. Ibid., pp. 90, 97.

51. Ibid., pp. 90, 94–95.

52. Ibid., p. 96.

53. Ibid., pp. 91, 97–98, 96, 110.

54. Mary Virginia Terhune [Marion Harland], *Loiterings in Pleasant Paths* (New York: Charles Scribner's Sons, 1880), p. 91; Terhune, *Autobiography*, pp. 7, 98–99; Kate Sanborn, "Mary Virginia Terhune," in *Our Famous Women*, p. 633.

55. Terhune, *Autobiography*, pp. 111–13.

56. Maria McIntosh, *Woman in America: Her Work and Her Reward* (New York: D. Appleton and Co., 1850), p. 23.

57. Diary of Catharine Maria Sedgwick, 20 Jan. 1811, Catharine Maria Sedgwick Papers, MHS; Sara Parton [Fanny Fern], "A Transition State," in *Ginger-Snaps* (New York: Carleton, 1870), p. 281; Mary Virginia Terhune [Marion Harland], *Alone* (Richmond: A. Morris, 1854), p. 12; Augusta Evans Wilson to Janie Tyler, 18 Jan. 1862, quoted in Fidler, *Wilson*, p. 66. The conviction that women and men were inherently different in mental organization and capacity was not unique to the nineteenth century. Nonetheless, as Barbara Welter suggests, Victorian America placed particular emphasis upon what had simply been presumed earlier, and developed as well as an elaboration that rendered female and male nature radically different. Women were endowed with intuition, men reason; women responded emotionaly, men thought analytically; to phrase it in terms familiar to the contemporaries of the literary domestics, women were associated with the "heart," men with the "head." Employed as a means by which a separate role and sphere for women were legitimated, this supposed difference had profound implications for female self-identity. See Welter's "Anti-Intellectualism and the American Woman" in *Dimity Convictions: The American Woman in the Nineteenth Century* (Athens: Ohio University Press), pp. 71–82. In contrast to Welter, Susan Phinney Conrad argues that the tenets of Romanticism, especially those stressing intuition as a source of knowledge, made possible a reconciliation between what it meant to be a woman and what it meant to be an intellectual. The evidence from the literary domestics, whom Conrad dismisses as " 'female scribblers,' " and who, she claims, straight-forwardly rejected the idea that women were intellectual, suggests that Welter's is the more convincing interpretation. See *Perish the Thought: Intellectual Women in Romantic America, 1830–1860* (New York: Oxford University Press, 1976), pp. 15–44. Linda K. Kerber and Mary Beth Norton allude to the relationship between

the supposed nature of women and the education they received in the early republic. See Kerber, *Women of the Republic*, pp. 189–231; Norton, *Liberty's Daughters*, pp. 256–94.

58. Mary Virginia Terhune [Marion Harland], *Eve's Daughters; or, Common Sense for Maid, Wife, and Mother* (New York: John R. Anderson and Henry S. Allen, 1882), p. 6; Sara Parton [Fanny Fern], "Gail Hamilton—Miss Dodge," in *Eminent Women of the Age* (S. M. Betts and Co., 1869), p. 219; idem, "To Gentlemen: A Call to Be a Husband," in *Fresh Leaves* (New York: Mason Bros., 1857), p. 305.

59. Maria McIntosh, *Woman in America*, pp. 23, 25.

60. Augusta Evans Wilson to Janie Tyler, 18 Jan. 1862, quoted in Fidler, *Wilson*, p. 66; Wilson, *Beulah* (New York: Derby and Jackson, 1859), pp. 256, 146, 198, 132.

61. Wilson, *Beulah*, pp. 141, 143, 273.

62. Ibid., pp. 353–54, 222, 355, 452, 397, 11, 508. As Anne Goodwyn Jones has noted, Wilson "found herself split between an inner vision and a desire to conform." See Jones's stimulating analysis of *Beulah*, in which she seeks to place the novel in a female Southern context while not denying the more general context of what I have termed literary domesticity, in *Tomorrrow Is Another Day: The Woman Writer in the South, 1859–1936* (Baton Rouge: Louisiana State University Press, 1981), pp. 51–91.

63. Mary Jane Holmes, *Meadow Brook* (New York: Mershon Co., n.d./1857), p. 42.

64. Augusta Evans Wilson, *St. Elmo* (New York: Carleton, 1866), pp. 90, 88.

65. Ibid., pp. 105, 193, 192.

66. Ibid., pp. 116, 87, 395, 394.

67. Harriet Beecher Stowe, *Oldtown Folks*, p. 408; idem, *The Pearl of Orr's Island* (Boston: Houghton Mifflin Co., 1896/1862), pp. 122–23.

68. Harriet Beecher Stowe to Georgiana May, undated, in Fields, *Life and Letters*, p. 86; Mary Virginia Terhune, homily dated 13 Oct. 1887, Simon Gratz Collection, HSP; Susan Warner [Elizabeth Wetherell], *Queechy*, 2 vols. (New York: George P. Putnam, 1852) 2:72–73; Terhune quoted in Sarah K. Bolton, *Successful Women* (Boston: D. Lothrop Co., 1888), p. 108.

CHAPTER 5. SECRET WRITERS

1. See Chapter Eight.

2. Mary Virginia Terhune [Marion Harland], *Marion Harland's Autobiography: The Story of a Long Life* (New York: Harper and Bros., 1910), p. 98.

3. Cotton Mather, *Manuductio ad Ministerium, or the Angels Preparing to Sound the Trumpets* (Boston: Hancock, 1726). I thank Annette Kolodny for calling the essay to my attention. The attitudes of New England Puritans toward imaginative literature, particularly poetry, have been analyzed by Perry Miller and Thomas R. Johnson. Their spirited defense of the Puritans' perspective on the arts notwithstanding, their commentary demonstrates that Mather was hardly alone in his concern about the pernicious effects of stimulating the imagination: see *The Puritans*, 2 vols. (New York: Harper Torchbooks, 1963/1938).

4. The Puritan perspective is presented in Perry Miller's two-volume study. See *The New England Mind: The Seventeenth Century*, vol. 1, pp. 239–79; *From Colony to Province*, vol. 2, pp. 417–36 (Boston: Beacon Press, 1961).

5. John Trumbull, "On Romances and Novels," in Alexander Cowie, "John Trumbull Glances at Fiction," *American Literature* 12 (March 1940): 72–73; Timothy Dwight, *Travels in New England and New York*, ed. Barbara Miller Solomon, 4 vols. (Cambridge: Harvard University Press, 1969/1821–22) 1:515, 518.

6. Samuel Miller, *Brief Retrospect of the Eighteenth Century*, 2 vols. (New York: T. and J. Swords, 1802) 2:155, 176–178. The striking popularity of Scottish Common Sense realists such as Thomas Reid and Dugald Stewart is documented in David Lundberg and Henry F. May, "The Enlightened Reader in America," *American Quarterly* 28 (Summer 1976): 262–89. The tenets of the philosophy and their impact are explored in Henry F. May, *The Enlightenment in America* (New York: Oxford University Press, 1976), esp. pp. 337–62. William Charvat was the first to emphasize that Scottish Common Sense philosophy was as influential as Puritanism in shaping the dominant American perspective on fiction. See *The Origins of American Critical Thought, 1810–1835* (Philadelphia: University of Pennsylvania Press, 1936), pp. 134–63. A thorough and persuasive analysis of the philosophy generally is found in Elizabeth Flower and Murray G. Murphey, *A History of Philosophy in America*, 2 vols. (New York: G. P. Putnam's Sons, 1977) 1:215–73.

7. "On Novels and Novel Reading," quoted in Charvat, *Origins*, pp. 138–39.

8. Miller, *Brief Retrospect* 2:174; Daniel Walker Howe notes Norton's perspective and quotes from his essays in *The Unitarian Conscience: Harvard Moral Philosophy, 1805–1861* (Cambridge: Harvard University Press, 1970), p. 181. For an excellent analysis of the Revolutionary generation's ambivalent perspective on the arts, see Joseph J. Ellis, *After the Revolution: Profiles in Early American Culture* (New York: W. W. Norton and Co., 1979). Ellis's portrait of Hugh Henry Brackenridge suggests the more specific ideological as well as social constraints on the development of an indigenous literature. See also Gordon S. Wood's insightful discussion of this subject in *The Rising Glory of America, 1760–1820* (New York: George Braziller, 1971), pp. 1–22. For a discussion of one such group's efforts to serve as a moral and literary elite, see Howe's study of the Unitarian moral philosophers at Harvard, esp. pp. 174–204. In his analysis of early nineteenth-century American literary criticism, Charvat investigates what he calls "a practically homogeneous upper class which felt itself competent to legislate, culturally, for other classes"; see his *Origins*, p. 1.

9. Mather, *Manuductio*; "On Novels and Novel Reading," quoted in Charvat, *Origins*, p. 139.

10. Noah Webster, "On the Education of Youth in America," in *A Collection of Essays and Fugitive Writings on Moral, Historical, Political and Literary Subjects* (Boston: L. Thomas and E. T. Andrews, 1790), p. 29. Excerpts from this essay are reprinted in Wood's *Rising Glory*, pp. 155–69. A recent study of Webster which highlights his metamorphosis from enthusiastic confidence about America's promise to a skeptical and highly contentious posture is Richard M. Rollins's *The Long Journey of Noah Webster* (Philadelphia: University of Pennsylvania Press, 1980). Ellis's chapter on Webster discusses the same change as a transition from exuberant

nationalism to disillusioned republicanism: see Ellis, *After the Revolution*, pp. 161–212.

11. Thomas Jefferson to Robert Skipwith, 3 Aug. 1771, in Julian P. Boyd, ed., *The Papers of Thomas Jefferson* (Princeton: Princeton University Press, 1950) 1:76–77. The letter and list of suggested volumes are reprinted in Wood's *Rising Glory*, pp. 170–74.

12. Thomas Jefferson to Nathaniel Burwell, 14 March 1818, printed in *Missouri Historical Society Collections* 4 (1923): 475–78. The intellectual and cultural milieu in which Jefferson's convictions found expression has been explored by Richard Beale Davis. In particular, Davis notes the dominant influence of Scottish Common Sense philosophy and its impact upon attitudes toward literature. See *Intellecutal Life in Jefferson's Virginia, 1790–1830* (Chapel Hill: University of North Carolina Press, 1964), esp. pp. 255–350.

13. Jefferson to Burwell, *Missouri Historical Society Collections* 4 (1923): 475–78. Concerns similar to those expressed by Webster and Jefferson are examined in Linda K. Kerber's commentary on women's reading in the early republic: see *Women of the Republic: Intellect and Ideology in Revolutionary America* (Chapel Hill: University of North Carolina Press, 1980), pp. 233–64.

14. *North American Magazine* 4 (May 1834): 358; Sara Parton [Fanny Fern], *Ruth Hall: A Domestic Tale of Our Time* (New York: Mason Bros., 1855), p. 31; Caroline Howard Gilman, *Love's Progress* (New York: Harper and Bros., 1840), p. 62. As late as 1942, literary critics René Wellek and Austin Warren pointed to the "lingering American popular view, disseminated by pedagogues, that the reading of nonfiction was instructive and meritorious, that of fiction harmful or at best self-indulgent": *Theory of Literature* (New York: Harcourt, Brace and World, 1956/1942), p. 201.

15. Mary Jane Holmes spoke to J. C. Derby of her youthful attachment to fiction. See Derby's *Fifty Years Among Authors, Books and Publishers* (New York: G. W. Carleton and Co., 1884), p. 571; Mary J. Holmes, *Meadow Brook* (New York: Mershon Co., n.d./1857), p. 136.

16. Biographical sketch of Harriet Beecher Stowe in n.a., *Eminent Women of the Age* (Hartford: S. M. Betts and Co., 1869), p. 301; Charles Beecher, ed., *Autobiography, Correspondence, Etc., of Lyman Beecher, D.D.*, 2 vols. (New York: Harper and Bros., 1864–65) 1:62, 526.

17. Beecher, *Autobiography* 1:526, 529.

18. Anna B. Warner, *Susan Warner* (New York: G. P. Putnam's Sons, 1909), pp. 90–91.

19. Ibid., p. 91; journal of Susan Warner, 19 July 1834, Susan Warner Papers, CIA.

20. Warner, *Susan Warner*, pp. 157–58; Warner journal, 21 Sept. 1839, CIA.

21. Mary Virginia Terhune to Dann Pratt, 21 Jan. 1889, Simon Gratz Collection, HSP; Terhune to Mr. Rideing, 7 Dec. 1889, Clifton Waller Barrett Library, Alderman-UVA.

22. Terhune, *Autobiography*, p. 98. Linda K. Kerber notes the same gingerly tasting of fiction on the part of late eighteeneth-century women. See *Women of the Republic*, pp. 233–64.

23. Derby, *Fifty Years*, p. 573; Mary Jane Holmes to J. C. Derby, undated, Clifton Waller Barrett Library, Alderman-UVA; Holmes, *Meadow Brook*, p. 4.

24. Holmes, *Meadow Brook*, p. 4.

25. Autobiographical sketch of Caroline Howard Gilman in John S. Hart, ed., *The Female Prose Writers of America* (Philadelphia: E. H. Butler and Co., 1852), pp. 51–52; autobiographical sketch of E.D.E.N. Southworth in Hart, *Female Prose Writers* (1855), p. 213; Harriet Beecher Stowe quoted in *Our Famous Women* (Hartford: A. D. Worthington, 1884), p. 588; Stowe to Charles Stowe, 1886, in Annie Fields, ed., *Life and Letters of Harriet Beecher Stowe* (Boston: Houghton Mifflin Co., 1897), pp. 43, 49.

26. Caroline Lee Hentz, *Ernest Linwood* (Boston: John P. Jewett, 1856), pp. 18, 36, 67.

27. Lyle H. Wright, *American Fiction, 1774–1850*, rev. ed. (San Marino, Calif.: Henry E. Huntington Library, 1948). The emergence of the *lady* as writer during the first quarter of the nineteenth century is commented upon in Janet Wilson James's "Changing Ideas about Women in the U.S., 1776–1825" (Ph.D. diss., Radcliffe College, 1954). Basing her commentary upon English as well as American writers, James notes that they generally published anonymously. Their eighteenth-century female predecessors in England, whether amateur or professional in their literary endeavors also published anonymously or adopted pseudonyms. Brief allusions to this phenomenon appear in Alison Adburgham, *Women in Print: Writing Women and Women's Magazines from the Restoration to the Accession of Victoria* (London: George Allen and Unwin, 1972) and J.M.S. Tompkins, *The Popular Novel in England, 1770–1800* (Westport, Conn.: Greenwood Press, 1976/1961).

28. Once the true identity was revealed of a longtime best-seller like Terhune, the continued use of a pseudonym was probably prompted in part by commercial motives. That is, it was the fiction of "Marion Harland" that sold, not that of Terhune. However, it no doubt was also due to reluctance or inability to discontinue a practice that had originally contributed to a sense of psychological security.

29. Harriet Beecher Stowe to Georgiana May, undated, in Fields, *Life and Letters*, p. 83. J. C. Derby claimed that Stowe published fifteen anonymous sketches in the *Ledger*. See *Fifty Years*, p. 203. Many English contemporaries of the literary domestics chose a similar path, either publishing anonymously or adopting pseudonyms. Generally, however, the pseudonyms were male and the reasons for their adoption apparently different. According to Elaine Showalter, novelists such as George Eliot cloaked their identity in order to have the issue of gender removed and their fiction judged on its merits alone. Concerned too that their novels would be considered autobiographical, they turned to the pseudonym to avoid having their private lives linked to their public prose. See Showalter's "Women Writers and the Double Standard," in Vivian Gornick and Barbara K. Moran, eds., *Woman in Sexist Society: Studies in Power and Powerlessness* (New York: New American Library, 1971), pp. 452–79, and idem, *A Literature of Their Own: British Women Novelists From Brontë to Lessing* (Princeton: Princeton University Press, 1977), esp. pp. 57–60. Sandra M. Gilbert and Susan Gubar also comment briefly upon British female strategies behind the adoption of a pseudonym, in their *The Madwoman in the Attic: The Woman Writer and the Nineteenth-Century Literary Imagination* (New Haven: Yale University Press, 1979).

30. Warner journal, 21, 23 April 1832, 8, 9 July 1834, CIA; Warner, *Susan Warner*, p. 119. References to Warner telling stories are sprinkled throughout her journals, but the "novels" to which her sister refers are not deposited with the Susan Warner Papers. Gordon Wood explores the reasons that many leaders of the Revolutionary generation chose to publish anonymously in "The Democratization of Mind in the American Revolution," in *Leadership in the American Revolution*, Papers presented at the Third Symposium, 9–10 May 1974 (Washington: Library of Congress, 1974).

31. Warner journal, 28 Oct. 1839, CIA; Warner to "My Dear Sir," 1 April 1851, Simon Gratz Collection, HSP.

32. Clippings of the notices cited are deposited with the Cummins Family Papers, EI.

33. Asahel Huntington to Maria Cummins, 6 March, 23 March 1854; John P. Jewett to Cummins, 13 Dec. 1854, ibid.

34. Henry Dwight Sedgwick to William Minot, [22 April 1822], Sedgwick Family Papers, Sedgwick IV, MHS.

35. Catharine Maria Sedgwick to Henry Dwight Sedgwick, [29 March 1822], Sedgwick Family Papers, Sedgwick II; Sedgwick to Susan Higginson Channing, 1822, in Mary E. Dewey, ed., *Life and Letters of Catharine M. Sedgwick* (New York: Harper and Bros., 1872), pp. 153–54; Sedgwick to Charles Sedgwick, 4 Jan. 1827, Catharine Maria Sedgwick Papers; Sedgwick to Henry Dwight Sedgwick, 24 August [1825], Frances James Child Papers, MHS.

36. Terhune, *Autobiography*, pp. 238–39, 242–43, 246.

37. Ibid., pp. 264, 88, 138; Terhune, *Loitering in Pleasant Paths* (New York: Charles Scribner's Sons, 1880), p. 132.

38. Terhune, *Autobiography*, pp. 240, 247; Terhune to Virginia Eppes Dance, 15 Oct. 1849, Perkins-Duke.

39. Terhune, *Autobiography*, pp. 240–41.

40. Mary Virginia Terhune to W. E. Mitchell, 22 July 1893. Clifton Waller Barrett Library, Alterman-UVA.

41. Mary Virginia Terhune to Kate Sanborn, undated, in *Our Famous Women*, p. 632.

42. Ibid., pp. v–vi.

43. Julia Deane Freeman [Mary Forrest], *Women of the South Distinguished in Literature* (New York: Charles B. Richardson, 1865), p. vi; John S. Hart, ed., *The Female Prose Writers of America* (Philadelphia: E. H. Butler and Co., 1852), pp. vii–viii.

44. Hart, *Female Prose Writers*, pp. 49–50, 56–57.

45. Ibid., p. 387; Susan Warner to John S. Hart, 17 March 1851, Maurice Family Papers, Southern Historical Collection–UNC; Warner journal, 22 Feb., 11 Jan. 1851, CIA; Warner, *Susan Warner*, p. 321.

46. Warner to Hart, 11 March 1851, Southern Historical Collection–UNC; Hart, *Female Prose Writers* (1855), p. 423; Warner [Elizabeth Wetherell], *Queechy*, 2 vols. (New York: George P. Putnam, 1852) 1:382–83.

47. Ellen Eldredge Parton to ? , 28 Feb. 1899, Sara Parton Papers, Sophia Smith Collection, Smith.

48. Hart, *Female Prose Writers* (1855), p. 470.

49. Elizabeth Bancroft Schlesinger, "Fanny Fern: Our Grandmothers' Mentor," *New York Historical Society Quarterly* 38 (October 1954):505; Sara Parton to Editor, 31 Jan. 1855, Clifton Waller Barrett Library, Alderman-UVA.

50. Biographical sketch of Mary Abigail Dodge in *Eminent Women of the Age*, pp. 204, 202; biographical sketch of Sara Parton in *Eminent Women*, pp. 84, 82; Sara Jane Lippincott to James Parton, 23 March 1868, James Parton Papers, Houghton-Harvard.

CHAPTER 6. NO HAPPY WOMAN WRITES

1. Sara Parton [Fanny Fern], *Ruth Hall: A Domestic Tale of the Present Time* (New York: Mason Bros., 1855), p. 333.

2. Ibid., pp. 332–33.

3. Ibid., p. 333.

4. Calvin Stowe to Harriet Beecher Stowe, 11 July 1853, Stowe-Day; Harriet Beecher Stowe to a sister, [1838], Beecher Family Papers, Sterling-Yale.

5. Drawing upon the personal papers of 450 eighteenth-century families, Mary Beth Norton has presented a detailed and cogent analysis demonstrating that the domestic realm circumscribed women's identity and status in all respects, including the economic. Although more descriptive then analytical, Julia Spruill's earlier examination of colonial women in the South corresponds to Norton's. Lyle Koehler's and Laurel Thatcher Ulrich's more recent studies complement Spruill's findings, extending them to women in colonial New England. Although their analyses diverge sharply in other respects, both Koehler and Ulrich agree that women were enveloped by the world of domesticity. See Norton, *Liberty's Daughters: The Revolutionary Experience of American Women* (Boston: Little, Brown and Co., 1980), esp. pp. 3–151; Spruill, *Women's Life and Work in the Southern Colonies* (New York: Russell and Russell, 1969/1938); Koehler, *A Search for Power: The "Weaker Sex" in Seventeenth-Century New England* (Urbana: University of Illinois Press, 1980); Ulrich, *Good Wives: Image and Reality in the Lives of Women in Northern New England, 1650–1750* (New York: Alfred A. Knopf, 1982). The traditional linkage between women's work and the home is explored in Carl N. Degler, *At Odds: Women and the Family in America from the Revolution to the Present* (New York: Oxford University Press, 1980), pp. 362–94.

6. Mary Beth Norton was the first to challenge premises concerning female economic status in colonial and revolutionary America. Her persuasive refutation was outlined in the aptly titled "Myth of the Golden Age" and further developed in *Liberty's Daughters*. See Carol Ruth Berkin and Norton, *Women of America: A History* (Boston: Houghton Mifflin Co., 1979), pp. 37–46. Although Joan Hoff Wilson has argued that women occupied a socioeconomic position of unprecedented importance during the colonial period, she attributes that position to their numerical scarcity and a critical labor shortage, and contends that it did not indicate any diminution of sexist attitudes or any change in sex-role economic stereotyping. See "The Illusion of Change: Women and the Revolution," in Alfred Young, ed., *The American Revolution: Explorations in the History of American Radicalism* (DeKalb: Northern Illinois University Press, 1976), esp. pp. 393–400.

7. Two recent studies are especially helpful in their analysis of women's education in nineteenth-century America. See Kathryn Kish Sklar, *Catharine*

Beecher: A Study in American Domesticity (New York: W. W. Norton, 1976/1973), and Anne Firor Scott, "That Ever Widening Circle: The Diffusion of Feminist Values from the Troy Female Seminary, 1822–1872," *History of Education Quarterly* 19 (1979): 3–27. Women's entrance into the classroom as students as well as teachers is examined in Maris Vinovski and Richard Bernard, "Beyond Catharine Beecher: Female Education in the Antebellum Period," *Signs: Journal of Women in Culture and Society* 3 (Summer 1978):856–69, and idem, "The Female School-teacher in Antebellum Massachusetts," *Journal of Social History* 10 (March 1977): 332–45.

8. Significant scholarship on the subject of women, work, and industrialization has only begun to appear. One of the most insightful analyses is found in Judith A. McGaw, "Women's Work in the American Past: Historians' Insights and Oversights," in Valerie Gill Couch, ed., *Women and the Workplace: Conference Proceedings* (Norman: University of Oklahoma Press, 1979), pp. 39–51. See also McGaw's recent survey of scholarship on the relationship between women and technology in *Signs: Journal of Women in Culture and Society* 7 (Summer 1982): 798–828. Also pertinent is Joan Wallach Scott's excellent article, "The Mechanization of Women's Work," *Scientific American*, Sept. 1982, pp. 167–87.

9. See David M. Katzman, *Seven Days a Week: Women and Domestic Service in Industrializing America* (New York: Oxford Univesity Press, 1978), as well as Scott's "Mechanization of Women's Work."

10. See Judith McGaw's "Technological Change and Women's Work: Mechanization in the Berkshire Paper Industry, 1820–1855," in Martha Moore Trescott, ed., *Dynamos and Virgins Revisited: Women and Technological Change in History* (Metuchen, N.J.: Scarecrow Press, 1979), pp. 77–99. See also McGaw's "Women and the History of American Technology" and Scott's "Mechanization of Women's Work."

11. Sara Parton [Fanny Fern], "Facts for Unjust Critics," in *Fresh Leaves* (New York: Mason Bros., 1857), p. 300.

12. E.D.E.N. Southworth to Robert Bonner, Dec. 1875, E.D.E.N. Southworth Papers, Perkins-Duke.

13. Maria McIntosh, *Woman in America: Her Work and Her Reward* (New York: D. Appleton and Co., 1850), pp. 22–24.

14. Maria McIntosh to Maria Cummins, 1 Oct. 1857, Clifton Waller Barrett Library, Alderman-UVA.

15. Catharine Maria Sedgwick to Kate Sedgwick Minot, 13 July 1851, Catharine Maria Sedgwick Papers, MHS.

16. Susan to Anna Warner, undated, in Anna B. Warner, *Susan Warner* (New York: George P. Putnam's Sons, 1909), pp. 305, 313.

17. Warner journal, 15, 26 Nov., 2 Dec. 1839, Susan Warner Papers, CIA; Warner, *Susan Warner*, pp. 178, 217.

18. Warner, *Susan Warner*, pp. 261, 263.

19. Susan Warner [Elizabeth Wetherell], *Queechy*, 2 vols. (New York: G. P. Putnam, 1852) 1:382–83; Warner journal, 30 Sept., 2 Nov. 1839, CIA.

20. Warner, *Susan Warner*, pp. 277, 279, 283.

21. Warner journal, [October] 1850, 2, 5 Nov. 1850, CIA.

22. Ibid., 6 Jan. 1851, 22, 25, 30 Nov. 1850.

23. George P. Putnam to Susan Warner, 3 April 1851, in Warner, *Susan Warner*, p. 346.

24. Warner, *Susan Warner*, pp. 351, 376, 403–4, 407, 438; Susan Warner to James T. Fields, 22 Dec. 1857, Houghton-Harvard.

25. James Parton, *Fanny Fern: A Memorial Volume* (New York: G. W. Carleton and Co., 1873), p. 43; Sara Parton [Fanny Fern], "Literary Aspirants," in *Ginger-Snaps* (New York: Carleton, 1870), p. 30.

26. James Parton, *Fanny Fern*, p. 50; Ethel Parton, "Fanny Fern: An Informal Biography," Sara Parton Papers, Sophia Smith Collection, Smith; Sara Parton, *Ruth Hall*, p. 220.

27. James Parton, *Fanny Fern*, p. 43; Parton, *Ruth Hall*, p. 39. What *Ruth Hall* omits of that part of Parton's life, *Rose Clark* provides. See Chapter Ten.

28. For a glimpse of Parton's relationship with her brother, see Chapter Eight.

29. Parton, *Ruth Hall*, p. 30.

30. Ibid., p. 115, 126, 136. Information concerning Hezekiah and Mary Eldredge is found in the Sara Parton Papers, Sophia Smith Collection, Smith.

31. Parton, *Ruth Hall*, pp. 155, 193, 252, 233, 240, 252–54; James Parton, *Fanny Fern*, pp. 50–52; J. C. Derby, *Fifty Years Among Authors, Books and Publishers* (New York: G. W. Carleton and Co., 1884), p. 209; Ethel Parton, "Fanny Fern," Sara Parton Papers, Sophia Smith Collection, Smith.

32. Parton, *Ruth Hall*, pp. 232, 240–41, 250.

33. Ibid., pp. 254–55.

34. Ibid., p. 268.

35. Ibid., 272, 276, 279, 280–81. (It is remarkable how much this fictional exchange between editor and writer parallels and foreshadows the real-life exchange between Robert Bonner and E.D.E.N. Southworth. See Chapter One.)

36. Ibid., pp. 298–99, 293, 310–11.

37. James Parton, *Fanny Fern*, pp. 50–54; Derby, *Fifty Years*, pp. 208–20.

38. Parton, *Ruth Hall*, p. 343; Sara Parton to Harriet Beecher Stowe, 14 Feb. 1868, Beecher-Stowe Collection, Schlesinger-Radcliffe; Sara Parton to "Dear Sir," undated, William Conant Church Papers, NYPL-Manuscripts.

39. The marriage certificate and agreement signed by Sara and James Parton are deposited with the James Parton Papers, Houghton-Harvard; Sara Parton's will is in the Sara Parton Papers, Sophia Smith Collection, Smith.

40. Parton, "My Old Ink-Stand and I; or, The First Article in the New House" in *Fresh Leaves*, pp. 103–5. See also "Literary Aspirants" in *Ginger-Snaps*, on Parton's pride regarding her economic accomplishments.

41. Parton, "Charlotte Brontë," in *Fresh Leaves*, p. 334; autobiographical sketch by E.D.E.N. Southworth in John S. Hart, *The Female Prose Writers of America* (Philadelphia: E. H. Butler and Co., 1855), p. 213; Southworth to her daughter Lottie, 22 June 1895, E.D.E.N. Southworth Papers, LOC.

42. Hart, *Female Prose Writers* (1855), p. 213; Southworth to daughter Lottie, 2 May 1894, 7 May 1894, 22 June 1895, Southworth Papers, LOC.

43. Hart, *Female Prose Writers* (1855), p. 214.

44. Autobiographical sketch written by Southworth at the request of S. T. Pickard, dated 17 June 1893, Houghton-Harvard; Southworth to daughter Lottie, 3 June 1894, Southworth Papers, LOC.

45. Hart, *Female Prose Writers*, pp. 214–15; *Saturday Evening Post*, 3 Nov. 1855; *Washington Post*, 2 Dec. 1894; E.D.E.N. Southworth, *The Curse of Clifton* (Philadelphia: T. B. Peterson, 1867/1853), pp. 276–77.

46. Hart, *Female Prose Writers*, p. 215; Southworth to daughter Lottie, 3 June 1894, Southworth Papers, LOC.

47. Southworth to Robert Bonner, 26 Dec. 1869, E.D.E.N. Southworth Papers, Perkins-Duke.

48. Southworth to Bonner, undated, ibid.

49. Southworth to Bonner, [June 1867], 25 Sept. 1867, 25 Dec. 1868, 29 March 1887, ibid.

50. Southworth to Abraham Hart, 15 Dec. 1852, BPL; Southworth to Robert Bonner [26 Dec. 1873], Southworth Papers, Perkins-Duke.

51. Southworth to Bonner, Oct. 1876, 18 May 1883, Southworth Papers, Perkins-Duke; Southworth to Bonner, 6 June 1887, reprinted in Donald Gallup, "More Letters of American Writers," *Yale University Library Gazette* 37 (July 1962): 32.

52. Southworth to Bonner, [29 Nov. 1875], Southworth Papers, Perkins-Duke; Southworth to Bonner, 13 Dec. 1881, in Gallup, "Letters," p. 30; *Washington Post*, 2 Dec. 1894.

CHAPTER 7. BUYING MY TIME

1. Caroline Lee Hentz to Abraham Hart, 13 Nov. 1851, Simon Gratz Collection, HSP; Harriet Beecher Stowe to Gamaliel Bailey, 18 April [1852], Houghton-Harvard.

2. Hentz is characterized as a "rolling stone" by his son in the "Autobiography of Charles A. Hentz," p. 10, Hentz Family Papers, Southern Historical Collection–UNC.

3. Diary of Caroline Lee Hentz, entry dated 11 Feb. 1836, Hentz Family Papers, Southern Historical Collection–UNC.

4. Caroline Lee Hentz diary, entry dated 30 May 1836; Hentz to Mrs. Stafford, 7 Jan. 1846; ibid.

5. Diary of Charles A. Hentz, entries dated 29 July, 26 Aug., 7 Sept. 1846; Charles A. Hentz autobiography, p. 56, ibid.

6. Edward Burgess, ed., *The Spiders of the United States: A Collection of the Arachnological Writings of Nicholas Marcellus Hentz* (Boston: Boston Society of Natural History, 1875), p. xi; Charles A. Hentz autobiography, p. 90; Charles A. Hentz diary, entries dated 29 Nov., 28 Dec. 1849, 7 Sept. 1850, Hentz Family Papers, Southern Historical Collection–UNC.

7. Caroline Lee Hentz to Abraham Hart, 7 March [1851], Simon Gratz Collection, HSP.

8. Caroline Lee Hentz to Abraham Hart, 13 Nov. 1851, ibid., Hentz to Hart, 30 Nov. 1851, BPL.

9. Charles A. Hentz autobiography, p. 133, Hentz Family Papers, Southern Historical Collection–UNC.

10. Caroline Lee Hentz to Abraham Hart, 18 Nov. 1852, Overbury Collection,

Barnard; M. H. Olmstead, "Personal Recollections of Mrs. Caroline Lee Hentz," *Beadle's Monthly*, June 1866, p. 521.

11. Caroline Lee Hentz to Abraham Hart, 14 Dec. 1852, Huntington; Hentz to Hart, 13 Feb. 1854, [1854], BPL.

12. Harriet Beecher Stowe to Eliza Cabot Follen, 16 Feb. 1853, Follen Miscellany, MHS.

13. Stowe to Sara Parton, 15 Feb. [1860s], Sara Parton Papers, Sophia Smith Collection, Smith; Stowe to Eliza Cabot Follen, 16 Feb. 1853, Follen Miscellany, MHS; Stowe to Carey and Hart, 1 Jan. 1840, Simon Gratz Collection, HSP.

14. Harriet Beecher Stowe to Calvin Stowe, 31 Aug.–3 Sept. 1844, Beecher-Stowe Collection, Schlesinger-Radcliffe; Harriet to Calvin, [Jan. or Feb. 1851], Calvin to Harriet, 22 July 1853, Stowe-Day.

15. Stowe to Calvin Stowe, 6 Nov. 1850, Stowe to Stowe, 21 Jan. [1851], Stowe-Day; Stowe to Stowe, 4 April [1860], Stowe to Hattie and Eliza Stowe, 5 Oct. 1863, Beecher-Stowe Collection, Schlesinger-Radcliffe.

16. Stowe to James T. Fields, undated, James T. Fields Papers, Huntington; Stowe to [Ticknor and Fields], 8 Sept. 1865, Berg-NYPL; Stowe to James R. Osgood, 16 Aug. [1865], Houghton-Harvard.

17. Stowe to Hattie and Eliza Stowe, 1 Aug. 1869, Beecher-Stowe Collection, Schlesinger-Radcliffe; Stowe to James T. Fields, undated, Stowe to James R. Osgood, [1869], James T. Fields Papers, Huntington; Stowe to Edward Everett Hale, 14 April 1869, Stowe-Day; Stowe to Calvin Stowe, 2 Sept. [1879], Beecher-Stowe Collection, Schlesinger-Radcliffe.

18. Stowe to Charley and Susy Stowe, 10 Sept. 1879, 8 March 1882, Beecher-Stowe Collection, Schlesinger-Radcliffe.

19. Stowe to "Mr. Houghton," 7 Oct. 1885, Houghton Mifflin Papers, Houghton-Harvard.

20. *Mobile* (Ala.) *Register*, 10 May 1909.

21. Augusta Evans Wilson to Mrs. J. H. Chrisman, 3 Feb. 1866, DAC.

22. Augusta Evans Wilson, *Beulah* (New York: Derby and Jackson, 1859), pp. 294–95.

23. Mary Virginia Terhune to Mr. Rideing, 7 Dec. 1889, Clifton Waller Barrett Library, Alderman-UVA.

24. Mary Virginia Terhune, *Marion Harland's Autobiography: The Story of a Long Life* (New York: Harper and Bros., 1910), pp. 363–64.

25. Terhune to Albert Bigelow Paine, 21 July, 24 July, 5 Aug. 1897, Huntington.

26. Terhune to Albert Bigelow Paine, 20 Nov. 1897, 15 Dec. 1901, ibid.

27. Samuel Gilman to Louisa Gilman Loring, undated, Samuel Gilman Papers, South Caroliniana–USC.

28. Caroline Howard Gilman to Harriet Fay, 30 Aug. [1845], Gilman Family Papers, AAS.

29. Sedgwick to Kate Sedgwick Minot, 14 Dec. 1830; Sedgwick to Charles Sedgwick, 4 Feb., 22 July 1836, Catharine Maria Sedgwick Papers, MHS; Sedgwick to Carey and Hart, 6 March 1836, Simon Gratz Collection, HSP.

30. Sedgwick to Mr. Harper, 13 May 1857, NYPL-Manuscripts; Sedgwick to

Mr. Harper, 24 March 1858, Harper Collection, Morgan.

31. Journal of C. M. Sedgwick, 18 May 1828, 16 July 1849, Catharine Maria Sedgwick Papers, MHS.

CHAPTER 8. A MAN'S CLOTHING

1. Caroline Howard Gilman to one of her daughters, 2 May 1874, in Mary Scott Saint-Amand, *A Balcony in Charleston* (Richmond: Garrett and Massie, 1941), p. 151; autobiographical sketch by Gilman in John S. Hart, ed., *The Female Prose Writers of America* (Philadelphia: E. H. Butler and Co., 1852), p. 55.

2. The successive definitions of culture cited in this paragraph derive from Raymond Williams's *Keywords: A Vocabulary of Culture and Society* (New York: Oxford University Press, 1976), pp. 76–82, and the *Oxford English Dictionary*. "Culture," of course, has myriad meanings and debate continues among scholars concerning interpretation and usage. The meaning employed here is the one currently agreed upon by many historians. It has been stated most succinctly by Daniel Walker Howe, who defines culture as "an evolving system of beliefs, attitudes, and techniques, transmitted from generation to generation, and finding expression in innumerable activities people learn." This definition draws upon those developed in anthropology; most influential in this regard has been the scholarship of Clifford Geertz. Beginning with the premise that the human being is "an animal suspended in webs of significance he himself has spun," Geertz defines "culture to be those webs, and the analysis of it to be therefore not an experimental science in search of law but an interpretative one in search of meaning." What is suggested is that the spinning of "webs of significance" involves both a conscious and an unconscious response to one's experience and environment. Geertz's exposition is particularly illustrative, for two reasons. The first is ironic and, even today, not uncommon. Inadvertently, he has highlighted the connection between *man* and culture, to the exclusion of woman. The designation I have chosen, "creator of culture," is not one which the literary domestics or their contemporaries, male or female, would have recognized. But there is no question that the society of the literary domestics would have shared the notion implicit in Geertz's definition, namely that men, and not women, are the creators of culture, that is, are recognized as the legitimate creators of consciously articulated "webs of significance." Secondly, Geertz's exposition is illustrative in its identification of ideology as a cultural system. Arguing that ideology is rooted in the chronic malintegration of society, he defines it as a " 'symbolic outlet' for emotional disturbances generated by social disequilibrium." The application to the literary domestics is illuminating. Their fiction, their letters, diaries, and journals, the whole cultural system they created was their response to a society characterized not by equilibrium but by asymmetrical divisions based on gender. See Howe, "American Victorianism as a Culture," *American Quarterly* 27 (December 1975): 507–32; Geertz, *The Interpretation of Cultures: Selected Essays* (New York: Basic Books, 1973).

3. Caroline Howard to Louisa Gilman, 5 Feb. 1813, Gilman Family Papers, AAS; Catharine Maria Sedgwick to Pamela Sedgwick, 6 Oct. 1803, Sedgwick Family Papers, Sedgwick IV, MHS; Virginia Woolf, *A Room of One's Own* (London: Granada Publishing, 1979/1929), pp. 72–73.

4. Caroline Howard Gilman to Mrs. Slade, 22 March 1878, South Caroliniana-USC; *Southern Rose-Bud*, 6 Sept. 1834. Maria Jane Jewsbury, Mrs. William Fletcher, contributed verse, stories, and miscellaneous essays to English annuals, especially in the 1820s. After Jewsbury's mother died in 1819 and she was left responsible for the household and the care of her siblings, Jewsbury found her time severely limited, as she later wrote a friend, and her life "became so painfully, laboriously domestic that it was an absolute duty to crush intellectual tastes." Obviously, however, Jewsbury did continue to write. She married Fletcher in 1830, three years before her death. See *Maria Jane Jewsbury: Occasional Papers, Selected with a Memoir* (London: Oxford University Press, 1932).

5. Susan Warner to John S. Hart, 17 March 1851, Maurice Family Papers, Southern Historical Collection–UNC.

6. Henry Wadsworth Longfellow to Mary Virginia Terhune, undated, in Terhune [Marion Harland], *Marion Harland's Autobiography: The Story of a Long Life* (New York: Harper and Bros., 1910), pp. 263–64.

7. Augusta Evans Wilson, *Beulah* (New York: Derby and Jackson, 1859), p. 293; J. C. Derby, *Fifty Years Among Authors, Books and Publishers* (New York: G. W. Carleton and Co., 1884), p. 394.

8. Harriet Beecher Stowe to Calvin Stowe, undated, in Annie Fields, *Life and Letters of Harriet Beecher Stowe* (Boston: Houghton Mifflin Co., 1897), p. 94; Stowe, *The Minister's Wooing* (Boston: Houghton Mifflin Co., 1896/1859), p. 346.

9. Stowe to Sarah Josepha Hale, 10 Nov. [1850], Huntington.

10. Sarah Josepha Hale, *Woman's Record; or, Sketches of All Distinguished Women From "The Beginning" until A.D. 1850* (New York: Harper and Bros., 1853), p. vii.

11. Mary Virginia Terhune to Virginia Eppes Dance, 9 Oct. 1848, Mary Virginia Terhune Papers, Perkins-Duke.

12. Terhune to Dance, 7 Nov. 1851, ibid.

13. Terhune to Dance, 15 Oct. 1849, ibid.; Terhune to Kate Sanborn, 3 March 1883, in *Our Famous Women* (Hartford: A. D. Worthington, 1886), p. 634; Terhune, *Autobiography*, p. 242.

14. Caroline Lee Hentz, "The Sex of the Soul," in *The Banished Son, and Other Stories of the Heart* (Philadelphia: T. B. Peterson, 1856), pp. 266–68.

15. Ibid., p. 269.

16. Sara Parton [Fanny Fern], *Fern Leaves from Fanny's Portfolio, First Series* (Auburn, N.Y.: Miller, Orton and Mulligan, 1854), p. 100. The same defensiveness can be seen among the original bluestockings a century earlier. Elizabeth Carter, the most highly educated of these late-eighteenth-century British women, was defended by her friend Dr. Johnson. Carter's domestic skills, he insisted, equaled her intellectual accomplishments: "My old friend, Mrs. Carter, could make a pudding as well as translate Epictetus from the Greek and work a handkerchief as well as compose a poem." Johnson is quoted in Alison Adburgham, *Women in Print: Writing Women and Women's Magazines from the Restoration to the Accession of Victoria* (London: George Allen and Unwin, 1972), pp. 134–35.

17. Augusta Evans Wilson, *St. Elmo* (New York: Carleton, 1866), pp. 85–86.

18. Ibid., pp. 86–87, 235. In Wilson's novel *At the Mercy of Tiberius*, a minor female character, aptly named Leo Gordon, is told by her aunt, " 'A woman

bedecked with rags and tags of far-fetched learning is about as attractive an object as if she had turned out a full beard and mustache. I am very sure you have heard me assert more than once, that I verily believe Venus herself would scare all the men into monasteries, if she wore blue stockings.' " In her last novel, *Devota*, published in 1907, Devota Lindsay, highly educated and erudite in the typical Wilson mold, declines a request made by the president of a female college to endow a chair of philology and etymology. Offering instead to endow a chair of "Household Economics, Sanitation and Decoration," Devota says, " 'If the stockings are blue, the petticoats must be long.' " This statement has been attributed to Francis Jeffrey, an editor of the *Edinburgh Review*. See *Notes and Queries 1*, ser. 11 (30 April 1910): 357; *At the Mercy of Tiberius* (New York: G.W. Dillingham, 1887), p. 227; *Devota* (New York: G.W. Dillingham, 1913/1907), pp. 42–43.

19. Wilson, *St. Elmo*, pp. 167, 234, 292, 235.

20. Ibid., pp. 437–38.

21. Ibid., p. 421.

22. Ibid., p. 428.

23. Mary Virginia Terhune [Marion Harland], *Phemie's Temptation* (New York: Carleton, 1869), pp. 19, 43.

24. Ibid., pp. 61–62, 150, 152–53.

25. Ibid., p. 215.

26. Ibid., pp. 180–81, 183.

27. Ibid., pp. 184–85.

28. Ibid., pp. 310, 186, 202, 197, 200–201.

29. Ibid., pp. 230, 249, 254.

30. Ibid., pp. 272–74, 277.

31. Ibid., pp. 302, 300, 308.

32. Ibid., pp. 221–22, 310.

33. Nathaniel Parker Willis to Sara Parton, undated, Sara Parton Papers, Sophia Smith Collection, Smith. See also Henry A. Beers, *Nathaniel Parker Willis* (Boston: Houghton Mifflin Co., 1885).

34. Sara Parton [Fanny Fern], *Ruth Hall: A Domestic Tale of the Present Time* (New York: Mason Bros., 1855), pp. 220–22.

35. Ibid., pp. 26, 156; biographical sketch of Willis, *Oxford Companion to American Literature*; undated newspaper clipping signed "Boston Correspondent, Cleveland Herald," James Parton Papers, Houghton-Harvard.

36. Calvin Stowe to Harriet Beecher Stowe, 30 April 1842, Stowe-Day; Caroline Lee Hentz to Mrs. Stafford, 5 March 1851, Southern Historical Collection–UNC.

37. Terhune, *Autobiography*, pp. 251–53.

38. See Chapter Nine.

39. Theodore Sedgwick to C. M. Sedgwick, 24 Dec. 1799, Sedgwick Family Papers, Sedgwick IV, MHS.

40. Henry Dwight Sedgwick to C.M. Sedgwick, 22 June 1812, ibid.

41. C. M. Sedgwick to a friend, Feb. 1821, in Mary E. Dewey, ed., *Life and Letters of Catharine M. Sedgwick* (New York: Harper and Bros., 1872), p. 150; Sedgwick to Theodore Sedgwick, [29 March 1822], Sedgwick II, MHS.

42. Henry Dwight Sedgwick to William Minot, 22 April, 6 May, Spring 1822,

Sedgwick IV, MHS; Theodore Sedgwick to C. M. Sedgwick, 6 May 1822, in Dewey, *Life and Letters*, p. 152.

43. C. M. Sedgwick to Susan Higginson Channing, 1822, in Dewey, *Life and Letters*, p. 154; Sedgwick to Channing, 15 June 1822, C. M. Sedgwick Papers; Henry Dwight Sedgwick to Sedgwick, 25 May 1822, Sedgwick Family Papers, Sedgwick IV, MHS.

44. Henry Dwight Sedgwick to William Minot, [28 Sept. 1822], Sedgwick IV; C. M. Sedgwick to Theodore Sedgwick, 2 June [1824], Sedgwick II, MHS.

45. Robert Sedgwick to C. M. Sedgwick, 17 July 1824, Henry Dwight Sedgwick to William Minot, 29 July 1824, Sedgwick IV, ibid.

46. C. M. Sedgwick to Henry Dwight Sedgwick, 1 June [1825], Frances James Child Papers, MHS.

47. C. M. Sedgwick to Charles Sedgwick, 4 Jan. 1827; journal of C.M. Sedgwick, July 1827, Catharine Maria Sedgwick Papers, MHS.

48. C. M. Sedgwick to "Dear Sir," 6 Nov. 1827, ibid.

49. Charles Sedgwick to C. M. Sedgwick, 1 June 1827, Sedgwick IV; Sedgwick journal, 31 Dec. 1828, Catharine Maria Sedgwick Papers, MHS.

50. C. M. Sedgwick to Mr. Wheaton, 15 March 1829, Morgan; Sedgwick to Charles Sedgwick, 7 March 1830; Sedgwick to Susan Higginson Channing, 14 March, 23 June 1830, Catharine Maria Sedgwick Papers, MHS.

51. Sedgwick journal, 14 May 1830, C. M. Sedgwick Papers, MHS; Sedgwick to Lydia Maria Child, 12 June 1820, BPL; Charles Sedgwick to Sedgwick, 21 June 1830, Sedgwick Family Papers, Sedgwick IV, MHS.

52. Sedgwick journal, 22 Dec. 1831, 23 Dec. 1832, Catharine Maria Sedgwick Papers; Sedgwick to Louisa Minot, Sedgwick IV, MHS.

53. C. M. Sedgwick to Louisa Minot, 26 Feb. 1835, Sedgwick IV; Sedgwick to Kate Sedgwick, 18 March 1835, Catharine Maria Sedgwick Papers, MHS.

54. C. M. Sedgwick to Louisa Minot, 14 Feb. 1857, Sedgwick IV; Sedgwick to Kate Sedgwick Minot, 12 April 1857, Catharine Maria Sedgwick Papers, MHS.

55. C. M. Sedgwick to William Minot, Jr., 20 July 1857; Sedgwick to Kate Sedgwick Minot, 20 July 1857, Catharine Maria Sedgwick Papers, MHS.

56. Mary Jane Holmes, *Meadow Brook* (New York: Mershon, n.d./1857), pp. 86–87.

57. Ibid., pp. 140–41.

58. Ibid., pp. 194, 37–38.

59. Ibid., p. 233.

60. Ibid., pp. 4, 278. The italics are Holmes's.

61. Ibid., pp. 288–91.

62. Mary Virginia Terhune to W. E. Mitchell, 22 July 1893, Clifton Waller Barrett Library, Alderman-UVA; autobiographical sketch by E.D.E.N. Southworth in *The Haunted Homestead* (Philadelphia: T. B. Peterson, 1860), p. 37; Augusta Evans Wilson to T. E. Cooke, 30 Oct. 1866, Augusta Evans Wilson Papers, LOC; Mary Virginia Terhune quoted in *Our Famous Women* (Hartford: A. D. Worthington and Co., 1866), p. 636; Caroline Howard Gilman to Harriet Fay, 13 April 1838, in Saint-Armand, *Balcony in Charleston*; Sara Parton [Fanny Fern], *Ruth Hall*, p. iii; James Parton, *Fanny Fern: A Memorial Volume* (New York: Carleton and Co., 1873), p. 76.

63. Mary Jane Holmes to J. C. Derby, undated, Clifton Waller Barrett Library, Alderman-UVA; Mary Virginia Terhune quoted in *Our Famous Women*, p. 636; interview with E.D.E.N. Southworth, *Washington Post*, 2 Dec. 1894; autobiographical sketch by Caroline Howard Gilman in John S. Hart, ed., *The Female Prose Writers of America* (Philadelphia: E. H. Butler and Co., 1852), p. 56; Journal of Susan Warner, 21 Sept. 1839, CIA.

64. Catharine Maria Sedgwick to Charles Sedgwick, 7 March 1830, C. M. Sedgwick Papers, MHS; Sedgwick, *Redwood*, 2 vols. (New York: E. Bliss and E. White, 1824), p. x; Sedgwick to Henry Dwight Sedgwick, 1 June [1825], Francis James Child Papers, MHS; Caroline Howard Gilman, *Recollections of a Southern Matron* (Philadelphia: John E. Potter and Co., 1867/1838), p. iii.

65. Sedgwick, "Cacoethes Scribendi," in *Tales and Sketches* (Philadelphia: Carey, Lea, and Blanchard, 1835), p. 165.

66. Ibid., pp. 166–67, 169.

67. Ibid., pp. 170, 169.

68. Ibid., pp. 170–71.

69. Ibid., pp. 172–73.

70. Ibid., pp. 174–75.

71. Ibid., pp. 176–77.

72. Ibid., pp. 179–81.

73. Sara Parton [Fanny Fern], "A Chapter on Literary Women," in *Fern Leaves from Fanny's Portfolio*, pp. 175–77.

CHAPTER 9. THE CRISIS OF DOMESTICITY:
A CRISIS OF BEING

1. Caroline Lee Hentz, *Ernest Linwood* (Boston: John P. Jewett, 1856), p. 69.

2. Ibid., pp. 5, 18, 10, 8–9.

3. Ibid., p. 69.

4. Ibid.

5. Susan Warner to Anna Warner, undated, in Anna B. Warner, *Susan Warner* (New York: G. P. Putnam's Sons, 1909), p. 272; E.D.E.N. Southworth to Robert Bonner, [1878], 24 March 1887, E.D.E.N. Southworth Papers, Perkins-Duke.

6. Mary Virginia Terhune [Marion Harland], *Eve's Daughters; or, Common Sense for Maid, Wife, and Mother* (New York: John R. Anderson and Henry S. Allen, 1882), p. 8; Sara Parton [Fanny Fern], *Ruth Hall: A Domestic Tale of the Present Time* (New York: Mason Bros., 1855), p. 332.

7. As Elaine Showalter has noted in her article on feminist criticism and women's writing, "Language and style are never raw and instinctual but are always the products of innumerable factors of genre, tradition, memory, and context." The anthropologist Sherry Ortner has argued that the fact of female biology combined with beliefs concerning women's supposedly distinctive nature and their prescribed role has led to the perception of women as engaged more in "natural" functions than in "cultural" ones. Both Nancy Cott and Barbara Welter have commented upon women's identification with the "heart" in nineteenth-century America. See Showalter, "Feminist Criticism in the Wilderness," *Critical Inquiry* 8 (Winter

NOTES 379

1981): 193; Ortner, "Is Female to Male as Nature Is to Culture?" in Michelle Rosaldo and Louise Lamphere, eds., *Woman, Culture, and Society* (Stanford: Stanford University Press, 1974), pp. 67–87; Cott, *The Bonds of Womanhood: "Woman's Sphere" in New England, 1780–1835* (New Haven: Yale University Press, 1977), esp. pp. 160–68; Welter, *Dimity Convictions: The American Woman in the Nineteenth Century* (Athens: Ohio University Press, 1976), pp. 71–82.

8. Hentz, *Ernest Linwood*, pp. 163–64.

9. Ibid., p. 164.

10. Ibid., p. 229. The italics are Hentz's.

11. The literary domestics—in this instance Hentz—provide a striking illustration of the degree to which women identified with and were affected by their prescribed role during the nineteenth century. If historians concerned with the impact of prescription upon behavior are to achieve a fuller understanding of this complicated issue, careful studies of individual marriages must be undertaken. Already completed examinations which reveal complex but strong identification with domesticity include Kirk Jeffrey, "Marriage, Career, and Feminine Ideology in Nineteenth-Century America: Reconstructing the Marital Experience of Lydia Maria Child, 1828–1874," *Feminist Studies* 2, no. 2/3 (1975): 113–30; Mary H. Grant, "Domestic Experience and Feminist Theory: The Case of Julia Ward Howe," and Elisabeth Griffith, "Elizabeth Cady Stanton on Marriage and Divorce: Feminist Theory and Domestic Experience" in Mary Kelley, ed., *Woman's Being, Woman's Place: Female Identity and Vocation in American History* (Boston: G. K. Hall, 1979), pp. 220–51.

12. Diary of Caroline Lee Hentz, 20 Feb., 27 April 1836, Hentz Family Papers, Southern Historical Collection–UNC.

13. Autobiography of Charles A. Hentz, pp. 12, 133; Diary of Charles A. Hentz, 28 Dec. 1849, ibid.

14. Hentz, *Ernest Linwood*, pp. 57, 167, 165, 80–81.

15. Ibid., pp. 201–2, 178, 184.

16. Ibid., pp. 100, 126, 189–90.

17. Ibid., pp. 202, 222–23, 225.

18. Nicholas Marcellus Hentz to Caroline Lee Hentz, 1 June 1830, in Charles A. Hentz autobiography, p. 11, Hentz Family Papers, Southern Historical Collection–UNC; Hentz, *Ernest Linwood*, pp. 266, 297.

19. Hentz, *Ernest Linwood*, pp. 295, 304, 298, 333, 337, 303, 370.

20. Charles A. Hentz autobiography, p. 17, Hentz Family Papers, Southern Historical Collection–UNC.

21. Ibid., pp. 17–18.

22. Hentz, *Ernest Linwood*, pp. 293, 297–98.

23. Ibid., p. 467.

24. Diary of Caroline Lee Hentz, 7 Feb. 1836, Hentz Family Papers, Southern Historical Collection–UNC.

25. Ibid., 22 Feb., 6 March, 12 March 1836.

26. Ibid., 27 April, 11, 26, 31 May, 11 August 1836.

27. Hentz to Elizabeth Peabody, undated, Simon Gratz Collection, HSP.

28. Hentz to Mrs. Stafford, 5 March 1851, Hentz Family Papers, Southern Historical Collection–UNC.

29. Terhune, *Eve's Daughters*, p. 406, 399. That marriage was also regarded as a

momentous affair by eighteenth-century white women and entailed a "crisis" in their lives is documented in Mary Beth Norton's *Liberty's Daughters: The Revolutionary Experience of American Women, 1750–1800* (Boston: Little, Brown and Co., 1980), pp. 40–64.

30. Mary Virginia Terhune to Virginia Eppes Dance, 16 Aug. 1856, in Terhune [Marion Harland], *Marion Harland's Autobiography: The Story of a Long Life* (New York: Harper and Bros., 1910), p. 305.

31. Mary Virginia Terhune to Virginia Eppes Dance, 16 Aug. 1856, Mary Virginia Terhune Papers, Perkins-Duke.

32. Ibid., 8 Nov. 1857.

33. Harriet Beecher Stowe to Georgiana May, 6 Jan. 1836, in Annie Fields, ed., *Life and Letters of Harriet Beecher Stowe* (Boston: Houghton Mifflin Co., 1897), pp. 91–92.

34. Susan Warner to Fanny Warner, 12 Jan. [1849], in Warner, *Susan Warner*, p. 248; E.D.E.N. Southworth, *The Wife's Victory, and Other Nouvellettes* (Philadelphia: T. B. Peterson, 1854), p. 27; Mary Virginia Terhune [Marion Harland], *Moss-Side* (New York: Derby and Jackson, 1857), pp. 449–50; Sara Parton [Fanny Fern], *Rose Clark* (New York: Mason Bros., 1856), p. 230.

35. Caroline Lee Hentz, *Marcus Warland; or, The Long Moss Spring* (Philadelphia: T. B. Peterson, 1856/1852), p. 131.

36. Hentz, *Marcus Warland*, p. 131; Catharine Maria Sedgwick, *Married or Single?*, 2 vols. (New York: Harper and Bros., 1857) 1:28.

37. Mary Virginia Terhune [Marion Harland], *Charybdis* (New York: Carleton, 1869), pp. 324, 314, 396.

38. Harriet Beecher Stowe, *We and Our Neighbors; or, the Records of an Unfashionable Street* (Boston: Houghton Mifflin Co., 1896/1873), p. 87; idem, *Pink and White Tyranny: A Society Novel* (Boston: Houghton Mifflin Co., 1896/1871), p. 514. The commentary on nineteenth-century divorce is based upon Department of Commerce and Labor, Bureau of the Census, *Special Reports: Marriage and Divorce, 1867–1906. Part I: Summary, Laws, Foreign Statistics* (1909), pp. 7–50; Paul H. Jacobson, *American Marriage and Divorce* (New York: Rinehart and Co., 1959), pp. 88–92; Nelson Manfred Blake, *The Road to Reno: A History of Divorce in the United States* (New York: Macmillan Co., 1962), esp. pp. 48–63; William L. O'Neill, *Divorce in the Progressive Era* (New Haven: Yale University Press, 1964). In a recent study of the subject, Elaine Tyler May has pointed to the dramatic increase in divorce in the decades following the Civil War, noting that in the years between 1867 and 1929 the nation's population increased 300 percent, the number of marriages rose 400 percent, and the rate of marriages ending in divorce increased 2,000 percent. See *Great Expectations: Marriage and Divorce in Post-Victorian America* (Chicago: University of Chicago Press, 1980).

39. Augusta Evans Wilson, *Vashti; or, "Until Death Do Us Part"* (New York: Carleton, 1869), p. 371; E.D.E.N. Southworth, "Sybil Brotherton; or, The Temptation" in *The Wife's Victory*, p. 136.

40. E.D.E.N. Southworth, *The Deserted Wife* (New York: D. Appleton and Co., 1850), p. 5; Southworth to Rose Lawrence, 2 June 1895, E.D.E.N. Southworth Papers, LOC.

41. Southworth to her daughter Lottie, 3 June 1894, E.D.E.N. Southworth

Papers, LOC; Augusta Evans Wilson, *Beulah* (New York: Derby and Jackson, 1859), p. 403–5.

42. Journal of Catharine Maria Sedgwick, August 1837, Catharine Maria Sedgwick Papers, MHS. Not surprisingly, single women like Segwick have been even more invisible than their married female contemporaries. Recently, however, these women have also been brought into the domain of historical inquiry. See, for example, Lee Chambers-Schiller, "The Single Woman: Family and Vocation among Nineteenth-Century Reformers," in Kelley, *Woman's Being, Woman's Place*, pp. 334–50; and Carl Degler, *At Odds: Women and the Family in America from the Revolution to the Present* (New York: Oxford University Press, 1980), pp. 144–77. For additional analysis of Sedgwick's life as a single woman, see my article "A Woman Alone: Catharine Maria Sedgwick's Spinsterhood in Nineteenth-Century America," *New England Quarterly* 51 (June 1978): 209–25.

43. Sedgwick, *Married or Single?* 1:vi.

44. Ibid., 2:81–82.

45. Sedgwick, *Means and Ends; or, Self-Training* (Boston: Marsh, Capen, Lyon, and Webb, 1839), dedication, pp. 19, 17; idem, "Old Maids," in *Tales and Sketches* (Philadelphia: Carey, Lea, and Blanchard, 1835), pp. 98–99, 107.

46. Sedgwick to Anna Jameson, 5 Nov. 1842; Sedgwick journal, 24 May 1834, Catharine Maria Sedgwick Papers, MHS.

47. Sedgwick to Kate Sedgwick Minot, 28 Nov. 1847; Sedgwick, "Notebook of Memories of Her Life, Dated 1853," pp. 116, 136; Sedgwick journal, 1849–54, entry undated, ibid.

48. Sedgwick Journal, 18 May 1828, ibid.; Sedgwick to Anna Barker Ward, 8 March 1850, Houghton-Harvard.

49. Sedgwick to Louisa Minot, Sept. 1841, Sedgwick (Minot); Sedgwick to Robert Sedgwick, 2 July 1813; Sedgwick to Charles Sedgwick, 2 Feb. 1829, Catharine Maria Sedgwick Papers, MHS.

50. Sedgwick to Robert Sedgwick, 24 March 1819, Dec. 1821, ibid.

51. Sedgwick to Kate Sedgwick Minot, 20 Feb. 1853, ibid.

52. Sedgwick to Susan Higginson Channing, 1822, in Mary E. Dewey, ed., *Life and Letters of Catharine Maria Sedgwick* (New York: Harper and Bros., 1872), p. 153; Robert Sedgwick to C. M. Sedgwick, 19 Aug. 1822, Sedgwick Papers (Minot); C. M. Sedgwick to Robert Sedgwick, 11 June 1823, Catharine Maria Sedgwick Papers, MHS.

53. C. M. Sedgwick to Frances Watson, 21 Jan. 1828, Sedgwick Family Papers, Sedgwick IV; Sedgwick journal, 18 May 1828, Catharine Maria Sedgwick Papers, MHS.

54. Sedgwick journal, 14 May, 7 June, 5 Aug. 1830, 29 Nov. 1832, Catharine Maria Sedgwick Papers, MHS.

55. Ibid., 1 Jan. 1833; Charles Sedgwick to Sedgwick, 29 Jan. 1821, Sedgwick to Louisa Minot, 16 Jan. 1842, Sedgwick to Kate Sedgwick Minot, [1856], Sedgwick Papers (Minot), MHS.

56. C. M. Sedgwick to Anna Jameson, 8 Sept. 1841, Sedgwick to Kate Sedgwick Minot, 4, 11 Aug. 1856, Catharine Maria Sedgwick Papers, MHS.

57. C. M. Sedgwick to Kate Sedgwick, 16 Feb. 1835; Sedgwick journal, 17 Dec. 1835, ibid.

58. Sara Parton's letter is quoted in Sara Jane Lippincott [Grace Greenwood], "Fanny Fern—Mrs. Parton," in *Eminent Women of the Age* (Hartford: S. M. Betts and Co., 1869), p. 84; Parton to Robert Bonner, undated, in Parton's obituary, *New York Ledger*, 9 Nov. 1872. Parton's affection for Effie is evident in a letter grandmother sent granddaughter: "I think of you all the time. I am afraid you won't get washed enough! or be hungry except for me. I look into all the shop windows and wonder what you would like." Undated letter deposited with Sara Parton Papers, Sophia Smith Collection, Smith.

59. Sara Parton [Fanny Fern], "Mrs. Washington's Eternal Knitting," in *Caper-Sauce* (New York: G. W. Carleton and Co., 1872), pp. 48–49; Parton, "Gail Hamilton—Miss Dodge," in *Eminent Women of the Age*, p. 219.

60. Harriet Beecher Stowe to Charles Beecher, undated, in Charles Beecher, ed., *Autobiography, Correspondence, Etc., of Lyman Beecher, D.D.*, 2 vols. (New York: Harper and Bros., 1864) 1:302; Stowe, undated memorandum, Beecher-Stowe Collection, Schlesinger-Radcliffe; Stowe to Georgiana May, [1848], in Fields, *Life and Letters*, pp. 115–16; Stowe to Annie Fields, 27 July 1868, James T. Fields Papers, Huntington.

61. Dewey, *Life and Letters*, p. 222; Robert Sedgwick to Catharine Maria Sedgwick, 15 March 1813; Charles Sedgwick to Sedgwick, 10 Dec. 1832, Sedgwick Papers (Minot); Jane Sedgwick to Sedgwick, June 1837, Sedgwick IV, MHS.

62. Mary Virginia Terhune quoted in biographical sketch in Sarah K. Bolton, *Successful Women* (Boston: D. Lothrop Co., 1888), p. 107; Augusta Evans Wilson, *Beulah* (New York: Derby and Jackson, 1860), p. 197; idem, *St. Elmo* (New York: Carleton, 1866), p. 438.

63. Harriet Beecher Stowe quoted in J. C. Derby, *Fifty Years Among Authors, Books and Publishers* (New York: G. W. Carleton and Co., 1884), p. 521; Mary Virginia Terhune quoted in biographical sketch in Bolton, *Successful Women*, p. 103; Terhune quoted in interview with Florine Thayer McCray, "Marion Harland at Home," *Ladies Home Journal* 4 (August 1887): 3; Terhune, *Autobiography*, pp. 239, 240, 244, 246, 485; autobiographical sketch of Caroline Howard Gilman in *The Female Prose Writers of America* (Philadelphia: E. H. Butler and Co., 1855), p. 56; Catharine Maria Sedgwick to Kate Sedgwick Minot, 18 March 1835, Catharine Maria Sedgwick Papers, MHS.

CHAPTER 10. THE GREAT QUESTION OF MORAL LIFE

1. *Independent*, 21 Feb. 1856. In fact, the same technological advances in printing along with improvements in transportation that contributed to the development of a national publishing industry also enabled the antislavery press to become an important instrument of reform, and Stowe herself benefited from that press in the form of the *National Era*, which first serialized *Uncle Tom's Cabin*.

2. I am suggesting here that the "parable of literary domesticity" should be regarded as illustrative of a public, historical phenomenon that went beyond the literary domestics, just as a women's rights convention, for example, was a public, historical phenomenon that went beyond women's rights activists. We have not been trained, as individuals or historians, to regard domestic life as historical.

3. As to a "secret alliance" I, for one, am referring to an alliance of *experience*. In an article that has had lasting influence upon historians engaged in the study of women, Carroll Smith-Rosenberg introduced the concept of a "female world," suggesting not only that it encompassed female values, institutions, and familial and friendship networks, but that it also provided women with intense, emotionally satisfying relationships. Nancy F. Cott also perceptively explores this subject in her study of New England women in the early republic. See Smith-Rosenberg, "The Female World of Love and Ritual: Relations Between Women in Nineteenth-Century America," *Signs: Journal of Women in Culture and Society* 1 (Autumn 1975): 1–30; Cott, *The Bonds of Womanhood: "Woman's Sphere" in New England, 1780–1835* (New Haven: Yale University Press, 1977), esp. 160–96.

4. Harriet Beecher Stowe to George Eliot, 15 April 1869, Berg-NYPL.

5. Susan Warner [Elizabeth Wetherell], *Queechy*, 2 vols. (New York: George P. Putnam, 1852) 2:129.

6. Maria McIntosh, *Woman an Enigma; or, Life and Its Revealings* (New York: Harper and Bros., 1843), p. 6.

7. Caroline Howard to Louisa Gilman, 5 Feb. 1813, Gilman Family Papers, AAS.

8. Caroline Howard Gilman to Harriet Fay, 6, 19 Jan. [1840], Gilman Family Papers, AAS.

9. Harriet Beecher Stowe to George Eliot, 25 May [1869], Berg-NYPL. A brilliant exposition of Stowe's struggle with her religious heritage is found in Charles H. Foster's *The Rungless Ladder*. Foster's analysis of Stowe's fiction demonstrates that New England Puritanism remained a vital force for Stowe, that she grappled with its implications in many of her novels, and that the confrontation resulted in her simultaneously saying yes and no to the legacy. As in so many facets of her life, Stowe experienced a deep and lasting ambivalence. See *The Rungless Ladder: Harriet Beecher Stowe and New England Puritanism* (Durham: Duke University Press, 1954). The varied but equally intense religiosity of the Beechers generally is explored in Marie Caskey, *Chariot of Fire: Religion and the Beecher Family* (New Haven: Yale University Press, 1978).

10. Harriet Beecher Stowe, *Oldtown Folks* (Cambridge: Harvard University Press, 1966/1869), p. 455. In describing Esther, Stowe had in mind, as she noted in the novel, the seventeenth-century metaphysical poetry of John Donne. Catharine Beecher's religious crisis receives penetrating analysis in Kathryn Kish Sklar's *Catharine Beecher: A Study in American Domesticity* (New York: W. W. Norton and Co., 1976/1973).

11. Stowe, *Oldtown Folks*, p. 456. As was suggested to me by Charles T. Wood, Stowe in referring to women's antipathy to Augustinian theology was probably thinking of Augustine's doctrine of infant damnation.

12. Ibid.

13. Mary Virginia Terhune [Marion Harland], *Eve's Daughters; or, Common Sense for Maid, Wife, and Mother* (New York: John R. Anderson and Henry S. Allen, 1882), pp. 1, 7.

14. Ibid., p. 7.

15. Ibid., pp. 76–77.

16. Harriet Beecher Stowe, *We and Our Neighbors; or, The Records of an*

Unfashionable Street (Boston: Houghton Mifflin Co., 1896/1873), p. 37; Maria McIntosh, *Woman in America: Her Work and Her Reward* (New York: D. Appleton and Co., 1850), pp. 19, 20, 26.

17. Catharine Maria Sedgwick to Susan Higginson Channing, 15 June 1822, Catharine Maria Sedgwick Papers, MHS; Harriet Beecher Stowe to an editor, 1 Nov. 1856, Clifton Waller Barrett Library, Alderman-UVA; Mary Virginia Terhune [Marion Harland], *Marion Harland's Autobiography: The Story of a Long Life* (New York: Harper and Bros., 1910), p. 481; Terhune, "Nobody to Blame" in *Husbands and Homes* (New York: Sheldon and Co., 1865), p. 47; Maria McIntosh, *Woman in America*, p. 131; Catharine Maria Sedgwick, *Home* (Boston: James Monroe and Co., 1835), p. 5. Katherine Ellis's commentary on nineteenth-century British literature suggests a similar domestic dream spawned by disillusionment. Portrayed as a peaceful, harmonious refuge from the world, the home is seen in actuality as a reservoir of conflict, particularly between wife and husband. Ellis, however, ignores the even greater conflict generated by the personal turmoil experienced by the woman. Using American popular literature as his source, Kirk Jeffrey also analyzes the image of the nineteenth-century family and, unlike Ellis, does suggest that the demand on woman to create a utopian retreat could lead not only to tension and anxiety but to attempts on her part to evade the challenge. See Ellis, "Paradise Lost: The Limits of Domesticity in the Nineteenth-Century Novel," *Feminist Studies* 2, no. 2/3 (1975): 55–63; Jeffrey, "The Family as Utopian Retreat from the City," *Soundings* 55 (Spring 1972): 21–41. For further elaboration of Jeffrey's ideas, see "Family History: The Middle-Class American Family in the Urban Context, 1830–1870" (Ph.D. diss., Stanford University, 1971).

18. Harriet Beecher Stowe to Charles Beecher, undated, in Charles Beecher, ed., *Autobiography, Correspondence, Etc., of Lyman Beecher, D.D.,* 2 vols. (New York: Harper and Bros., 1864) 1:319; Maria McIntosh quoted in a biographical sketch, *The Living Female Authors of the South* (Philadelphia: Claxton, Remsen and Haffelfinger, 1872), p. 224; Catharine Maria Sedgwick, *Hope Leslie* (New York: Harper and Bros., 1862/1827), p. 20.

19. Augusta Evans Wilson, *At the Mercy of Tiberius* (New York: G. W. Dillingham, 1887), pp. 225–26.

20. Terhune, *Eve's Daughters*, p. 284; E.D.E.N. Southworth, *Her Mother's Secret* (New York: A. L. Burt Co., n.d./1882), p. 10.

21. Catharine Maria Sedgwick, *Married or Single?,* 2 vols. (New York: Harper and Bros., 1857) 1:120; Mary Virginia Terhune [Marion Harland], *Jessamine* (New York: G. W. Carleton and Co., 1873), p. 214.

22. Maria Cummins, *Haunted Hearts* (Boston: J. E. Tilton and Co., 1864), pp. 435–36.

23. Stowe, *We and Our Neighbors*, pp. 306–7.

24. Sara Parton [Fanny Fern], "Woman," in *Fern Leaves from Fanny's Portfolio* (Auburn: Miller, Orton and Mulligan, 1854), p. 133; Catharine Maria Sedgwick to Kate Sedgwick Minot, 20 March 1853, Catharine Maria Sedgwick Papers, MHS.

25. Terhune, *Eve's Daughters*, p. 413.

26. Autobiographical sketch by E.D.E.N. Southworth in John S. Hart, ed., *The Female Prose Writers of America* (Philadelphia: E. H. Butler and Co., 1855), p.

213; autobiography by Southworth in *The Haunted Homestead* (Philadelphia: T. B. Peterson, 1860), p. 36.

27. E.D.E.N. Southworth to her daughter Lottie, 19 Jan. 1894, E.D.E.N. Southworth Papers, LOC.

28. Ibid., 3 June 1894, 22 June 1895.

29. Autobiographical sketch by E.D.E.N. Southworth in Hart, *Female Prose Writers*, p. 213; Southworth, *Retribution; or, The Vale of Shadows, A Tale of Passion* (New York: Harper and Bros., 1849), preface.

30. Southworth, *Retribution*, pp. 62, 67, 69, 108.

31. Charles Eldredge to Sara Willis 23 Jan. [1837?], Sara Parton Papers, Sophia Smith Collection, Smith.

32. Ellen Parton to "Dear Sir," 28 Feb. 1899, ibid.

33. The documents are deposited with the Sara Parton Papers, ibid., as is Ethel Parton's "Fanny Fern: An Informal Biography."

34. Ellen Parton to "Dear Sir," 28 Feb. 1899, ibid.; James Parton to Ellen Eldredge, 6 Oct. 1873, James Parton Papers, Houghton-Harvard.

35. Sara Parton [Fanny Fern], *Rose Clark* (New York: Mason Bros., 1856), pp. 230–31.

36. Ibid., pp. 231–32, 235, 253.

37. Ibid., pp. 281, 345.

38. Sara Parton [Fanny Fern], "Gail Hamilton—Miss Dodge," in *Eminent Women of the Age* (Hartford: S. M. Betts and Co., 1869), p. 212.

39. Maria McIntosh, *Woman an Enigma*, p. 219.

40. Harriet Beecher Stowe, *Pink and White Tyranny: A Society Novel* (Boston: Houghton Mifflin Co., 1896/1871), pp. x, 366.

41. Augusta Evans Wilson to Rachel Lyons Heustis, undated, in William Perry Fidler, *Augusta Evans Wilson* (University: University of Alabama Press, 1951), p. 77; Wilson, *At the Mercy of Tiberius*, p. 560. It is this quest for self-respect and for significance and purpose in the woman's life that probably led Nina Baym to suggest that these "tales [are] about the triumph of the feminine will." That is to simplify and distort the meaning of this literature. It is to overlook the myriad strains of conflict and contradiction. See Baym, *Woman's Fiction: A Guide to Novels by and about Women in America, 1820–1880* (Ithaca: Cornell University Press, 1978), p. 14.

42. Catharine Maria Sedgwick, *The Linwoods; or, "Sixty Years Since" in America*, 2 vols. (New York: Harper and Bros., 1835) 2:215; Sedgwick, *Married or Single?* 1:148–49; Augusta Evans Wilson, *Macaria; or, The Altars of Sacrifice* (Richmond: West and Johnston, 1864).

43. Maria McIntosh, *Two Pictures; or, What We Think of Ourselves, and What the World Thinks of Us* (New York: D. Appleton and Co., 1863), pp. 358–59; Maria Cummins, *Mabel Vaughan* (Boston: John P. Jewett and Co., 1857), pp. 9–10; E.D.E.N. Southworth, *The Curse of Clifton* (Philadelphia: T.B. Peterson and Bros., 1867/1853), p. 309.

44. Mary Virginia Terhune [Marion Harland], *Alone* (Richmond: A. Morris, 1855), p. 347; Caroline Howard Gilman, *Love's Progress* (New York: Harper and Bros., 1840), p. 95.

45. E.D.E.N. Southworth, *Vivia; or, The Secret of Power* (Philadelphia: T. B. Peterson, 1857), p. 540; Susan Warner [Elizabeth Wetherell], *Queechy*, 2 vols.

(New York: George P. Putnam, 1852), 1:348; Catharine Maria Sedgwick, *Home* (Boston: James Munroe and Co., 1835), pp. 122–23.

46. Harriet Beecher Stowe, *We and Our Neighbors,* p. 399; idem, *My Wife and I; or, Harry Henderson's History* (Boston: Houghton Mifflin Co., 1896/1870), pp. x–xi; Stowe to Hattie and Eliza Stowe, 8 March 1859, Beecher-Stowe Collection, Schlesinger-Radcliffe.

47. Caroline Lee Hentz, *Robert Graham: A Sequel to Linda* (Philadelphia: T. B. Peterson, 1856/1855), pp. 94–95.

48. Harriet Beecher Stowe, *Poganuc People: Their Loves and Lives* (Boston: Houghton Mifflin Co., 1896/1878), p. 262; Sara Parton, *Rose Clark,* p. 352; Susan Warner [Elizabeth Wetherell], *Daisy,* 2 vols. (Philadelphia: J. B. Lippincott and Co., 1869) 1:382; Maria McIntosh, *The Lofty and the Lowly; or, Good in All and None All Good,* 2 vols. (New York: D. Appleton and Co., 1852) 1:186.

49. Mary J. Holmes, *Hugh Worthington* (New York: G. W. Dillingham, 1865), p. 228; Stowe, *My Wife and I,* pp. 33–34.

50. Mary J. Holmes, *Hugh Worthington,* p. 130; Maria McIntosh, *Two Pictures,* preface, p. 3.

51. Caroline Lee Hentz, *Lovell's Folly* (Cincinnati: Hubbard and Edmonds, 1833), p. 84.

52. Harriet Beecher Stowe to Hattie and Eliza Stowe, 8 March 1859, Beecher-Stowe Collection, Schlesinger-Radcliffe; Catharine Maria Sedgwick to Kate Sedgwick Minot, 2 April, 11 Nov. 1844, Catharine Maria Sedgwick Papers, MHS; Caroline Howard Gilman [Clarissa Packard], *Recollections of a Housekeeper* (Philadelphia: John E. Potter and Co., 1867/1834), p. 363; Gilman to her daughter Eliza, 17 Sept. 1863, Samuel Gilman Papers, South Caroliniana–USC.

53. Sara Parton [Fanny Fern], "A Mother's Soliloquy," in *Fern Leaves from Fanny's Portfolio,* p. 157; Parton, *Ruth Hall: A Domestic Tale of the Present Time* (New York: Mason Bros., 1855), p. 39.

54. Mary Virginia Terhune [Marion Harland], "A Christmas Talk with Mothers" in *The Christmas Holly* (New York: Sheldon and Co., 1867), p. 54; Terhune, *Eve's Daughters,* p. 425.

55. E.D.E.N. Southworth, *The Discarded Daughter* (Philadelphia: T. B. Peterson, 1852), p. 342; Charles Sedgwick to Catharine Maria Sedgwick, 2 Feb. 1821, Sedgwick Family Papers, Sedgwick IV, MHS; Caroline Howard Gilman to Harriet Fay, 5 June [1838], Gilman Family Papers, AAS.

56. Harriet Beecher Stowe to James T. Fields, undated, James T. Fields Papers, Huntington.

57. Sara Parton, *Ruth Hall,* p. 36; Anna B. Warner, *Susan Warner* (New York: G. P. Putnam's Sons, 1909), p. 380; Maria McIntosh, *Two Pictures,* p. 15; Mary Virginia Terhune [Marion Harland], *Ruby's Husband* (New York: Sheldon and Co., 1869), p. 355.

58. Undated document, E.D.E.N. Southworth Papers, LOC.

59. Mary Virginia Terhune to Mr. Rideing, 7 Dec. 1889, Clifton Waller Barrett Library, Alderman-UVA; Terhune, "Nobody to Blame," in *Husbands and Homes,* pp. 125–26; Sara Parton [Fanny Fern], "Two Kinds of Wives," in *Caper-Sauce* (New York: G. W. Carleton and Co., 1872), p. 55; idem, "Sauce for the Gander," in *Caper-Sauce,* p. 296; idem, "Blue Monday," in *Ginger-Snaps* (New York: Carleton, 1870), p. 70; Stowe, *My Wife and I,* p. 40. Carroll Smith-Rosenberg offers a

compelling analysis of the tension and conflict experienced by nineteenth-century women. See "The Hysterical Woman: Sex Roles and Role Conflict in Nineteenth-Century America," *Social Research* 39 (Winter 1972): 652–78.

60. Caroline Howard Gilman, *Recollections of a Southern Matron* (New York: Harper and Bros., 1838), p. 256; Harriet Beecher Stowe, *The Pearl of Orr's Island: A Story of the Coast of Maine* (Boston: Houghton Mifflin Co., 1896/1862) p. 315; Sara Parton, "Two Kinds of Women," in *Ginger-Snaps*, p. 128.

61. Caroline Howard Gilman [Mrs. Clarissa Packard], *Recollections of a Housekeeper* (New York: Harper and Bros., 1834), pp. 154–55; Mary Virginia Terhune, "Two Ways of Keeping a Wife," in *Husbands and Homes*, pp. 125–26; Maria McIntosh, *Woman in America*, pp. 136–37.

62. E.D.E.N. Southworth, *The Deserted Wife* (New York: D. Appleton and Co., 1850) pp. 6–7; Sara Parton, "Mothers of Many Children," in *Caper-Sauce*, p. 152; idem, "Blue Monday," in *Ginger-Snaps*, p. 70.

63. Mary Virginia Terhune to Mr. Holt, 27 Dec. 1899, Clifton Waller Barrett Library, Alderman-UVA.

64. Harriet Beecher Stowe to Calvin Stowe, [July 1844], Beecher-Stowe Collection, Schlesinger-Radcliffe. A more extended analysis of Stowe's experience as a wife and mother can be found in my article "At War with Herself: Harriet Beecher Stowe as Woman in Conflict within the Home," *American Studies* 19 (Fall 1978):23–40.

65. Calvin Stowe to Harriet Beecher Stowe, 24 May [1835], Stowe-Day.

66. Calvin Stowe to Harriet Beecher Stowe, 7 Aug., 20 June 1836, Stowe-Day. Harriet Beecher Stowe to Calvin Stowe, 4 Sept. [1842], Beecher-Stowe Collection, Schlesinger-Radcliffe. Harriet and Calvin's sexual relationship provides a vehicle for the examination of various hypotheses concerning the decline of fertility during the nineteenth century and whether the female or the male was the primary determinant. Daniel Scott Smith has argued that the female tended to be the controlling party. Women were practicing "domestic feminism," as Smith has termed it, and thereby exercising significant power and autonomy within the family. Carl Degler has argued along similar lines, suggesting that "as women became more conscious of themselves as individuals, they also sought to control their fertility." In contrast, Gerda Lerner has noted that the lowered birth rates can be attributed just as easily to the male's desire, motivated by economic considerations, to limit the number of children in his family. The evidence from Harriet and Calvin's correspondence suggests not only the complexity of sexual relationships but also the tenuousness of broad generalizations about the most intimate of human experiences. See Smith, "Family Limitation, Sexual Control and Domestic Feminism in Victorian America," *Feminist Studies* 1 (Winter-Spring 1973):40–57; Degler, *At Odds: Women and the Family in America From the Revolution to the Present* (New York: Oxford University Press, 1980), esp. pp. 178–248; Lerner, "Placing Women in History," in Berenice A. Carroll, ed., *Liberating Women's History* (Urbana: University of Illinois Press, 1976), pp. 357–67.

67. Calvin Stowe to Harriet Beecher Stowe, 1 Nov., 30 June 1846, Stowe-Day.

68. Calvin Stowe to Harriet Beecher Stowe, 20 Aug. 1846, ibid.

69. Calvin Stowe to Harriet Beecher Stowe, 22 Nov. 1846, [1847]; Calvin Stowe to Hepzibah Stowe, 7 Feb. 1847, Stowe-Day.

70. Harriet Beecher Stowe to Calvin Stowe, 1 Jan. 1847, Beecher-Stowe Collection, Schlesinger-Radcliffe.

71. Harriet Beecher Stowe to George Eliot, 25 May [1869], 3 August 1869, 8 Feb. 1872, NYPL-Berg.

CHAPTER 11. PREACHERS OF THE FICTIONAL PAGE

1. Journal of Catharine Maria Sedgwick, 19 May 1836, Catharine Maria Sedgwick Papers, MHS. In her entry Sedgwick did not indicate the source for Mackintosh's comments, but the first and second editions of the posthumously published *Memoirs of the Life of the Right Honorable Sir James Mackintosh,* edited by his son Robert James Mackintosh, had appeared in 1835 and 1836 respectively. Mackintosh's statements on fiction and Coleridge appear in vol. 2, pp. 20 and 200. See *Memoirs,* 2 vols. (London: Edward Moxon, 1836).

2. Catharine Maria Sedgwick to Theodore Sedgwick, [12 May 1826], Catharine Maria Sedgwick Papers, MHS. Sedgwick's reference is to her brother's collections of essays, *Hints to My Countrymen,* issued in 1826. As previously noted, the educational fare of the literary domestics included the fiction of eighteenth- and nineteenth-century British women. For an examination of Maria Edgeworth and other female fictional moralists, see Vineta Colby, *Yesterday's Woman: Domestic Realism in the English Novel* (Princeton: Princeton University Press, 1974). Other studies from a variety of perspectives include J.M.S. Tompkins, *The Popular Novel in England, 1770–1800* (Westport, Ct.: Greenwood Press, 1976/1961), and Jenni Calder, *Women and Marriage in Victorian Fiction* (New York: Oxford University Press, 1976).

3. Journal of Catharine Maria Sedgwick, 10 June 1827, 31 March 1837; Sedgwick to Charles Sedgwick, 21 May 1836, Catharine Maria Sedgwick Papers, MHS; Sedgwick to Lydia Maria Child, 12 June 1830, BPL.

4. Obituary of Sara Parton, *New York Ledger,* 9 Nov. 1872; Parton to Robert Bonner, [January 1868], in J. C. Derby, *Fifty Years Among Authors, Books and Publishers* (New York: G. W. Carleton and Co., 1884), p. 215; Nathaniel Hall, Sermon preached 8 Oct. 1866, Cummins Family Papers, EI; Susan Warner to Mrs. Smith, 1 July 1852, Overbury Collection, Barnard. In nineteenth-century American society, laden as it was with moralists of all stripes, the literary domestics were obviously not alone in their posture. But it was their perception of the nature of womanhood that enabled them to regard and justify their literature ipso facto as moral in purpose. Similar attitudes can be seen in other nineteenth-century female professionals. Regina Markell Morantz notes that women doctors justified their practice of medicine in part on the premise that morality itself was medically curative and that women as inherently moral were best able to promote morality among their patients. As R. Lawrence Moore shows, even female mediums rationalized their practice in moral terms, portraying themselves as the self-sacrificing instruments of others. See Morantz, "'The Connecting Link': The Case for the Woman Doctor in Nineteenth-Century American Medicine," in Judith Walzer Leavitt and Ronald Numbers, eds., *Sickness and Health in America: Readings in the History of Medicine and Public Health* (Madison: University of Wisconsin Press, 1978), pp.

117–28; Moore, "The Spiritualist Medium: A Study of Female Professionalism in Victorian America," *American Quarterly* 27 (May 1975):200–221.

5. Augusta Evans Wilson to J.L.M. Curry, 9 Jan. 1867, J.L.M. Curry Papers, LOC, reprinted in William Perry Fidler, *Augusta Evans Wilson* (University: University of Alabama Press, 1951), p. 137; Wilson, *St. Elmo* (New York: Carleton, 1866), pp. 168, 238, 457.

6. Mary Virginia Terhune [Marion Harland], *Phemie's Temptation* (New York: Carleton, 1869), pp. 178, 276.

7. Mary J. Holmes quoted in William M. Griswold, comp., *Descriptive Lists of American International Romantic and British Novels* (New York: Burt Franklin Bibliography and Reference Series, no. 135, 1968), pp. 63–64; Caroline Howard Gilman to Harriet Fay, 28 June [1838], Gilman Family Papers, AAS.

8. Autograph of E.D.E.N. Southworth, NYPL-Manuscripts. Within the context of a historiography primarily concerned with a male past, it was almost inevitable that the social philosophy of individualism would receive much more consideration than that of selflessness. Perhaps the most astute commentary on individualism remains John William Ward's "The Ideal of Individualism and the Reality of Organization," in *Red, White and Blue: Men, Books and Ideas in American Culture* (New York: Oxford University Press, 1969), pp. 227–66. See also Ward's *Andrew Jackson: Symbol for an Age* (New York: Oxford University Press, 1955). In addition to his focus upon the triumph of individualism in nineteenth-century America, Fred Somkin does note the inherent conflict between individualism and the ideology of republicanism, particularly in its emphasis upon virtue. See *Unquiet Eagle: Memory and Desire in the Idea of American Freedom, 1815–1860* (Ithaca: Cornell University Press, 1967). The flaw in these analyses does not lie primarily in their explications of individualism. But they fail to explore the fact that the countervailing ideology, namely selflessness, still existed and had come to be applied primarily to women. Selflessness as a critical value in an age supposedly dominated by individualism has only begun to be explored by historians. Kathryn Kish Sklar, one of the first to explore the principle of self-sacrifice as it was applied to women, demonstrates that the principle was defined as a positive good and made the vehicle for female fulfillment. See *Catharine Beecher: A Study in American Domesticity* (New York: W. W. Norton, 1976/1973).

9. Augusta Evans Wilson, *At the Mercy of Tiberius* (New York: G. W. Dillingham, 1887), p. 526; Journal of Catharine Maria Sedgwick, 16 May 1834, Catharine Maria Sedgwick Papers, MHS; Harriet Beecher Stowe, undated, Beecher Family Papers, Sterling-Yale.

10. The most insightful study of nineteenth-century Protestantism remains Sidney E. Mead's *The Lively Experiment.* See also Sydney E. Ahlstrom's thorough and comprehensive analysis of American religion generally. The impact of the Enlightenment is astutely analyzed in Henry F. May's *Enlightenment in America,* while nineteenth-century theological developments receive extended consideration in studies by Mead and H. Shelton Smith as well as in Ahlstrom's survey. See Mead, *The Lively Experiment: The Shaping of Christianity in America* (New York: Harper and Row, 1963) and idem, *Nathaniel William Taylor: Connecticut Liberal* (Chicago: University of Chicago Press, 1942); Ahlstrom, *A Religous History of the American People* (New Haven: Yale University Press, 1972); May, *The Enlightenment in America* (New York: Oxford University Press, 1976); Smith, *Changing*

Conceptions of Original Sin: A Study in American Theology Since 1750 (New York: Charles Scribner's Sons, 1955).

11. Catharine Maria Sedgwick to Mr. Wheaton, 15 March 1829, Morgan; Sedgwick to Leonard Sismondi, 15 March 1828, Catharine Maria Sedgwick Papers, MHS. Sedgwick left the Congregationalists and became a Unitarian in 1821. Daniel Walker Howe's is an especially persuasive analysis of Unitarianism in antebellum America. See *The Unitarian Conscience: Harvard Moral Philosophy, 1805–1861* (Cambridge: Harvard University Press, 1970).

12. The material in this paragraph is drawn from the Sara Parton Papers, Sophia Smith Collection, Smith. See also the biographical sketch of Edward Payson in Dumas Malone, ed., *Dictionary of American Biography*, 20 vols. (New York: Charles Scribner's Sons, 1934) 14:333–34.

13. Stowe's recollection is found in Ethel Parton, "Fanny Fern: An Informal Biography"; Catharine Beecher to Nathaniel and Hannah Willis, 27 May 1829, Sara Parton Papers, Sophia Smith Collection, Smith.

14. Sara Parton [Fanny Fern], "Notes on Preachers and Preaching," in *Folly As It Flies* (New York: G. W. Carleton, 1869), pp. 89–90, 97.

15. Harriet Beecher Stowe to Isabella Beecher Hooker, 1 Feb. 1883, Stowe-Day; E.D.E.N. Southworth, *The Discarded Daughter* (Philadelphia: T. B. Peterson, 1852), p. 26; Stowe to Hattie and Eliza Stowe, Beecher-Stowe Collection, Schlesinger-Radcliffe. Of course Stowe's own brother, Henry Ward Beecher, became by midcentury the foremost spokesperson for the emphasis upon God's benevolence, compassion, and mercy as expressed in the phrase "God is Love." The most insightful analysis of Beecher is Clifford E. Clark, *Henry Ward Beecher: Spokesman for a Middle-Class America* (Urbana: University of Illinois Press, 1978). Also useful is William McLoughlin, *The Meaning of Henry Ward Beecher* (New York: Alfred A. Knopf, 1970).

16. Henry Warner to Anna Warner, 7 Sept. 1822, in Anna B. Warner, *Susan Warner* (New York: G. P. Putman's Sons, 1909), p. 53. Also see pp. 203, 221.

17. Mary Virginia Terhune to Virginia Eppes Dance, 18 Oct. 1855, Mary Virginia Terhune Papers, Perkins-Duke; E.D.E.N. Southworth, *Em's Husband* (New York: Robert Bonner's Sons, 1892/1876), p. 11; autograph of Harriet Beecher Stowe, Stowe-Day; August Evans Wilson to Rachel Lyons Heustis, 2 Feb. 1860; in Fidler, *Augusta Evans Wilson*, p. 51. Timothy L. Smith was one of the first historians to explore the connection between nineteenth-century Protestantism and social reform. Since his influential study appeared in 1957, there has been a continuing debate about the character of that interaction. The foremost exponent of the thesis that those lay and clergy who were engaged in reform and especially in benevolent societies were motivated by their fear of an increasingly egalitarian and secular society is Charles S. Griffin. A convincing refutation is made by Lois Banner, who argues that this more negative stimulus was only part of a complex motivation that was characterized as well by the more positive hope that lay and clergy might contribute to the success of the republican experiment and simultaneously hasten the millennium. Recent scholarship, including that of James Moorhead, Carroll Smith-Rosenberg, Robert Handy, and Martin Marty, reflects this broader perspective, as does the interpretation presented here. See Smith, *Revivalism and Social Reform: American Protestantism on the Eve of the Civil War* (Nashville: Abington Press, 1957); Griffin, *Their Brother's Keepers: Moral Stewardship in the United States,*

1815-1865 (Brunswick: Rutgers University Press, 1964); Banner, "Religious Benevolence as Social Control," *Journal of American History* 60 (June 1973): 23–41; Moorhead, "Social Reform and the Divided Conscience of Antebellum Protestantism," *Church History* 48 (December 1979):416–430; Smith-Rosenberg, *Religion and the Rise of the American City: The New York City Mission Movement, 1812–1870* (Ithaca: Cornell University Press, 1971); Handy, *A Christian America: Protestant Hopes and Historical Realities* (New York: Oxford University Press, 1971); Marty, *Righteous Empire: The Protestant Experience in America* (New York: Dial Press, 1970).

18. Susan Warner to Dorothea Dix, 27 Aug. 1852, Houghton-Harvard; Warner, *Susan Warner*, p. 264; Maria Cummins to Annie Fields, 16 Sept. 1862, Houghton-Harvard; E.D.E.N. Southworth to her daughter Lottie, 27 May 1892, E.D.E.N. Southworth Papers, LOC.

19. Catharine Maria Sedgwick to William Ellery Channing, 24 Aug. 1837, Catharine Maria Sedgwick Papers, MHS; Harriet Beecher Stowe, *Pink and White Tyranny: A Society Novel* (Boston: Houghton Mifflin Co., 1896/1871), Preface, x; Mary Virginia Terhune to Virginia Eppes Dance, 28 Jan. 1854, in Mary Virginia Terhune [Marion Harland], *Marion Harland's Autobiography: The Story of a Long Life* (Harper and Bros., 1910), p. 246; Caroline Lee Hentz to Mrs. Stafford, 5 March 1851, Hentz Family Papers, Southern Historical Collection–UNC. There is, of course, an inherent paradox in women being restricted to the private sphere of activity and yet simultaneously responding to the call to do God's work in public. Janet Wilson James was the first to explore the contradictory message provided by early nineteenth-century Protestantism. While women were told in unequivocal terms that the domestic was the sole sphere appropriate for them, they were simultaneously urged to engage in benevolent activities beyond the home. See "Changing Ideas about Women in the United States, 1776–1825" (Ph.D. diss., Radcliffe College, 1954).

20. Maria Cummins, *Mabel Vaughan* (Boston: John P. Jewett, 1857), p. 11; Harriet Beecher Stowe, *The Minister's Wooing* (Boston: Houghton Mifflin Co., 1896/1859), pp. 567–68; Mary Virginia Terhune quoted in a biographical sketch in Sara K. Bolton, *Successful Women* (Boston: D. Lothrop Co., 1888), p. 108; Terhune, *Autobiography*, p. 344. The idea of a "feminization" of religion in the nineteenth century was first raised by Barbara Welter. Others such as Nancy F. Cott and Richard D. Shiels have discussed the fact of women's numerical domination of Protestant congregations. But the actual impact of women's involvement in Protestantism has yet to be fully explored. See Welter, "The Feminization of American Religion," in *Dimity Convictions: The American Woman in the Nineteenth Century* (Athens: Ohio University Press, 1976), pp. 83–102; Cott, *The Bonds of Womanhood: "Woman's Sphere" in New England, 1780–1835* (New Haven: Yale University Press, 1977), pp. 126–59; Shiels, "The Feminization of American Congregationalism, 1730–1835," *American Quarterly* 33 (Spring 1981): 46–61.

21. Journal of Susan Warner, 31 Dec. 1873, in Warner, *Susan Warner*, p. 485.

22. Autobiographical sketch of Caroline Howard Gilman in John S. Hart, *The Female Prose Writers of America* (New York: E. H. Butler and Co., 1855), pp. 54–55. Like Alexis de Tocqueville before him, Michael Kammen has pointed to the paradoxical character of a society that exalted individualism while its members

actively and persistently joined a multitude of voluntary societies. See *People of Paradox: An Inquiry into the Origins of American Civilization* (New York: Alfred A. Knopf, 1972). Women's involvement in such societies has been persuasively analyzed in Mary P. Ryan, *Cradle of the Middle Class: The Family in Oneida County, New York, 1790–1865* (New York: Cambridge University Press, 1981). See also Barbara Leslie Epstein, *The Politics of Domesticity: Women, Evangelism and Temperance in Nineteenth-Century America* (Middletown: Wesleyan University Press, 1981).

23. The most important source for the reaction of male elites to what he has called the nineteenth century's "democratic, socially unstructured society" is Stow Persons's *The Decline of American Gentility* (New York: Columbia University Press, 1973). Another valuable source is Gordon S. Wood's introduction to *The Rising Glory of America, 1760–1820* (New York: George Braziller, 1971), pp. 1–22. Persons refers to the new American gentry elite as descendants of the colonial gentry, while Wood notes the transition of the republican gentleman to the Christian democrat. However, both suggest that the social transformation encountered was perhaps the greatest in American history.

24. Catharine Maria Sedgwick, "Notebook of Memories of Her Life Dated 1853," p. 99, Catharine Maria Sedgwick Papers, MHS.

25. Ibid., pp. 105–6. Whether Sedgwick the historian knew it or not, her commentary looked back in particular to the 1790s, when the Federalist party became increasingly apprehensive regarding popular power. She may not have realized either that her childhood memories of her father's and his colleagues' aspersions concerning the Jeffersonian Republicans referred more to the New England branch of the opposition than to the Southern base of the Virginia Dynasty that began with Jefferson's election in 1800. A broader and more critical analysis than Sedgwick's is found in two studies of early Massachusetts politics. See James M. Banner, Jr., *To the Hartford Convention: The Federalists and the Origins of Party Politics in Massachusetts, 1789–1815* (New York: Alfred A. Knopf, 1970) and Paul Goodman, *The Democratic-Republicans of Massachusetts: Politics in a Young Republic* (Cambridge: Harvard University Press, 1964). The ideology described by Sedgwick receives more dispassionate consideration in Linda K. Kerber's *Federalists in Dissent: Imagery and Ideology in Jeffersonian America* (Ithaca: Cornell University Press, 1970). The Jeffersonian counterpart is explored in Lance Banning, *The Jeffersonian Persuasion: Evolution of a Party Ideology* (Ithaca: Cornell University Press, 1978).

26. Sedgwick, "Notebook of Memories," p. 105.

27. Sedgwick to James Parton, 25 February 1865, Clifton Waller Barrett Library, Alderman-UVA.

28. Catharine Maria Sedgwick, *The Linwoods; or, "Sixty Years Since" in America*, 2 vols. (New York: Harper and Bros., 1835) 1:42; preface, p. xi–xii. Regarding the novel, Sedgwick wrote to Louisa Minot, "I have an advantage in the book I have now nearly finished in the period I have chosen (our revolutionary war) which gives the effect of picturesque position and lights and shadows to common characters and domestic affections. I have meddled very little with the war—that is not a woman's forte I think—certainly not mine—I have now and then attempted to give dignity to my pictures by gracing them with historical characters and have

endeavored to be true to the characteristics of my country." Sedgwick to Minot, 26 Feb. 1835, Sedgwick Family Papers, Sedgwick IV, MHS.

29. Caroline Howard Gilman to Harriet Fay, 4 March 1821, in Mary Scott Saint-Amand, *A Balcony in Charleston* (Richmond: Garrett and Massie, 1941), p. 16. The Gilmans, husband *and* wife, were maintaining a tradition. Stow Persons has noted that from the sixteenth century onward many writers on gentility were clergymen who, as he observed, made gentlemen "their secular allies by endowing gentility with the cluster of values which permitted it to bring moral standards into social relations." See Persons's *The Decline of American Gentility.* Donald M. Scott's primary concern is the change in the Congregational ministers' position, but he does note that the clergy, through moral societies, were still seeking to exercise influence upon the rest of the community. See his exemplary analysis in *From Office to Profession: The New England Ministry, 1750–1850* (Philadelphia: University of Pennsylvania Press, 1978). In a chapter titled "Gentility" Bertram Wyatt-Brown has perceptively analyzed the values shared by southern and northern gentlemen as well as the differing emphases within the southern ideal. See *Southern Honor: Ethics and Behavior in the Old South* (New York: Oxford University Press, 1982), esp. pp. 88–114.

30. A comprehensive study of America's politics from the Revolution through the nineteenth century is found in Robert Kelley's path-breaking *The Cultural Pattern in American Politics: The First Century* (New York: Alfred A. Knopf, 1979). Edward Pessen provides a particularly astute analysis of antebellum politics and its successful practitioners. It is complemented by Marvin Meyers's commentary on the ambivalent response to the emerging order and values. See Pessen, *Jacksonian America: Society, Personality, and Politics* (Homewood, Ill.: Dorsey Press, 1978/1969), esp. pp. 149–96; Meyers, *The Jacksonian Persuasion: Politics and Belief* (Stanford: Stanford University Press, 1966/1957), esp. pp. 57–100.

31. Henry Warner to Anna Warner, June 1821, Feb. 1822, in Warner, *Susan Warner,* pp. 39, 46.

32. Henry Warner to Anna Warner, 1 Sept. 1822, 8 Sept. 1822, ibid., pp. 48, 55.

33. Maria McIntosh, *Woman in America: Her Work and Her Reward* (New York: D. Appleton and Co., 1850), p. 59.

34. Ibid., p. 60.

35. Ibid., pp. 60–61. Anne Scott MacLeod and R. Gordon Kelley note that Americans' ambivalence about their society's values and their anxiety regarding its stability even found its way into children's literature of the period. See MacLeod, *A Moral Tale: Children's Fiction and American Culture, 1820–1860* (Hamden, Ct.: Archon, 1975), and Kelley, *Mother Was a Lady: Self and Society in Selected Children's Periodicals, 1865–1890* (Westport, Ct.: Greenwood Press, 1974).

36. McIntosh, *Woman in America,* pp. 11, 128.

37. Ibid., pp. 152–53, 155.

38. Augusta Evans Wilson, *St. Elmo,* pp. 465–66.

39. Ibid., pp. 467.

40. Caroline Howard Gilman to Louisa Gilman Loring, 17 Jan. 1833, Caroline Howard Gilman Papers, SCHS.

41. Caroline Howard Gilman to Eliza Gilman, 13 Sept. 1865, ibid.; Harriet

Beecher Stowe to Eunice Beecher, 30 June 1860, Beecher Family Papers, Sterling-Yale. Despite the character of Hattie's intended she never did marry him, or anyone else.

42. Catharine Maria Sedgwick to Kate Sedgwick Minot, 28 Aug. 1859, Catharine Maria Sedgwick Papers, MHS; Augusta Evans Wilson, *At the Mercy of Tiberius*, p. 10.

43. Sedgwick journal, 23 May 1837, Catharine Maria Sedgwick Papers, MHS.

44. Maria McIntosh, *The Lofty and the Lowly; or, Good in All and None All Good*, 2 vols. (New York: D. Appleton and Co., 1852) 1:120; Mary J. Holmes, *Cousin Maude* (Akron: Saalfield Publishing Co., 1860/1903), p. 136; Caroline Lee Hentz, *Robert Graham* (Philadelphia: T. B. Peterson, 1856/1855), p. 105.

45. Caroline Lee Hentz, *Ernest Linwood* (Boston: John P. Jewett and Co., 1856), p. 88; Harriet Beecher Stowe, *The Minister's Wooing*, p. 53.

46. Catharine Maria Sedgwick, *The Linwoods* 2:221; Caroline Lee Hentz, *Eoline; or, Magnolia Vale* (Philadelphia: T. B. Peterson, 1852), p. 197.

47. Susan Warner [Elizabeth Wetherell], *Queechy*, 2 vols. (New York: George P. Putnam, 1852) 1:128, 207; Maria McIntosh, *Charms and Counter-Charms* (New York: D. Appleton and Co., 1862/1848) p. 352; Augusta Evans Wilson, *Beulah* (New York: Derby and Jackson, 1859), pp. 507, 510.

48. Harriet Beecher Stowe, *The Pearl of Orr's Island: A Story of the Coast of Maine* (Boston: Houghton Mifflin Co., 1896/1862), pp. 195–96.

49. Ibid., pp. 230–31, 229, 389–91.

50. Warner, *Queechy* 2:96–97.

51. Catharine Maria Sedgwick, *Redwood,* 2 vols. (New York: E. Bliss, E. White, 1824) 1:266, 2:157.

52. Caroline Lee Hentz, *Rena; or, The Snowbird* (Philadelphia: A. Hart, 1852), pp. 264–66.

53. Sara Parton [Fanny Fern], "Gail Hamilton—Miss Dodge," in *Eminent Women of the Age* (Hartford: S. M. Betts and Co., 1869), p. 210; Diary of Caroline Lee Hentz, 20 May 1836, Hentz Family Papers, Southern Historical Collection–UNC.

54. Harriet Beecher Stowe, *My Wife and I; or, Harry Henderson's History* (Boston: Houghton Mifflin Co., 1896/1871), p. 76; Mary J. Holmes, *Millbank* (New York: Grosset and Dunlap, n.d./1871), p. 290.

55. E.D.E.N. Southworth, *The Deserted Wife* (New York: D. Appleton and Co., 1850), p. 5.

56. Catharine Maria Sedgwick to Frances Sedgwick Watson, April 1821, Catharine Maria Sedgwick Papers, MHS; Mary Virginia Terhune [Marion Harland], *Husks* (New York: Sheldon and Co., 1863), p. 32; Sara Parton [Fanny Fern], "A Glance at a Chameleon Subject," in *Fresh Leaves* (New York: Mason Bros., 1857), p. 295.

57. Maria Cummins, *The Lamplighter* (Chicago: Rand McNally and Co., n.d./1854), pp. 398–400.

58. Augusta Evans Wilson, *Macaria; or, Altars of Sacrifice* (Richmond: West and Johnston, 1864), p. 163.

59. Caroline Lee Hentz, *Lovell's Folly* (Cincinnati: Hubbard and Edmonds, 1833), pp. 49–50; Catharine Maria Sedgwick, "Second Thoughts Best," in *Tales*

and Sketches, Second Series (New York: Harper and Bros., 1844), p. 360; Stowe, *Pink and White Tyranny,* p. 326; Terhune, *Husks,* p. 233; Parton, "To the Ladies: A Call To Be A Wife," in *Fresh Leaves,* pp. 307–8; idem, "Rag-Tag and Bob-Tail Fashions," in *Ginger-Snaps* (New York: Carleton, 1870), p. 96.

60. Augusta Evans Wilson, *Beulah* (New York: Derby and Jackson, 1859), p. 454–55.

CHAPTER 12. A RIGHT REGARD FOR WOMANHOOD:
A WORD OR TWO ON ALL SIDES

1. Elizabeth Cady Stanton, Susan B. Anthony, and Matilda Joslyn Gage, eds., *History of Woman Suffrage,* 6 vols. (Rochester, N.Y.: Charles Mann, 1881–1922) 1:70.

2. Ibid. 1:71.

3. The first phase of the nineteenth-century women's rights movement has received the most perceptive consideration from Ellen Carol Du Bois and Blanche Glassman Hersh. Du Bois's *Feminism and Suffrage: The Emergence of an Independent Women's Movement in America, 1848–1869* (Ithaca: Cornell University Press, 1978) focuses upon the evolution of the movement, while Hersh's *The Slavery of Sex: Feminist-Abolitionists in America* (Urbana: University of Illinois Press, 1978) provides a collective biography of the participants.

4. Harriet Beecher Stowe to Edward Everett Hale, 14 April 1869, Stowe-Day.

5. Catharine Maria Sedgwick to Anna Jameson, 27 July 1845, Catharine Maria Sedgwick Papers, MHS. In her discussion of the nine married-women's property laws enacted by state legislatures before the Civil War, Joan Hoff Wilson has noted that legislators voted for these acts "on the basis of conservative economic reasoning designed to protect, not to liberate women" and that lower courts interpreted these acts accordingly. However, she also points out that by 1900 statutory reform of American law constituted a significant tool in the advancement of women's marital property rights. See Albie Sachs and Joan Hoff Wilson, *Sexism and the Law: A Study of Male Beliefs and Legal Bias in Britain and the United States* (New York: Free Press, 1978), esp. pp. 67–111.

6. Catharine Maria Sedgwick to [Anna Jameson], 10 Aug. 1846, Catharine Maria Sedgwick Papers, MHS.

7. Harriet Beecher Stowe to George Eliot, 25 May [1869], NYPL-Berg; Sara Parton [Fanny Fern], "Out on the End of Cape Ann," "The Old Maid of the Period," "Woman's Millennium" in *Ginger-Snaps* (New York: Carleton, 1870), pp. 266, 147, 81.

8. Harriet Beecher Stowe to Sara Parton, [1860s], Sara Parton Papers, Sophia Smith Collection, Smith.

9. Caroline Howard Gilman to Louisa Gilman Loring, 8 July [1830s], Gilman Family Papers, AAS; Catharine Maria Sedgwick to Anna Jameson, 12 Nov. 1840, Catharine Maria Sedgwick Papers, MHS; Mary Virginia Terhune [Marion Harland], *Marion Harland's Autobiography: The Story of a Long Life* (New York: Harper and Bros., 1910), p. 285.

10. Susan Warner to Anna Warner, [early 1840s], in Anna B. Warner, *Susan*

Warner (New York: G. P. Putnam's Sons, 1909), p. 232; Catharine Maria Sedgwick to Kate Sedgwick Minot, 25 Nov. 1849, Catharine Maria Sedgwick Papers, MHS.

11. *New York Ledger*, 26 Nov. 1859; Sara Parton [Fanny Fern], *Ruth Hall: A Domestic Tale of the Present Time* (New York: Mason Bros., 1855), p. 328.

12. E.D.E.N. Southworth to Robert Bonner, undated, [1863], E.D.E.N. Southworth Papers, Perkins-Duke; Southworth, *Retribution; or, The Vale of Shadows, A Tale of Passion* (New York: Harper and Bros., 1849), p. 62.

13. E.D.E.N. Southworth to Robert Bonner, [1863], E.D.E.N. Southworth Papers, Perkins-Duke.

14. Ibid., [1863], [December 1875].

15. E.D.E.N. Southworth, *Ishmael; or, In the Depths* (New York: Grosset and Dunlap, n.d./1876), Preface; *New York Ledger*, 5 March 1864, 10 Nov. 1877.

16. Southworth, *Ismael*, pp. 121, 199, 274.

17. Ibid., pp. 443, 471.

18. Catharine Maria Sedgwick, *The Linwoods; or, "Sixty Years Since" in America*, 2 vols. (Harper and Bros., 1835) 2:259–60; Catharine Maria Sedgwick to Theodore Sedgwick, 1 March 1812, Catharine Maria Sedgwick Papers, MHS.

19. Terhune, *Autobiography*, pp. 107, 244, 44, 365, 158; Mary Virginia Terhune [Marion Harland], *Eve's Daughters; or, Common Sense for Maid, Wife, and Mother* (New York: John R. Anderson and Henry S. Allen), p. 59.

20. Maria McIntosh, *Woman in America: Her Work and Her Reward* (New York: D. Appleton and Co., 1850), pp. 23, 22, 25, 70, 109.

21. Catharine Maria Sedgwick, *Means and Ends; or, Self-Training* (Boston: Marsh, Capen, Lyon, and Webb, 1839), p. 270; Sedgwick, *Married or Single?*, 2 vols. (New York: Harper and Bros., 1857) 2:81; E.D.E.N. Southworth, *The Mother-In-Law: A Tale of Domestic Life* (Philadelphia: T. B. Peterson, 1860/1851), p. 167; Augusta Evans Wilson, *St. Elmo* (New York: Carleton, 1866), pp. 525–26.

22. Harriet Beecher Stowe, *My Wife and I; or, Harry Henderson's History* (Houghton Mifflin Co., 1899/1871), pp. vii, 36. Stowe's son Charles, who held the copyright for Houghton Mifflin's sixteen-volume edition of his mother's fiction, was probably the author of the introductory note.

23. Ibid., pp. 36–37.

24. Augusta Evans Wilson to Walter Clopton Harriss, 1856, in William Perry Fidler, *Augusta Evans Wilson* (University: University of Alabama Press, 1951), p. 54; Catharine Maria Sedgwick to Louisa Minot, 26 Nov. 1836; Sedgwick to "Committee on Libraries for the Ward Schools of New York," 14 Dec. 1859, Sedgwick Papers (Minot), MHS.

25. Mary Virginia Terhune [Marion Harland], *The Hidden Path* (New York: J. C. Derby, 1855) pp. 221–22.

26. Ibid., p. 222.

27. Ibid., pp. 313–14, 315, 318.

28. Ibid., p. 318.

29. Mary Virginia Terhune, *Autobiography*, p. 484; Terhune to a friend, 24 Dec. 1911, NL; Terhune quoted in an interview in Francis Whiting Halsey, ed., *Women Authors of Our Day in Their Homes* (New York: James Pott and Co., 1903), pp. 25, 29.

30. The roots of the contrasting premises employed to legitimate female suffrage are explored in Linda K. Kerber, *Women of the Republic: Intellect and Ideology in Revolutionary America* (Chapel Hill: University of North Carolina Press, 1980). See also Du Bois's *Feminism and Suffrage* for the phase of the women's rights movement in which the demand for suffrage was based primarily upon the conviction that females were human beings first and women second, and Aileen Kraditor's *The Ideas of the Woman Suffrage Movement, 1890–1920* (New York: Columbia University Press, 1965) for the later phase in which the shift in emphasis occurred.

31. Mary Virginia Terhune, *Eve's Daughters*, p. 424; Sara Parton [Fanny Fern], "Women and Their Discontents," in *Folly As It Flies* (New York: G. W. Carleton and Co., 1869), pp. 65–66; idem, "Getting To Rights," in *Caper-Sauce* (New York: G. W. Carleton and Co., 1872), p. 161.

32. Wilson, *St. Elmo,* pp. 393–94; Harriet Beecher Stowe to Sara Parton, 25 July [1869], Sara Parton Papers, Sophia Smith Collection, Smith.

33. Mary Virginia Terhune, Homilies dated 1 May 1883, 13 Oct. 1887, Simon Gratz Collection, HSP; Sara Parton [Fanny Fern], "Two Kinds of Women," in *Ginger-Snaps*, pp. 127–28.

34. Caroline Howard Gilman, unpublished poem, Samuel Gilman Papers, South Caroliniana–USC.

35. Catharine Maria Sedgwick to Susan Higginson Channing, 12 Feb. 1833, Catharine Maria Sedgwick Papers, MHS.

Epilogue

1. Mary J. Holmes, *The English Orphans; or, A Home in the New World* (New York: D. Appleton and Co., 1860/1855), pp. 43, 45, 47, 48. As will be seen, Crazy Sal is in some respects Sandra M. Gilbert and Susan Gubar's "madwoman in the attic." She is the "woman who seeks the power of self-articulation." See Gilbert and Gubar, *The Madwoman in the Attic: The Woman Writer and the Nineteenth-Century Literary Imagination* (New Haven: Yale University Press, 1979).

2. Holmes, *English Orphans*, pp. 58–59.

3. Ibid., pp. 63, 60–61. In the text of the novel Holmes merely notes that Mary has been studying "Smith." The reference undoubtedly is to Roswell Chamberlain Smith's variously titled *The Productive Grammar, Smith's New Grammar,* and *English Grammar on the Productive System,* which was widely used in nineteenth-century America and appeared in multiple editions.

4. Ibid., pp. 63, 105, 108, 211, 65, 82.

5. Ibid., pp. 82, 85, 83.

6. Ibid., pp. 90, 78, 63.

7. Ibid., pp. 91, 110.

8. Ibid., pp. 119, 121.

9. Ibid., pp. 137, 176.

10. Ibid., pp. 307–08.

11. Ibid., p. 329.

BIBLIOGRAPHICAL NOTE

One of my greatest rewards in the process of research has been in first detecting the presence of historical personages and then reconstructing them from multiple and disparate materials and sources. That is an experience that has been shared by countless scholars, but a distinguishing feature of my experience has been that these historical personages have been thought by many not to exist. There are a variety of explanations, but I will suggest only a few.

I would begin with the familiar fact that until little more than a decade ago women were thought not to exist in history. Since then historians have come a long distance, and the many books on women before this one have put that thought to rest. Although much remains to be done in recovering the history of women, we can anticipate that it will be a stimulating and valuable journey. Initially the literary domestics, or the "scribbling women" as they were often called, were primarily studied by literary critics, and it is the practice of some critics to restrict themselves to analysis of texts. While that is of course a legitimate practice in many respects, it is not one that has heretofore served the literary domestics particularly well, for their texts have frequently been studied only to be rejected, which has had the effect of rejecting the literary domestics themselves or of removing them from historical consideration. And if one went no further than the stories that were rejected, this guaranteed that no other stories would be found. As I have found to my own satisfaction, however, and have attempted to show, there is much in those texts themselves, ironically, that relates in significant ways to the personal stories of the literary domestics. I first sensed that when I began this study a decade ago with my initial reading of the approximately two hundred volumes of the literary domestics' prose.

In truth, it was not my original intention to go far beyond the literary domestics' published writings. Perhaps that was due to my own inability to imagine that the sentimentalists—for so I too thought of them originally—existed apart from their printed pages. Perhaps I was influenced as well by the thought that primary evidence pertaining to the personal histories of women was not as plentiful as that for men. Had not women's experiences been basically private and thus publicly unrecorded? What then would be left behind? But I did make an initial foray to a number of manuscript depositories, and long before I made the many more such forays on which this book is based—to a total of more than twenty-five depositories from Massachusetts to South Carolina to Illinois to California—I recognized, as many other scholars had recognized before me regarding many other women, that the literary domestics had left behind a significant and varied body of personal material. Thousands of letters and dozens of diaries, journals, and miscellaneous papers later, it is difficult for me to recall the blank page with which I myself began. It is not difficult for me to recognize that those primary documents constitute as a whole the single most important resource upon which this study rests.

It has always been my intention to place the literary domestics within their historical context in a manner I thought necessary and appropriate, initially the literary domestics as represented by their public texts and subsequently the literary domestics as represented by both their public texts and their private papers. In that regard I am indebted to those whose scholarship has explored various dimensions of the past, including intellectual, social, cultural, literary, political, religious, and economic. Most important has been the scholarship of individuals whose primary focus has been upon the history of American women.

In terms of the primary and secondary sources I have drawn upon from this and past centuries, including most especially the nineteenth century, the most important are cited in the endnotes. Not every source I have investigated, of course, has been cited. Obviously, too, only those private papers and published texts of the literary domestics referred to in the study have been noted in the citations.

However, it seems appropriate to add one last citation in reference to a subject that is paradoxical in nature. As is well known, for the last decade or more intellectual history has been a discipline that has had to weather a storm. That is to say that the study of intellectual history has not been regarded as a fashionable undertaking in a number of circles. In part, that is because intellectual history has traditionally been associated with the study of elites, and it has been thought by some that it is a far better thing to study the unnamed, the unheard, the unspoken, and the unknown. On the one hand, had I agreed with that thought I might never have undertaken this study, for it represents in part an effort to contribute to intellectual history and it is to an extent a study of elites. On the other hand, it is a study of women, traditionally among the unnamed, the unheard, the unspoken, and the unknown. That is to say, once again, that the literary domestics in a peculiar fashion relate to both traditions. It is also to say, in an unscholarly fashion, that things are not always what they seem. And so the last citation is of the recorded thoughts of a historical personage who represents perhaps the most important single figure in this study, and who in my judgment proved herself to be a compelling and profound writer in her private prose, namely, Catharine Maria Sedgwick. The following are her thoughts in full regarding a conversation that she had recently had with the British writer Harriet Martineau. Except to note that her thoughts relate to the subjects of intellectual history, elites, and nonelites, and to observe that Sedgwick in other places and other times contradicted in some fashion practically every one of her thoughts, I offer them unedited and without further comment:

> Miss M—asked me when I began to write and what induced me to it—she seemed surprised and a little displeased with my want of frankness or rather communicativeness on the subject—said she likes to talk over her literary course (well she may!) and she had always found others so disposed—that "out of the abundance of the heart the mouth speaketh" and that it was impossible any one should be an author without having the matter deeply at heart—This is true and still it is true that in my case it is not affectation—nor a parade of modesty the worst of all parades—I have as much pleasure in success (and certainly as much in the *consciousness* of deserving it) as others—but I early took a disgust to hearing people talk of themselves— common place people I suppose they were—besides my vanity forbids it—I see that most persons soon weary of listening to these self-glorifiers, self- expounders, or whatever they may be—We are in danger of self-exaggeration.

> Journal of Catharine Maria Sedgwick
> 8 October 1834
> Massachusetts Historical Society

Index

Abolitionism, 317
Adventure schools, 58, 64, 182
Advertising: in publishing, 4–5, 9–10
Alexander, George W., 25
Alger, Horatio, 323
Alone. See Terhune, Mary Virginia: Works
American Monthly Magazine, 33
American Publishers' Circular, 26
American Revolution. *See* Republicanism
American Union, 24
Anonymity, writers'. *See* Writers: women writers
Appleton, D., publishers, 16, 19, 24
Appleton, Daniel, 24
Atlantic, 19, 36, 171
At the Mercy of Tiberius. See Wilson, Augusta Evans: Works
Aunt Patty's Scrap-Bag. See Hentz, Caroline Lee: Works
Authors. *See* Writers

Bailey, Gamaliel, 164, 170
Baltimore Sunday Visitor, 20, 160
Bancroft, George, 4, 36
Banner of Light. See Stowe, Harriet Beecher: Works
Bartlett, Anna. *See* Warner, Anna Bartlett
Batcheller, Mr. (editor), 176
Beecher, Catharine, 44, 46, 48, 78, 80, 107, 126, 320; and Hartford Female Seminary, 60, 74–76, 84, 123, 153
Beecher, Esther, 46, 48
Beecher, Eunice, 305
Beecher, George, 48, 81, 119
Beecher, Harriet. *See* Stowe, Harriet Beecher
Beecher, Henry Ward, 4, 33, 289, 305
Beecher, Isabella. *See* Hooker, Isabella Beecher
Beecher, Lyman, 32, 43–49, 78–79, 81–85, 119, 170, 250, 254, 292; autobiography, 43; school, 47

Beecher, Roxana Foote, 32–33, 43–49, 79, 81, 119
Beecher, Sarah, 81
Beecher, William, 46
Beulah. See Wilson, Augusta Evans: Works
Blackwell, Elizabeth, 334
Bleecker, Ann Eliza, 125
Blind Alice. See McIntosh, Maria: Works
Bliss and White, publishers, 12, 13, 18
Bluestocking, defined, 190. *See also* Literary domestics; Writers: women writers
Bolton, Sarah K., 107
Bonheur, Rosa, 334
Bonner, Robert, 3–6, 10, 19, 21–24, 36, 157, 158, 161–63, 198, 220, 247, 287, 321–23
Book sales. *See* Publishing industry; *financial subhead under* Literary domestics *and individual writers;* Works *Subhead under individual writers.*
Bookselling, 9. *See also* Publishing industry
Boston, as publishing center, 8
Boston *Gazette,* 24
Boston Recorder, 33
Brace, John, 80–81
Breck family, 34
Brontë, Charlotte, 112; *Villette,* 121
Brown, Charles Brockden, 11
Brown, William Hill: *Power of Sympathy,* 11
Brownwood Collegiate Institute for the Education of Young Ladies, 72
Bryant, William Cullen, 4
Bunyan, [John]: *The Pilgrim's Progress,* 113
Burney, Frances, 112; *Evalina,* 45
Burr, Aaron, 298

Calhoun family, 34
Calvert, Leonard, 33
Calvinism, 85, 289–90. *See also* Puritanism; *names of other denominations*

Caper-Sauce. See Parton, Sara: Works
Carey, Mathew, 7
Carey and Hart, publishers, 169, 178
Carey and Lea, publishers, 13
Carleton, G. W., 24, 25, 26
Carter, Elizabeth, 375 n.16
Carter, Robert, 19
Cave, Mehitable. *See* Cummins, Mehitable Cave
Cervantes, [Miguel]: *Don Quixote,* 113
Channing, Susan Higginson, 201, 204, 243, 258, 334
Channing, William E., 241, 294
Charms and Counter-Charms. See McIntosh, Maria: Works
Charybdis. See Terhune, Mary Virginia: Works
Chicago *Tribune,* 331
Child, Lydia Maria, 15, 204, 319–20
Children's literature, 393 n.35; children's newspapers, 14
Civil War: effect on family life, 237; effect on publishing, 25
Clarence. See Sedgwick, Catharine Maria: Works
Clay, [Henry], 325
Coleridge, [Samuel Taylor], 285
Colman, S., 14, 15
Common Sense in the Household. See Terhune, Mary Virginia: Works
'Common Sense' philosophers, 113–14, 117
Confalonieri, Federico, 306
Congregationalism, 82, 83. *See also* Puritanism; *names of denominations*
Cooper, James Fenimore, 13; *The Spy,* 11–12, 18
Copyright, 8, 10; and Cummins, 24; and Gilman, 16; and Parton, 157, 158
Cousin Maude. See Holmes, Mary Jane: Works
"Crazy Sal," 336–42
Crenshaw family, 34
Critic, 121
Crowfield, Christopher (pseud.). *See* Stowe, Harriet Beecher
Culture. *See* Literary domestics: as creators of culture
Cummins, David, 31, 129
Cummins, Isaac, 31
Cummins, Maria, 7, 26, 124, 126, 239, 320; early life, 31; and McIntosh, 147; marital status, 34; religion, 293, 294; values, 313–14; on woman's role and status, 270, 287. Works: *El Fureidis,* 24; *Haunted Hearts,* 24, 260–61; *The Lamplighter,* 24, 27, 128–29, 313–14; *Mabel Vaughan,* 24, 270, 294–95
Cummins, Mehitable Cave, 31
Curry, J.L.M., 287
Curse of Clifton. See Southworth, E.D.E.N.: Works

Daisy. See Warner, Susan: Works
Dame schools, 57–58
Dance, Virginia Eppes, 17, 130, 186, 188, 233–34, 252, 293, 294

Danforth, Orpah. *See* Whiting, Orpah Danforth
Davenport, John, 32
Defoe, Daniel, 113
De Leon, T. C., 77
Democracy. *See* Republicanism
Derby, J. C., 17, 18, 25, 122, 157, 184, 210, 249
Derby and Jackson, publishers, 25
The Deserted Wife. See Southworth, E.D.E.N.: Works
Devota. See Wilson, Augusta Evans: Works
Dickens, [Charles], 4, 112
The Discarded Daughter. See Southworth, E.D.E.N.: Works
Divorce, 237–38, 319. *See also* Parton, Sara; Southworth, E.D.E.N.
Dix, Dorothea, 293
Dixon, James, 238
Dodge, Mary Abigail, 101, 136–37, 247
Domesticity. *See* Literary domestics; Women: role and status
Doolady, Michael, 25
Drake, Dr., 229
Dred; a Tale of the Dismal Swamp. See Stowe, Harriet Beecher: Works
Duty, as fiction subject, 269 *ff.*
Dwight, Abigail Williams, 32, 50, 52
Dwight, Joseph, 32
Dwight, Pamela. *See* Sedgwick, Pamela Dwight
Dwight, Timothy, 113
Dyer, Oliver, 154, 156, 157, 158

Eastern Argus, 33, 291
Economic development: effect on publishing, 7–8
Edgeworth, Maria, 112; *Frank,* 44
Education: Colonial, 57–59; role of family, 59; post-Revolutionary, 59 *ff.*; and social values, 303. *See also* Women: education; *names of individual writers.*
Edwards, Jonathan, 292
Egalitarianism. *See* Republicanism
Eldredge, Charles H., 36, 154, 264
Eldredge, Ellen, 23, 135–36, 158, 265, 266
Eldredge, Hezekiah, 36, 153
Eldredge, Mary, 153, 154
El Fureidis. See Cummins, Maria: Works
Eliot, George, 80, 252, 254, 283, 284, 319
Emerson Ladies Seminary, 76
Em's Husband. See Southworth, E.D.E.N.: Works
The English Orphans. See Holmes, Mary Jane: Works
Eoline. See Hentz, Caroline Lee: Works
Episcopalianism, 79, 83. *See also names of other denominations*
Ernest Linwood. See Hentz, Caroline Lee: Works
Evans, Augusta. *See* Wilson, Augusta Evans: Works
Evans, Matthew Ryan, 34, 173
Evans, Sarah Skrine Howard, 34, 173

Eve's Daughters. See Terhune, Mary
   Virginia: Works

"Fanny Fern" (railroad car), 3, 6–7, 24, 27.
   See also Parton, Sara
Farrington, Samuel P., 36, 264–66
Farrington, Thomas, 265
Fay, Harriet, 14, 177, 253–54, 299
Federalism, 82–83, 298–99
Fern, Fanny (pseud.). *See* Parton, Sara
Fern Leaves from Fanny's Portfolio. See
   Parton, Sara: Works
Fiction, 7–8, 12; autobiographical, 37–40;
   British, effect on American publishing,
   7–8, 13; serialization, 20; value of,
   112–22, 285 *ff. See also* Publishing
   industry; *names of individual writers*
Fielding, [Henry], 112
Fields, Annie, 248
Fields, James T., 9, 10, 26, 151, 171, 276.
   See also Ticknor and Fields
Fletcher, William, Mrs., 182
Follen, Eliza Cabot, 26, 168
Folly As It Flies. See Parton, Sara: Works
Foote, Eli, 33, 44
Foote, Harriet, 45, 46, 79, 84
Foote, Roxana. *See* Beecher, Roxana Foote
Foote, Samuel, 48
Forrest, Mary (pseud.). *See* Freeman, Julia
   Deane
Freeman, Julia Deane, 42; *Women of the
   South,* 133
Fresh Leaves. See Parton, Sara: Works
Fuller, Margaret, 318

Galaxy, 157
Georgia Female College, 72
Gerry, Elbridge, 69
Gilman, Caroline Howard, 7, 27, 123; on
   anonymity, 126, 134, 187, 221; on
   Lydia M. Child, 319–20; and children's
   literature, 14; early life, 34–35; education,
   59, 68–73, 76, 181–82; financial
   situation, 145, 176–77; and religion,
   299–300, 304; and social service, 296;
   on woman's role and status, 181–82, 210,
   249, 253–54, 288, 333–34. Works:
   "Household Woman," 333–34; *The
   Ladies Annual Register,* 15; *Love's
   Progress,* 14, 16, 118, 270, 276; *The
   Poetry of Travelling in the United States,*
   14, 15, 16; *Recollections of a
   Housekeeper,* 14–16, 27, 70–72, 275,
   279; *Recollections of a Southern Matron,*
   14–16, 211, 278; *Southern Rose-Bud*
   [various names], 14, 72, 73, 176, 182;
   Tales and Ballads, 16; *Verses of a
   Lifetime,* 15
Gilman, Caroline Howard (daughter). *See*
   Jervey, Caroline Howard Gilman
Gilman, Eliza, 305
Gilman, Louisa. *See* Loring, Louisa Gilman
Gilman, Samuel, 15, 35, 176, 177,
   299–300, 304; "Fair Harvard," 35
Ginger-Snaps. See Parton, Sara: Works
*Godey's Lady's Book. See Godey's Lady's
   Magazine*

Godey's Lady's Magazine, 19, 131
Good Times, 182
Graham, George R., 19
Graham's Magazine, 9, 10
Grant, Zilpah, 76
Greenwood, Grace (pseud.). *See* Lippincott,
   Sara Jane
Griswold, Rufus Wilmot, 9, 15, 16

Hale, Edward Everett, 171–72, 318
Hale, Sarah Josepha: *Woman's Record,* 185
Hall, Nathaniel, 24, 287
Hamilton, Gail (pseud.). *See* Dodge, Mary
   Abigail
Harland, Marion (pseud.). *See* Terhune,
   Mary Virginia
Harper, publisher, 7, 12–16, 18
Harper's, 19, 20
Hart, Abraham, 162–64, 167, 168
Hart, John S., 134–36, 159–60, 183, 210,
   287; *The Female Prose Writers of
   America,* 133, 180
Hartford Courant, 4
Hartford Female Seminary, 74–76, 84–85,
   123, 153. *See also* Beecher, Catharine
Haunted Hearts. See Cummins, Maria:
   Works
Haunted Homestead. See Southworth,
   E.D.E.N.: Works
Hawes, Fanny Olds, 34
Hawes, Herbert, 95
Hawes, Joel, 34
Hawes, Judith Anna Smith, 32, 93, 94
Hawes, Mary Jane. *See* Holmes, Mary Jane
Hawes, Mary Virginia. *See* Terhune, Mary
   Virginia
Hawes, Mea, 95
Hawes, Preston, 34
Hawes, Samuel Pierce, 17, 32, 93–99, 199,
   325
Heger, M., 121
Henshaw, Joshua L., 33, 76, 159
Hentz, Caroline Lee, 7, 14, 26, 124, 126,
   198; early life, 31–32; financial status,
   145, 164–68; marriage, 35, 164, 224–32;
   and religion, 294; school, 164–66; and
   slavery, 168; and Terhune, 96; values,
   306–8, 312, 314; on woman's role and
   status, 188–89, 222–32, 235–36,
   272–73, 311–12. Works: *Aunt Patty's
   Scrap-Bag,* 14, 165; *Eoline,* 307–8;
   Ernest Linwood, 14, 31, 37–40, 42, 124,
   217–19, 222–28, 229–30, 231, 232,
   307; *Lovell's Folly,* 14, 165, 314;
   Marcus Warland, 166–67, 168, 235–36;
   The Planter's Northern Bride, 168; *Rena,
   or the Snowbird,* 166, 198, 311–12;
   "Reubens and the Unknown Artist," 224,
   230; *Robert Graham,* 272–73, 306–7;
   "The Sex of the Soul," 188–89
Hentz, Charles, 165–68, 224–25, 227,
   229
Hentz, Julia, 167
Hentz, Nicholas Marcellus, 35–36, 164–68,
   224–29, 231, 232; *Spiders of the United
   States,* 36; *Tadeuskund,* 36

Hentz, Thaddeus, 167–68
Her Mother's Secret. See Southworth,
  E.D.E.N.: Works
Heustis, Rachel Lyons, 269, 293
The Hidden Hand. See Southworth,
  E.D.E.N.ʻ Works
The Hidden Path. See Terhune, Mary
  Virginia: Works
Hill, William, 70
Holmes, Daniel, 36
Holmes, Mary Jane, 7, 24, 26, 126,
  337–38; early life, 34, 36; marriage, in
  fiction, 207–9; reading, 122; religion,
  295–96; and social values, 312; and
  temperance, 295; on woman's role and
  status, 206–9. Works: *Cousin Maude,*
  306; *The English Orphans,* 24, 336–42;
  Hugh Worthington, 273, 274; *Meadow
  Brook,* 104, 118, 122–23, 206–9;
  Millbank, 312; *Tempest and Sunshine,*
  24
Holmes, Oliver Wendell, 198
Home. See Sedgwick, Catharine Maria:
  Works
Home, as fiction subject, 270–73
Home Journal, 33, 36, 197
Hooker, Isabella Beecher, 292
Hope Leslie. See Sedgwick, Catharine
  Maria: Works
Hopkins, Mark, 32
Hopkinson, Francis: *A Pretty Story,* 11
Hopper, Isaac T., Home, 296
Hosmer, Harriet, 334
Houghton Mifflin, publishers, 172
House and Home Papers. See Stowe,
  Harriet Beecher: Works
Howard, Anna Lillie, 34
Howard, Anna Maria. *See* White, Anna
  Maria Howard
Howard, Caroline. *See* Gilman, Caroline
  Howard
Howard, John, 34
Howard, Nehemiah, 34
Howard, Samuel, 34
Howard, Sarah Skrine. *See* Evans, Sarah
  Skrine Howard
Howison, Robert Reid, 98; *History of
  Virginia,* 97; *The Student's History of
  the United States,* 97
Hubbard, Mary, 46
Hugh Worthington. See Holmes, Mary
  Jane: Works
Huntington, Asahel, 128–29
Husbands and Homes. See Terhune, Mary
  Virginia: Works
Husks. See Terhune, Mary Virginia: Works
Hussey, B.B., 15

Independent, 250
Independent Chronicle, 33
Inez. See Wilson, Augusta Evans: Works
Insanity, in women, 279, 280
Intuition, as female characteristic, 102
Ipswich Female Seminary, 76
Irving, Washington, 11, 13
Ishmael. See Southworth, E.D.E.N.: Works

Jacksonianism, 299. *See also* Republicanism
Jameson, Anna, 241, 246, 318, 319–20
Jay, [John], 298
Jefferson, Thomas, 116–17, 297
Jeffersonianism, 82, 83. *See also*
  Republicanism
Jervey, Caroline Howard Gilman, 334
Jessamine. See Terhune, Mary Virginia:
  Works
Jewett, John P., 16, 24, 26, 129, 147, 232
Jewsbury, Maria Jane, 375 n.4
Johnson, [Samuel], 375 n.16

Kemble, Fanny, 334
Kilbourne, Ma'am (school), 79
King, Col., 229, 231
Kittridge, Thomas, 31

Lacy, Drury, 42
Ladies Almanac, 182
Ladies Annual Register, 15
The Ladies' Wreath, 134
Lady of the Isle. See Southworth,
  E.D.E.N.: Works
The Lamplighter. See Cummins, Maria:
  Works
Lawrence, Rose, 238, 263
Layton and Company, publishers, 22
Libraries, subscription, 10
Lillie, Anna. *See* Howard, Anna Lillie
Lillie, Theophilos, 34
The Linwoods. See Sedgwick, Catharine
  Maria: Works
Lippincott, publishers, 12, 19, 25
Lippincott, Sara Jane, 137
Literacy, in the U.S., 10
Literary domestics, 7; and anonymity,
  126–37, 221–22; as creators of culture,
  111, 181–214, 219, 334–35; and
  education, 42, 112, 122; and fashion,
  314–15; and fiction, 118, 220, 285 *ff.*;
  financial responsibility, 111, 138–79;
  moral influence, 250*ff.*, 285*ff.*; and
  suffrage, 332–33; and woman's role and
  status, 100–107, 251 *ff.*, 270; and
  women's rights movement, 317*ff. See
  also* Writers: women writers; *names of
  individual writers*
*Little Fern Leaves for Fanny's Little
  Friends. See* Parton, Sara: Works
Live and Let Live. See Sedgwick, Catharine
  Maria: Works
The Lofty and the Lowly. See McIntosh,
  Maria: Works
Longfellow, Henry Wadsworth, 4, 183
Loring, Louisa Gilman, 15, 176, 181, 253,
  304, 319
Lothrop, Amy (pseud.). *See* Warner, Anna
Love, as fiction subject, 268–69, 274, 279
Lovell's Folly. See Hentz, Caroline Lee:
  Works
Love's Progress. See Gilman, Caroline
  Howard: Works
Lowell, James Russell, 10
Lyon, Mary, 60, 76

Mabel Vaughan. See Cummins, Maria: Works
Macaria. See Wilson, Augusta Evans: Works
McCray, Florine Thayer, 96
McIntosh, James M., 34
McIntosh, Lachlan, 33–34, 146
McIntosh, Maria, 7, 34, 239; and anonymity, 126; on democracy, 301–3; and duty, 270; early life, 33–34; education, 99–100; financial situation, 145–48; marital status, 34–35; on woman's role and status, 257–58, 308; and women's rights movement, 325–26. Works: "Aunt Kitty's Tales," 16, 147; *Blind Alice,* 16, 147; *Charms and Counter-Charms,* 16, 308; *The Lofty and the Lowly,* 273, 306; *Two Lives,* 16; *Two Pictures,* 270, 274, 277; *Woman an Enigma,* 253, 268; *Woman in America,* 100, 102, 257–58, 279, 301, 325–26
McIntosh, Mary Moore Maxwell, 33
Mackintosh, James, Sir, 285, 286, 288
Male leadership, as fiction subject, 306 *ff.*
Manufacturing, effects on women's status, 143–44
Manville, P.O., Mrs., 125
Marcus Warland. See Hentz, Caroline Lee: Works
Marriage, 207 *ff.,* 233 *ff.,* 260 *ff.,* as fiction subject, 207–9, 259; post-Revolutionary, 317. *See also* Women: role and status
Married in Rage. See Southworth, E.D.E.N.: Works
Married or Single? See Sedgwick, Catharine Maria: Works
Marshall, John, 27
Mason Brothers, publishers, 10, 154
Mason, Misses (school), 70
Materialism, 295–315
Mather, Cotton, 112–13, 115, 117, 118, 120, 291–92
Maxwell, Mary Moore. *See* McIntosh, Mary Moore Maxwell
May, Georgiana, 107, 234–35, 247
The Mayflower. See Stowe, Harriet Beecher: Works
Mayhew, Elizabeth, 51
Meadow Brook. See Holmes, Mary Jane: Works
Means and Ends. See Sedgwick, Catharine Maria: Works
Memoirs of the Life of the Right Honorable Sir James Mackintosh, 285
Merchant's Ledger, 4. *See also New York Ledger*
Millbank. See Holmes, Mary Jane: Works
Miller, Orton and Company, publishers, 24
Miller, Samuel, 114, 115
The Minister's Wooing. See Stowe, Harriet Beecher: Works
Minot, Alice, 49–50, 54, 55, 62, 65, 67, 241, 297, 298
Minot, Catharine Maria Sedgwick [Kate], 49, 129, 147, 205, 206, 241, 244–46, 249, 261, 274–75, 305
Minot, Louisa, 201, 205, 206, 328
Minot, William, 12, 49, 129, 201, 202, 206
Minot, William Jr., 206
Mitchell, Maria, 334
Monroe, James, president, 323
Morris, Adolphus, 16–17, 188, 199
Morton, James, 96
Moss-Side. See Terhune, Mary Virginia: Works
The Mother-in-Law. See Southworth, E.D.E.N.: Works
Mother's Assistant, 155
Munroe, James, 13, 15
Musical World and Times, 33, 154, 157
My Wife and I. See Stowe, Harriet Beecher: Works

Nation, 26
National Era, 20, 160, 161, 164, 170
"Natural History" (game), 149, 150
Nevitte, Charles Lecompte, 33
Nevitte, E[mma] D[orothy] E[liza]. *See* Southworth, E.D.E.N.
A New England Tale. See Sedgwick, Catharine Maria: Works
New York (City), as publishing center, 8
New York Evening Mirror, 4
New York Evening Post, 17
New York Herald, 4
New York Journal, 20
New York Ledger, 3–6, 10, 19, 21–23, 36, 126, 157, 158, 161–62, 198, 220, 287, 321–23
New York Mirror, 33
New York Times, 20
New York Tribune, 4
New York Weekly, 19
North American Magazine, 117–18
North American Review, 19, 36, 201
Norton, Andrews, 115
Novels, *See* Fiction

Old and New, 171–72, 318
An Old-Field School-girl. See Terhune, Mary Virginia: Works
Old Neighborhoods. See Southworth, E.D.E.N.: Works
Olds, Fanny. *See* Hawes, Fanny Olds
Oldtown Folks. See Stowe, Harriet Beecher: Works
Olive Branch, 23, 155, 157
"On Novels and Novel Reading," 114, 115
Opie, Amelia, 112
Osgood, James R., 171
Our Church Music, 33

Packard, Clarissa (pseud.). *See* Gilman, Caroline Howard
Paine, Albert Bigelow, 175, 176
Panic of 1837, 14, 15, 35, 147, 148, 176
Parker, E. P.: *Eminent Women of the Age,* 119

Parker, Hannah. *See* Willis, Hannah Parker
Parton, Ethel, 75, 76, 153, 247, 266
Parton, Grace, 247, 265
Parton, James, 4, 9–10, 36, 74, 76, 137, 152–55, 157, 158, 210, 267, 298
Parton, Sara, 3, 5, 16, 23, 26, 36, 45; and anonymity, 126, 135–37, 221; divorce, 152, 285–86, 319; early life, 33, 41, 43; education, 74–76, 153; financial situation, 138–40, 146, 152–58; marriage, 158, 235, 264–66; on men, 100, 101; relations with in-laws, 154; and religion, 290–91; and Stowe, 74, 169; on suffrage, 332; values, 313, 314–15; on woman's role and status, 155, 189–90, 197–98, 210, 240–47, 287. Works: on Aaron Burr, 298; *Caper-Sauce*, 278, 279, 332; "A Chapter on Literary Women," 214; "Fanny Ford: A Story of Everyday Life," 6; *Fern Leaves from Fanny's Portfolio*, 5, 138, 145, 261; *Folly As It Flies*, 332; *Fresh Leaves*, 145; *Ginger-Snaps*, 278, 279, 319; "A Glance at a Chameleon Subject," 313; "Great Original Tale," 23; *Little Fern Leaves for Fanny's Little Friends*, 5; "A Mother's Soliloquy," 275; "My Old Ink-Stand and I," 158; "Notes on Preachers and Preaching," 291–92; "The Old Maid of the Period," 319; "A Practical Blue-Stocking," 189–90; "Rag-Tag and Bob-Tail Fashions," 314; *Rose Clark*, 23, 235, 266–68, 273; *Ruth Hall*, 5, 9–10, 76, 118, 136, 138–39, 145, 153–57, 197–98, 210, 221, 264, 266, 275, 277, 321; "To the Ladies," 314; "Two Kinds of Women," 333; "Women's Millennium," 319
Patterson, Mrs., 125
Payne, Mrs. (school), 64–65
Payson, Edward, 291
Peabody, Elizabeth, 232
The Pearl of Orr's Island. See Stowe, Harriet Beecher: Works
"Peculiar circumstances." *See* Literary domestics
Periodical publishing, 10, 19–20
Peterson, Henry, 20–22, 161
Peterson, Theophilius B., 12, 22, 162, 321
Phemie's Temptation. See Terhune, Mary Virginia: Works
Philadelphia, as publishing center, 8
Philadelphia *North American*, 331
Pierce, George F., 72
Pierce, Sarah, 47, 80, 84, 123
Pink and White Tyranny. See Stowe, Harriet Beecher: Works
The Planter's Northern Bride. See Hentz, Caroline Lee: Works
The Poetry of Travelling in the United States. See Gilman, Caroline Howard: Works
Poganuc People. See Stowe, Harriet Beecher: Works
Polk, [James K.], president, 325
Pomeroy, Eliza Sedgwick, 65, 241–42
Pomeroy, Thaddeus, 65

The Poor Rich Man, and the Rich Poor Man. See Sedgwick, Catharine Maria: Works
Powers, Prof., 293–94
Printing, technological advances, 8
Proctor and Worthington, publishers, 232
Property, 312, 319. *See also* Women's rights movement
Protestantism, 290, 292, 293, 317. *See also* Puritanism; Selflessness; *names of denominations*
Pseudonyms, use of. *See* Literary domestics: anonymity; *names of individual writers*
Publishers Weekly, 26
Publishing industry, 7–10, 15, 17, 125; competition, 22–23; fiction, 117; growth, 11–13, 144–45, 177, 219–20, 250, 288; and periodicals, 19; and women writers, 27
"Puffing." *See* advertising: in publishing
Puritanism, 112, 113, 254, 256, 289–90. *See also* Protestantism; *names of denominations*
Putnam, George Haven, 19
Putnam, George Palmer, 12, 13, 18, 19, 148, 150, 151
Putnam's, 19, 20

Queechy. See Warner, Susan: Works

Railroads, and publishing, 8
Recollections of a Housekeeper. See Gilman, Caroline Howard: Works
Reading. *See subhead* education *under names of individual writers*
Recollections of a Southern Matron. See Gilman, Caroline Howard: Works
Recorder, 33, 291
Redwood. See Sedgwick, Catharine Maria: Works
Reeve, Judge, 47, 80
Reid, Thomas, 114
Remer, Robert (pseud.). *See* Terhune, Mary Virginia
Rena, or the Snowbird. See Hentz, Caroline Lee: Works
Republicanism, 59 *ff.*, 112, 114–15, 296–98, 300–303, 306, 313, 317; "Virtue," 59–60
Retribution. See Southworth, E.D.E.N.: Works
Revolution, American. *See* Republicanism
Rice, Aunt, 96–99
Rice, John Holt, 96
Richardson, [Samuel]: *Pamela*, 113
Robert Graham. See Hentz, Caroline Lee: Works
Rose-Bud, or Youth's Gazette, 14, 176. *See also Southern Rose; Southern Rose-Bud*
Rose Clark. See Parton, Sara: Works
Rowson, Susanna, 125; *Charlotte Temple*, 11
Ruby's Husband. See Terhune, Mary Virginia: Works
Ruth Hall. See Parton, Sara: Works

Sabbath School and Benevolent Society, 296

St. Elmo. See Wilson, Augusta Evans: Works

Sanborn, Kate, 41, 96, 187–88; *Our Famous Women,* 132–33

Sartain's Union Magazine, 134–35

Saturday Evening Post, 19, 20–22, 159–61

Scott, [Sir Walter], 11, 13, 112

"Secret writers." *See* Literary domestics: anonymity; *names of individual writers*

Royalties. *See* Copyright; Publishing industry; *financial subhead under* Literary domestics *and individual writers;* Works *subhead under individual writers*

Sedgwick, Catharine Maria, 7, 14, 112, 52, 249, 276; and anonymity, 129 *ff.,* 181, 184; on children, 274–75; on democracy, 297–99, 306; early life, 32, 49–55; education, 59, 62–68, 73, 76, 102, 181; on fiction, 285–86; financial situation, 13, 177–79; marital status, 34; on marriage, 239 *ff.;* and prisons, 296; and religion, 290, 294; on sexuality, 261–62; social concerns, 307, 313, 314; and Warner, 147–48; on woman's role and status, 29–30, 181, 199–206, 210, 219 *ff.,* 248, 258–59, 289, 305, 310–11, 318–19, 320–21, 324–26, 328, 334. Works: "Cacoethes Scribendi," 211–14; *Clarence,* 13, 148, 178, 204–5, 210, 244, 245; *Home,* 13, 26–27, 30, 66–67, 205, 258, 271, 286; *Hope Leslie,* 13, 29, 202, 203, 259, 286, 290; *The Linwoods,* 13, 30, 246, 249, 269, 298, 307, 324; *Live and Let Live,* 13, 205, 286; *Married or Single?,* 126, 178, 206, 236, 239–40, 260, 270, 326; *Means and Ends,* 205, 240, 326; *A New England Tale,* 12, 18, 26, 67–68, 130, 178, 200, 201, 211, 243, 258, 286; "Notebook of Memories of Her Life," 297; "Old Maids," 240–41; *The Poor Rich Man, and the Rich Poor Man,* 13, 178, 205, 328; *Redwood,* 148, 178, 202, 211, 310–11; "Second Thoughts Best," 314; *Tales and Sketches,* 30, 126, 205, 211

Sedgwick, Catharine Maria [Kate] (niece). *See* Minot, Catharine Maria Sedgwick

Sedgwick, Charles, 13, 130, 177–78, 199, 203–6, 242–46, 248, 276, 286, 313

Sedgwick, Eliza. *See* Pomeroy, Eliza Sedgwick

Sedgwick, Elizabeth, 76, 243

Sedgwick, Ellery, 178

Sedgwick, Frances, 241–42, 243–44, 313

Sedgwick, Henry Dwight, 12, 129, 130, 178, 184, 199–202, 203–4, 205, 211, 219, 248, 276

Sedgwick, Jane, 248

Sedgwick, Pamela Dwight, 32, 49, 50–55, 64–65

Sedgwick, Robert, 29, 178, 199, 202, 205, 206, 242–43, 245, 248

Sedgwick, Robert (grandfather), 32

Sedgwick, Theodore, 32, 50–55, 64, 66, 178, 199, 200, 297, 324

Sedgwick, Theodore Jr., 130, 199, 200, 201, 205, 286

Sedgwick, Theodore (nephew), 178

Selflessness, 268–73, 285–95. *See also* Protestantism

Self-Raised. See Southworth, E.D.E.N.: Works

Sentimentalists. *See* Literary domestics; Writers: women writers; *names of individual writers*

Sexuality, 260–62; as fiction subject, 260–68

Sheldon, Blakeman, publishers, 232

Sigourney, Lydia, 134–35, 150

Sismondi, Leonard, 290

Slade, Mrs. (editor), 182

Slavery, 168, 250, 317

Smith, John, 32

Smith, Judith, 41

Smith, Judith Anna. *See* Hawes, Judith Anna Smith

Smith, William Sterling, 32

Southern Era, 131, 132

Southern Literary Messenger, 17

Southern Rose, 14, 72, 73, 176. *See also* Rose-Bud; Southern Rose-Bud

Southern Rose-bud, 14, 182. *See also* Rose-Bud; Southern Rose

Southworth, E.D.E.N., 4, 7, 14, 16, 20, 26, 123, 161–63; and Robert Bonner, 21–23; and divorce, 238, 264; early life, 33; education, 76, 313; and fiction, 220, 322–24; and financial responsibility, 145, 146, 152, 159–63; marriage, 35, 159, 235, 238, 262–64; and religion, 292–94; and *Saturday Evening Post,* 20–22, 159; as teacher, 159–60; on woman's role and status, 210, 235, 277, 289, 311, 313, 321, 326. Works: *The Curse of Clifton,* 163, 270; *The Deserted Wife,* 238, 264, 279, 294, 313; *The Discarded Daughter,* 276, 292; *Em's Husband,* 293; *Haunted Homestead,* 210; *Her Mother's Secret,* 259–60; *The Hidden Hand,* 22, 27, 163; "The Irish Refugee," 20; *Ishmael,* 321–24; "Island Princess," 5; *Lady of the Isle,* 5; *Married in Rage,* 163; "The Married Shrew," 235; *The Mother-in-Law,* 326; *Old Neighborhoods,* 163; *Retribution,* 20, 152, 160, 161, 263–64, 321; "Self-Made," 321; *Self-Raised,* 321–24; "Sybil Brotherton," 237–38, 311; *The Wife's Victory,* 235

Southworth, Frederick Hamilton, 35, 159, 238, 262–63

Southworth, Lottie, 159–61, 238, 262–63, 294

Southworth, Richmond, 20, 159, 160, 162, 163

A Speckled Bird. See Wilson, Augusta Evans: Works

Spinsters. *See* Women, unmarried

Stafford, Mrs., 198, 232

Stanton, Elizabeth Cady, 316

Stewart, Dugald, 114
Stone, Lucy, 320–21
Stowe, Calvin, 35, 82, 140, 164, 169–70,
    172, 184, 198, 254, 255; marriage,
    280–83; *Report on Elementary
    Instruction in Europe,* 35
Stowe, Charley, 170, 172
Stowe, Eliza, 170, 172, 271, 274, 292
Stowe, Fred, 170, 172
Stowe, Georgiana, 170, 172
Stowe, Harriet Beecher, 4, 7, 14, 119, 123,
    252, 266, 276, 284; and children, 274;
    early life, 32–33, 43–49; education,
    77–83; financial responsibilities, 26, 140,
    145, 164, 168–72, 312; marriage, 35,
    198, 234–35, 280–83; and Parton, 74,
    157, 169; and religion, 289 *ff.*; on slavery,
    250; values, 305, 307, 314; on woman's
    role and status, 184–86, 210, 247–49,
    254–58, 269, 289 *ff.*; 309–10, 318 *ff.*,
    327–28, 333. Works: *Dred; a Tale of the
    Dismal Swamp,* 170; *House and Home
    Papers,* 171; *The Mayflower,* 26; *The
    Minister's Wooing,* 26, 184–85, 294,
    307; *My Wife and I,* 271, 273–74, 278,
    312, 327–28; *Oldtown Folks,* 26, 80–83,
    106, 171, 254–56, 283–84; *The Pearl of
    Orr's Island,* 106, 278, 309–10; *Pink
    and White Tyranny,* 171, 237, 269, 294,
    314, 318; *Poganuc People,* 80, 83–84,
    273; *Uncle Tom's Cabin,* 14, 26, 126,
    164, 169, 250, 293; *We and Our
    Neighbors,* 257, 261, 271
Stowe, Hattie, 170, 271, 292, 305
Stowe, Susy, 172
Subscription libraries, 10
Suffrage, 316, 331 *ff. See also* Women's
    rights movement

Tales and Ballads. See Gilman, Caroline
    Howard: Works
Tales and Sketches. See Sedgwick,
    Catharine Maria: Works
Taylor, Mandy, 159
Taylor, Zachary, president, 301
Tempest and Sunshine. See Holmes, Mary
    Jane: Works
Tennyson, [Alfred], 9
Terhune, Edward Payson, 35, 175, 233
Teaching, as women's profession, 61–62,
    143. *See also* Eduation
Terhune, Mary Virginia, 4, 7, 16, 27, 107,
    112, 124, 140, 199, 320; and anonymity,
    132–33, 184; early life, 32, 41; education,
    77–78, 93–99; 121–22; financial
    situation, 17, 145, 174–76; marriage, 35,
    233–36; and religion, 293–94; on
    suffrage, 332; on teaching, 61–62; values,
    313, 314; on woman's role and status,
    183, 186–88, 192–96, 209, 248–49, 252,
    256–59, 287–88, 325; on woman writers,
    328–31. Works: *Alone,* 17, 100, 130–31,
    183, 186, 188, 199, 210, 270, 294;
    Autobiography, 41–42, 43, 93, 132, 175,

    233, 258, 331; *Charybdis,* 236; "A
    Christmas Talk with Mothers," 275;
    Common Sense in the Household, 17,
    175; *Eve's Daughters,* 42–43, 101, 220,
    233, 256–57, 259, 275–76, 280, 325,
    332; *The Hidden Path,* 17, 328–31;
    Husbands and Homes, 258, 279; *Husks,*
    313, 314; *Jessamine,* 260; "Kate
    Harper," 131–32; "Marrying Through
    Prudential Motives," 131; *Moss-Side,*
    235; "Nobody to Blame." 278; *An Old-
    Field School-Girl,"* 95; *Phemie's
    Temptation,* 9, 192–96, 287–88; *Ruby's
    Husband,* 277; "The Woman with the
    Suds," 280
Thackeray, [William], 112
Thayer, Caroline Maltilda, 125
Theology, and women, 255–56, 291 *ff.*
Thomas, John, 51
Thompson, John R., 17
Thomson, Grace Ethel, 158
Ticknor and Fields, 9, 12, 24, 171, 172.
    See also Fields, James T.
Tilton, J.E., 24
Town and Country, 33
True Flag, 23, 155, 157
Trumbull, John, 113
Tucker, Sarah, 65
Two Lives. See McIntosh, Maria: Works
Two Pictures. See McIntosh, Maria: Works
Tyler, Janie, 100, 102
Tyler, John, president, 100

Uncle Tom's Cabin. See Stowe, Harriet
    Beecher: Works
Union Theological Seminary, 96
Unitarianism, 290. *See also* Puritanism;
    names of denominations
Unmarried women. *See* Women, unmarried

Vale, Mary (pseud.). See Terhune, Mary
    Virginia
Vashti. See Wilson, Augusta Evans: Works
Verses of a Lifetime. See Gilman, Caroline
    Howard: Works
"Virtue" (political theory). *See*
    Republicanism
Voluntary societies, 295–97

Ward, Andrew, 33, 44
Ward, Anna Barker, 242
Ward, John Elliot, 34
Warner, Anna, 19, 85, 86, 89, 90, 92,
    120, 126, 148–49, 277, 292, 293, 320;
    and anonymity, 135; *Dollars and Cents,*
    91; "Natural History," 149, 150
Warner, Anna Bartlett, 31, 86, 147, 292,
    301
Warner, Henry Whiting, 18, 31, 85–87,
    90–91, 120, 121, 147–48, 199; *Discourse
    on Legal Science,* 31; financial situation,
    90–91, 148–49, 151; *Liberties of
    America,* 31; and politics, 301; and
    religion, 292–93

Warner, Jason, 31
Warner, Susan, 7, 16, 26, 27, 89–90, 199, 210, 277, 239, 301; and anonymity, 126–27, 134–36, 183; on Catharine Beecher, 320; early life, 31; education, 77–78, 85–93, 120–21; financial situation, 90–93, 145, 146, 148–52; marital status, 35; on marriage, 235; and religion, 292–93; and Sedgwick, 148; values, 308; on woman's role and status, 28–29, 287, 310. Works: *Daisy*, 273; *Queechy*, 18, 28, 107, 135, 149, 150, 252–53, 271, 308, 310; *The Wide, Wide World*, 17–18, 19, 28, 89, 134, 147–51, 220, 293
Warner, Thomas, 31
Warner, William, 31
Washington Post, 160, 163
Washington Star, 20, 22
Watson, Frances, 63
We and Our Neighbors. *See* Stowe, Harriet Beecher: Works
Webster, Daniel, 33, 76
Webster, Noah, 115, 116, 117
Weekly Messenger, 200
West and Johnston, publishers, 25, 173
Wetherell, Elizabeth (pseud.). *See* Warner, Susan
Whigs, 325
White, Anna Maria Howard, 59, 73
White, Lucy, 59
White, Gallaher and White, publishers, 13
Whiting, Caroline Lee. *See* Hentz, Caroline Lee
Whiting, Henry, 32
Whiting, John, 31
Whiting, Orpah Danforth, 31, 37
Whiting, Samuel, 32
The Wide, Wide World. *See* Warner, Susan: Works
The Wife's Victory. *See* Southworth, E.D.E.N.: Works
Wildman, Dr., 198, 232
Wiley, Charles, 11, 18
Wiley and Halsted, publishers, 11, 12
Willard, Emma, 60
Williams, Abigail. *See* Dwight, Abigail Williams
Williams, Ephraim, 32
Williams College, 32
Willis, George, 33, 41
Willis, Hannah, 291
Willis, Hannah Parker, 33, 41
Willis, Nathaniel, 33, 153, 291, 292

Willis, Nathaniel Parker, 9, 10, 76, 153, 197–98
Willis, Richard Storrs, 33
Willis, Sara. *See* Parton, Sara
Wilson, Augusta Evans, 7, 24, 27, 112, 124, 320; and anonymity, 126; on art, 328; early life, 34, 42; education, 76–77, 100; financial situation, 145, 173–74; marriage, 36, 174, 237–39; and religion, 293; social concerns, 303–6, 314, 315; on suffrage, 332–33; on woman's role and status, 190–92, 210, 249, 259, 269, 270, 287, 289, 308, 311; on women's rights movement, 326. Works: *At the Mercy of Tiberius*, 259, 269, 289, 305–6; *Beulah*, 25, 30, 40–41, 43, 77, 102–3, 104, 173, 174, 184, 190, 238–39, 308, 314; *Devota*, 174; *Inez*, 25, 173; *Macaria*, 25, 26, 173, 270, 314; *St. Elmo*, 25, 26, 27, 77, 104–6, 174, 190–92, 287, 303–4, 326, 332; *A Speckled Bird*, 174; *Vashti*, 26, 174, 237, 311
Wilson, Lorenzo M., 36, 174
Wirt, William, 323
Woman an Enigma. *See* McIntosh, Maria: Works
Woman in America. *See* McIntosh, Maria: Works
The Woman's Story, 25
Women: education of, 31, 42, 56–62, 68–70, 77, 116, 122, 143, 256–57, 318–19; and financial independence, 139–45, 152; in public affairs, 60–61, 132; role and status, 17, 27, 29, 34–35, 45, 65, 111, 140, 217–49, 278 *ff.*, 304 *ff.* *See also* Literary domestics; Women's rights movement; Women, unmarried; Writers: women writers
Women, unmarried, 238 *ff.*; in fiction, 211–14
Women teachers. *See* Teaching
Women's Prison Association, 296
Women's rights movement, 316 *ff.*, 331–32
Woolf, Virginia, 182
Writers, 7, 10–11, 19, 20; and anonymity, 126–27; British writers in the U.S., 8, 11, 13; as fictional characters, 30, 122 *ff.*, 214, 217, 328–31; women writers, 26–27, 37, 125, 137, 138–79, 180, 181. *See also* Literary domestics; Publishing industry
Young Ladies School, 76
Youth and Home, 175
Youth's Companion, 33, 152

H75172

PS374
W6K4

$24.95

Kelley, Mary.
    Private woman, public stage.

6 7/92

7 7/06